KEY TO SYMBOLS USED ON

STATION - on some large scale maps actual shape MAY be shown

HALT/UNSTAFFED STATION - shown as at map date, unless recently ⸱ ⸱⸱ still open - then current position shown.

JUNCTION - may be named - or 'J' followed by number; for details see facing gazetteer.

JI

VIADUCT OR BRIDGE - if 'V' and number, identified in gazetteer.

S2

LINE SUMMIT - Number refers to gazetteer where height may be given

P3

SIDING - may be shown by letter - for details see facing gazetteer

W

WATER TROUGHS

G6 C1 E10

GOODS DEPOTS, ENGINE SHEDS, COMPANY WORKS - code letter shows which and colour indicates ownership. This style used on large scale plans and for Goods Depots on most maps.

E11

ENGINE SHEDS, COMPANY WORKS, GOODS DEPOTS - small scale maps. These features are sometimes indicated by code letter and number only

T8

TUNNEL - number refers to gazetteer, where length may be shown

EXETER	OPEN TO PASSENGERS
(CROSSFLATTS)	Opened post-grouping or post main map date and still open (may apply to part of name added later).
KEIGHLEY	Open and used by both BR and preserved line services.
Tiverton	Closed.
Norton Fitzwarren	Closed but line still open for all traffic.
Elland	Closed but line still open for goods only.
Oxenhope	Closed by BR but now open for preserved line services only
(Halberton Halt)	Opened post-grouping or post main map date and now closed (underline shows current line position as above)

Page of Continuation Map   At same scale

At a larger scale   } Only shown if there
At a smaller scale   } is no continuation at
   } the same scale

NV	NW
SA	SB

Green letters in pairs - National Grid reference.

Abbreviations used for features on the map sometimes shown in code, and colour codes used on maps and/or gazetteers. Entry in main colour used. (Variations in brackets):

A	STATION/HALT (Gazetteer entries not on map)		Railway Names on maps
B	SIGNAL BOX	P	SIDINGS (sometimes blue or black)
C	RAILWAY WORKS	S	LINE SUMMIT
E	ENGINE SHED	T	TUNNEL
G	GOODS DEPOT (sometimes in black)	V	BRIDGE OR VIADUCT
J	JUNCTION (sometimes in black)	W	WATER TROUGHS (sometimes darker blue)
L	NAME FOR SECTION OF LINE *dotted arrows may indicate limits*		Water features, canals thus ⊢⊢⊢⊢⊢⊢⊢⊢

Area surrounded by a fine dotted line in red and dotted number in red shows there is an enlargement of the area on the map page indicated by the number.

Other symbols used occasionally - explained on appropriate map or gazetteer

JOWETT'S
RAILWAY ATLAS
of Great Britain and Ireland

JOWETT'S

RAILWAY ATLAS

of Great Britain and Ireland

from pre-Grouping to the present day

Alan Jowett

Patrick Stephens Limited

First published in 1989

British Library Cataloguing in Publication Data

Jowett, Alan
   Jowett's railway atlas of Great Britain and
   Ireland: From pre-grouping to the present
   day
   1. Great Britain. Railways, history. Maps,
   atlases
   I. Title
   912'. 1385 '0941

ISBN 1-85260-086-1

The grid used in these maps is the National Grid
taken from Ordnance Survey maps with the permission
of the Controller of Her Majesty's Stationery Office

Patrick Stephens Limited is part of the
Thorsons Publishing Group, Wellingborough,
Northamptonshire NN8 2RQ, England.

Lithographic Reproduction by Beeby & Willcocks Ltd, Northampton
Printed in Great Britain by Butler & Tanner Limited, Frome, Somerset

10 9 8 7 6 5 4 3 2 1

CONTENTS

Publisher's note

The author and publishers have made every effort to ensure as far as possible the accuracy of this Atlas, but it should be noted that, although the maps incorporate much information about the current status of lines and stations, they are based on the situation at or between the pre-Grouping source date(s) stated on each, and are therefore not able to offer a finite picture of a constantly changing scene. Thus, all formations, nomenclature, spellings and other details are, unless otherwise specified, as at the map date(s) and are those as given on maps and/or used by the railway companies at that time. However, Patrick Stephens Limited would be pleased to hear from anyone who can offer further relevant information or correction to the Atlas, bearing in mind the above circumstances.

FOREWORD
by
David Shepherd, OBE, FRSA.

As a railway artist and steam enthusiast, I was delighted when I was asked to write the foreword to this book.

I believe we live, in many respects, in an all too ugly and functional age. I live, for example, in an Elizabethan farmhouse, all oak beams and inglenook fireplaces; I believe this will stand up long after architectural horrors such as multi-storey car parks will have crumbled into dust. I contend that the man who designed 'Flying Scotsman' was an artist as well as an engineer; his philosophy being that it should not only do it's job, but that it should look right. So much of this seems now to be forgotten in an age of built in obsolescence.

Maps need not be entirely functional; they should surely please the eye, too. What an opportunity there is with, in particular, railway maps, for here there is the element of adventure; for here, railways have a romance all of their own.

For nearly two centuries Great Britain has not only had a complex network of main arterial trunk routes, but also countless branch lines threading their way through our green and pleasant land. The sleepy country branch line is a part of our heritage. Now the motor vehicle has almost taken over but, if one searches, one can still find sleepy stations and junctions which have their own unique appeal; to those who appreciate these things there is a challenge in looking at such maps to find out how to get from A to B, not always in the shortest way possible.

Such a beautiful atlas of the railway system of the United Kingdom as this is a work of art in itself and it goes a long way to bringing together the joint interests of map-reading and travelling on trains.

I was particularly pleased when it was suggested that, in keeping with the whole flavour of this magnificent volume, I should write my foreword with a fountain pen. All too often in the mad rush of life these days, we reach for our ball-points. The fountain pen, like the beautiful maps in this atlas, reflects perhaps a more leisurely age which, like so much of our railway heritage, is so nearly gone.

I believe passionately that we must fight for and preserve a quality of life which can be an inspiration for future generations, and I am honoured to be associated with this lovely work of art.

David Shepherd

Winkworth Farm, Surrey.

AUTHOR'S INTRODUCTION

My interest in cartography and in railways both date back to my very early years. My first map was in fact produced at the age of eight. It was a plan of the street in which I lived. That map turned out to be the first of a series with each succeeding map encompassing a slightly increased area including additional details. Subsequent projects followed and have, most recently, included a triangulated plan of a local area and a 1:25000 scale model in balsa wood of 'The Lakes'.

Railway interest also dates back to this pre-war period. But from the outset my interest was mainly operations and signalling, in both prototype and model aspects.

The two interests were brought together from the early '80s when I had the good fortune to be able to obtain a complete set of the folding maps issued by the Railway Clearing House covering Great Britain and Ireland. These maps were rich in fascinating detail but were cumbersome and somewhat inconvenient as a regular reference source. So the idea of an all-embracing historical atlas was born.

In making the atlas, a full six months was devoted to planning, with careful thought being directed to the avoidance of annoying features to which in general atlases are prone. This planning then dictated the development of the final format. In the first instance I wanted a reference system which gave each place a unique reference quite independent of its page number. This led logically to the utilisation of the National Grid and its extension to cover Ireland, but also led to the first problems. On Ordnance Survey maps the grid forms precise squares parallel to the edges of the page; on the RCH and other maps this was not the case. Not only did the grid not form squares, they were not parallel to the edges and differed both from map to map and page to page. Thus a mammoth task had from the outset presented itself in transferring the grid onto the source maps to form the basis of the often re-scaled copies to be undertaken. At this time also the arrangement of working from north-west to south-east with end-on matching was decided on, to give easier reference in following east-west routes. Avoidance of all but very marginal overlaps would save paper and time, quite apart from the fear that in overlapping I might produce overlaps that did not precisely duplicate each other.

Turning to more general considerations, I wanted the maps themselves to be as informative as possible and not only did I want to give a clear indication of the situation in the '80s but also to include a lot of additional information not included on the RCH maps. This in turn presented a problem in lack of space particularly as I had also resolved that stations must not be number coded on the maps. Of course these difficulties were solved by the combination of two features. First the different styles for the presentation of stations enabled me without extra space being used to distinguish between stations open and closed, old and new and to distinguish LT and Metro systems. In addition, the line situation could also be shown, distinguishing lines open for all traffic, goods only, preserved railways or completely closed. Secondly, the facing page gazetteers meant that other features could be coded and additional information included without sacrificing the basic clarity of the maps.

The main index also presented a problem in maintaining a strictly alphabetical sequence. The solution was first to list on sheets of paper every station from a pre-grouping Bradshaw. After each gazetteer had been prepared the page number was entered against the station name. Any additions not in Bradshaw were cross-checked and inserted on the sheets. Finally, items on the sheets left without number were checked to ensure they were not in fact open as at the main map date. The advantage of this treatment was to bring to light as the work progressed mis-spellings on maps and/or gazetteers. There was the disadvantage, however, that Bradshaw was not always itself strictly alphabetical.

Although the RCH maps are the most accurate railway maps ever produced and were used by all railways in setting rates, in looking at them in detail surprising errors and omissions were noted. In addition to this they were not always to scale. Other source references also contain their quota of errors. This atlas cannot therefore claim to be 100% accurate since in cases of conflict an arbitrary decision has had to be made by the author in some odd errors in styles and spellings of stations. Spellings do very often give rise

to difficulty particularly in Ireland and Scotland. For example, it is very easy to write POLLOKSHAWS as POLLOCKSHAWS or to omit an R when writing FORRESTFIELD. But if there is difficulty in Scotland and in Ireland, in Wales the situation becomes an impossible nightmare. One example concerns a small railway in South Wales with a local area name included in its title. This was spelt one way in its Certificate of Incorporation and another way on the company seal. It was spelt yet another way on its headed note-paper!!

Once the preliminary work had been undertaken, the actual production was entirely completed in only about 15 months. Even on a working day, four hours would be devoted to the atlas but more often eight to nine hours. At weekends and holidays 12 hours was a normal minimum but sometimes absorption in the project became so complete that 18 hours or even more might be spent. One thing that did help the comparatively speedy completion was the detail and planning done first. This proved very worth-while since only very minor variations to the original had to be made. The index maps, for example, were finished very early in the project and never required amendment.

I hope you get as much enjoyment from this atlas as I have had in making it.

Alan Jowett
Bingley, 1989

PREFACE

The primary objective of this work is to show clearly in an uncluttered series of maps, the railways of the British Isles from the pre-grouping era. The primary source of reference has been the general and district maps of the Railway Clearing House. The dates of issue of the maps referred to are listed in the Bibliography, together with all the other sources of information utilised.

Although the main purpose has been to show line ownership and passenger stations in the pre-grouping era, it has been possible, by utilising distinctive styles of station indication, to show also the more up-to-date position on both maps and gazetteers. It has also been possible to show many additional features such as Goods Depots, Engine Sheds, Water Troughs, Viaducts, Bridges, Tunnels, Summits, Works, Private Sidings and Junctions. These additional features are regarded as supplementary and are sometimes omitted or identified only in code to ensure that the line and passenger station situation remains clearly defined. A unique feature of the atlas is the facing page gazetteers, identifying all the features shown, their owning company, and locating them on the map. The main index lists passenger stations only.

Most atlases of the British Isles illogically start in the south, and, on occasions, in the east as well. Also because of the peculiar shape of Britain it can be extremely frustrating when attempting to follow a route from east to west. This atlas therefore starts in the north-west. The first maps cover Ireland, then Scotland is covered, and finally England and Wales. Each map in a strip from west to east has its right-hand page margin matching precisely the left-hand page margin of its continuation. Where full page enlargements are used, these occur immediately after the most appropriate smaller scale area map. It is thus easier to move from map to map in this atlas.

The scale of the maps varies according to the intensity of the network in the area covered. The maps covering Great Britain are linked to the National Grid system. A similar system has also been assigned to Ireland. The whole of Ireland and the northern part of Scotland is covered at a uniform scale of $7\frac{1}{2}$ miles to the inch. The remainder of Scotland and the whole of England and Wales is covered at a uniform scale of approximately 5 miles to the inch (except South Wales and London — in these two areas the maps are at 2 miles to the inch). In areas of high density network, the area is also covered at 2 miles to the inch. Throughout the atlas, insets are used together with full-page enlargements at scales of 1 mile, $\frac{1}{2}$ mile and $\frac{1}{4}$ mile to the inch to enable extra detail to be shown at complex and interesting railway locations. As the maps utilised bear widely differing dates, the principal map date is shown in the bottom left-hand corner of each map. Subsequent dates in brackets indicate the dates of other railway maps referred to for additional information.

As indicated in the Introduction although every effort has been made to ensure the maps are accurate, some errors may have inevitably been perpetuated. In the first place, although the Railway Clearing House was renowned for its attention to detail, its maps, the primary source documents, are not free from inaccuracy. In some cases these errors remained uncorrected through several editions of the maps extending over very many years — usually because such errors were not relevant to the users. For example:
  (1) The West of England map of 1889 shows the Tiverton Branch of the Great Western Railway as Broad Gauge. In fact it had been converted to Standard between 28 and 30 July 1884 in readiness for the opening of the Exe Valley route a few days later, this latter line having been built 'narrow'.
  (2) The England & Wales (Large) 1926 shows a triangular junction at Adderbury on the Banbury and Cheltenham branch of the Great Western — the line southwards is a fiction.
  (3) Scotland 1907 — on the West Highland line of the North British, Corrour is misplaced. Although at the map date the station was not officially open — it in fact existed as a passing place, line summit and private station — its position has never changed. It is shown at the head of Loch Treig when in fact it is over three miles away opposite the head of Loch Ossian. This was discovered the hard way — by walking to the station. Incidentally, the error remains unaltered on the 1926 map.
  (4) Incidental features such as villages, mountains etc are often misplaced and/or misnamed. It is obvious of course that such features are irrelevant to the railway situation.

Secondly, station and junction names do change, so the name utilised on these maps will be the pre-grouping name. Sometimes, however, a note is appended in the facing page gazetter regarding a subsequent change of name. This is particularly the case with Irish stations which have remained open into the 1980's. With junctions, the situation is more complex. On Railway Clearing House maps, emphasis is placed on the inter-company junctions together with what were inter-company junctions of older companies prior to amalgamation in the nineteenth and early twentieth century. At times, junctions can be named after local topographical features and/or the signal box working them. Sometimes a single junction can have different names allocated by different authorities. In yet other cases, two authorities can allocate an identical name to two different junctions which are at closely adjoining sites. An example of the further confusion that can arise relates to RED POSTS JUNCTION near Andover. Records, at least since the early 'forties, show Red Post Junction (no's') to be at the intersection of the ex-Midland & South Western Junction line with the main line of the ex-London & South Western just outside Andover Junction station. This is supported by the very clear photographic evidence of the wartime signal box at this site with its extremely large sign. Such an eminent authority as R.A. Cooke has been sufficiently misled as to issue an amendment to the appropriate Track Layout Diagram altering the name. What I imagine has happened is this. At some stage, someone has made a mistake when having the sign made, since all older plans and Railway Clearing House maps show not only RED POSTS JUNCTION, but also show it as an end-on junction some chains to the west of the line convergence. So in this atlas you will find RED POSTS JUNCTION, and in its proper place. Where alternatives exist, therefore, an arbitrary decision has had to be made and in most cases the Railway Clearing House alternative will have been selected. Where no official or unofficial name is known, junctions are described by their location.

Thirdly, some features are of a transient nature. This does mean that on occasions features may be omitted, or two features may be shown on the map when in fact at any one time they never co-existed. Thus the indication of a feature on a map can only be taken as indication that it did exist at some period of time in the early part of the twentieth century, unless otherwise specified, and also that during that period it was known by the name indicated by at least one authority.

Some deliberate omissions, together with some possible inconsistencies on the maps, should be noted:

(1) ACTUAL LINES - Although new lines (post-grouping) are often shown, these are NOT shown if:
   (a) They are new London Underground lines outside the Central area.
   (b) Any alteration consists only of an altered junction alignment.
   They MAY NOT be shown if the new line has been subsequently closed.

(2) STATIONS - The map sources utilised cover a fairly wide period, and the date of the principal source reference is quoted on the map. Full updating has not always been possible. Therefore:
   (a) Some features indicated may in fact be inter-war additions.
   (b) Some features attributable to the inter-war period but abandoned prior to the nationalisation of the railways may be omitted.
   (c) No account is taken of stations which are open now and were also open in the pre-grouping period, but were closed for a time in between.
   (d) Where a station has been rebuilt on a closely adjoining site, this is not indicated - but name changes are usually recorded.
   (e) Stations closed in the nineteenth century are not shown. Neither are some stations which closed in the early twentieth century. This will depend upon the principal source reference date.
   (f) Some features shown may have been up-graded or down-graded. The indication of, say, a halt on a map is an indication only that at sometime in the early twentieth century it was just that — even though it was something else for a much longer period, e.g. a passing place, siding or station.

(3) COLOURING OF LINES - Jointly owned lines are normally coloured in accordance with the colour code utilised to define the owning partners. This does mean that on occasions colour-coding will fail to distinguish two different railways in one area owned by the same partners. When practicable an appropriate note states the situation. Where a railway was totally worked by a non-owning company, the former's colour-code is often adapted, e.g. The Didcot, Newbury and Southampton, worked by the Great Western, is shown in the Great Western colour code. In other cases there

may have been a change in the working company. In this case the owning but non-working company is allocated its own colour code, and a note about working may be appended.

(4) LONDON TRANSPORT and METRO SYSTEMS — Modern names are shown and, with the exception of some London Transport lines, a clear indication is given of pre-grouping ownership.

(5) JUNCTIONS — In case of doubt or conflict, the Railway Clearing House nomenclature is the one normally given preference. At worst, a junction will bear a name applied to it by at least one authority at some time during the early twentieth century. Alternatively, the name may be just a simple identification of the location.

(6) OTHER FEATURES — As mentioned earlier, 'other features' are sometimes deliberately omitted to leave the line and station situation clearly defined. In other cases the information is selective only.

(7) THE UP TO DATE SITUATION — This is shown as at the mid-'eighties or sometimes a little later, depending on when the map was drawn.

THE FACING PAGE GAZETTEERS

Besides listing all stations and railway companies, these include many other coded features which are identified and named together with a note of the owning company and/or other information, eg height of summit, length of tunnel.

In addition, each feature is identified in its location on the map. The entire area covered by the maps has been divided into squares measuring 100km x 100km and allocated two letters based on the National Grid (a similar system has been assigned to Ireland). The edges of these squares are outlined in green and they are designated at their intersections on the maps. Sometimes additional green lines are drawn on the maps to make it easier to locate a feature within its square. Where the whole of a map is within one square, the letters of the square are shown in the top left corner of the map.

Each of these large squares is divided into 100 (10x10). In reading the reference, the eastwards figures are read first (bottom or top margin) followed by northwards figures (side margin).

For example: LONDONDERRY - WATERSIDE Map 2 Reference NV66

STEP 1   The map shows parts of four squares: NV, NW, SA and SB. It is clear which part of the map is within NV.

STEP 2   Go along the bottom (or top) margin to identify the limits of square 6 in NV

STEP 3   Go along the side margin to identify the limits of northwards squares 6. Where the two coincide is 66 where you will find LONDONDERRY - WATERSIDE.

On some maps at larger scales, a further subdivision of squares may occur. If this were done with WATERSIDE we should need to imagine one-tenths along each margin of square NV66, thus NV6768. Both eastwards figures precede the northwards figures. The large figures show how the shorter reference fits into the longer one.

The indication of a grid reference on the maps is for identification purposes only. Due to different projections and minor inaccuracies on source maps the reference will not always coincide precisely with the actual National Grid reference.

IRELAND

Map	Area	Ref	Size in kms	NOTES
1	DONEGAL + COLLOONEY	RE 5070	80 × 130	1. SCALE – All main maps are at the uniform scale of 7½ miles to an inch. The insets are at various scales
	Collooney			
2	LONDONDERRY + STRABANE	SA 3070	80 × 130	
3	BELFAST + NEWRY	SB 1070	80 × 130	2. DATE – The main maps are all based on the position in 1912. The insets are various dates – crosschecked for new information as at 1928
	Belfast			
	Newry			
4	BALLINA + WESTPORT	RJ 7050	80 × 120	
5	CLAREMORRIS, ATHLONE + ATHENRY	RK 5050	80 × 120	3 REF – South West corner
6	NAVAN + MARYBOROUGH	SF 3050	80 × 120	4 SIZE – Eastwards distance first
7	DUNDALK + DUBLIN	SG 1050	80 × 120	
	Dublin			
8	KILRUSH + TRALEE	RO 7030	80 × 120	
	Tralee			
9	LIMERICK + MALLOW	RP 5030	80 × 120	
10	KILKENNY + WATERFORD	SL 3030	80 × 120	
	Waterford			
11	WICKLOW, WEXFORD + ROSSLARE	SM 1030	80 × 120	
12	CORK + BALTIMORE	RU 1050	120 × 80	
	Cork			

MAP INDEX - IRELAND

Note: Towns underlined in red have enlargements later

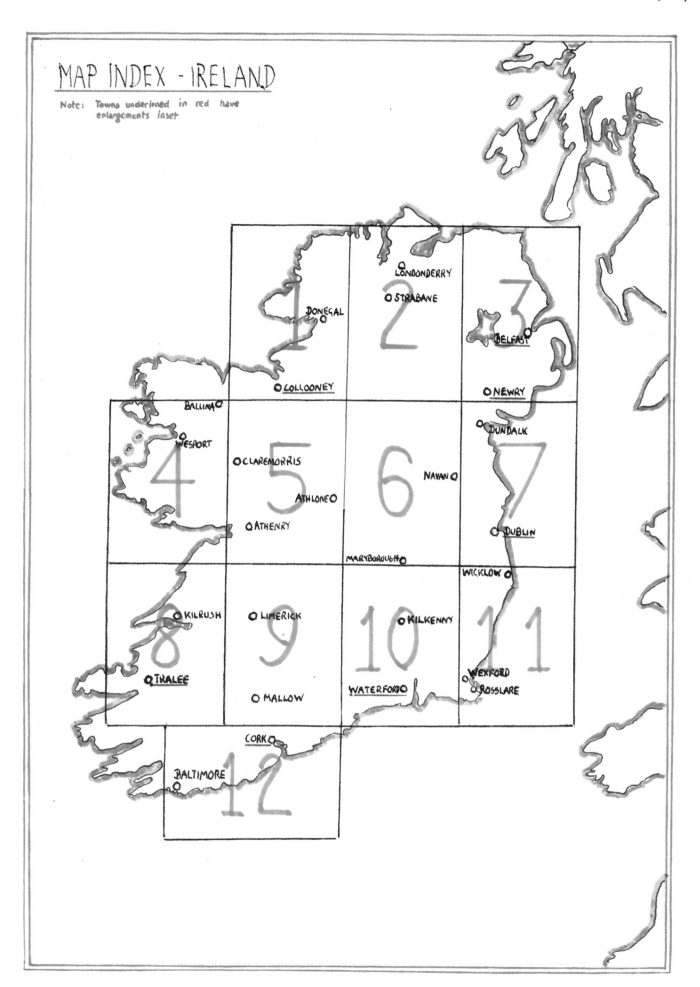

NORTH BRITAIN

Map Page	Area	Scale	Ref	Size
13	THURSO, WICK + THE MOUND	7½	NH5570	85x110
14	INVERNESS, KYLE OF LOCHALSH + MALLAIG	7½	NM6090	130x80
	Inverness			
15	ABERDEEN	7½	NN9090	130x80
	Aberdeen			
16	FORT WILLIAM, OBAN + CRIANLARICH	7½	NM6010	130x80
	Fort William			
	Crianlarich			
17	MONTROSE, DUNDEE + PERTH	7½	NN9010	130x80
	Montrose			
	Dundee			
	Perth			
18	GREENOCK, GLASGOW + KILMARNOCK	5	NS1530	55x80
19	GLASGOW + PAISLEY	2	NS3855	32x20
20A	GLASGOW	½	NS5562	7.5x5.5
20B	GREENOCK + FIRTH OF CLYDE	2	NS1058	32x22
21	ARDROSSAN, KILMARNOCK + TROON	2	NS2030	30x20
22	STIRLING, DUNFERMLINE + MOTHERWELL	5	NS7030	50x80
23A	STIRLING + ALLOA	2	NS7590	20x10
23B	FALKIRK	2	NS7875	20x10
23C	DUNFERMLINE	2	NT0080	20x12
24	AIRDRIE + MOTHERWELL	2	NS7040	20x32
25	EDINBURGH + GALASHIELS	5	NT2030	50x80
26	EDINBURGH	2	NT0860	32x20
27	BERWICK-ON-TWEED + KELSO	5	NT7030	55x80
28	AYR, GIRVAN + STRANRAER	5	NX0040	50x90
	KINTYRE	5	NR5817	20x20
	Ayr			
29	CUMNOCK + DUMFRIES	5	NX5050	50x80
	Dumfries			
30	CARLISLE + MOFFAT	5	NY0050	50x80
31	CARLISLE	¼	NY3953	2x3
32	JEDBURGH + HEXHAM	5	NY5050	50x80
33	MORPETH, NEWCASTLE + SUNDERLAND	5	NZ0050	50x80
	Morpeth			
34	NEWCASTLE, SOUTH SHIELDS + SUNDERLAND	2	NZ1550	35x22
	Newcastle			

Map Page	Area		Scale	Ref	Size
35	WHITEHAVEN, BARROW + CARNFORTH	§	5	SC9565	55x85
	Barrow				
	Carnforth				
36	WHITEHAVEN + WORKINGTON		2	NX9000	22x41
37	PENRITH + KENDAL		5	SD5068	50x82
38	DURHAM, MIDDLESBROUGH + NORTHALLERTON		5	SE0070	50x80
	Northallerton				
39A	STOCKTON + MIDDLESBROUGH		2	NZ4008	20x22
39B	DURHAM		2	NZ2028	15x22
40	WHITBY + MALTON		5	SE5070	50x80
	SCARBOROUGH + FILEY		5	TA0070	30x30
41	ISLE OF MAN		4	SC1060	40x60
42	CARNFORTH, WIGAN + BOLTON		5	SD2500	55x70
	Carnforth				
	Lancaster				
	Morecambe				
43	SOUTHPORT + FORMBY	*	2	SD2800	20x32
	Southport				
44	PRESTON + WIGAN	*	2	SD5000	20x32
	Wigan				
45	BOLTON, BURY + OLDHAM		2	SD7000	25x35
46	SKIPTON, LEEDS + OLDHAM		5	SD8000	50x70
47	BRADFORD + GREENFIELD		2	SD9500	25x40
	Bradford, Shipley + Laisterdyke				
48	HORSFORTH, LEEDS + GARFORTH		2	SE1930	22x10
	Leeds				
49	BARNSLEY, BATLEY + METHLEY		2	SE2000	20x32
	Barnsley				
	Batley				
	Methley				
50	HARROGATE, YORK + DONCASTER		5	SE3000	50x70
51	PONTEFRACT + DONCASTER		2	SE4000	25x30
52	YORK + SELBY		2	SE5030	20x30
	York				
53	HUMBERSIDE		5	SE8000	50x70
54	HULL		1	TA0020	20x12

NOTES:

(1) Scale is miles to an inch and is approximate – insets at various scales – if in CAPITALS same scale as main map

(2) Reference is at South West corner of map

(3) Size is in kms – The distance eastwards is always given first

(4) * On the maps so marked there is an ADDITIONAL overlap to the south

(5) § The southward continuation which includes BARROW is not shown on the index map

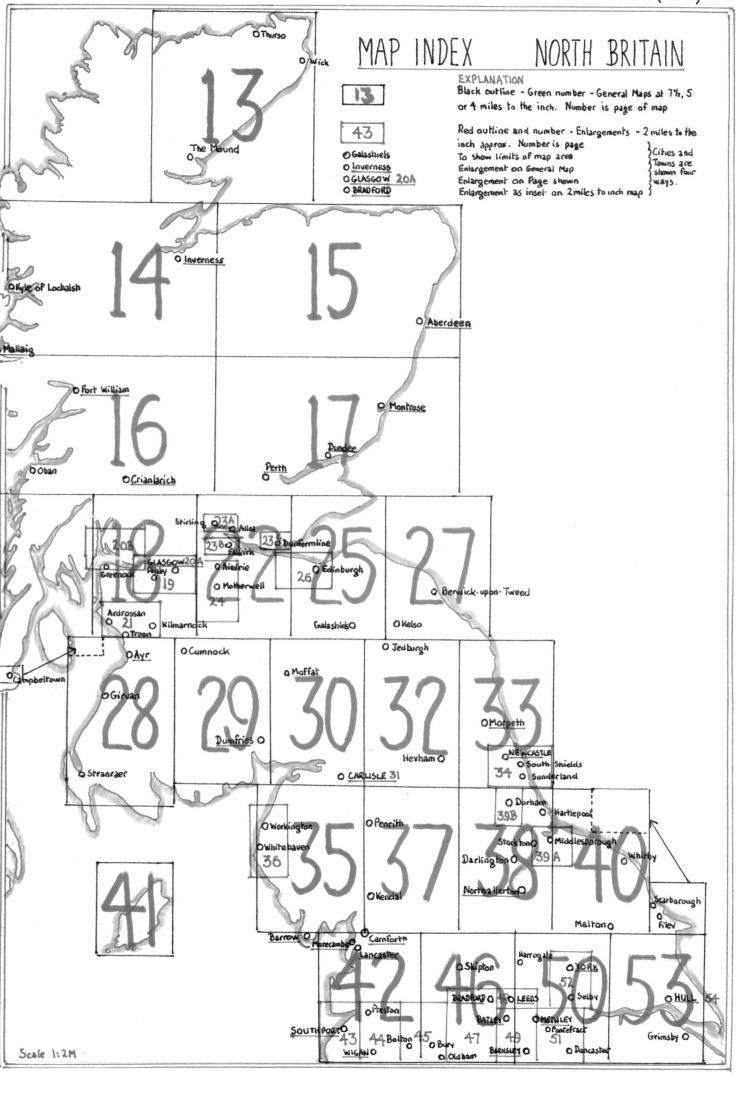

MAP INDEX   NORTH BRITAIN

EXPLANATION

Black outline - Green number - General Maps at 7½, 5 or 4 miles to the inch. Number is page of map

Red outline and number - Enlargements - 2 miles to the inch approx. Number is page

To show limits of map area

Enlargement on General Map

Enlargement on Page shown

Enlargement as inset on 2 miles to inch map

} Cities and Towns are shown four ways.

Scale 1:2M

SOUTH BRITAIN

Map	Area	Scale	Ref	Size
55 ANGLESEY + SNOWDONIA		5	SH2020	50x80
56 NORTH WALES		5	SH7020	50x80
57 LIVERPOOL, OSWESTRY + CREWE		5	SJ2020	50x80
58B BIRKENHEAD + LIVERPOOL		2	SJ2895	16x16
A BIRKENHEAD		1	SJ2888	*
B LIVERPOOL		1	SJ3587	6x12
59 CHESTER + WREXHAM		2	SJ3545	24x32
Chester				
60 WIDNES + WARRINGTON		2	SJ5018	30x22
Widnes				
Warrington				
Altrincham †				
61 CREWE + STOKE		2	SJ6040	40x22
62 MANCHESTER + STAFFORD		5	SJ7020	50x80
63 MANCHESTER + MACCLESFIELD		2	SJ8070	25x30
Stockport				
Macclesfield				
64 MANCHESTER		1	SJ8090	20x12
65 SHEFFIELD, DERBY + NOTTINGHAM		5	SK2020	50x80
66 SHEFFIELD + ROTHERHAM		2	SK3077	40x23
67 CHESTERFIELD + MANSFIELD		2	SK3053	40x24
68 DERBY + NOTTINGHAM		2	SK3030	40x23
Nottingham				
69 BURTON 1928		1	SK2020	10x10
Burton 1984				
70 LINCOLN, NEWARK + SLEAFORD		5	SK7020	50x80
71 LINCOLN 1904		½	SK9469	6x3
Lincoln 1984				
72 SKEGNESS, SPALDING + KING'S LYNN		5	TF2020	50x80
Spalding				
King's Lynn				
73A WELLS-NEXT-THE-SEA + FAKENHAM		5	TF7020	50x40
73B CROMER + NORTH WALSHAM		5	TG2020	50x40
Cromer				
North Walsham				
74 ABERYSTWYTH		5	SN2040	50x80
HAVERFORDWEST		5	SR9090	30x50
Aberystwyth				
75 BUILTH + CENTRAL WALES		5	SN7040	50x80
Builth				
76 WELSHPOOL, WELLINGTON + HEREFORD		5	SO2040	50x80

Map	Area	Scale	Ref	Size
77 WELSHPOOL + OSWESTRY		2	SJ3304	22x35
78 SHREWSBURY + WELLINGTON		2	SO4298	30x22
Shrewsbury				
Wellington				
79A CRAVEN ARMS + LUDLOW *		2	SO4070	21x22
79B HEREFORD		½	SO4837	6x6
80 WOLVERHAMPTON + EVESHAM		5	SO7040	50x80
81 BIRMINGHAM + WOLVERHAMPTON		2	SO8080	40x35
82 LEICESTER, RUGBY + BANBURY		5	SP2040	50x80
83 LOUGHBOROUGH, LEICESTER + RUGBY		3	SP4938	22x70
Leicester + Wigston				
Rugby				
84 NUNEATON, COVENTRY + LEAMINGTON		2	SP2058	22x35
85 PETERBORO', N'HAMPTON + BEDFORD		5	SP7040	50x80
86A PETERBOROUGH		½	TL1095	8x10
B BEDFORD		¼	TL0347	2x4
C NORTHAMPTON		3	SP6845	22x30
D WELLINGBOROUGH		3	SP9060	10x10
87 WISBECH + CAMBRIDGE		5	TL2040	50x80
88A HUNTINGDON + ST IVES		2	TL2065	20x10
B WISBECH + MARCH		2	TL4095	10x20
C CAMBRIDGE		2	TL4050	10x20
89 WYMONDHAM + IPSWICH		5	TL7040	50x80
90 NORWICH, YARMOUTH + LOWESTOFT		5	TM2040	50x80
Norwich				
Yarmouth				
Lowestoft				
91 SOUTH WALES INDEX SHEET		7½	SS2060	130x80
110 BRISTOL + CHELTENHAM		5	ST5060	50x80
111 FOREST OF DEAN		2	ST5095	24x37
112 GLOUCESTER + CHELTENHAM		2	ST9795	24x37
113 BRISTOL + BATH		3	ST5060	30x30
Bristol				
114 BANBURY, SWINDON + NEWBURY		5	SU0060	50x80
115A SWINDON + SAVERNAKE		2	SU1060	15x30
B BANBURY + ANNHO JUNCTION		2½	SP4025	20x30
116 VERNEY JUNCTION, DIDCOT + READING		5	SU5060	50x80
Reading		5	SU5060	50x80
117 VERNEY JUNCTION, AYLESBURY + PRINCES RISBOROUGH		2	SP6598	22x35
118A OXFORD		2	SP4800	6x15

Map	Area	Scale	Ref	Size
118B NEWBURY		2	SU4060	10x10
C DIDCOT		2	SU5088	10x10
D READING		2	SU6872	12x10
E ST ALBANS		2	TL1303	5x10
119A HITCHIN + ST ALBANS		2	SO4070	30x40
119B LONDON INDEX SHEET		5	TL0000	50x40
132 CHELMSFORD + ROCHESTER		5	TQ0060	50x80
Rochester			TQ5060	
133 COLCHESTER + FELIXSTOWE		5	TR0060	50x80
Felixstowe				
Manningtree				
Colchester				
134 LAUNCESTON, HALWILL + BIDEFORD		5	SX0080	50x80
135 BARNSTAPLE + EXETER		5	SS5080	50x80
Barnstaple				
Exeter				
136 HIGHBRIDGE, TAUNTON + EXMOUTH		5	SY0080	50x80
Highbridge				
Bridgwater				
137 WESTBURY + WEYMOUTH		5	ST5075	50x85
138A WESTBURY + FRAME		2	ST7845	10x10
B YEOVIL		2	ST5410	10x8
C DORCHESTER + WEYMOUTH		2	ST6861	11x35
D WIMBORNE, POOLE + BOURNEMOUTH		2	SY9790	12x20
139 ANDOVER + SOUTHAMPTON		5	ST0010	50x90
140A ANDOVER		2	SU2345	15x10
B WINCHESTER		2	SU4525	5x10
C SALISBURY		2	SU2810	10x6
D SOUTHAMPTON		2	SU3505	20x20
141 GUILDFORD + PORTSMOUTH		6	SZ5070	50x90
142 DORKING + BRIGHTON		5	TV0080	50x80
Shoreham, Brighton + Lewes				
143 GUILDFORD + DORKING		2	SU8540	32x20
144 DORKING, REIGATE + EDENBRIDGE		2	TQ1840	32x20
145 MAIDSTONE, TUNBRIDGE + HASTINGS		5	TV5080	50x80
Maidstone				
Tunbridge Wells				
146 MARGATE, ASHFORD + DOVER		5	TR0000	50x80
Margate + Ramsgate				
Dover				

Map	Area	Scale	Ref	Size
147 REDRUTH, TRURO + PENZANCE		5	SW4800	32x80
148A BODMIN + PLYMOUTH		5	SX0040	30x40
148B TOTNES + NEWTON ABBOT		5	SX5040	50x40
149 PLYMOUTH		¾	SX4452	11x6

NOTES:

(1) SCALE is miles to the inch and is approximate only

(2) REF is South West corner of the map and is to the nearest km

(3) SIZE is in kms and the eastward figure is always given first - relates to the overall maximum distances (approximate)

(4) INSETS CAPITALS Same scale as main map, other are at various scales.

(5) † Not shown on index map

(6) INDEX MAPS:
  a) 91 South Wales - covers maps 79B and 92 to 109 inclusive - Gazetteer for these sheets see facing page 91
  b) 119B London - covers maps 120 to 151 incl. Gazetteer for these sheets see facing Map 119

(7) IRREGULAR SHAPE *

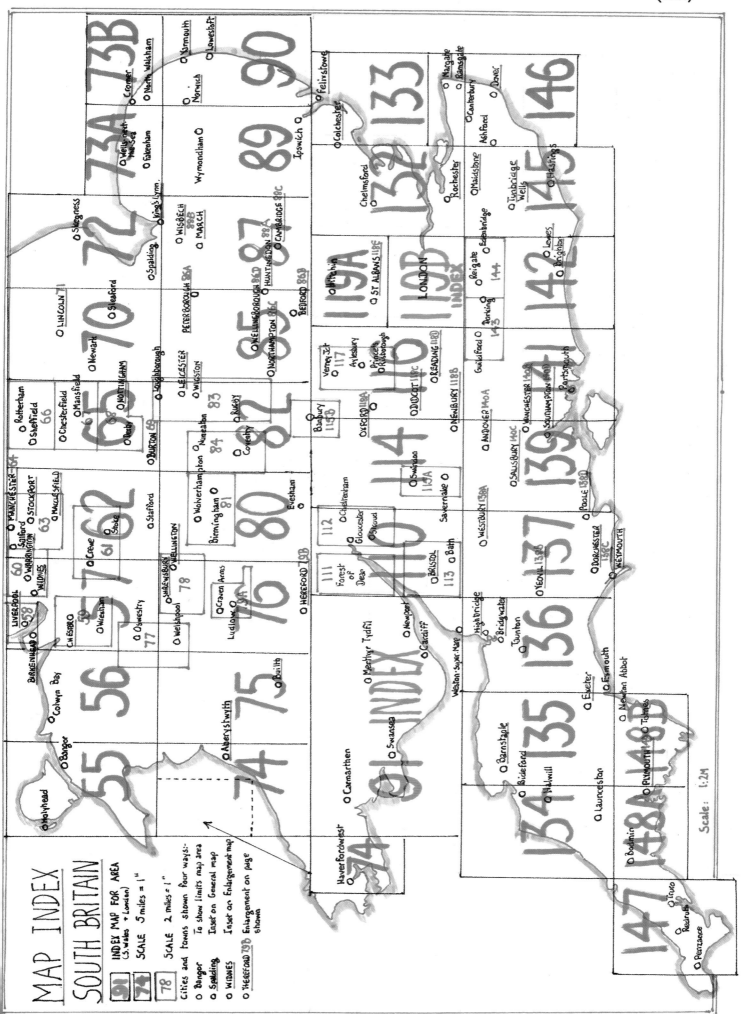

MAP INDEX
SOUTH BRITAIN

INDEX MAP FOR AREA
(S. Wales + London)
SCALE 5 miles = 1"

SCALE 2 miles = 1"

Cities and towns shown four ways:-
o Bangor   To show limits map area
o Spalding   Inset on General map
o WIDNES   Inset an Enlargement map
o HEREFORD 79B Enlargement on page shown

Scale: 1:2M

1

RAILWAYS

No	Company	Gauge	Owners
R 1	LONDONDERRY + LOUGH SWILLY	3'	
2	COUNTY DONEGAL JOINT	3'	3+7
3	GREAT NORTHERN (IRELAND)		
4	SLIGO, LEITRIM + NORTHERN COUNTIES		
5	MIDLAND GREAT WESTERN		
6	GREAT SOUTHERN + WESTERN		
7	Northern Counties Committee (Midland)		

STATIONS + HALTS

DONEGAL + COLLOONEY

No	Name	Ry Ref
A 1	Ardara Road	
2	Ballinamore	
3	Ballintogher	
4	Ballintra	
5	BALLYMOTE	
6	Ballyshannon	
7	Ballyshannon	
8	Ballysodare	
9	Barnesmore Halt	
10	Belcoo	
11	Belleek	
12	Bridgetown	
13	Bruckless	
14	Bundoran	
15	Burtonport	
16	Carrowmore	
17	Cashelnagore	
18	Castle Caldwell	
19	Clarbridge Halt	
20	Cloghan	2 NV25
21	Collooney	4 RE97
22	COLLOONEY	5 RE87
23	Collooney	6 RE87
24	Creeslough	1 NV28
25	Creevey Halt	2 NV01
26	Crolly	1 NV07
27	Donegal	2 NV13
28	Dooran Road	2 NV02
29	Dromahair	4 SA08
30	Drumbar Halt	2 NV12
31	Dunfanachy Road	1 NV28
32	Dungloe	1 MZ96
33	Dunkineely	2 MZ92
34	Falcarragh	1 NV18
35	Fintown	2 NV15
36	Glenfarne	4 SA28
37	Glenmore	2 NV34
38	Glenties	2 NV04
39	Gweedore	1 NV07
40	Inver	2 NV03
41	Killybegs	2 MZ92
42	Kilkymard Halt	2 NV13
43	Laghey	2 NV12
44	Leyny	5 RE87
45	Lough Eske	2 NV23
46	Manorhamilton	4 SA19
47	Mountcharles	2 NV12
48	Port Halt	2 NV02
49	Rossnowlagh	2 NV11
50	SLIGO	5 RE98

Ry Ref (stations 1–19):
1	2	MZ93
2	2	NV15
3	4	RE97
4	2	NV12
5	5	RE87
6	2	NV11
7	3	NV11
8	5	RE88
9	2	NV23
10	4	SA39
11	3	NV11
12	2	NV12
13	2	MZ93
14	3	NV01
15	1	MZ97
16	6	RE77
17	1	NV17
18	3	NV21
19	2	NV13

GOODS

No	Location	Ry Ref
G 1	SLIGO QUAY	5 RE98

JUNCTIONS

No	Name / Location	Ry Ref
J 1	Carrignagat	46 RE87
2	Collooney West	6 RE87
3	Collooney North	56 RE87
4	Collooney East	46 RE97
5	Donegal	2 NV13
6	Sligo Docks Branch	5 RE98

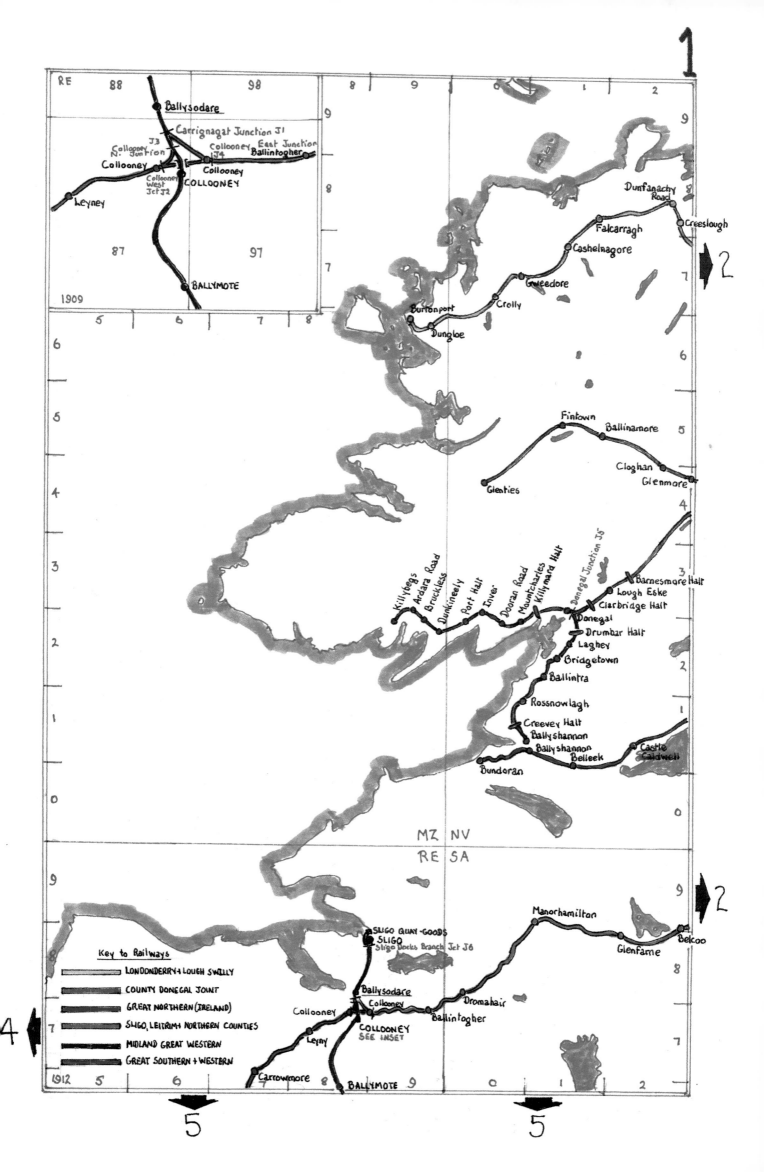

LONDONDERRY + STRABANE

RAILWAYS

No.	Company	Notes
R 1	LONDONDERRY + LOUGH SWILLY	N
2	COUNTY DONEGAL JOINT	N (4)
3	GREAT NORTHERN (IRELAND)	S
4	SLIGO, LEITRIM + NORTHERN COUNTIES	S
5	CLOGHER VALLEY	N
6	NORTHERN COUNTIES COM. (MIDLAND)	(2)
7	GIANT'S CAUSEWAY + PORTRUSH	O
8	CASTLEDERG + VICTORIA BRIDGE	N

NOTES:

(1) GAUGE: S Standard 5'3"; N Narrow 3'0"; O Not known

(2) NCC (MIDLAND) is Standard except where shown narrow on map

(3) NAME CHANGE § NEW § OLD

(4) COUNTY DONEGAL JOINT - Owners Gt. Northern(I) + NCC (Midland)

(5) DOWNGRADED STATIONS - Those shown ✱ thus downgraded to Halt status only by 1923

(6) LONDONDERRY - Stations are indexed both under Londonderry and under individual names

(7) OTHER RAILWAYS - Londonderry Harbour, Port Stewart Tramway — gauge not known

STATIONS + HALTS

No.	Station	Co	Ref
A 1	Aghadowey	6	NW07
2	Ardmore	6	NV97
3	Armagh	3	SB09
4	Armagh - Irish St Halt	3	SB09
5	Augher	5	NV70
6	Aughnacloy	5	NV80
7	Ballinamallard	3	NV40
8	Ballindrait	2	NV55
9	Ballyards	3	SB08
10	Ballybay	3	SA97
11	Ballybofey	2	NV34
12	Ballygawley	5	NV80
13	Ballykelly	6	NV87
14	Ballyliffin	1	NQ60
15	Ballymagan	1	NV58
16	Ballymagorry	6	NV55
17	Belcoo	4	SA39
18	BELLARENA	6	NV88
19	Beragh	3	NV71
20	Bridge End	1	NV67
21	Broighter	6	NV87
22	Brookeborough	5	SA69
23	Buncrana	1	NV58
24	Bundoran Junction	3	NV50
25	Burnfoot	1	NV67
26	Caledon	5	SA99
27	Carnagh	3	SB07
28	Carndonagh	1	NV69
29	Carrichue	6	NV87
30	Carrickmore	3	NV82
31	Carrigans	3	NV66
32	Carrowen	1	NV57
33	Castleblayney	3	SB06
34	Castlederg	8	NV43
35	Castlefin	2	NV44
36	CASTLEROCK	6	NV98
37	Churchill	1	NV36
38	Clady	2	NV54
39	Clogher	5	NV70
40	Clones	3	SA77
41	Clonmany	1	NV69
42	Coalisland	3	NW01
43	Colebrooke	5	SA69
44	COLERAINE	6	NW08
45	Convoy	2	NV45
46	Cookstown	3+6	NW02
47	Coolaghy ✱	2	NV55
48	Cornagillagh Halt	2	NV45
49	Creaghanroe	3	SB07
50	Creeslough	1	NV28
51	Crew	8	NV53
52	CROMORE §	6	NW08
53	Cullion	6	NV65
54	Culmore	6	NV77
55	Derryork	6	NV96
56	Desertmartin	6	NW04
57	Desertstone ✱	6	NV65
58	(DHU VARREN)	6	NW09
59	Donemana	6	NV65
60	Donaghmore	3	NV91
61	Downhill	6	NV98
62	Draperstown	6	NW04
63	Dromore Road	3	NV51
64	Drumsurn	6	NV96
65	Drumfries	1	NV69
66	Dungannon	3	NW01
67	Dungiven	6	NV96
68	Eglinton	6	NV77
69	Enniskillen	3	SA49
70	Fahan	1	NV57
71	Fintona	3	NV61
72	Fintona Junction	3	NV61
73	Fivemiletown	5	SA69
74	Florencecourt	4	SA49
75	Foxhall	1	NV36
76	Foyle Rd. - Londonderry	3	NV66
77	Fyfin	8	NV53
78	Gallagh Road	1	NV67
79	Garvagh	6	NW06
80	Glasslough	3	SA99
81	Glenmaquin	2	NV45
82	Glenmore	2	NV34
83	Graving Dock, Londonderry	1	NV66
84	Inch Road	1	NV57
85	Irvinestown	3	NV40
86	Irish Street Halt - Armagh	3	SB09
87	Keady	3	SB08
88	Kesh	3	NV11
89	Killygordon	2	NV44
90	Killylea	3	SB09
91	Kilmacrenan	1	NV07
92	Kilrea	6	NW15
93	Knockloughrim	6	NW04
94	Letterkenny	(2) 1	NV46
95	Lifford Halt	2	NV55
96	Limavady	6	NV97
97	Limavady Junction	6	NN87
98	Lisbellaw	3	SA59
99	Liscooly	2	NV44
100	Lisnaskea	3	SA58
	LONDONDERRY		NV66
101	Foyle Road	3	NV66
102	Graving Dock	1	NV66
103	Victoria Road	6	NV66
104	WATERSIDE	6	NV66
105	Macfin	6	NW17
106	Maghera	6	NW05
107	Magherafelt	6	NW04
108	MAGILLIGAN	6	NV98
109	Maguiresbridge	3	SA58
110	Maguiresbridge	5	SA58
111	Manorcunningham	1	NV46
112	Meen Glas ✱	2	NV34
113	Milford	3	SB09
114	Monaghan	3	SA88
115	Monaghan Road	3	SA87
116	Moneycarrie ✱	6	NW06
117	Moneymore	6	NW03
118	Newbliss	3	SA77
119	New Buildings	6	NV66
120	New Mills	1	NV36
121	Newtownbutler	3	SA67
122	Newtowncunningham	1	NV56
123	Newtownstewart	3	NV65
124	Old Town	1	NV36
125	Omagh	3	NV62
126	Pettigo	3	NV31
127	Pluck	1	NV46
128	Pomeroy	3	NV92
129	Porthall	3	NV55
130	PORTRUSH	6	NW09
131	Portrush	7	NW09
132	PORT STEWART §	6	NW08
133	Raphoe	2	NV45
134	Rashenny	1	NQ60
135	Redhills	3	SA66
136	Rockcorry	3	SA86
137	St Johnston	3	NV56
138	Sallybrook	1	NV56
139	Sion Mills	3	NV54
140	Sixmilecross	3	NV71
141	Smithsborough	3	SA88
142	Spamount	8	NV53
143	Stewartstown	3	NW02
144	Strabane	2	NV55
145	Strabane	3	NV55
146	Stranolar	2	NV34
147	Tassagh	3	SB08
148	Tooban Junction	1	NV57
149	Trew + Moy	3	NW01
150	Trillick	3	NV50
151	Tynan	3	SA99
152	Tynan	5	SA99
153	(UNIVERSITY)	6	NW08
154	Upperlands	6	NW05
155	Vernersbridge	3	NW00
156	Victoria Bridge	3	NV54
157	Victoria Bridge	8	NV54
158	Victoria Road, Londonderry	6	NV66
159	WATERSIDE, LONDONDERRY	6	NV66

JUNCTIONS

No	Junction	Co	Ref
J 1	Castleblayney	3	SB06
2	Shantona	3	SA97
3	Clones East	3	SA77
4	Clones West (Cavan Bch)	3	SA77
5	Enniskillen	(4) 3	SA49
6	Bundoran	3	NV50
7	Fintona	3	NV61
8	Omagh	3	NV62
9	Dungannon	3	NV91
10	Magherafelt East	6	NW14
11	Magherafelt West	6	NW04
12	Stranolar	2	NV34
13	Letterkenny	(2) 1	NV46
14	Tooban	1	NV57
15	Limavady	6	NV87
16	Coleraine	6	NW08
17	Macfin	6	NW17
18	Cookstown	3 6	NW02
19	Armagh East	3	SB09
20	Armagh West	3	SB09

TUNNELS

No	Name	Co	Ref
T 1	Castlerock	6	NV98

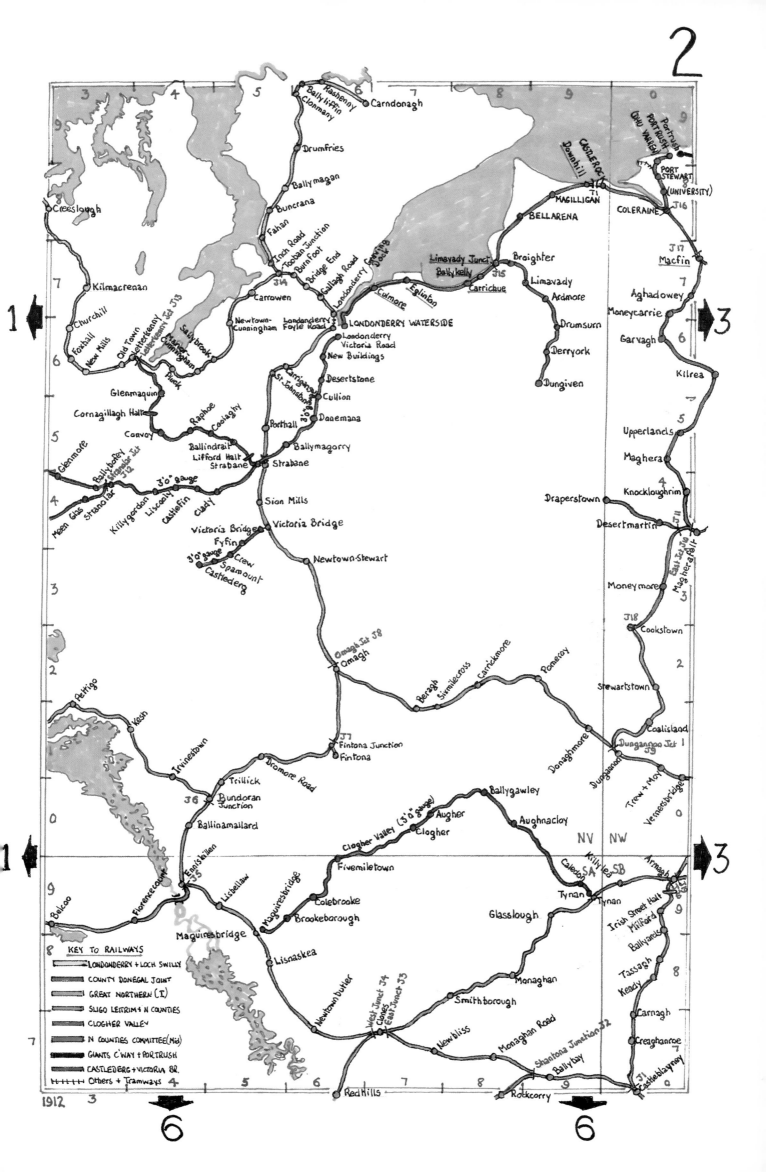

RAILWAYS

No	Company	Notes
R1	GIANTS CAUSEWAY + PORTRUSH	
2	BELFAST + COUNTY DOWN	
3	BALLYCASTLE	✳
4	GREAT NORTHERN (IRELAND)	
5	NORTHERN COUNTIES COMMITTEE (L.MIDLAND)	
5A	BALLYMENA CUSHENDALL + RED BAY	✳
5B	BALLYMENA + LARNE	✳
6	DUNDALK NEWRY + GREENORE	‡
7	BELFAST HARBOUR TRAMWAYS	

STATIONS + HALTS

No	Name	Ry Ref
A1	Adavoyle	4 B27
2	Adelaide + Windsor	4 W52
3	Aghadowey	5 W07
4	Aldergrove	4 W33
5	Annaghmore	4 W10
6	ANTRIM	45 W33
7	Ardglas	2 B18
8	Armagh	4 B09
9	Armoy	3 W28
10	BALLINDERRY	4 W31
11	Ballyboley	5B W74
12	BALLYCARRY	5 W64
13	Ballycastle	3 W39
14	Ballyclare	5 W44
15	Ballyclare	5B W44
16	Ballyclare Junction	5 W53
17	Ballycloughan	5A W35
18	Ballydogherty Halt	4 B28
19	Ballygarvey	5A W35
20	Ballygowan	2 W61
21	BALLYMENA	55AB W35
22	BALLYMONEY	35 W17
23	Ballynahinch	2 W50
24	Ballynahinch Junction	2 W60
25	Ballynashee	5B W44
26	Ballynoe	2 B79
27	Ballynure	5B W54
28	Ballyrobert Halt	5 W43
29	Ballyroney	4 B48
30	Ballyward	4 B48
31	BALMORAL	4 W52
32	Banbridge	4 B39
33	BANGOR	2 W73
34	(BANGOR WEST)	2 W63
	BELFAST	W52
35	(BOTANIC)	4 W52
36	(BRIDGE END)	4 W52
37	CENTRAL	4 W52
38	Great Victoria Street	4 W52
39	Queens Bridge	4 W52
40	(VICTORIA PARK)	2 W52
41	YORK ROAD	5 W52
42	BELFAST CENTRAL	4 W52
43	Bessbrook §	4 B28
44	Bloomfield	2 W52
45	(BOTANIC)	4 W52
46	(BRIDGE END)	4 W52
47	Bridge Street Newry	6 B27
48	Brookmount	4 W31
49	Bushmills	1 W19
50	Capecastle	3 W28
51	Cargan	5A W36
52	CARNALEA	2 W63
53	CARRICKFERGUS	5 W63
54	Castle Dawson	5 W14
55	Castlewellan	24 B58
56	Clough Road	5A W36
57	Collin	5 W45
58	Comber	2 W62
59	Cookstown Junction	5 W34
60	Corbet	2 B39
61	CRAIGAVAD	2 W63
62	(CRAWFORDSBURN)	2 W63
63	CRUMLIN	4 W32
64	Crossgar	2 W60
65	Crossroads	5A W36
66	CULLYBACKEY	5 W25
67	CULTRA	2 W63
68	DERRIAGHY HALT	4 W41
69	Dervock	5 W18
70	Doagh	5 W43
71	Doagh	5B W44
72	Donaghadee	2 W73
73	(DOWNSHIRE)	5 W64
74	Downpatrick	2 B79
75	Dromore	4 W30
76	Dublin Bridge Newry	4 B37
77	Dunadry	5 W33
78	Dundonald	2 W62
79	Dundrum	2 B68
80	Dunloy	5 W27
81	DUNMURRY	4 W42
82	Edward Street Newry	4 B27
83	FINAGHY HALT	4 W52
84	Giants Causeway	1 W19
85	Glarry Ford	5 W26
86	GLENAVY	4 W32
87	GLYNN	5 W65
88	(GOODYEAR)	4 W21
89	Goragh Wood	4 B28
90	Gracehill	3 W28
91	Great Victoria Street	5 W52
92	Greencastle	5 W53
93	GREENISLAND	5 W53
94	Groomsport Road	2 W73
95	Hamilton's Brawn	4 B19
96	Harryville	5B W35
97	Headwood	5B W54
98	HELEN'S BAY	2 W63
99	Hillsborough	4 W41
100	HILDEN HALT	4 W41
101	HOLYWOOD	2 W63
102	JORDANSTOWN	5 W53
103	Katesbridge	4 W49
104	Kells	5 W35
105	Kellswater	5B W34
106	Killagan	5 W26
107	Killough	2 B68
108	Kilrea	5 W16
109	Kilroot	5 W64
110	Kilwaughter Halt	5B W55
111	Kinnegar Halt	2 W63
112	Knock	2 W52
113	Knockanally	5 W36
114	Knockloughrim	5 W04
115	LAMBEG	4 W41
116	LARNE HARBOUR	55B W65
117	LARNE TOWN	55B W65
118	Laurencetown	4 B39
119	Leitrim	4 W58
120	Lenaderg	4 W39
121	LISBURN	4 W41
122	Lisnalinchy	5 W44
123	Loughgilly	4 B28
124	LURGAN	4 W21
125	Macfin	5 W17
126	Magherafelt	5 W14
127	MAGHERAMORNE	5 W65
128	MARINO	2 W63
129	Markethill	4 B19
130	Maze	4 W61
131	MOIRA	4 W31
132	Monkstown Halt	5 W53
133	Moorfields	5B W35
134	Mossley	5 W53
135	Muckamoor Halt	5 W33
136	Mullafernaghan	4 W30
137	Narrow Water	4 B37
138	Neill's Hill	2 W53
139	Newcastle	2 B58
	NEWRY	B
140	Bessbrook §	4 B28
141	Bridge Street	6 B27
142	Dublin Bridge	4 B37
143	Edward Street	4 B27
144	NEWRY §	4 B28
145	Newtownards	2 W62
146	Omeath	6 B36
147	Parkmore	5A W37
148	PORTADOWN	4 W20
149	Portrush	1 W09
150	Poyntzpass	4 B29
151	Queens Bridge	1 W19
152	Randal's Town	5 W34
153	Rathkenny	5A W36
154	Richhill	4 W10
155	Saintfield	2 W61
156	Scarva	4 B29
157	(SEAHILL)	2 W63
158	Staffordstown	5 W23
159	Stranocum	3 W28
160	SYDENHAM	2 W52
161	Tandragee	4 B29
162	Templepatrick	5 W43
163	Tillysburn	2 W52
164	Toome	5 W24
165	TROOPERS LANE	5 W53
166	Tullmurry	2 B69
167	Upperlands	5 W05
168	Vernersbridge	4 W01
169	(VICTORIA PARK)	2 W52
170	Warrenpoint	4 B36
171	WHITEABBEY	5 W53
172	WHITEHEAD	5 W64
173	Whitehouse	5 W53
174	YORK ROAD	5 W52

7 Antrim 45 W36

ADDITIONAL STATION

No	Name	Ry Ref
A55A	(CLIPPERSTOWN)	5 W53

GOODS

No	Name	Ry Ref
G1	Grosvenor Street	4 W52
2	QUEENS QUAY	2 W52
3	Albert Basin	4 B27
4	Retreat	5A W37
5	Mayfields Sidings	4 W52
6	Ballymena	55AB W35

TUNNELS

No	Name	Ry Ref
T1	Whitehead	5 W64

JUNCTIONS

No	Name/Location	Ry Ref
J1	Knockmore	4 W41
2	Ballyclare	5 W53
3	Central (Belfast)	4 W52
4	East Bridge Street	4 W52
5	Ballymaccarret Jcts	24 W52
6	King Street	4 B27
7	Bridge Street	46 B27
8	Portadown	4 W20
9	Castlewellan	24 B58
10	Ballynahinch	2 W60
11	Macfin	5 W17
12	Cookstown	5 W34
13	Comber	2 W62
14	Antrim	45 W33
15	Ballyboley	5B W54
16	Donegal Quay	47 W52
17	Queens Dock	57 W52
18	Downpatrick Jcts	2 B79
19	Banbridge	4 B39
20	Scarva	4 B29
21	Grosvenor Goods Branch	4 W52
22	York Road	5 W52
23	Goraghs Wood North	4 B28
24	Goraghs Wood South	4 B28

NOTES:

(1) Standard Gauge is 5'3"
(2) Narrow Gauge 3'0" ✳
(3) Owned LNWR ‡
(4) NEWRY (1984 Station) §
(5) on site of Bessbrook §
(6) REF in 5B or NW, the Sor N is omitted in the reference column
(7) Dual ownership of stations is indicated by appropriate combination of railway nos.
(8) Continuation Northwards to Kintyre: see Inset on map 28 (North of the area where Belfast enlargement is located)
(9) For full details at Portrush, Magherafelt and Armagh see MAP 2

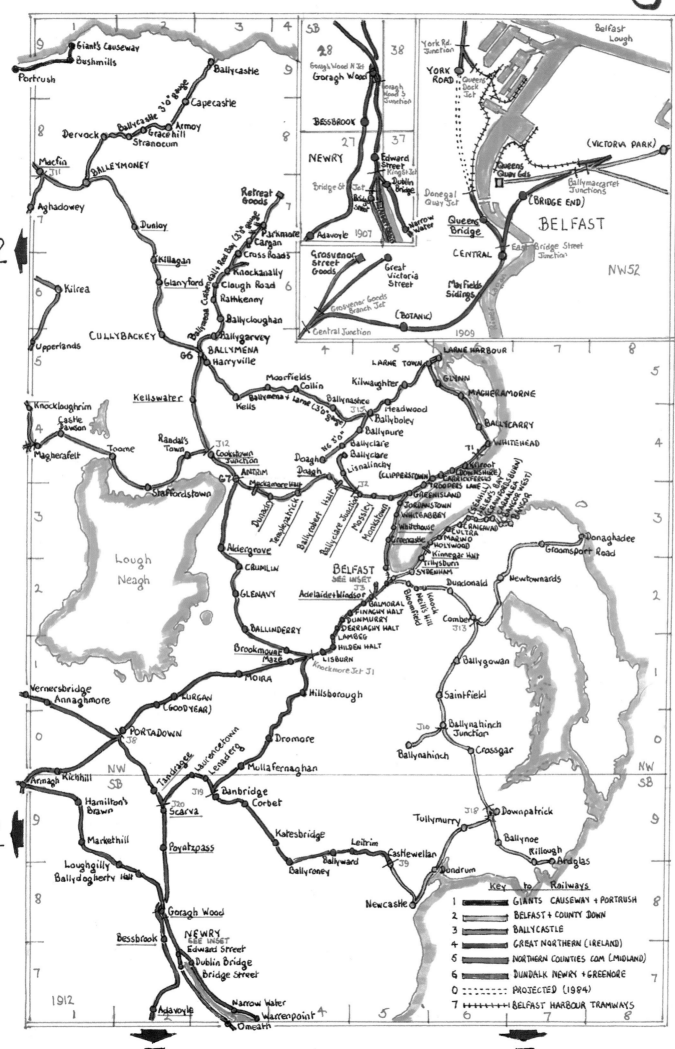

Giant's Causeway
Bushmills
Portrush
Ballycastle
Capecastle
Ballycastle 3'0" gauge
Dervock
Armoy
Gracehill
Stranocum
Macfin
J11
BALLYMONEY
Aghadowey
Dunloy
Killagan
Kilrea
Glanyford
Clough Road
Rathkenny
Upperlands
Ballycloughan
CULLYBACKEY
Ballygarvey
BALLYMENA
G6
Harryville
Knockloughrim
Castle Dawson
Toome
Randal's Town
Magherafelt
Cookstown Junction
J12
Staffordstown
ANTRIM
Mackamore Halt
G7
Dunadry
Templepatrick
Aldergrove
CRUMLIN
GLENAVY
BALLINDERRY
Brookmount
Maze
Lough Neagh

Retreat Goods
Parkmore
Cargan
Cross Roads
Knockanally
Ballymena Cushendall & Red Bay 3'0" gauge

Moorfields
Collin
Ballynashee
Kells
Ballymena & Larne (3'0" gauge)
Kellswater
J15
Headwood
Ballyboley
Ballynure
Ballyclare
NG 3'0"
Ballyclare
Doagh
Lisnalinchy
(CLIPPERSTOWN)
Doagh
Ballyrobert Halt
Ballyclare Junction
J2
Massley
Mossley
Monkstown

LARNE HARBOUR
LARNE TOWN
Kilwaughter
GLYNN
MAGHERAMORNE
BALLYCARRY
WHITEHEAD
T1
Kilroot
(DOWNSHIRE)
CARRICKFERGUS
TROOPERS LANE
GREENISLAND
JORDANSTOWN
WHITEABBEY
Whitehouse
Greencastle
GREENHILL
HELEN'S BAY
(CRAWFORDSBURN)
CRAIGAVAD
CULTRA
MARINO
HOLYWOOD
Kinnegar Halt
Tillysburn
SYDENHAM
BANGOR
(BANGOR WEST)
CARNALEA
Donaghadee
Groomsport Road
Newtownards
Dundonald
Knock
Neill's Hill
Bloomfield
Comber
J13
Ballygowan
Saintfield
Ballynahinch Junction
J16
Ballynahinch
Crossgar

BELFAST
SEE INSET
J3
Adelaide & Windsor
BALMORAL
FINAGHY HALT
DUNMURRY
DERRIAGHY HALT
LAMBEG
HILDEN HALT
LISBURN
Knockmore Jct J1

Vernersbridge
Annaghmore
LURGAN
(GOODYEAR)
MOIRA
Hillsborough
PORTADOWN
J8
NW
SB
Armagh
Richhill
Hamilton's Bawn
Tandragee
Laurencetown
Lenaderg
Mullafernaghan
J19
Banbridge
Corbet
J20
Scarva
Markethill
Poyntzpass
Katesbridge
Loughgilly
Ballydogherty Halt
Dromore
Leitrim
Ballyward
J9
Ballyroney
Castlewellan
Tullymurry
J18
Downpatrick
Ballynoe
Killough
Ardglas
Goragh Wood
Bessbrook
NEWRY
SEE INSET
Edward Street
Dublin Bridge
Bridge Street
1912
Adavoyle
Narrow Water
Warrenpoint
Omeath
Dundrum
Newcastle

SB
28   38
Goragh Wood N Jct
Goragh Wood
Goragh Wood S Junction
BESSBROOK
27   37
NEWRY
Edward Street
Bridge St Jct
Kingst Jct
Dublin Bridge
Bridge Street
Adavoyle   1907
Narrow Water

York Rd. Junction
YORK ROAD
Queens Dock Jct
Belfast Lough
(VICTORIA PARK)
Queens Quay Gds
Ballymaccarret Junctions
Donegal Quay Jct
(BRIDGE END)
Queens Bridge
BELFAST
CENTRAL
East Bridge Street Junction
NW52
Mayfields Sidings
Grosvenor Street Goods
Great Victoria Street
Grosvenor Goods Branch Jct
(BOTANIC)
Central Junction
1909
River Lagan

2

Key to Railways

1	GIANTS CAUSEWAY & PORTRUSH
2	BELFAST & COUNTY DOWN
3	BALLYCASTLE
4	GREAT NORTHERN (IRELAND)
5	NORTHERN COUNTIES COM (MIDLAND)
6	DUNDALK NEWRY & GREENORE
0	PROJECTED (1984)
7	BELFAST HARBOUR TRAMWAYS

BALLINA + WESTPORT

RAILWAYS

No	Company	Gauge
R 1	MIDLAND GREAT WESTERN	S - 5'3"

STATIONS

No	Station	Ry Ref
A 1	Achill	1 RD94
2	Balla	1 RE43
3	BALLINA	1 RE46
4	Ballinrobe	1 RE41
5	Ballynahinch	1 RK09
6	Ballyvary	1 RE94
7	CASTLEBAR	1 RE34
8	Clifden	1 RD90
9	Foxford	1 RE95
10	Hollymount	1 RE91
11	Killala	1 RE48
12	Maam Cross	1 RK29
13	Mallaranny	1 RE04
14	Manulla	1 RE93
15	Moycullen	1 RK48
16	Newport	1 RE24
17	Oughterard	1 RK30
18	Recess	1 RK09
19	Ross	1 RK38
20	Westport Quay	1 RE23
21	WESTPORT TOWN	1 RE23

JUNCTIONS

No	Location	Ry Ref
J 1	Manulla	1 RE93
2	Westport Quay Branch	1 RE23

GOODS DEPÔTS

No	Location	Ry Ref
G 1	BALLINA	1 RE46
2	CASTLEBAR	1 RE34
3	WESTPORT	1 RE23

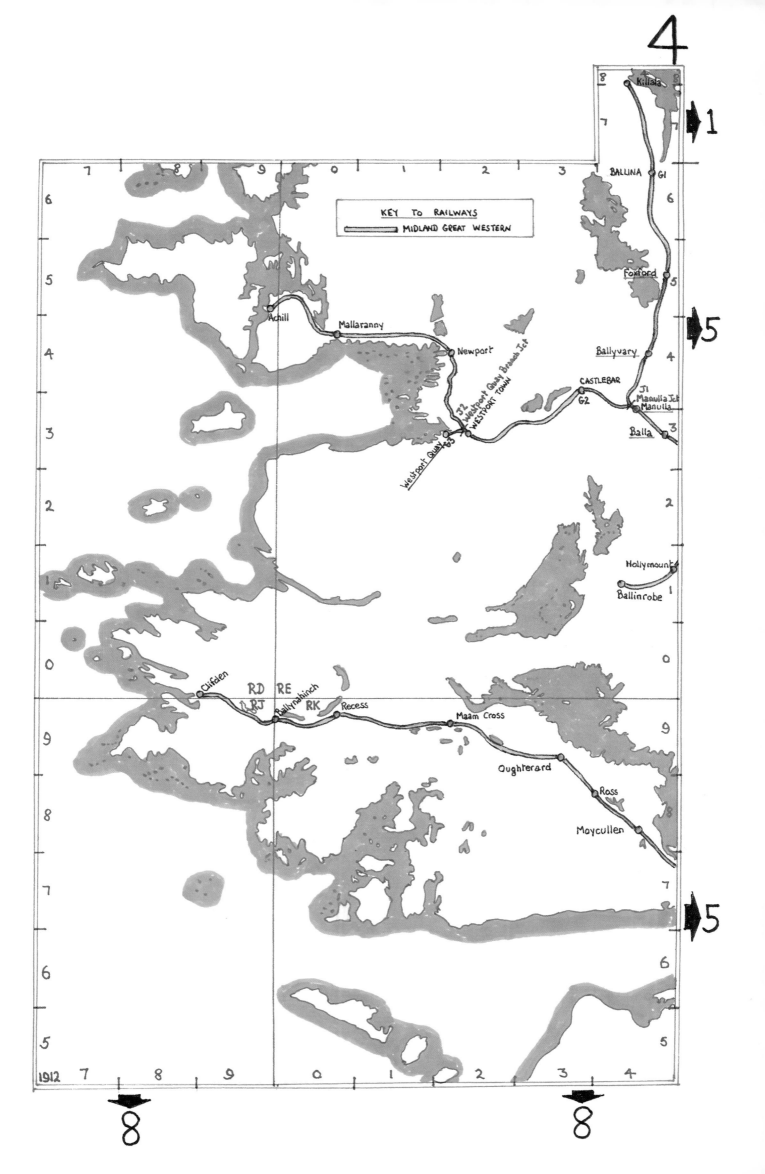

5 CLAREMORRIS ATHLONE + ATHENRY

RAILWAYS

No	Company	Gauge
R 1	GREAT SOUTHERN + WESTERN	5'3"
2	MIDLAND GREAT WESTERN	5'3"
3	CAVAN + LEITRIM	3'0"

STATIONS

No	Station	Ry	Ref
A 1	Annadale	3	SA26
2	Ardrahan	1	RK66
3	Arigna	3	SA16
4	ATHENRY	(1) 2	RK77
5	(ATHLONE)	1	SF29
6	Athlone	(1) 2	SF29
7	ATTYMON (JUNCTION)	2	RK87
8	Ballaghaderreen	2	RE84
9	BALLINASLOE	2	SF08
10	Ballindine	1	RE51
11	Ballinlough	2	RE82
12	Ballyduff	3	SA36
13	Ballyglunin	1	RK69
14	BALLYHAUNIS	2	RE72
15	Ballymoe	2	RE92
16	BALLYMOTE	2	RE86
17	Ballymurry	2	SA11
18	Banagher	1	SF26
19	Bekan	2	RE62
20	Belmont + Cloghan	1	SF37
21	Birr	1	SF25
22	BOYLE	2	SA05
23	CARRICK-ON-SHANNON	2	SA14
24	Carrowmore	1	RE77
25	Castlegrove	1	RE60
26	CASTLEREA	2	RE93
27	Charlestown	1	RE75
28	CLAREMORRIS	2	RE52
29	Cornabrone	3	SA26
30	Craughwell + Loughrea	1	RK76
31	Creagh	3	SA26
32	Curry	1	RE75
33	Dereen	3	SA34
34	Donamon	2	SA01
35	DROMOD	2	SA24
36	Deomod	3	SA24
37	Drumshambo	3	SA16
38	Drumsna	2	SA24
39	Dunsandle	2	RK87
40	Edmondstown	2	RE84
41	GALWAY	2	RK57
42	Gort	1	RK65
43	Hollymount	2	RE41
44	Island Road	2	RE94
45	Kilfree	2	RE95
46	Kiltimagh	1	RE54
47	Kiltoom	2	SA20
48	Kiltubrid	3	SA26
49	Knockcroghery	2	SA10
50	Loughrea	2	RK88
51	Milltown	1	RE61
52	Oranmore	2	RK67
53	ROSCOMMON	2	SA11
54	Swinford	1	RE65
55	Tuam	1	RE60
56	Tubbercurry	1	RE67
57	WOODLAWN	2	RK98

JUNCTIONS

No	Location	Ry	Ref
J 1	Kilfree	2	RE95
2	Claremorris North	21	RE52
2A	Claremorris Central	2	RE52
3	Claremorris South	21	RE52
4	Athenry West	21	RK77
5	Athenry East	21	RK77
6	Attymon	2	RK87
7	Athlone West	2	SF29
8	Athlone E	21	SF29

ENGINE SHEDS

No	Shed	Ry	Ref
E 1	Athlone	2	SF29

GOODS DEPOTS

No	Location	Ry	Ref
G 1	Claremorris	1	RE52
2	Tuam	1	RE60
3	Athenry	12	RK77
4	Ballinasloe	2	SF08
5	Athlone	1	SF29
6	Roscommon	2	SA11
7	Castlerea	2	RE93
8	Boyle	2	SA05
9	Ardrahan	1	RK66

NOTES:-
(1) Stations in brackets — opened post map date.
(2) Part of title in brackets indicates that portion of name added after map date.

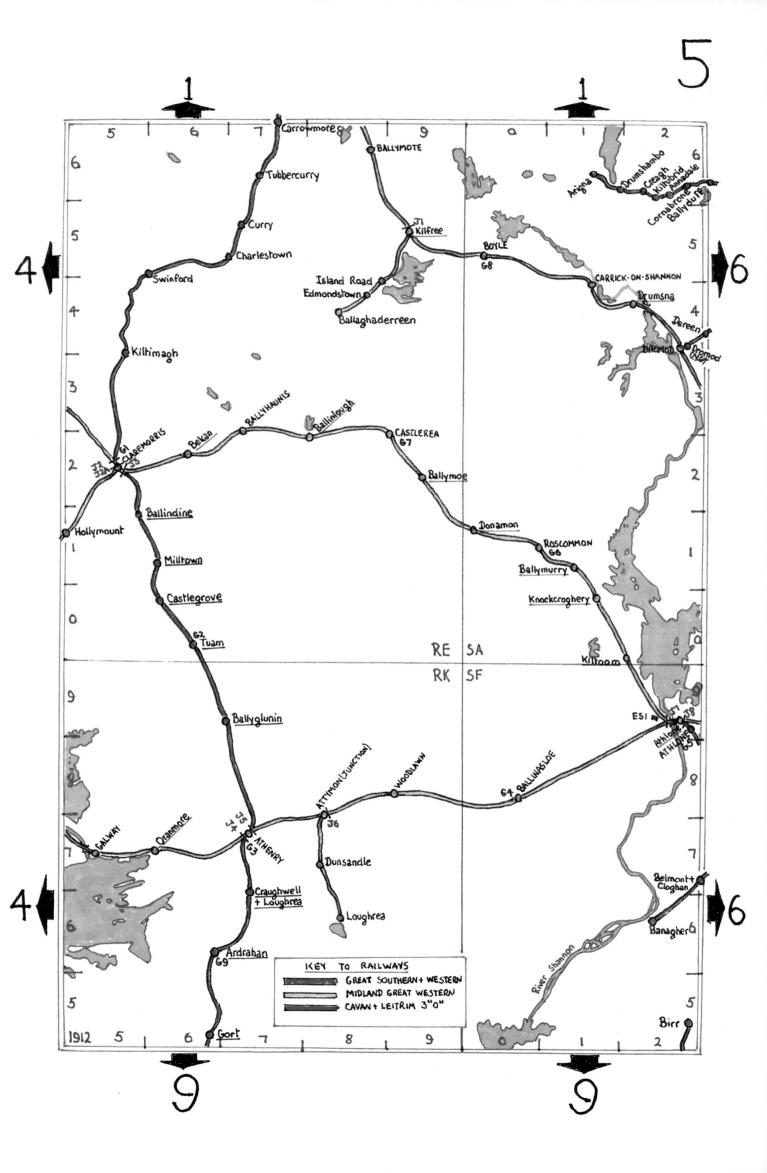

NAVAN + MARYBOROUGH

RAILWAYS

No.	Company	Gauge
R 1	MIDLAND GREAT WESTERN	5'3"
2	GREAT SOUTHERN + WESTERN	5'3"
3	GREAT NORTHERN (IRELAND)	5'3"
4	CAVAN + LEITRIM	3'0"

STATIONS

No.	Station	Ry	Ref
A 1	Adoon	4	SA35
2	Arva Road	1	SA55
3	Athboy	1	SA91
4	Ballinamore	4	SA36
5	Ballybeg	3	SB02
6	Ballyconnell	4	SA46
7	Ballycumber	2	SF48
8	Ballyduff	4	SA36
9	Ballyhaise	3	SA66
10	Ballyheady	4	SA46
11	Ballywillan	1	SA63
12	Bawnboy Rd + Templeport	4	SA46
13	Bective	1	SB01
14	Belmont + Cloghan	2	SF37
15	Belturbet	3	SA56
16	Belturbet	4	SA56
17	Carbury	1	SF98
18	Carrickmacross	3	SB05
19	CASTLETOWN	1	SF50
20	Cavan	13	SA65
21	Clara	1	SF48
22	CLARA	2	SF48
23	Clonhugh	1	SA61
24	Colbinstown	2	SG04
25	Cootehill	3	SA86
26	Crossdoney	1	SA55
27	Culloville	3	SB06
28	(CURRAGH) ✱	2	SF96
29	Dereen	4	SA34
30	DROICHEAD NUA §72	2	SG06
31	Drumhowna	1	SA54
32	Dulavin	2	SG05
33	Edenderry	1	SF88
34	EDGEWORTHSTOWN §64	1	SA42
35	Enfield	1	SG09
36	Essexford	3	SB15
37	Fenagh	4	SA35
38	Ferbane	2	SF37
39	Fernslock	1	SG09
40	Float	1	SA52
41	Garadice	4	SA36
42	Geashill	2	SF66
43	Gibbstown	1	SB02
44	Harristown	2	SG16
45	Hill of Down	1	SF89
46	Horseleap	1	SF58
47	Inny Junction	1	SA51
48	Kells	3	SA92
49	Kilcock	1	SG09
50	Kildangan	2	SF85
51	KILDARE	2	SF96
52	Killeshandra	1	SA55
53	Killucan	1	SA70
54	Killyran	4	SA46
55	Kilmainham Wood	1	SB04
56	Kilmessan	1	SB10
57	Kingscourt	1	SB04
58	Lawderdale	4	SA36
59	LONGFORD	1	SA32
60	MARYBOROUGH §77	2	SF65
61	MOATE	1	SF49
62	Mohill	4	SA34
63	Manasterven	2	SF86
64	MOSTRIM §34	1	SA42
65	Mountmellick	2	SF65
66	Moyvalley	1	SF99
67	MULLINGAR	1	SA60
68	Multyfarnham	1	SA61
69	Naas	2	SG17
70	Navan	1	SB01
71	Navan	3	SB01
72	NEWBRIDGE §30	2	SG06
73	Newtown Forbes	1	SA33
74	Nobber	1	SB03
75	Old Castle	3	SA73
76	PORTARLINGTON	2	SF75
77	PORTLAOISE §60	2	SF65
78	Redhills	3	SA66
79	Rockcorry	3	SA86
80	Rosharry	4	SA35
81	Sallins	2	SG17
82	Streamstown	1	SF59
83	Street + Rathowen	1	SA51
84	Tomkin Road	4	SA65
85	Trim	1	SB00
86	TULLAMORE	2	SF57
87	Virginia Road	3	SA83
88	Wilkinstown	1	SB02

GOODS

No.	Location	Ry	Ref
G 1	Portlaoise	2	SF65
2	Newbridge	2	SG06
3	Mullingar	1	SA60
4	Kingscourt	1	SB04
5	Longford	1	SA32
6	Curragh	2	SF96
7	Navan	3	SB02

JUNCTIONS

No.	Name/Location	Ry	Ref
J 1	Ballinamore	4	SA36
2	Ballyhaise	3	SA66
3	Crossdoney	1	SA55
4	Inny	1	SA51
5	Navan	13	SB01
6	Kilmessan	1	SB10
7	Mullingar	1	SA60
8	Streamstown	1	SF59
9	Banagher Branch	2	SF48
10	Clara South	12	SF58
11	Nesbitt	1	SF99
12	Portarlington	2	SF76
13	Cherryville	2	SF86
14	Sallins	2	SG17
15	Maryborough	2	SF64
16	Conniberry	2	SF64
17	Cavan	13	SA65

NOTES:

(1) Change of Name:-

§ Map date name - number gives reference to modern name

§ New name - number gives reference to map date name.

(2) ✱ At map date this station was a goods siding.

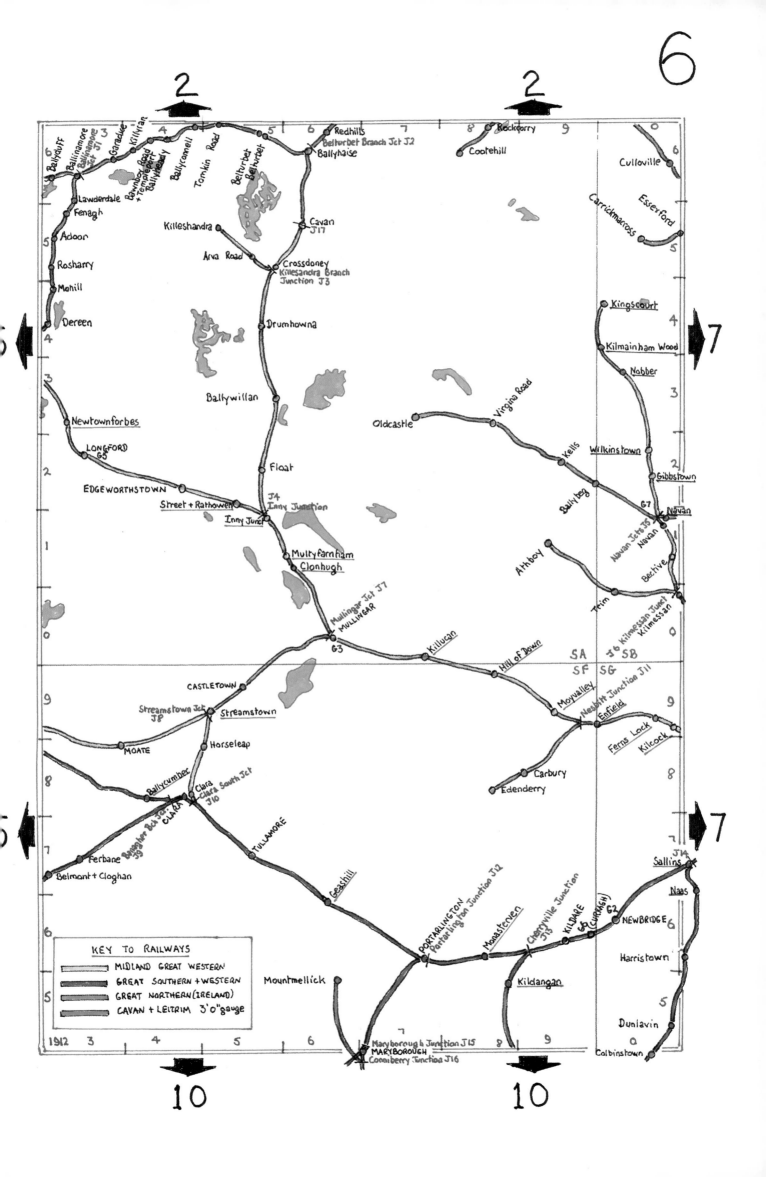

Ballyduff
Ballinamore
Ballinamore Jct J1
Garadice
Killyran
Bawnboy Road + Templeport
Ballyheady
Ballyconnell
Tomkin Road
Belturbet
Belturbet
Redhills
Belturbet Branch Jct J2
Ballyhaise
Rockcorry
Cootehill
Culloville
Carrickmacross
Esserford

Lawderdale
Fenagh
Adoon
Rosharry
Mohill
Dereen

Killeshandra
Cavan J17
Arva Road
Crossdoney
Killesandra Branch Junction J3
Drumhowna
Kingscourt
Kilmainham Wood
Nobber

Ballywillan

Newtownforbes
LONGFORD G5
EDGEWORTHSTOWN
Street + Rathowen
Float
J4
Inny Junction
Inny Junc
Oldcastle
Virginia Road
Kells
Ballybeg
Wilkinstown
Gibbstown
G7
Navan
Navan Jcts J5
Navan

Multyfarnham
Clonhugh
Athboy
Bective

Mullingar Jct J7
MULLINGAR
G3
Killucan
Hill of Down
Trim
J6 Kilmessan Junct
Kilmessan

SA   SB
SF   SG

CASTLETOWN
Streamstown Jct J8
Streamstown
Moyvalley
Nesbitt Junction J11
Enfield

MOATE
Horseleap
Ballycumber
Clara South Jct
Clara J10
Ferns Lock
Kilcock

Banagher Old Jct J9
CLARA
Carbury
Edenderry

Ferbane
Belmont + Cloghan
TULLAMORE
Geashill
Sallins J14
Naas

PORTARLINGTON
Portarlington Junction J12
Monasterevan
Cherryville Junction J13
KILDARE
G6 (CURRAGH)
G2
NEWBRIDGE
Harristown

Mountmellick
Kildangan
Dunlavin

1912

KEY TO RAILWAYS
MIDLAND GREAT WESTERN
GREAT SOUTHERN + WESTERN
GREAT NORTHERN (IRELAND)
CAVAN + LEITRIM 3'0" gauge

DUNDALK + DUBLIN

RAILWAYS

No	Company	Gauge
R 1	MIDLAND GREAT WESTERN	5
2	GREAT SOUTHERN + WESTERN	5
3	GREAT NORTHERN (IRELAND)	5
4	DUBLIN + SOUTH EASTERN	5
5	CITY OF DUBLIN JUNCTION	5
6	DUNDALK NEWRY + GREENORE	5
7	CITY of DUBLIN STEAM PACKET	5
8	LONDON + NORTH WESTERN	5
9	DUBLIN + BLESSINGTON	?
10	DUBLIN + LUCAN	3'6"
11	LUCAN, LEIXLIP + CELBRIDGE	3'0"

STATIONS

No	Station	Ry	Ref
A 1	Adavoyle	3	SB26
2	Amiens Street	5	3884
3	AMIENS STREET JUNCTION §27	3	3884
4	Ardee	3	SB14
5	ASHTOWN	1	SG38
6	Baldoyle + SUTTON §113A	3	SG48
7	BALBRIGGAN	3	SB14
8	Batterstown	1	SG19
9	(BAYSIDE)	3	SG48
10	Beauparc	3	SB12
11	Bective	1	SB01
12	Bellurgan	6	SB36
13	BLACKROCK	4	SG47
14	Blanchardstown	1	SG28
15	Blessington	9	SG16
16	BOOTERSTOWN	4	SG38
17	BRAY	4	SG47
18	Brittas	9	SG27
19	Broadstone	1	3684
20	Bush	6	SB35
21	Carlingford	6	SB36
22	Carrickmines	4	SG47
23	Castlebellingham	3	SB24
24	Clondalkin	2	SG28
25	CLONSILLA	1	SG28
26	Clontarf	3	3986
27	(CONNOLLY) §3	5	3884
28	Culloville	3	SB06
29	DALKEY	4	SG47
30	DONABATE	3	SG49
31	DROGHEDA	3	SB22
32	Dromin	3	SB24
33	Drumree	1	SB10

DUBLIN

No	Station	Ry	Ref
34	Amiens Street	3	3884
35	AMIENS ST. JCT §38	5	3884
36	Broadstone	1	3684
37	Clontarf	3	3986
38	(CONNOLLY) §35	5	3884
39	Harcourt Street	4	3781
40	(HEUSTON) §41	2	3463
41	KINGSBRIDGE §40	2	3463
42	LANSDOWNE ROAD	4	3981
43	Liffey Junction	1	3587
44	Milltown	4	3778
45	North Wall	7/8	3863
46	(PEARSE) §51	45	3882
47	Rathmines + Ranelagh	4	3779
48	TARA ST + George's Quay	5	3753
49	Templeogue	9	3687
50	Terenure	9	3678
51	WESTLAND ROW §46	45	3882
52	Duleek	3	SB22
52A	Dunboyne	1	SG29
53	DUNDALK	3	SB25
54	Dundalk Quay Street	6	SB25
55	Dundrum	4	SG37
56	(DUN LAOGHAIRE) §80	4	SG47
57	DUNLEER	3	SB23
58	Embankment	9	SG27
59	Essexford	3	SB15
60	Foxrock	4	SG47
61	GLENAGEARY	4	SG47
62	GORMANSTON	3	SB31
63	Greenore	6	SB46
64	GREYSTONES + Delganey	4	SG46
65	Harcourt Street	4	3781
66	(HARMONSTOWN)	3	SG38
67	Harristown	2	SG16
68	Hazlehatch + Celbridge	2	SG28
69	(HEUSTON) §79	2	3463
70	HOWTH	3	SG48
71	HOWTH JUNCTION	3	SG48
72	Inniskeen	3	SB15
73	(KILBARRACK)	3	SG49
74	Kilcock	1	SG09
75	KILCOOL	4	SG55
76	(KILLESTER)	3	SG48
77	KILLINEY	4	SG47
78	Kilmessan	1	SB10
79	KINGSBRIDGE §69	2	3463
80	KINGSTOWN §56	4	SG47
81	Lamb (The) *	9	SG26
82	LANSDOWNE ROAD	4	3981
83	LAYTOWN	3	SB32
84	LEIXLIP	1	SG28
85	Liffey Junction	1	3587
86	Lucan	1	SG28
87	Lucan	2	SG28
88	MALAHIDE	3	SG49
89	MAYNOOTH	1	SG18
90	Milltown	4	3778
91	(MOSNEY)	3	SB37
92	Mount Pleasant	3	SB26
93	Naas	2	SG16
94	Navan	1	SB01
95	Navan	3	SB01
96	Newcastle	4	SG55
97	North Wall	7/8	3863
98	Omeath	6	SB63
99	(PEARSE) §120	45	3882
100	PORTMARNOCK	3	SG49
101	Poulaphouca	9	SG11
102	RAHENY	3	SG48
103	Rathmines + Ranelagh	4	3779
104	RUSH + LUSK	3	SB40
105	Sallins	2	SG17
106	SALTHILL	4	SG47
107	SANDYCOVE	4	SG47
108	SEAPOINT +	4	SG47
109	(SHANKHILL)	4	SG46
110	Shankhill	4	SG47
111	SKERRIES	3	SB41
112	Straffan	2	SG17
113	Stillorgan	4	SG47
113A	SUTTON §6	3	SG48
114	SYDNEY PARK	4	SG38
115	TARA ST + George's Quay	5	3783
116	Tallaght	9	SG27
117	Templeogue	9	3678
118	Terenure	9	3678
119	The Lamb *	9	SG26
120	WESTLAND ROW §99	45	3882

GOODS

No	Name/Location	Ry	Ref
G 1	Kingsbridge	2	3483
2	Dublin (Lucan)	10	3483
3	Broadstone Cattle	1	3684
4			
5	North Wall	1	3883
6	North Wall	8	3883
7			
8	North Wall Cattle	8	3883
9	North Wall Cattle	2	3983
10	Harcourt Street	4	3781
11	Amien Street	3	3883
12	Sallins	2	SG17
13	Drogheda	3	SB22
14	Barrack Street	3	SB25
15	Lucan	10/11	SG28
16	Leixlip	11	SG28

SIDINGS

No.	Name/Owner	Ry	Ref
P 1	Cabra Cattle	2	3486
2	North City Mills	1	3686
3	Cunliffe Mills	1	3786
4	Dublin Warehousing Co	2	3984
5	East Wall	2	
6	Fitzsimon's	2	
7	Guinness'	2	3483
8	Inchimore (Co. Stores)	2	

TUNNELS

No	Name	Ry	Ref
T 1	Phoenix Park	2	3483
2	Dalkey	4	SG47
3	Bray Head	4	SG46
4	Cross Guns	1	3687

JUNCTIONS

No	Name/Location	Ry	Ref
J 1	Liffey	1	3588
2	Cabra Sidings	2	3587
3	City Mills	1	3587
4	Drumcondra	2	3587
5	Glasnevin	12	3687
6	Newcomen Bridge	15	3885
7	North Strand Road	2	3885
8	East Wall	3	3885
9	Church Road North	23	3885
10	Church Road South	28	3885
11	Dublin Warehouse	2	3984
12	Sheriff Street	17	3884
13	Amiens Street	25	3885
14	Cattle Branch	1	3685
15	Island Bridge	2	3483
16	Clonsilla	1	SG28
17	Sallins	2	SG17
18	Shankhill	4	SG47
19	Navan	13	SB01
20	Dromin	3	SB24
21	Windmill Road	36	SB25
22	Dundalk West	3	SB25
23	Inniskeen	3	SB15
24	Greenore	6	SB45
25	Drogheda	3	SB22
26	Howth	3	SG48
27	Sutton	3	SG48
28	Dundalk Station	3	SB25
29	Kilmessan	1	SB00
30	West Street	12	3885

NOTES:

(1) Name changes:
   § Map date } Number indicates refence to the other name
   § Modern }

(2) Dublin stations:- Indexed under Dublin and the individual station name

(3) References Dublin inset are four figure numbers. Map not to scale

(4) * Other double index station

(5) + Now known as: MONKSTOWN + SEAPOINT

(6) 5 Standard gauge - 5'3"

(7) ? Gauge not known

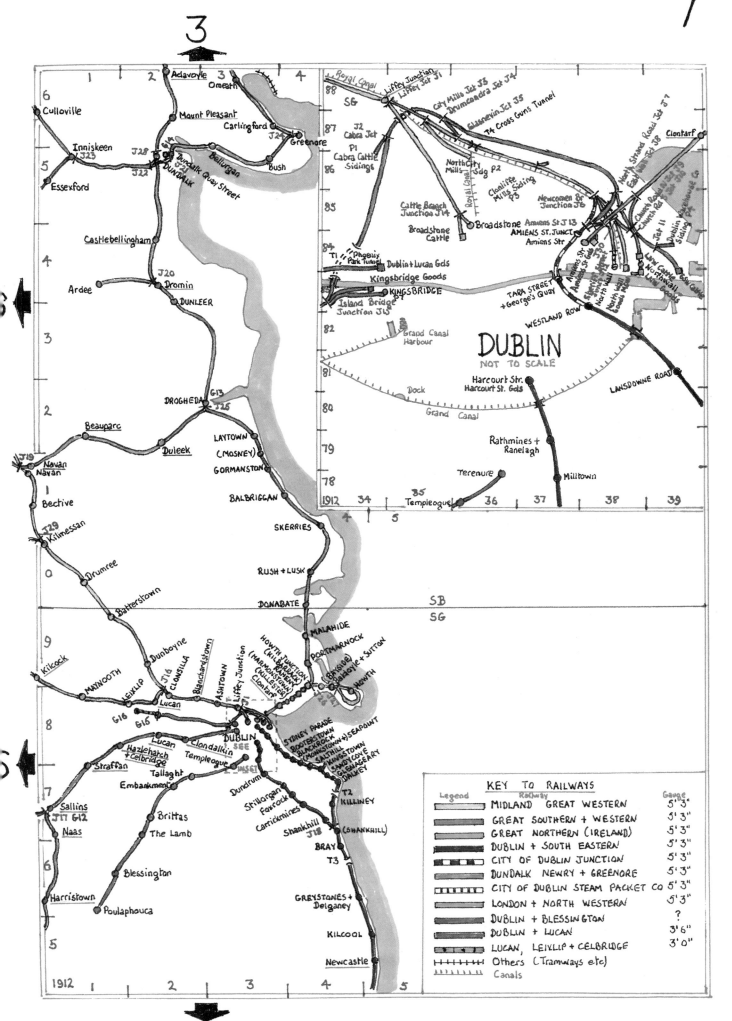

KILRUSH + TRALEE

RAILWAYS

No	Company	Gauge
R1	GREAT SOUTHERN + WESTERN	S
2	WEST CLARE	3'0"
3	TRALEE + DINGLE	3'0"
4	LISTOWEL + BALLYBUNION †	Mono Rail

STATIONS

No	Name	Ry	Ref
A 1	Ardfert *	1	RP07
2	Abbeydorney	1	RP07
3	Abbeyfeale	1	RP37
4	Ardagh	1	RP58
5	Aughacasla	3	RO86
6	Aunascaul	3	RO85
7	Ballineesteenig	3	RO75
8	Ballinasare	3	RO85
9	Ballybrack	1	RP14
10	Ballybunion †	4	RP09
11	Barnagh	1	RP48
12	Basin (Tralee) *	3	RP06
13	Blackweir	2	RK11
14	Blennerville *	3	RP06
15	Cahirciveen	1	RO62
16	Caragh Lake	1	RO94
17	Castlegregory	3	RO86
18	Castlegregory Junction	3	RO96
19	Castleisland	1	RP26
20	Castlemaine	1	RP05
21	Corrofin	2	RK53
22	Craggaknock	2	RK22
23	Curraheen	3	RO96
24	Deelis	3	RO86
25	Derrymore	3	RO96
26	Devon Road	1	RP37
27	Dingle	3	RO65
28	Dooks	1	RO94
29	Doonbeg	2	RK11
30	Emalough	3	RO85
31	Ennistymon	2	RK33
32	FARRANFORE	1	RP15
33	Fenit	1	RO96
34	Foynes	1	RK40
35	Garrynadur	3	RO75
36	Glenbeigh	1	RO84
37	Glenmore	3	RO85
38	Glounagalt Bridge	3	RO95
39	Gortatlea *	1	RP16
40	Headford	1	RP23
41	Kells	1	RO73
42	Kilfenora	1	RO96
43	Kilkee	2	RK11
44	KILLARNEY	1	RP14
45	Killorglin	1	RO94
46	Kilmorna	1	RP28
47	Kilmurry	2	RK22
48	Kilrush	2	RK20
49	Lahinch	2	RK33
50	Liselton	† 4	RP18
51	Lispole	3	RO75
52	Listowel	1	RP28
53	Listowel	† 4	RP28
54	Lixnaw	1	RP18
55	Loo Bridge	1	RP23
56	Millstreet	1	RP44
57	Milltown	1	RP05
58	Milltown Malbay	2	RK23
59	Molahiffe	1	RP15
60	Mountain Stage	1	RO83
61	Moyasta Junction	2	RK11
62	Newcastle	1	RP58
63	Quilty	2	RK22
64	RATHMORE	1	RP34
65	Spa *	1	RP06
66	TRALEE *	1	RP06
67	Tralee *	3	RP06
68	Valentia Harbour	1	RO26
69	Willbrook	2	RK43

GOODS

No	Name/Location	Ry	Ref
G1	Killarney	1	RP14
2	Tralee *	13	RP06
3	Fenit Pier	1	RO96
4	Foynes Pier	1	RK40
5	Cappa Pier, Kilrush	2	RK20

TUNNELS

No	Name/Location	Ry	Ref
T1	Barnagh	1	RP48

JUNCTIONS

No	Name/Location	Ry	Ref
J1	Moyasta	2	RK11
2	Tralee *	1	RP06
3	Castleisland Branch *	1	RP16
4	Farranfore	1	RP15
5	Castlegregory Branch	3	RO96
6	Headford	1	RP23
7	Newcastle	1	RP58

NOTES:

(1) The strange layout at Tralee is shown in detail on the inset. It is not known if both stations were used for passengers. Items in the gazetteer also on Inset are marked *. Exchange sidings at Tralee appear to have existed.

(2) † Elevated Monorail - The first in the world !?

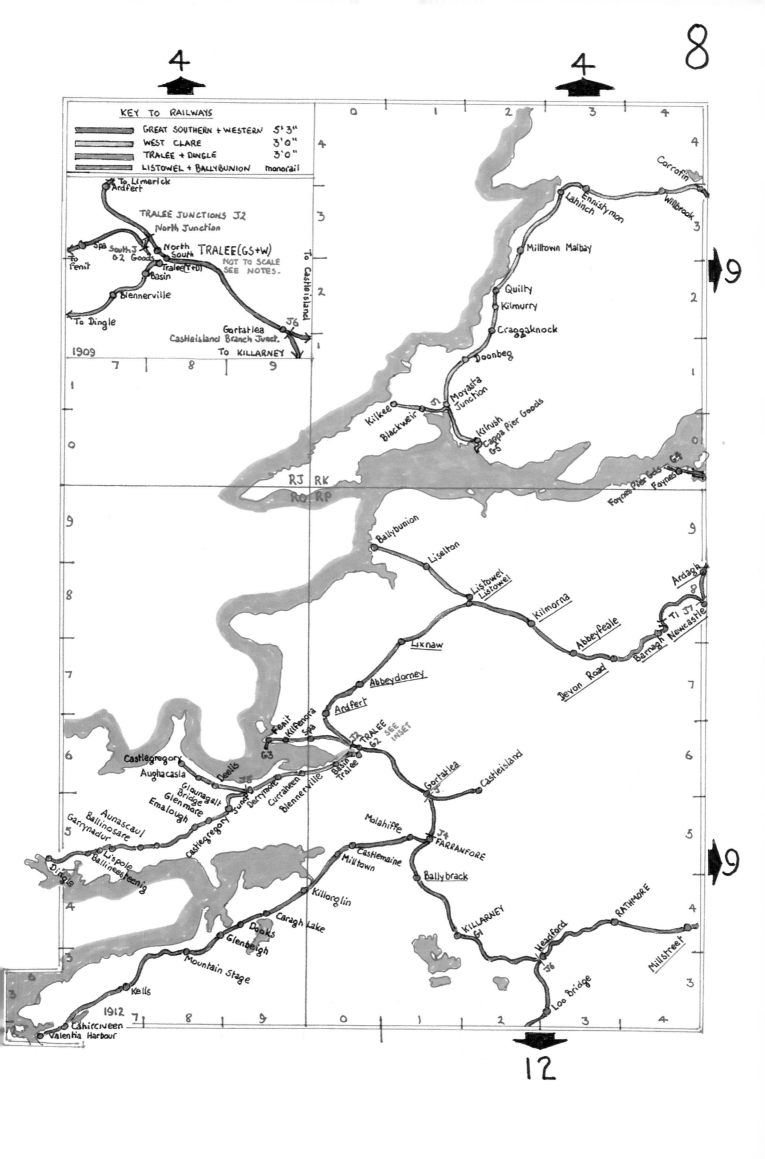

KEY TO RAILWAYS

GREAT SOUTHERN + WESTERN   5'3"
WEST CLARE   3'0"
TRALEE + DINGLE   3'0"
LISTOWEL + BALLYBUNION   monorail

TRALEE JUNCTIONS J2
North Junction

To Limerick
Ardfert
Spa South J. North TRALEE(GS+W)
To   J2 Goods South NOT TO SCALE
Fenit   Tralee(T+D) SEE NOTES.
Basin
Blennerville
To Dingle
1909   Gortatlea   J6
              Castleisland Branch Junct.
To Castleisland
                    TO KILLARNEY

Corrofin
Ennistymon
Lahinch
Willbrook
Milltown Malbay
Quilty
Kilmurry
Craggaknock
Doonbeg
Moyasta Junction
Kilkee   J1
Blackweir
Kilrush Cappa Pier Goods
         GS
RJ RK
RO RP
Faynes Pier Gds   G4
              Faynes
Ballybunion
Liselton
Listowel
Listowel
Kilmorna
Abbeyfeale
Lixnaw
Devon Road   Barnagh Newcastle
Abbeydorney   TI J7
Ardfert   Ardagh
Fenit Kilfenora
       Spa
       G3
Castlegregory
Aughacasla   Deelis
Glounagalt Derrymore J5 Basin
Bridge   Curraheen J2 Tralee TRALEE
Glenmore   Blennerville G2 SEE
Emalough   INSET
Aunascaul   Gortatlea Castleisland
Ballinosare   J3
Garrynadur
Lispole   Malahiffe
Ballinasteenig   J4
Dingle   Castlemaine FARRANFORE
             Milltown   Ballybrack
             Killorglin
Caragh Lake   KILLARNEY Headford RATHMORE
Dooks   G1   Millstreet
Glenbeigh
Mountain Stage   J6
                        Loo Bridge
Kells
1912
Cahirciveen
Valentia Harbour

LIMERICK + MALLOW

RAILWAYS

No.	Company	Gauge
R1	GREAT SOUTHERN + WESTERN†	5'3"
2	WEST CLARE	3'0"
3	CORK + MUSKERRY	3'0"

STATION

No	Station	Ry	Ref
A1	Ardare	1	RP69
2	Ardagh	1	RP58
3	Ardmayle	1	SL29
4	Ardsollus + Quin	1	RK62
5	Askeaton	1	RK50
6	Ballindangan	1	RP95
7	Ballingrane	1	RP59
8	Ballycar + Newmarket	1	RK61
9	Ballyduff	1	SL14
10	Ballyhooly	1	RP94
11	Bansha	1	SL18
12	BANTEER	1	RP54
13	BIRDHILL	1	RK91
14	Boher	1	RK90
15	Bruree	1	RP77
16	Buttevant	1	RP75
17	CAHIR	1	SL27
18	Cashel	1	SL29
19	Castleconnell	1	RK81
20	Castletownroche	1	RP84
21	CHARLEVILLE §	1	RP77
22	Clare Castle	1	RK52
23	Clondulane	1	SL04
24	CLOUGHJORDAN	1	SF13
25	Corrofin	2	RK53
26	Cratloe	1	RK61
27	Croom	1	RP79
28	Crusheen	1	RK63
29	Donoughmore	3	RP73
30	Dromkeen	1	RP99
31	Dundrum	1	SL19
32	Emly	1	RP98
33	Ennis	1	RK52
34	Ennis	2	RK52
35	Fermoy	1	SL04
36	Firmount	3	RP73
37	Foynes	1	RK40
38	Glanworth	1	RP95
39	Goold's Cross	1	SL29
40	Kanturk	1	RP55
41	Killaloe	1	RK92
42	Killanan	1	RK80
43	Kilmallock	1	RP87
44	Knockane	3	RP73
45	Knocklong	1	RP97
46	LIMERICK	1	RK70
47	LIMERICK JUNCTION	1	SL08
48	Lismore	1	SL24
49	Lisnagry	1	RK80
50	Lombardstown	1	RP64
51	Longpavement	1	RK70
52	MALLOW	1	RP74
53	Mitchelstown	1	SL06
54	Mourne Abbey	1	RP74
55	NENAGH	1	SF03
56	Newcastle	1	RP58
57	Newmarket	1	RP55
58	Oola	1	SL09
59	Pallas	1	RP99
60	Patrick's Well	1	RK70
61	Rathduff	1	RP83
62	Rathkeale	1	RP59
63	(RATHLUIRIC) §	1	RP77
64	Rosstemple	1	RP78
65	Ruan	2	RK53
66	Shallee	1	SF02
67	Sixmilebridge	1	RK61
68	Tallow Road	1	SL14
69	THURLES	1	SF30
70	TIPPERARY	1	SL09
71	Tubber	1	RK64

GOODS

No	Name/Location	Ry	Ref
G1	Ennis	1	RK52
2	Limerick	1	RK70
3	Foynes Pier	1	RK40
4	Charleville	1	RP77
5	Buttevant	1	RP75
6	Mallow	1	RP74
7	Tipperary	1	SL09
8	Cahir	1	SL27
9	Limerick Junction	1	SL08
10	Thurles	1	SF30
11	Nenagh	1	SF03
12	Killaloe Pier	1	RK92

JUNCTIONS

No	Name/Location	Ry	Ref
J1	Newmarket Branch	1	RP54
2	Mallow South	1	RP74
3	Mallow North	1	RP74
4	Mitchelstown Branch	1	SL04
5	Charleville	1	RP77
6	Newcastle	1	RP58
7	Foynes	1	RP59
8	Patrick's Well	1	RP79
9	Station Jcts (Limerick)	1	RK70
10	Killanan	1	RK80
11	Limerick Jct North	1	SL08
12	Limerick Jct South	1	SL08
13	Cashel Branch	1	SL29
14	Killaloe Branch	1	RK91
15	Thurles	1	SF30

NOTES:

(1) Change of name:-
§ Map date name
§ Modern name

(2) † 5'3" is standard gauge in Ireland

(3) Thurles is further East than shown

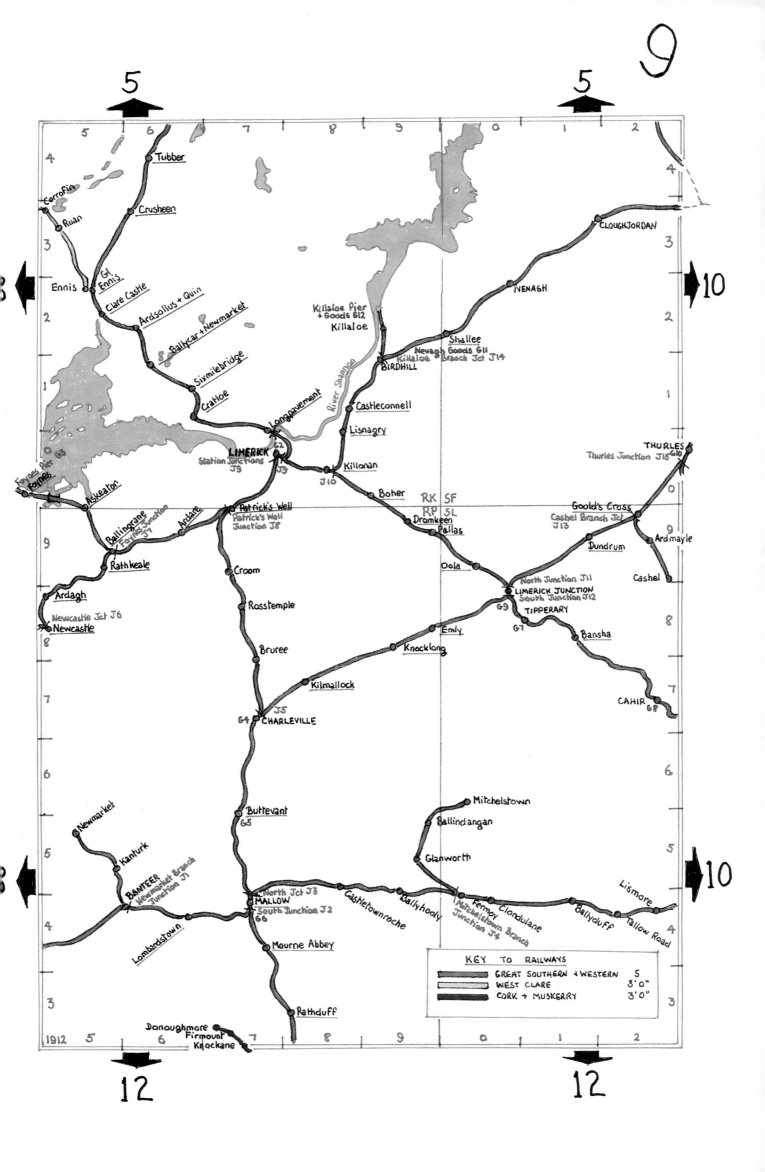

KILKENNY + WATERFORD

RAILWAYS

No.	Company
R 1	GREAT SOUTHERN + WESTERN (GSW)
2	DUBLIN + SOUTH EASTERN (DSE)
3	GSW + DSE JOINT
4	WATERFORD + TRAMORE

STATIONS

No.	Station	Ry	Ref
A 1	Abbeykix	1	SF63
2	ATHY	1	SF94
3	Attanagh	1	SF62
4	BAGENALSTOWN §44	1	SF91
5	BALLYBROPHY	1	SF43
6	BALLYCULLANE	1	SM06
7	Ballyhale	1	SL78
8	Ballyragget	1	SF62
9	Ballywilliam	1	SM08
10	Baltinglass	1	SG03
11	Bennettsbridge	1	SF70
12	Barris	1	SF90
13	CAMPILE	1	SL96
14	Cappagh	1	SL44
15	Cappaquin	1	SL34
16	CARLOW	1	SF92
17	CARRICK-ON-SUIR	1	SL67
18	Carroll's Cross	1	SL65
19	Cashel	1	SL39
20	CLONMEL	1	SL47
21	Colbinstown	1	SG04
22	Dungarvan	1	SL44
23	Durrow	1	SL54
24	Farranalleer	1	SL49
25	Fethard	1	SL48
26	Fiddown	1	SL67
27	Glenmore + Aylwardstown	1	SL87
28	Goresbridge	1	SF90
29	Gowran	1	SF80
30	Grange	1	SL76
31	Grange Con	1	SG04
32	Horse + Jockey	1	SF30
33	KILKENNY	1	SF70
34	Kilmacow	1	SL87
35	Kilmacthomas	1	SL65
36	Kilmeaden	1	SL76
37	Kilsheelan	1	SL57
38	Laffan's Bridge	1	SL49
39	Lisduff	1	SF42
40	Mageney	1	SF93
41	MARYBOROUGH §48	1	SF64
42	Milford	1	SF92
43	Mountrath	1	SF54
44	(MUINE BHEAG) §4	1	SF91
45	Mullinavat	1	SL77
46	New Ross	2	SL97
47	Palace East	2	SM08
48	(PORTLAOISE) §41	1	SF64
49	Rathgarogue	2	SM08
50	Rathvilly	1	SG03
51	ROSCREA	1	SF34
52	TEMPLEMORE	1	SF32
53	The Manor, Waterford ✳	4	SL86
54	THOMASTOWN	1	SL89
55	THURLES	1	SF30
56	Tramore	4	SL85
57	Tullow	1	SG02
58	WATERFORD North ✳	1	SL86
59	Waterford, The Manor ✳	4	SL85
60	WELLINGTON BRIDGE	1	SM06
61	Youghal	1	SL32

TUNNELS

No.	Name/Location	Ry	Ref
T 1	Snowhill	1	SL86

GOODS

No.	Name/Location	Ry	Ref
G 1	Waterford ✳ †	1	SL86
2	New Ross	1	SL97
3	Bennettsbridge	1	SF70
4	Kilkenny	1	SF70
5	Carlow	1	SF92
6	Maryborough	1	SF64

7	Thurles	1	SF30
8	Clonmel	1	SL47
9	Lisduff	1	SF42
10	Youghal	1	SL32

JUNCTIONS

No.	Name/Location		Ry	Ref
J 1	Abbey	✳	123	SL85
2	Joint Line	✳	13	SL85
3	New Wharf	✳	1	SL85
4	Suir Bridge	✳	1	SL85
5	New Rath	✳	1	SL85
6	Palace East		21	SM08
7	Kilkenny		1	SF70
8	Clonmel		1	SL47
9	Thurles		1	SF30
10	Birr Branch		1	SF34
11	Conniberry		1	SF64
12	Maryborough		1	SF64
13	Bagenalstown		1	SF91
14	Ballybrophy		1	SF43

NOTES:

(1) Name changes:

§ Map date } Number after symbol gives reference to
§ Modern } the other name.

(2) † Two Goods stations (see inset).

(3) ✳ Items shown in inset map.

9 11

KEY TO RAILWAYS
GREAT SOUTHERN + WESTERN (GSW)
DUBLIN + SOUTH EASTERN (DSE)
GSW + DSE JOINT
WATERFORD + TRAMORE

Birr Branch Jct J10
ROSCREA
Mountrath
BALLYBROPHY J14
G9 Lisduff
TEMPLEMORE
THURLES Thurles Jct J9 G7
Horse + Jockey
Laffan's Bridge
Cashel
Farranalleen
Fethard
Kilsheelan
CARRICK-ON-SUIR
CLONMEL Clonmel Jct J8 G8
Cappoquin
Cappagh
Dungarvan
Durrow
Youghal G10
River Blackwater
1912

MARYBOROUGH
Maryborough Jct J12
Conniberry Jct J11
Abbeyleix
Attanagh
Ballyragget
KILKENNY Kilkenny Jct J7 G4
Gowran
G3 Bennettsbridge
THOMASTOWN
Ballyhale
Mullinavat
Kilmacow
Fiddown
Grange
River Suir
Kilmacthomas
Carroll's Cross
Kilmeadan
Tramore
River Suir

Colbinstown
Grange Con
Baltinglass
Rathvilly
ATHY
Mageney
CARLOW G5
Milford
Tullow
BAGENALSTOWN J13
Goresbridge
Barris
SF SG
SL SM
Ballywilliam
New Ross G2
Rathgarogue
Palace East Jct J6
Glenmore + Aylwardstown
WATERFORD DSE (WEST)
T1
CAMPILE
BALLYCULLANE
WELLINGTON BRIDGE
Waterford The Manor
River Barrow

1913
SL86
New Rath Junct. J5
Suir Bridge Jct J4
Suir Bridge Goods IA
WATERFORD NORTH
New Wharf Jct J3
Joint Line Jct J2
Abbey Junction J1
Waterford Goods CI
Waterford The Manor
River Suir

WICKLOW, WEXFORD + ROSSLARE

RAILWAYS

No	Company
R1	GREAT SOUTHERN + WESTERN
2	DUBLIN + SOUTH EASTERN

STATIONS

No	Station	Ry	Ref
A1	ARKLOW	2	SG42
2	Aughrim	2	SG32
3	(AVOCA) §	2	SG43
4	Ballinglen	2	SG22
5	Baltinglass	1	SG03
6	BRIDGETOWN	1	SM26
7	Camolin	2	SG20
8	Chapel	2	SM18
9	Duncormick	1	SM16
10	Edermine Ferry	2	SM18
11	ENNISCORTHY	2	SM19
12	Ferns	2	SM29
13	Glenealy	2	SG44
14	GOREY	2	SG31
15	Inch	2	SG41
16	Killinick	1	SM26
17	Killurin	2	SM17
18	Kilrane	1	SM36
19	Macmine	2	SM18
20	OVOCA §	2	SG43
21	RATHDRUM	2	SG43
22	Rathnew	2	SG44
23	Rathwilly	1	SG03
24	(ROSSLARE HARBOUR MAINLAND)	1	SM36
25	ROSSLARE HARBOUR PIER	1	SM36
26	ROSSLARE STRAND	1	SM36
27	Shillelagh	2	SG21
28	Tinahely	2	SG22
29	Tullow	1	SG02
30	WEXFORD	2	SM27
31	Wexford South	1	SM27
32	WICKLOW	2	SG54
33	Woodenbridge	2	SG42

SHEDS

No	Location	Ry	Ref
E1	Rosslare Harbour	1	SM36

GOODS

No	Location	Ry	Ref
G1	Wexford	2	SM27
2	Enniscorthy	2	SM19
3	Arklow	2	SG42
4	Rosslare Harbour	1	SM36

JUNCTIONS

No	Name/Location	Ry	Ref
J1	Felthouse	1	SM26
2	Killinick	1	SM26
3	Strand	1	SM36
4	GSW/DSE Wexford	12	SM27
5	Macmine	2	SM18
6	Woodenbridge	2	SG42

TUNNELS

No	Name/Location	Ry	Ref
T1	Ferrycarrig	2	SM27
2	Killurin	2	SM17
3	Enniscorthy	2	SM19
4	Rathdrum	2	SG43

NOTES:

(1) Gauge: Both railways shown on this map are standard gauge 5'3"

(2) Change of name
§ Map name
§ Modern name possible mis-spelling

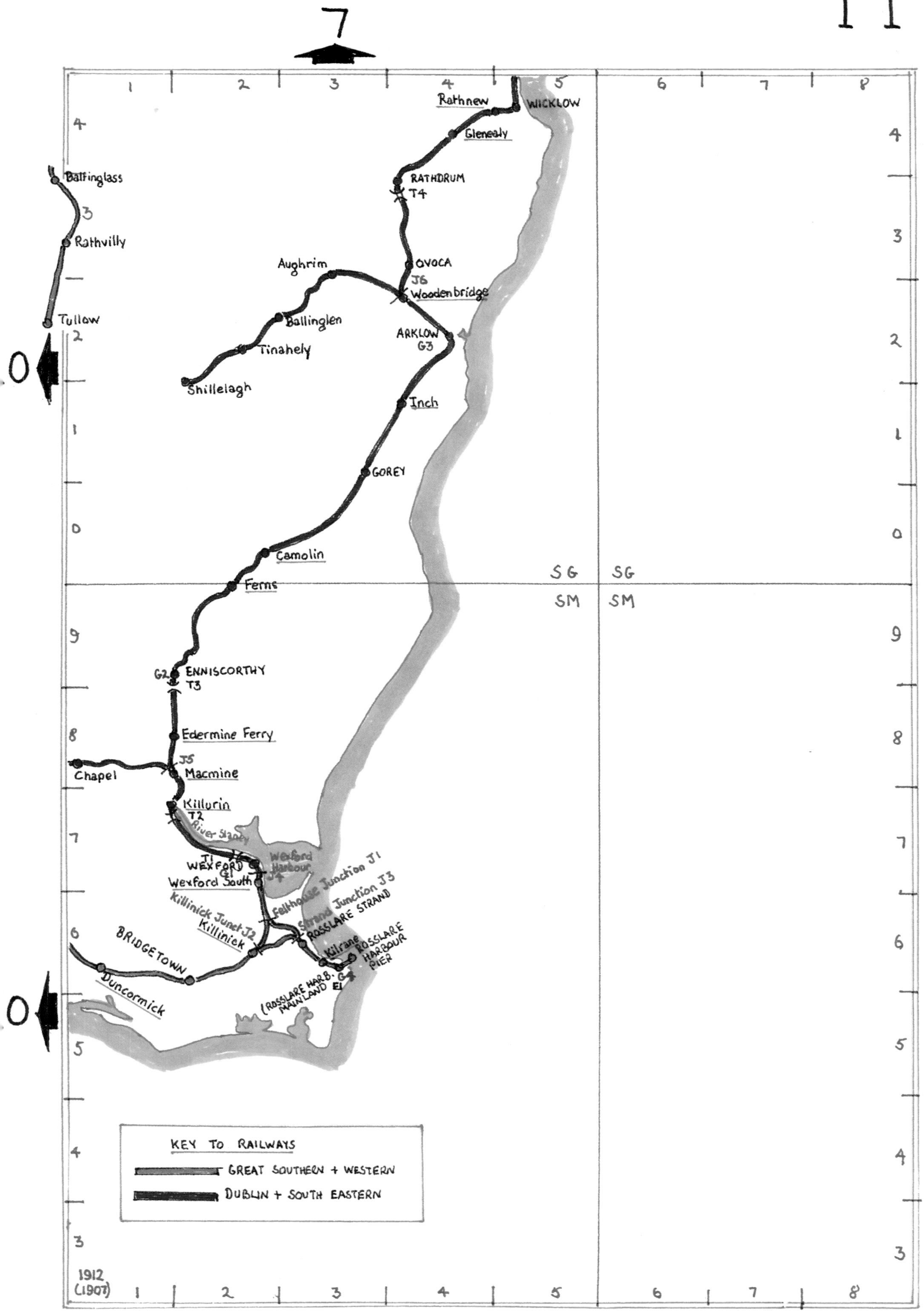

Baltinglass

Rathvilly

Tullow

0

Ballinglass

Rathvilly

Rathnew

Glenealy

RATHDRUM
T4

WICKLOW

OVOCA
J6
Woodenbridge

Aughrim

Ballinglen

Tinahely

ARKLOW
G3

Shillelagh

Inch

GOREY

Camolin

Ferns

SG | SG
SM | SM

G2 ENNISCORTHY
T3

Edermine Ferry

Chapel

J5

Macmine

Killurin
T2

River Slaney

T1
WEXFORD
G4

Wexford South

Killinick Junct J2

Killinick

BRIDGETOWN

Duncormick

Wexford
Harbour

Felthouse Junction J1

Strand Junction J3
ROSSLARE STRAND

Kilrane

ROSSLARE
HARBOUR
PIER

(ROSSLARE HARB. G.
MAINLAND E.)

0

KEY TO RAILWAYS

———————— GREAT SOUTHERN + WESTERN

———————— DUBLIN + SOUTH EASTERN

1912
(1907)

CORK + BALTIMORE

NOTES:
(1) † Gauge: S = Standard - 5'3"
(2) Change of name:
   § Mapdale } number gives ref.
   § Modern } to other name in the gazetteer
(3) * Gazetteer items shown on the inset (May also be on the main map).
(4) Cork stations are indexed both under Cork and individual names.

RAILWAYS

No	Company	† Gauge	Ry Ref
R1	GREAT SOUTHERN + WESTERN	S	
2	CORK BANDON + SOUTH COAST	S	
3	CORK + MACROOM	S	
4	CORK CITY RAILWAYS	S	
5	CORK BLACKROCK + PASSAGE	3'0"	
6	CORK + MUSKERRY	3'0"	
7	SCHULL + SKIBBEREEN	3'0"	
8	TIMOLEAGUE + COURTMACSHERRY	S	

STATIONS

No	Name		Ry	Ref
A1	Albert Street	*	5	RP92
2	Albert Quay	*	2	RP92
3	Ballincollig		3	RP82
4	Ballinhassig		2	RP81
5	Ballinscarthy		2	RU69
6	Ballydehob		7	RU28
7	Ballymartle		2	RP80
8	Ballyneen Enniskean		2	RP50
9	Baltimore		2	RU27
10	Bandon		2	RP70
11	Blackrock		5	RP92
12	Blarney		1	RP82
13	Blarney		6	RP82
14	Bantry		2	RU29
15	Burnt Mill		6	RP72
16	Capwell			
17	Carrigaline		5	
18	CARRIGALOE		5	
19	Carrigrohane		S	
20	Carrigtohill		S	
21	Church Cross		S	
22	Cloghroe		6	RP72
23	Clonakilty		2	RU59
24	Clonakility Junction		2	RP60
26	Coachford		6	RP62
	Coachford Junction		6	RP82
27	(COBH) §77		1	SLO1
28	(COBH JUNCTION) §78		1	SLO2

CORK

29	Albert Quay	*	2	RP92
30	Albert Street	*	3	RP82
31	Capwell	*	2	RP81
32	GLANMIRE ROAD	*	1	RP92
33	Western Road	*	6	RP82
34	Courtmacsherry		8	RU79
35	Creagh		2	RP71
36	Crookstown Road		3	RP61
37	Crosshaven		5	SLO1
38	Desert		2	RP60
39	Donoughmore		6	RP73
40	Dooniskey		3	RP61
41	Drimoleague		2	RU39
42	Dripsey		6	RP72
43	Dunkettle	*	3	RP92
44	Dunmanway		5	RP91
45	Durrus Road		1	SLO1
46	Farrangalway		6	RP82
47	Firmount		1	SLO2
48	FOTA		7	RU28
49	Fox's Bri		6	RP72
50	GLANMIRE ROAD		2	RU59
51	Glenbrook		2	RP60
52	Gurteen		6	RP62
53	Healy's Bridge		6	RP82
54	Hollyhill		1	SLO1
55	Kenmare		1	SLO2
56	Kilcoe			
57	Kilcrea		2	RP92
58	Kilgarvan		5	RP92
59	Killeagh		3	RP92
60	Kilmurry		1	RP92
61	Kilumney		6	RP82
62	Kinsale		8	RU79
63	Kinsale Junction		2	RU38
64	Knockane		3	RP61
65	Knockbue		5	SLO1
66	Lee Mount		2	RP60
67	LITTLE ISLAND		6	RP73
68	Macroom		3	RP61
69	Madore		2	RU39
70	Midleton		6	RP72
71	Mogeely		1	RP92
72	Monkstown		2	RP40
73	Morley's Bridge		2	RU29
74	Newcourt		2	RP80
75	Passage		6	RP73
76	Peake		1	SLO2
77	QUEENSTOWN §27		6	RP72
78	QUEENSTOWN JUNCTION §28		1	SLO2
79	Raffeen		5	RP91
80	Rochestown		6	RP72
81	Rushbrooke		6	RP82
82	St. Anne's		1	RP12
83	Schull		7	RU28
84	Skeaf		3	RP71
85	Skibbereen		1	RP22
86	Skibbereen		7	SL22
87	Timoleague		5	RP72
88	Tivoli		3	RP71
89	Tower Bridge		2	RP80
90	Upton + Inishannon		2	RP71
91	Victoria		6	RP82
92	Waterfall		2	RP49
93	Western Road	*	6	RP87
94	Woodlands		7	RU18
95	Youghal		1	SL32
96			2	RU39
97			1	SLO2

GOODS

No	Name/Location		Ry	Ref
G1	Kilbarry Cattle		5	RP91
2	Rathpeacon		7	RP38
3	Albert Quay	*	5	RP91
4	Western Road	*	6	RP67
5	Albert Street	*	1	SLO1
6	Youghal		1	SLO2

SIDINGS

No	Name/Co/Location		Ry	Ref
S1	Penrose Quay	*	1	SLO1
2	Anderson's Quay	*	6	RP82
3	Lapp's Quay		7	RU18
4	Victoria Quay	*	8	RU79

TUNNELS

No	Name		Ry	Ref
T1	Cork	*	1	RP92

JUNCTIONS

No	Name/Location		Ry	Ref
P1	CORK CITY		6	RP82
2	Penrose Quay	*	2	RP81
3	Anderson's Quay	*	7	RU18
4	Lapp's Quay	*	1	SL32
5	Victoria Quay		24	RP92
6	Coachford Junction		6	RP82
7	St. Anne's		6	RP82
8	Queenstown Junction		1	SLO1
9	Kinsale Junction		2	RP71
10	Clonakilty		2	RP60
11	Ballinscarthy		28	RU69
12	Drimoleague		2	RU39
13	Albert Quay	*	42	RP92

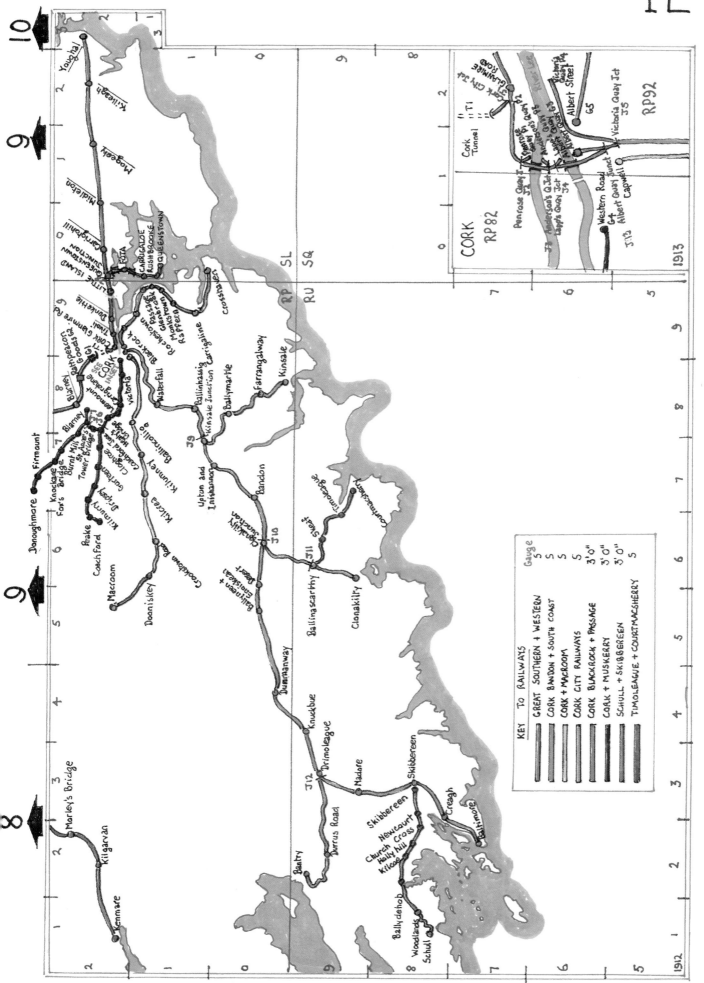

12

KEY TO RAILWAYS

		Gauge
GREAT SOUTHERN + WESTERN		5
CORK BANDON + SOUTH COAST		5
CORK + MACROOM		5
CORK CITY RAILWAYS		5
CORK BLACKROCK + PASSAGE		3'0"
CORK + MUSKERRY		3'0"
SCHULL + SKIBBEREEN		3'0"
TIMOLEAGUE + COURTMACSHERRY		5

13

THURSO, WICK + THE MOUND

RAILWAYS

No.	Company	
R 1	HIGHLAND	
2	DORNOCH (Light)	} worked by HIGHLAND
3	WICK + LYBSTER (Light)	

STATIONS + HALTS

No	Name	Ry	Ref
A 1	ALTNABREAC	1	NC94
2	(ARDGAY) §	1	NH59
3	Bilbster	1	ND25
4	BONAR BRIDGE §	1	NH59
5	Borrobol Platform	1	NC82
6	Bower	1	ND15
7	BRORA	1	NC80
8	Cambusavie Platform	2	NH79
9	CULRAIN	1	NH59
10	Delney	1	NH77
11	Dornoch	2	NH78
12	Dunrobin ✳	1	NC80
13	Edderton	1	NH68
14	Embo	2	NH79
15	FEARN	1	NH77
16	FORSINARD	1	NC84
17	GEORGEMAS	1	ND16
18	GOLSPIE	1	NH89
19	Halkirk	1	ND16
20	HELMSDALE	1	ND01
21	Hoy	1	ND16
22	INVERSHIN	1	NH59
23	Kildary	1	NH77
24	KILDONAN	1	NC82
25	KINBRACE	1	NC83
26	LAIRG	1	NC50
27	Loth	1	NC91
28	Lybster	3	ND23
29	Mid·Clyth	3	ND23
30	Mound, The	12	NH79
31	Nigg	1	NH77
32	Occumster	3	ND23
33	ROGART	1	NC70
34	SCOTSCALDER	1	ND50
35	Skelbo	2	NH79
36	TAIN	1	NH78
37	The Mound	12	NH79
38	THURSO	1	ND16
39	Thrumster	3	ND34
40	Ulbster	3	ND34
41	WICK	13	ND35
42	Watten	1	ND25

GOODS

No	Location	Ry	Ref
G1	Thurso	1	ND16
2	Wick	13	ND35
3	Lairg	1	NC50
4	Bonar Bridge	1	NH59
5	Fearn	1	NH77
6	Dornoch	2	NH78

ENGINE SHEDS

No	Location	Ry	Ref
E 1	Wick	1	ND35
2	Helmsdale	1	ND01

SUMMITS

No	Name / Location	Ht	Ref
S 1	County March	708'	NC94
2	Lairg	488'	NC60

JUNCTIONS

No	Location	Ry	Ref
J1	Georgemas	1	ND16
2	Wick	13	ND35
3	The Mound	12	NH79

NOTES:

(1) Name change: Old § New §

(2) Private Station ✳

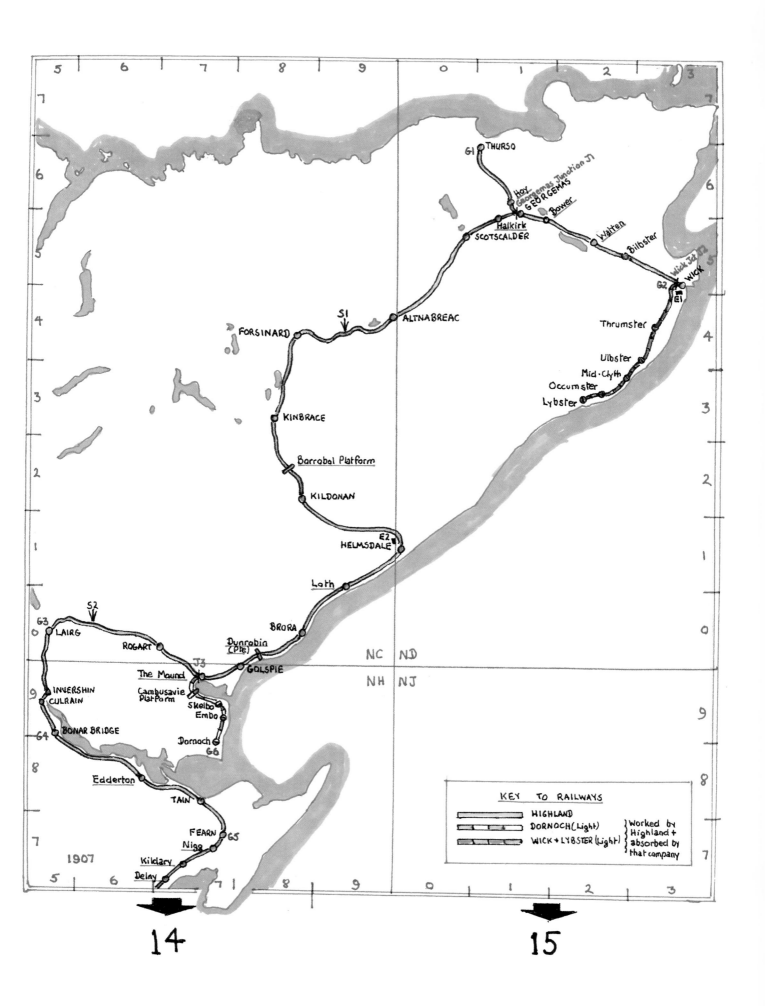

13

KEY TO RAILWAYS

HIGHLAND

DORNOCH (Light)

WICK + LYBSTER (Light)

Worked by Highland + absorbed by that company

THURSO
G1
Hoy
Georgemas Junction Jt
GEORGEMAS
Bower
Halkirk
SCOTSCALDER
Watten
Bilbster
Wick Jct T2
WICK
G2
E1
Thrumster
Ulbster
Mid-Clyth
Occumster
Lybster
S1
ALTNABREAC
FORSINARD
KINBRACE
Barrobal Platform
KILDONAN
E2
HELMSDALE
Loth
BRORA
Dunrobin (Pte)
S2
G3
LAIRG
ROGART
The Mound
J3
GOLSPIE
NC   ND
NH   NJ
INVERSHIN
CULRAIN
Cambusavie Platform
Skelbo
Embo
BONAR BRIDGE
G4
Dornoch
G6
Edderton
TAIN
FEARN
G5
Nigg
1907
Kildary
Delny

14

15

RAILWAYS

No.	Company	Note	Ry Ref
R 1	HIGHLAND		
2	CROMARTY + DINGWALL	(1)	
3	INVERGARRY + FORT AUGUSTUS	(2)	
4	NORTH BRITISH	(3)	

STATIONS

No.	Name	Ry Ref
A 1	Aberchalder	3 NH30
2	ACHANALT	1 NH26
3	ACHNASHEEN	1 NH15
4	Achterneed	1 NH45
5	Alcaig	2 NH55
6	Allanfearn	1 NH74
7	Allangrange	1 NH55
8	ALNESS	1 NH66
9	ATTADALE	1 NG93
10	AUCHNASHELLACH	1 NG94
11	AVIEMORE	1 NH81
12	Avoch	
13	Beauly	
14	Bunchrew	
15	CARR BRIDGE	
16	Clacknaharry	
17	Clunes	
18	Conon	
19	Cromarty	
20	Culbokie	
21	CULLODE MOOR	
22	Dalcross	
23	Daviot	
24	DINGWALL	
25	Drumcudden	
26	DUIRINISH	
27	Fort Augustus	
28	Fort Augustus Pier	
29	Fort George	
30	Fortrose	
31	Fowlis	
32	GARVE	1 NH65
33	Glencarron Platform	1 NH55
34	Gollanfield Junction	1 NH64
35	Invergarry	1 NH82
36	INVERGORDON	1 NH64
37	INVERNESS	1 NH54
38	Kincraig	12 NH55
39	KINGUSSIE	2 NH76
40	KYLE OF LOCHALSH	2 NH66
41	Lentran	1 NH74
42	LOCHLUICHART	1 NH74
43	MALLAIG	1 NH74
44	MORAR	1 NH55
45	May	2 NH66
46	MUIR OF ORD	1 NG72
47	Munlochy	3 NH30
48	NAIRN	3 NH31
49	Newhall	1 NH75
50	NEWTONMORE	1 NH75
51	Novar	1 NH56
52	PLOCKTON	1 NH36
53	Redcastle	1 NH05
54	STRATHCARRON	1 NH15
55	Strathpeffer	3 NN29
56	STROME FERRY	1 NH66
57	Tomatin	1 NH64

GOODS

No.	Name/Location	Ry Ref
G 1	Inverness	1 NH54
2	Inverness Docks	1 NH36
3	Mallaig	4 NM69
4	Kyle of Lochalsh	4 NM69
5	Invergordon	1 NH73
6	Novar	1 NH55
7	Dingwall	1 NH65

ENGINE SHEDS

No.	Name/Location	Ry Ref
E 1	Inverness	1 NH94
2	Kyle of Lochalsh	1 NH45
3	Dingwall	1 N683
4	Aviemore	1 NH72
4	Millburn	1 NH64
5	Harbour Branch	1 NH64
6	Muir of Ord	1 NH55
7	Conon	12 NH55
8	Dingwall	1 NH55
9	Fodderty	1 NH55
10	Gollanfield	1 NH75
11	Aviemore	1 NH81

SUMMITS

Ry Ref	No.	Name/Location	Alt.	Ry Ref
1 NH64	S 1	Luib	646'	1 NH15
1 NH64	2	Corriemoillie	429'	1 NH36
4 NM69	3	Raven's Rock	458'	1 NH46
1 NG72	4	Schlod	1315'	1 NH82

JUNCTIONS

No.	Name/Location	Ry Ref
		1 NH66
		1 NH56
		1 NH55

INVERNESS

No.	Name/Location	Ry Ref
J 1	Station	1 NH64
2	Rose Street	1 NH64
3	Welsh's Bridge	1 NH64

WORKS

No.	Name/Location	Ry Ref
W 1	Lochgorm - Inverness	1 NH56

NOTES:

(1) Light Railway (Highland)
(2) Worked by Highland, then by North British
(3) West Highland Line

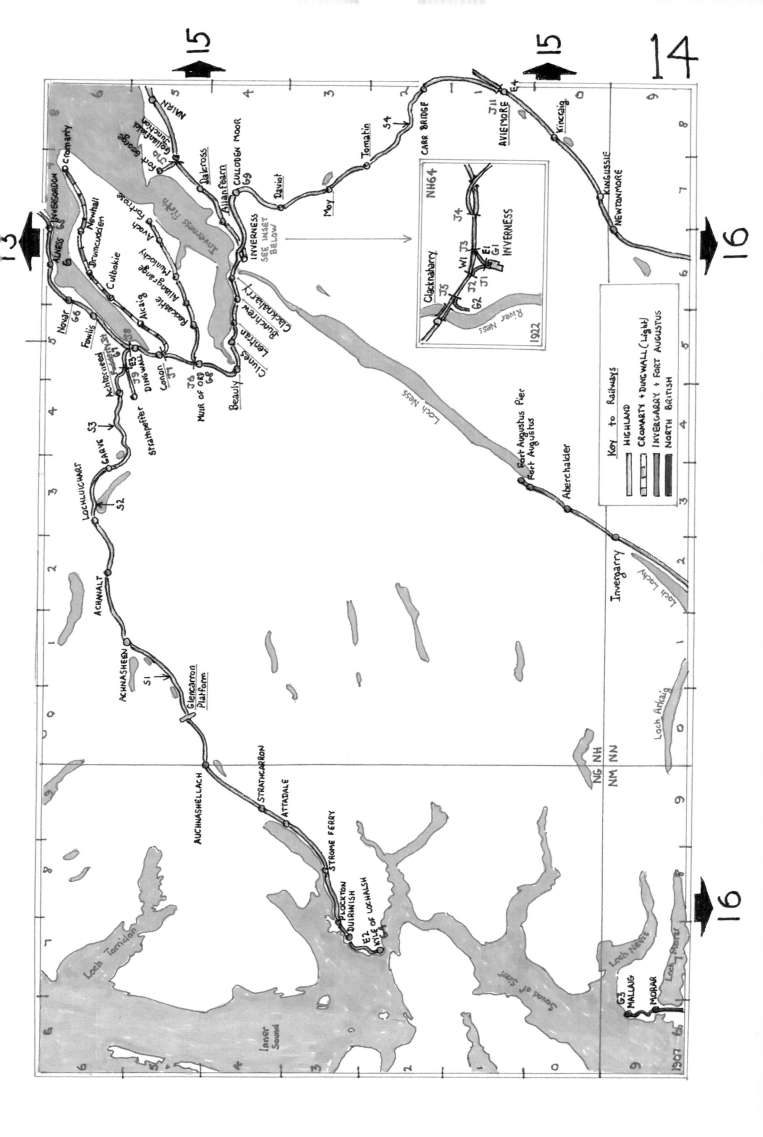

ABERDEEN

RAILWAYS

No.	Company	Notes
R 1	HIGHLAND	
2	CALEDONIAN	
3	GREAT NORTH OF SCOTLAND	GNoS
4	ST COMBS (Light)	
5	HARBOUR TRUSTEES	Aberdeen Tramways

STATIONS

No.	Name	Ry Ref
A	ABERDEEN	23
1	JOINT	3 NJ90
2	Don Street	3 NJ90
3	Holburn Street	3 NJ90
4	Hutcheon Street	3 NJ90
5	Kittybrewster	3 NJ90
6	Schoolhill	3 NJ90
7	Aberlour	3 NJ24
8	Aboyne	3 NO59
9	Advie	3 NJ13
10	Alford	3 NJ51
11	Alves	1 NJ16
12	Arnage	3 NJ93
13	Auchindachy	3 NJ34
14	Auchmacoy	3 NJ93
15	Auchnagatt	3 NJ94
16	Auchterless	3 NJ74
17	Auldearn	1 NH95
18	Aultmore	1 NJ35
19	Ballater	3 NO39
20	Ballindalloch	3 NJ13
21	Balnacoul	1 NJ35
22	Banchory	3 NO69
23	Banff Bridge	3 NJ66
24	Banff Harbour	3 NJ66
25	Bankhead	3 NJ81
26	Bieldside	3 NJ80
27	Birchfield Platform	3 NJ25
28	Blacksboat	3 NJ15
29	Boat of Garten	13 NH91
30	Baddam	3 NK14
31	Brockley	3 NJ96
32	Brodie	1 NH95
33	Broomhill	1 NH92
34	Buckie	1 NJ46
35	Buckie	3 NJ46
36	Buckpool	3 NJ36
37	Bucksburn	3 NJ80
38	Bullers o' Buchan Platf.	3 NKO3
39	Burghead	1 NJ16
40	Cairnbulg	4 NKO6
41	Cairnie Junction	3 NJ44
42	Calcots	3 NJ26
43	Cambus o' May	3 NO49
44	Carron	3 NJ24
45	Coleburn	3 NJ25
46	Coltfield	1 NJ16
47	Cornhill	3 NJ55
48	Cruden Bay	3 NKO3
49	Cove	2 NJ90
50	Craigellachie	3 NJ24
51	Crathes	3 NO79
52	Cramdale	3 NJ02
53	Cullen	3 NJ46
54	Culter	3 NJ80
55	Cults	3 NJ80
56	Dandaleith	3 NJ24
57	Dava	1 NJ03
58	Dess	3 NJ50
59	Dinnet	3 NO49
60	Don Street	3 NJ90
61	Drum	3 NO79
62	Drummuir	3 NJ34
63	Drybridge	1 NJ46
64	Dufftown	3 NJ34
65	Dumphail	1 NJ04
66	Dyce	3 NJ81
67	ELGIN	1 NJ26
68	Elgin	3 NJ26
69	Ellon	3 NJ93
70	Enzie	1 NJ36
71	Esslemont	3 NJ92
72	Findochty	3 NJ46
73	Fingask Platform	3 NJ72
74	Fochabers-on-Spey	1 NJ35
75	FORRES	1 NJ05
76	Fraserburgh	3 NJ76
77	Fyvie	3 NJ73
78	Garmouth	3 NJ36
79	Garffy	3 NJ53
80	Glassel	3 NO69
81	Glenbarry	3 NJ55
82	Glasshaugh	3 NJ80
83	Grange	3 NKO3 §
84	Grantown	1 NJ16
85	Grantown	4 NKO6
86	Hatton	3 NJ44
87	Holburn Street	3 NJ26
88	Hutcheon Street	3 NO49
89	Hopeman	3 NJ24
90	HUNTLY	3 NJ25
91	INSCH	1 NJ16
92	Inveramsay	3 NJ55
93	Inverugie	3 NKO3
94	INVERURIE	2 NJ90
95	KEITH	3 NJ24
96	Keith Town	3 NO79
97	Kemnay	3 NJ02
98	(Kennethmont)	3 NJ46
99	Kinaldie	3 NJ80
100	King Edward	3 NJ80
101	Kinloss	3 NJ24
102	Kintore	1 NJ03
103	Kittybrewster	3 NJ50 §
104	Knack	3 NO49
105	Knockando	3 NJ90
106	Lady's Bridge	3 NO79
107	Lethenty	3 NJ34
108	Lhanbryde	1 NJ46
109	Logierieve	3 NJ34
110	Longhaven	1 NO14
111	Longmorn	3 NJ81
112	Langside	1 NJ26
113	Lanmay	3 NJ26
114	Lossiemouth	3 NJ93
115	Lumphanan	1 NJ36
116	Macduff	3 NJ92
117	Maud	3 NJ46
118	Millimber	3 NJ80
119	Minlaw	3 NJ94
120	Monymusk	3 NJ61
121	Mormond	3 NJ95
122	Mosstowie	3 NJ76
123	Muchalls	3 NJ36
124	Mulben	3 NJ53
125	Murtle	3 NO69
126	Nethy Bridge	3 NJ55
127	New Machar	3 NJ56
128	Newseat	3 NJ44
129	Newtonhill	1 NJ02
130	Old Meldrum	3 NJ02
131	Orbliston	3 NKO3
132	Orden's Platform	3 NJ90 §
133	Orton	3 NJ90 §
134	Oyne	1 NJ16
135	Pack	3 NJ25
136	Parkhill	3 NJ62
137	Persley	3 NJ72
138	Peterhead	3 NKO4
139	Philorth	3 NJ72
140	Pittaple	(1) 3 NJ46
141	Pitfodels	3 NJ44
142	Pitlurg	3 NJ71
143	Pitmedden	3 NJ52
144	Plaidy	3 NJ81
145	Port Elphinstone	3 NJ15
146	Portessie	1 NO06
147	Portessie	3 NJ71
148	Port Gordon	3 NJ90 §
149	Portknackie	3 NJ55
150	Porthlethen	3 NJ24
151	Portsoy	3 NJ66
152	Rathen	3 NJ72
153	Rathven	1 NJ26
154	Rothes	3 NJ92
155	Rothie Norman	3 NK14
156	Rothiemay	3 NJ25
157	Ruthrieston	3 NKO4
158	St Combs	3 NJ95
159	Schoolhill	3 NJ16
160	Stoneywood	3 NJ50
161	Strichen	3 NJ66
162	Tillyfourie	3 NJ94
163	Tillynaught	3 NJ80
164	Tochieneal	3 NJ94
165	Torphins	3 NJ61
166	Turriff	3 NJ95
167	Udny	1 NJ16
168	Urquhart	2 NO89
169	Wardhouse	1 NJ35
170	Wartle	3 NJ80
171	West Cults	3 NH92
172	Whitehouse	3 NJ81
173	Woodside	3 NKO4

Stations (cross-referenced, marked *)

No.	Name	Ry Ref	
7	Kinfore	3 NJ71	
8	Ellon	3 NJ80	
9	Maud	3 NJ81	
10	Fraserburgh	3 NJ90	
11	Elgin (High + GNoS)	13 NJ26	*
12	Elgin South	3 NJ26	*
13	Elgin North	3 NJ26	
14	Alves	1 NJ16	
15	Forres West	3 NJ05	*
16	Forres East	1 NJ05	*
17	Forres South	1 NJ05	*
18	Boat of Garten	13 NH91	
19	Craigellachie	3 NJ24	
20	Keith West	1 NJ45	
21	Keith East	3 NJ45	
22	Grange-Station	3 NJ44	*
23	Grange-North	3 NJ44	*
24	Grange-Cairnie	3 NJ44	*
25	Tillynaught	3 NJ56	
26	Inveramsay	3 NJ72	
27	Inverurie	3 NJ72	

GOODS

No.	Name/Location	Ry Ref	
G	ABERDEEN		
§ 1	Waterloo	1 NJ25	
§ 2	Guild Street	3 NO66	
3	Deeside	1 NJ35	
4	Towiemore	3 NJ62	
5	Coltfield	3 NO79	
6	Burghead	3 NJ81	
7	Keith	3 NJ82	
8	Peterhead Pier	3 NKO4	
9	Banff Harbour	3 NJ96	

SUMMITS

No.	Name/Location	Ht	Ry Ref
S 1	Dava	1052'	1 NJ03
2	Dufftown		3 NJ34
3	New Machar		3 NJ82

ENGINE SHEDS

No.	Name/Location		Ry Ref
E 1	Aberdeen		2 NO99
2	Kittybrewster	* §	3 NJ90
3	Inverurie	§	3 NJ72
4	Keith		3 NJ45
5	Elgin	*	3 NJ26
6	Forres		1 NJ05

COMPANY WORKS

No.	Name/Location		Ry Ref
W 1	Inverurie	§	3 NJ72

JUNCTIONS

No.	Name/Location		Ry Ref
J 1	Ferryhill	†	2.5 NJ90
2	Goods Branch	†	2 NJ90
3	Deeside Goods Bcht	†	23 NJ90
4	Denburn	†	23 NJ90
5	Kittybrewster	† *	5 NJ90
6	Dyce		3 NJ81

NOTES:

(1) Items in Gazetteer marked * are not fully located on the map.

(2) Junctions marked † are located at Aberdeen

(3) Stations marked § are located at Aberdeen and indexed also under Aberdeen.

(4) Engine Shed & Company Works at Inverurie are on the same site.

(5) Goods Stations underlined in blue thus Waterloo are still in use for goods traffic (1985)

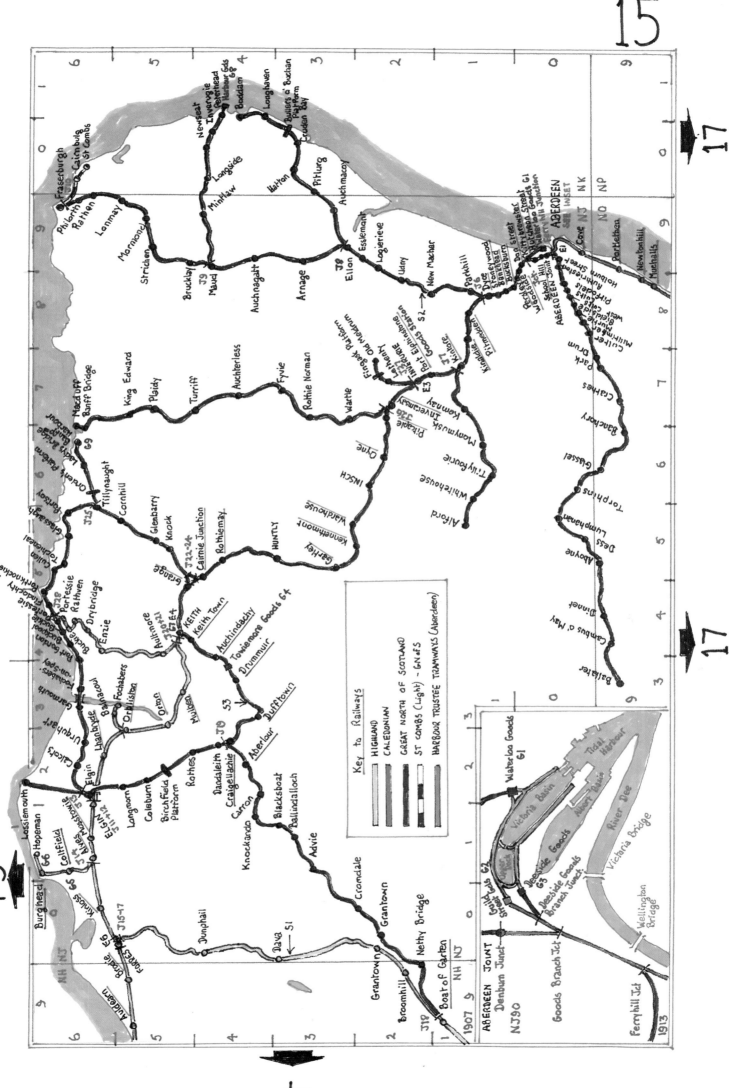

16 — FORT WILLIAM, OBAN + CRIANLARICH

RAILWAYS

No.	Company
R1	HIGHLAND
2	NORTH BRITISH
3	CALEDONIAN
4	INVERGARRY + FORT AUGUSTUS (worked by 2, then 3)

STATIONS

No.	Name	Ry Ref
A1	Aberfeldy	1 NN85
2	Ach-na-Cloiche	3 NM93
3	Appin	3 NM94
4	ARDLUI	2 NN31
5	ARISAIG	2 NM68
6	Ballachulish + Glencoe	3 NM05
7	Ballachulish Ferry	3 NM05
8	Balquhidder	3 NN52
9	BANAVIE	2 NN17
10	Banavie Pier	2 NN17
11	(BEASDALE)	
12	Benderloch	
13	BLAIR ATHOLL	
14	BRIDGE OF ORCHY	
15	Comrie	
16	CONNEL FERRY	
17	CORPACH	
18	(CORROUR)	
19	Creagan	
20	CRIANLARICH	
21	Crianlarich	
22	Crieff	
23	DALMALLY	
24	Dalnaspidal	
25	DALWHINNIE	
26	Duror	
27	FORT WILLIAM	
28	Gairlochy	
29	GLENFINNAN	
30	(Gorton)	
31	Grandtully	2 NM77
32	Highlandman	3 NN93
33	Innerpeffray	1 NM96
34	Kentallen	2 NN33
35	Killin	3 NN72
36	Killin Junction	3 NM93
37	Kingshouse	2 NN17
38	LOCHAILORT	2 NN36
39	Loch Awe	3 NM94
40	Lochearnhead	2 NM32
41	LOCHEILSIDE	3 NM32
42	Loch Tay	3 NN82
43	Luib	3 NN12
44	Muthill	1 NN67
45	North Connel	1 NN68
46	OBAN	3 NM95
47	RANNOCH	2 NN17
48	ROY BRIDGE	4 NN18
49	St Fillans	2 NM88
50	SPEAN BRIDGE	2 NN35
51	Strathyre	1 NN85
52	Struan	3 NN81
53	TAYNUILT	3 NN82
54	TYNDRUM (LOWER)	3 NN05
55	TYNDRUM (UPPER)	3 NN53
56	TULLOCH	3 NN52

BRIDGES + VIADUCTS

No.	Name/Location	Ry Ref
V1	Connel Ferry Bridge	3 NM93
2	Glenfinnan Viaduct	2 NM88

SUMMITS

No.	Name/Location	Ht	Ry Ref
S1	West Highland – County March	1024	2 NN67
2	Gorton		2 NN35
3	Corrour	1350	2 NN36
4	Glenoglehead	941	3 NN52
5	Tyndrum	840	3 NN33
6	Druimuachdar	1484	1 NN67
7	Glencruitten	301	3 NM83

GOODS

No.	Location/Name	Ry Ref
G1	Fort William	3 NN12
2	Banavie Pier	2 NN07
3	Oban	3 NN53
4	Crianlarich	3 NN42

JUNCTIONS

No.	Name/Location	Ry Ref
J1	Ft. William Goods	2 NN17
2	Mallaig / Banavie Bch	2 NN17
3	Banavie Oban Line	2 NN17
4	Crianlarich Oban Line	2 NN32
5	Glasgow	3 NN32
6	Crieff	3 NN82
7	Balquhidder	3 NN52
8	Killin	3 NN52
9	Connel Ferry	3 NM93
10	Spean Bridge	2 NN28

SIDINGS

No.	Name/Location	Ry Ref
P1	Annat	2 NN45

ENGINE SHEDS

No.	Name/Location	Ry Ref
E1	Oban	3 NM82

NOTE:

* Private station – never shown in public timetables

16 17 22 11 18 11

Blair Atholl
Struan
Dalnaspidal
56
Dalwhinnie
Loch Ericht
Loch Laggan
Grandtully
Aberfeldy
Loch Tay
Loch Rannoch
Rannoch
52 (Gorton)
53 (Corrour)
Corrour
Tulloch
Roy Bridge
Spean Bridge
Gairlochy
J10
Mallaig Jct
Fort William SEE INSET BELOW
Corpach
Banavie Pier
Caledonian Canal
Lochielside
Glenfinnan
J9 Y2
Lochailort
Beasdale
Arisaig
Bridge of Orchy
51
Tyndrum (Upper)
64
35 J4
Tyndrum (Lower)
55
Crianlarich SEE INSET ABOVE
Ardlui
Loch Awe
Dalmally
Loch Awe
Taynuilt
Ach-na-Cloich
Connel Ferry
V1
North Connel
Benderloch
Creagan
Appin
Duror
Kentallen
Ballachulish
Ballachulish Ferry
Ballachulish + Glencoe
Firth Lorne
Loch Linnhe
57
Oban
J3 G3
Killin
54
Lochearnhead
J7 Balquhidder
Kingshouse
Strathyre
Killin
Loch Tay
J8 Killin Junction
Luib
Innerpeffray
J6
Crieff
Highlandman
Comrie
St. Fillans
Muthill

INSET (1904):
Crianlarich
64
35 J4
Tyndrum (Upper)
Tyndrum (Lower)
NN32
Crianlarich

INSET (1909):
Banavie Goods
Canal
G2
J3
Banavie Pier
BANAVIE
Corpach
Pt. Corpach
NN17
Mallaig
Other J2
J1
G1
B1
Ft William Goods
Fort William
Loch Linnhe

Key to Railways
HIGHLAND
NORTH BRITISH
CALEDONIAN
INVERGARRY + FORT AUGUSTUS

NN NM
1907

MONTROSE, DUNDEE + PERTH

RAILWAYS

No	Company	work by
R1	HIGHLAND	
2	CALEDONIAN	
3	NORTH BRITISH	
4	DUNDEE + ARBROATH JT	2+3
4A	CARMYLLIE (Light)	2+3
5	DUNDEE HARBOUR LINE	2+3
6	BANKFOOT (Light)	2

STATIONS

No	Station/Halt	Ry Ref
A1	Abercairney	2 NN92
2	Abernethy	3 NO11
3	Almond Bank	2 NO22
4	Alyth	2 NO24
5	Alyth Junction	2 NO24
6	Arbirlot	4A NO53
7	ARBROATH	4 NO64
8	Ardler	2 NO23
9	Auchterarder	2 NN91
10	Auchterhouse	2 NO33
11	Auchtermuchty	3 NO21
12	Auldbar Road	2 NO45
13	Baldovan	2 NO33
14	Baldragon	2 NO33
15	Balgowan	2 NN92
16	Ballinluig	1 NN95
17	(BALMOSSIE)	4 NO43
18	Bankfoot	6 NO03
19	Barnhill	2 NO43
20	BARRY LINKS	4 NO53
21	Bernie	3 NO87
22	Birnie Road	3 NO77
23	Blackford	2 NN80
24	Blairgowrie	2 NO14
25	Boarhills	3 NO51
26	Brechin	2 NO56
27	Bridge of Don	2 NO66
28	Bridge of Earn	3 NO11
29	BROUGHTY FERRY	4 NO43
30	Broughty Ferry Pier	3 NO43
31	Boddon	4 NO53
32	Careston	2 NO56
33	Cargill	2 NO15
34	Carmyllie	4A NO54
35	CARNOUSTIE	4 NO53
36	Cauldcots	2+3 NO64
37	Clocksbriggs	2+3 NO45
38	Collessie	2+3 NO21
39	Colliston	2 NO64
40	Coupar Angus	2 NO23
41	Craigo	2 NO66
42	CRIEFF JUNCTION §	2 NN91
43	CUPAR	3 NO31
44	Cuthlie	4A NO54
45	Dairsie	3 NO41
46	Dalguise	1 NN94
47	Denhead	4A NO54
48	Dronley	2 NO33
49	Drumlithie	2 NO78
50	Dubton Junction	2 NO66
51	DUNDEE TAYBRIDGE	3 NO33
52	Dundee East	42 NO43
53	Dundee Esplande	3 NO21
54	Dundee West	2 NO35
55	DUNKELD + Birnam	2 NO33
56	Donning	2 NO33
57	Eassie	2 NN92
58	East Haven	1 NN95
59	East Newport	4 NO45
60	Edzell	6 NO03
61	Elliot	2 NO45
62	Elliot Junction	4 NO53
63	ERROL	3 NO87
64	Esplande (Dundee)	3 NO77
65	Farnell Road	2 NN80
66	Fordoun	2 NO14
67	Forfar	3 NO51
68	Forgandenny	2 NO05
69	Forteviot	2 NO06
70	Friockheim	3 NO11
71	Glamis	4 NO43
72	Glasterlaw	3 NO45
73	Glencarse	4 NO53
74	(GLENEAGLES)	2 NO56
75	Glenfarg	2 NO15
76	(GOLF STREET)	4A NO54
77	Gourdon	4 NO53
78	Grandtully	3 NO64
79	Guard Bridge	2 NO45
80	Guay	3 NO21
81	Guthrie	2 NO64
82	Hillside	2 NO25
83	Inchbare	2 NO66
84	Inchture	2 NN91
85	Inchture Village	3 NO31
86	INNERGOWRIE	4A NO54
87	Inverkeilor	3 NO41
88	Johnshaven	1 NN94
89	Jordanstone	4A NO54
90	Justinhaugh	2 NO33
91	Killiecrankie	2 NO78
92	Kilmany	2 NO66
93	Kinfauns	3 NO33
94	Kingennie	4A NO43
95	Kingsbarns	3 NO52
96	Kingsmuir	2 NO35
97	Kirkbuddo	1 NO04
98	Kirriemuir	2 NO01
99	LADYBANK	2 NO34
100	Laurencekirk	4 NO53
101	Lauriston	3 NO42
102	Letham Grange	2 NO56
103	LEUCHARS JUNCTION	4A NO53
104	Leuchars Old	4A NO65
105	Leysmill	2 NO22
106	Liff	3 NO32
107	Lindores	2 NO65
108	Lochee	2 NO77
109	Lochee West	2 NO45
110	Longforgan	2 NO01
111	Lunan Bay	2 NO01
112	Luncarty	2 NO55
113	Luthrie	2 NO34
114	Madderty	3 NO55
115	Magdalene Green	3 NO12
116	Markirk	2 NN91
117	Meigle	3 NO11
118	Methven	4 NO55
119	MONIFIETH	3 NO87
120	Monikie	1 NN85
121	MONTROSE	3 NO41
122	Montrose	1 NN94
123	Mount Melville	2 NO55
124A	Murthly	3 NO66
125	Newburgh	2 NO35
126	Newtyle	2 NO22
127	North Water Bridge	2 NO32
128	PERTH-GENERAL	2 NO32
129	Perth-Princes Street	3 NO65
130	PITLOCHRY	3 NO76
131	Rosemount	2 NO24
132	Ruthven Road	2 NO45
133	St Andrews	1 NN96
134	St Cyrus	3 NO52
135	St Fort	2 NO12
136	SORNEFIELD	2 NO43
137	Stanley	3 NO51
138	STONEHAVEN	2 NO45
139	Strathmiglo	2 NO44
140	Strathord	2 NO35
141	Strathvithie	3 NO21
142	Tannadice	2 NO67
143	Tayport	3 NO76
144	Tibbermuir	3 NO64
145	Tullibardine	3 NO41
146	West Ferry	3 NO41
147	West Newport	2 NO54
148	Woodside + Burrelton	2 NO33
149	Wormit	3 NO02

JUNCTIONS

No	Name/Location	Ry Ref
1	Perth – Hilton	2 NO24
2	– Harbour	2 NO02
3	– D+P	4 NO43
4	– NB Goods	2 NO45
	Montrose Area	
5	Kinnaber	3 NO65
6	Dubton	2 NO75
7	Broomfield North	3 NO41
8	Broomfield South	3 NO21
9	Cal Goods	2 NO24
10	South Harbour	3 NO76
11	North Station	2 NO02
11A	Bridge of Don	2 NO12
	Dundee Area	
12	Ninewells	2 NO14
13	Buckingham West	2 NO02
14	Buckingham East	3 NO41
15	Camperdown East	6 NO76
16	Broughty Ferry Pier	3 NO42
17	Forfar Line	3 NO31
18	St Fort – North	2 NO13
19	St Fort – South	2 NO88
20	St Fort – Newburgh	3 NO21
21	Tay Bridge South	2 NO03
	Others	
22	Bridge of Earn	3 NO51
23	Ladybank – South	3 NO44
24	Ladybank – North	2 NO02
25	Leuchars – North	2 NN91
26	Leuchars – South	4 NO43
27	Almond Valley	3 NO21
28	Methven	2 NO13
29	Aberfeldy	3 NO32
30	Blairgowrie	2 NO33
31	Alyth – West *	2 NO23
32	Alyth – South *	2 NO24
33	Alyth – Branch *	2 NO24
34	Kirriemuir	2 NO84
35	Forfar – East	2 NO65
36	Forfar – West	2 NO55

GOODS

No	Name/Location	Ry Ref
G1	Perth – Harbour	2 NO55
2	– NB	2
3	– Dovecotland	3
4	Montrose – N Harbour	4
5	– S Harbour	5
6	Dundee	6

No		Ry Ref
37	Glasterlaw *	2 NO33
38	Guthrie *	2 NO55
39	Friockheim *	2 NO55
40	Brechin – Station	2 NO56
41	– West *	2 NO56
42	– East *	2 NO56
43	– Edzell *	2 NO56
44	St Vigens	254 NO64
45	Elliot	AAA NO63
46	Stanley	12 NO13
47	Bankfoot	26 NO03
48	Crieff (Gleneagles)	2 NN91
49	Inchture	2 NO22
50	Glenburnie	2 NO21

SIDINGS

No		Ry Ref
P1	Kirkton	3 NO21
2	Barnhill	3 NO41
3	Friarton	3 NO41
4	Morton	2 NO02

ENGINE SHEDS

No		Ry Ref
E1	Perth	1 NN95
2	Dundee	2 NO23
3	Dundee	2 NO24
4	Forfar	2 NO24

TUNNELS

No		Ry Ref
T1	Moncreiffe	2 NO84
2	Kingswood	2 NO65
3	Inver	2 NO04

Notes:
2 NO33
2 NO02 * Junctions not precisely
2 NO35 § CRIEFF JUNCTION (+2) Map
2 NO33 name is now known as :§74
3 NO65 GLENEAGLES (modern name)
2 NO02 * Junctions not precisely
3 NO52 located on the map - usually
2 NN92 groups of 2,3 or 4.

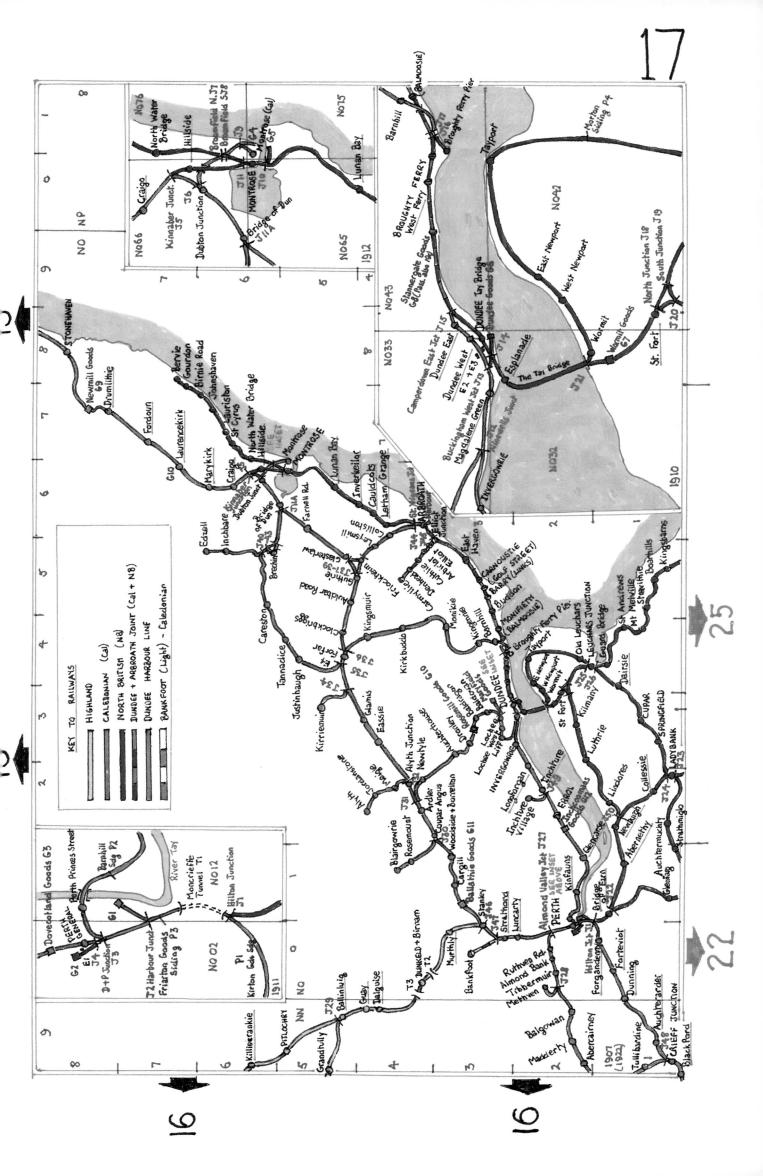

RAILWAYS

No.	Company
R1	NORTH BRITISH
2	NB + CAL JOINT
3	CALEDONIAN
4	CAL + GSW JOINT
5	GLASGOW + SOUTH WESTERN

STATIONS (SEE NOTES)

No	Name	Ry	Ref
A1	Aberfoyle	1	NN 50
(19)	ALEXANDRA PARK	1	66
2	ALEXANDRIA	2	37
	ARDROSSAN:		
3	Ardrossan	5	24
4	PIER	3	24
5	Pier	5	24
6	SOUTH BEACH	5	24
7	ARROCHAR + TARBET	1	NN 30
8	Auchenmade	3	34
9	Baillieston	3	66
10	Balfron	1	58
11	BALLOCH CENTRAL	2	38
12	BALLOCH PIER	2	38
13	Balmore	1	57
14	BARASSIE	5	33
15	Bardowie	1	57
16	Bargeddie	1	66 (20B)
(19)	BARNHILL	1	66
17	BARRHEAD	4	45
(19)	Barrhead Central	3	55
18	Barrmill	4	35
19	BEARSDEN	1	57
(19)	Bellahouston	4	56
(19)	BELLGROVE	1	66
20	Bieth	4	35
21	Bieth	5	35
22	BISHOPBRIGGS	1	66
23	BISHOPTON	3	47
24	Blanefield	1	57
25	BLANTYRE	3	65
26	Bogside	3	34
27	Bogside	5	34
28	BOGSTON	3	37
(19)	Botanic Gardens	3	56
29	Bothwell	1	65
(19)	Bothwell	3	65
30	BOWLING	1	47
31	Bowling	3	47
32	Brackenhills	3	35
33	(BRANCHTON)	3	27
34	Bridge of Weir	5	36
(19)	BRIDGETON	3	66
35	Broomhouse	1	66
36	Broomhouse	3	66
37	Buchlyvie	1	59
38	(Burnbank) §	1	65
39	BURNSIDE	3	66
40	BUSBY	3	55
41	Caldarvan	1	48
42	Caldwell	4	45
42A	Callander	3	NN 60
43	CAMBUSLANG	3	66
(19)	CARDONALD	4	56
44	Campsie Glen	1	67
45	CARDROSS	1	37
46	Carmyle	3	66
47	CARNTYNE	1	66
48	CARTSDYKE	3	27
49	CATHCART	3	56
50	CATHCART STREET	3	27
(19)	CHARING CROSS	1	56
51	CLARKSTON	3	55
52	Clydebank	3	46
53	CLYDEBANK Central	1	46
(19)	Clydebank East	3	56
(19)	Cowlairs	1	38
54	CRAIGENDORAN	3	66
(19)	(CROFTFOOT	5	56
(19)	Crookstown	5	56
(19)	CROSSHILL	5	34
55	Crosshouse	4	56
(19)	CROSSMYLOOF		
56	Cunninghamhead	5	34
57	DALMUIR	1	47
58	Dalmuir	3	47
59	DALREOCH	2	37
60	DALRY	5	24
61	Darvel	1	NN 30
62	Dreghorn	5	53
63	Drybridge	5	33
64	DRUMCHAPEL	1	57
65	Drumclog	3	63
66	DRUMRY	1	57
67	Drymen	1	48
(19)	DUKE STREET	1	66
68	DUMBARTON Central	2	37
(20B)	DUMBARTON EAST	3	47
69	Dumgoyne	1	58
70	DUNLOP	4	44
71	EASTERHOUSE	1	66
72	EAST KILBRIDE	3	65
73	Eglinton Street	3	56
74	Eiderslie	5	46
75	FAIRLIE	5	25
76	Fallside	3	66
77	FORT MATILDA	3	27
78	Gailes	5	33
79	Galston	1	79
80	Gargunnock	1	29
81	GARGLOCHHEAD	1	66
82	Garnkirk	1	66
83	Gartcosh	1	66
84	Gartmore	1	59
85	Gartness	1	48
86	Gatehead	5	33
87	Gavell	1	67
88	Giffen	3	35
89	GIFFNOCK	3	55
	GLASGOW:		
90	Buchanan Street	3	56
	CENTRAL	1	66
	CHARING CROSS	3	66
91	Eglinton Street	1	59
	HIGH STREET	1	65
92	QUEEN STREET	3	66
93	St Enoch's	3	55
94	Glengarnock	1	48
95	GLENGARNOCK	4	45
96	GOUROCK	3	NN 60
97	Govan	3	66
98	Greenfield §	4	56
99	GREAT WESTERN ROAD	1	67
	GREENOCK:		
100	CATHCART STR. §	3	66
100A	CENTRAL §	1	66
101	Prince's Pier	3	27
102	WEST	3	56
103	HAIRMYRES	3	27
(19)	Hawkhead	1	56
104	HELENSBURGH CENTRAL	3	55
105	HELENSBURGH UPPER	3	46
106	High Blantyre	1	46
107	HILLFOOT	3	56
(19)	(HILLINGTON EAST)	1	56
(19)	(HILLINGTON WEST)	1	38
108	Houston	3	66
109	Houston	5	56
110	Howwood	5	56
111	Hurlford	5	34
(19)	HYNDLAND	4	56
112	Ibrox	5	34
113	Inch Green	1	47
114	INVERKIP	3	47
115	Irvine	2	37
116	IRVINE	5	24
117	Jamestown	5	53
118	JOHNSTONE	5	33
(19)	JORDANHILL	5	33
(19)	Kelvin Bridge	1	57
119	KENNISHEAD	3	63
120	Kilbarchan	1	57
121	Kilbirnie	1	48
122	Kilbirnie	1	66
123	KILBOWIE	2	37
(19)	Kilbowie (Road)	3	47
124	Killearn	1	58
125	Kilmalcolm	4	44
126	KILMARNOCK	1	66
127	KILMAURS	3	65
128	KILPATRICK	3	56
129	Kilwinning	5	46
130	KILWINNING	5	25
(19)	King's Inch	3	66
(19)	(KING'S PARK)	3	27
131	Kippen	5	33
(19)	KIRKHILL	5	43
132	Kirkintilloch	1	79
(19)	Kirklee	1	29
133	LANGBANK	1	66
(19)	LANGSIDE	3	66
134	LARGS	1	66
135	Lennoxtown	3	66
136	LENZIE	1	59
(19)	Lochburn	1	48
137	LOCHSIDE	5	33
138	Lochwinnoch	1	67
139	Loudon hill	3	35
140	Lugton	3	55
141	Lugton		
142	Lynedoch	3	56
143	Lynedoch Upper	3	56
144	Maryhill	1	56
(19)	Maryhill	3	56
(19)	Maryville	1	56
(19)	MAXWELL PARK	1	56
145	Meikle Earnock	5	56
145A	Milliken Park	3	35
146	MILNGAVIE	5	35
147	Milton	3	37
148	Montgreenan	4	56
(19)	MOUNT FLORIDA	1	65
149	Mount Vernon	1	56
150	MUIREND		
151	NEILSTON	3	27
152	Neilston	3	27
153	Newmilns	5	27
154	NEWTON	3	27
155	NITSHILL	3	65
156	North Johnstone	5	46
157	Old Kilpatrick	1	28
	PAISLEY:	1	28
158	Abercorn	3	65
159	Canal	1	57
(19)	GILMOUR STREET	4	56
160	ST JAMES	4	56
161	West	3	46
162	Parkhead	5	46
(19)	Parkhead	5	46
(19)	PARTICK	5	43
(19)	Partick Central	1	65
(19)	Partick West	4	56
163	PATTERTON	5	37
(19)	POLLOKSHAWS EAST	3	27
(19)	POLLOKSHAWS WEST	3	33
(19)	POLLOKSHIELDS EAST	5	33
(19)	POLLOKSHIELDS WEST	1	38
164	PORT GLASGOW	5	46
165	Port Glasgow Upper	1	56
166	Port of Montieth	3	56
167	Potterhill	4	56
168	Prince's Pier	5	46
(19)	QUEEN'S PARK	3	35
169	QUEEN STREET	5	35
(19)	POSSIL PARK	1	47
170	Ravenscraig	3	46
	Renfrew:	1	58
171	Fulbar Street	5	37
(19)	Potterfield	5	43
172	South	4	44
173	Wharf	1	47
174	RENTON	3	24
(19)	Robroyston	5	24
175	Row	4	56
176	RUTHERGLEN	3	56
177	Ryeland	1	69
178	St Marnock's	3	66
(19)	St Rollox	1	67
179	Saltcoats	1	56
180	SALTCOATS	3	37
(19)	Scotstoun	3	56
(19)	SCOTSTOUNHILL	5	25
181	Shandon	1	67
(19)	SHAWLANDS	1	57
182	SHETTLESTON	1	56
183	Springside	5	35
184	Stepps Road	5	35
185	Stevenston	5	53
186	STEVENSON	3	45
187	STEWARTON	4	45
(19)	Stobcross	5	27
188	Strathaven Central	3	27
189	Strathblane	1	56
190	Summerston	3	56
191	THORNLIEBANK	1	66
192	THORNTONHALL	3	56
(19)	Tollcross	3	63
193	Torrance	5	46
194	TROON	1	57
195	Uddingston	1	67
196	UDDINGSTON	5	34
(19)	Uddingston West	3	56
197	Uplawmoor	1	66
(19)	Victoria Park	3	55
198	WEMYSS BAY	3	45
(19)	WESTERTON	4	45
199	WEST KILBRIDE	5	53
200	Whistlefield	3	66
201	WHITECRAIGS	4 56	3 55
(19)	Whiteinch	5 46	1 56
(19)	Whiteinch	3 47	3 56
(19)	(WILLIAMWOOD)		3 55
202	(WOODHALL)	5 46	3 37
(19)	Yorkhill	5 46	1 66
203	YOKER	4 46	1 56
(19)	Yoker	3 46	3 56

GOODS

No.	Name/Location	Ry	Ref
61	Gree	3	35
2	Fairlie Harbour	5	25
3	Barmill	3	35

SIDINGS

No	Name	Ry	Ref
P1	Swinlees Branch	5	25

JUNCTIONS

No	Name/Location	Ry	Ref
J1	Buchlyvie	1	59
2	Gartness	2	48
3	Todhills	5	35
4	Lugton North	34	45
5	Lugton South	4	45
6	East	3	45
7	County Boundary	35	63
8	Giffen South	3	35
9	Giffen North	3	35
10	Barmill	34	33
11	Swinlees Branch	5	25
12	Fairlie Pier	5	25

NOTES:

(1) All references in square NS except three (in NN and so marked).

(2) All stations in the area covered by the map are listed with the exception of some located in Glasgow Central area (see 20A). Those named on 18 are in black. Those not located are in blue and the map on which they are shown is given in blue in the No. column.

(3) Goods, Junctions etc are included ONLY if they do not appear on an enlargement.

§ Map name } NAME CHANGE
§ Modern name }

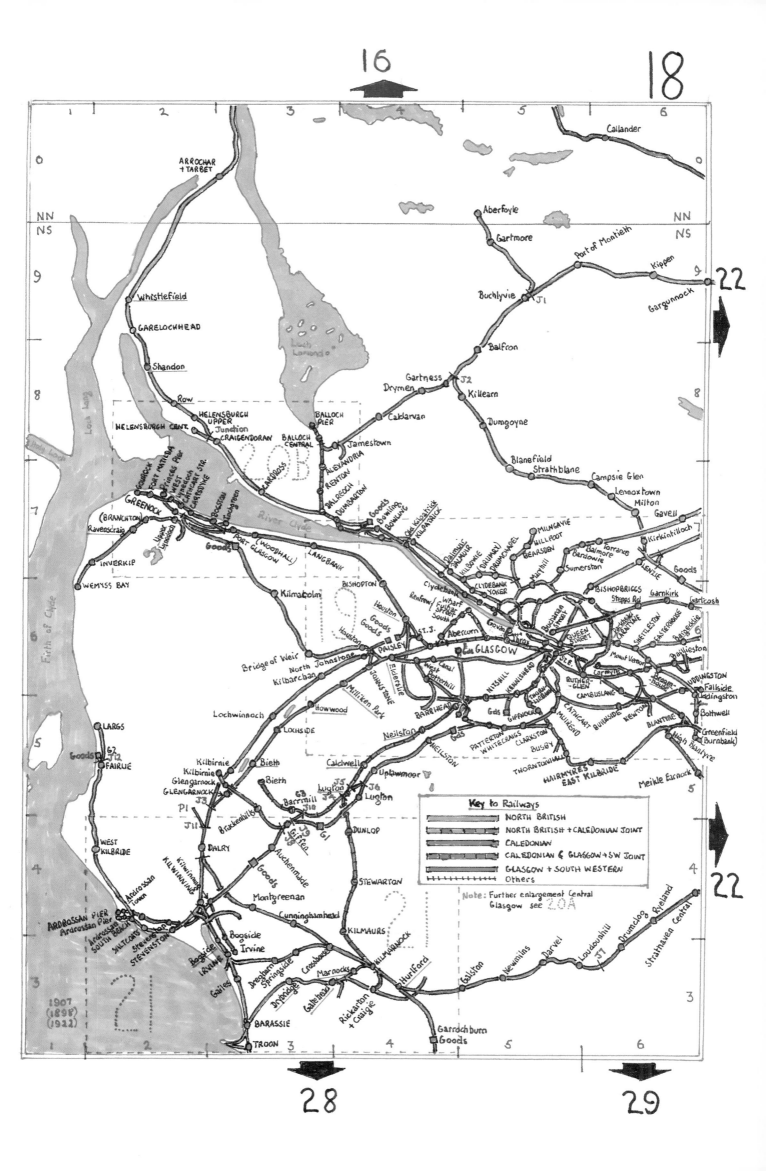

GLASGOW + PAISLEY

RAILWAYS

No	Company
R1	NORTH BRITISH
2	NORTH BRITISH & CALEDONIAN JOINT §14
3	CALEDONIAN
4	CALEDONIAN & GLASGOW & S W JOINT
5	GLASGOW & SOUTH WESTERN

STATIONS

No	Name	Ry	Ref
A1	ALEXANDRA PARK	*1	66
2	Baillieston	3	66
3	Balmore	1	57
4	Bardowie	1	57
5	Bargeddie	1	66
6	BARNHILL	*1	66
7	BARRHEAD	4	45
8	Barrhead Central	3	55
9	BEARSDEN	1	57
10	Bellahouston	*4	56
11	BELLGROVE	*1	66
12	BISHOPBRIGGS	1	66
13	BISHOPTON	3	47
14	BLANTYRE	3	65
15	Botanic Gardens	*3	56
16	Bothwell	1	65
17	Bothwell	3	65
18	BOWLING	1	47
19	Bowling	3	47
20	Bridge of Weir	5	36
21	BRIDGETON	*3	66
22	Broomhouse	1	66
23	Broomhouse	3	66
24	Burnbank	1	65
25	BURNSIDE	3	66
26	BUSBY	3	55
27	Caldwell	4	45
28	CAMBUSLANG	3	66
29	CARDONALD	4	56
30	Carmyle	3	66
31	CARNTYNE	*1	66
32	CATHCART	3	56
33	CHARING CROSS	*1	56
34	CLARKSTON (for Eaglesham)	3	55
35	Clydebank	3	46
36	CLYDEBANK (Central)	1	46
37	Clydebank East	3	56
38	Cowlairs	1	56
39	(CROSSFOOT)		
40	Crookston		
41	CROSSHILL	3	66
42	CROSSMYLOOF	4	56
43	DALREOCH	1	57
44	DALMUIR	1	57
45	Dalmuir	1	66
46/47	DRUMCHAPEL / DRUMRY	*1	66
48	DUKE STREET	3	66
49	DUMBARTON (CENTRAL)	1	57
50	DUMBARTON (EAST)	1	57
51	EASTERHOUSE	1	66
52	EAST KILBRIDE	*1	66
53	Eglinton Street	4	45
54	Elderslie	3	55
55	Fallside	1	57
56	Garngad	*4	56
57	Garnkirk	*1	66
58	(GARROWHILL)	1	66
59	Gartosh	3	47
60	GIFFNOCK	3	65
	GLASGOW:		
61	Buchanan Street	1	65
62	CENTRAL	3	65
63	CHARING CROSS	1	47
64	Eglinton Street	3	47
65	HIGH STREET	5	36
66	QUEEN STREET	*3	66
67	St Enoch's	1	66
68	Govan	3	66
69	GREAT WESTERN ROAD	1	65
70	HARMYRES	3	66
71	Hawkhead	3	55
72	High Blantyre	4	45
73	HILLFOOT	3	66
7A	(HILLINGTON-EAST)	4	56
75	(HILLINGTON-WEST)	3	66
76	Houston	1	66
77	Houston	3	56
78	Harwood	*1	56
79	HYNDLAND	3	55
80	Ibrox	3	46
81	JOHNSTONE	1	46
82	JORDANHILL	3	56
82A	Kelvin Bridge		
83	KENNISHEAD	*1	56
84	Kilbarchan	3	66
85	KILBOWIE	5	56
86	Kilbowie (Road)	3	56
87	KILPATRICK	4	56
88	King's Inch	2	37
89	(King's Park)	1	47
90	KIRKHILL	3	47
91	Kirkintilloch	1	57
92	Kirklee	1	57
93	LANGBANK	*1	66
94	LANGSIDE	2	37
95	LENZIE	3	47
96	Lochburn	1	66
97	Maryhill	3	65
98	Maryhill	*3	56
99	Maryville	5	46
100	MAXWELL PARK	3	66
101	Milliken Park	*1	66
102	MILNGAVIE	3	66
103	MOUNT FLORIDA	1	66
104	Mount Vernon	3	66
105	MUIREND	3	55
106	NEILSTON		
107	Neilston	*3	56
108	NEWTON	*3	56
109	NITSHILL	*1	56
110	North Johnstone	*3	56
111	Old Kilpatrick	*1	56
	PAISLEY:	1	56
112	Abercorn	5	56
113	Canal	4	56
114	GILMOUR STREET	1	56
115	ST JAMES	3	65
116	West	5	46
117/118	Parkhead / Parkhead	3	65
119	PARTICK	4	56
120	Partick Central	4	56
121	Partick West	3	46
122	PATTERTON	5	46
123	POLLOKSHAWS EAST	5	46
124	POLLOKSHAWS WEST	*1	65
125	POLLOKSHIELDS EAST	1	56
126	POLLOKSHIELDS WEST	*4	56
127	Potterhill	1	57
127A	Possil Park	*3	56
128	QUEEN'S PARK	*1	56
129	QUEEN'S STREET	5	46
130	Renfrew-Fulbar Street	1	47
131	-Porterfield	3	46
132	-South	1	47
133	-Wharf	4	56
134	Robroyston	3	56
135		3	66
	RUTHERGLEN	3	66
136	St Rollox	1	67
137	Scotstoun	1	57
137	Scotstoun	*3	56
138	SCOTSTOUNHILL	3	37
139	SHAWLANDS	3	56
140	SHETTLESTON	1	57
141	(SUNFER) §85	1	56
142	Stepps Road	1	56
143	Stobcross (Note 6)	3	56
144	Summerston	*1	66
145	THORNLIEBANK	*3	56
146	THORNTONHALL	5	46
147	Tollcross	1	57
148	Torrance	3	56
149	Uddingston	1	66
150	UDDINGSTON	3	55
151	Uddingston West	3	45
152	Victoria Park	4	45
153	WESTERTON	3	66
154	WHITEINCH	*5	46
155	Whiteinch	5	46
156	Whiteinch	3	47
157	(WILLIAMWOOD)	1	56
158	YOKER	5	46
159	Yoker	5	46
160	Yorkhill	4	46

GOODS DEPOTS

Ry	Ref	No	Name / Location
5	46	14	Cart
5	46	16	Canal
3	46	17	Blackstone
A5	46	21	Wallneuk
A5	46	22	Arkleston
5	46	23	Corsebar
5	46	24	Potterhill
5	46	25	Meiklerigs
34	56	31	Busby
4	56	33	Cardonald North
3	56	3A	Partick West - West
3	46	35	Partick West - North
3	66	36	Partick West - East
3	66	37	Bellshaugh
3	56	38	Kelvinside
3	56	39	Kelvinside North
1	56	42	Cowlairs
2	37	43	Cathcart West
3	47	AA	Cardonald South
4	56	48	Cathcart North
1	56	49	Cathcart East
1	56	51	Ruthglen West
4	55	52	Ruthglen North
5	46	53	Ruthglen Central
1	67	54	Ruthglen East
1	67	58	Kirkhill
3	66	60	Hunthill
5	46	61	Auchencraith
3	46	62	Strathaven
5	46	65	Bridgend
4	65	66	Waterside
4	56	67	Middlemuir/Monkland
1	67	69	Campsie Branch
1	56	73	Shettleston
3	55	7A	Clarkston West
3	55	75	Clarkston East
3	55	76	Lyon Cross
1	65	77	Goods

Ry	Ref	No	Name / Location
5	56	61	Burnbank
4	46	2	Uddingston
5	46	3	Newton
5	56	4	Netherton
3	66	5	Barrhead South
3	66	6	Gleniffer
3	56	7	Glenfield
3	56	8	Paisley King Street
1	56	9	Paisley
3	56	10	Paisley East
1	66	11	Rutherglen
1	47	12	Kennyhill
3	66	13	Springburn Park
1	56	14	Possil
1	57	15	Possil Park
3	55	16	Dumbarton
3	55	17	Dumbarton
3	66	18	Deanside
1	67	19	Yoker
1	66	20	Whiteinch
3	66	21	Thornliebank
1	66	22	Sautel
3	56	23	Basin - Kirkintilloch
1	57	24	Bridgend
3	55	25	Cambusland
1	56	26	Paisley Canal
3	56	27	Linwood
3	55	28	Linwood
1	56	29	Barrhead
3	56	30	Pollokshaws West

COMPANY WORKS

No	Name	Ry	Ref
C1	Cowlairs	1	56
2	St Rollox	3	56

JUNCTIONS

No.	Name	Ref
6	Milngavie	1 57
7	Knightswood North	1 56
8	Maryhill	1 56
9	Knightswood South	1 56
10	Whiteinch - West	1 56
11	Whiteinch - North	3 56
12	Whiteinch - East	1 56

NOTES

(1) REF - All in square N5
(2) * - Detail see 20A
(3) § - Name changed
(4) § - Modern name
(5) Brackets round part of name - if in CAPITALS indicates modern addition - if in small letters it shows that part now dropped.
(6) Stobcross shown on maps in the 157. Joint Goods - See 20A for full details
(7) Some omissions in 20A area due to lack of space

Jcts in the Dumbarton area see Map 20B
Jcts in the Glasgow Central area See Map 20A

NOTE
Due to lack of space Junctions are named selectively in Gazetteer

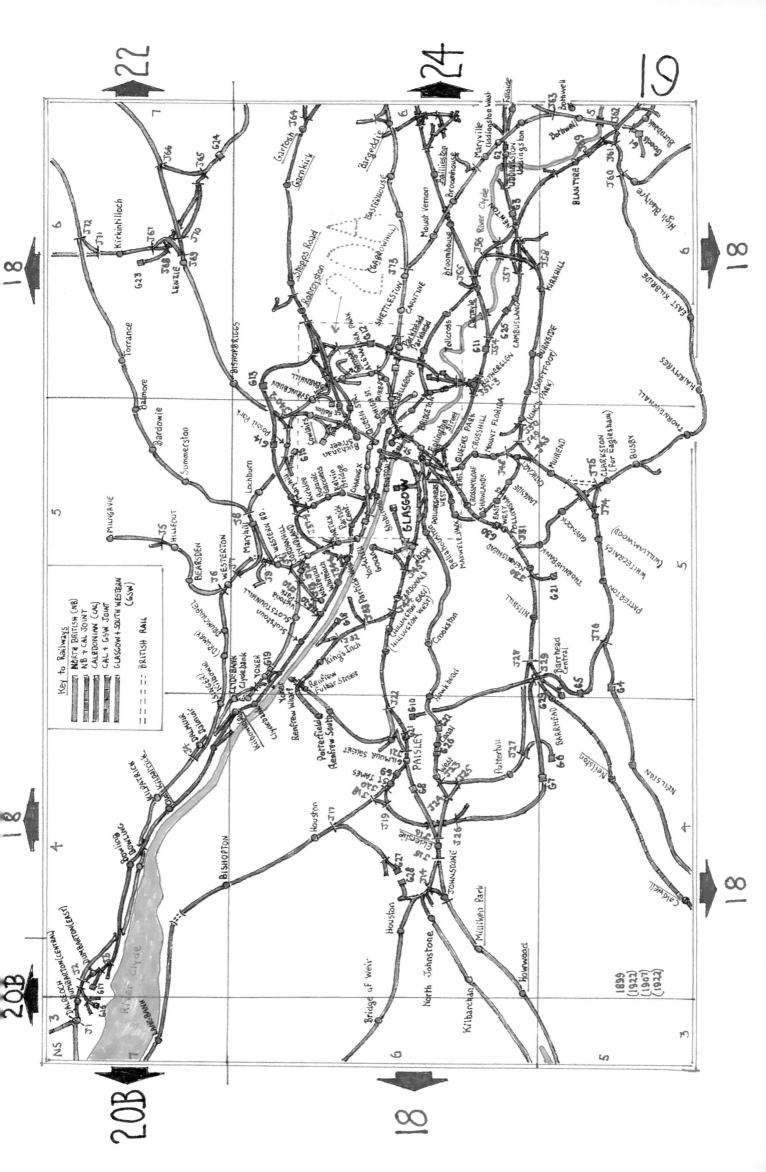

20A GLASGOW

RAILWAYS

No.	Company
R 1	NORTH BRITISH
2	CALEDONIAN
3	CALEDONIAN + GLASGOW & S.W. JT.
4	GLASGOW + SOUTH WESTERN
5	PRINCE'S DOCK JOINT (1,2+4)
6	GLASGOW SUBWAY (4' gauge)

STATIONS

No.	Name	Ry Ref
A 1	ALEXANDRA PARADE	§ 1 6165
2	ALEXANDRA PARK	§ 1 6165
3	ANDERSTON CROSS	2 5865
4	(ARGYLE STREET)	2 5965
5	BARNHILL	1 6067
6	Bellahouston	4 5564
7	BELLGROVE	1 6065
8	Botanic Gardens	2 5667
9	BRIDGE STREET	§ 6 5864
9A	Bridge Street	§ 2 5864
10	Bridgeton Central	§ 1 6064
11	Bridgeton Cross	§ 1 6064
12	BRIDGETON CROSS	2 6064
13	Buchanan Street	2 5966
14	BUCHANAN STREET	6 5865
15	CARNTYNE	1 6265
16	CENTRAL HIGH LEVEL	2 5865
17	Central Low Level	2 5865
18	CESSNOCK	6 5564
19	CHARING CROSS	1 5765
20	COPLAND ROAD	§43 6 5564
21	COWCADDENS	6 5866
22	Cowlairs	1 5967
23	Crow Road	2 5567
24	Cumberland Street	4 5863
25	DALMARNOCK	2 6063
26	DUKE STREET	1 6165
27	Eglinton Street	2 5863
28	Finnieston	1 5765
29	(FINNIESTON)	§70 2 5765
30	Gallowgate	4 5965
31	Gallowgate Central	1 6064
32	Garngad	1 6066
33	Glasgow Cross	2 5965
34	Glasgow Green	2 5964
35	Gorbals	3 5864
36	Govan	3 5565
37	GOVAN	6 5565
38	HIGH STREET	1 5965
39	HILLHEAD	6 5766
40	Hyndland	4 5564
41	(HYNDLAND)	1 5567
42	Ibrox	6 5564
43	(IBROX)	6 5864
44	Kelvin Bridge	2 5864
45	KELVINBRIDGE	1 6064
46	KELVIN HALL	1 6064
47	Kelvinhaugh	2 6064
48	KINNING PARK	2 5966
49	Kirklee	6 5865
50	MAXWELL PARK	1 6265
51	Parkhead	2 5865
52	Parkhead	2 5865
53	PARTICK	6 5664
54	PARTICK	1 5765
55	Partick Central	6 5564
56	Pollokshields	6 5866
57	POLLOCKSHIELDS EAST	1 5967
58	POLLOCKSHIELDS WEST	2 5567
59	QUEEN STREET · HIGH LEVEL	1 5965
60	QUEEN STREET · LOW LEVEL	1 5965
61	St. Enoch's	6 5865
62	ST ENOCH'S	6 5865
63	ST GEORGE'S CROSS	6 5866
64	St. Rollox	2 6066
65	Shields	4 5965
66	Shields Road	1 6064
67	SHIELDS ROAD	1 6066
68	SPRINGBURN	2 5965
69	Strathbungo	2 5964
70	STOBCROSS	3 5864
71	Tollcross	3 5565
72	WEST STREET	6 5565
73	Yorkhill	1 5965

TUNNELS

No	Name	Ry Ref
38	Prince's Dock	2 6167
T1	Stobcross	2 6166
2	Anderston	2 6066
3	Canning Street	1 6066
4	Dalmarnock Road	1 6165
5	Finnieston	1 5765
6	Charing Cross	2 6164
7	High Street	2 6063 †
8	Bellgrove	2 6063
9	Duke Street	2 6062
10	Blochairn	4 5964
11	Eglinton Street	4 5964

No	Name	Ry Ref
3	Balornock	2 5864
4	Provan Mill	3 5664
5	Robroyston	2 5966
6	Blackhill	2 5966
7	Blochairn	1 6066
8	Sighthill East	3 5863
9	Sighthill	12 5765
10	Haghill	2 5864
11	Sydney Street	3 5564
12	Parkhead Forge	2 5765
13	London Road	2 5865
14	Strathclyde	2 5965
15	Clyde	2 6064
16	Saltmarket	2 6063
17	Clyde Street	1 5765
18	West Street	1 5865
19	Langside	1 5965
20	Cathcart Road	1 6065
21	Gushetfaulds	1 6065
22	Central Station	1 6066
23	Muirhouse South	2 5863
24	Muirhouse Central	
25	Muirhouse North	
26	Maxwell	
27	Shields	
28	Scotland Street	
29	Kelvinside	
30	Partick	
31	Eglinton Street	
32	Bridge Street	
33	Bellahouston	
34	Terminus	

SIDINGS

No.	Company / Name 1900	Ry Ref
P1	Provan Gas Works In	2 5765 §19
2	Provan Gas Works	2 6263
3	Blochairn Iron	6 5864
4	Blochairn Iron	1 5566
5	Port Dundas Distillery	
6	Dyewood Mills	1 6264
7	Carntyne Iron & Steel	1 6264
8	Parkhead Forge	3 5664
9	(Cook Street Branch	2 6063 §20
10	Eglinton Foundry	1 6164

GOODS

No.	Name / Location	Ry Ref
1	BELLAHOUSTON	3 5564
2	Bridgeton	2 6063
3	CAMLACHIE	2 5666
4	College	6 5766
5	Craighall	6 5866
6	Eglinton Street	1 5665
7	GENERAL TERMINUS	6 5564
8	GUSHETFAULDS	2 5667
9	Haghill	2 5662
10	HIGH STREET (College)	1 6164
11	Kennyhill	2 6164
12	Kinning Park	1 5566
13	LONDON ROAD	6 5566
14	PARTICK	2 5566
15	Pinkston North	3 5764
16	Pinkston South	2 5763
17	Port Dundas	2 5762
18	PORT EGLINTON	1 5965
19	Prince's Dock	
20	ST ROLLOX EAST	4 5865
21	St Rollox West	6 5865
22	Sighthill	6 5866
23	Southside	2 6066
24	Stobcross	4 5763
25	West Street	4 5764

RAILWAY WORKS

No.	Name / Location	Ry Ref
C1	St Rollox	2 5764
2	Parkhead	2 5664

ENGINE SHEDS

No.	Name / Location	Ry Ref
E1	St Rollox	2 6165
2	Parkhead	2 5664

JUNCTIONS

No.	Name / Location	Ry Ref
J1	Germiston High	1 5966
2	Germiston Low	2 5966

NOTES:

(1) Name changes §1920's name   §Modern name

Part name in small letters — that portion dropped from title

Name or part in brackets shows modern addition

(2) †Also known as ~ High Street, College East or Stoney Street at various times

(3) References are all in NS

(4) Stations in RED - Subway

(5) Goods in CAPITALS - Open in 1985

(6) Junctions un-named on the map

~ official name not known.

35 5564

20A

20B   GREENOCK + FIRTH OF CLYDE

NOTES:
(1) NAME CHANGE: Old & (New) $
(2) REFERENCES: All in NS

RAILWAY

No.	Company
R 1	NORTH BRITISH
2	DUMBARTON + BALLOCH JOINT (1+3)
3	CALEDONIAN
4	GLASGOW + SOUTH WESTERN

STATIONS

No.	Name	Ry Ref
A 1	ALEXANDRIA	2 37
2	BALLOCH CENTRAL	2 38
3	BALLOCH PIER	2 38
4	BOGSTON	5 37
5	(BRANCHTON)	3 27
6	CARDROSS	1 37
7	CARTSDYKE	3 27
8	CATHCART STREET	3 27
9	CRAIGENDORAN	1 38
10	DALREOCH	2 37
11	DUMBARTON (CENTRAL)	2 37
12	DUMBARTON (EAST)	3 47
13	FORT MATILDA	3 27
14	GOUROCK	3 27
	GREENOCK:	
15	CATHCART STREET §	3 27
16	(CENTRAL) §	3 27
17	Prince's Pier	4 27
18	WEST	3 27
19	HELENSBURGH CENTRAL	2 37
20	HELENSBURGH UPPER	2 38
21	Inch Green	2 38
22	INVERKIP	5 37
23	Jamestown	3 27
24	Kilmalcolm	1 37
25	LANGBANK	3 27
26	Lynedoch	3 27
27	Lynedoch Upper	1 38
28	PORT GLASGOW	2 37
29	Port Glasgow - Inch Green	4 37
30	Port Glasgow - Upper	4 37
31	Prince's Pier	4 27
32	Ravenscraig	3 27
33	RENTON	2 37
34	Row	1 28
35	Shandon	1 28
36	WEMYSS BAY	3 16
37	(WOODHALL)	3 37

No.	Name	Ry Ref
4	Dumbarton	2 37
5	Dumbarton	3 47
7	Craigendoran	2 37
	DUMBARTON:	
8	Goods	2 37
9	Joint Line	123 47
10	Dock Yard	2 37
11	Leven	3 47
12	Harbour Branch	3 37
13	James Watt Dock Dock Jcts	4 37
14	Wemyss Bay	3 37
15	Port Glasgow	4 27
16	Overton	3 27

SIDINGS

No.	Company / Location	Ry Ref
P 1	Dalmonach	1 38
2	Ferryfield Print	1 28
3	Dillichip Dye	3 16
4	Cordale Print	3 37
5	Overton Paper	

ENGINE SHEDS

No.	Name / Location	Ry Ref
E 1	Helensburgh	4 37

GOODS

No.	Name / Location	Ry Ref
G 1	Greenock	4 27
2	Bogston	3 27
3	Port Glasgow	3 37

JUNCTIONS

No.	Name / Location	Ry Ref
J 1	Forth + Clyde	1 28
2	Dalmonach	2 38
3	Alexandria North	2 37
4	Alexandria South	2 37
5	Cordale Branch	2 37
6	Dalreoch	3 37

TUNNELS

No.	Name	Ry Ref
T 1	Newton Street	1 38
2		2 38
3		2 37
4	Bishopton No.1 + No.2	2 37
5	Dalreoch	12 37

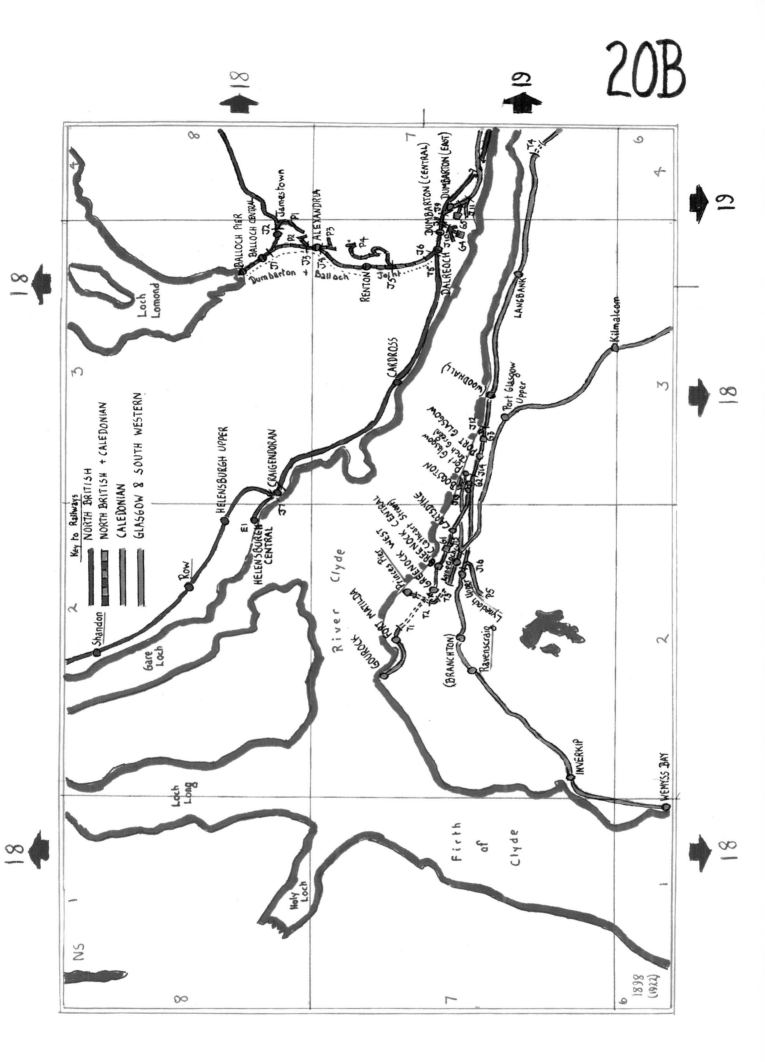

20B

ARDROSSAN, KILMARNOCK + TROON

RAILWAYS

No	Company	Ry Ref
R1	CALEDONIAN	3 35
2	CALEDONIAN & GLASGOW + SOUTH WESTERN	3 43
3	GLASGOW + SOUTH WESTERN	3 43

STATIONS

No	Name	Ry Ref
A	ARDROSSAN:	
1	Ardrossan	3 24
2	(HARBOUR)	1 24
3	Montgomerie Pier	1 24
4	SOUTH BEACH	3 24
5	Town	1 24
6	Winton Pier	3 24
7	Auchenmade	1 34
8	BARASSIE	3 33
9	Bogside	1 34
10	Bogside	3 34
11	Crosshouse	
12	Cunninghamhead	
13	DALRY	
14	Dreghorn	
15	Drybridge	
16	DUNLOP	
17	Gailes	
18	Galston	
19	Gatehead	
20	Hurlford	
21	Irvine	3 24
22	IRVINE	1 24
23	KILMARNOCK	3 24
24	KILMAURS	3 24
25	Kilwinning	1 24
26	KILWINNING	3 24
27	MONTGOMERIE PIER §2	1 34
28	Montgreenan	3 33
29	St Marnocks	1 34
30	Saltcoats	3 34
31	SALTCOATS	3 34
32	Springside	3 34
33	Stevenston	3 24
34	STEVENSTON	3 33
35	STEWARTON	3 33
36	TROON	2 44
37	WEST KILBRIDE	3 33
38	Winton Pier	3 43

JUNCTIONS

No	Name/Location	Ry Ref
1	Ardrossan - Parkhouse	1 24
2	- Holm	3 33
3	- Castlehill	3 34
4	- Harbour	BR 25
5	- Winton	BR 25
6	Dubbs	3 24
7	Longford	3 43
8	Byrehill	1 24
9	Kilwinning	3 33
10	Dalry	
11	Irvine	
12	Barassie North	3 43
13	Middle	3 43
14	South	3 24
15	Templehill	
16	Town + Harbour	
17	Lochgreen	
18	Perceton Branch	3 43
19	Crosshouse	3 35
20	Kilmarnock - West (Note 3)	3 43
21	- Central	3 43
22	- East	3 43
23	- Key Park	3 43
24	Fairlie Branch	3 33
25	Moorfield	3 24
26	Bellfield	3 24
27	Garrieth Branch (Note 1)	3 34
28	Craigie	3 24
29	Mayfield Branch	3 24
30	Kilwinning	3 33

SIDINGS + GOODS BRANCHES

No	Name of Company or Location	Ry Ref
P1	Araeer Iron	1 24
2	Fairlie Branch	3 24
3	Fergushill Pits Branch	2 44
4	Hunterston Ore	3 33
5	Hunterston Ore	3 24
6	Longford Chemicals	3 24
7	Mayfield Branch	3 43
8	Nobel's Siding	1 24
9	Perceton Branch	3 33

ENGINE SHEDS

No	Location	Ry Ref
E1	Kilmarnock	3 43
2	Ardrossan	1 34

TUNNELS

No	Name	Ry Ref
T1	Mossgiel	3 33

GOODS DEPOTS

No	Name/Location	Ry Ref
G1	Garrochburn	1 33
2	Irvine Harbour	3 43
3	Kilmarnock	2 44
4	Kilmarnock	1 24
5	Lissens	3 24
6	Riccarton + Craigie	1 34
7	Stewarton	3 34
8	Troon	3 43
9	Troon Harbour	1 24

NOTES:

(1) Also known as Galston Branch Jn

(2) REF - All in square NS

(3) NAME CHANGE -
§ 1920's name
⸭ Modern name

(4) GOODS - Red underline indicates
line on which station is open (1985)

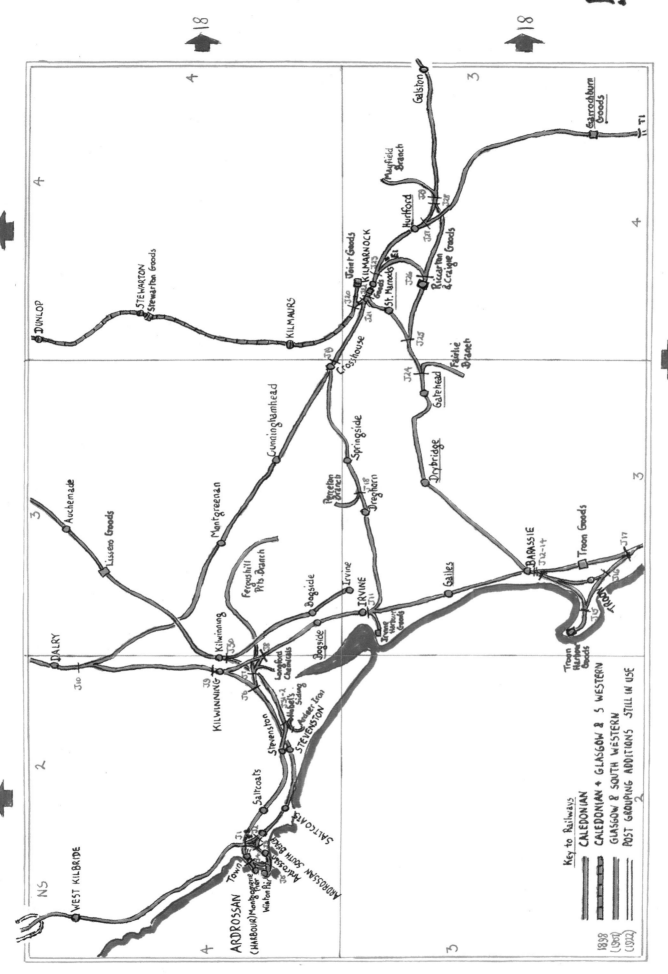

21

Key to Railways
CALEDONIAN + GLASGOW & S WESTERN
GLASGOW & SOUTH WESTERN
POST GROUPING ADDITIONS STILL IN USE

1898
(1907)
(1912)

STIRLING, DUNFERMLINE + MOTHERWELL

No.	Company
R1	NORTH BRITISH
2	NORTH BRITISH + CALEDONIAN JOINT
3	CALEDONIAN
4	FORTH BRIDGE see Note 4

NOTES:
(1) ALL STATIONS in the area covered by the map are listed. Those indicated AND named on the map are shown in BLACK. Those not located are in BLUE and the enlargement map where they are to be found is indicated in the number column. OTHER features listed only if not on enlargements

(2) REFERENCES - Are in NN, NO, NS and NT. The initial N is omitted.

(3) NAME CHANGES - § map date name § modern (or later) name.

(4) FORTH BRIDGE - Owned by GREAT NORTHERN, NORTH EASTERN, NORTH BRITISH + MIDLAND. Worked NB

STATIONS

No.	Name	Ry Ref
A1	ABERDOUR	1 T18
2	ADDIEWELL	3 S96
3	AIRDRIE	1 S76
(24)	Airdrie	3 S76
4	Airth	3 S88
5	Alloa	1 S89
6	Alva	1 S89
7	Armadale	1 S96
8	Auchengray	3 S95(24)
9	Auchenheath	3 S84(24)
10	Avon Bridge	1 S97(24)
11	Balado	1 O00(24)
12	Balerno	3 T17
13	Bangour	1 T07(24)
14	Bankhead	1 S94
15	Banknock	2 S77
16	Bannockburn	3 S89
17	Bargeddie	1 S76
18	Bantan	3 T16
19	Bathgate Lower	1 S96
20	Bathgate Upper	1 S96
(24)	Bellshill	1 S76
21	BELLSHILL	3 S75
22	Bents	1 S96
23	Biggar	3 T03
24	Blackford	3 N80
25	Blackston(e)	1 S97
26	Blackwood	3 S84
27	Blairadam	1 T19
(24)	BLAIRHILL + Gartsherrie	1 S76
28	Bogside	1 S99
28A	Bo'ness	1 T08
29	Bonnybridge	1 S87
30	Bonny bridge	3 S87
31	Bonnybridge Central	2 S88
32	Bothwell	1 S75
33	Bothwell	3 S75
34	Bowhouse	1 S97
35	Braidwood	3 S84
36	BREICH	3 S96
37	Broomlee	1 T15
38	Broughton	3 T13
39	(Burnbank) §	1 S75
40	Bridge of Allan	3 S79
41	Brocketsbrae	3 S84
42	Calder	3 S76
43	Calderbank	3 S76
44	Caldercruix	1 S86(24)
45	Cambus	1 S89
(24)	Cambusnethan	3 S85
46	Cairneyhill	1 T08
47	Camelon	1 S88
48	CARDENDEN	1 T29
49	(CARFIN)	3 S75
50	CARLUKE	3 S84
51	Carnwath	3 S94
52	CARSTAIRS	3 S94
53	Castlecary	1 S77
54	Causewayend	1 S97
55	Causewayhead	1 S89
56	Chapelhall	3 S76

No.	Name	Ry Ref
57	Charlestown	1 T08
58	Clackmannan (+ Kennet)	1 S99
59	Clackmannan Road	1 S99
60	Clarkston	1 S76
61	Cleghorn	3 S88
62	Cleland	1 S89
63	(CLELAND) §166	1 S89
64	Coalburn	1 S87
	COATBRIDGE	1 O00(24)
65	Cobbinshaw	3 T17
65A	Calzium	2 S77
66	Commonhead	3 S89
67	Coulter	1 S76
68	Cowdenbeath New	3 T16
69	COWDENBEATH Old	1 S96
70	CRIEFF JUNCT §109	1 S96
71	Crook of Devon	1 S76
72	Crossgates	3 S75
73	CROY	1 S96
74	Culross	3 T03
75	CUMBERNAULD	3 N80
76	Currie	1 S97
77	Currie Hill	3 S84
78	DALMENY	1 T19
79	Dalserf	3 S88
80	Denny	1 S99
81	Dennyloanhead	1 T08
82	Dollar	1 S87
83	Dolphinton	3 S87
84	Dolphinton	2 S88
85	Douglas	1 S75
86	Douglas West	3 S75
87	Doune	1 S97
88	Drumshoreland	3 S84
89	Dullatur	3 S96
90	DUNBLANE	1 T15
91	DUNFERMLINE Lower	3 T13
92	Dunfermline Upper	1 S75
93	Dunsyre	3 S79
94	Eastgrange	3 S84
	FALKIRK	1 S88
95	GRAHAMSTOWN	1 S87
96	HIGH STREET	1 S86(24)
97	Fallside	1 S89
98	Ferniegair	3 S85
99	Flemington	1 T08
100	Forest Mill	1 S99
101	Forrestfield	3 S75
102	Gargunnock	3 S84
103	Gartcosh	3 S94
104	Gartsherrie	3 S94
105	Gateside	1 S77
106	Gavell	1 S97
107	Glassford	1 S89
108	Glenboig	3 S76
109	(GLENEAGLES) §70	3 N91

No.	Name	Ry Ref
110	Gogar	1 T08
111	Grangemouth	1 S99
112	Greenhill	1 S99
113	Greenloaning	1 S76
114	Halbeath	3 S94
115	HAMILTON CENTRAL	3 S85
116	Hamilton	3 S85
117	Hamilton Peacock Cross	3 S83
118	HAMILTON WEST	
119	Harburn	3 S76
120	HARTWOOD	1 S76
121	Haywood	1 S76
122	HOLYTOWN	1 S76
123	INVERKEITHING	3 T05
124	Juniper Green	3 S85
125	Kelty	2 S77
126	Kilbagie	1 S76
127	Kilsyth	3 T03
128	Kinbuck	1 T19
129	Kincardine	1 T19
130	Kinniel	3 N91
131	Kinross	1 O00
132	Kirkliston	1 T18
133	(KIRKNEWTON) §153	1 S77
134	Lamington	1 S98
135	LANARK	3 S77
136	Langloan	3 T16
137	LARBERT	3 T16
138	Larkhall East	4 T17
139	Larkhall Central	3 S75
140	Law	3 S88
141	Lesmahagow	2 S87
142	LINLITHGOW	1 S99
143	Livingston	1 T14
144	LOCHGELLY	3 T14
145	Loch Leven	3 S83
146	Longriggend	3 S83
147	Macbie Hill	3 N70
148	Manuel Lower	1 T07
149	Manuel Upper	1 S77
150	Mawcarse	3 N70
151	Meikle Earnock	1 T08
152	Menstrie	1 T08
153	MIDCALDER §133	3 T04
154	Milnathort	1 T08
155	Morningside	
156	Morningside	1 S88
157	Mossend	1 S87
158	MOTHERWELL	3 S75
159	Netherburn	3 S96
160	Newbigging	3 S75
161	Newhouse	3 S75
162	Newmains	1 S99
163	Newpark	3 S86
164	NORTH QUEENSFERRY	1 S79
165	Oakley	3 S76
166	OMOA §63	3 S76
167	Overtown	1 O10
168	Phillipstoun	1 S77
169	Plains	3 S74
170	Plean	3 S76
171	POLMONT	3 N91
172	Ponfeigh	1 T17

No.	Name	Ry Ref
173	Quarter Road	3 S98
174	Ratho	3 S87
175	(Ravelrig)	3 N80
176	Rawyards	1 T18
177	(ROSYTH)	1 T09
178	Rumbling Bridge	1 S75
179	Sandilands	1 S75
180	Sauchie	3 S75
181	Saughton	3 T06
182	Shielmuir	3 S85
183	SHOTTS	3 S95
184	Slamannan	3 S75
185	Stirling	1 T18
186	STIRLING	3 T16
187	Stobo	1 T19
188	Stonehouse	1 S99
189	Strathaven Central	2 S77
190	Strathaven North	3 N70
191	Symington	1 S98
192	Thankerton	1 S98
193	Throsk Platform	1 O10
194	Tillicoultry	1 T17
195	Tillietudlem	3 T16
196	Tarryburn	3 S93
197	Turnhouse	3 S84
198	Uddingston	3 S76
199	Uphall	3 S88
200	WEST CALDER	3 S75
201	Westcraigs	3 S75
202	Westfield	3 S85(24)
203	Whifflet High	3 S84(24)
204	Whifflet Low	1 T07(24)
205	Whifflet (NB)	1 T06
206	Whitburn	1 T19
207	Whiterigg	1 O10
208	Wilsontown	1 S86
	Winchburgh	1 T15
	WISHAW Central	1 S97
	Wishaw South	1 S97

GOODS

No	Name/Location	Ry Ref
G 1	Crofthead	1 S89
2	Addiewell	3 T16
3	East Calder	1 O10
4	Holygate	1 S85
5	Greengairs	3 S85
6	Gartshore	3 S76
7	Lochmill	3 S75
8	South Queensferry	3 S84
9	Steelend	3 T04
	SIDINGS	
No	Name/Location/Camp	Ry Ref
P1	Spireslack Pit	3 T06
2	Climpey Colliery	4 T18
3	Cleuch Lower	1 T08
4	Pool Colliery	3 S85
5	Tarbrax Oil	3 S85
6	Cobbinshaw Pit	1 T07
7	Benhar East Branch	1 S86
8	Benhar West Branch	3 S88
9	Benhar No.2	1 S97
10	Woodend Colliery	3 S83
11	Armadale Branch	1 S96
12	Coulston Branch	1 S96
13	Broxburn Oil	1 T07
14	Jawcraig Branch	1 S87
15	West Plean Pit	3 S88
16	East Plean Pit	3 S88
17	Oakley Colliery	1 T09
18	Cowglen Quarry	1 T09
19	Lettians Colliery	1 T09
20	Lathalmond Lime	1 T09
21	Blairenbathie Siding	1 T19
22	Lochore Mines	1 T19
25	Glencraig Colliery	1 T19

ENGINE SHEDS

No	Location	Ry Ref
E1	Bathgate	1 S96
2	Carstairs	3 S94

BRIDGES

No.	Name	Ry Ref
V1	Forth Bridge	4 T17

SUMMITS

No	Name/Location	Ry Ref
S1	Cobbinshaw	3 T05

JUNCTIONS

No	Name/Location	Ry Ref
J1	Dunblane	3 N70
2	Kinross	1 O10
3+4	Kelty North	1 T19
7	Lumphinnans	1 T19
9	Cowdenbeath North	1 T19
10	Slamannan	1 S87
11	Blackstone	1 S97
12	Bangour	1 T07
13	Uphall Branch	1 T07
15	Winchburgh	1 T07
16	Westcraigs	1 S96
17	Woodend	1 S96
18	Armadale	1 S96
19	Bathgate West	1 S96
20	Polkemmet (N)	1 S96
21	Polkemmet (S)	1 S96
22	Bathgate East	1 S96
23	West Calder Branch	1 S96
24	Addiewell Branch	1 S96
25	Benhar	3 S96
26	West Benhar Branch	1 S96
27	Woodmuir	3 S96
28	Limefield	3 T06
29	Auchengray (N, W) §S	3 T05
30	Tarbrax	3 T05
31-2	Lawhead + Pool	3 S95
33	Silvermuir South	3 S94
36	Dolphinton Branch	3 S94
37	Strawfrank	3 S94
38	Dolphinton	13 T14
39	Alton Heights	3 S83
40	Coatburn Branch	3 S83
41	Poneil	3 S83
42	Symington	3 S93
43	Kelty South	1 T19
44	Plean Branch	3 S88
45	Alloa Branch	3 S88

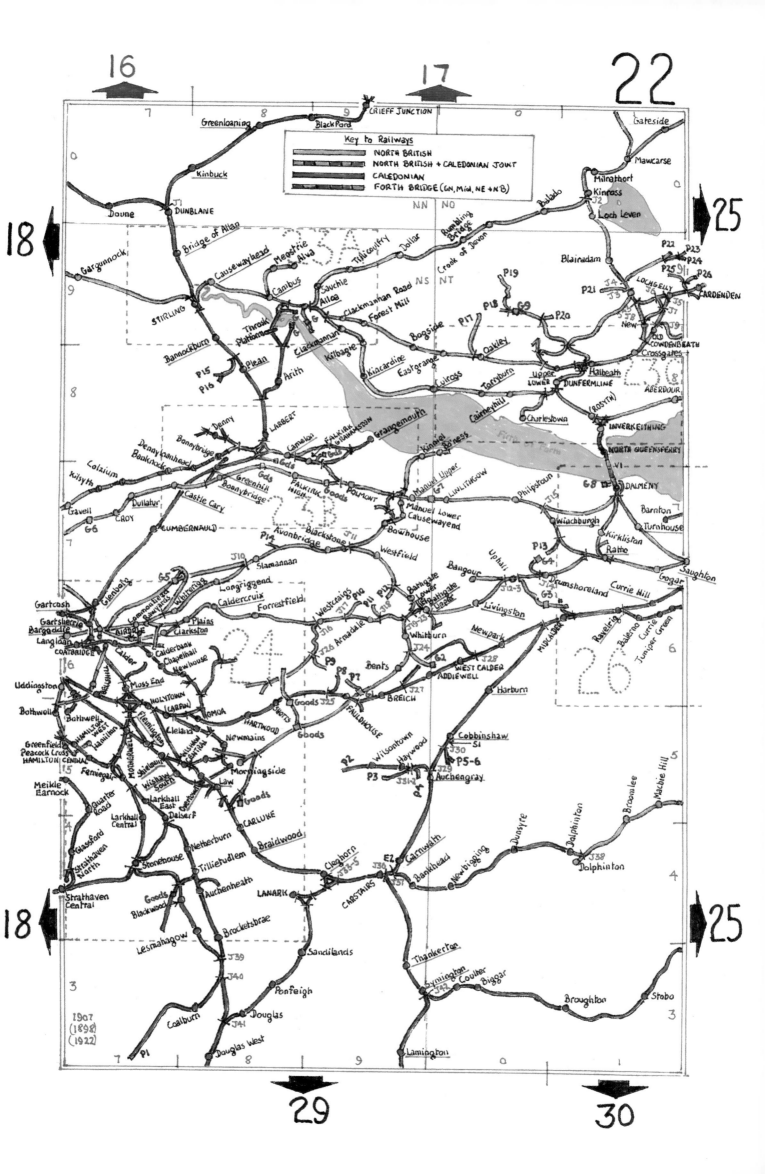

STIRLING + ALLOA   FALKIRK   DUNFERMLINE

RAILWAYS

No.	Company
R 1	NORTH BRITISH
2	NB + CALEDONIAN JOINT
3	CALEDONIAN
4	FORTH BRIDGE (See Note 2)
5	ADMIRALTY LINE - ROSYTH

STATIONS

No.	Name	Ry Ref
A 1	ABERDOUR	1 C 18
2	Alloa	1 A 89
3	Alva	1 A 89
4	Banknock	2 B 77
5	Bannockburn	3 A 89
6	Bonnybridge	1 B 87
7	Bonnybridge	3 B 87
8	Bonnybridge Central	2 B 88
9	Bowhouse	1 B 97
10	Bridge of Allan	3 A 79
11	Cambus	1 A 89
12	Cairneyhill	1 C 08
13	Camelon	1 B 88
14	Castlecary	1 B 77
15	Causewayend	1 B 97
16	Causewayhead	1 A 89
17	Charlestown	1 C 08
18	Clackmannan (+ Kennet)	1 A 99
19	Clackmannan Road	1 A 99
20	Cowdenbeath New	1 C 19
21	COWDENBEATH Old	1 C 19
22	Crossgates	1 C 18
23	Denny	3 B 88
24	Dennyloanhead	2 B 87
25	DUNFERMLINE (Lower)	1 C 08
26	DUNFERMLINE Upper	1 C 08
27	Eastgrange	1 C 08
	FALKIRK:	
28	GRAHAMSTON	1 B 88
29	HIGH STREET	1 B 87
30	Forest Mill	1 A 99
31	Grangemouth	3 B 98
32	Greenhill	3 B 87
33	Halbeath	1 C 18
34	INVERKEITHING	1 C 18
35	Kilbagie	1 A 99
36	Kinniel	1 B 98
37	LARBERT	3 B 88
38	Manuel High Level	1 B 97
39	Manuel Low Level	1 B 97
40	Menstrie	1 A 89
41	NORTH QUEENSFERRY	4 C 18
42	Oakley	1 C 08
43	POLMONT	1 B 97
44	(ROSYTH)	1 C 18
45	Sauchie	1 A 89
46	Stirling	1 A 89
47	STIRLING	3 A 79
48	Throsk Platform	3 A 89
49	Tillicoultry	1 A 99
50	Torryburn	1 C 08

GOODS

No.	Name/Location	Ry Ref
G 1	Stirling Shore Road	1 A 89
2	Alloa	1 A 89
3	Alloa	3 A 89
4	South Alloa	3 A 89
5	Stoneywood	3 B 78
6	Ingliston	3 B 88
7	Camelon	1 B 87
8	Camelon	3 B 88
9	Falkirk - Daldecse	1 B 88
10	Springfield	1 B 88
11	Redding	1 B 97
12	Rough Castle	1 B 87
13	Lime Road	1 B 87
14	Charlestown	1 C 08
15	Netherton	1 C 08
16	North Queensferry	1 C 18
17	Inverkeithing	1 C 18

SIDINGS

No.	Branch / Company	Ry Ref
P 1	Alloa Dock	1 A 89
2	Kilbagie	1 A 99
3	Carronrigg Colliery	3 B 78
4	Brick Works	3 B 88
5	Iron Co	3 B 98
6	Harbour	3 B 98
7	Falkirk Iron	1 B 98
8	Shieldhill Branch	1 B 97
9	Roughrigg Colliery	1 B 97
10	Lowglen Quarry	1 C 09
11	Steelend Goods	1 C 09
12	Lassodie + Gask	1 C 19
13	Balmule Collieries	1 C 09
14	Victoria Pit	1 C 08
15	Colton	1 C 08
16	Charlestown Harbour	1 C 08
17	Admiralty Sidings	5 C 18
18	Inverkeithing Harbour	1 C 18

No.		Ry Ref
19	Oakley Colliery	1 C 08

BRIDGES

No.	Name	Ry Ref
V 1	Alloa Bridge	1 A 89
2	Forth Bridge	1 A 89

ENGINE SHEDS

No.	Name/Location	Ry Ref
E 1	Stirling	3 A 89
2	Polmont	1 B 97
3	Dunfermline	1 C 18

TUNNELS

No.	Name	Ry Ref
T 1	Kippenross	3 A 79

JUNCTIONS

No.	Name/Location	Ry Ref
J 1	Balloch Line	31 A 79
2	Dunfermline Line	31 A 89
3	Alva Line	1 A 89
4	Alloa Longarse	31 A 89
5	West	1 A 89
6	Kincardine	1 A 99
7	East	1 A 89
8	Goods	1 A 89
9	Dunmore	3 A 89
10	Stoneywood	3 B 88
11	Ingliston	3 B 88
12	Denny Branch North	3 B 88
13	West	3 B 88
14	South	3 B 88
15	Carmuirs North	31 B 88
16	East	1 B 88
17	West	31 B 88
18	Swing Bridge	1 B 88
19	Bainsford	13 B 98
20	Grahamston Goods	3 B 98
21	Grangemouth Branch	13 B 88
22	Dalerse	1 B 88
23	Fauldubs	3 B 98
24	Grangemouth Docks	3 B 98
25	Bonnybridge Station	3 B 87
26	Greenhill Upper	13 B 87
27	Greenhill Lower	13 B 87
28	Camelon	3 B 88
29	Rough Castle Branch	1 B 87
30	Falkirk High - Goods	1 B 87
31	Polmont	1 B 97
32	Coatbridge Line	1 B 97
33	Bowness Low	1 B 97
34	Bowness High	1 B 97
35	Shieldhill Branch	1 B 97
36	Causewayend	1 B 97
37	Standburn Branch	1 B 97
38	Bonnywater	32 B 88
39	Streamhouse	3 B 88
40	Cowglen	1 C 09
41	Gask	1 C 09
42	Lassodie	1 C 19
43	Cowdenbeath	1 C 19
44	Auchtertool	1 C 19
45	Lilliehill North	1 C 19
46	South	1 C 09
47	Oakley	1 C 08
48	Touch North	1 C 18
49	South	1 C 18
50	Townhill	1 C 18
51	Charlestown Branch	1 C 08
52	Elbowend	1 C 08
53	Inverkeithing North	1 C 18
54	East	1 C 18
55	Central	1 C 18
56	South	14 C 18
57	Rosyth Line	15 C 18
58	Charlestown Dock	1 C 08
59	Charlestown Goods	1 C 08
60	Torryburn Line	1 C 08
61	Charlestown	1 C 08
62	Wellstood + Eglin	1 C 08

NOTES:

(1) As the three maps are closely adjoining a combined gazetteer is used. For simplicity the Grid letters are NOT used. Maps A and B are both entirely within NS, map C is entirely within NT.

(2) The Forth Bridge Railway was owned jointly by the Gt. Northern, North Eastern, North British and Midland. It was worked by the North British.

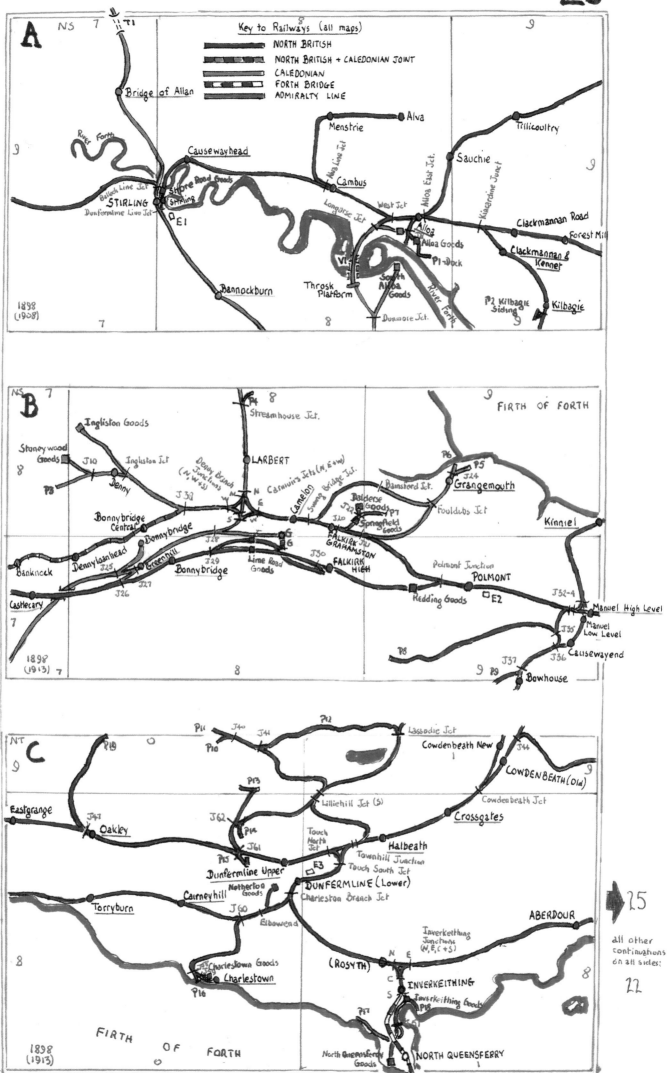

A

NS 7 T1

Key to Railways (all maps)
- NORTH BRITISH
- NORTH BRITISH + CALEDONIAN JOINT
- CALEDONIAN
- FORTH BRIDGE
- ADMIRALTY LINE

Bridge of Allan

River Forth

Alva
Menstrie
Tillicoultry
Alloa Line Jct.
Sauchie
Causewayhead
Cambus
Alloa East Jct.
Kincardine Junct.
Balloch Line Jct
Shore Road Goods
Longarse Jct.
West Jct
Clackmannan Road
STIRLING
Stirling
Dunfermline Line Jct
Alloa
Forest Mill
E1
Alloa Goods
P1-Dock
Clackmannan & Kennet
Vic
Bannockburn
Throsk Platform
South Alloa Goods
River Forth
P2 Kilbagie Siding
Kilbagie
Dunmore Jct.

1898 (1908)
7
8

B

NS 7
FIRTH OF FORTH

Ingliston Goods
Streamhouse Jct.
P4 8
Stoneywood Goods
J10
Ingliston Jct.
LARBERT
P6
P5
Denny Branch Junctions (N, W & S)
Carmuirs Jcts (N, E & W)
Bainsford Jct.
J24
Grangemouth
P3
Denny
Camelon
Swing Bridge Jct.
Balderse Goods
P7
Fouldubs Jct
Kinniel
Bonnybridge Central
J38
J12
Springfield Goods
J10
Bonnybridge
Banknock
Dennyloanhead
Greenhill
J28
J29
FALKIRK Jct
GRAHAMSTON
J30
FALKIRK HIGH
Polmont Junction
J25
Lime Road Goods
J26 J27
Bonnybridge
POLMONT
J32-4
Manuel High Level
Castlecary
Redding Goods
E2
J35
Manuel Low Level
P8
J37
J36
Causewayend
1898 (1913) 7
8
9 P9
Bowhouse

C

NT
P11
J40 J41
Lassodie Jct.
P10
P19
Cowdenbeath New
J44
P10
COWDENBEATH (Old)
Eastgrange
P13
Lilliehill Jct (S)
Cowdenbeath Jct
J47
Oakley
J62
Touch North Jct
Cowdenbeath Jct
Crossgates
P14
J61
Halbeath
P15
Townhill Junction
Dunfermline Upper
E3
Touch South Jct
Netherton Goods
DUNFERMLINE (Lower)
Cairneyhill
Charleston Branch Jct
Torryburn
J60
Elbowend
ABERDOUR
Inverkeithing Junctions (N, E, C + S)
Charlestown Goods
N E
Charlestown
P16
P17
(ROSYTH)
C
INVERKEITHING
S
Inverkeithing Goods
P18

FIRTH OF FORTH

North Queensferry Goods
NORTH QUEENSFERRY
V2

1898 (1913)

25

all other continuations on all sides:

22

RAILWAYS

No.	Company
R1	NORTH BRITISH
2	N. BRITISH + CALEDONIAN JOINT
3	CALEDONIAN

STATIONS

No	Name	Ry	Ref
A 1	AIRDRIE	1	76
2	Airdrie	3	76
3	Auchenheath	3	84
4	Bargeddie	1	76
5	Bellshill	1	76
6	BELLSHILL	3	75
7	Blackwood	3	84
8	BLAIRHILL + Gartsherrie	1	76
9	Bothwell	1	75
10	Bothwell	3	75
11	Braidwood	3	84
12	Burnbank §	1	75
13	Brocketsbrae	3	84
14	Calder	3	76
15	Calderbank	3	76
16	Caldercruix	1	86
17	Cambusnetham	3	85
18	(CARFIN) §	3	75
19	CARLUKE	3	84
20	Chapelhall	3	76
21	Clarkston	1	76
22	Cleghorn	3	94
23	Cleland	3	85
24	(CLELAND) §61	3	85

COATBRIDGE:

No	Name	Ry	Ref
25	Coatbridge	3	76
26	CENTRAL	1	76
27	SUNNYSIDE	1	76
28	COATDYKE	1	76
29	Coltness *	3	85
30	Commonhead	1	76
31	Dalserf	3	75
32	Fallside	3	75
33	Ferniegair	3	75
34	Flemington	3	75
35	Forrestfield	3	86
36	Gartcosh	3	76
37	Gartsherrie	3	76
38	Glassford	3	74
39	Glenboig	3	76

HAMILTON:

No	Name	Ry	Ref
40	CENTRAL	3	75
41	Hamilton	1	75
42	Peacock Cross	1	75
43	WEST	3	75
44	HARTWOOD	3	85
45	HOLYTOWN	3	75
46	LANARK	3	84
47	Langloan	3	76
48	Larkhall East	3	75
49	Larkhall Central	3	75
50	Law	3	85
51	Lesmahagow	3	84
52	Longriggend	1	86
53	Meikle Eanock	3	75
54	Morningside	1	85
55	Morningside	3	85
56	Mossend	3	76
57	MOTHERWELL	3	75
58	Netherburn	3	84
59	Newhouse	3	76
60	Newmains	3	85
61	OMOA §24	3	85
62	Overtown	3	85
63	Plains	1	86
64	Quarter Road	3	75
65	Rawyards	1	76
66	Shielmuir	3	75
67	SHOTTS	3	85
68	Stonehouse	3	74
69	Strathaven Central	3	74
70	Strathaven North	3	74
71	Tillietudlem	3	84
72	Uddingston	1	76
73	Westcraigs	1	96

WHIFFLET:

No	Name	Ry	Ref
74	High	3	76
75	Low	3	76
76	Whifflet	1	76
77	Whiterigg	1	76
78	Wishaw South	3	75
79	WISHAW Central	3	75

GOODS

No	Name/Location	Ry	Ref
G1	Airdrie	1	76
2	Auchenbeath	3	84
3	Bellshill	3	75
4	Blackhall	1	85
5	Blackwood	1	74
6	Burnbank §	1	75
7	Castlehill	1	85
8	Cuilhill Basin	1	76
9	Ferniegair	3	75
10	Greenfield §	1	75
11	Greengairs	1	77
12	Motherwell	3	75
13	Newarthill §	3	75
14	Shotts	1	85
15	Whifflet	3	76

SIDINGS + GOODS ONLY

No	Name / Location / Company	Ry	Ref
P1	Barton Colliery	1	86
2	Benbar Colliery	1	86
3	Cadzow Colliery	3	75
4	Calderbank a)Iron b)Steel	3	76
5	Castlehill Iron	3	85
6	Craigenhill Lime	3	84
7	Dewshill Pit	3	86
8	Dundoff Quarry	3	74
9	Duniston Colliery	3	86
10	Duntillan Pit	3	86
11	Dykehill Branch	1	{76 / 77}
12	Eddlewood Colliery	3	75
13	Fairhill Colliery	3	75
14	Graystone Lee	1	85
15	Hallcraig Pit	3	85
16	Hamilton Palace Colliery	2	75
17	Hassockrigg Colliery	1	86
18	Jerviston Branch	3	75
19	Law Pits	3	85
20	Legbrannock Cols.	3	86
21	Littlegill Colliery	3	84
22	Motherwell Iron Co	3	75
23	Newmains Col	1	85
24	Plains Branch	1	86
25	Rosehall Pits	3	76
26	Shawburn Colliery	3	74
27	Shawfield Colliery	3	85
28	Springbank Pit	3	86
29	Tennochside	3	76
30	Woodhall Branch	3	76

ENGINE SHEDS

No	Name/Location	Ry	Ref
E1	Motherwell	3	76
2	Hamilton West	3	78

JUNCTIONS

No	Name/Location	Ry	Ref
J1	Gartcosh	3	76
2	Garnqueen North	3	76
3	South	13	76
4	Gartsherrie North	13	76
5	South	3	76
7	Breddish	3	76
8	Drumpellier	3	76
9	Tennochside	3	76
13	Langloan South	3	76
14	North	3	76
15	Airdrie Branch	3	76
16	Whifflet North	3	76
17	South	31	76
22	Woodhall Branch West	3	76
23	Mossend North	3	76
24	Woodhall Branch East	3	76
25	Airdrie West	3	76
26	North	3	76
27	East	3	76
28	Calderbank Steel Works	3	76
29	Commonhead	1	76
30	Raebog	1	76
31	Dykehead Branch	1	76
33	Springwell Branch	1	76
34	Calderbank Iron	3	76
38	Slamannan	1	87
40	Turdees Branch	3	86
41	Dewshill Branch	3	86
42	North Lanridge	3	86
45	Westcraigs	1	86
46	West Benhar Branch	1	86
47	Hartwood Hill	1	86
51	Bothwell	3	75
52	Bothwell	1	75
53	Strathaven	3	75
55	Fairhill Coly	3	75
56	Eddlewood	3	75
57	Ross	3	75
58	Haughead	3	75
59	Ferniegair	3	75
60	Merryton	3	75
61	Lesmahagow	3	75
66	Fullwood	3	75
70	Shielmuir	3	75
71	Wishaw Central	3	75
73	Omoa	3	75
76	Drumbowie	3	85
78	Lanridge	3	85
79	Blackhall	1	85
80	Castlehill Branch	1	85
82	Carriongill	3	85
85	Hallcraig	3	85
86	Castlehill Iron Wks	3	85
88	Stonehouse North	3	74
89	South	3	74
93	Dunduff Branch	3	74
94	Littlegill	3	84
95	Southfield	3	84
96	Craigenhill	3	84
97	Silvermuir North	3	94
98	for Lanark	3	94
99	South	3	94
100	Douglas West	3	84
101	South	3	84
102	East	3	84
103	Sunnyside	1	76
106	Stonehouse	3	75

NOTES: (1) NAME CHANGES Burnbank § previously Greenfield §; following the closure of Cleland OMOA § now (CLELAND) §; (CARFIN) § is on the approximate site of Newarthill §.

(2) Coltness * appears to have been a works stopping place only.

(3) REFERENCES - all in square NS

(4) JUNCTIONS not all listed - unlisted take names from location.

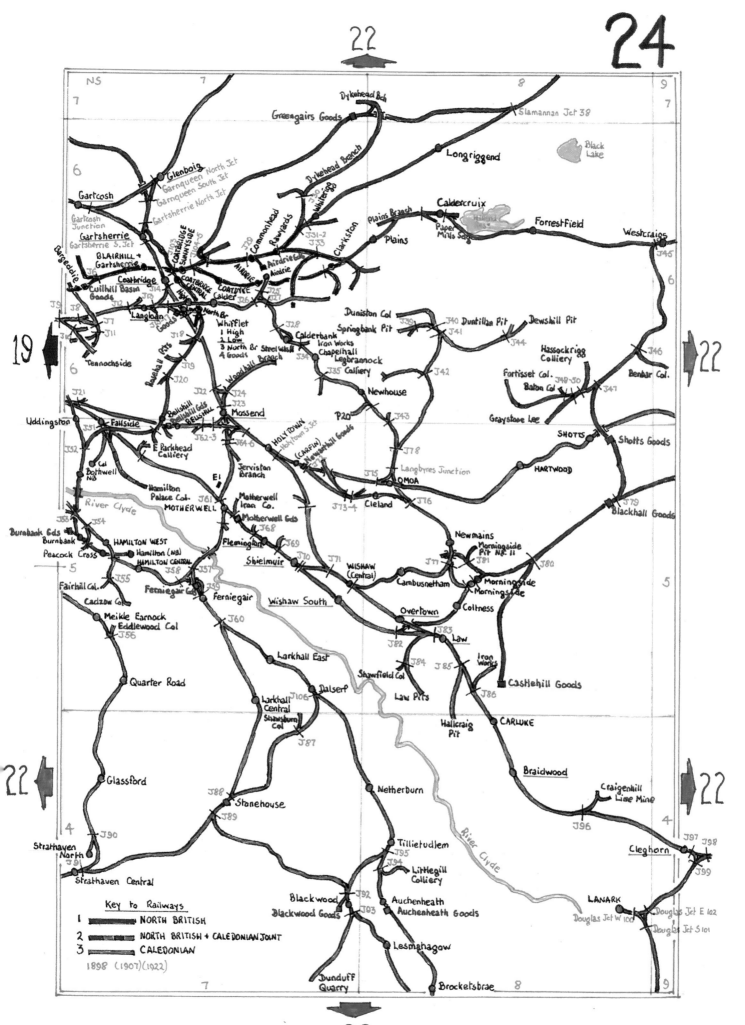

NS

7

6

Gartcosh

Gartcosh
Junction

Bargeddie

BLAIRHILL +
Gartsherrie

Gartsherrie
Gartsherrie S. Jct

Coatbridge

Cuilhill
Goods

Langloan
Goods

J9 J8

J7

J10

J11 J12

J14

J13

J6

Tennochside

Glenboig

Garnqueen North Jct
Garnqueen South Jct
Gartsherrie North Jct
Gartsherrie North Jct

COATBRIDGE
SUNNYSIDE

COATBRIDGE
CENTRAL

Calder

COATDYKE

North Br

Whifflet
1 High
2 Low
3 North Br Steel Works
4 Goods

Rosehall Pit

J18

J19

J20

Greengairs Goods

Dykehead Bch

Whitterigg

Commonhead
Rawyards

ALDRIG

Airdrie Sth

Airdrie

J31-2
J33

Clarkston

Calderbank
Iron Works

Chapelhall
Legbrannock

J34 J35 Colliery

Dykehead Branch

Plains Branch

Plains

Slamannan Jct 38

Longriggend

Caldercruix

Paper
Mills Sdg

Dunbar Col.

Springbank Pit

J40 Duntillan Pit

J39

J41

Black
Lake

Forrestfield

J42

Dewshill Pit

J44

Hassockrigg
Colliery

Fortissat Col.
Baton Col

J48-50

J47

Graystone Lee

Westcraigs

J45

J46

Benhar Col.

19

6

Uddingston

J21

Fallside

J51

J52

Col
Bothwell
NB

Hamilton
Palace Col.

MOTHERWELL

J61

Motherwell
Iron Co.

Motherwell Gds

J68

Bellshill
Bellshill Gds
BELLSHILL

J22

J23

J24

E Parkhead
Colliery

E1

Jerviston
Branch

J62-3

J64-6

Mossend

HOLYTOWN

Holytown S Jct

(CAAFIN)

Newarthill Goods

J75

P20

J43

J78

Langbyres Junction

OMOA

J73-4

Cleland

J16

J77

SHOTTS

HARTWOOD

Newhouse

Shotts Goods

Blackhall Goods

J79

5

Burnbank Gds

Burnbank

Peacock Cross

Fairhill Col.

J53

J54

J55

Cadzow Col

Meikle Earnock
Eddlewood Col

J56

HAMILTON WEST

Hamilton (NB)

HAMILTON CENTRAL

J58

J57

J59

Ferniegair Col

Ferniegair

Flemington

Shielmuir

J69

J70

J71

WISHAW
(Central)

Wishaw South

River Clyde

Cambusnethan

Newmains

Morningside
Pit No. 11

J81

J80

Morningside

Morningside

Coltness

Overtown

J82

J83

Law

5

Quarter Road

J60

Larkhall East

Dalserf

J106

Larkhall
Central

Shawsburn
Col

J87

Shawfield Col

Law Pits

J84

J85

Iron
Works

J86

CARLUKE

Hallcraig
Pit

Castlehill Goods

22

Glassford

J88

Stonehouse

J89

Netherburn

River Clyde

Braidwood

Craigenhill
Lime Mine

22

4

Strathaven
North

J90

J91

Strathaven Central

Blackwood

Blackwood Goods

J92

J93

Tillietudlem

J95

J94

Littlegill
Colliery

Auchenheath

Auchenheath Goods

Cleghorn

J96

LANARK

J97 J98

J99

Lesmahagow

Dunduff
Quarry

Brocketsbrae

Douglas Jct W100

Douglas Jct E 102

Douglas Jct S 101

Key to Railways

1 ——————— NORTH BRITISH

2 ——————— NORTH BRITISH + CALEDONIAN JOINT

3 ——————— CALEDONIAN

1898 (1907)(1922)

22

22

22

22

22

7

8

9

RAILWAYS

No	Company
R 1	NORTH BRITISH
3	CALEDONIAN

EDINBURGH + GALASHIELS

STATIONS (See Note!)

No	Name	Ry Ref
A 1	Abbeyhill	1 NT27
2	Abbotsford Ferry	1 NT43
3	ABERDOUR	1 NT18
4	Aberlady	1 NT47
5	Anstruther	1 NO50
6	Auchendinny	1 NT26
7	Auchtermuchty	1 NO21
8	Barnton for Cramond Brig	3 NT17
*	Barnton Gate	3 NT27
*	Blackford Hill	1 NT27
*	Bonnington	1 NT27
9	Bonnyrigg	1 NT36
10	Bowland	1 NT43
11	Buckhaven	1 NT39
12	BURNTISLAND	1 NT28
13	Broomieknowe	1 NT36
14	Cameron Bridge	1 NO30
15	CARDENDEN	1 NT29
16	Cardrona	1 NT33
17	Clovenfords	1 NT43
18	Colinton	3 NT26
19	Corstophine	1 NT27
*	Craigleith	3 NT27
*	Craiglockhart	1 NT27
20	Crail	1 NO50
21	Dalhousie	1 NT36
22	Dalkeith	1 NT36
*	Dalry Road	3 NT27
23	Dirleton	1 NT59
24	DREM	1 NT57
25	Duddingston	1 NT27
26	DUNBAR	1 NT67
27	Dysart	1 NT29
28	Earlston	1 NT53
*	Easter Road	1
29	East Fortune	1 NT57
30	East Linton	1 NT57
31	Eddleston	1 NT24
	EDINBURGH	NT27
	Abbeyhill	1 NT27
*	Dalry Road	3 NT27
32	HAYMARKET	1 NT27
*	Leith Walk	1 NT27
33	Merchiston	3 NT27
34	Murrayfield	3 NT27
*	Powderhall	1 NT27
35	Prince's Street	3 NT27
36	WAVERLEY	1 NT27
37	Elie	1 NO40
38	Eskbank	1 NT36
39	Esk Bridge	
40	Falkland Road	
41	Fountainhall Junction	1 NT44
42	Fushiebridge	1 NT36
43	Galashiels	1 NT43
44	Gifford	1 NT56
45	Gilmerton	1 NT36
46	Glencorse	1 NT26
47	Gordon	1 NT64
48	Gorebridge	1 NT36
*	Gorgie	1 NT27
*	Gorgie	3 NT27
49	Granton	1 NT27
*	Granton Road	3 NT27
50	Greenlaw	1 NT64
51	Gullane	1 NT48
52	Haddington	1 NT57
53	Hawthornden + Rosewell	1 NT26
54	HAYMARKET	1 NT27
55	Heriot	1 NT45
56	Humbie	1 NT46
57	Innerleithen	1 NT33
58	Inveresk	1 NT57
59	Joppa	1 NT37
*	Junction Road	1 N27
60	Kilconquhar	1 NO40
61	KINGHORN	1 NT28
62	Kingskettle	1 NO30
63	KINGSKNOWE	3 NT27
64	KIRKCALDY	1 NT29
65	LADYBANK	1 NO31
66	Lamancha	1 NT25
67	Largo	1 NO40
68	Lasswade	1 NT36
69	Lauder	1 NT54
70	Leadburn	1 NT25
	Leith:	
*	Junction Road	1 NT27
71	Leith Central	1 NT27
72	North	1 NT27
73	North	3 NT27
74	South	1 NT27
*	Leith Walk	1 NT27
75	Leslie	1 NO20
76	Leven	1 NO30
77	Lindean	1 NT43
78	Loanhead	1 NT26
79	LONGNIDDRY	1 NT47
80	Lundin Links	1 NO40
81	Lyne	3 NT23
82	Macmerry	1 NT47
83	MARKINCH	1 NO20
84	Maxton	1 NT62
85	Melrose	1 NT53
86	Merchiston	3 NT27
87	Methil	1 NT39
88	Millerhill	1 NT36
*	Morningside Road	1 N27
89	Murrayfield	3 N27
90	Musselburgh	1 NT37
91	New Hailes	1 NT37
*	Newhaven	3 NT27
92	Newington	1 N27
93	NORTH BERWICK	1 NT59
94	North Leith	1 NT27
95	North Leith	3 NT27
96	Ormiston	1 NT46
97	Oxton	1 NT45
98	Peebles	1 NT24
99	Peebles	3 NT23
100	Pencaitland	1 NT46
101	Penicuik	1 NT25
102	Piershill	1 NT27
103	Pittenweem	1 NO50
104	Polton	1 NT26
105	Pomathorn	1 NT25
106	Portobello	1 NT37
*	Powderhall	1 NT27
107	PRESTONPANS	1 NT37
108	Prince's Street	3 NT27
109	Roslin	1 NT26
110	Rosslyn Castle	1 NT26
111	Rosslynlee	1 NT26
112	Roxburgh	1 NT62
113	Rutherford	1 NT63
114	St Boswells	1 NT53
115	St Monan's	1 NO50
116	Saltoun	1 NT46
117	Selkirk	1 NT42
118	Sinclairtown	1 NT29
119	SLATEFORD	3 NT27
120	Smeaton	1 NT36
121	South Leith	1 NT27
122	Stow	1 NT44
123	Strathmiglo	1 NO20
124	Thornielee	1 NT43
125	Thornton (Junction) see note	1 NT39
126	Tynehead	1 NT35
127	Walkerburn	1 NT33
128	WAVERLEY	1 NT27
129	Wemyss Castle	1 NT39
130	West Wemyss	1 NT39
131	Winton	1 NT47

GOODS

No	Name	Ry Ref
G 1	Auchtertool	1 NT29
2	Beltonford	1 NT67
3	Falahill	1 NT35
4	Kennoway	1 NO30
5	Largoward	1 NO40
6	Lochty	1 NO50
7	Montrave	1 NO30

SUMMITS

No	Name	Ry Ref
S 1	Falahill	1 NT35

SHEDS

No	Name/Location	Ry Ref
E 1	Dunbar	1 NT67
2	Galashiels	1 NT43
3	Thornton	1 NT39

JUNCTIONS

No	Name	Ry Ref
J 1	Markinch	1 NO20
2	Auchmuty Mills	1 NO20
3	Lochty Branch	1 NO30
4	Leven	1 NO30
5	Dock Line	1 NT39
6	Thornton - North	1 NT39
7	Thornton - West	1 NT39
7A	Thornton - Central	1 NT39
8	Thornton - South	1 NT39
9	Thornton - East	1 NT39
10	Craighead Branch	1 NT29
11	Glencraig	1 NT29
12	Inverhel	1 NT28
12A	Kirkcaldy Harbour	1 NT29
14	Longniddry	1 NT47
15	Aberlady	1 NT47
16	Drem	1 NT57
17	Ormiston	1 NT46
18	Leadburn	1 NT25
19	Peebles	13 NT23
20	Peebles	1 NT24
21	Fountainhall	1 NT44
22	Kilnknowe	1 NT43
23	Galafoot	1 NT53
24	Ravenswood	1 NT53
25	Kelso	1 NT53
26	Roxburgh	1 NT62

SIDINGS

No	Name	Ry Ref
P 1	Kirkness Col	1 NT29
2	Kinninmonth Col	1 NT29
3	Craighead	1 NT29
4	Muiredge Col	1 NT39
5	Kirkcaldy Harbour	1 NT29

NOTES

(1) Stations shown in * Blue are NOT named on this map although they MAY be indicated. See the enlargement sheet 26. Goods, Summits, Sheds, Junctions and Sidings are only shown outside the area covered by 26.

(2) Some Edinburgh and Leith stations are indexed both under Edinburgh and Leith, and under individual station name.

(3) Thornton station had Junction added to name early in the 20th century.

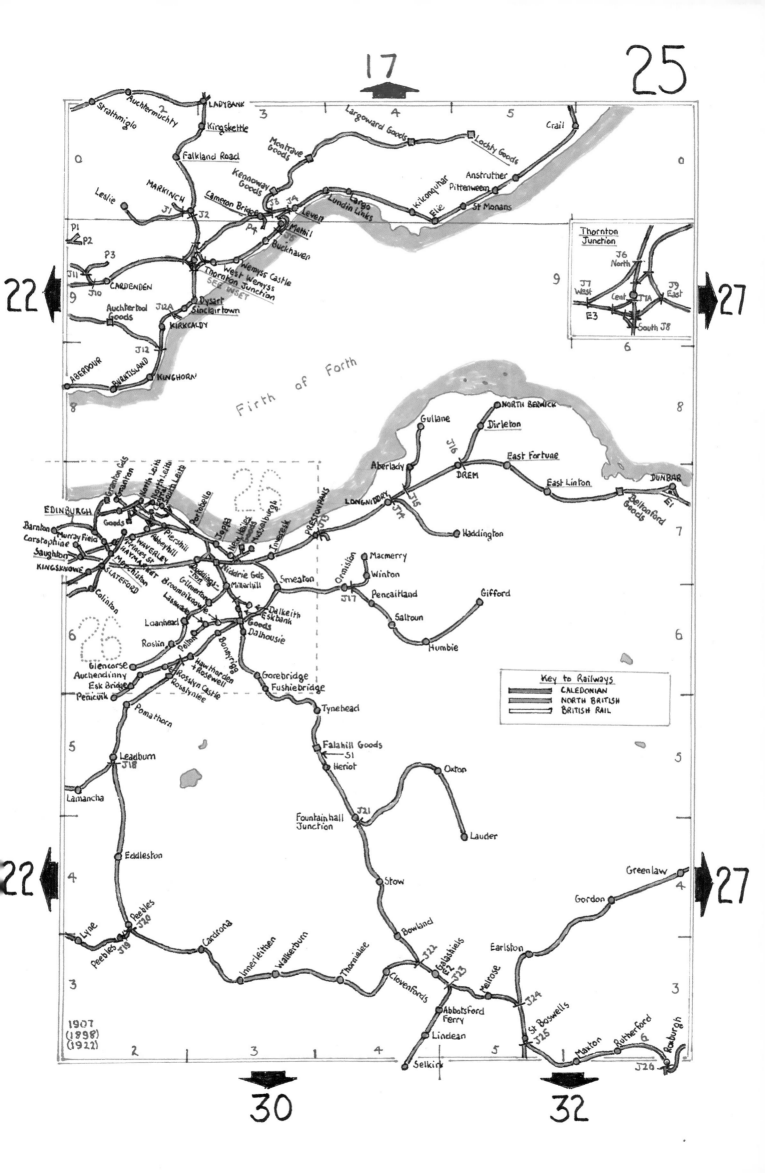

EDINBURGH

RAILWAYS

No.	Company
R 1	NORTH BRITISH
3	CALEDONIAN
4	FORTH BRIDGE (See Note 1)

STATIONS

No.	Name	Ry Ref
A 1	Abbeyhill	1 27
2	Auchendinny	1 26
3	Balerno	3 16
4	Barnton for Cramond Br.	3 17
5	Barnton Gate	3 27
6	Blackford Hill	1 27
7	Bonnington	1 27
8	Bonnyrigg	1 36
9	Broomieknowe	1 36
10	Colinton	3 26
11	Corstorphine	1 27
12	Craigleith	3 27
13	Craiglockhart	1 27
14	Currie	3 16
15	Currie Hill	3 16
16	Dalhousie	1 36
17	Dalkeith	1 36
18	DALMENY	4 17
19	Dalry Road	3 27
20	Drumshoreland	1 07
21	Duddingston	1 27
22	Easter Road	1 27
EDINBURGH		
23	Abbeyhill	1 27
24	Dalry Road	3 27
25	HAYMARKET	1 27
26	Leith Walk	1 27
27	Merchiston	3 27
28	Murrayfield	3 27
29	Powderhall	1 27
30	Prince's Street	3 27
31	WAVERLEY	1 27
32	Eskbridge	1 26
33	Fushiebridge	1 36
34	Gilmerton	1 27
35	Glencorse	1 26
36	Gogar	3 17
37	Gorebridge	1 36
38	Gorgie	3 22
39	Gorgie	1 27
40	Granton	1 27
41	Granton Road	1 36
42	Hawthornden + Rosewell	1 36
43	HAYMARKET	3 26
44	Inveresk	1 27
45	Joppa	3 27
46	Junction Road	1 27
47	Juniper Green	3 16
48	KINGSKNOWE	3 16
49	Kirkliston	1 36
50	(KIRKNEWTON)	1 36
51	Lasswade	4 17
Leith		3 27
52	Central	1 07
53	Junction Road	1 27
54	North	1 27
55	North	
56	South	1 27
57	Leith Walk	3 27
58	Loanhead	1 27
59	Merchiston	1 27
60	MIDCALDER	3 27
61	Millerhill	3 27
62	Morningside Road	1 27
63	Murrayfield	3 27
64	Musselburgh	1 27
65	New Hailes	1 26
66	Newhaven	1 36
67	Newington	1 36
68	North Leith	1 26
69	North Leith	1 17
70	NORTH QUEENSFERRY	4 18
71	Penicuik	1 25
72	Piershill	3 27
73	Polton	1 27
74	Pomathorn	3 27
75	Portobello	1 26
76	Powderhall	1 27
77	PRESTON PANS	1 37
78	Princes Street	1 37
79	Ratho	1 27
80	Ravelrig	3 26
81	Roslin	3 27
82	Rosslyn Castle	1 17
83	Rosslynlee	3 16
84	Saughton	1 30
85	SLATEFORD	3 27
86	Smeaton	1 36
87	South Leith	1 27
88	Trinity	1 27
89	Turnhouse	3 27
90	WAVERLEY	1 27
91	Winchburgh	1 27

GOODS

No.	Name/Location	Ry Ref
G 1	South Leith Dock	1 37
2	South Leith	1 27
3	Restalrig	3 27
4	Leith Walk	1 37
5	Bonnington	1 37
6	Bonnington	3 27
7	Granton Harbour	1 27
8	Granton Breakwater	3 27
9	Leith Walk	3 27
10	Scotland Street	4 18
11	Lothian Road	1 25
12	St. Leonards	1 27
13	Gogar	1 26
14	Camps	1 25
15	Camps	1 37
16	Holygate	1 27
17	North Queensferry	1 37
18	South Queensferry	3 27
19	Balerno	1 17
20	West Mill	3 17
21	Fisherrow	1 26
22	Niddrie	1 26
23	Hardengreen	1 26
24	East Calder	1 27
25	Dalmeny	3 27

SIDINGS

No.	Company/Location	Ry Ref
P 1	Broxburn Oil	1 17
2	Broxburn Oil	1 27
3	Ingliston Colliery	1 17
4	Camps Lime	1 07
5	Oakbank Oil	3 06
6	Tranent	3 16
7	Penicuik Gasworks	3 27
8	Lady Victoria Pit	1 36

BRIDGES

No.	Name	Ry Ref
V 1	Forth Bridge	3 27

ENGINE SHEDS

No.	Name/Location	Ry Ref
E 1	Piershill	1 27
2	Leith	3 27
3	Haymarket	1 27

JUNCTIONS

No.	Name/Location	Ry Ref
J 1	Dalmeny North	1 07
2	South	1 18
3	Winchburgh	1 07
4	Broxburn Branch	3 16
5	Holygate Branch	3 26
6	Oakbank	1 37
7	Midcalder	1 37
8	Camps East + West	3 16
9	Camps Branch	1 06
10	Ravelrig	1 17
11	Balerno Goods Branch	3 16
12	Bathgate Branch	1 17
13	Ingliston Branch	1 07
14	Newbridge	1 07
15	Saughton	1 27
16	Balerno	1 17
17	Haymarket West	3 06
18	Barnton	3 06
19	Crewe	1 37
20	Pilton East	1 26
21	West	1 36
22	Breakwater	
23	Trinity	
24	Bonnington North	1 27
25	Newhaven	1 27
26	Warriston	1 27
27	Bonnington South	1 27
28	Abbeyhill	1 27
29	Easter Road	1 27
30	Piershill	3 27
31	Lochend	1 27
32	Seafield	3 27
33	Dalry East	1 27
34	Coltbridge	3 27
35	Haymarket Central	1 27
36	Gorgie	1 27
37	Granton	1 07
38	Dalry West	1 07
39	Duddingston	1 07
40	Portobello West	3 06
41	East	3 04
42	Niddrie West	3 16
43	North	3 16
44	Millerhill	3 16
45	South	3 16
46	East	1 37
47	Fisherrow	1 17
48	Monktonhall	1 17
49	Tranent	1 27
50	Smeaton	3 27
51	Millerhill	3 27
52	Glenesk	1 36
53	Hardengreen	1 36
54	Esk Valley	1 36
55	Hawthornden	1 36
56	Lady Victoria	1 36
57	Bonnington East	1 27
58	New Hailes	1 37

NOTES:

(1) FORTH BRIDGE RAILWAY owned jointly by Gt. Northern, North Eastern, North British and Midland. Worked by North British.

(2) REFERENCES - All in NT

(3) CHANGE OF NAME:
§ Map date
§ Modern
May be a different station but on a closely adjoining site.

(4) EDINBURGH & LEITH: Some of the stations are double indexed both under Edinburgh or Leith and under individual name.

(5) JUNCTIONS - Some layouts have been expanded out of scale, and goods lines are sometimes omitted in the Granton - Leith - Edinburgh area.

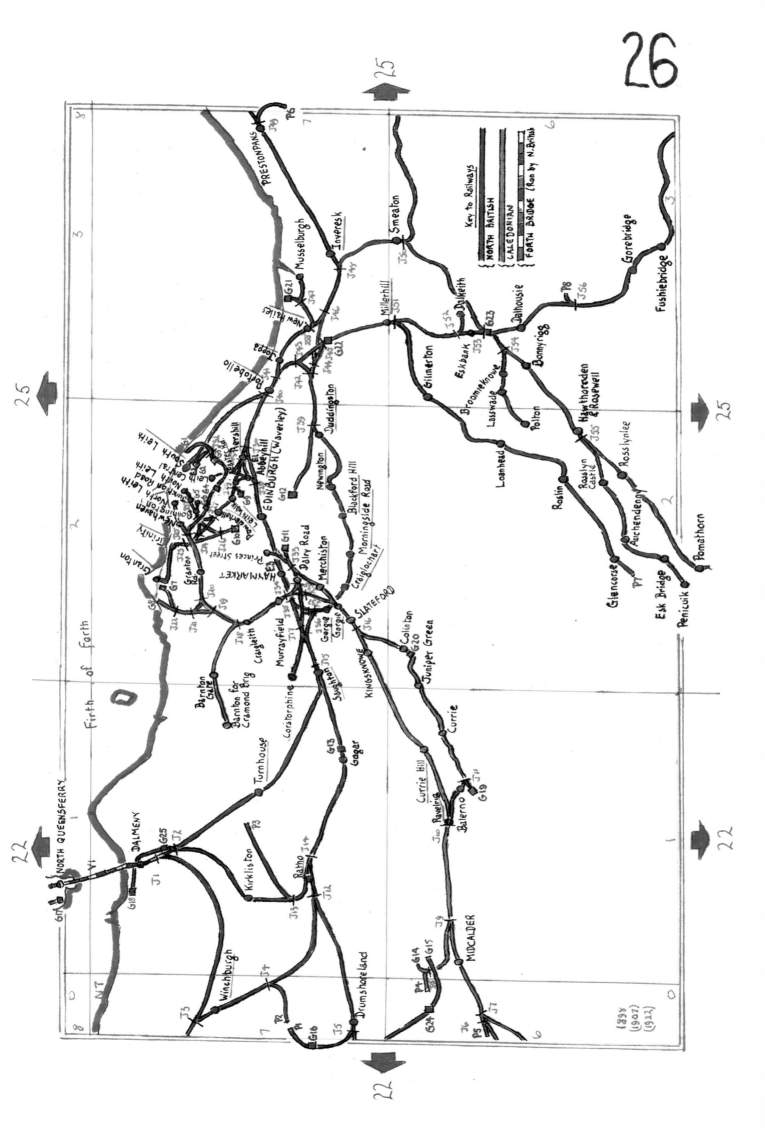

BERWICK·UPON·TWEED + KELSO

RAILWAYS

No.	Company
R 1	NORTH BRITISH
2	NORTH EASTERN

STATIONS

No.	Name	Ry Ref
A 1	Ayton	1 NT95
2	Beal	2 NU04
3	Belford	2 NU13
4	BERWICK·UPON·TWEED	12 NU05
5	Burnmouth	1 NT96
6	Carham	2 NT73
7	Chirnside	1 NT85
8	Cockburnspath	1 NT77
9	Coldstream	2 NT83
10	Duns	1 NT75
11	Edrom	1 NT85
12	Eyemouth	1 NT96
13	Goswick	2 NU04
14	Granthouse	1 NT86
15	Greenlaw	1 NT64
16	Innerwick	1 NT77
17	Kelso	1 NT73
18	Lucker	1 NU13
19	Marchmont	1 NT74
20	Mindrum	2 NT83
21	Norham	2 NT84
22	North Sunderland	2 NU23
23	Reston	1 NT86
24	Scremerston	2 NU04
25	Seahouses	2 NU23
26	Smeafield	2 NU13
27	Sprouston	2 NT73
28	Sunilaws	2 NT83
29	Tweedmouth	2 NU05
30	Twizell	2 NT84
31	Velvet Hall	2 NT94

JUNCTIONS

No.	Name / Location	Ry Ref
J 1	Tweedmouth - Goods	2 NU05
2	Tweedmouth - Coldstream Branch	2 NU05
3	Coldstream	2 NT83
4	Sprouston	12 NT73
5	Burnmouth	1 NT96
6	Reston	1 NT86
7	Berwick Station	12 NU05

GOODS

No.	Name / Location	Ry Ref
G 1	Tweedmouth	2 NU05

ENGINE SHEDS

No	Name / Location	Ry Ref
E 1	Tweedmouth	2 NU05

BRIDGES

No	Name	Ry Ref
V 1	Royal Border Bridge	2 NU05

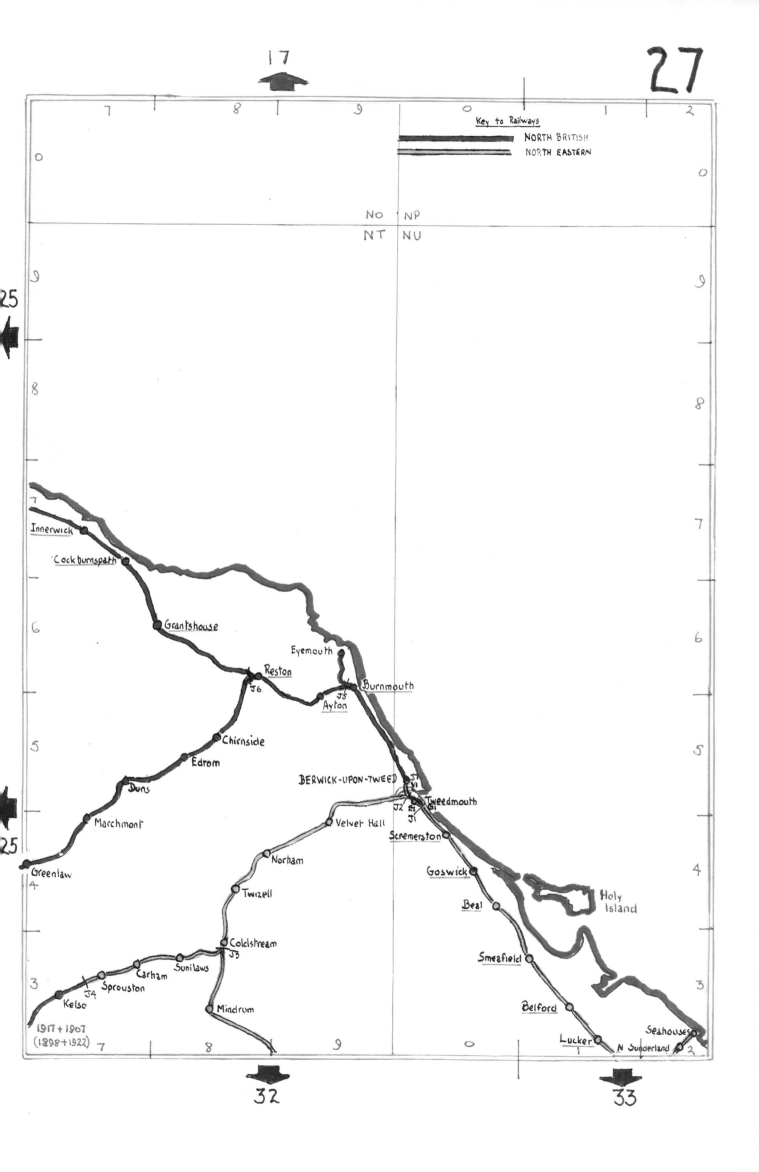

Key to Railways
NORTH BRITISH
NORTH EASTERN

NO | NP
NT | NU

Innerwick

Cockburnspath

Grantshouse

Eyemouth

Reston

J6

Burnmouth

J5

Ayton

Chirnside

Edrom

BERWICK-UPON-TWEED

J7

Y1

Duns

Tweedmouth

J2

E1

G1

J1

Marchmont

Velvet Hall

Scremerston

Greenlaw

Norham

Goswick

Twizell

Beal

Holy Island

Colclstream

J3

Smeafield

Sunilaws

Carham

Sprouston

J4

Kelso

Mindrum

Belford

Lucker

Seahouses

N Sunderland

1917 + 1907
(1898 + 1922)

NOTES: (1) Worked by Glasgow + South Western

No	Company	Notes
R 1	GLASGOW + SOUTH WESTERN	(1)
2	MAIDENS + DUNURE (Light)	(1)
3	PORTPATRICK + WIGTOWNSHIRE (2) + (3)	
4	CAMPBELTOWN + MACHRIHANISH (Light) (6)	

(2) Owned by London + North Western, Midland, Caledonian + Glasgow & South Western
(3) Worked by Glasgow + South Western (+ Caledonian)
(4) Not used after 1900 — but re-opened as Exchange platforms only in 1920's until final closure
(5) (Town) part of title not used until post World-War II.
(6) Gauge - 2'3"

STATIONS + HALTS

No	Name	Ry Ref		No	Name	Ry Ref		No	Name	Ry Ref
A 1	Alloway	2 NS31		26	Killochan	1 NS20		54	Tarbolton	1 NS42
2	Annbank	1 NS42		27	Kirkcowan	3 NX36		55	Trabboch	1 NS42
3	Auchincruive	1 NS32		28	Kirkinner	3 NX45		56	Trodigal Halt	4 NR63
4	AYR	1 NS32		29	Knoweside	2 NS21		57	Turnberry	2 NS10
5	BARRHILL	1 NX28		30	Linkmill Halt	4 NR63		58	Waterside	1 NS40
6	Campbeltown	4 NR73		31	Macrihanish	4 NR63		59	Whauphill	3 NS44
7	Cassillis	1 NS31		32	Macrihanish Farm Halt	4 NR63		60	Whithorn	3 NS44
8	Castle Kennedy	3 NX15		33	Maidens	2 NS20		61	Wigtown	3 NX45
9	Colfin	3 NX05		34	Mauchline	1 NS42				
10	Creetown	3 NX46		35	MAYBOLE	1 NS20			GOODS	
11	Dailly	1 NS20		36	Millisle	3 NX44		No	Name / Location	Ry Ref
12	Dalmellington	1 NS40		37	Monkton	1 NS32		G 1	Ayr	1 NS32
13	Dalrymple	1 NS31		38	Moss Road Halt	4 NR63		2	Ayr - Cattle + Minerals	1 NS32
14	Drongan	1 NS41		39	New Luce	3 NX16		3	Greenan Castle	2 NS21
15	Drumlemble Halt	4 NR63		40	NEWTON-ON-AYR	1 NS32		4	Dipple	2 NS10
16	Dunragit	3 NX15		41	Newton Stewart	3 NX46		5	Garliestown	3 NX44
17	Dunure	2 NS21		42	Palnure	3 NX46				
18	GIRVAN	1 NX19		43	Patna	1 NS41			SIDINGS	
19	Glenluce	3 NX15		44	Pinmore	1 NX19		P 1	Ayr Old Harbour	1 NS32
20	Glenside	2 NS20		45	Pinwherry	1 NX18		2	Ayr New Harbour	1 NS32
21	Glenwhilly	1 NX17		46	Plantation Halt	4 NR73		3	Girvan Harbour	1 NX19
22	Heads of Ayr	2 NS21		47	Portpatrick	3 NW95				
23	(Holehouse) NOTE 4	1 NS41		48	PRESTWICK	1 NS32			SHEDS	
24	Hollybush	1 NS31		49	Rankinston	1 NS41		E 1	Ayr	1 NS32
25	Kilkerran	1 NS20		50	Sorbie	3 NS44		2	Stranraer	1 NX05
				51	Stewarton (Plantation) Halt	4 NR73				
				52	STRANRAER HARBOUR	3 NX06			SUMMITS	
				53	Stranraer (Town) NOTE 5	3 NX05		S 1	Chirmorie	1 NX17

JUNCTIONS

No	Name / Location	Ry Ref
J	AYR + DISTRICT: ✳	NS32
1	Falkland	1 NS32
2	Harbour Lines	1 NS32
3		1 NS32
4	Goods + New Harbour	1 NS32
5	Station	1 NS32
6	Blackhouse	1 NS32
7	Hawkhill	1 NS32
8	Monkton	1 NS32
9	Mossblown	1 NS42
10	Dromley Pit	1 NS42
11	Mauchline	1 NS42
12	Alloway	1 NS31
13	Dalrymple	1 NS31
14	Belston	1 NS41
15	Holehouse	1 NS41
16	Girvan North	12 NX19
17	Girvan South	1 NX19
18	Stranraer Harbour	3 NX05
19	Challoch	31 NX15
20	Newton Stewart	3 NX46
21	Millisle	3 NX44

✳ There is also a rail level-crossing at Ayr just outside the station   NS32

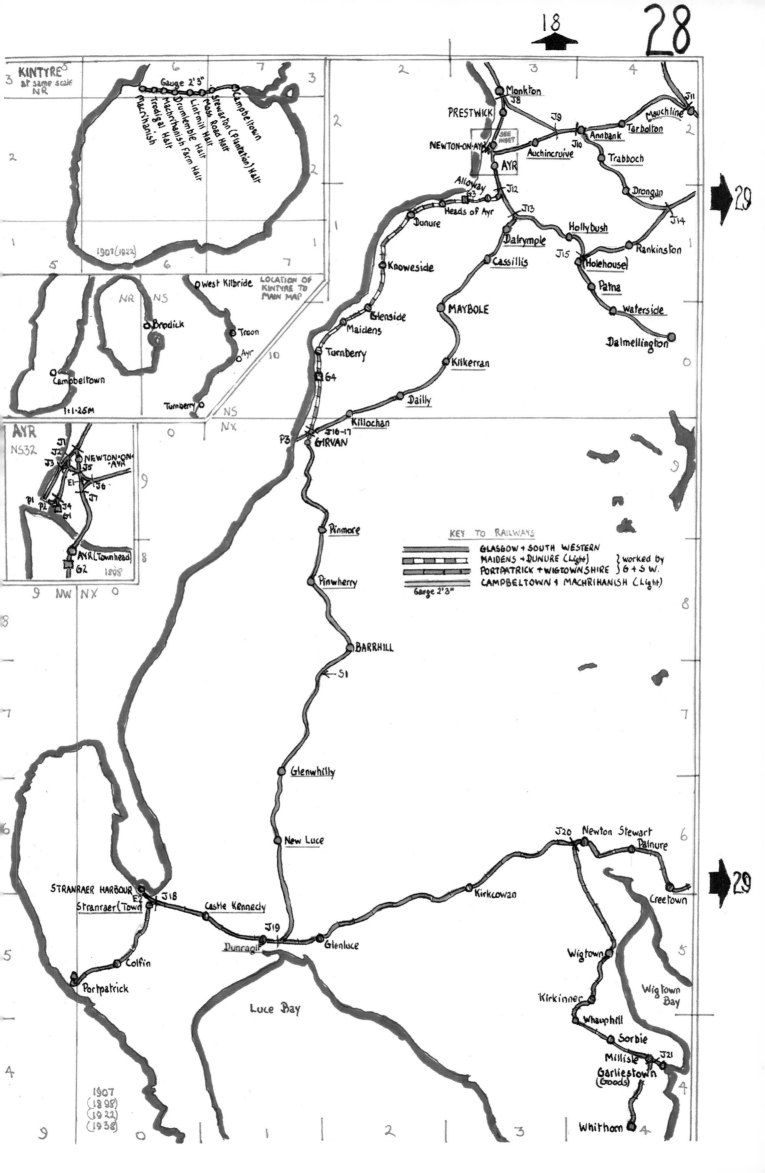

KINTYRE
at same scale
NR

Gauge 2'3"
Campbeltown
Stewarton (Plantation) Halt
Moss Road Halt
Drumlemble Halt
Lintmill Halt
Machrihanish Farm Halt
Tiradigal Halt
Machrihanish

1907 (1922)

29

West Kilbride
LOCATION OF
KINTYRE TO
MAIN MAP

NR   NS

Brodick

Troon
Ayr

Campbeltown

1:1.25M

Turnberry

NS
Nx

AYR
NS32

J1
J2
J3   NEWTON-ON-AYR
J5
E1   J6
P1   J7
P2   34
G1

AYR (Townhead)
G2
1898

9   NW   NX   0

Monkton
J8

PRESTWICK

J11

Muchline

Tarbolton

NEWTON-ON-AYR   SEE INSET

AYR   J9   Annbank
Auchincruive   J10   Trabboch

Alloway   J12   Drongan
G3   J13
Heads of Ayr   Hollybush
Dunure   Dalrymple   J14
Knoweside   Cassillis   J15   Rankinston
(Holehouse)
Glenside   Patna
MAYBOLE   Waterside
Maidens
Turnberry   Kilkerran   Dalmellington
G4
Daily
Killochan
P3   J16-17
GIRVAN

Pinmore

Pinwherry

BARRHILL

S1

KEY TO RAILWAYS

GLASGOW + SOUTH WESTERN
MAIDENS + DUNURE (Light)   } worked by
PORTPATRICK + WIGTOWNSHIRE   } G + S W.
CAMPBELTOWN + MACHRIHANISH (Light)

Gauge 2'3"

Glenwhilly

New Luce

J20   Newton Stewart
Palnure

Kirkcowan   Creetown

STRANRAER HARBOUR   J18
E2   Castle Kennedy
Stranraer (Town)   J19
Dunragit   Glenluce

Colfin   Wigtown

Portpatrick   Kirkinner   Wigtown
Bay
Whauphill

Luce Bay   Sorbie
Millisle   J21
Garlieston
(Goods)

1907
(1898)
(1922)
(1938)

Whithorn

No	Company	
R 1	CALEDONIAN	
3	GLASGOW + SOUTH WESTERN	(1)
4	PORTPATRICK + WIGTOWNSHIRE JT	(2)

CUMNOCK → DUMFRIES

NOTES: (1) Line from Dumfries to Moniaive known Cairn Valley Light Railway – owned + worked by G+SW.

(2) Owned by London + North Western, Midland, Caledonian and Glasgow + South Western and was worked by Glasgow + South Western (and Caledonian)

(3) Gatehouse of Fleet – this station previously named Dromore.

STATIONS + HALTS

No	Station/Halt	Ry Ref
A 1	Abington	1 NS92
2	Amisfield	1 NX98
3	AUCHINLECK	3 NS52
4	Auldgirth	3 NS98
5	Bridge of Dee	3 NX76
6	Carronbridge	3 NS80
7	Castle Douglas	3 NX76
8	Catrine	3 NS52
9	Closeburn	3 NX99
10	Commondyke	3 NS52
11	Crawford	1 NS92
12	Cronberry	3 NS62
13	Crossford	3 NX88
14	Crossmichael	4 NX76
15	Cumnock	3 NS52
16	Dalbeattie	3 NX86
17	DUMFRIES	3 NX97
18	Dumfries House	3 NS52
19	Dunscore	3 NX88
20	Elvanfoot	1 NS91
21	Gatehouse-of-Fleet (NOTE 3)	4 NX56
22	Glenbuck	1 NS72
23	Holywood	3 NX98
24	Inches	1 NS72
25	Irongray	3 NX98
26	Killywhan	3 NX86
27	KIRKCONNEL	3 NS71
28	Kirkcudbright	3 NX65
29	Kirkgunzeon	3 NX86
30	Kirkland	3 NX89
31	Leadhills	1 NS81
32	Lochanhead	3 NX97
33	Locharbriggs	1 NX98
34	Loch Skerrow Halt	4 NX66
35	Lugar	3 NS52
36	Maxwelltown	3 NX97
37	Moniaive	3 NX79
38	Muirkirk	3 NS62
39	New Cumnock	3 NS61
40	New Galloway	4 NX67
41	Newtonairds	3 NX88
42	Ochiltree	3 NS51
43	Old Cumnock	3 NS52
44	Parton	4 NX67
45	Sanquhar	3 NS71
46	Skares	3 NS51
47	Southwick	3 NX86
48	Stepford	3 NX88
49	Tarff	3 NX65
50	Thornhill	3 NX89
51	Wanlockhead	3 NX81

GOODS

No.	Location	Ry Ref
G 1	Dumfries	1 NX97
2	Dumfries	3 NX97

SIDINGS

No	Name	Ry Ref
P 1	Gilmilnscroft Branch	3 NS52
2	Gasworks Branch	3 NS62

SHEDS

No	Location	Ry Ref
E 1	Dumfries	3 NX97
2	Muirkirk	3 NS72

VIADUCTS

No	Name	Ry Ref
V 1	Water of Fleet	4 NX56

WATER-TROUGHS

No	Location	Ry Ref
W 1	New Cumnock	3 NS61

JUNCTIONS

No	Name/Location	Ry Ref
J 1	Brackenhill	3 NS52
2	Auchinleck	3 NS52
3	Gilmilnscroft Branch	3 NS52
4	Old Cumnock	3 NS52
5	Logan	3 NS52
6	Cronberry	3 NS62
7	Gasworks Branch	3 NS62
8	Muirkirk	13 NS62
9	Elvanfoot	1 NS91
	DUMFRIES:	NX97
10	Cairn Valley	3 NX97
11	Goods	1 NX97
12	(Level Crossing)	31 NX97
13	Caledonian + G+SW	31 NX97
14	Castle Douglas Branch	3 NX97
15	Portpatrick Line	34 NX76

SUMMITS

No	Name	Ht	Ry Ref
S 1	Dromore		4 NX56
2	Polquhap		3 NS51

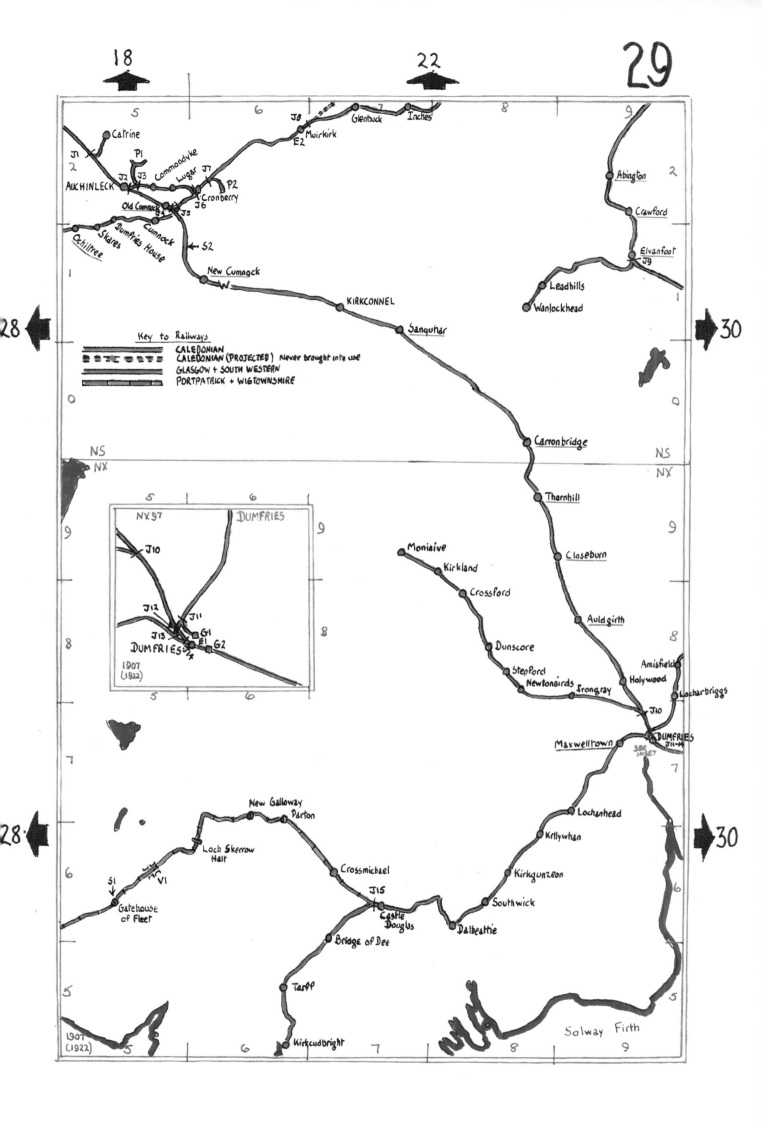

Key to Railways

CALEDONIAN
CALEDONIAN (PROJECTED) Never brought into use
GLASGOW + SOUTH WESTERN
PORTPATRICK + WIGTOWNSHIRE

NX 97   DUMFRIES

J10

J12   J11

J13   G1
E1   G2

DUMFRIES

1907
(1922)

18   22

Catrine
J1
P1
Commondyke
Auchinleck   J2   J3   Lugar   J7   P2
Cronberry
Old Cumnock   J5   J6
J4
Cumnock
Dumfries House
Skares
Ochiltree
S2
New Cumnock
KIRKCONNEL
Sanquhar

J8   Muirkirk   Glenbuck   Inches
E2

Abington
Crawford
Elvanfoot
J9
Leadhills
Wanlockhead

28   30

Carronbridge

Thornhill

Moniaive
Kirkland
Crossford
Closeburn
Auldgirth

Dunscore
Stepford
Newtonairds   Irongray
Amisfield
Holywood
Locharbriggs
J10
DUMFRIES
J11-14
Maxwelltown   SEE INSET

New Galloway
Parton
Loch Skerrow
Halt
Crossmichael
J15
Castle
Douglas
Bridge of Dee
Tarff
Kirkcudbright

S1
V1
Gatehouse
of Fleet

28   30

Lochanhead
Killywhan
Kirkgunzeon
Southwick
Dalbeattie

Solway Firth

1907
(1922)

CARLISLE + MOFFAT

RAILWAYS

No	Company
R1	NORTH BRITISH
2	NORTH EASTERN
3	CALEDONIAN
4	LONDON + NORTH WESTERN
5	GLASGOW + SOUTH WESTERN
6	MIDLAND
7	MARYPORT + CARLISLE
8	OTHERS - Details see 31

STATIONS + HALTS

No	Name	Ry	Ref
A1	Abbeyholme	1	NY15
2	Abbey Junction	3	NY15
3	Abbey Town	1	NY15
4	Annan	3	NY16
5	ANNAN	5	NY16
6	Beattock	3	NT00
7	Black Dyke *	1	NY15
8	Bowness	3	NY26
9	Burgh	1	NY35
10	Canonbie	1	NY47
11	CARLISLE CITADEL	8	NY35
12	Cummersdale	7	NY35
13	Cummertrees	5	NY16
14	Cumwhinton	6	NY45
15	DALSTON	7	NY35
16	Dinwoodie	3	NY19
17	Dornock	5	NY26
18	Drumburgh	1	NY25
19	Ecclefechan	3	NY17
20	Floriston	3	NY36
21	Gilnockie	1	NY37
22	Glasson *	1	NY26
23	Gretna	1	NY36
24	Gretna	3	NY36
25	Gretna Green	5	NY36
26	Harker	1	NY36
27	Hawick	1	NT51
28	Kershope Foot	1	NY48
29	Kirkandrews	1	NY35
30	Kirkbride	1	NY25
31	Kirkpatrick	3	NY27
32	Kirtlebridge	3	NY27
33	Langholm	1	NY38
34	Lochmaben	3	NY08
35	LOCKERBIE	3	NY18
36	Longtown	1	NY36
37	Lyneside	1	NY36
38	Moffat	3	NT00
39	Nethercleugh	3	NY18
40	Newcastleton	1	NY48
41	Penton	1	NY47
42	Port Carlisle	1	NY26
43	Racks	5	NY07
44	Riddings	1	NY47
45	Rigg	5	NY26
46	Rockcliffe *	3	NY36
47	Ruthwell	5	NY06
48	Scotby	2	NY45
49	Scotby	6	NY45
50	Scotch Dyke	1	NY37
51	Selkirk	1	NT42
52	Shieldhill	3	NY08
53	Silloth	1	NY15
54	Stobs	1	NT50
55	Whamphray	3	NY19
56	WETHERAL	2	NY45
57	Whitrigg	3	NY25

* Reduced to Halt status by 1922

GOODS

No	Location	Ry	Ref
G1	Port Carlisle Dock	1	NY26

SIDINGS

No	Company	Ry	Ref
P1	Convalescent Institute	1	NY15
2	Solway Chemical	1	NY15
3	Grimsdale Siding	1	NY35

SHEDS

No	Location	Ry	Ref
E1	Beattock	3	NT00
2	Hawick	1	NT51

SUMMITS

No	Name	Ht	Ry	Ref
S1	Beattock	1015'	3	NT01

BRIDGES

No	Location	Ry	Ref
V1	Solway Viaduct	3	NY26
2	Esk Viaduct	3	NY36

JUNCTIONS

No	Name / Location	Ry	Ref
J1	Moffat Branch	3	NT00
2	Lockerbie	3	NY18
3	Shawhill	3	NY16
4	Annan (Cal + G&SW)	53	NY16
5	Dumfries Line	35	NY36
6	Longtown Line	31	NY36
7	Goods	1	NY36
8	Longtown	1	NY36
9	Riddings	1	NY47
10	Abbey (2)	13	NY15
11	Kirkbride	13	NY25
12	Dock	1	NY26
13	Drumburgh	1	NY25
14	Kirtlebridge	3	NY27

NOTES:

(1) In the Carlisle area - full details of lines, junctions, goods and sidings and of engine sheds - see map 31. This maps also shows some additional features.

(2) Also known as Abbeyholme

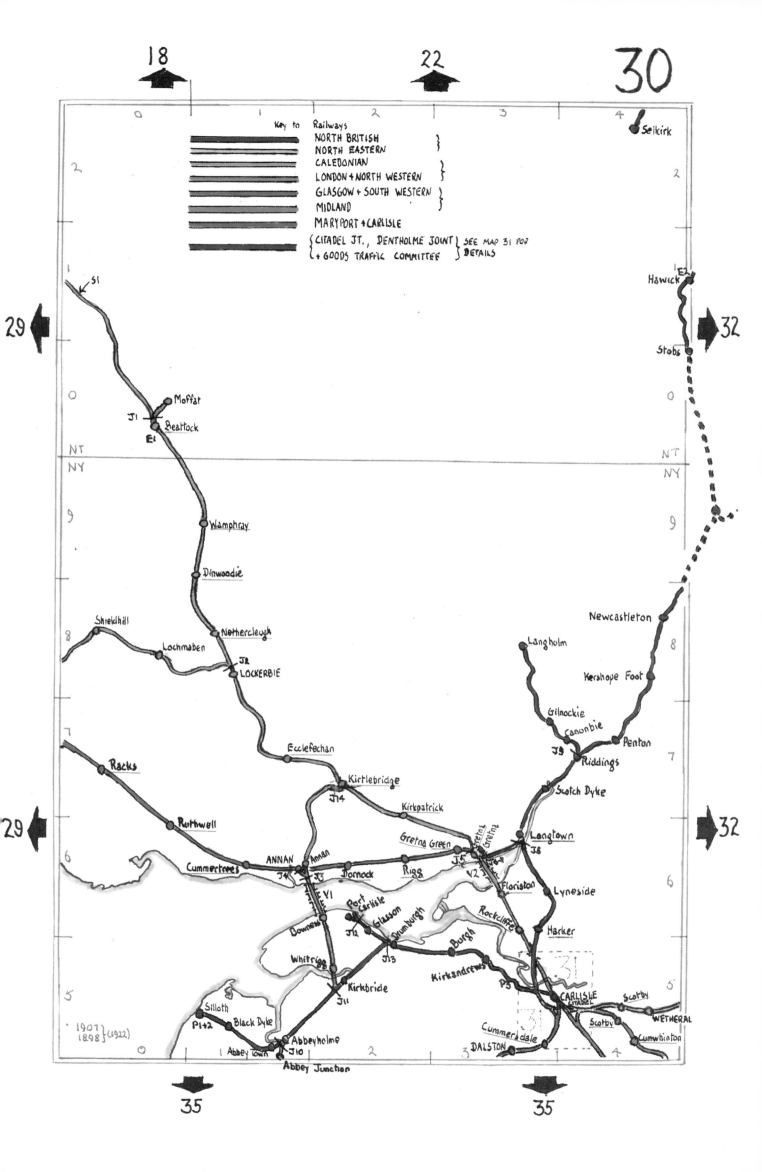

Key to Railways
NORTH BRITISH
NORTH EASTERN   }
CALEDONIAN
LONDON + NORTH WESTERN }
GLASGOW + SOUTH WESTERN }
MIDLAND
MARYPORT + CARLISLE
{ CITADEL JT., DENTHOLME JOINT } SEE MAP 31 FOR
{ + GOODS TRAFFIC COMMITTEE   } DETAILS

Selkirk

Hawick E2

29   32

Stobs

Moffat
J1
Beattock
E1

NT
NY

Wamphray

Dinwoodie

Newcastleton

Shieldhill
Nethercleugh
Langholm

Lochmaben
J2
LOCKERBIE
Kershope Foot

Gilnockie
Canonbie
Ecclefechan
Penton
J9
Racks
Riddings
Kirtlebridge
Scotch Dyke
J14
Kirkpatrick

Ruthwell
Gretna Green Gretna Langtown
29   32
J5 V3
Greina J8
Cummertrees ANNAN Annan
J4 J3 Dornock Rigg V2 Floriston Lyneside
V1
Port Glasson
Carlisle Rockcliffe
Downess J12 Drumburgh Burgh Harker
J13
Whitrigs Kirkandrews P5
Kirkbride
J11 31
Silloth
P1+2 Black Dyke CARLISLE Scotby
CITADEL
1907 (1922) Abbeyholme Scotby WETHERAL
1898 J10 31 Cumwhinton
Abbey Town Cummersdale
Abbey Junction DALSTON

31

RAILWAYS

No	Company	Owners of Joint Lines
R 1	CALEDONIAN	
2	LONDON + NORTH WESTERN	
3	CITADEL STATION COMMITTEE	1 + 2
4	MIDLAND	
5	GLASGOW + SOUTH WESTERN	
6	GOODS TRAFFIC COMMITTEE	1, 2, 4 + 5
7	NORTH EASTERN	
8	NORTH BRITISH	
9	DENTHOLME JOINT COMMITTEE	4, 5 + 8
10	MARYPORT + CARLISLE	
11	Others	

NOTES:

(1) MAP REFERENCES These are four figure references all in NY

(2) RAILWAY PARTNERS - Certain English + Scottish Companies had close associations, these were

CALEDONIAN	LONDON + NORTH WESTERN
GLASGOW + S WESTERN	MIDLAND
NORTH BRITISH	NORTH EASTERN

(3) LINES IN USE - Most of this network in use except N.B + NE betweens Jcts. 5 and 30.

(4) SIGNAL BOXES Nos. 1-4, 4A, 5-13 were also known as Carlisle No.1 etc. Signal Box information - circa 1900

(5) SCALE The map is not to scale. Distances are sometimes exagerated in order to aid clarity of layout

STATIONS

No	Name	Ry	Ref
A 1	CARLISLE CITADEL	3	4054
2	Cumersdale	10	3953

SIGNAL BOXES

No	Name	No. of Levers	Ref
B 1	Willowholme Jct.		3955
2	Port Carlisle Bch Jct		4054
3	Caldew Junction		4054
4	(Citadel North)		4054
4A	(Citadel Station)		4054
5	(Citadel South)		4054
6	Bog Goods Jct		4054
7	London Road Jct		4053
8	Currock Junction		4053
9	Forks Junction		4054
10	Bog Junction		4054
11	Rome Street Junction		4054
12	Upperby Junction		4053
13	Upperby Bridge Jct		4053
14	Dentholme South Jct		4054
15	Kingmoor Jct	25	3955
16	Etterby Junction		3955
17	Canal Junction	85	3955
18	Dentholme Goods North	28	4054
19	Dalston Road	16	4054
20	Dentholme Goods South	20	4054
21	Petteril Bridge Jct	66	4053
22	Petteril Goods	30	4153
23	Durran Hill Junction	30	4153
24	Durran Hill	54	4153
25	Dentholme North Jct	55	4054

ENGINE SHEDS

No	Name	Ry	Ref
E 1	Kingmoor	1	3955
2	Upperby	2	4053
3	Durran Hill	4	4153
4	(Near Currock Jct)	5	4053
5	London Road	7	4054
6	Canal	8	3955
7	M+C	10	4053

GOODS DEPÔTS

No	Name	Ry	Ref
G 1	Viaduct	1	4054
2	Crown Street	2	4054
3	LNW Cattle	2	4053
4	Petteril	4	4053
5	Dentholme ✳	58	4054
6	Canal	8	3955
7	London Road	7	4054
8	Bog	10	4054

JUNCTIONS

No	Name / Location	Ry	Ref
J 1	Kingmoor	1	3955
2	Etterby	1	3955
3	Canal Shed	8	3955
4	Canal	8	3955
5	Port Carlisle	18	3955
6	Goods Station Branch	8	3954
7	Biscuit Works	8	3954
8	Port Carlisle Branch	1	4054
9	Caldew	16	4054
10	Caldew South	6	4054

JUNCTIONS (continued)

No	Name / Location	Ry	Ref
J 11	Viaduct Goods	16	4054
12	Dentholme North	69	4054
13	Dentholme Goods	9	4054
14	Dentholme South	69	4054
15	Gas Works	611	4054
16	Canal	78	4054
17	Citadel South - (N)	3	4054
18	Citadel South - (S)	3	4054
19	M+C and Citadel	103	4054
20	Bog Goods	10	4054
21	Rome Street	1076	4054
22	Forks	10	4054
23	Bog	106	4054
23A	(Bog North)	107	4054
24	Currock	10	4053
24A	Shed	105	4053
25	Upperby Shed	2	4053
26	Upperby West	2	4053
27	Upperby Middle	2	4053
28	Upperby East	2	4053
28A	Upperby Sidings	2	4053
29	Upperby Bridge	2	4053
30	London Road West	7	4053
31	London Road East	27	4053
32	Petteril Bridge	47	4053
33	Shed + Goods (L.Rd)	7	4054
34	Durran Hill (NE)	7	4153
35	Durran Hill (Mid)	4	4153
36	Durran Hill Goods	4	4153
37	Durran Hill Shed	4	4153
38	Citadel North	13	4054

JUNCTIONS (continued)

No	Name / Location	Ry	Ref
J 39	Citadel + North Eastern	73	4054
40	Citadel + LNW	23	4054
41	Willowholme	16	3955

SIDINGS

No	Name / Co / Location	Ry	Ref
P 1	Kingmoor	1	3955
2	Carr's Biscuits	8	3954
3	Dentholme North	9	4054
4	Dentholme South	9	4054
5	Dalston Road	78	4054
6	Gas Works	11	4054
7	London Road	7	4154
8	Upperby	8	4053
9	Petteril	4	4153
10	Durran Hill ‡	4	4153
11	Corporation	6	§
12	Cowan Sheldon + Co	247	§
13	Creighton's	28	§
14	Electric Lighting Sta	6	§
15	Etterby	1	§
16	Guaranteed Manure Co	8	§
17	John Hewitson	47	§
18	T Niven	8	§
19	South End Co-op	4	§
20	Timber Yard	8	§
21	Lonsdale ‡	4	§
22	Carlisle Farmers ‡	8	§
✳	Originally G+SW only		
‡	Outside map area		
§	Location uncertain		

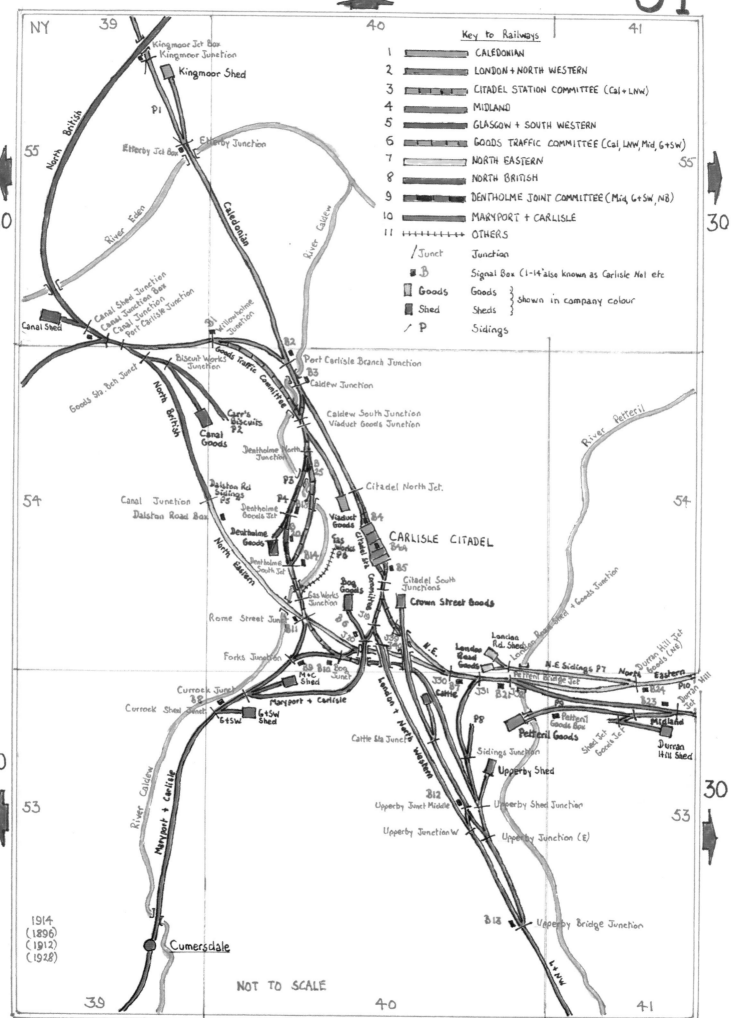

NY

30

39   40   41

55   55

30   30

Key to Railways

1 CALEDONIAN
2 LONDON + NORTH WESTERN
3 CITADEL STATION COMMITTEE (Cal + LNW)
4 MIDLAND
5 GLASGOW + SOUTH WESTERN
6 GOODS TRAFFIC COMMITTEE (Cal, LNW, Mid, G+SW)
7 NORTH EASTERN
8 NORTH BRITISH
9 DENTHOLME JOINT COMMITTEE (Mid, G+SW, NB)
10 MARYPORT + CARLISLE
11 OTHERS

/ Junct   Junction
B Signal Box (1-14 also known as Carlisle No.1 etc
Goods Goods
Shed   Sheds   } shown in company colour
/ P   Sidings

Kingmoor Jct Box
Kingmoor Junction
Kingmoor Shed
P1

North British
River Eden
Caledonian
River Caldew

Etterby Jct Box
Etterby Junction

Canal Shed Junction
Canal Junction Box
Canal Junction
Port Carlisle Junction
Canal Shed
B1
Willowholme Junction
B2
Port Carlisle Branch Junction
B3
Caldew Junction

Goods Traffic Committee

Biscuit Works Junction
Goods Sta. Bch Junct
North British
Carr's Biscuits P2
Canal Goods

Caldew South Junction
Viaduct Goods Junction

Dentholme North Junction
B15
P3
Citadel North Jct.

River Petteril

Canal Junction
Dalston Rd Sidings P5
Dalston Road Box
Dentholme Goods Jct
P4
Viaduct Goods
B4
B4A

CARLISLE CITADEL

Dentholme Goods
B10
Dentholme South Jct
B14
Gas Works P6
Citadel Jct
B5
Citadel South Junctions

Gas Works Junction
Bog Goods
Crown Street Goods

54   54

Rome Street Junct
B11
London Rd Shed
London Road & Petteril Goods Junction

Forks Junction
B9 B16 Bog Junct
M+C Shed
J19
J30
B6
J39
N.E.
London Road Goods
N-E Sidings P7
North Eastern
Durran Hill Jct Goods (NE)

Currock Junct
B8
Currock Shed Junct
G+SW Shed
G+SW
Maryport + Carlisle
J30
Cattle
J31
B22
Petteril Bridge Jct
B9
Petteril Goods Box
Durran Hill Jct
B23
B24
Midland
Durran Hill Shed

London + North Western

Cattle Sta Junct
P8
Sidings Junction
Upperby Shed
Petteril Goods
Shed Jct Goods Jct

River Caldew

30   30

53   53

B12
Upperby Junct Middle
Upperby Junction W
Upperby Shed Junction
Upperby Junction (E)

1914
(1896)
(1912)
(1928)

Cumersdale

B13
Upperby Bridge Junction

L+NW

NOT TO SCALE

39   40   41

30

JEDBURGH + HEXHAM

RAILWAYS

No	Company
R1	NORTH BRITISH
2	NORTH EASTERN
3	Col. Railways

STATIONS

No	Name	Ry Ref
A1	Akeld	2 NT92
2	Allendale	2 NY85
3	BARDON MILL	2 NY76
4	Barrasford	1 NY97
5	Bellingham	1 NY88
6	Belses	1 NT52
7	BRAMPTON Junction	2 NY55
8	Brampton Town	2 NY55
9	Chollerford ✳	1 NY96
10	Chollerton	1 NY97
11	Coanwood	2 NY65
12	CORBRIDGE	2 NZ06
13	Deadwater	1 NY69
14	Elrington	2 NY86
15	Falstone	1 NY78
16	Featherstone Park	2 NY66
17	Fourstones	2 NY86
18	Gilsland	2 NY66
19	Greenhead	2 NY66
20	HALTWHISTLE	2 NY76
21	Hassenden	1 NT52
22	Hawick	1 NT51
23	HAYDON BRIDGE	2 NY86
24	Heads Nook	2 NY55
25	HEXHAM	2 NY96
26	How Mill	2 NY55
27	Jedburgh	1 NT62
28	Jedfoot	1 NT62
29	Kielder	1 NT69
30	Kirkbank	1 NT72
31	Kirknewton	2 NT92
32	Knowesgate	1 NZ08
33	Lambley	2 NY65
34	Langley	2 NY86
35	Low Row	2 NY56
36	Maxton	1 NT62
37	Naworth	2 NY56
38	Nisbet	1 NT62
39	Plashetts	1 NY68
40	Reedsmouth	1 NY88
41	Riccarton Junction	1 NY59
42	Roxburgh	1 NT72
43	Rutherford	1 NT63
44	St Boswells	1 NT53
45	Saughtree	1 NY59
46	Shankend	1 NT50
47	Slaggyford	2 NY65
48	Staward	2 NY85
49	Steele Road	1 NY59
50	Stobs	1 NT50
51	Tarset	1 NY88
52	Thorneyburn	1 NY78
53	Wall	1 NY96
54	Wark	1 NY87
55	Woodburn	1 NY98

✳ Closed before 1922

SIDINGS

No (PRIVATE)	Col	Ref
P1	(Coal Staith)	3 NY55
2	Blacksike Col	3 NY55
3	Howgill Col	3 NY55
4	Bishophill Col	3 NY56
5	Lambley Cols.	3 NY56

SHEDS

No	Location	Ry Ref
E1	Hawick	1 NT51
2	St Boswells	1 NT53

TUNNELS

No	Name/Location	Ry Ref
T1	Haltwhistle	2 NY76
2	Whitrope	1 NT50

SUMMITS

No	Name/Location	Ry Ref
S1	Gilsland	2 NY66
2	Whitrope	1 NT50

JUNCTIONS

No	Name/Location	Ry Ref
J1	Brampton	2 NY55
2	Haltwhistle	2 NY76
3	Allendale Branch	2 NY96
4	Reedsmouth Line	2 1 NY96
5	Reedsmouth	1 NY88
6	Riccarton	1 NY59
7	Kelso	1 NT53
8	Roxburgh	1 NT72

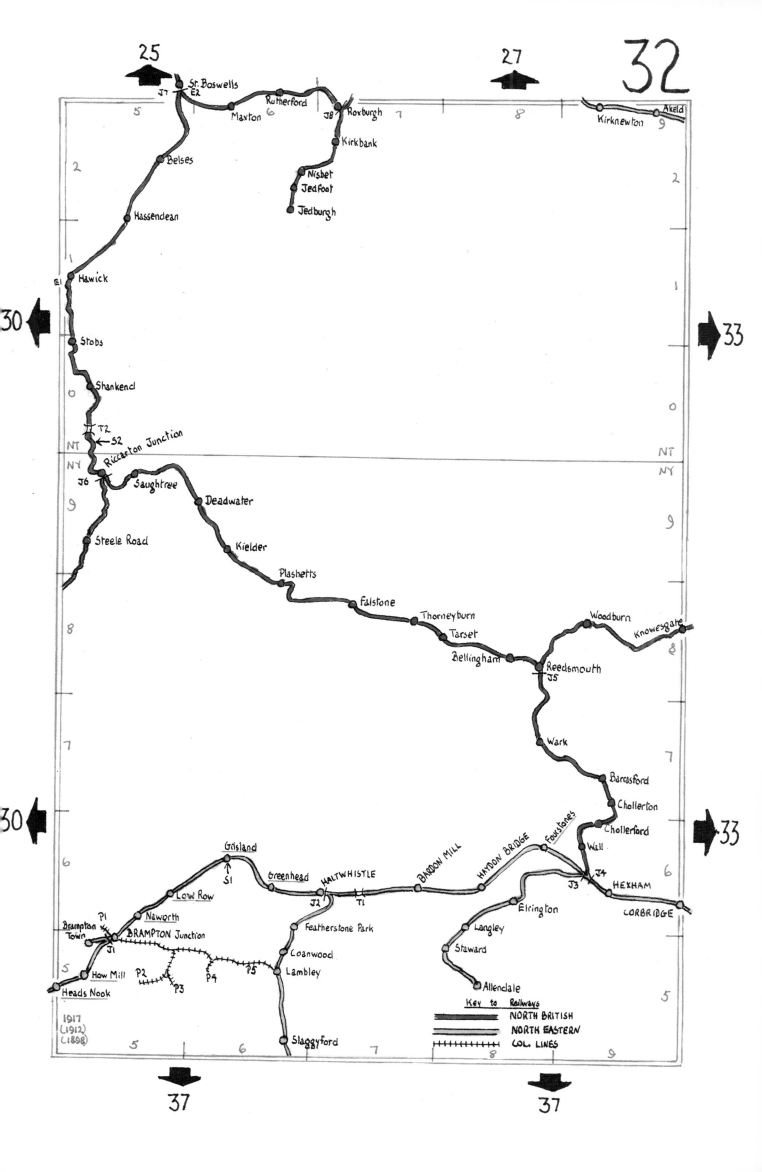

25

27

St. Boswells
J7
E2
Maxton
Rutherford
J8
Roxburgh
7
8
Kirknewton
9
Akeld

Kirkbank

Belses

Nisbet
Jedfoot
Jedburgh

Hassendean

Hawick
E1

30

33

Stobs

Shankend

T2
←52
Riccarton Junction

NT
NY

J6
Saughtree
Deadwater

Steele Road
Kielder

Plashetts

Falstone
Thorneyburn
Woodburn
Knowesgate

Tarset
Bellingham
Reedsmouth
J5

Wark

Barrasford

Chollerton

Chollerford

30

33

Grisland
S1
Greenhead
HALTWHISTLE
BARDON MILL
HAYDON BRIDGE
Fourstones
Wall
J4
HEXHAM

Low Row
J2
T1

Naworth
Featherstone Park
CORBRIDGE

P1
BRAMPTON Junction
Coanwood
Elrington
J3

Brampton Town
J1
Langley

How Mill
P2
P4
P5
Lambley
Staward

Heads Nook
P3
Allendale

1917
(1912)
(1898)

Slaggyford

Key to Railways

NORTH BRITISH

NORTH EASTERN

COL. LINES

37

37

RAILWAYS

No.   Company
R 1 NORTH BRITISH
2 NORTH EASTERN
3 SOUTH SHIELDS, MARSDEN + WHITBURN COL.
4 TYNE + WEAR METRO (ex NE) see Notes

NOTES:
(1) STATIONS: In BLUE not named on map; see map 34※. All stations, old and new are listed
(2) METRO : Station styles giving additional Information - see end of this gazetteer
(3) NAME CHANGES   §Old   §(New). Sometimes on different but nearby site
(4) OTHER FEATURES: Only listed in area not covered by the enlargement.
(5) REFERENCES: In NU or NZ the initial N is omitted.
(6) DURHAM TURNPIKE - Works station closed about 1901 ※

STATIONS

No.	Name	Ry	Ref
A 1	ACKLINGTON	2	U20
2	ALNMOUTH	2	U21
3	Alnwick	2	U11
4	Amble	2	U20
5	Angerton	1	Z08
6	Annfield Plain	2	Z15
7	Annitsford	2	Z27
8	Ashington	2	Z28
9	BACKWORTH §119	4	Z37
※	(BANKFOOT) §61	4	Z26
10	Beamish	2	Z25
11	Bebside	2	Z28
※	(BEDE)	4	Z36
12	Bedlington	2	Z28
13	Bensham	2	Z26
14	BENTON	4	Z26
15	Benton Square	24	Z27
16	Birtley	2	Z25
17	Blackhill	2	Z15
18	BLAYDON	2	Z16
19	Blyth	2	Z38
20	(BOLDON COLLIERY) §22	2	Z36
21	Brinkburn	1	U00
22	BROCKLEY WHINS §20	2	Z36
23	Broomhill	2	U20
※	Byker	2	Z26
※	(BYKER)	4	Z26
24	Callerton	2	Z17
※	Carville	2	Z36
25	CHATHILL	2	U12
26	CHESTER-LE-STREET	2	Z25
27	Chevington	2	Z29
28	Choppington	2	Z28
※	(CHICHESTER)	4	Z36
29	Christon Bank	2	U22
30	Consett	2	Z15
31	CORBRIDGE	2	Y96
32	Cox Green	2	Z35
33	COXLODGE §FAWDON	4	Z26
34	CRAMLINGTON	2	Z27
35	CULLERCOATS	4	Z37
36	Darras Hall	2	Z17
※	(DUNSTON)	2	Z26
37	Dunston-on-Tyne	2	Z26
38	Durham Turnpike ※Note6	2	Z25
39	EAST BOLDON	2	Z36
40	Ebchester	2	Z15
41	Edlington	2	U10
42	Elswick	2	Z26
43	Ewesley	1	Z09
※	FAWDON §33	4	Z26
44	FELLING	4	Z26
45	Fence Houses	2	Z35
46	Fontburn	1	Z09
47	Forest Hall	2	Z27
※	FOUR LANE ENDS	4	Z26
48	Gateshead	2	Z26
※	(GATESHEAD)	4	Z26
※	(GATESHEAD STADIUM)	4	Z26
49	Glanton	2	U01
※	(HADRIAN ROAD)	4	Z36
50	Hartley	2	Z37
※	(HAYMARKET)	4	Z26

	Name	Ry	Ref
※	Heaton		
51	HEBBURN		
52	Heddon-on-the-Wall		
53	Hedgeley		
54	Hepscott		
※	(HEWORTH)		
55	High Shields		
56	High Westwood		
57	HOWDON-on Tyne		
58	Hylton		
59	Ilderton		
※	(ILFORD ROAD)	4	Z26
60	JARROW		
※	Jesmond		
※	(JESMOND)	4	Z26
61	KENTON §BANKFOOT (2)	4	Z26
62	Killingworth		
※	(KINGSTON ROAD)	4	Z26
63	Knitsley		
64	Lamesley		
64A	Leadgate		
65	Lemington		
66	Lintz Green		
67	Little Mill		
※	(LONGBENTON)		
68	Longhurst		
69	Longhoughton		
70	Long Witton		
71	Low Fell		
72	Lucker		
73	MANORS		
	(MANORS)		
74	Marsden		
75	Marsden Cottage		
76	Meldon		
77	Middleton		
78	Millfield		
79	MONKSEATON		
80	Monkwearsmouth		
81	MORPETH		
※	(MONUMENT)		
82	Newbiggin-by-the-Sea		
83	Newburn		
	NEWCASTLE		
84	CENTRAL		
※	(HAYMARKET)		
85	Heaton		
86	MANORS		
	(MANORS)		
※	(MONUMENT)		
※	(ST JAMES)		
87	Newham		
88	Newsham		
89	North Seaton		
90	NORTH SHIELDS		
91	North Sunderland		
92	North Wylam		
93	Pallion		
94	PEGSWOOD		
95	PELAW	4	Z26
96	Pelton	4	Z26
97	Penshaw		
98	PERCY MAIN		
99	Plessey		
※	Point Pleasant	4	Z26

	Name	Ry	Ref
100	Ponteland	2	Z17
101	PRUDHOE	4	Z36
※	(REGENT CENTRE) §134	2	Z16
102	RIDING MILL	2	U01
103	Rothbury	2	Z28
104	Rowlands Gill	24	Z26
105	Rowley	2	Z36
106	Ryhope	2	Z15
107	Ryhope East	4	Z36
108	Ryton	2	Z35
※	St. Anthonys	2	U02
※	(ST JAMES)	4	Z26
※	St Peters	4	Z36
109	Scotsgap	4	Z26
110	Scotswood	2	Z26
111	(SEABURN)	4	Z26
112	SEAHAM	2	Z27
113	Seaham Colliery	4	Z26
114	Seaham Hall (Private)	2	Z14
115	Seahouses	2	Z25
116	Seaton Delaval	2	Z15
117	Seghill	2	Z16
118	Shield Row	2	U21
119	(SHIREMOOR) §89	2	Z26
120	Shotley Bridge	2	Z28
※	(SMITHS PARK)	2	U21
121	SOUTH GOSFORTH	1	Z09
122	SOUTH SHIELDS	2	Z25
123	Stannington	2	U13
124	STOCKSFIELD	2	Z26
125	SUNDERLAND Central	2	Z26
126	Swalwell	3	Z46
127	TYNE DOCK	3	Z46
128	TYNEMOUTH	1	Z18
129	Usworth	1	Z08
※	Walker	2	Z35
130	WALKERGATE	4	Z37
131	WALLSEND	2	Z45
※	(WANSBECK ROAD)	2	Z28
132	Warkworth	2	Z38
133	Washington	4	Z26
134	WEST GOSFORTH § REGENT CENTRE	24	Z26
135	Westhoe Lane	2	Z26
136	WEST JESMOND	4	Z26
137	WEST MONKSEATON	2	Z26
138	WHITLEY BAY	2	Z26
139	Whittingham	4	Z26
140	WIDDRINGTON	4	Z26
141	Willington Quay	4	Z26
142	Wooler	2	U12
143	Wooperton	2	Z57
144	WYLAM	2	Z28

GOODS

No.	Name/Location	Ry	Ref
G 1	Morpeth	2	Z28
2	North Blyth	2	Z38

SIDINGS

No.	Name/Company/Location	Ry	Ref
P 1	Crowton Crofton Mill Col	2	Z38
2	Widdrington Colliery	2	Z29
3	Unton Colliery	2	Z29
4	Ellington Colliery	2	Z29
5	Ashington Colliery Line	2	Z28

		Ry	Ref
6	Barmoor West Colliery	2	Z28
7	Radcliffe Colliery	2	U20

BRIDGES + VIADUCTS

No	Name/Location	Ry	Ref
V 1	Wansbeck-Morpeth	2	Z28

WATER TROUGHS

		Ry	Ref
W 1	Lucker	2	U13

ENGINE SHEDS

No.	Name/Location	Ry	Ref
E 1	Alnmouth	2	U21
2	North Blyth	2	Z38
3	Blyth	2	Z38

JUNCTIONS

No.	Name/Location	Ry	Ref
J 1	Chathill	2	U12
2	Alnwick	2	U11
3	Alnmouth	2	U21
4	Amble Branch	2	Z29
5	Morpeth - NB+NE	21	Z28
6	Reedsmouth Branch	2	Z28
7	Bedlington Branch	2	Z28
8	Goods Branch	2	Z28
9	Ashington Colliery	2	Z28
10	Scotsgap	1	Z08
11	Marchey's House	2	Z28
12	West Sleekburn -South	2	Z28
13	West Sleekburn -East	2	Z28
14	Bedlington	2	Z28
15	Hartley	2	Z37
16	Consett North+South	2	Z05
17	Consett East	2	Z15
18	Hownesgill	2	Z04
19	Newsham	2	Z27
20	West Wylam	2	Z16

KEY TO STATION STYLES IN THIS GAZETTER GIVING ADDITIONAL INFORMATION

(1) NEWCASTLE
  BR + Metro station on map
(2) ※ (HEWORTH)
  BR + Metro station not on map
(3) MONKSEATON
  Metro only (ex N.E) on map
(4) ※ (MANORS) [4] indicates NEW line
  New Metro only station -not on map
(5) ※ (KINGSTON ROAD)
  New Metro (on ex NE line) not on map
(6) PELAW
  Metro (ex NE) and line used by all traffic
(7) HEBBURN
  Metro (ex NE), line Goods only.
(8) Names in brackets ( ) indicate that Station open past map date.
(9) All Metro stations   RED
  All Other stations   BLACK
(10) Where new station is unnumbered and has changed its name. The new name is given after §
thus:
  WEST GOSFORTH § REGENT CENTRE
  Old (map) Name   New name

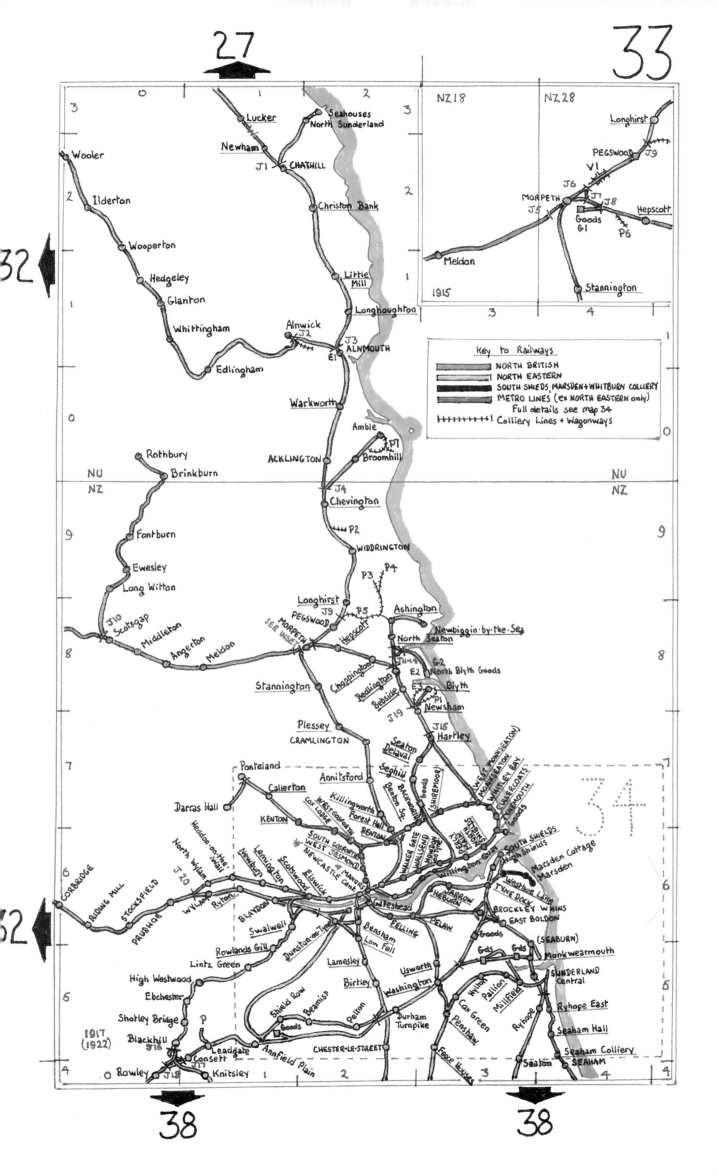

NOTES: (1) METRO STATIONS – Shown in RED. Where there has been a change of name, the modern name is shown on this map. A cross reference to the old name is given. Other information see key map 33
(2) REFERENCES – All in square NZ – therefore figures only shown
(3) OTHER LINES – A full selection of colliery lines is included – position shown is as at 1898; subsequent extensions or closures ARE NOT noted
(M) ENGINE SHEDS – All still open in 1955 included – but location relative to railway lines is not shown.

RAILWAYS

No	Company
R2	NORTH EASTERN
3.5	SHIELDS, MARSDEN + WHITBURN COL (BY N EASTERN)
4	TYNE+WEAR METRO (BY N EASTERN)
0	TYNE+WEAR NEW LINES

STATIONS

No	Ry Ref	Name
A1	2 15	Annfield Plain
2	0 26	(BANKFOOT) §48
3	2 15	Beamish
4	4 36	(BEDE)
5	2 26	Bensham
6	2 26	BENTON
7	24 17	Benton Square
8	2 15	Birtley
9	24 37	BACKWORTH §31
10	2 16	BLAYDON
11	2 36	BOLDON COLLIERY §12
12	2 36	BROCKLEY WHINS §11
13	2 16	Byker
14	0 26	(BYKER)
15	2 17	Callerton
16	2 36	Carville
17	2 25	CHESTER-LE-STREET
18	4 36	(CHICHESTER)
19	4 26	Cox Green
20	2 35	COXLODGE §28
21	4 26	CULLERCOATS
22	2 17	Darras Hall
23	2 26	(DUNSTON)
24	2 26	Dunston-on-Tyne
25	2 25	Durham Turnpike
26	2 36	EAST BOLDON
27	2 46	Elswick
28	4 26	(FAWDON) §20
29	4 26	FELLING
30	2 35	Fence Houses
31	2 27	Forest Hill
32	4 26	(FOUR LANE ENDS)
33	2 26	Gateshead
34	0 26	(GATESHEAD STADIUM)
35	0 26	(GATESHEAD) STADIUM
36	4 36	(HADRIAN ROAD)
37		(HAYMARKET)
38	2 26	Heaton
39	2 15	HEBBURN
40	0 26	(HEWORTH)
41	2 15	High Shields
42	4 36	HOWDON-on-Tyne
43	2 26	Hylton
44	4 26	(ILFORD ROAD)
45	2 26	JARROW
46	2 15	Jesmond
47	24 37	(JESMOND)
48	2 16	KENTON §2
49	2 36	Killingworth
50	2 36	(KINGSTON ROAD)
51	2 16	Lamesley
52	0 26	Lemington
53	2 17	(LONG BENTON)
54	2 36	Low Fell
55	2 25	MANORS
56	4 36	(MANORS)
57	2 35	Marsden
58	4 26	Marsden Cottage
59	4 37	Millfield
60	2 17	MONKSEATON
61	2 26	Monkwearmouth
62	2 26	(MONUMENT)
63	2 25	Newburn
64	2 46	NEWCASTLE CENTRAL
65	4 26	(HAYMARKET)
66	4 26	Heaton
67	2 35	MANORS
68	2 27	(MANORS)
69	4 26	(MONUMENT)
70	2 26	(ST JAMES)
71	0 26	NORTH SHIELDS
72	0 26	Pallion
73	4 36	Pelton
74	0 26	(PELAW)
75	2 26	Penshaw
76	4 36	PERCY MAIN
77	24 26	Point Pleasant
78	2 36	Ponteland
79	4 36	(REGENT CENTRE) §105
80	2 35	Rowlands Gill
81	4 26	Ryhope
82	4 36	Ryhope East
83	4 26	Ryton
84	0 26	St. Anthony's
85	2 26	(ST JAMES)
86	2 27	St Peter's
87	4 26	Scotswood
88	2 25	(SEABURN)
89	2 16	Seaham Hall (Private) §9
90	4 26	Shield Row
91	2 25	(SHIREMOOR)
92	2 26	(SMITHS PARK)
93	0 26	SOUTH GOSFORTH
94	3 46	SOUTH SHIELDS
95	5 46	SUNDERLAND Central
96	2 35	Swalwell
97	4 37	TYNE DOCK
98	2 45	TYNEMOUTH
99	0 26	Usworth
100	2 16	Walker
101	26 26	WALKERGATE
102	0 26	WALLSEND
103	2 26	(WANSBECK ROAD)
104	2 26	Washington
105	2 26	WEST GOSFORTH §79
106	0 26	Westhoe Lane – S.Shields
107	0 26	(WEST JESMOND)
108	0 26	(WEST MONKSEATON)
109	4 26	WHITLEY BAY
110	2 35	Willington Quay
111	2 36	

JUNCTIONS

Ry Ref	No	Name/Location
27	J1	West
27	2	Castle
37	3	High Level Bridge
37	4	Gateshead
36	5	King Edward Bridge E
26	6	King Edward Bridge W
26	7	Oakwellgate
2 36	8	Gateshead Goods
2 36	9	Manors
36	10	Jesmond
26	11	New Bridge Street Goods
26	12	Byker – Riverside
3 46	13	Collywell
35	14	Backworth
2 26	15	Gosforth – West
2 26	16	Gosforth – South
2 26	17	Gosforth – East
2 26	18	Benton – West
2 26	19	Benton – East
2 26	20	Benton – South Jets
2 26	21	Percy Main – West
2 26	22	Percy Main – North
2 26	23	Percy Main – East
2 26	24	Monkseaton North
2 26	25	Monkseaton South
2 35	26	Scotswood
2 35	27	Derwenthaugh N+5
2 16	28	Forth Goods Branch
2 26	29	Low Fell
2 26	30	Redheugh
2 26	31	Bowes Bridge
2 26	32	Tanfield
2 26	33	West Stanley
2 26	34	South Pelaw
2 26	35	Stanley
2 26	36	Washington
2 26	37	Southwick
2 26	38	Pelaw West East
2 26	39	Brockley Whins West
2 26	40	Brockley Whins West
2 26	41	Brockley Whins South
2 26	42	South
2 37	43	Brockley Whins East
2 37	44	East Boldon
2 26	45	Green Lane South
2 26	46	Green Lane North
2 26	47	Tyne Goods
2 26	48	Tyne Dock-Marsden
23 36	49	North Easter/Marsden
2 26	50	Penshaw
2 36	51	Sunderland-West
2 36	52	Millfield
2 35	53	Dock Branch
2 45	54	South Dock
2 37	55	Ryhope
2 16	56	Castletown
2 17	57	Ponteland
2 16	58	Scotswood Bridge
2 26	59	Greenfield
2 26	60	Tynemouth Goods

GOODS DEPOTS

Ry Ref	No	Name/Location
4 26	1	Boldon
2 36	2	Forth
2 17	3	Gateshead
4 26	4	Holywell
2 15	5	Hylton Lane
2 45	6	New Bridge Street
2 45	7	Redeugh
2 16	8	South Shields
2 26	9	Southwick
0 26	10	Tyne Dock
2 26	11	Tynemouth
2 26	12	West Stanley
4 26	21	Dinnington Colliery
2 35	22	Burradon Colliery
2 26	23	Backworth Church Pit
2 26	24	East Holywell Colliery
4 26	25	Follingsby Colliery
2 37	26	Teams Colliery Wagonway
2 35	27	Heworth Colliery
2 26	28	Whitburn Colliery
2 26	29	Southwick Quarries
2 36	30	Quayside Branch
2 35	31	Depôts
2 36	32	Oakwellgate Sidings
2 36	33	Iron Works Siding
2 15	34	Tyne Main Colliery
2 35	35	Cement Works Siding
2 45	36	Brick Works Siding
2 15	37	Glass Works Siding
2 26	38	Oakwellgate Sidings
45 39	39	Chemical Works Siding
35	40	Chemical Works Siding
35	41	Lady Ann Pit

SIDINGS GOODS ONLY & COLLIERY LINES

No	Name (Colliery/Company)	Ry Ref
P1	Ryhope Colliery	4 36
2	Silksworth Colliery	4 26
3	New Herrington Colliery	4 36
4	Dorothea – Newbottle	2 45
5	Margaret – Newbottle	2 16
6	Houghton Colliery	4 36
7	Washington Colliery	4 36
8	Lumley Pit	2 35
9	Waldbridge New Pit	2 26
10	S Moor Colliery New Pit	4 26
11	Hedley Pit	4 36
12	S Moor Colliery (Charlie)	2 35
13	East Pontop Colliery	4 26
14	Urpeth Colliery	2 26
15	Ouston E Colliery	4 36
16	Berwicke Main Pit	4 26
17	Tanfield Branch	4 37
18	Blaydon Burn	4 37
19	Gateshead + Chopfield Lane	2 36
20	Seatonburn Wagonway	

SIDINGS, GOODS ONLY + COLLIERY LINES (cont)

No	Name	Ry Ref
43	Marley Mill Colliery	25
44	Victoria-Garesfield Col	16
45	Twizell Colliery	25
46	Usworth Colliery	35
47	New Lambton Colliery	35
48	Mount Moor Colliery	25
49	Stargate Colliery	16
60	Killingworth Colliery	27
61	Teams Colliery	15
62	South Garesfield	PJ 15
63	Springwell Colliery	25
43	North Walbottle Colliery	16
44	Maria Colliery	25
45	Preston Colliery	35
46	Northumberland Dock Goods	35
47	Teams Colliery Wagonway	25
48	Derwenthaugh Goods	16
49	Esther Pit	27
50	Dipton Delight Col	15
51	North Dock Branch	15
52	Caroline Pit	25

BRIDGES

No	Name	Ry Ref
V1	King Edward Bridge	2 26
2	High Level Bridge	2 26
3	Ouseburn Viaduct	2 26
4	Scotswood Bridge	2 16

ENGINE SHEDS

No	Location	Ry Ref
E1	Gateshead	2 15
2	Bowes Bridge	25
3	Heaton	25
4	Blaydon	25
5	Percy Main	2 25
6	South Garesforth	16
7	Sunderland	16
8	Tyne Dock	27

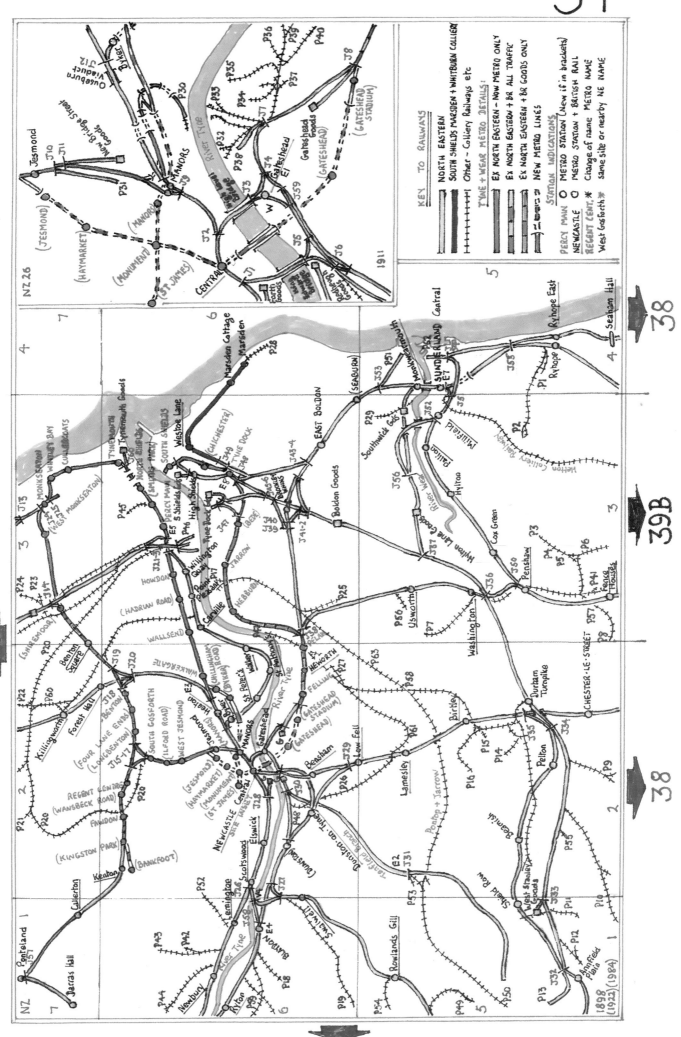

KEY TO RAILWAYS

NORTH EASTERN
SOUTH SHIELDS MARSDEN + WHITBURN COLLIERY
Other - Colliery Railways etc

TYNE + WEAR METRO DETAILS:
EX NORTH EASTERN - Now METRO ONLY
EX NORTH EASTERN + BR ALL TRAFFIC
EX NORTH EASTERN + BR GOODS ONLY
NEW METRO LINES

STATION INDICATIONS
PERCY MAIN   ○ METRO STATION (New if in brackets)
NEWCASTLE   ◑ METRO STATION + BRITISH RAIL
REGENT CENT, * Change of name METRO NAME
West Gosforth * Same site or nearby NE NAME

RAILWAYS

WHITEHAVEN, BARROW + CARNFORTH

No	Company
R 1	MIDLAND
2	MIDLAND + FURNESS JOINT
3	FURNESS
4	FURNESS + LNW JOINT
5	WHITEHAVEN, CLEATOR + EGREMONT (Furness + LNW Joint)
6	LONDON + NORTH WESTERN
7	COCKERMOUTH, KESWICK + PENRITH
8	CLEATOR + WORKINGTON JUNCTION
9	MARYPORT + CARLISLE
10	ROWRAH + KELTON FELL
11	CALEDONIAN
22	RAVENGLASS + ESKDALE (3'0" Gauge)

STATIONS + HALTS

No	Name	Ry Ref
A 1	Armathwaite	1 NY54
2	ARNSIDE	3 SD47
3	ASKAM	3 SD17
4	ASPATRIA	9 NY14
5	Baggrow	9 NY14
6	BARROW Central	3 SD16
7	Bassenthwaite Lake	7 NY12
8	Beckermet	5 NY00
9	BECKFOOT	22 SD19
10	Blencow	7 NY42
11	Bolton-le-Sands	6 SD46
12	BOOT	22 NY10
13	BOOTLE	3 SD08
14	Braithwaite	7 NY22
15	BRANSTY (Whitehaven)	36 NX92
16	Branthwaite	5 NY02
17	BRAYSTONES	3 NX90
18	Brayton	9 NY14
19	Bridgefoot	5 NY02
20	Brigham	69 NY03
21	Broomfield	11 NY14
22	Broughton-(in-Furness)	3 SD28
23	Bullgill	9 NY03
24	BURNESIDE	6 SD59
25	Calthwaite	6 NY43
26	Camerton	6 NY03
27	CARK + CARTMEL	3 SD37
28	CARNFORTH	1246 SD46
29	Cleator Moor	5 NY01
30	Cleator Moor	8 NX91
31	Cockermouth	76 NY13
32	Conishead Priory	3 SD37
33	Coniston Lake	3 SD29
34	CORKICLE	3 NX91
35	Catehill	1 NY44
36	Curthwaite	9 NY34
37	DALEGARTH	22 NY10
38	DALTON	3 SD27
39	Dearham	9 NY03
40	Dearham Bridge	9 NY03
41	Distington	58 NY02
42	DRIGG	3 SD09
43	Egremont	5 NY01
44	Embleton	7 NY12
45	ESKDALE (DALEGARTH)	22 NY10
46	ESKDALE GREEN	22 SD19
47	Eskmeals	3 SD08
48	FLIMBY	6 NY03
49	FOXFIELD	3 SD28
50	Frizington	5 NY01
51	Furness Abbey	3 SD27
52	GRANGE (OVER-SANDS)	3 SD47
53	Great Broughton	8 NY03
54	Greenodd	3 SD38
55	GREEN ROAD	3 SD18
56	HARRINGTON	6 NX92
57	Harrington-Church Rd Halt	8 NX92
58	Haverthwaite	3 SD38
59	Hest Bank	6 SD46
60	Heversham	3 SD48
61	High Blaithwaite	9 NY24
62	High Harrington	8 NX92
63	IRTON ROAD	22 SD19
64	KENTS BANK	3 SD37
65	Keswick	7 NY22
66	KIRKBY (in FURNESS)	3 SD28
67	Lakeside Windermere	3 SD38
68	Lamplugh	5 NY02
69	Leegate	9 NY24
70	Lindal	3 SD27
71	Lonsdale Cross	3 SD27
72	Lowca	8 NX92
73	MARYPORT	9 NY03
74	Mealsgate	9 NY24
75	Micklam	8 NX92
76	MILLOM	3 SD17
77	Moor Row	5 NX91
78	Moresby Parks	8 NX91
79	MUNCASTER MILL	22 SD09
80	NETHERTOWN	3 NX90
81	(Newby Bridge)	3 SD38
82	Oatlands	8 NY01
83	Papcastle	9 NY03
84	PARTON	6 NX92
85	PENRITH	6(7) NY52
86	Penruddock	7 NY42
87	Piel	3 SD26
88	Plumpton	6 NY43
89	Rampside	3 SD26
90	Ramsden Dock	3 SD16
91	RAVENGLASS	3 SD09
92	RAVENGLASS	22 SD09
93	ROOSE	3 SD26
94	Rosehill	8 NX92
95	Rowrah	5 NX01
96	ST BEES	3 NX91
97	Sandside	3 SD47
98	SEASCALE	3 NY00
99	Seaton	8 NY03
100	SELLAFIELD	3 NY00
101	Siddick	6 NX93
102	SILECROFT	3 SD18
103	SILVERDALE	3 SD47
104	Southwaite	6 NY44
105	STAVELEY	6 SD49
106	Threlkeld	7 NY32
107	Torver	3 SD29
108	Troutbeck	7 NY32
109	Ullock	5 NY01
110	ULVERSTON	3 SD27
111	WHITEHAVEN	36 NX92
112	Whitehaven	6 NX92
113	WIGTON	9 NY24
114	Winder	5 NY01
115	WINDERMERE	6 SD40
116	Windermere Lakeside	3 SD38
117	Woodend	5 NY01
118	Woodland	3 SD28
119	WORKINGTON	6 NX92
120	Workington Bridge	6 NY02
121	Workington Central	8 NY02
122	Wreay	6 NY44
123	Yeathouse	5 NY01

GOODS

No	Name / Location	Ry Ref
G 1	Barrow	3 SD16
2	Carnforth	613 SD46
3	Park	3 SD27
4	Millom	3 SD17
5	Seascale	3 NY00
6	Lindal Goods	3 SD27
7	Lindal Ore	3 SD27
8	Coniston	3 SD29
9	Ulverston	3 SD27
10	Broughton-in-Furness	3 SD28
11	Linefoot	89 NY03
12	Crossfield	5 NY01

WORKS

No	Location	Ry Ref
C 1	Barrow	3 SD16

SIDINGS + COLLIERY LINES

No	Name / Company / Location	Ry Ref
P 1	Hawcoat Branch	3 SD16
2	Sandscale Branch	3 SD17
3	Stainton Branch	3 SD27
4	Stank Branch	3 SD26
5	Millom Iron Works	3 SD17

SHEDS

No	Location	Ry Ref
E 1	Penrith	6 NY52
2	Coniston	3 SD29
3	Carnforth	1 SD46
4	Carnforth	3 SD46
5	Carnforth	6 SD46
6	Barrow	3 SD16

BRIDGES

No	Name / Location	Ry Ref
V 1	Kent Viaduct	3 SD47
2	Leven Viaduct	3 SD37

JUNCTIONS

No	Name / Location	Ry Ref
J 1	Buccleuch Dock	3 SD16
2	Salthouse	3 SD26
3	St Lukes	3 SD16
4	Goods	3 SD16
5	Hawcoat	3 SD16
6	Ormsgill	3 SD17
7	Sandscale	3 SD17
8	Oak Lea	3 SD27
9	Thwaite Flat	3 SD27
10	Goldmire North	3 SD27
11	Goldmire South	3 SD27
12	Millwood	3 SD27
13	Dalton	3 SD27
14	Crooklands	3 SD27
15	Carnforth	346 SD46
16	Joint + Furness	34 SD46
17	Station (South)	23 SD46
18	Furness + Midland	23 SD46
19	Furness + Midland	23 SD46
20	Goods	23 SD46
21	East Junction	2 SD46
22	Bullgill	9 NY03
23	Aspatria	9 NY14
24	Brayton	911 NY14
25	Aikbank	9 NY24
26	Penrith	76 NY52
27	Eamont Bridge	NE+ 6 NY52
28	Redhills	NE+ 7 NY42
29	Coniston Goods	3 SD29
30	Broughton Goods	3 SD28
31	Foxfield	3 SD28
32	Lindal Goods	3 SD27
33	Plumpton West	3 SD37
34	Plumpton North	3 SD37
35	Plumpton East	3 SD37
36	Arnside	3 SD47
37	Hest Bank North	6 SD46
38	Millom (for Iron Works)	3 SD17
39	Ulverston Goods	3 SD27
40	Seascale Goods	3 SD09

NOTES:

(1) STATIONS - All stations are located on the map including the area covered by the enlargement - Map 36

(2) OTHER FEATURES - These are shown and included in the gazetteer, in the main ONLY if they are shown on the map in the area not covered by the enlargement (Map 36)

(3) CARNFORTH - Enlargement Inset - Also Inset on Map 42

(4) BARROW - Inset to show layout of Junctions. All lines on this inset are Furness Railway

(5) ESKDALE RAILWAY - Stations shown in CAPITALS. Has more or less remained open. Unlike the normal preserved line which is closed and then subsequently opened. Eg:- on this map the Lakeside - Haverthwaite.

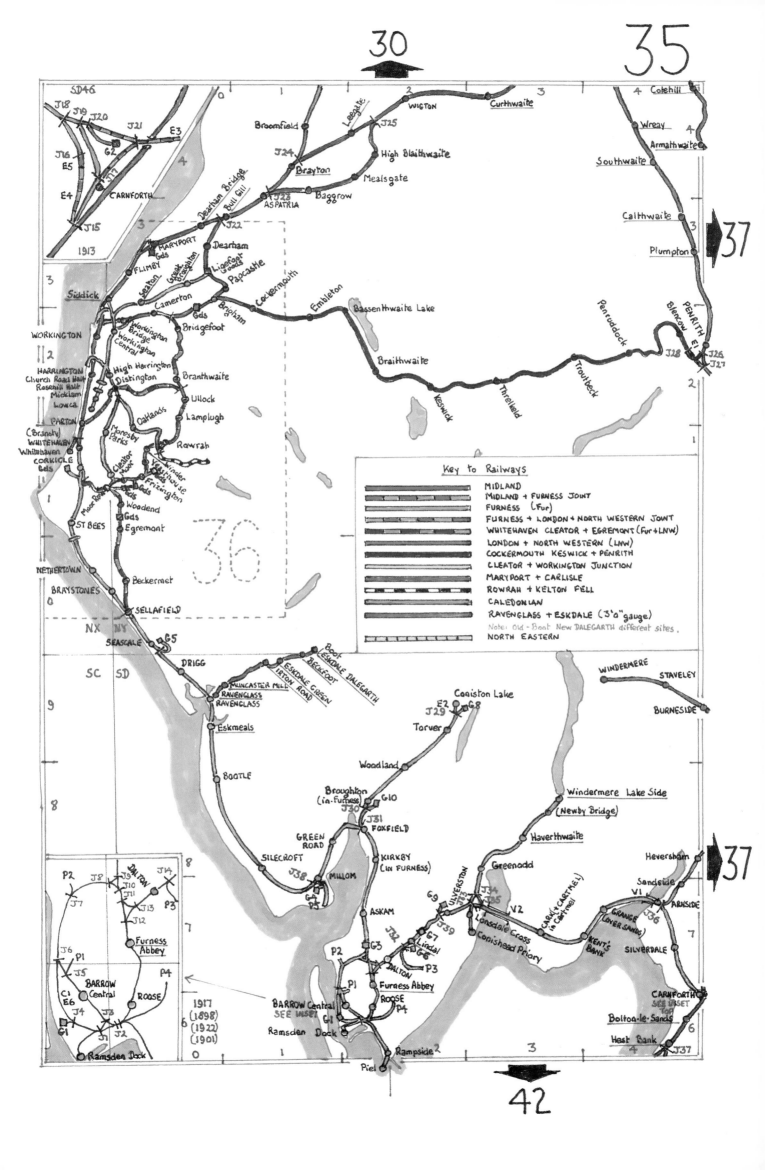

WHITEHAVEN + WORKINGTON

RAILWAYS

No	Company
R 3	FURNESS
5	WHITEHAVEN, CLEATOR + EGREMONT
	(Furness and LNW Joint)
6	LONDON + NORTH WESTERN
67	LNW + C, KESWICK + PENRITH
7	COCKERMOUTH, KESWICK + PENRITH
8	CLEATOR + WORKINGTON JUNCTION
9	MARYPORT + CARLISLE
10	ROWRAH + KELTON FELL (Goods)

STATIONS + HALTS

No	Name	Ry Ref
A 1	Beckermet	5 NY00
2	BRANSTY (Whitehaven 36	NX92
3	Branthwaite	5 NY02
4	BRAYSTONES	3 NX90
5	Bridgefoot	5 NY02
6	Brigham	69 NY03
7	Bullgill	9 NY03
8	Camerton	6 NY03
9	Cleator Moor	5 NY01
10	Cleator Moor	8 NX91
11	Cockermouth	67 NY13
12	CORKICLE	3 NX91
13	Dearham	9 NY03
14	Dearham Bridge	9 NY03
15	Distington	58 NY02
16	Egremont	5 NY01
17	FLIMBY	6 NY03
18	Frizington	5 NY01
19	Great Broughton	8 NY03
20	HARRINGTON	6 NX92
21	Harrington- Church Rd *	8 NX92
22	High Harrington	8 NX92
23	Lamplugh	5 NY02
24	Lowca	8 NX92
25	MARYPORT	9 NY03
26	Micklam	8 NX92
27	Moor Row	5 NX91
28	Moresby Parks	8 NX91
29	NETHERTOWN	3 NX90
30	Oatlands	8 NY01
31	Papcastle	9 NY03
32	PARTON	6 NX92
33	Rosehill Halt *	8 NX92
34	Rowrah	5 NY01
35	ST BEES	3 NX91
36	Seaton	8 NY03
37	SELLAFIELD	3 NY00
38	Siddick	6 NX93
39	Ullock	5 NY01
40	WHITEHAVEN	36 NX92
41	Whitehaven	6 NX92
42	Winder	5 NY01
43	Woodend	5 NY01
44	WORKINGTON	6 NX92
45	Workington Bridge	6 NY02
46	Workington Central	8 NY02
47	Woodend	5 NY01

GOODS

No	Name/Location	Ry Ref
G 1	Arlecdon	8 NY01
2	Bigrigg	5 NY01
3	Broughton Cross (4)	6 NY03
4	Cockermouth	67 NY13
5	Crossfield	5 NY01
6	Eskett	5 NY01
7	Gillfoot	5 NY01
8	Linefoot	89 NY03
9	Maryport	9 NY03
10	Parton	6 NX92
11	Preston Street	3 NX91

SIDINGS, COLLIERY LINES + GOODS LINES

No	Line/Company/Location	Ry Ref
P 1	Lowther Pit	NY03
2	Lonsdale Pit	NY03
3	Nelson Pit (Broughtonmoor)	NY03
4	Bertha Pit	NY03
5	Seatonmoor No 2	NY03
6	Seatonmoor No 3	NY03
7	Flimby Col - Robinhood Pit	NY03
8	Senhouse Dock	96 NY03
9	Phoenix Foundry	9 NY03
10	Lonsdales Dock	NX92
11	Lord Lonsdales Lines	P+8 NX93
12	Merchants Quay	6 NX92
13	Derwent Hematite	8 NX92
14	Harbour Branch	8 NX92
15	John Pit	NX92
16	Saltom Pit	NX91
17	Kells Pit	NX91
18	Ladysmith Pit	NX91
19	Distington Iron Works	5 NY02
20	Moresby Parks Siding	NY01
21	Lonsdale Mining	P+5 NY01
22	Mowbray Branch	5 NY01
23	Rowrah New Limestone	8 NY01
24	Kirkland Goods	10 NY01
25	Kelton Iron	10 NY01
26	Bairds - Knockmurton	10 NY01
27	Gillfoot Branch	5 NY01
28	Stirlings Pit	NY01
29	Beckermet Mine	NY00
30	Buckhill Pit	8 NY03

ENGINE SHEDS

No	Location	Ry Ref
E 1	Whitehaven	3 NX91
2	Moor Row	5 NY01
3	Distington	5 NY02
4	Siddick	6 NY03
5	Workington	6 NX92

JUNCTIONS

No	Name/Location	Ry Ref
J 1	Senhouse + Elizabeth	9 NY03
2	Docks Branch	9 NY03
3	Goods	9 NY03
4	Docks Bra	6 NY03
5	Dearham Bridge	9 NY03
6	Bullgill	9 NY04
7	Linefoot	98 NY03
8	Cockermouth Goods	67 NY13
9	L+NW and CK+P	67 NY13
10	Marron	65 NY03
11	Workington Bridge	68 NY02
12	Clappock's	8 NY02
13	Calva	8 NY03
14	Workington + Docks	6 NX92
15	Cockermouth + Workington	6 NX92
16	Merchant's Quay Line	6 NX92
17	Siddick	68 NX93
18	Siddick + Docks	8 NX93
19	} Colliery Lines	6 NY03
20		
21	Dock Lines	8 NX92
22	Jct of Railways 3+4	8 NX92
23	Distington West	58 NY02
24	Iron Works Branch	5 NY02
25	Distington South	8 NY02
26	Ullock	5 NY02
27	Kelton Fell Line	510 NY01
28	Arlecdon	8 NY01
29	C+W Jct and R+KF	810 NY01
30	Eskett	5 NY01
31	Mowbray	5 NY01
32	Birks Bridge	5 NY01
33	Moor Row North	58 NY01
34	Moor Row West	58 NY01
35	Bigrigg	5 NY01
36	Gillfoot Branch	5 NY01
37	Mirehouse	35 NX91
38	Moor Row Line South	3 NX91
39	Moor Row Line North	3 NX91
40	Preston Street	3 NX91
41	Corkicle	3 NX91
42	Bransty	G3 NX91
43	Distington Line	65 NX92
44	Goods Line	6 NX92

45	Parton Goods	65 NX92
46	John Pit	8 NX92
47	Beckermet Mine Branch	5 NY00
48	Sellafield	35 NY00
49	M+C and L+NW	96 NY03

NOTES:

(1) REFERENCES - Stations and Halts are identical to those on General Map 35. The Grid line between 0 +1 is therefore somewhat east of its proper position

(2) Linefoot + Crossfield Stations may have had passenger facilities at one time - but if so these had gone before 1904.

(3) * indicates Halt

(4) Also passenger station for a time

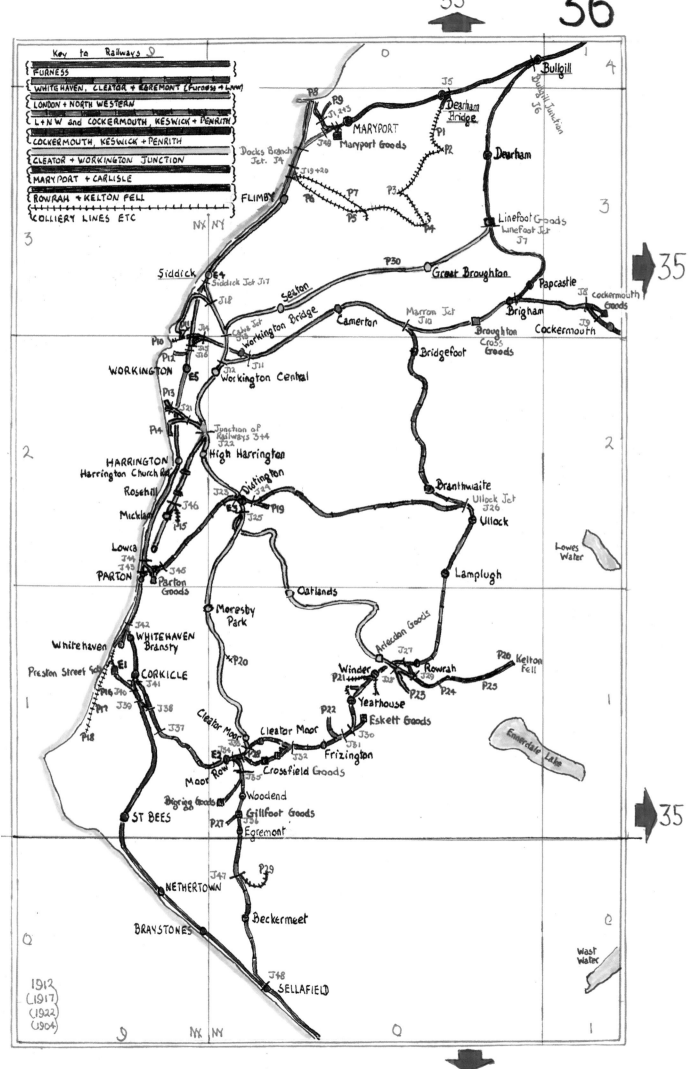

Key to Railways

FURNESS
WHITEHAVEN, CLEATOR + EGREMONT (Furness + LNW)
LONDON + NORTH WESTERN
L + NW and COCKERMOUTH, KESWICK + PENRITH
COCKERMOUTH, KESWICK + PENRITH
CLEATOR + WORKINGTON JUNCTION
MARYPORT + CARLISLE
ROWRAH + KELTON FELL
COLLIERY LINES ETC

Bullgill
Bullgill Junction 36
J5
Dearham Bridge
P8
P9
J1,2+3
J48
MARYPORT
Maryport Goods
P1
P2
Dearham
Docks Branch Jct. J4
J19+20
P7
P3
P6
FLIMBY
P5
P4
Linefoot Goods
Linefoot Jct
J7
NX NY
3
P30
Great Broughton
Papcastle
J8 Cockermouth Goods
Siddick E4
Siddick Jct J17
Seaton
Marron Jct J10
Brigham
Cockermouth
J9
J18
Cocke Jct
Workington Bridge
Camerton
Broughton Cross Goods
J13
Pio
J14
P12
J15 J16
J11
Workington Central
Bridgefoot
WORKINGTON E5
J12
P13
J21
2
P14
Junction of Railways 3+4
J22
High Harrington
Branthwaite
HARRINGTON
Harrington Church Rd
Distington
Ullock Jct
J26
Rosehill
J23 J24
Ullock
J46
E3
Pig
Micklam
J15
J25
Lowca
Lamplugh
Lowes Water
J44
J43
PARTON
J45
Parton Goods
Oatlands
Moresby Park
Arlecdon Goods
J27
J42
Rowrah
P20
P26 Kelton Fell
Whitehaven
WHITEHAVEN Bransty
Winder
J29
P25
Preston Street Sdgs
E1
CORKICLE
P21
J28
P23 P24
J41
P22
Yearhouse
P16 J40
Eskett Goods
P17 J39
J38
Cleator Moor
Frizington
P18
J37
Cleator Moor
J31 J30
J35
1
Ennerdale Lake
E2
J34 J33
J32
Moor Row
Crossfield Goods
J35
Bigrigg Goods
Woodend
Gillfoot Goods
ST BEES
P27
J36
Egremont
J47
P29
NETHERTOWN
Beckermeet
BRAYSTONES
West Water
1912
(1917)
(1922)
(1904)
NX NY
J48
SELLAFIELD
0

PENRITH + KENDAL

RAILWAYS

No.	Company
R 1	LONDON + NORTH WESTERN
2	NORTH EASTERN
3	MIDLAND
4	MIDLAND + FURNESS JOINT
5	FURNESS
6	COCKERMOUTH KESWICK + PENRITH
7	NIDD VALLEY (Light)

STATIONS

No.	Name	Ry Ref
A 1	Alston	2 NX74
2	Appleby	2 NX62
3	APPLEBY (West)	3 NX62
4	Arkholme	4 SD57
5	Armathwaite §	3 NX54
6	Askrigg	2 SD99
7	Barbon	1 SD68
8	Barras	2 NX81
9	BENTHAM	3 SD66
10	Borwick	4 SD57
11	Bowes	2 NZ01
12	BURNESIDE	1 SD59
13	Burton + Holme	1 SD57
14	CARNFORTH	1345 SD47
15	CLAPHAM	3 SD76
16	Cliburn	2 NX52
17	Clifton	2 NX52
18	Clifton + Lowther	1 NX52
19	Crosby Garrett	3 NX70
20	Culgaith	3 NX62
21	Dent §	3 SD78
22	Eastgate	2 NX93
23	Gaisgill	2 NX60
24	Grayrigg	1 SD59
25	Hawes	23 SD88
26	Hawes Jct + Garsdale §	3 SD79
27	Heversham	5 SD48
28	Hornby	3 SD56
29	Horton (-in-Ribblesdale) §	3 SD87
30	Ingleton	1 SD67
31	Ingleton	3 SD67
32	KENDAL	1 SD59
33	Kirkby Lonsdale	1 SD87
34	Kirkby Stephen	2 NX70
35	Kirkby Stephen + Ravenstonedale §	3 NX70
36	Kirkby Thore	2 NX62
37	Langwathby §	3 NX53
38	Lazonby + Kirkoswald §	3 NX53
39	Little Salkeld	3 NX53
40	Lofthouse-in-Nidderdale	7 SD97
41	Long Marton	3 NX62
42	Low Gill	1 SD69
43	Melling	4 SD57
44	Mickleton	2 NX92
45	Middleton	1 SD68
46	Middleton-in-Teesdale	2 NX92
47	Milnthorpe	1 SD58
48	Musgrave	2 NX71
49	New Biggin	3 NX62
50	Ormside	3 NX61
51	OXENHOLME	1 SD59
52	PENRITH (26)	1 NX52
53	Ravenstonedale	2 NX60
54	Ribblehead §	3 SD77
55	Romaldkirk	2 NX92
56	St John's Chapel	2 NX83
57	Sedbergh	1 SD69
58	Shap	1 NX51
59	Smardale	2 NX70
60	Stanhope	2 NZ03
61	Tebay	12 NX60
62	Temple Sowerby	2 NX62
63	Warcop	2 NX71
64	Wearhead	2 NX83
65	WENNINGTON	34 SD66
66	Westgate-in-Weardale	2 NX93
3	Tebay	1 NX60
4	Tebay	2 NX60
5	Bentham (Low)	3 SD66
6	Low Gill	1 SD69
7	Kendal	1 SD59

ENGINE SHEDS

No	Name/Location	Ry Ref
E 1	Oxenholme	1 SD58
2	Penrith	1 NX52
3	Kirkby Stephen	2 NX70
4	Tebay	1 NX60
5	Ingleton	3 SD67

GOODS

No	Name/Location	Ry Ref
G 1	Parkhead	2 NZ04
2	Stanhope	2 NZ03
3	Tebay	1 NX60
4	Tebay	2 NX60
5	Eamont Bridge	12 NX52
6	Eden Valley	12 NX52
7	Appleby	3 NX62
8	Midland/North Eastern	23 NX62
9	Kirkby Stephen	2 NX70
10	Tebay North	12 NX60
11	Tebay South	1 NX60
12	Tebay Station	12 NX60
13	Goods	2 NX60
14	Hawes	3 SD79
15	Ingleton Mid-LNW	13 SD67
16	Wennington	34 SD66
17	Clapham	3 SD76
18	Hincaster	15 SD58
19	Oxenholme	1 SD59
20	Low Gill	1 SD69
21	Hawes Station	23 SD89
22	Bolts Burn	0 NX94

SIDINGS + MINERAL LINES

No.	Location/Company	Ry Ref
P 1	Stanhope Lime	2 NX94
2	Rookhope Smelting	NX94
3	Groove Rake Mine	NX84
4	Rispey Mines	NX94
5	Slit Mines	NX93
6	Middlehope	NX84

TUNNELS

No	Name	Length	Ry Ref
T 1	Armathwaite	330	3 NX54
2	Baron Wood No.2	251	3 NX54
3	Baron Wood No.1	207	3 NX54
4	Lazonby	99	3 NX53
5	Waste Bank	164	3 NX53
6	Culgaith	661	3 NX62
7	Helm	571	3 NX71
8	Crosby Garrett	181	3 NX70
9	Birkett	424	3 NX70
10	Shotlock Hill	106	3 SD79
11	Moorcock	98	3 SD79
12	Rise Hill	1213	3 SD78
13	Blea Moor	2629	3 SD78
14	Moss Dale Head	245	3 SD89

BRIDGES + VIADUCTS

No.	Name	Ry Ref
V 1	Ribblehead Viaduct	3 SD77
2	Dent Head Viaduct	3 SD78
3	Moorcock Viaduct	3 SD79
4	Aisgill Viaduct	3 SD79
5	Belah Viaduct	2 NY81

JUNCTIONS

No.	Name/Location	Ry Ref
J 1	Rookhope Branch	2 NZ04
2	Stanhope Goods	2 NZ03
3	Penrith	17 NX52
4	Redhills	27 NX52

SUMMITS

No	Name/Location	Ht	Ry Ref
S 1	Shap	916'	1 NX51
2	Aisgill	1166'	3 SD79
3	Stainmoor	1370'	2 NX91

NOTES:

(1) CARNFORTH - Junctions, Lines, Goods, Engine Sheds are shown in detail in the insets on maps 35 and 42

(2) SETTLE-CARLISLE LINE - A fairly full selection of the engineering features of this line is shown. Tunnel length is in yards.

(3) § Station re-opened since map drawn

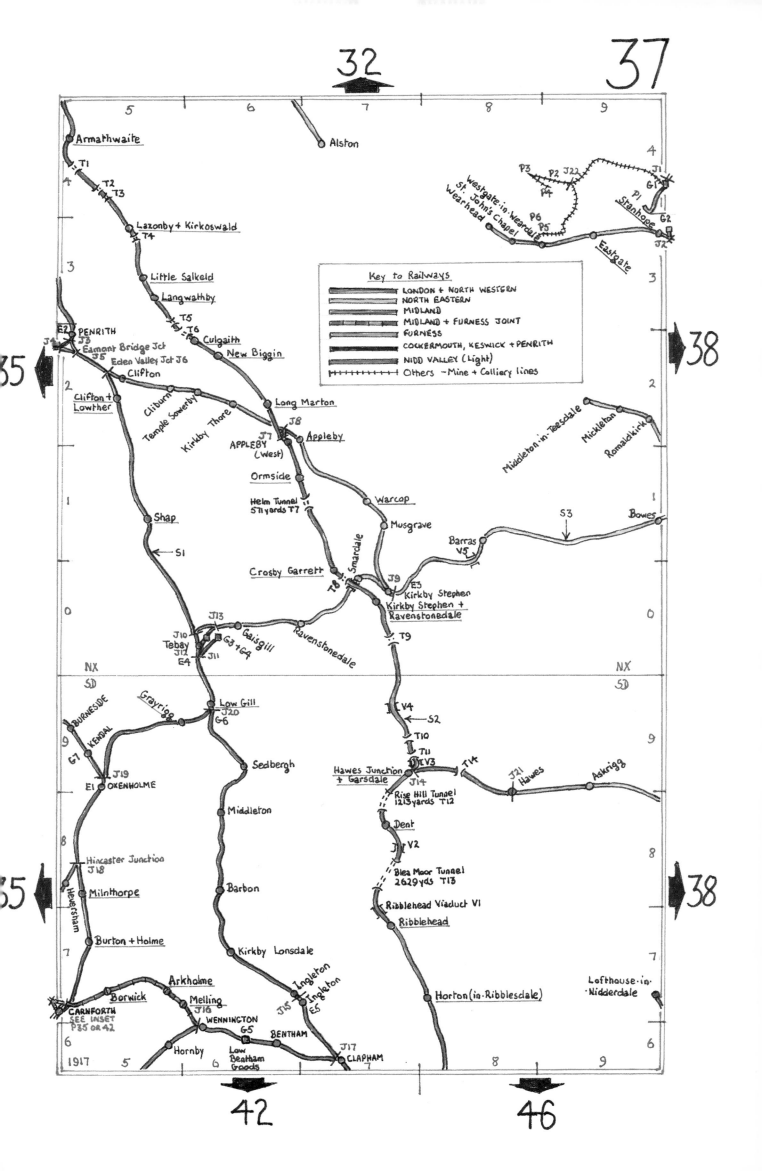

Key to Railways

	LONDON + NORTH WESTERN
	NORTH EASTERN
	MIDLAND
	MIDLAND + FURNESS JOINT
	FURNESS
	COCKERMOUTH, KESWICK + PENRITH
	NIDD VALLEY (Light)
+++++	Others — Mine + Colliery lines

Armathwaite
T1
T2
T3
Lazonby + Kirkoswald
T4
Little Salkeld
Langwathby
T5
T6
Culgaith
New Biggin

E2 PENRITH
J4 J3
Eamont Bridge Jct
J5
Eden Valley Jct J6
Clifton
Clifton +
Lowther
Cliburn
Temple Sowerby
Kirkby Thore
J8
APPLEBY Long Marton
J7 Appleby
APPLEBY
(West)
Ormside
Helm Tunnel
511 yards T7
Warcop
Shap Musgrave
S1
Crosby Garrett
Smardale Barras
T8 V5
J9
E3
Kirkby Stephen
Kirkby Stephen +
Ravenstonedale
J13
J10 Gaisgill
Tebay G3 + G4 Ravenstonedale
J12 J11
E4 T9

NX
SD

Burneside
Grayrigg Low Gill
KENDAL J20
G6
G7 V4
J19 S2
E1 OXENHOLME T10
T11
Sedbergh V3
Hawes Junction T14
+ Garsdale J21 Hawes Askrigg
J14
Middleton Rise Hill Tunnel
1213 yards T12
Hincaster Junction Dent
J18 J V2
Heversham Milnthorpe Barbon Blea Moor Tunnel
2629 yds T13
Ribblehead Viaduct V1
Burton + Holme Ribblehead
Kirkby Lonsdale
Lofthouse-in-
Arkholme Ingleton Nidderdale
Borwick Ingleton
Melling J15
CARNFORTH J16 E5
SEE INSET WENNINGTON Horton (in Ribblesdale)
P35 OR 42 G5
BENTHAM
1917 Hornby Low J17
Beatham CLAPHAM
Goods

Alston

Westgate-in-Weardale
P3 P2 J22 J1
St. John's Chapel P4 G1
Wearhead P6 P1
P5 Stanhope
G2
Eastgate J2

Middleton-in-Teesdale Mickleton
Romaldkirk

S3 Bowes

38

RAILWAYS

No.	Company
R 1	NORTH EASTERN
2	NIDD VALLEY (Light)

STATIONS

No.	Name	Ref
A 1	Ainderby	SE39
2	Aldin Grange	NZ24
3	(ALLEN'S WEST)	NZ41
4	Aycliffe	NZ22
5	Aysgarth	SE08
6	Baldersby	SE37
7	BANK TOP (DARLINGTON)	NZ21
8	Barnard Castle	NZ01
9	Bedale	SE28
10	Beechburn	NZ13
11	BILLINGHAM	NZ42
12	BISHOP AUCKLAND	NZ22
13	Blackhall Rocks	NZ43
14	Bowes	NZ01
15	Bradbury	NZ32
16	Brancepeth	NZ23
17	Brandon Colliery	NZ23
18	Brompton	SE39
19	Broomielaw	NZ01
20	Burnhill	NZ04
21	Byers Green	NZ23
22	Carlton	NZ32
23	Castle Eden	NZ43
24	Catterick Bridge	NZ20
25	Cockfield	NZ12
26	Constable Burton	SE19
27	Cotherstone	NZ01
28	Coundon	NZ23
29	Cowton	NZ30
30	Coxhoe Bridge	NZ33
31	Crakehall	SE28
32	Croft Spa	NZ20
33	Crook	NZ13
34	Croxdale	NZ23
35	Danby Wiske	SE39
	DARLINGTON	
36	BANK TOP	NZ21
37	NORTH ROAD	NZ21
38	DINSDALE	NZ31
39	DURHAM	NZ24
40	EAGLESCLIFFE	NZ41
41	Easington	NZ44
42	Elvet	NZ24
43	Etherley	NZ13
44	Evenwood	NZ12
45	Ferry Hill	NZ33
46	Finghall Lane	SE19
47	Frosterley	NZ03
48	Gainford	NZ11
49	GREATHAM	NZ42
50	Harperley	NZ13
51	Hart	NZ43
52	Hartlepool	NZ53
53	HARTLEPOOL (West)	NZ53
54	Haswell	NZ34
55	Haverton Hill	NZ42
56	HEIGHINGTON	NZ22
57	Hetton	NZ34
58	Harden	NZ44
59	Hunwick	NZ13
60	Hurworth Burn	NZ43
56A	Hesledon	NZ43

No.	Name	Ref
61	Jervaulx	SE28
62	Knitsley	NZ14
63	Lanchester	NZ14
64	Lartington	NZ01
65	Leamside	NZ34
66	Leeming Bar	SE28
67	Leyburn	SE19
68	Lofthouse-in-Nidderdale 2	SE07
69	Masham	SE28
70	Melmerby	SE37
71	MIDDLESBROUGH	NZ42
72	Moulton	NZ20
73	Murton	NZ34
74	Newby Wiske	SE38
75	Newport	NZ42
76	(NEWTON AYCLIFFE)	NZ22
77	NORTHALLERTON	SE39
78	NORTH ROAD - Darlington	NZ21
79	Norton-on-Tees	NZ42
80	Otterington	SE38
81	Pickhill	SE38
82	Picton	NZ40
83	Piercebridge	NZ21
84	Pilmoor	SE47
85	Pittington	NZ34
86	Plawsworth	NZ24
87	Potto	NZ40
88	Ramsgill	2 SE07
89	Redmire	SE09
90	Richmond	NZ10
91	Ripon	SE37
92	Rowley	NZ04
93	Scorton	NZ20
94	Scruton	SE39
95	SEAHAM	NZ44
96	Seaton	NZ34
97	SEATON CAREW	NZ52
98	Sedgefield	NZ32
99	Sessay	SE47
100	Sexhow	NZ40
101	Sherburn Colliery	NZ34
102	Sherburn House	NZ34
103	SHILDON	NZ22
104	Shincliffe	NZ33
105	Shotton Bridge	NZ34
106	Sinderby	SE38
107	South Hetton	NZ34
108	Spennithorne	SE19
109	Spennymoor	NZ23
110	Stanhope	NZ03
111	Stillington	NZ32
112	STOCKTON (on-Tees)	NZ41
113	Tanfield	SE27
114	(TEES-SIDE AIRPORT)	NZ31
115	THIRSK	SE48
116	THORNABY	NZ41
117	Thornley	NZ43
118	Thorpe Thewles	NZ42
119	Topcliffe	SE37
120	Tow Law	NZ13
121	Trenholme Bar	NZ40
122	Trimdon	NZ43
123	Ushaw Moor	NZ24
124	Waterhouses	NZ14
125	Wear Valley Junction	NZ13
126	Welbury	NZ40
127	Wellfield	NZ43
128	Wensley	SE09

No.	Name	Ref
129	West Auckland	NZ12
130	(West) HARTLEPOOL	NZ53
131	West Cornforth	NZ33
132	West Rounton Gates	NZ40
133	Willington	NZ23
134	Wingate	NZ43
135	Winston	NZ11
136	Witton Gilbert	NZ24
137	Witton-le-Wear	NZ13
138	Wolsingham	NZ03
139	Wynyard	NZ42
140	Yarm	NZ41

GOODS

No.	Name/Location	Ref
G 1	Parkhead	NZ04
2	Stanhope	NZ03
3	Waskerley	NZ04
4	High Stoop	NZ14
5	Waterhouses	NZ14
6	Wingate	NZ33
7	Butterknowle	NZ12
8	Barnard Castle	NZ01
9	Shildon	NZ22
10	Forcett	NZ11
11	Barton	NZ20
12	Fighting Cocks	NZ31
13	Eryholme	NZ30
14	Town (Northallerton)	SE39
15	Thirsk	SE48

SIDINGS ETC

No.	Name/Company	Ref
P 1	Rookhope Branch	NZ04
2	Wooley Colliery	NZ13
3	Wooley Colliery	NZ13
4	Forcett Quarry	NZ11
5	Melsonby Quarry	NZ20
6	Quarry	NZ20
7	Thornley Colliery	NZ34
8	Wheatley Hill Lime	NZ34
9	Croft Depot	NZ21

SHEDS

No.	Location	Ref
E 1	Bank Top - Darlington	NZ21
2	Northallerton	SE39
3	West Auckland	NZ12

NOTES

(1) All stations in the area are included in this gazetteer. But other features are included + identified only if not also on the enlargements

(2) Only N.E.R represented except two Nidd Valley - marked 2

(3) Northallerton Inset shows - junctions layout and also the lines still in use - all traffic or goods only (1984)

(4) Name changes - small letters now dropped — CAPITALS are modern addition - Part of name in brackets - eg (West)HARTLEPOOL shows West now dropped

JUNCTIONS

No.	Name/Location	Ref
J 1	Consett North	NX05
2	Consett South	NX05
3	Hownesgill	NX04
4	Consett East	NZ15
5	Burnhill	NZ04
6	Rookhope Branch	NZ04
7	Murton	NZ34
8	Stanhope Goods	NZ03
9	Wooley Colliery Branch	NZ13
10	Wear Valley	NZ13
11	Goods	NZ13
12	Thornley	NZ43
13	Wellfield	NZ43
14	Hutton Henry	NZ43
15	Castle Eden	NZ43
16	Wingate	NZ43
17	Hart	NZ43
18	Hartlepool - North	NZ53
19	Hartlepool - North	NZ53
20	Hartlepool - East	NZ53
21	Hartlepool - South	NZ53
	BISHOP AUCKLAND	
22	West	NZ22
23	North	NZ22
24	Station	NZ22
25	East	NZ22
26	Barnard Castle Line	NZ22
27	Adelaide	NZ22
28	Spring Gardens	NZ22
29	Shildon Goods	NZ22
30	Sim Pasture	NZ22
31	Stillington	NZ32
32	Middleton	NZ01
33	Auckland	NZ01
34	Forcett	NZ11
35	Merrybent	NZ21
	DARLINGTON	
36	Stooperdale	NZ21
37	Charity	NZ21
38	Albert Hill	NZ21
39	South	NZ21
40	Geneva	NZ21
41	Croft Goods	NZ21
42	Dinsdale	NZ31
43	Eryholme	NZ30
44	Picton	NZ40
	NORTHALLERTON	
45	West	SE39
46	North	SE39
47	Low	SE39
48	High	SE39
49	Boroughbridge Gates	SE39
50	Longlands	SE39
51	Cordio	SE39
52	Ripon Line	SE48
53	Croods	SE47
54	Melmerby North	SE37
55	Melmerby South	SE37
56	Pilmoor	SE47
57	Sessay Wood	SE47
58	Sunbeck	SE47
59	Bishophouse	SE47
60	Docks Branch	NZ53

WORKS

No.	Location	Ref
C 1	Darlington	NZ21

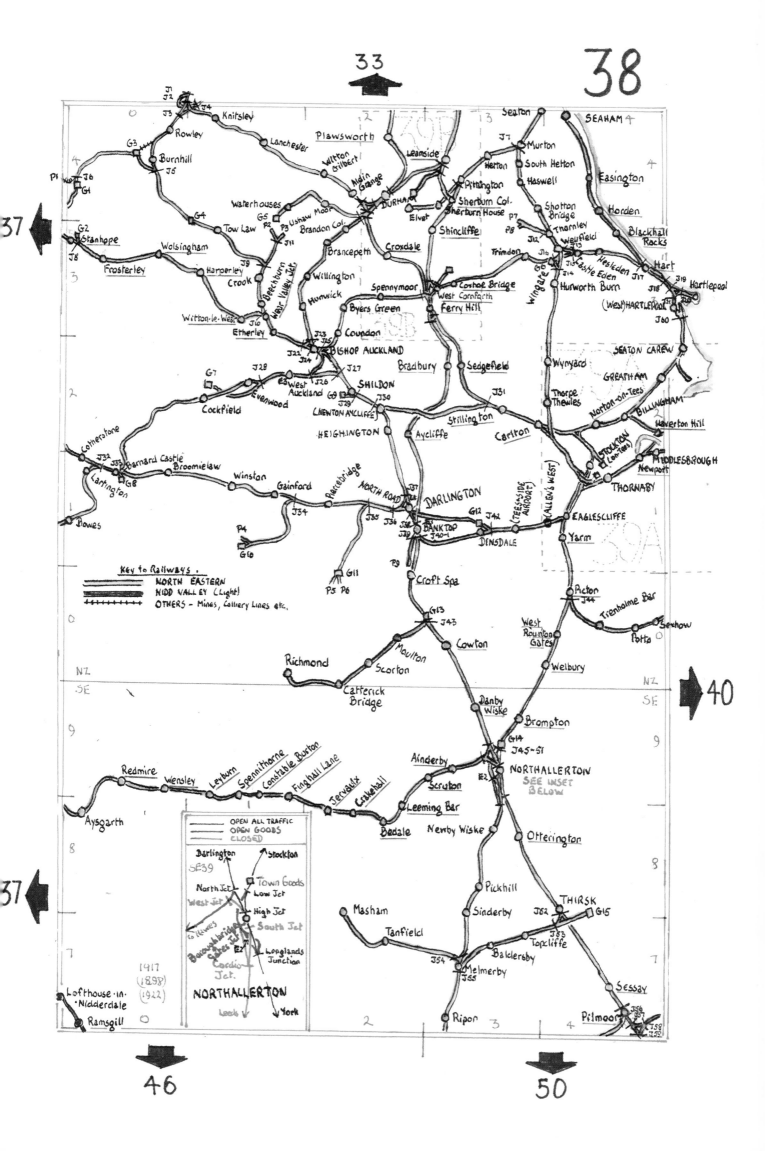

37

40

37

46

50

Key to Railways.

NORTH EASTERN
NIDD VALLEY (Light)
OTHERS - Mines, Colliery Lines etc.

OPEN ALL TRAFFIC
OPEN GOODS
CLOSED

Darlington   Stockton
SE39
North Jct.   Town Goods
West Jct.   Low Jct.
              High Jct.
              South Jct.
Boroughbridge Gates Jct.
Cordio Jct.   Longlands Junction

NORTHALLERTON
1917
(1898)
(1922)

Leeds   York

Lofthouse-in-Nidderdale
Ramsgill

Seaton   SEAHAM
Murton
South Hetton   Easington
Hetton   Haswell   Horden
Pittington
Sherburn Col.   Blackhall Rocks
Sherburn House   Shotton Bridge
Elvet   Thornley
Shincliffe   Weetfield
                 Hesleden   Hart
Trimdon   Hartlepool
          Wingate Castle Eden
                 Hurworth Burn (West) Hartlepool
Coxhoe Bridge
West Cornforth   SEATON CAREW
Ferry Hill   Wynyard GREATHAM
Bradbury Sedgefield   Norton-on-Tees BILLINGHAM
              Thorpe Thewles   Haverton Hill
         J31
Stillington   STOCKTON (on-Tees)
Carlton   (Allen's West) MIDDLESBROUGH
Aycliffe   Newport
                 (TEESSIDE AIRPORT) THORNABY
Darlington   EAGLESCLIFFE
BANK TOP   G12   Yarm
DINSDALE
Croft Spa   Picton
                 Trenholme Bar
                 Potto   Sexhow
                 West Rounton Gates
Cowton
                 Welbury
Richmond
Scorton   Danby Wiske
Catterick Bridge Brompton
                 NORTHALLERTON
Redmire Wensley Leyburn Spennithorne Constable Burton Finghall Lane
                 Ainderby
Aysgarth   Jervaulx Crakehall Scruton
                 Leeming Bar   Otterington
                 Bedale Newby Wiske
                 Pickhill
Masham   Sinderby   THIRSK
Tanfield   Balderby Topcliffe
                 Melmerby   Sessay
Ripon   Pilmoor

Knitsley
Rowley
Burnhill
Lanchester
Plawsworth
Leamside
Witton Gilbert
Aldin Grange
Waterhouses
Tow Law   Ushaw Moor
Stanhope   Brandon Col.
Wolsingham   DURHAM
Frosterley   Brancepeth   Croxdale
Harperley Crook Willington
                 Hunwick
Witton-le-Wear   Byers Green Spennymoor
Etherley   Coundon
West Auckland   BISHOP AUCKLAND
Cockfield Evenwood   SHILDON
                 Newton Aycliffe
                 HEIGHINGTON
Cotherstone   NORTH ROAD
Barnard Castle
Lartington Broomielaw
Bowes   Winston Gainford Piercebridge
Northallerton

NOTES:

(1) CURRENT SITUATION – As only one Pre-Grouping Railway the North Eastern operated this area it has been possible to show the up to date situation on all lines.

(2) REFERENCES – All in square NZ, so letter A or B used to indicate on which map features are to be found in this combined gazetteer.

(3) NAME CHANGE – Ormesby now known as MARTON

Collieries / Works

No	Name	Ref
9	Eston Brick Works	A51
10	Teesdale Iron Works	A41
11	Greatham Creek Branch	A52
12	Newton Quarries	A51
13	Roseberry Mines	A51
14	Ayton Quarry	A51
15	Chaloner Mines	A51
20	Kimblesworth Colliery	B24
21	Framwellgate Collieries	B24
22	Little Town Colliery	B34
23	Sherburn Hill Colliery	B34
24	Sherburn House Colliery	B34
25	North Hetton Colliery	B34
26	Rainton Bridge Pits	B34
27	Bearpark Colliery	B24
28	Tudhoe Colliery	B23
29	South Brancepeth Col.	B33
30	Westerton Col + Lime Wks	B23
31	Chilton Colliery	B23
32	Leasingthorne Colliery	B23
33	Adelaide Colliery	B22
34	Auckland Park Col.	B22
35	South Durham + Eldon Col	B33
36	Chilton Lime Works	B34
37	Bowburn Colliery	B34
38	Tursdale Colliery	B34
39	To East Hetton Col	B34
40	Middleham Quarry	B24
41	Fishburn Colliery Line	B23
42	Brancepeth Cols.	B33
43	Browney Colliery	B23
44	Littleburn Colliery	B23

JUNCTIONS

No	Name / Location	Ref
J1	Carlton West	A50
2	Carlton North	A41
3	Carlton East	A42
4	Carlton South	B24
5	Norton West	B35
6	Norton South	B24
7	Norton East	A42
8	} North Shore Jcts	A41
9	}	
10	Billingham	Ref
11	Seaton Snook	A41
12	Middlesbrough Goods	A41
13	Guisborough	A42
14	Eston	A52
15	Hartburn	A52
16	Eaglescliffe North	B24
17	} Bowesfield Junctions	B33
18	}	
19	Eaglescliffe South	A51
20	Flatts Lane	A40
21	Nunthorpe	Ref
22	Picton	A41
23	Battersby North	A42
24	Battersby South	(B12)
25	Tod Point	A52
30	Durham – Knitsley N	B24
31	Durham – Knitsley S	Ref
32	Durham – Brancepeth N	B24
33	Durham – Brancepeth S	B24
34	Durham – Ferryhill	B24
35	Relly Mill Jcts	B24
36	Aykley	B24
37	Leamside	B24
38	Belmont	B24
39	Broomside Branch	B24
40	Sherburn Colliery	B24
41	West Cornforth North	B35
42	Auckland Line	B35
43	West Cornforth Station	B33
44	Ferryhill North	B33
45	Ferryhill Station	B33
46	{ Ferryhill South	B35
47	{ Ferryhill South }	B33
48	Chilton	B33
49	Bishop Auckland West	B22
50	Bishop Auckland North	B22
51	Bishop Auckland Station	B22
52	Barnard Castle Line	B22
53	Adelaide	B22
54	Fishburn	B22
55	Bishop Middleham	B32

GOODS

No	Name / Location	Ref
G1	Stockton North Shore	A50
2	Stockton South	B34
3	Middlesbrough	A51
4	Seaton Snook	A42
5	Tod Point	A41
6	Durham	A42
7	Coxhoe	A51

SHEDS

No	Location	Ref
E1	Stockton	A51
2	Middlesbrough	B34
3	West Auckland	A52

BRIDGES

No	Location	Ref
VI	Yarm – Tees Viaduct	B34

SIDINGS ETC

No	Name (Company / Location)	Ref
P1	Billingham Beck Branch	A50
2	Haverton Salt Works	A50
3	Iron Works Sidings	A52
4	Tees North Breakwater	B24
5	Redcar Wharf	B24
6	Iron Works Sidings	B24
7	Cleveland Steel	B24
8	Eston Mines	B24

STATIONS

No	Name	Ref
A1	Aldin Grange	A51
2	(ALLEN'S WEST)	A52
3	BATTERSBY	A41
4	BILLINGHAM	A50
5	BISHOP AUCKLAND	A42
6	Bradbury	B22
7	Brancepeth	B32
8	Brandon Colliery	B23
9	(BRITISH STEEL – REDCAR)	A52
10	Byers Green	B23
11	CARGO FLEET	A53
12	Carlton	A42
13	Coundon	B23
14	Coxhoe Bridge	B33
15	Crowdale	B23
16	DURHAM	B24
17	EAGLESCLIFFE	A41
18	Elvet	B24
19	Eston	A51
20	Ferry Hill	B33
21	GRANGETOWN	A52
22	GREAT AYTON	B24
23	GREATHAM	A41
24	(GYPSY LANE)	A50
25	Haverton Hill	A42
26	Ingleby	B22
27	Leamside	B32
28	(MARTON) §33	B23
29	MIDDLESBROUGH	B35
30	Newport	B23
31	Norton-on-Tees	A52
32	NUNTHORPE	B23
33	ORMESBY §28	A53
34	Picton	A42
35	Pinchinthorpe	B23
36	Pittington	B33
37	Plawsworth	B23
38	Port Clarence	B24
39	SEATON CAREW	A52
40	Sedgefield	A41
41	Sherburn Colliery	B24
42	Sherburn House	A51
43	Shincliffe	B33
44	Spennymoor	A52
45	SOUTH BANK	A52
46	STOCKTON	A44
47	Stokesley	A50
48	THORNABY	A41
49	Thorpe Thewles	A42
50	Ushaw Moor	B24
51	West Cornforth	B35
52	Witton Gilbert	B24
53	Wynyard	A42
54	Yarm	A41

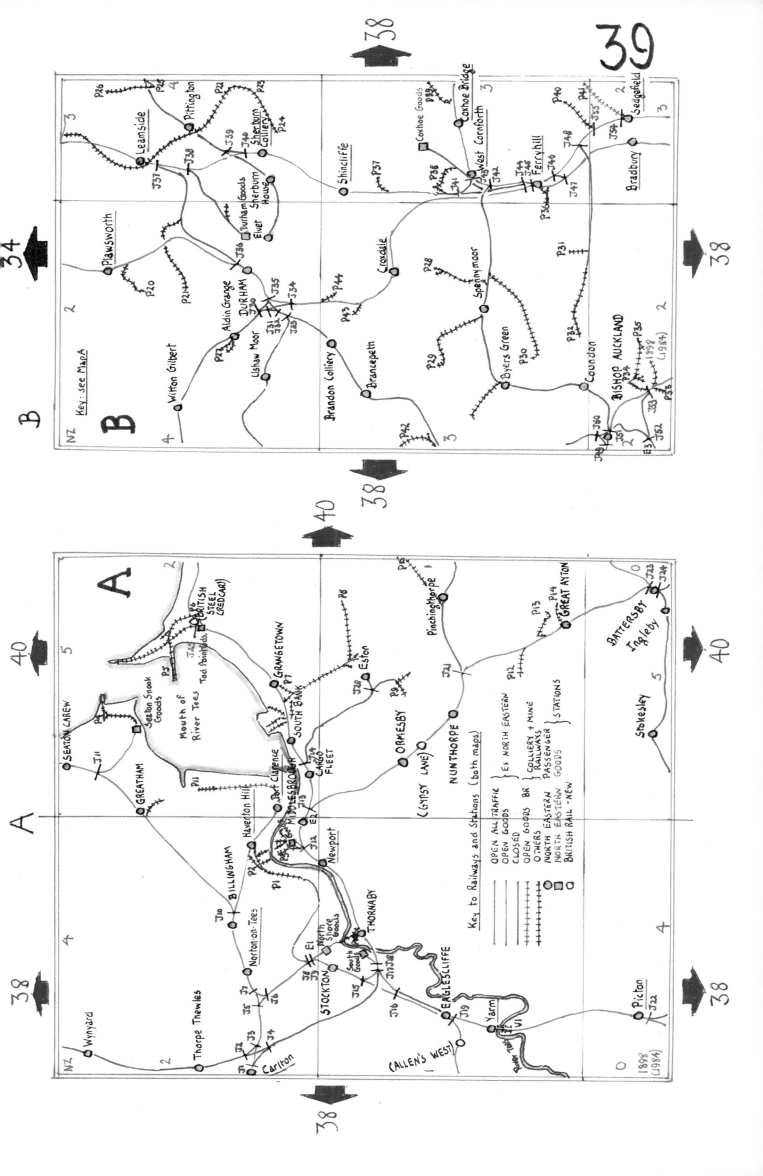

WHITBY + MALTON   SCARBOROUGH + FILEY

RAILWAYS

No	Company
R 1	NORTH EASTERN

STATIONS + HALTS

No	Name	Ref
A 1	Amotherley	SE77
2	Ampleforth	SE57
3	Barton-le-Street	SE77
4	BATTERSBY	NZ50
5	Bempton	TA17
6	Boosbeck	NZ61
7	(BRITISH STEEL (REDCAR))	NZ52
8	Brotton	NZ62
9	CARGO FLEET	NZ52
10	CASTLETON (MOOR)	NZ60
11	Cayton	TA08
12	Cloughton	TA09
13	COMMONDALE	NZ61
14	Coxwold	SE57
15	DANBY	NZ70
16	Ebberston	SE88
17	EGTON	NZ80
18	Eston	NZ51
19	FILEY	TA18
20	Forge Valley	SE98
21	Fyling Hall	NZ90
22	Ganton	SE97
23	Gilling	SE67
24	GLAISDALE	NZ70
25	Goathland	NZ80
26	GRANGETOWN	NZ52
27	GREAT AYTON	NZ51
28	GREATHAM	NZ52
29	Grinkle	NZ71
30	Gristhorpe	TA08
31	GROSMONT	NZ80
32	Guisborough	NZ61
33	(GYPSY LANE)	NZ51
34	Hartlepool	NZ53
35	HARTLEPOOL, West	NZ53
36	Hayburn Wyke	TA09
37	Helmsley	SE68
38	Hawsker	NZ90
38A	Heslerton	SE97
39	Hinderwell	NZ81
40	Hovingham Spa	SE67
41	HUNMANBY	TA17
42	Husthwaite Gate	SE57
43	Hutton Gate	NZ61
44	Ingleby	NZ50
45	Kettleness	NZ81
46	KILDALE	NZ60
47	Kirby Moorside	SE68
48	Knapton	SE87
49	LEAHOLM	NZ70
50	Levisham	SE89
51	Loftus	NZ71
52	MALTON	SE77
53	MARSKE	NZ62
54	(MARTON) §61	NZ51
55	MIDDLESBROUGH	NZ52
56	Nawton	SE68
57	(Newtondale Halt)	SE80
58	North Skelton	NZ61
59	Nunnington	SE67
60	NUNTHORPE	NZ51
61	ORMESBY §54	NZ51
62	Pickering	SE88
63	Pinchingthorpe	NZ51
64	Port Clarence	NZ52
65	Ravenscar	NZ90
66		
	REDCAR	
67	(BRITISH STEEL)	NZ52
68	CENTRAL	NZ62
69	(EAST)	NZ62
70	Rillington	SE87
71	Robin Hood's Bay	NZ90
72	RUSWARP	NZ80
73	SALTBURN	NZ62
74	Sandsend	NZ81
75	Sawdon	SE98
76	Scalby	TA09
77	SCARBOROUGH	TA08
78	SEAMER	TA08
79	SEATON CAREW	NZ52
80	Sinnington	SE78
81	Skinningrove	NZ72
52A	Marishes Road	E87
82	SLEIGHTS	NZ80
83	Slingsby	SE17
84	Snainton	SE98
85	SOUTH BANK	NZ52
86	Speeton	TA17
87	Staintondale	TA09
88	Staithes	NZ72
89	Stokesley	NZ50
90	Thornton Dale	SE88
91	Weaverthorpe	SE97
92	West Cliff Whitby	NZ81
93	West HARTLEPOOL	NZ53
94	WHITBY Town	NZ81
95	Wykeham	SE98

GOODS

No	Name / Location	Ref
G 1	Scarborough	TA08
2	Rosedale	SE79

SIDINGS ETC

No	Name / Company / Location	Ref
P 1	Lingdale Mines	NZ61
2	Beckhole Branch	NZ80
3	Kilton Mines	NZ61
4	East Rosedale Mines	NZ70
5	Hartlepool Docks	NZ53

JUNCTIONS

No	Name / Location	Ref
J 1	Scarborough	TA08
2	Seamer	TA08
3	Hartlepool North	NZ53
4	Hartlepool South	NZ53
5	Hartlepool East	NZ53
6	Battersby North	NZ50
7	Battersby South	NZ50
8	Saltburn Exten⁵	NZ62
9	North Skelton	NZ62
10	Brotton	NZ62
11	Lumpsey	NZ62
12	Priestcrofts	NZ62
13	Hutton	NZ62
14	Prospect	NZ81
15	Boghall	NZ80
16	Deviation	NZ80
17	Blakey	SE69
18	Pickering Junctions	SE88
19	Malton West	SE77
20	Malton East	SE87
21	Gilling	SE67
22	Rillington	SE87

SHEDS

No	Location	Ref
E 1	Scarborough	TA08
2	Saltburn	NZ62
3	Malton	SE77
4	Whitby	NZ81

NOTES:

(1) ENLARGEMENT - In the area of the enlargement all stations are indicated on this map and included in gazetteer, but no other features are shown or included.

(2) NAME CHANGE - ORMESBY § now known as MARTON § 61 Other changes - in small letters, now dropped from the title - e.g West HARTLEPOOL now just HARTLEPOOL. In the case of REDCAR, only one station pregrouping. Is now known as REDCAR CENTRAL

(3) TEES MOUTH - dotted blue line shows old coast line; modern coast is a continous line to the north. The area between is now a network of Goods lines!

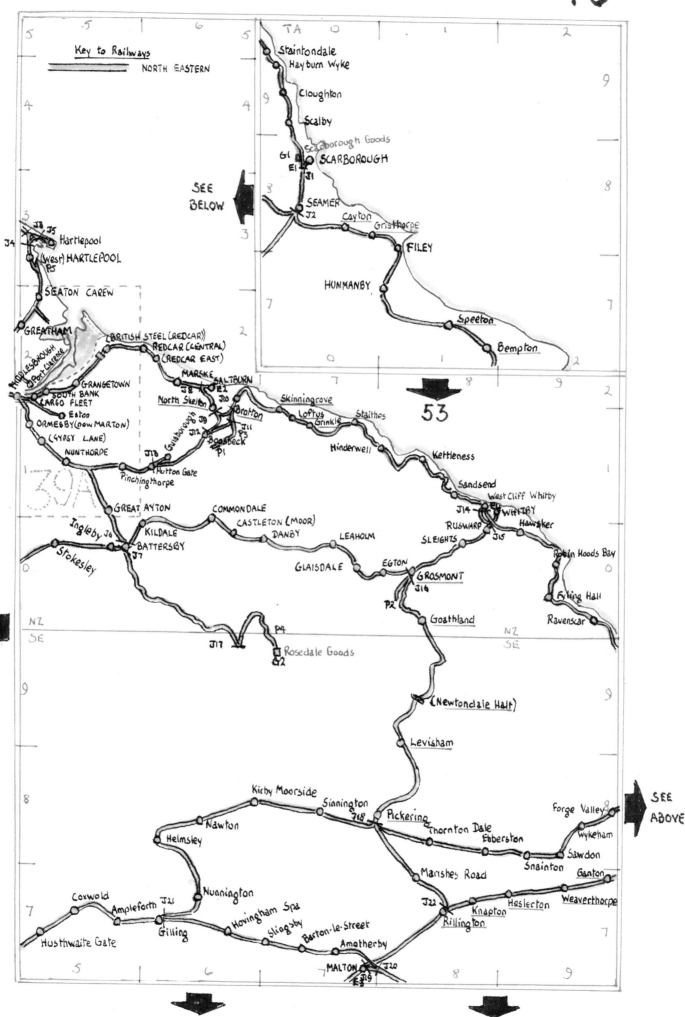

Key to Railways

———————— NORTH EASTERN

Staintondale
Hayburn Wyke
Cloughton
Scalby
Scarborough Goods
G1 SCARBOROUGH
E1
J1
SEAMER
J2
Cayton
Gristhorpe
FILEY
HUNMANBY
Speeton
Bempton

SEE BELOW

53

J3 J5 Hartlepool
J4
(West) HARTLEPOOL
P5
SEATON CAREW
GREATHAM
MIDDLESBROUGH
Port Clarence
(BRITISH STEEL (REDCAR))
REDCAR (CENTRAL)
(REDCAR EAST)
MARSKE SALTBURN
GRANGETOWN
J8 J21
North Skelton
SOUTH BANK
CARGO FLEET
J10
Eston Brotton
ORMESBY (now MARTON)
Guisborough J9 J11
(GYPSY LANE)
J12 P3
NUNTHORPE
Boosbeck
P1
J13
Hutton Gate
Pinchingthorpe
Skinningrove
Loftus
Grinkle
Staithes
Hinderwell
Kettleness
Sandsend
West Cliff Whitby
GREAT AYTON
COMMONDALE
J14
WHITBY
Ingleby J6
KILDALE
CASTLETON (MOOR)
DANBY
RUSWARP
Hawsker
BATTERSBY
LEAHOLM
SLEIGHTS
J15
Stokesley
J7
GLAISDALE
EGTON
Robin Hoods Bay
GROSMONT
J16
Fyling Hall
P2
Ravenscar
Goathland
J17
P4
Rosedale Goods
G2
(Newtondale Halt)
Levisham
38
Kirby Moorside
Sinnington
Pickering
Forge Valley
SEE ABOVE
Nawton
J18
Thornton Dale
Wykeham
Helmsley
Ebberston
Sawdon
Marishes Road
Snainton
Ganton
Coxwold
Ampleforth J21
Nunnington
J22
Heslerton
Weaverthorpe
Gilling
Hovingham Spa
Slingsby
Knapton
Rillington
Husthwaite Gate
Barton-le-Street
Amotherby
MALTON J20
E19

50

53

ISLE OF MAN

NOTES: (1) INFORMATION - Not available except for Map date – some halts therefore may be missing

(2) RAILWAYS - Only the Isle of Man Railway can properly be so classified. Full information on tramways not available, exact location of some stations uncertain

(3) INDEX - IoM Stations only included in Main Index

(4) REFERENCES - All in SC

(5) OTHER - Facilities –no information. Only Railways (and tramways) + Stations are listed.

RAILWAYS

No	Name	Gauge	Traction
R1	ISLE OF MAN	3' 0"	Steam
2	MANX ELECTRIC	3' 0"	Electric
3	LAXEY - SNAEFELL	3' 6"	Electric
4	DOUGLAS CORP TRAMS	3' 0"	Horses

STATIONS

No	Name	Ry Ref
A1	BALDRINE	2
2	BALLABEG	1
3	BALLABEG (Laxey)	2
4	BALLASALLA	1
5	BALLAGLASS	2
6	BALLAJORA	2
7	BALLARGH	2
8	Ballaugh	1
9	BELLE VUE	2
10	BUNGALOW	3
11	CASTLETOWN	1
12	COLBY	1
13	CORNAA	2
14	Crosby	1
15	DERBY CASTLE	24
16	DHOON	2
17	DOUGLAS	1
18	DOUGLAS PIER	4
19	DREEMSKERRY	2
20	FAIRY COTTAGE	2
21	Foxdale	1
22	GARWICK GLEN	2
23	GLEN MONA	2
24	GROUDLE GLEN	2
25	HOWSTRAKE	2
26	Kirk Michael	1
27	LAXEY	23
28	LEWAIGUE	2
29	Lezayre	1
30	MINORCA	2
31	ONCHAN HEAD	2
32	Peel	1
33	Peel Road	1
34	PORT ERIN	1
35	PORT ST MARY	1
36	PORT SODERICK	1
37	Ramsey	1
38	RAMSEY	2
39	St Germains	1
40	St John's	1
41	SANTON	1
42	SNAEFELL	3
43	SOUTH CAPE	2
44	Sulby Bridge	1
45	Sulby Glen	1
46	Union Mills	1
47	Waterfall	1

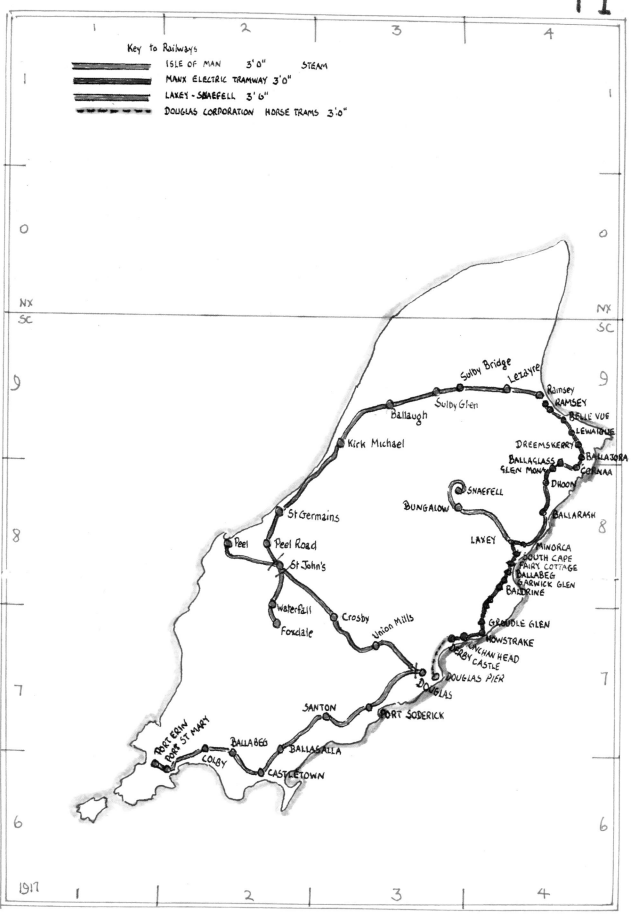

41

Key to Railways

ISLE OF MAN   3'0"   STEAM
MANX ELECTRIC TRAMWAY 3'0"
LAXEY - SNAEFELL   3'6"
DOUGLAS CORPORATION HORSE TRAMS 3'0"

1917

Sulby Bridge
Lezayre
Ramsey
RAMSEY
BELLE VUE
LEWAIGUE
DREEMSKERRY
BALLAGLASS
GLEN MONA
BALLAJORA
CORNAA
DHOON
SNAEFELL
BUNGALOW
BALLARASH
LAXEY
MINORCA
SOUTH CAPE
FAIRY COTTAGE
BALLABEG
GARWICK GLEN
BALDRINE
GROUDLE GLEN
HOWSTRAKE
ONCHAN HEAD
DERBY CASTLE
Douglas Pier
DOUGLAS

Sulby Glen
Ballaugh
Kirk Michael
St Germains
Peel
Peel Road
St John's
Waterfall
Foxdale
Crosby
Union Mills

SANTON
PORT SODERICK
PORT ERIN
PORT ST MARY
BALLABEG
COLBY
BALLASALLA
CASTLETOWN

CARNFORTH, WIGAN + BOLTON

RAILWAYS

No.	Company
R	ILANCASHIRE + YORKSHIRE (LY)
12A	LANCASHIRE UNION
12B	NORTH UNION JOINT
12C	PRESTON + LONGRIDGE
12D	PRESTON + WYRE
12	LY + LNW JOINT — Others
2	LONDON + NORTH WESTERN (LNW) (44) Chowbent
23	LNW + FURNESS JOINT
3	FURNESS
34	FURNESS + MIDLAND JOINT
4	MIDLAND
456	CHESHIRE LINES COMMITTEE
5	GREAT CENTRAL
6	GREAT NORTHERN
7	KNOTT END
O	CORPORATION OF PRESTON

STATIONS

No.	Name	Ry Ref
A 1	ACCRINGTON	1 72
2	ADDLINGTON	1 61
3	Agecroft	1 70
4	AINSDALE	1 31
5	Ainsdale Beach	456 31
6	Altcar + Hillhouse	456 30
7	Altcar Rifle Range	1 30
8	ANSDELL + FAIRHAVEN	12 32
9	APPLEY BRIDGE	1 50
10	Aspull (see Dicconson)	1 60
11	Atherton	2 60
12	ATHERTON Central	1 60
13	(AUGHTON PARK)	1 40
14	Balshaw Lane + Euxton	2 51
15	BAMBER BRIDGE	1 52
16	Bamfurlong	2 60
17	Banks	1 32
18	BARE LANE	2 46
19	Barton	1 30
20	Barton + Broughton	2 53
21	Baxenden	1 72
22	Bay Horse	2 45
23	BENTHAM	4 66
24	BESCAR LANE	1 31
25	Bickershaw (+ Abram)	5 60
26	BIRKDALE	1 31
27	Birkdale Palace	4563 1
28	BISPHAM	12 53
29	BLACKBURN	1 62
30	Black Lane	1 70
	BLACKPOOL	
31	Central	12 33 (43)
32	NORTH §	12 33
33	SOUTH Shore	12 33
34	TALBOT ROAD §	12 33
35	Waterloo Road	12 33
36	BLACKROD	1 61
(43)	Blowick	1 31
37	Boars Head	12A 50
38	BOLTON	1 70
39	Bolton - Gt Moor St.	2 70
40	Bolton-le-Sands	2 46
41	Bradley Fold	1 70
42	Brinscall	12A 62
43	Brock	2 54
44	BROMLEY CROSS	1 71
45	BRYNN §	2 50
46	BURSCOUGH BRIDGE	1 41
47	BURSCOUGH JUNCTION	1 41
(43)	Butts Lane Halt	1 31
(44)	Butler Street	1 52
48	BURY High Level	1 71
49	CARNFORTH	234 47
50	Caton	4 56
51	CHAPEL STREET	1 31
52	Chatburn	1 74
53	Chequerbent	2 60
54	CHERRY TREE	1 62
55	CHORLEY	1 51
(44)	Chowbent	2 60
56	CHURCH + OSWALDTWISTLE	1 72
57	Churchtown	1 31
58	CLAPHAM	4 76
59	CLIFTON Junction	1 70
60	Clitheroe	1 74
61	Conder Green	2 45
62	Coppull	2 51
63	Crossens	1 31
64	CROSTON	1 41
65	Daisyfield	1 62
66	DAISY HILL	1 60
67	Darcy Lever	1 70
68	DARWEN	1 62
69	Deepdale	12C 53
70	Dicconson Lane + Aspull	1 60
71	Dixon Fold	1 70
72	Ellenbrook	2 70
73	ENTWISTLE §	1 71
74	Euxton	1 52
75	Ewood Bridge + Edenfield	1 72
76	Farington	12B 52
77	FARNWORTH + Halshaw Moor	1 70
78	Feniscowles	12A62
79	FISHERGATE §	12B 52
80	Fleetwood	12D 34
81	FORMBY	1 20
82	FRESHFIELD	1 20
83	Galgate	2 45
84	Garstang	7 44
85	Garstang + Catterall	2 54
86	GATHURST	1 59
87	GIGGLESWICK	4 76
88	Glasson Dock	2 45
89	Great Harwood	1 73
90	Gt Moor St - Bolton	2 70
91	Greenmount	1 71
91A	Grimsargh	12C 53
92	HALL ROAD	1 30
93	Halsall	1 30
94	Halton	4 56
95	HAPTON	1 73
96	Haslingden	1 72
97	Heapey	1 61
(43)	Healthy Lane Halt	1 31
98	Helmshore	1 72
99	Hesketh Bank	1 42
100	Hesketh Park	1 31
101	Hest Bank	2 46
102	Heysham	4 45
103	HIGHTOWN	1 30
104	(HILLSIDE)	1 31
105	Hilton House	1 60
106	HINDLEY	1 60
107	Hindley + Platt Bridge	5 60
108	Hindley Green	2 60
109	Haghton	1 62
110	Halcombe Brook	1 71
111	Hoole	1 42
112	Harnby	4 56
113	Horwich	1 61
114	HOSCAR	1 41
115	HUNCOAT	1 73
116	Hundred End	1 42
117	Hutton + Howick	1 52
118	INCE	1 50
119	KEARSLEY + Stoneclough	1 70
120	Kew Gardens	1 31
121	KIRKHAM + WESHAM	12D 43
122	Knott End	7 34
123	LANCASTER Castle	2 46
124	Lancaster - Green Ayre	4 46
125	Langho	1 73
126	Lea Road	12D 43
127	Leight + Bedford	2 60
128	LEYLAND	12B 52
129	Longridge	12C 53
130	Langton Bridge	1 42
131	Lord Street	456 31
132	LOSTOCK HALL	1 52
133	Lostock Junction	2 60
134	Lower Darwen	1 62
(44)	Lower Ince	5 50
135	Lydiate	1 30
136	LYTHAM	12 32
137	MAGHULL	1 30
138	MEOLS COP	1 31
139	Middleton Road	4 45
140	Midge Hall	1 52
141	MILL HILL	1 62
(45)	Molyneux Brow	1 70
(45)	MOORSIDE + Wardley	1 70
142	MORECAMBE	4 46
143	Morecambe	2 46
144	MOSES GATE	1 70
145	Mossbridge	456 30
146	MOSS SIDE	12 32
147	Nateby	7 44
(43)	New Cut Lane Halt	1 31
148	NEW LANE	1 41
149	Oaks, The	1 71
150	ORMSKIRK	1 40
151	ORRELL	1 50
152	Padiham	1 73
153	PARBOLD	1 41
154	PEMBERTON	1 50
(45)	Pendlebury	1 70
155	Pilling	7 44
(44)	Platt Bridge	2 60
156	PLEASINGTON	1 52
(43)	Plex Moss Lane Halt	1 30
(46)	Plodder Lane	2 70
157	POULTON (·LE·FYLDE)	12D33
158	Preescall	7 34
	PRESTON	
(44)	Butler Street	1 52
159	FISHERGATE (JT)	12B52
160	West Lancs	1 52
161	Preston Junction	1 52
162	RADCLIFFE	1 70
163	Radcliffe Bridge	1 70
164	RAINFORD Junction	1 40
(43)	Rainford Junction	2 40
165	Rainford Village	2 40
166	Ramsbottom	1 71
167	Red Rock	1 60
168	Ribbleton	12C53
169	Rimington	1 74
170	Ringley Road	1 70
171	RISHTON	1 72
172	RUFFORD	4 56
(44)	Rumworth + Daub Hill	2 60
173	ST.ANNES (·ON·THE·SEA)	12 32
(43)	St Lukes (Road)	1 31
175	SALWICK	12D 43
176	Scorton	2 44
177	Sefton	456 30
178	Shirdley Hill	1 31
179	Simonstone	1 73
180	Singleton	12D 33
181	Skelmersdale	1 40
	SOUTHPORT	
182	Birkdale Palace	456 31
183	BIRKDALE	1 31
(43)	Blowick	1 31
(43)	Butts Lane Halt	1 31
184	CHAPEL STREET	1 31
185	Hesketh Park	1 31
186	Lord Street	4563 1
187	MEOLS COP	1 31
(43)	St Lukes (Road)	1 31
188	Spring Vale	1 62
189	(SQUIRES GATE)	1 33
190	Standish	2 51
191	Stubbins	1 71
192	Summerseat	1 71
193	SWINTON	1 70
194	TALBOT ROAD §	12 33
195	The Oaks	1 71
196	Thornton	12D 34
197	Tottington	1 71
198	TOWN GREEN + Aughton	1 40
199	Turton	1 71
200	Tyldesley	2 60
201	UPHOLLAND	1 50
202	WALKDEN	2 46
203	Walkden	2 70
204	Waterloo Road	12 33
205	WENNINGTON	4 66
206	WEST HOUGHTON	1 60
207	West Lancs - Preston	1 52
208	West Leigh	2 60
209	Whalley	1 73
210	White Bear	12A 51
	WIGAN	
(44)	Central	5 50
211	LNW	2 50
212	WALLGATE	1 50
213	Wilpshire for Ribchester	1 63
214	Withnell	12A 62
215	Woodvale	456 31
216	Woolford	1 71
217	Worsley	2 70
218	Wrea Green	12 33
219	Wyre Dock	12D 34

GOODS

No.	Name/Location	Ry Ref
G1	Morecambe Pier	4 46
2	Morecambe	4 46
3	Lancaster	2 46
4	Carnforth	234 47
5	Low Bentham	4 66
6	Wyre Dock	12D 34
7	Poulton	12D 34
8	Blackpool Lytham Rd	12 33
9	Lytham Dock	12 32

ENGINE SHEDS

No.	Name/Location	Ry Ref
E1	Carnforth	2 47
2	Carnforth	3 47
3	Carnforth	4 47
4	Lancaster	4 46
5	Fleetwood	1 34
6	Blackpool South	1 33
7	Blackpool North	1 33

SIDINGS

No.	Name/Co/Location	Ry Ref
P1	Earl Derby's	12C 63
2	Longridge Quarry	12C 63
3	Lancaster Quay	2 46

JUNCTIONS

No.	Name/Location	Ry Ref
JA)	MORECAMBE AREA	
1	Harbour	4 46
2	Hest Bank	24 46
3	Station	2 46
4	Torrisholme West	4 46
5	Torrisholme East	4 46
6	Bare Lane	2 46
7	Hest Bank South	2 46
8	Hest Bank North	2 46
B)	LANCASTER DISTRICT	
9	Quay Branch	2 46
10	Glasson Dock Branch	2 46
11	Castle	24 46
12	Green Ayre	4 46
13	Goods Branch	2 46
C)	CARNFORTH	
15	Carnforth	234 47
16	Joint + Furness	233 47
17	Station South	334 47
18	Furness + Midland	334 47
19	Furness + Midland	334 47
20	Goods	334 47
21	East Junction	34 47
14	Wennington	344 66
22	Clapham	4 76
23	Wyre Dock	12D 34
24	Poulton North	12D 34
25	Poulton West	12D 33
26	Poulton East	12D 33
27	Poulton Goods	12D 33
28	Direct Line	12D 33
29	Catterall	27 54
30	Horrocks Ford	1 74
31	Goods Branch	12 32
32	Wyre + Lytham	12D 43
33	Waterloo Road	12 33
34	Longridge	1 53

NOTES:

(1) Several places show variation in spelling and style
ENTW(h)ISTLE
BRYN(n)
TALBOT ROAD/NORTH
In other cases part of the title shown may be a later addition or deletion. In the gazetteer such alterations are SOMETIMES indicated by enclosing part of the title in brackets, or, with open stations, showing deletions in small letters. Eg: MOORSIDE+Wardley shows Wardley now dropped.

(2) Some stations are indexed — under both town and individual designation Eg: WIGAN

(3) Stations in blue not named on map. Full details see numbered enlargement shown in No. col.

(4) Other features are included only in the unenlarged area.

(5) Other notes - see enlargement gazetteers

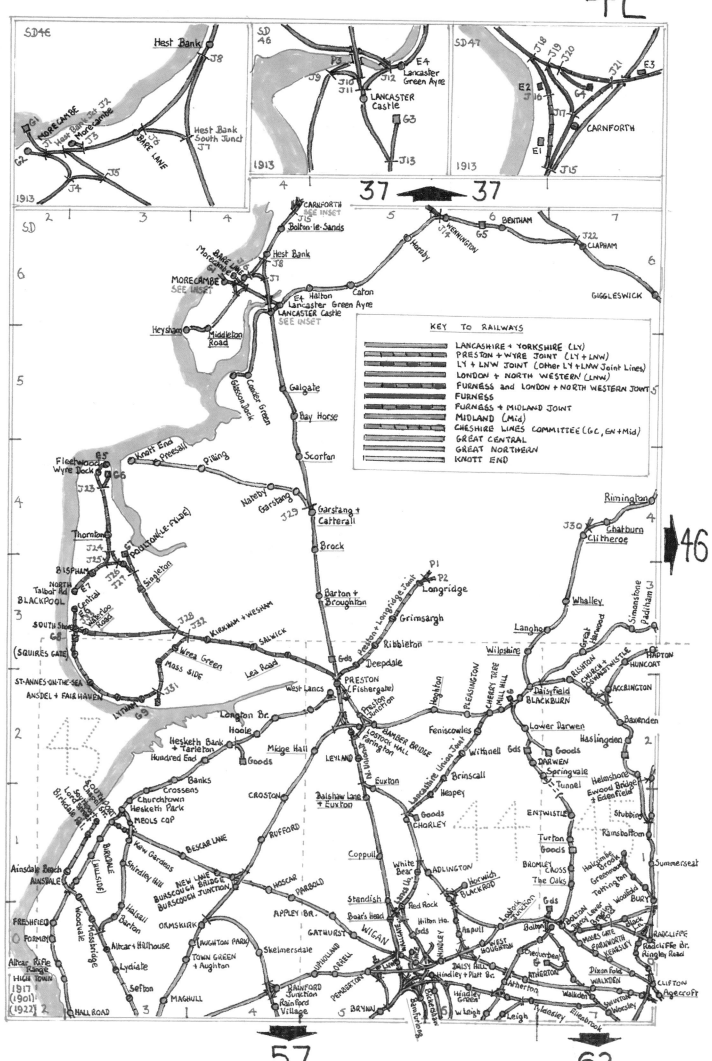

SD4E

Hest Bank
J8

MORECAMBE
G1
Hest Bank Jct J2
Morecambe
J1   J3
G2   BARE LANE
J6
Hest Bank
South Junct
J7
J5
J4
1913

SD2   3   4
SD

SD46

P3
J9
J10
J12
Lancaster
Green Ayre
E4
J11
LANCASTER
Castle
G3
1913
J13
4

SD47

J18 J19 J20
J21
E3
E2
J16
G4
J17
CARNFORTH
E1
1913
J15

37   37
57

CARNFORTH
SEE INSET
J15
Bolton-le-Sands

Hest Bank
J8
J7

MORECAMBE
SEE INSET

E4 Halton
Lancaster Green Ayre
LANCASTER Castle
SEE INSET

Heysham
Middleton
Road

WENNINGTON
J14
BENTHAM
G5

Hornby
Caton
Galgate
Bay Horse
Scorton

Clapham
J22

GIGGLESWICK

KEY TO RAILWAYS

LANCASHIRE + YORKSHIRE (LY)
PRESTON + WYRE JOINT (LY+LNW)
LY + LNW JOINT (Other LY+LNW Joint Lines)
LONDON + NORTH WESTERN (LNW)
FURNESS and LONDON + NORTH WESTERN JOINT
FURNESS
FURNESS + MIDLAND JOINT
MIDLAND (Mid)
CHESHIRE LINES COMMITTEE (GC, GN+Mid)
GREAT CENTRAL
GREAT NORTHERN
KNOTT END

Fleetwood
Wyre Dock
E5
G6
J23
Knott End
Preesall
Piling

Thornton
J24
J25
BISPHAM
J26
NORTH
Talbot Rd E7 J27 Singleton
BLACKPOOL Central
J33 Waterloo
SOUTH SHORE Road
G8
(SQUIRES GATE)
ST-ANNES-ON-THE-SEA
ANSDEL + FAIRHAVEN
LYTHAM
G9

Nateby
Garstang
J29
Garstang +
Catterall
Brock

Barton +
Broughton

POULTON-LE-FYLDE

KIRKHAM + WESHAM
SALWICK
J28 J32
Wrea Green
Moss SIDE
Lea Road
J31
West Lancs

Longton Br.
Hoole
Hesketh Bank
+ Tarleton
Hundred End
Goods

Banks
Crossens
Churchtown
Hesketh Park
MEOLS COP

SOUTHPORT
Chapel St
Seaforth
Lord St
Birkdale Rd

Ainsdale Beach
AINSDALE

FRESHFIELD
FORMBY

Altcar Rifle
Range
HIGH TOWN
1917
(1901)
(1922)

2   3

BIRKDALE
(HILLSIDE)
Shirdley Hill
Halsall
Barton
Lydiate
Sefton
MAGHULL

HALL ROAD

P1
P2
Longridge
Grimsargh
Ribbleton
Deepdale
Gds

PRESTON
(Fishergate)
Preston
Junction

BAMBER BRIDGE
Farington
LEYLAND

Midge Hall
Goods

Kew Gardens
NEW LANE
BURSCOUGH BRIDGE
BURSCOUGH JUNCTION

BESCAR LANE

RUFFORD

CROSTON

Hoscar
APPLEY BR.

ORMSKIRK
(AUGHTON PARK)
TOWN GREEN
+ AUGHTON

Skelmersdale

Balshaw Lane
+ Euxton
Euxton
Goods
CHORLEY

Coppull

White
Bear ADLINGTON
Standish
Red Rock
Boar's Head
Hilton Ho.

RAINFORD
Junction
Rainford
Village

GATHURST
WIGAN
UPHOLLAND
ORRELL
PEMBERTON
BRYN
Bickershaw
W.Leigh

Feniscowles
Withnell
Heapey

Brinscall

Goods

Horwich
BLACKROD

Bromley
Cross
The Oaks

Aspull
Gds

Lostock
Junction
West
Houghton

DAISY HILL
Hindley + Platt Br.
Hindley
Green

Woburn
Pleasington
Cherry Tree
Mill Hill
Wilpshire

Hoghton

Whalley
Langho

RISHTON
CHURCH +
OSWALDTWISTLE

Daisyfield
BLACKBURN

Lower Darwen

Gds
DARWEN
Springvale
Tunnel

ENTWISTLE

Turton
Goods

Holcombe
Brook
Greenmount
Tottington

HAPTON
HUNCOAT
ACCRINGTON
Baxenden
Haslingden
Helmshore
Ewood Bridge
+ Edenfield

Stubbins
Rainsbottom

Summerseat

BURY

Rimington
J30
Chatburn
Clitheroe
46

Simonstone
Padiham
Great Harwood

4

BOLTON
Dixon Lever
Bradley
Fold
MOSES GATE
FARNWORTH
KEARSLEY
Chequerbent
ATHERTON
Atherton
WALKDEN
Walkden
Tyldesley
Leigh
Ellenbrook
SWINTON
Worsley

Dixon Fold
RADCLIFFE
Radcliffe Br.
Ringley Road

CLIFTON
Agecroft

2

1

57   62

43

RAILWAYS

No	Company
R 1	LANCASHIRE + YORKSHIRE
12	L+Y AND L+NW JOINT LINES
2	LONDON + NORTH WESTERN
4	MIDLAND
456	CHESHIRE LINES COMMITTEE (Midland, Great Central and Great Northern Joint)

SOUTHPORT + FORMBY

NOTES:

(1) REFERENCES: All in square SD. However there is an overlap to the South into part of the area covered by Map 57. Those places which are in square SJ are indicated in the gazetteer by ✳

(2) NAME CHANGES – Sometimes just in spelling. In other cases part of the title has been dropped or added. This <u>may</u> be indicated by part of title in brackets ( ) or part in CAPITALS + the rest in small letters

(3) SOUTHPORT Main map –1901. Inset shows later developments – about 1914

(4) ORMSKIRK + KIRKBY – Although both these stations are open for all traffic – British Rail have cut the line in the middle of the station. In each case the station is worked as TWO back-to-back terminal stations !! Yes it really is.

STATIONS

No	Name	Ry	Ref
A 1	AINSDALE	1	31
2	Ainsdale Beach	456	31
3	Altcar + Hillhouse	456	30
4	Altcar Rifle Range	1	30
5	ANSDELL + FAIRHAVEN	12	32
6	(AUGHTON PARK)	1	40
7	Banks	1	32
8	Barton	1	30
9	BESCAR LANE	1	31
10	BIRKDALE	1	31
11	Birkdale Palace	456	31
12	Blowick	1	31
13	BLUNDELLSANDS + CROSBY	1✳	39
14	BURSCOUGH BRIDGE	1	41
15	BURSCOUGH JUNCTION	1	41
16	Butts Lane Halt	1	31
17	CHAPEL STREET	1	31
18	Churchtown	1	31
19	Crossen	1	31
20	CROSTON	1	41
21	FORMBY	1	20
22	FRESHFIELD	1	20
23	HALL ROAD	1	30
24	Halsall	1	30
25	Healthy Lane Halt	1	31
26	Hesketh Bank (+Tarleton)	1	42
27	Hesketh Park	1	31
28	HIGHTOWN	1	30
29	(HILLSIDE)	1	31
30	Hoole	1	42
31	HOSCAR	1	41
32	Hundred End	1	42
33	Kew Gardens	1	31
34	KIRKBY (see Note 4)	1✳	40
35	KIRKHAM + WESHAM	12	43
36	Lea Road	12	43
37	Longton Bridge	1	42
38	Lord Street	456	31
39	Lydiate	456	30
40	LYTHAM	12	32
41	MAGHULL	1	30
42	MEOLS COP	1	31
43	Mossbridge	456	30
44	MOSS SIDE	12	32
45	New Cut Lane Halt	1	31
46	NEW LANE	1	41
47	(OLD ROAN)	1✳	39
48	ORMSKIRK (see Note 4)	1	40
49	PARBOLD	1	41
50	Plex Moss Lane Halt	1	30
51	RAINFORD JUNCTION	1	40
52	Rainford Junction	2	40
53	Rainford Village	2	40
54	Roakery	1✳	49
55	RUFFORD	1	41
56	ST·ANNES·(ON·THE·SEA)	12	32
57	St Lukes (Road)	1	31
58	SALWICK	12	43
59	Sefton	456	30
60	Shirdley Hill (+Scarisbrick)	1	31
61	Skelmersdale	1	40

SOUTHPORT   31

No	Name	Ry	Ref
62	BIRKDALE	1	31
63	Birkdale Palace	456	31
64	Blowick	1	31
65	Butts Lane Halt	1	31
66	CHAPEL STREET	1	31
67	Hesketh Park	1	31
68	Lord Street	456	31
69	MEOLS COP	1	31
70	St Lukes (Road)	1	31
71	(SQUIRES GATE)	12	33
72	TOWN GREEN (+Aughton)	1	40
73	Wrea Green	12	33
74	Woodvale	456	31

GOODS

No	Name / Location	Ry	Ref
G 1	Central (Kensington St)	1	31
2	Ash Street	1	31
3	Lytham	12	32
4	Lord Street	456	31
5	Tarleton Canal Depot	1	42

SIDINGS

No	Company	Ry	Ref
P 1	Wesham Mill Siding	12	43

SHEDS

No	Location	Ry	Ref
E 1	Southport	1	31

WATER TROUGHS

No	Location	Ry	Ref
W 1	Kirkby	1✳	49

JUNCTIONS

No	Name / Location	Ry	Ref
J	SOUTHPORT		31
1	Chapel Street	1	31
2	Liverpool Line	1	31
3	Wigan Line	1	31
4	St Lukes	1	31
5	Goods + Shed	1	31
6	Ash Street	1	31
7	Roe Street	1	31
8	Meols Cop	1	31
9	Butt Lane	1	31
10	(New Line)	1	31
10A	(Proposed Line)	1	31
11	Lytham Goods	12	32
12	Wyre + Lytham	12	43
13	Wesham Mill	12	43
14	Tarleton Branch	1	42
15	Lord Street Goods	456	31
16	Hillhouse	1456	30
17	Ormskirk	1	40
18	Randle	2	40
19	Rainford North	1	40
20	Rainford East Jcts	12	40
21	Burscough Bridge W	1	41
22	Burscough Bridge E	1	41
23	Burscough North	1	41
24	Burscough South	1	41
25	Rainford LNW + LY	12	40

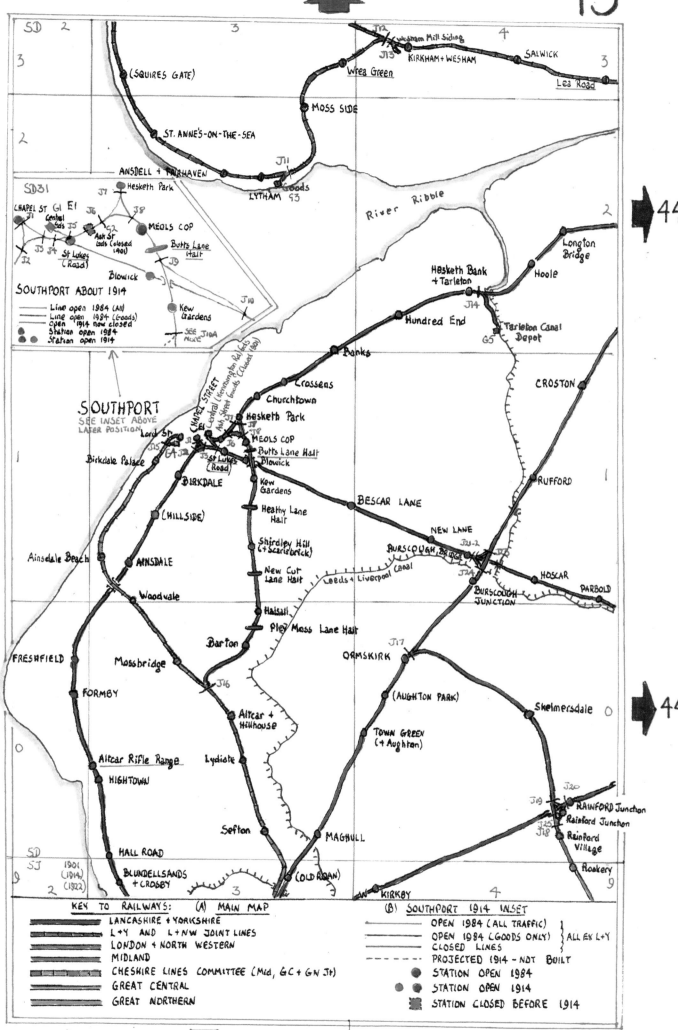

SD 2 3 4

(SQUIRES GATE)

J12 Wesham Mill Siding
J13 KIRKHAM + WESHAM SALWICK 3
Wrea Green Lea Road

MOSS SIDE

ST. ANNE'S-ON-THE-SEA

River Ribble 2

ANSDELL + FAIRHAVEN

SD31 J11
Hesketh Park J7
CHAPEL ST GI E1 J6 J8 Goods
J1 Central LYTHAM 93
Sds
J5 G2 MEOLS COP
Ash St Sds (closed
J3 J4 1901) J8
St Lukes Butts Lane
(Road) J9 Halt
Blowick JF

SOUTHPORT ABOUT 1914 J10
Kew
Gardens

Longton
Bridge
Hesketh Bank Hoole
+ Tarleton
J14
Hundred End Tarleton Canal
G5 Depot
CROSTON
Banks

Crossens
Churchtown RUFFORD
SOUTHPORT Hesketh Park 1
SEE INSET ABOVE MEOLS COP
LATER POSITION Lord St. Butts Lane Halt BESCAR LANE
Birkdale Palace St Lukes Blowick NEW LANE
Road Kew J21-2
Gardens BURSCOUGH BRIDGE
BIRKDALE Heathy Lane HOSCAR
Halt J24 PARBOLD
(HILLSIDE) Shirdley Hill BURSCOUGH
(+ Scarisbrick) JUNCTION
Ainsdale Beach New Cut Leeds + Liverpool Canal
AINSDALE Lane Halt
Halsall
Woodvale Pley Moss Lane Halt
Barton J17
ORMSKIRK
FRESHFIELD Mossbridge
(AUGHTON PARK)
FORMBY J16 Skelmersdale 0
Altcar + TOWN GREEN
Hillhouse (+ Aughton)
Altcar Rifle Range Lydiate
HIGHTOWN J19 J20
RAINFORD Junction
Rainford Junction
Sefton J25 J18 Rainford
SD MAGHULL Village
HALL ROAD Rookery
SJ 1901
9 (1914) BLUNDELLSANDS
2 (1922) + CROSBY (OLD ROAN)
3 KIRKBY 4 9

KEY TO RAILWAYS: (A) MAIN MAP
LANCASHIRE + YORKSHIRE
L+Y AND L+NW JOINT LINES
LONDON + NORTH WESTERN
MIDLAND
CHESHIRE LINES COMMITTEE (Mid, GC + GN Jt)
GREAT CENTRAL
GREAT NORTHERN

(B) SOUTHPORT 1914 INSET
OPEN 1984 (ALL TRAFFIC)
OPEN 1984 (GOODS ONLY) ALL EX L+Y
CLOSED LINES
PROJECTED 1914 - NOT BUILT
STATION OPEN 1984
STATION OPEN 1914
STATION CLOSED BEFORE 1914

PRESTON + WIGAN

RAILWAYS

No.	Company
R1	LANCASHIRE + YORKSHIRE (LY)
12A	LANCASHIRE UNION (LY+LNW)
12B	NORTH UNION JOINT (LY+LNW)
12C	PRESTON + LONGRIDGE (LY+LNW)
12D	PRESTON + WYRE (LY+LNW)
12	LY + LNW JOINT - Others
2	LONDON + NORTH WESTERN (LNW)
5	GREAT CENTRAL
O	CORPORATION OF PRESTON

STATIONS

No.	Name	Ry Ref
A1	ADLINGTON	1 61
2	APPLEY BRIDGE	1 60
3	Aspull (see Dicconson Lane)	1 60
4	Atherton	2 60
5	ATHERTON Central	1 60
6	Balshaw Lane + Euxton	2 51
7	BAMBER BRIDGE	1 52
8	Bamfurlong	2 60
9	Bickershaw	5 60
10	BLACKBURN	1 62
11	BLACKROD	1 61
12	Boar's Head	12A 50
13	Brinscall	12A 62
14	BRYNN (BRYN)	2 50
15	Butler Street	1 52
16	Chequerbent	2 60
17	CHERRY TREE	1 62
18	CHORLEY	1 51
19	Chowbent	2 60
20	Coppull	2 51
21	Daisyfield	1 62
22	DAISY HILL	1 62
23	DARWEN	1 62
24	Deepdale	12C 53
25	Dicconson Lane + Aspull	1 60
26	Euxton	1 52
27	Farington	12B 52
28	Feniscowles	12A 62
29	FISHERGATE	12B 52
30	GARSWOOD	1*59
31	GATHURST	1 50
32	Golborne	5*69
33	Heapey	12A 61
34	Hilton House	1 60
35	HINDLEY	1 60
36	Hindley + Platt Bridge	5 60
37	Hindley Green	2 60
38	Hoghton	1 62
39	Horwich	1 61
40	Hutton + Howick	1 52
41	INCE	1 50
42	Leigh + Bedford	2 60
43	LEYLAND	12B 52
44	LOSTOCK HALL	1 52
45	Lostock Junction	2 60
46	Lower Darwen	1 62
47	Lower Ince	5 50
48	Midge Hall	1 52
48A	MILL HILL	1 62
49	ORRELL	1 50
50	PEMBERTON	1 50
51	Pennington	2*69
52	Platt Bridge	2 60
53	PLEASINGTON	1 52
	PRESTON (see note 3)	
54	Butler Street	1 52
55	FISHERGATE	12B 52
56	West Lancs	1 52
57	Red Rock	12A 50
58	Ribbleton	12C 53
59	Rumworth + Daubhill	2 60
60	Spring Vale	1 62
61	Standish	2 51
62	Tyldesley	2 60
63	UPHOLLAND	1 50
64	WEST HOUGHTON	1 60
65	West Lancs	1 52
66	West Leigh	2 60
67	West Leigh + Bedford	5*69
68	White Bear	12A 51
	WIGAN	
69	Central	5 50
70	LNW	2 50
71	WALLGATE	1 50
72	Wilpshire for Ribchester	1 63
73	Withnell	12A 62

GOODS

No.	Name	Ry Ref
G1	Atherton	2 60
2	Blackburn King Street	1 62
3	LNW	2 62
4	Mill Hill	1 62
5	Chorley	2 51
6	Coppull	2 51
7	Farington	12B 52
8	Hindley + Amberswood	2 60
9	Hindley + Platt Bridge	5 60
10	Hollins	1 62
	PRESTON	
11	Butler Street	1 52
12	Christian Street	2 52
13	Deepdale	12C 52
14	Maudlands	12D 52
15	Oxheys	2 53
16	Rumworth	2 70
17	West Houghton	1 60
18	West Leigh	2 60
19	Whelley	2 50
20	Wigan Central	5 50
21	Wigan LNW	2 50

SIDINGS

No.	Name/Co/Location	Ry Ref
P1	Ellersbeck Colliery	12A 51
2	Springs Branch	2 60
3	Roundhouse Colliery	2 60
4	Norley Colliery	2 50
5	West Leig Colliery	2 60
6	Diggles South Colliery	2*69

WORKS

No.	Name	Ry Ref
C1	Horwich	1 61

ENGINE SHEDS

No.	Name/Location	Ry Ref
E1	Preston	2 52
2	Springs Branch	2 50
3	Horwich	1 61
4	Lostock Hall	1 52
5	Lower Darwen	1 62
6	Wigan	1 50

TUNNELS

No.	Name/Location	Ry Ref
T1	Upholland	2 50

JUNCTIONS

No.	Name/Location	Ry Ref
J1	Preston + Wyre	12D2 52
2	Preston + Longridge	12C2 52
3	P+W Goods Branch	12CD 52
4	Deepdale Goods Branch	12C 53
5	Penwortham	1 52
6	Ribble	1 52
7	Middleforth	1 52
8	Goods	12B2 52
9	Whitehouse West	1 52
10	Whitehouse North	1 52
11	Whitehouse South	1 52
12	Farington West	1 52
13	Farington West-New	1 52
14	Moss Lane	1 52
15	New	1 52
16	Farington	12B 52
17	Farington East	12B1 52
18	Lostock Hall West	1 52
19	Lostock Hall East	1 52
20	Lostock Hall North	1 52
21	Bamber Bridge	12A1 62
22	Cherry Tree	12 62
23	LY + LNW Goods	1 62
24	King Street	1 62
25	Daisyfield West	1 62
26	Daisyfield East	1 62
27	Hoddlesden	1 62
28	Euxton	12B21 52
29	Chorley	12A1 51
30	Coppull Goods	2 51
31	Ellerbeck	1212A1 51
32	Horwich West	1 61
33	Horwich East	1 61
34	Horwich South	1 60
35	Red Moss	1 60
36	Standish	2 51
37	Haigh	12A2 50
38	Boar's Head	12A2 50
39	Whelley (Standish Line)	2 50
40	Roundhouse Branch	2 50
41	Kirkless	2 60
42	Pemberton	12 50
43	Goose Green	2 50
44	Park Lane	2 50
45	Crow Nest	1 60
46	Aspull	1 60
47	Dobbs Brow	1 60
48	Lostock	1 60
49	Goods Line	2 60
50	Bamfurlong	2 60
51	Ince Moss South	2 50
52	Ince Moss North	2 50
53	Manchester Line (S)	2 50
54	Platt Bridge	2 60
55	Manchester Line (N)	2 50
56	St Helens Line	2 50
57	Springs Branch	2 50
58	Goods Branch	2 50
59	Goods Branch	5 50
60	Warrington Line	1 50
61	LNW + LY	12 50
62	Liverpool Line	2 50
63	Southport Line	1 60
64	Amberswood West Jcts.	25 60
65	Strangeways West	5 60
66	Strangeways Middle	5 60
67	Strangeways East	25 60
68	Goods Branch	5 60
69	Amberswood East	25 60
70	De Trafford	2 60
71	Bickershaw West	2 60
72	Bickershaw East	2 60
73	Bickershaw South	2 60
74	Plank Lane	25 60
75	Bedford	5 60
76	Pennington South	2*69
77	Pennington North	2*69
78	Diggles Branch	2*69
79	Chowbent West	2 60
80	Chowbent East	2 60
81	Chowbent North	2 60
82	Atherton Goods	2 60
83	Rose Bridge	2 60

CANALS

There are many canals in the area covered by the map, but just one is shown, the LEEDS + LIVERPOOL. There was interchange goods traffic between rail and canal at various points but particularly at WIGAN

NOTES:

(1) REFERENCES - All in square SD. However, there is an overlap to the South into part of the area covered by Map 57. Places in square SJ are indicated in gazetteer by *

(2) NAME CHANGES - Sometimes just in spelling but in other cases part of the title has been dropped or added. This MAY be indicated by part of title in brackets ( ) or a mixture of CAPITALS and small letters.

(3) PRESTON - Butler Street and West Lancs closed by 1910 except for Goods. Oxhey also had a passenger service until about 1905

(4) WIGAN - Inset shows the junction layout in the area.

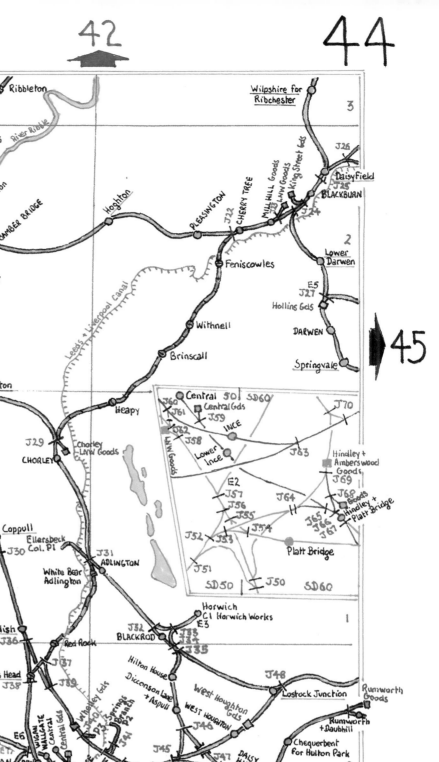
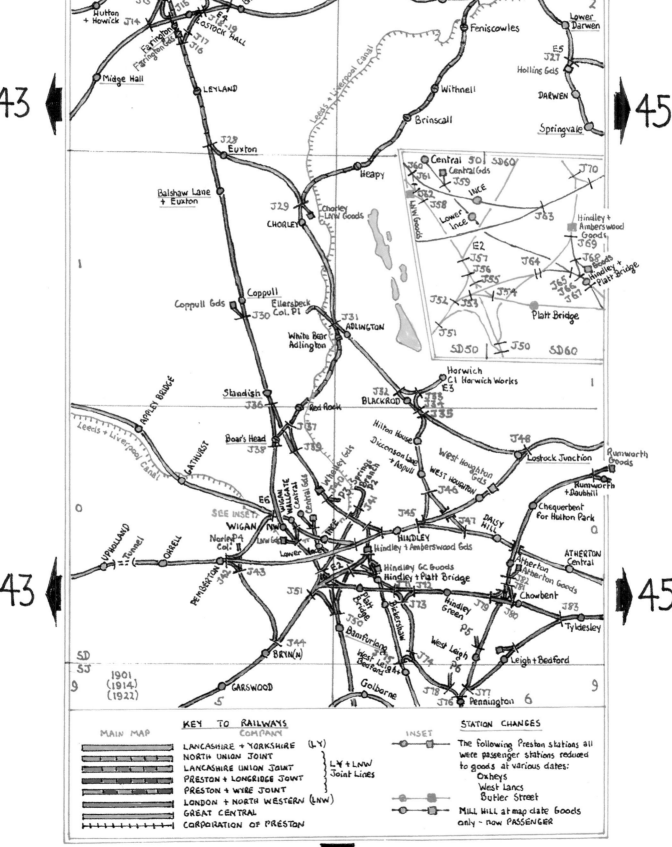

BOLTON, BURY + OLDHAM

NOTES: (1) REFERENCES - ALL in square SD
(2) NAME CHANGES - Shown by part of name (brackets) or mixture of CAPITALS and small letters
(3) EXTENSION - Map has been extended to the east. 47 is extended to the west to give a continuation without a break at this scale
(4) AGECROFT - Closed very early 20th century as a passenger station
(5) ENTW(H)ISTLE - In early 20th century, spelling has varied.

RAILWAYS

No	Company
R 1	LANCASHIRE + YORKSHIRE
2	LONDON + NORTH WESTERN
25	OLDHAM, ASHTON + GUIDE BRIDGE (G.C. and L+NW Jt)
5	GREAT CENTRAL

STATIONS

No	Name	Ry	Ref
A 1	ACCRINGTON	1	72
2	Agecroft	1	70
3	Bacup	1	82
4	BANK TOP (CENTRAL)	1	83
5	BARRACKS	1	80
6	Baxenden	1	72
7	(BESSES · O' · TH' · BARN)	1	80
8	Black Lane	1	70
9	BOLTON	1	70
10	Bolton - Gt Moor Street	2	70
11	(BONKER VALE)	1	80
12	Bradley Fold	1	70
13	Britannia	1	82
14	Broadfield	1	80
15	Broadley	1	81
16	BROMLEY CROSS	1	71
	BURNLEY		83
17	BANK TOP - CENTRAL	1	83
18	BARRACKS	1	83
19	Manchester Road	1	83
20	BURY High Level	1	71
21	Bury Low Level	1	81
22	CASTLETON	1	81
23	CHURCH + OSWALDTWISTLE	1	72
24	Clegg Street	25	90
25	CLIFTON	1	70
26	Clough Fold	1	82
27	Cornholme	1	92
28	CRUMPSALL	1	80
29	Darcy Lever	1	70
30	DEAN LANE	1	80
31	Dixon Fold	1	70
32	Ellenbrook	2	70
33	ENTWISTLE	1	71
34	Ewood Bridge	1	72
35	Facit	1	81
36	FAILSWORTH	1	80
37	FARNWORTH (+ Halshaw Moor)	1	70
38	Gladwick Road	2	90
39	Great Harwood	1	73
40	Great Moor Street	2	70
41	Greenmount	1	71
42	HAPTON	1	73
43	Haslingden	1	72
44	HEATON PARK	1	80
45	Helmshore	1	72
46	Heywood	1	80
47	Holcombe Brook	1	71
48	HOLLINWOOD	1	80
49	Holme	1	82
50	HUNCOAT	1	73
51	KEARSLEY (+Stoneclough)	1	70
52	Langho	1	73
53	Lees	2	90
54	LITTLEBOROUGH	1	91
55	Little Hulton	2	70
56	Manchester Road	1	83
57	Middleton	1	82
58	Middleton Junction	1	80
59	(MILLS HILL)	1	
60	MILNROW	1	91
61	Molyneux Brow	1	70
62	MOORSIDE + Wardley	1	70
63	MOSES GATE	1	70
64	MOSTON	1	80
65	MUMPS	1	90
66	NEW HEY	1	91
67	Newton Heath	1	80
68	Oaks, The	1	71
	OLDHAM		90
69	Central	1	90
70	Clegg Street	25	90
71	MUMPS	1	90
72	WERNETH	1	90
73	Padiham	1	73
74	Park Bridge	25	90
75	Pendlebury	1	70
76	Plodder Lane for Farnworth	2	70
77	Portsmouth	1	82
78	PRESTWICH	1	80
79	RADCLIFFE	1	70
80	Radcliffe Bridge	1	70
81	Ramsbottom	1	71
82	Rawtenstall	1	82
83	Ringley Road	1	70
84	RISHTON	1	72
85	ROCHDALE	1	81
86	ROSE GROVE	1	83
87	Royton	1	90
88	ROYTON Junction	1	90
89	Rumworth + Daubhill	2	60
90	SHAW + Crompton	1	90
91	Shawclough + Healey	1	81
92	Shawforth	1	82
93	Simonstone	1	73
94	SMITHY BRIDGE	1	91
95	Spring Vale	1	62
96	Stacksteads	1	82
97	Stansfield Hall	1	92
98	Stubbins	1	71
99	Summerseat	1	71
100	SWINTON	1	70
101	The Oaks	1	71
102	TODMORDEN	1	92
103	Tottington	1	71
104	Towneley	1	83
105	Turton	1	71
106	WALKDEN	1	70
107	Walkden	2	70
108	Walsden	1	92
109	Wardleworth	1	91
110	Waterfoot for Newchurch	1	82
111	WERNETH	1	90
112	WHITFIELD	1	80
113	Whitworth	1	81
114	WOODLANDS ROAD (H&H)	1	80
115	Woolfold	1	71
116	Worsley	2	70
117			
118			

GOODS

No	Name / Location	Ry	Ref
G 1	Astley Bridge	1	71
	BOLTON		70
2	Craddock Lane	1	70
3	Crook Street	2	70
4	Deansgate	2	70
5	Brindle Heath	1	80
6	Grane Road	1	72
7	Halliwell	1	71
8	Hartford Works	1	90
9	Heap Bridge	1	81
10	Hoddlesden	1	72
11	King William	1	71
12	Little Hulton Mineral	2	70
13	Oldham LNW	2	90
14	Oldham Scottfield	5	90
15	Rumworth	2	70

SIDINGS

No	Name/Location/Co	Ry	Ref
P 1	Stonehill		70
2	Kearsley Moss		70

SHEDS

No	Name/Location	Ry	Ref
E 1	Accrington	1	72
2	Rose Grove	1	83
3	Newton Heath	1	80
4	Agecroft	1	70
5	Bolton	1	70
6	Bury	1	81
7	Lees	2	90

TUNNELS

No	Name/Location		Ry	Ref
T 1	Sough	2015	1	71
2	Brooksbottom		1	71
3	Brooksbottom		1	71
4	Waterfoot		1	82
5	Townley		1	83
6	Holme		1	82
7	Cornholme - Kitson Wood		1	92
8	Millwood		1	92
9	Castlehill		1	92
10	Winterbuttee		1	92
11	Standedge	2285	1	91
12				

SUMMITS

No	Name	Ht	Ry	Ref
S 1	Copy Pit	749	1	82

JUNCTIONS

No	Name/Location	Ry	Ref
J 1	Daisyfield East	1	62
2	Accrington West	1	72
3	Accrington South	1	72
4	Accrington East	1	72
5	Rose Grove	1	82
6	Gannow	1	82
7	Whiteplatts	1	92

JUNCTIONS (continued)

No	Name/Location	Ry	Ref
J 8	Todmorden	1	92
9	Hall Royd	1	92
10	Bacup	1	82
11	Stubbins	1	71
12	Holcombe Brook Branch	1	71
13	Bury South	1	70
14	Bury East	1	80
15	Heap Bridge	1	80
16	Castleton East	1	80
17	Castleton North	1	80
18	Castleton South	1	80
19	Rochdale	1	90
20	Royton	1	90
21	Oldham Joint	125	90
22	Werneth	1	90
23	Clegg Street	25	90
24	Goods	25	90
25	Thorps Bridge West	1	80
26	Thorps Bridge East	1	80
27	Middleton	1	80
28	Cheetham Hill	1	80
29	Radcliffe - Bury	1	70
30	Radcliffe - Bolton	1	70
31	Radcliffe - Manchester	1	70
32	Molyneux	12	70
33	Clifton	1	70
34	Agecroft	1	70
35	Brindle Heath	1	70
36	Worsley	2	70
37	Stonehill	1	70
38	Kearsley Goods Line	1	70
39	Mineral Branch	2	70
40	Red Moss South	1	70
41	Red Moss East	1	70
42	Red Moss North	1	70
43	Bolton	2	70
44	Rumworth Goods	2	60
45	Astley Bridge	1	70
46	Bury High Level	1	71
47	Bury Low Level	1	80
48	Bolton Station West	1	70
49	Bolton Station South	1	70
50	Bolton Station East	1	70
51	Scottfield Goods	255	90

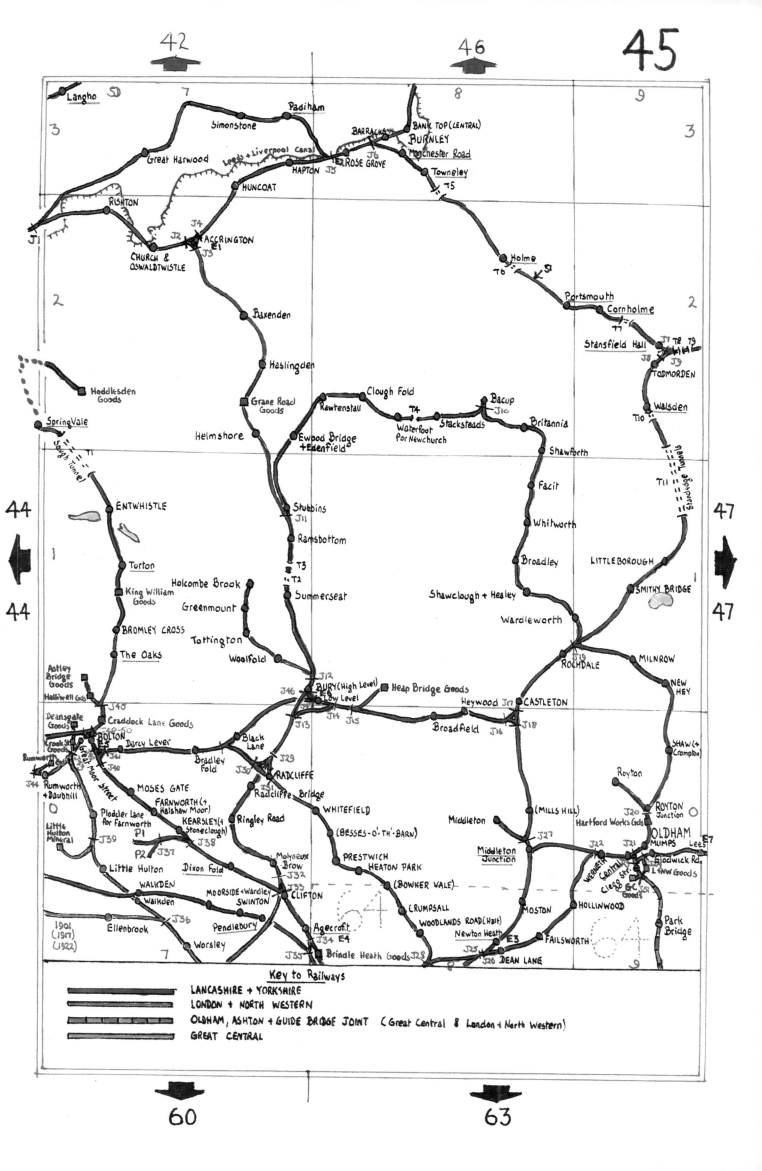

Key to Railways

| | LANCASHIRE & YORKSHIRE |
| LONDON & NORTH WESTERN |
| OLDHAM, ASHTON & GUIDE BRIDGE JOINT (Great Central & London & North Western) |
| GREAT CENTRAL |

RAILWAYS

No Company

R1 LANCASHIRE + YORKSHIRE
16 L+Y and GN JOINT
2 LONDON + NORTH WESTERN
25 OLDHAM, ASHTON + GUIDE BRIDGE
3 NORTH EASTERN
34 OTLEY + ILKLEY JOINT (Mid + NE)
4 MIDLAND
5 GREAT CENTRAL
6 GREAT NORTHERN
7 NIDD VALLEY (Light)

SKIPTON, LEEDS + OLDHAM

NOTES: (1) Gazetteer includes ALL stations in the area covered by the map. Those shown IN BLUE have not been included on the map - but are shown on an enlargement (49) shown thus.
(2) Other details apart from stations + railways are only shown if not covered by an enlargement
(3) References are in SD or SE - the initial S is omitted in the reference column
(4) § Map name   § Modern name   ‡ Unstaffed Halt (1986) where known   7 projected, never opened.

STATIONS + HALTS

No	Name	Ry Ref
A1	Addingham	4 E04
2	Apperley Br. + Rawdon	4 E13
3	Armley + Wortley	6 E23
(48)	Armley Canal Road	4 E23
4	Arthington	3 E24
5	Bacup	1 D82
6	BAILDON ‡	4 E13
7	Bailiff Bridge	1 E12
8	BANK TOP §47	1 D83
9	Barnoldswick	4 D84
10	BARRACKS	1 D83
11	BATLEY	2 E22
12	Barley	6 E22
(49)	Batley Carr	6 E22
13	Battyeford	2 E12
14	Beeston	6 E32
15	Bell Busk	4 D85
16	BEN RHYDDING ‡	34 E14
17	Berry Brow	1 E11
18	(BESSES·O'·TH·BARN)	1 D80
19	BINGLEY	4 E13
20	Birkenshaw + Tong	6 E22
(46)	Birstall	2 E22
21	Birstwith	3 E25
22	Bolton Abbey	4 E05
23	(BOWKER VALE)	1 D80
24	Bowling Junction	1 E12
	BRADFORD	
25	Bowling Junction	1 E12
26	Dudley Hill	6 E12
27	EXCHANGE §31	1 E13
28	FORSTER SQUARE	4 E13
29	Great Horton	6 E13
30	Horton Park	6 E13
31	INTERCHANGE §27	1 E13
32	Laisterdyke	6 E13
33	Manchester Road	6 E13
34	Manningham	4 E13
(47)	St Dunstan's	6 E13
35	Bradley	2 E11
36	BRAMLEY ‡	6 E23
37	BRIERFIELD ‡	1 D83
38	Brighouse - Clifton Rd	1 E12
39	Brighouse for Rastrick	1 E12
40	Britannia	1 D82
41	Broadfield	1 D80
42	Broadley	1 D81
43	BROCKHOLES ‡	1 E11
44	BURLEY (IN WHARFEDALE) ‡	34 E14
	BURNLEY	D83
45	BANK TOP §47	1 D83
46	BARRACKS ‡	1 D83
47	CENTRAL §45	1 D83
48	Manchester Road	1 D83
49	Bury Low Level	1 D81
50	Calverley + Rodley	4 E23
(49)	Carlinghow	2 E22

No	Name	Ry Ref
51	CASTLETON	1 D81
(49)	Churwell	2 E22
52	Clayton	6 E13
53	Clayton West	1 E21
54	Cleckheaton	1 E12
55	Cleckheaton	2 E12
(45)	Clegg Street	25 D90
56	Clifton Road	1 E12
57	Clough Fold	1 D82
58	COLNE ‡	14 D84
59	Cononley	4 D94
60	Cooper Bridge	1 E12
61	Copley	1 E02
62	Cornholme	1 D92
63	Crookrise ?	4 E05
64	(CROSSFLATTS) ‡	4 E13
65	CRUMPSALL	1 D80
66	Cullingworth	6 E03
67	Dacre	3 E16
68	Damens	4 E03
69	Darley	3 E16
70	DEAN LANE ‡	1 D80
71	DEIGHTON ‡	2 E11
72	Delph	2 D90
73	DENBY DALE + Cumberworth ‡	1 E20
74	Denholme	6 E03
75	DEWSBURY	2 E22
(49)	Dewsbury	1 E22
(49)	Dewsbury	6 E22
76	Diggle	2 E00
77	Drighlington + Adwalton	6 E22
78	Dudley Hill	6 E12
79	Dunford Bridge	5 E10
80	Earby	4 D94
81	Earlsheaton	1 E30
82	Eastwood	1 D92
83	Eccleshill	6 E13
84	Elland	1 E12
85	Elslack	4 D94
86	Embsay	4 D94
87	Esholt	4 E13
88	Facit	1 D81
89	FAILSWORTH ‡	1 D90
90	Farnley + Wortley	2 E23
91	Fenay Bridge + Lepton	2 E11
92	Flushdyke	6 E22
93	FORSTER SQUARE	4 E13
94	Foulridge	4 D84
95	Friezland	2 D90
96	Frizinghall	6 E13
97	GARGRAVE ‡	4 D95
98	GIGGLESWICK ‡	4 D76
99	Gildersome	2 E22
100	Gildersome	6 E22
101	Gisburn	1 D84
(45)	Glodwick Road	2 D90
102	Golcar	2 E01
103	Gomersal	2 E22
104	Grassington + Threshfield	E00
105	Great Horton	6 E13
106	GREENFIELD	2 D90
107	Greenside Pudsey	6 E23
108	Greetland	1 E02
109	Grotton + Springhead	2 D90
110	GUISELEY ‡	4 E14

No	Name	Ry Ref
	HALIFAX	E02
111	HALIFAX §113	1 E02
112	North Bridge	16 E02
113	OLD §111	1 E02
114	Pellon	16 E02
115	St Pauls	16 E02
116	Hampsthwaite	3 E25
117	HARROGATE	3 E36
118	Haworth	4 E03
119	Hazlehead Bridge	5 E10
120	HEADINGLEY ‡	3 E23
121	Healey House	1 E11
122	HEATON PARK	1 D80
123	HEBDEN BRIDGE	1 D92
124	Heckmondwike	1 E22
(49)	Heckmondwike	2 E22
125	HELLIFIELD ‡	4 D85
126	Heywood	1 D80
127	Hipperholme	1 E12
(48)	Holbeck High Level	6 E23
(48)	Holbeck Low Level	4 E23
128	HOLLINWOOD	1 D90
129	Holme	1 D82
130	Holmfield	16 E02
131	Holm Firth	1 E10
132	HONLEY ‡	1 E11
133	Horbury + Ossett	1 E21
134	HORSFORTH ‡	3 E23
135	Horton Park	6 E13
(49)	Howden Clough	6 E22
136	HUDDERSFIELD	1 E13
137	Idle	6 E13
138	ILKLEY	34 E14
139	Ingrow (East)	6 E03
140	Ingrow West	4 E03
141	KEIGHLEY	4 E04
142	Kildwick + Crosshills	4 E04
143	Kirkburton	2 E11
144	Kirkheaton	2 E11
145	Kirkstall	4 E23
146	Laisterdyke	6 E13
	LEEDS	E23
147	Armley + Wortley	6 E23
(48)	Armley Canal Rd	4 E23
148	Beeston	6 E23
149	Central 123	6 E23
150	Farnley + Wortley	2 E23
151	HEADINGLEY ‡	3 E23
(48)	Holbeck High Level	6 E23
(49)	Holbeck Low Level	4 E23
152	Kirkstall	4 E23
153	LEEDS (New)	23 E23
(49)	Wellington	4 E23
154	Lees	2 D90
155	Lightcliffe	1 E12
156	LITTLEBOROUGH	1 D91
(47)	Liversedge	1 E12
157	Liversedge	2 E22
158	LOCKWOOD ‡	1 E11
159	LONG PRESTON ‡	4 D85
159A	Longwood + Milnsbridge	2 E11
160	Low Moor	1 E12
161	Luddenden Foot	1 E02
162	M'chester Rd. Bfd	6 E13
163	M'chester Rd. Burnley	1 D83
164	Manningham	4 E13
165	MARSDEN ‡	2 E01

No	Name	Ry Ref
166	Meltham	1 E11
167	MENSTON ‡	4 E14
168	Micklehurst	2 D90
169	Middlestown	4 E21
170	Middleton	1 D80
171	Middleton Junction	1 D80
172	MILES PLATTING ‡	1 D80
173	(MILLS HILL) ‡	1 D80
174	MILNROW ‡	1 D91
175	MIRFIELD	1 E20
176	MORLEY	2 E22
(49)	Morley Top	6 E22
177	MOSSLEY	2 D90
178	MOSTON	1 D80
179	MUMPS	1 D80
180	MYTHOLMROYD	1 E02
181	NELSON	1 D83
182	Netherton	1 E11
183	NEW HEY ‡	1 D91
184	Newlay + Horsforth	4 E23
185	(NEW PUDSEY)	6 E23
186	Newsholme	1 D85
(45)	Newton Heath	1 D80
187	Nidd Bridge	3 E26
(49)	Northorpe	1 E22
(49)	Northorpe	2 E22
188	Oakworth	4 E03
	OLDHAM	D90
189	Central	1 D90
(46)	Clegg Street	25 D90
(45)	Gladwick Road	2 D90
190	MUMPS	1 D90
191	WERNETH ‡	1 D90
192	Ossett	6 E22
193	Otley	34 E14
194	Ovenden	16 E02
195	Oxenhope	4 E03
196	PANNAL ‡	3 E35
197	Park Bridge	25 D90
198	Pateley Bridge	3 E16
199	Pateley Bridge	7 E16
200	Pellon	16 E02
201	PENISTONE ‡	51 E20
202	Pool	3 E24
203	Portsmouth	1 D82
204	PRESTWICH	1 D80
	PUDSEY	E23
205	Greenside	6 E23
206	Lowtown	6 E23
207	(NEW)	6 E23
208	Queensbury	6 E13
(49)	Ravensthorpe	1 E22
209	RAVENSTHORPE	2 E22
210	Rawtenstall	1 D82
211	Rimington	1 D24
212	Ripley Valley	3 E26
213	Rippondent Barkisland	1 E01
214	Rishworth	1 E11
215	ROCHDALE	1 D81
216	Rochdale Rd. Br Halt	1 E02
217	ROSE GROVE ‡	1 D83
218	Royton	1 D90
219	ROYTON Junction ‡	1 D90
220	Rylstone	4 D95
221	Saddleworth	2 D90
(47)	St Dunstan's	6 E13

No	Name	Ry Ref
222	St Pauls	16 E02
223	SALTAIRE ‡	4 E13
224	SETTLE	4 D86
225	SHAW + Crompton ‡	1 D90
226	Shawclough + Healey	1 D81
227	Shawforth	1 D82
228	SHEPLEY ‡	1 E11
229	SHIPLEY ‡	4 E13
230	Shipley + Windhill	6 E13
231	SILKSTONE ‡	5 E20
232	Skelmanthorpe	1 E21
233	SKIPTON	4 D95
234	SLAITHWAITE ‡	2 E01
235	SMITHY BRIDGE	1 D91
236	SOWERBY BRIDGE	1 E02
237	Stacksteads	1 D82
(49)	Staincliffe + Batley Carr	2 E22
238	Stainland + Holywell Gr.	1 E01
(48)	Stanningley	6 E23
239	Stansfield Hall	1 D92
240	Steeton + Silsden	4 E04
241	STOCKSMOOR	1 E11
242	Thackley	6 E13
243	Thongs Bridge	1 E10
(49)	Thornhill	1 E22
244	Thornton - Bradford	6 E03
245	Thornton - Craven	4 D94
246	Thwaites	4 E04
247	Tingley	6 E22
248	TODMORDEN	1 D92
249	Towneley	1 D83
250	Triangle	1 E02
(49)	Upper Batley	6 E22
(49)	Upper Birstall	2 E22
251	Uppermill	2 D90
252	Walsden	1 D92
253	Wardleworth	1 D91
254	Waterfoot for Newchurch	1 D82
255	Wath-in-Nidderdale	7 E16
256	WEETON	3 E24
(48)	Wellington	4 E23
257	WERNETH	1 D90
258	West Vale	1 E02
259	WHITFIELD	1 D80
260	Whitworth	1 D81
261	Wilsden	6 E03
262	Woodkirk	6 E22
263	WOODLANDS ROAD ‡	1 D90
264	Wormald Green	3 E36
265	Wyket Norwood Green	1 E12
266	Yeadon see note on MAP 47	4 E23

SHEDS

No	Name	Ry Ref
E1	Hellifield	1 D85
2	Hellifield	4 D85
3	Skipton	4 D95

TUNNELS

No	Name		Ry Ref
T1	Bramhope	3761 yds.	3 E24

JUNCTIONS

No	Name	Ry Ref
J1	Settle	4 D86
2	Hellifield	41 D85
10	Milnerwood	344 E14
13	Arthington	3 E24
14	Bilton Road	3 E25
15	Dragon	3 E25
16	Nidd	3 E25
17	NE/Nidd Valley	37 E16

KEY TO RAILWAYS

No.	Legend	Company
1		LANCASHIRE + YORKSHIRE
16		HALIFAX + OVENDEN JOINT (Lancashire + Yorkshire & Great Northern)
16		HALIFAX HIGH LEVEL JOINT (Lancashire + Yorkshire & Great Northern)
2		LONDON + NORTH WESTERN
25		OLDHAM ASHTON + GUIDE BRIDGE JOINT (London + North Western & Great Central)
3		NORTH EASTERN
34		OTLEY + ILKLEY JOINT (Midland + North Eastern)
4		MIDLAND
5		GREAT CENTRAL
6		GREAT NORTHERN
7		NIDD VALLEY (Light)
0		Other Joint Lines — At LEEDS — See Map 48 for full detail

1917 (1921, 1923, 1901, 1922)

47

BRADFORD + GREENFIELD

NOTES:

(1) REFERENCES: All in squares SD or SE. 'S' is not included.

(2) NAME CHANGE: § Map name / § Modern name

(3) GOODS STATIONS (3) were originally passenger stations.

(4) CLOSED TO PASSENGERS. The following sections were closed to passenger traffic prior to 1939
A) Shipley - Laisterdyke (GN)
B) Dudley Hill - Low Moor (GN)
C) Holmfield - St Pauls (GN + LY)
D) Greetland - Stainland (LY)
E) Sowerby Bridge - Rishworth (LY)

(5) Yeadon ♀ only ever used for holiday passenger traffic - but used this way for many years. Principal use as Goods only.

(6) LMS connection J42 to J43

(7) FRIZINGHALL ‡ Station has now been re-opened.

(8) EXTENDED - Map is extended to the west to adjoin 45 at this scale without a break.

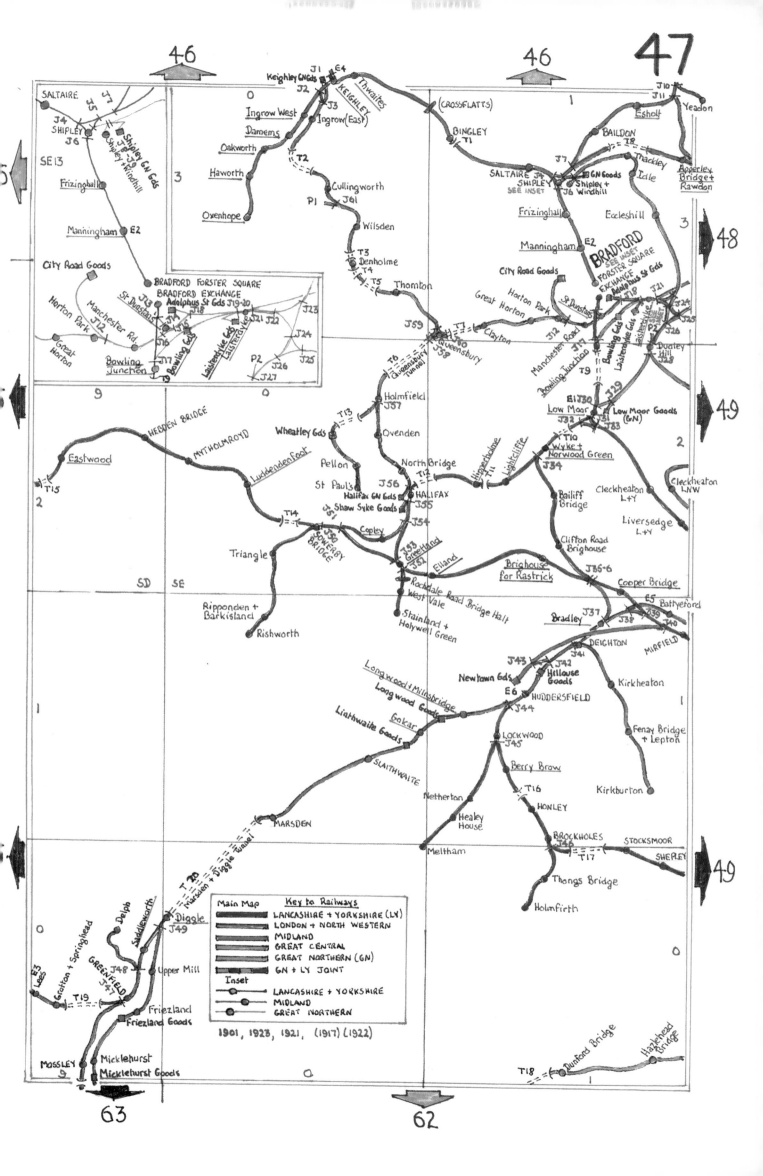

SALTAIRE
J7
J5
J4 SHIPLEY
J6
Shipley GN Gds
Shipley + Windhill
J8-J9
SE13
Frizinghall
Manningham E2
City Road Goods

Keighley GN Gds J1 E4
J2
KEIGHLEY
Ingrow West J3
Ingrow (East)
Damems
Oakworth
T2
Haworth
Cullingworth
P1 J61
Oxenhope
Wilsden

(CROSSFLATTS)
BINGLEY T1

J10
J11
Yeadon
Esholt
BAILDON J8
Thackley
J7
SALTAIRE J4 GN Goods Idle Apperley Bridge + Rawdon
SHIPLEY Shipley + Windhill
SEE INSET J6
Frizinghall Eccleshill
Manningham E2 BRADFORD
SEE INSET
FORSTER SQUARE
City Road Goods EXCHANGE
St Dunstans Adolphus St Gds
Horton Park J18 J21
Great Horton J12 J17
Manchester Road J9
Bowling Junction
E1 J30
Low Moor J32 J31 Low Moor Goods (GN)
J33 T10
Wyke + Norwood Green
J34

BRADFORD FORSTER SQUARE
BRADFORD EXCHANGE
Adolphus St Gds J19-20
St Dunstans J13
J3
Manchester Rd J18 J21 J22 J23
J14 Laisterdyke Gds
Bowling Gds J16
Horton Park J12 J17 P2 J24
Great Horton Bowling Junction J26 J25
J9 J27

HEBDEN BRIDGE
Eastwood
T15
MYTHOLMROYD
Wheatley Gds
Luddendenfoot
Pellon
St Paul's
Halifax GN Gds
Shaw Syke Goods
T13 J57
Holmfield
Ovenden
North Bridge
J56 HALIFAX
T12 J55
J54

Queensbury
T7 J60
J58 J59
Clayton
T6
Queensbury Tunnel

Manchester Road
J17
Bowling Junction
T9
J29
Hipperholme T11 Lightcliffe
Bailiff Bridge
Cleckheaton L+Y
Cleckheaton LNW
Liversedge L+Y

Triangle
T14 J50
SOWERBY BRIDGE
J51
Copley
Greetland J52
J53 Elland
Ripponden + Barkisland
Rishworth
Rochdale Road Bridge Halt
West Vale
Stainland + Holywell Green

Clifton Road Brighouse
Brighouse for Rastrick
J36-6
Cooper Bridge
E5 Battyeford
Bradley J37 J39 J40
J38 MIRFIELD

Longwood + Milnsbridge
Longwood Goods
Linthwaite Goods
Golcar
Slaithwaite

Newtown Gds
J43 J41
J42
Hillhouse Goods
E6 HUDDERSFIELD
J44
LOCKWOOD
J45
Berry Brow
Netherton
Healey House
HONLEY
T16
BROCKHOLES
J46
T17
Meltham
Thongs Bridge
Holmfirth

DEIGHTON
Kirkheaton
Fenay Bridge + Lepton
Kirkburton
STOCKSMOOR
SHEPLEY

MARSDEN
T20
Marsden + Diggle Tunnel

Delph
Saddleworth
Diggle
J49
Greenfield
J48
J47 Upper Mill
E3 Leeds
Grotton + Springhead
T19
Friezland
Friezland Goods
MOSSLEY
Micklehurst
Micklehurst Goods

Dunford Bridge
T18
Hazlehead Bridge

Key to Railways

Main Map	
▆▆▆	LANCASHIRE + YORKSHIRE (LY)
▆▆▆	LONDON + NORTH WESTERN
▆▆▆	MIDLAND
▆▆▆	GREAT CENTRAL
▆▆▆	GREAT NORTHERN (GN)
▆▆▆	GN + LY JOINT

Inset	
●—●	LANCASHIRE + YORKSHIRE
●—●	MIDLAND
●—●	GREAT NORTHERN

1901, 1923, 1921, (1917) (1922)

RAILWAYS

No.	Company
R1	LANCASHIRE + YORKSHIRE (LY)
12&6	LY + LNW JOINT
12&6	LY, LNW, NE + GN JOINT
16	GN + LY JOINT
2	LONDON + NORTH WESTERN (LNW)
23	LNW + NE JOINT
3	NORTH EASTERN (NE)
36	NE + GN JOINT
4	MIDLAND
6	GREAT NORTHERN (GN)
X	Monkbridge Iron (Private)

STATIONS

No.	Name	Ry Ref
A1	Apperley Bridge + Rawdon	4 13 23
2	Armley + Wortley	4 23
3	Armley Canal Road	4 23
4	Beeston	6 23
5	BRAMLEY	6 23
6	Calverley + Rodley	4 23
7	CROSS GATES	3 33 37
8	Dudley Hill	6 13 38
9	Eccleshill	6 13 39
10	Farnley + Wortley	2 23
11	GARFORTH	3 33
12	Greenside - Pudsey	6 23
13	HEADINGLEY	3 23 43
14	Holbeck High Level	6 23
15	Holbeck Low Level	4 23
16	HORSFORTH	3 23
17	Hunslet	4 33
18	Kirkstall	4 23
19	Laisterdyke	6 13
	LEEDS	
20	Armley + Wortley	6 23
21	Armley Canal Road	4 23
22	Beeston	1236 23
23	Central	3 33
24	Farnley + Wortley	2 23
25	Holbeck High Level	6 23
26	Holbeck Low Level	4 23
27	HEADINGLEY	4 33
28	Hunslet	6 23
29	Kirkstall	4 23
30	Marsh Lane	3 33
31	LEEDS New	23 23
32	Wellington	4 23
33	Lowtown - Pudsey	6 23
34	Marsh Lane	4 23
35	Newlay + Horsforth	6 23
36	(NEW PUDSEY)	6 23
	PUDSEY	
37	Greenside	4 23
38	Lowtown	6 13
39	(NEW)	6 13
40	Scholes	3 33
41	Stanningley	6 23
42	Wellington	6 23
43	Yeadon ♀	3 23

(see note 3)

GOODS

No.	Name/Location	Ry Ref
G1	Balm Road	6 13
2	Cardigan Road	6 23
3	Copley Hill	6 23
4	Crossgates	4 23
5	Hunslet	6 23
6	Hunslet	1236 23
7	Hunslet Lane	2 23
8	Kirkstall Forge ‡(8)	6 23
9	Wellington Street	4 23
10	Wellington Street	4 23
11	Wellington Street	4 33
12	Whitehall Road	4 23

SIDINGS

No.	Company	Ry Ref
P1	Monkbridge Iron	6 23

ENGINE SHEDS

No.	Name/Location	Ry Ref
E1	Neville Hill	6 23
2	Copley Hill	6 23
3	Farnley Junction	6 23
4	Leeds Holbeck	6 23
5	Stourton	3 33

TUNNELS

No.	Name	Length	Ry Ref
T1	Thackley	1496	4 13
2	Hillfoot	450	6 13
3	Headingley		3 23

BRIDGES + VIADUCTS

No.	Name	Ry Ref
V1	Farnley Viaduct	4 33

JUNCTIONS

No.	Name/Location	Ry Ref
J1	Holbeck	3 33
2	Whitehall	6 33
3	Curve	4 23
4	Monkbridge Iron Works	4 23
5	Armley Exchange Sdgs	12 23
6	Armley Exchange Sdgs	3 23
7	Wortley	6 23
8	Joint Line	12 23
9	Goods	3 33
10	Geldard (Jcts)	
11	Joint Line + GN	4 23
12	Three Signal Bridge E.	3612 23 X 23
13	Three Signal Bridge W	1236 23
14	Holbeck South	4 23
15	Wortley West	6 23
16	Wortley South	3 33
17	Copley Hill	6 23
18	Leeds South	2 23
19	Leeds North	4 23
20	Engine Shed	4 32
21	Canal	23(4)23
22	Joint Line	235 23
23	Neville Hill (Hunslet Bch)	4 13
24	Neville Hill (Hunslet Bch)	4 13
25	Goods	6 13
26	Siding	3 23
27	Exchange Sidings	6 33
28	Joint Sidings South	36 33
29	Joint Sidings North	36 33
30	Balm Lane Goods	4 33
31	Stourton	49 33
32	Wetherby Line	3 33
33	Goods	3 33
34	Garforth	3 43
35	Cardigan Road Goods	3 23
36	Bramley West	6 23
37	Apperley	4 23
38	Dudley Hill	6 13
39	Robson's Siding	6 13
40	Broad Lane	6 13
41	Tyersal	6 13
42	Cutlers North	6 13
43	Quarry Gap	6 13
44	Laisterdyke Station (E)	6 13
45	Shipley + Dudley Hill Lines	6 13
46	Farnley	2 23

NOTES:

(1) REFERENCES: All in square SE.

(2) STATIONS: Leeds inner suburb- an stations indexed also under LEEDS

(3) Yeadon ♀ only ever used for holiday passenger traffic — but used this way for many years. Principal use was as a Goods only station.

(4) BR LINES: Added about 1967 when Central and Wellington Street were closed. Neville Hill is BR motive-power Depot on site of ex-NE Shed.

(5) BRAMLEY was closed but re-opened in 1980's as an unstaffed halt.

(6) Wellington which adjoins (New) is still open but for parcels and stabling only.

(7) HARROGATE LINE - uses Armley Exchange deviation not Wortley as some authorities suggest. This is now a split scissors crossover between two sets of double track. Wortley Jct taken out of use.

(8) Kirkstall Forge ‡ previously also a passenger station.

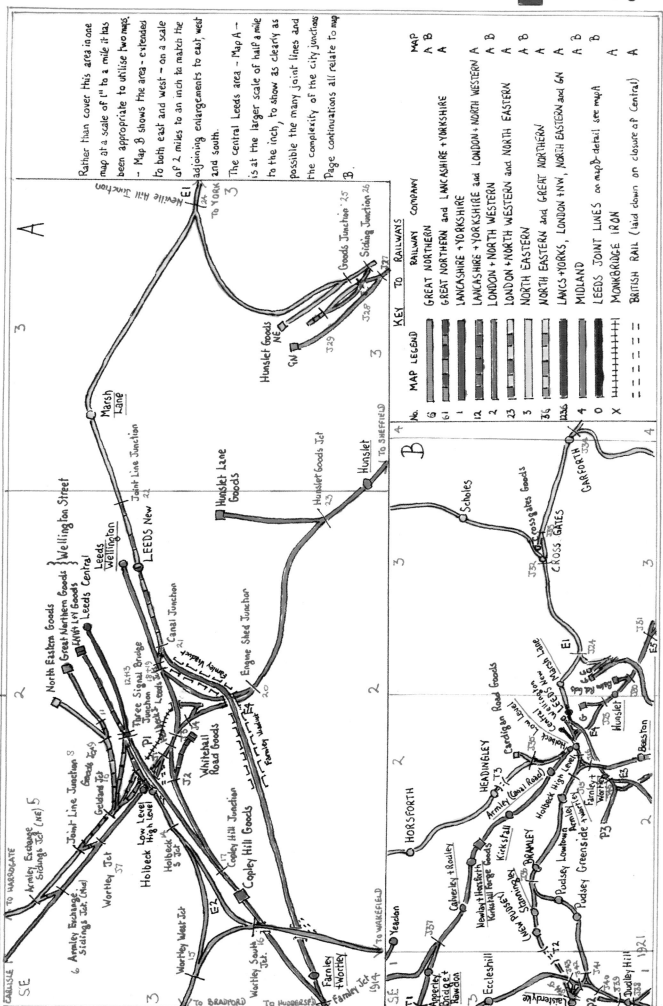

Rather than cover this area in one map at a scale of 1" to a mile it has been appropriate to utilise two maps. — Map B shows the area — extended to both east and west — on a scale of 2 miles to an inch to match the adjoining enlargements to east, west and south.

The central Leeds area — Map A — is at the larger scale of half a mile to the inch, to show as clearly as possible the many joint lines and the complexity of the city junctions. Page continuations all relate to map B.

A

3

3

3

Neville Hill Junction
TO YORK
E1

Goods Junction 25
Siding Junction 26
Hunslet Goods NE
GN
J29
J28
J27
3

Marsh Lane

Joint Line Junction
LEEDS New
Leeds Wellington
Wellington Street
Hunslet Lane Goods
Hunslet Goods Jct 23
Hunslet
TO SHEFFIELD

North Eastern Goods
Great Northern Goods
LNWR Goods
Wellington Street
Leeds Central

Canal Junction
Engine Shed Junction

Farnley Viaduct
Whitehall Road Goods

CARLISLE
TO HARROGATE
SE
Armley Exchange Sidings Jct (NE) 5
Joint Line Junction 8
Geldard Jct
Goods Jct 9
Wortley Jct
Holbeck Low Level High Level
Wortley West Jct
Wortley South Jct
Copley Hill Junction
Copley Hill Goods
E2
TO BRADFORD
TO HUDDERSFD
Farnley + Wortley
Farnley Jct
TO WAKEFIELD

KEY TO RAILWAYS

MAP LEGEND		RAILWAY COMPANY	MAP
No.			A B
6		GREAT NORTHERN	A B
61		GREAT NORTHERN and LANCASHIRE + YORKSHIRE	A
1		LANCASHIRE + YORKSHIRE	A B
12		LANCASHIRE + YORKSHIRE and LONDON + NORTH WESTERN	A
2		LONDON + NORTH WESTERN	A B
23		LONDON + NORTH WESTERN and NORTH EASTERN	A
5		NORTH EASTERN	A B
36		NORTH EASTERN and GREAT NORTHERN	A
1236		LANCS + YORKS, LONDON + NW, NORTH EASTERN and GN	A
4		MIDLAND	A B
0		LEEDS JOINT LINES on mapB detail see mapA	A B
X		MONKBRIDGE IRON	A
		BRITISH RAIL (laid down on closure of Central)	A

B

4

3

Scholes

Crossgates Goods
J35
CROSS GATES
Cross Gates
GARFORTH
J34
4

3

2

HORSFORTH
HEADINGLEY
J.T3
Cardigan Road Goods
Marsh Lane
Leeds New
Wellington
Central Low Level
E1
J24
Holbeck High Level
Bean Rd Goods
Hunslet
Beeston
E57

Yeadon
Calverley + Rodley
Newlay + Horsforth
Kirkstall Forge Goods
Kirkstall
New Stanningley
BRAMLEY
Armley (Canal Road)
Pudsey Lowtown
Armley
Farnley + Wortley
P3
E3

Eccleshill
(NEW PUDSEY)
J37
J2
Pudsey Greenside + Stanningley
Laisterdyke
Dudley Hill
1921
P2

SE
T1
Apperley Bridge
Rawdon
2

47
49

49 RAILWAYS

NOTES: (1) EXTENDED to the North with overlap onto 48
(2) REFERENCES All in square SE
(3) INSETS Barnsley, Methley, Batley - to show junction layouts more clearly
(4) BARNSLEY The present Quarry Junction, though close to the old junction, is different site.

Company

No	Company
R 1	LANCASHIRE + YORKSHIRE
2	LONDON + NORTH WESTERN
3	NORTH EASTERN
4	MIDLAND
5	GREAT CENTRAL
136	METHLEY JOINT (L+Y, NE and GN)
56	WEST RIDING + GRIMSBY JT (GN+GC)
6	GREAT NORTHERN
7	HULL + BARNSLEY
8	DEARNE VALLEY
9	EAST + WEST YORKSHIRE UNION
0	Colliery Lines

STATIONS + HALTS

No	Name	Ry	Ref
A 1	ALTOFTS + Whitwood	4	32
2	Alverthorpe	6	32
3	Ardsley	6	32
4	BARNSLEY	1	30
5	Barnsley Court House	4	30
6	BATLEY	2	22
7	Batley	6	22
8	Batley Carr	6	22
9	Battyeford	2	12
10	Beeston	6	32
11	Birdwell + Hoyland Common	5	30
12	Birkenshaw + Tong	6	22
13	Birstall	2	22
14	Carlinghow	2	22
15	Churwell	2	22
16	Clayton West	1	21
17	Cleckheaton	2	22
18	Crigglestone (West)	1	21
19	Crofton	1	31
20	Cudworth	4	30
21	DARTON	1	31
22	DENBY DALE + Cumberworth	1	20
23	DEWSBURY	2	22
24	Dewsbury	1	22
25	Dewsbury Central	6	22
26	Dodworth	5	30
27	Dovecliffe	5	30
28	Drighlington + Adwalton	6	22
29	Earlsheaton	6	22
30	ELSECAR + Hoyland	4	30
31	Flushdyke	6	22
32	Gildersome	2	22
33	Gildersome	6	22
34	Gomersal	2	22
35	Grimethorpe Halt	8	30
36	Haigh	1	21
37	Hare Park + Crofton	56	31
38	Heckmondwike	1	22
39	Heckmondwike	2	22
40	Horbury + Ossett	1	21
41	Horbury Junction	1	31
42	Howden Clough	6	22
43	Liversedge	1	22
44	Liversedge	2	22
45	Lofthouse + Outwood	6	32
46	Methley	1	32
47	Methley	4	32
48	Methley Joint	136	32
49	Middlestown	4	21
50	MIRFIELD	1	22
51	Monk Bretton	4	30
52	MORLEY	2	22
53	Morley Top	6	22
54	NORMANTON	4	32
55	Northorpe	1	22
56	Northorpe	2	22
57	Nostell	56	31
58	Notton + Royston	5	31
59	Ossett	6	22
60	PENISTONE	51	20
61	Ravensthorpe	1	22
62	RAVENSTHORPE	2	22
63	Royston + Notton	4	31
64	Ryhill	5	31
65	Ryhill Halt	1	31
66	Sandal	56	31
67	Sandal + Walton	4	31
68	Sharlston	1	31
69	SILKSTONE	5	20
70	Skelmanthorpe	1	21
71	Staincliffe + Batley Carr	2	22
72	Staincross for Mapplewell	5	30
73	Stairfoot for Ardsley	5	30
74	Stanley	136	32
75	Summer Lane	5	30
76	Thornhill	1	22
77	Tingley	6	22
78	Upper Batley	6	22
79	Upper Birstall	2	22
80	WAKEFIELD KIRKGATE	1	32
81	WAKEFIELD WESTGATE	6	32
82	WOMBWELL	4	30
83	Wombwell	5	30
84	Woodkirk	6	22
85	WOODLESFORD	4	32

GOODS

No	Name / Location	Ry	Ref
G 1	Barnsley	5	30
2	Birdwell + Pilley	4	30
3	Crigglestone	4	31
4	Cudworth	7	31
5	Dewsbury	4	22
6	Dewsbury	6	22
7	Elsecar	5	30
8	Healey Mills	1	21
9	Moor End	5	20
10	Oakenshaw	4	31
11	Oakwell	5	30
12	Old Mill Lane	5	30
13	Penistone	5	20
14	Robin Hood	9	32
15	Rothwell	9	32
16	Wakefield	56	32
17	Warsboro	5	30
18	Stourton	9	32

SIDINGS ETC

No	Company / Name / Location	Ry	Ref
P 1	Howley Pk + Gt Finsdale Q	6	22
2	Woodkirk Quarry	6	22
3	Pawson Brothers	6	22
4	Thorpe Quarries	9	32
5	Beeston Colliery	9	32
6	Rothwell Haigh	0	32
7	Newmkt Silkstone Col	90	32
8	Hodroyd Colliery	5	31
9	Wombwell Main Col	40	30
10	Oaks Colliery (4)	0	30
11	Silkstone Siding	1	30
12	New Monckton Main Col	4	31
13	New Monckton Main Col	7	31
14	Don Pedro Colliery	40	32
15	Whitwood Colliery	0	32
16	Denby Grange Col Lines	0	21
17	Denby Grange Col Lines	0	21
18	New Oaks Colliery	7	30
19	Wharncliffe Silkstone Col	4	30
20	Thurgoland Siding	5	20

ENGINE SHEDS

No	Location	Ry	Ref
E 1	Stourton	4	32
2	Normanton	4	32
3	Mirfield	1	21
4	Wakefield	1	32
5	Barnsley	1	30
6	Ardsley	6	32

TUNNELS

No	Name / Location	Length	Ry	Ref
T 1	Morley	3369	2	22
2	Gildersome	2331	2	22
3	Gomersal	819	2	22
4	Wooley	1745	1	21
5	Cumberworth	906	1	20
6	Wellhouse	415	1	20

JUNCTIONS

No	Name / Location	Ry	Ref
J 1	Farnley	2	23
2	Balm Road Goods	4	33
3	Stourton	49	33
4	Adwalton	6	22
5	Beeston North	6	22
6	Beeston South	6	22
7	Tingley East	6	22
8	Tingley West	6	22
9	Heckmondwike	1	22
10	Batley Lower North	6	22
11	Batley Lower South	6	22
12	Birstall	2	22
13	Batley GN North	2	22
14	Batley GN South	2	22
15	Batley LNW	6	22
16	Dewsbury North	6	22
17	Dewsbury South	6	22
18	Headfield North	16	22
19	Headfield South	1	22
20	Dewsbury East	1	21
21	Dewsbury West	1	22
22	Thornhill	1	22
23	Dewsbury	12	21
24	Mirfield	1	21
25	Chickenley Heath Branch	6	22
26	Ardsley	6	32
27	Robin Hood Jcts	9	32
28	Lofthouse North	136	32
29	Lofthouse South	136	32
30	Lofthouse East	136	32
31	Wrenthorpe West	6	32
32	Wrenthorpe North	6	32
33	Wrenthorpe South	6	32
34	Balne Lane	56	32
35	West Riding	656	32
36	King Road	16	32
37	Kirkgate West	1	32
38	Kirkgate East	1	32
39	Kirkgate South	1	32
40	Snydale	4	32
41	Goose Hill	41	32
42	Altofts	43	32
43	NE + Methley Line	3136	32
44	Methley NE + Mid	43	32
45	Methley L+Y and Mid	14	32
46	Lofthouse	1136	32
47	Whitwood	3	42
48	Whitwood Branch	3	42
49	St John's Colliery Sidings	4	32
50	Thornhill Midland	14	21
51	Middlestown	4	21
52	Horbury + Ossett	1	21
53	Crigglestone	1	21
54	Horbury	1	31
55	Clayton West Branch	1	21
56	Gadds	4	31
57	Sandal	56	31
58	Oakenshaw Mid + LY	41	31
59	Oakenshaw - Crofton	561	31
60	Oakenshaw - West	1	31
61	Oakenshaw - South	1	31
62	Oakenshaw - East	1	31
63	Hare Park	56	31
64	Nostell North	5	31
65	Nostell South + Colliery	5	31
66	Wintersett	5	31
67	Royston	4	31
68	Monckton Colliery	4	31
69	Monckton Colliery	7	31
70	Brierley Junction	78	31
71	Shafton	18	31
72	Cudworth	7	31
73	Carlton Ev Sidings	7	31
74	Penistone	15	20
75	For Barnsley	5	20
76	West Silkstone	5	20
77	East Silkstone	5	20
81	Cudworth North	4	30
82	Cudworth West	4	30
83	Cudworth South	4	30
84	Cudworth Station South	74	30
85	Cudworth Station South	4	30
86	Cudworth West Junction	74	30
87	Storr's Mill	4	30
88	Monk Spring	4	30
89	Barnsley Goods	5	30
90	Barnsley Station	15	30
91	Barnsley West	45	30
92	Chapeltown Line	5	30
93	Mount Osborne	5	30
94	Quarry	54	30
95 6	Oaks Colliery	454	30
97	New Oaks	5	30
98	Monk Spring	4	30
99	New Oaks	5	30
100	Manchester + London	5	30
101	Aldam	5	30
104	Wharncliffe Branch	4	30
107	Hoyland	4	30

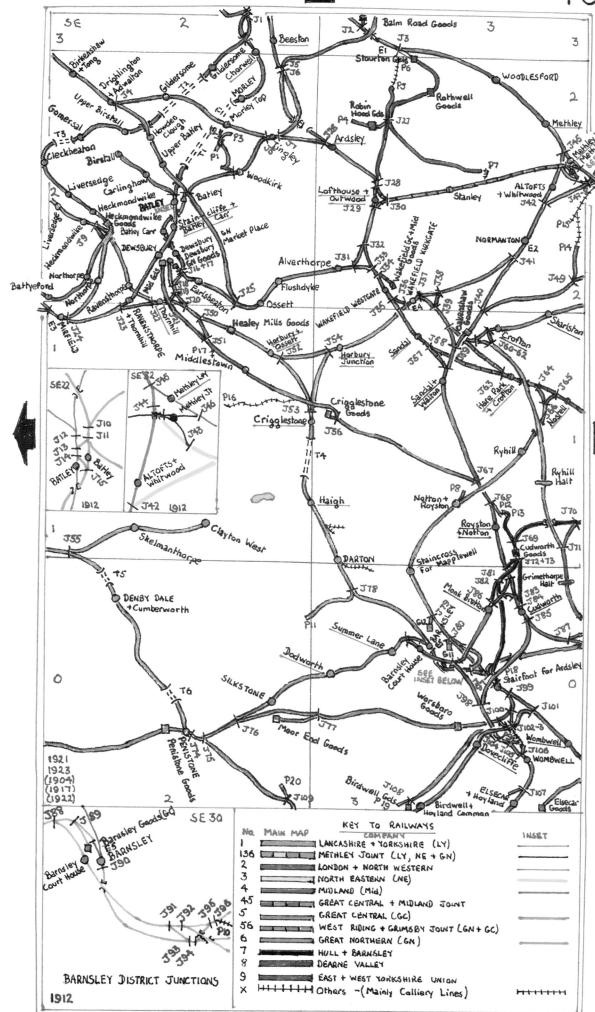

48 49
47
51
62 66

HARROGATE, YORK + DONCASTER

RAILWAYS + JOINT RAILWAYS

No.	Company (Owning Partners)
R 1	LANCASHIRE + YORKSHIRE
13	AXHOLME JOINT (LY + NE)
136	METHLEY JOINT (LY, NE + GN)
13456	SOUTH YORKSHIRE JOINT (LY, NE, Mid, GC + GN)
23	LONDON + NORTH WESTERN and NORTH EASTERN JOINT
3	NORTH EASTERN
‡	EASINGWOLD (Light) Alne to Easingwold (shown as NE on map)
34	NORTH EASTERN + MIDLAND JOINT
4	MIDLAND
45	MIDLAND + GREAT CENTRAL
457	MIDLAND, GREAT CENTRAL and HULL + BARNSLEY
5	GREAT CENTRAL
56	WEST RIDING + GRIMSBY JOINT (GC + GN)
57	GREAT CENTRAL and HULL + BARNSLEY JOINT
6	GREAT NORTHERN
611	GREAT NORTHERN + GREAT EASTERN JOINT
7	HULL + BARNSLEY
8	DEARNE VALLEY
9	EAST + WEST YORKSHIRE UNION (Goods only)
22	DERWENT VALLEY (Light)
33	BRACKENHILL (Light)
O	BRITISH RAILWAYS (New Main Line)

STATIONS

No	Name	Ry Ref
A1	Ackworth	34 41
2	Airmyn + Rawcliffe	3 62
3	Allerton	3 45
4	Alne	‡3 56
5	ALTOFTS + Whitwood	4 32
6	Alverthorpe	6 32
7	Ardsley	6 32
8	Arksey	6 50
9	Askern	1 51
10	BAGHILL	34 42
11	Balne	3 51
12	Bardsey	3 34
13	Barlow	3 62
14	Barmby	7 62
15	Barnby Dun	5 60
16	BARNSLEY	(5) 1 30
17	Barnsley Court House	4 30
18	Barton Hill	3 76
19	Belton	13 70
20	Beningbrough	3 55
21	(Bessacar Halt)	611 60
22	Birdwell + Hoyland Common	5 30
23	BOLTON·ON·DEARNE	34 40
24	Bolton Percy	3 54
25	Boroughbridge	3 36
26	Brafferton	3 46
27	Bubwith	3 73
28	Burton Salmon	3 42
29	Carcroft + Adwick·le·Street	56 50
30	Carlton	7 62
31	Castleford (Cutsyke)	1 42
32	CASTLEFORD	3 42
33	Castle Howard	3 76
34	CATTAL	3 45
35	Cawood	3 63
36	CHURCH FENTON	3 53
37	Cliff Common	3 63
38	Cliff Common	22 63
39	Collingham Bridge	3 34
40	Copgrove	3 36
41	Copmanthorpe	3 54
42	Cottingwith	22 64
43	Crigglestone	1 21
44	Crofton	1 31
45	Crowle	13 71
46	CROWLE Central	5 71
47	CROSS GATES	3 33
48	Cudworth	4 30
49	Darfield	4 40
50	DARTON	1 31
51	Denaby Halt	8 50
52	Dodworth	5 30
53	DONCASTER	6 50
54	Dovecliffe	5 30
55	Drax	7 62
56	Drax Hales	3 62
57	Dunnington	22 65
58	Dunnington Halt (Kexby)	22 65
59	Earswick	3 65
60	Easingwold	‡ 56
61	Eastoft	13 71
62	EASTRINGTON	3 72
63	Eastrington	7 73
64	ELSECAR + Hoyland	4 30
65	Elvington	22 64
66	Epworth	13 70
67	Escrick	3 64
68	Fangfoss	3 75
69	Featherstone	1 42
	PANNAL	
135	Pickburn + Brodsworth	34 42
136	Pocklington	611 60
	PONTEFRACT	
137	BAGHILL	3 66
138	MONKHILL	3 73
139	Tanshelf	34 40
140	POPPLETON	3 43
141	Raskelf	5 71
142	RAWCLIFFE	3 35
143	Reedness	
144	Riccall	8 40
145	Royston + Notton	8 40
146	Ryhill	8 40
147	Ryhill Halt	3 53
148	SALTMARSHE	3 46

No	Name	Ry Ref
70	Ferrybridge (for Knottingley)	34 42
71	Finningley	611 60
72	(FITZWILLIAM)	56 41
73	Flaxton	3 66
74	Foggathorpe	3 73
75	Frickley	34 40
76	GARFORTH	3 43
77	Godnow Bridge	5 71
78	Goldsborough	3 35
79	GOOLE	(1) 3 72
80	Great Houghton Halt	22 63
81	Grimethorpe Halt	8 40
82	Hambleton	3 53
83	Hammerton	3 45
84	Hampole	56 50
85	Hare Park + Crofton	56 31
86	Harlington	8 40
87	HARROGATE	3 35
88	Haxby	3 65
89	Haxey Town	13 70
90	Heck	3 51
91	Hemingbrough	3 63
92	Hemsworth	56 41
93	Hemsworth + S Kirkby	7 41
94	HENSALL	1 52
95	Hessay	3 55
96	Hickleton + Thurnscoe	7 40
97	High Field	3 73
98	Holme	3 73
99	Holtby	3 65
100	Horbury Junction	1 31
101	HOWDEN	3 72
102	Howden	7 72
103	Hunslet	4 33
104	Huttons Ambo	3 76
105	Kippax	3 42
106	Kirkham Abbey	3 76
107	Kirk Smeaton	7 51
108	KNARESBOROUGH	3 35
109	KNOTTINGLEY	1 42
110	Layerthorpe	22 65
111	Ledston	3 42
112	LEEDS New	23 23
113	Lofthouse + Outwood	6 32
114	Marsh Lane	3 33
115	Marston Moor	3 55
116	Medge Hall	5 71
117	Menthorpe Gate	3 63
118	Methley	1 32
119	Methley	4 32
120 (49)	Methley Joint	136 32
120	MICKLEFIELD	3 43
121 (51)	Monk Bretton	4 30
121	Monk Fryston	3 53
122	MONKHILL	1 42
123	Moorhouse + S Elmsall	7 40
124	MOORTHORPE + South Kirkby	34 41
125	Moss	3 51
126	Murton Lane	22 65
127	Naburn	3 64
128	Newton Kyme	3 44
129	Nidd Bridge	3 26
130	NORMANTON	4 32
131	Norton	1 51
132	Nostell	56 41
133	Notton + Royston	5 31
134	PANNAL	3 35

No	Name	Ry Ref
149	Sandal	56 31
150	Sandal + Walton	4 31
151	Scholes	3 35
152	SELBY	3 63
153	Sharleston	1 31
154	Sherburn·in·Elmet	3 53
155	Skipwith	22 63
156	SNAITH	1 62
157	Snaith + Pollington	57 62
158	SOUTH ELMSALL	56 41
159	SOUTH MILFORD	3 43
160	Spofforth	3 35
161	Sprotborough	7 50
162	Staincross for Mapplewell	5 30
163	STAINFORTH + HATFIELD	5 61
164	Stairfoot for Ardsley	5 30
165	Stamford Bridge	3 75
166	Stanley	136 32
167	STARBECK	3 35
168	Strensall	3 66
169	Summer Lane	5 30
170	Sykehouse	57 61
171	Tadcaster	3 44
172	Tanshelf	1 42
173	Temple Hirst	3 62
174	Thorganby	22 64
175	THORNE NORTH	3 61
176	Thorner	3 34
177	THORNE SOUTH	5 61
178	Thorp Arch	3 44
179	Thorpe·in·Balne	57 61
180	Tollerton	3 56
181	ULLESKELF	3 54
182	Upton + North Elmsall	7 41
183	WAKEFIELD KIRKGATE	1 32
184	WAKEFIELD WESTGATE	6 32
185	Warthill	3 65
186 (51)	Wath + Bolton	40
186	Wath·on·Dearne	5 40
187	Wath·on·Dearne	7 40
188	Wetherby	3 34
189	Wheldrake	22 64
190	WHITLEY BRIDGE	1 52
191	Wistow	3 53
192	WOMBWELL	4 30
193	Wombwell	5 30
194	Womersley	1 51
195	WOODLESFORD	4 32
196	Wormald Green	3 36
197	WRESSLE	3 73
198	YORK	3 55
199	York - Layerthorpe	22 65

GOODS

No.	Name/Location	Ry Ref
G1	Harrogate	3 35
2	Knaresborough	3 35
3	Wilstrop	3 45
4	Wetherby	3 44
5	Stutton	3 44
6	Goole Docks	1 72
7	Maud's Bridge	5 71
8	Hatfield Moor	13 70
9	Sandtoft	13 70
10	Thorp Gates	3 53
11	York	3 55
12	Foss Islands	3 65

JUNCTIONS

No	Name/Location	Ry Ref
J1	Alne	‡ 3 55
2	Pateley Bridge Line	3 35
3	Bilton Road	3 35
4	Dragon	3 35
5	Starbeck North	3 35
6	Starbeck South	3 35
7	Crimple	3 35
8	Pannal	3 35
9	Knaresborough Goods	3 35
10	York + Pilmoor	3 35
11	Wetherby West	3 34
12	Wetherby South	3 34
13	Wetherby East	3 44
14	Oakhill	1 72
15	Goole Docks	31 72
16	Potters Grange West	31 72
17	Booth Ferry Road	3 72
18	Marshland	313 72
19	Reedness	13 71
20	Thorne GC + NE	53 61
21	Goole Line	5 61
22	Epworth	13 70
23	Colton	30 54
24	Hambleton North	30 53
25	Hambleton West	30 53
26	Hambleton South	30 53
27	Hambleton East	30 53
28	Temple Hirst	30 53

ENGINE SHEDS

No.	Name/Location	Ry Ref
E1	Starbeck	3 35

NOTES:

(1) REFERENCES: All in square SE

(2) RAILWAYS — EASINGWOLD (Light) Alne to Easingwold shown on map as North Eastern

(3) JUNCTIONS in red are new British Rail junctions laid in when new MAIN LINE built.

(4) Stations - Closed but still used by passengers on an ad hoc basis

(5) Stations in blue not named on the map. For full details see numbered enlargement.

(6) OTHER FEATURES - may not be included EXCEPT in the area not covered by enlargements.

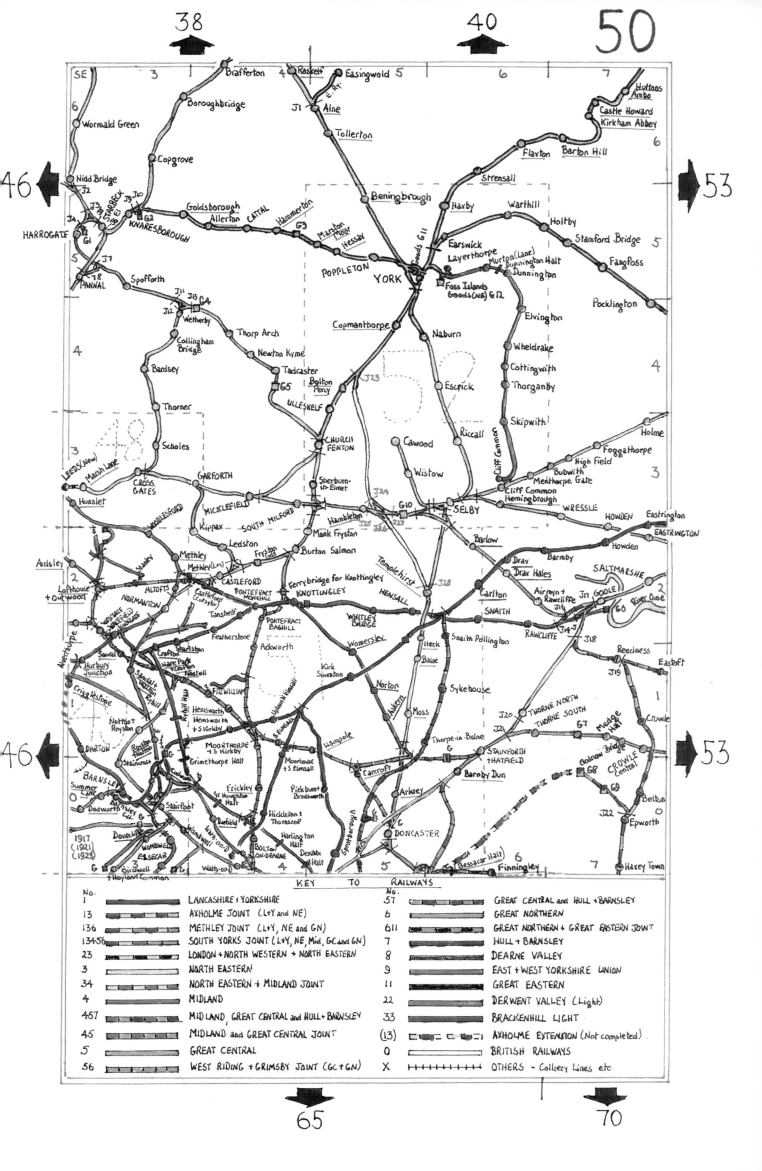

51

RAILWAYS

No	Company
R 1	LANCASHIRE + YORKSHIRE
13456	SOUTH YORKS UNION (L+Y, NE, Mid, GC, GN)
3	NORTH EASTERN
34	NORTH EASTERN + MIDLAND JOINT
4	MIDLAND
45	MIDLAND + GREAT CENTRAL JOINT
5	GREAT CENTRAL
56	WEST RIDING + GRIMSBY JT (GC+GN)
57	GREAT CENTRAL + HULL and BARNSLEY JT.
6	GREAT NORTHERN
611	GREAT NORTHERN + GREAT EASTERN JT.
7	HULL + BARNSLEY
8	DEARNE VALLEY
33	BRACKENHILL (Light) - Goods only
O	BRITISH RAIL (New Works)
X	OTHERS - Colliery lines etc

STATIONS + HALTS

No	Name	Ry Ref
A 1	Ackworth	34 41
2	Arksey	6 50
3	Askern	1 51
4	BAGHILL	34 42
5	Balne	3 51
6	Barlow	3 62
7	Barnby Dun	5 60
8	(Bessacar Halt)	611 60
9	BOLTON·ON·DEARNE	34 40
10	Burton Salmon	3 42
11	Carcroft + Adwick-le-Street	56 50
12	Carlton	7 62
13	Castleford (Cutsyke)	1 42
14	CASTLEFORD	3 42
15	Darfield	4 40
16	Denaby Halt	8 50
17	DONCASTER	(5) 6 50
18	Featherstone	1 42
19	Ferrybridge for Knottingley	34 42
20	(FITZWILLIAM)	56 41
21	Frickley	34 40
22	Goldthorpe + Thurnscoe Halt	8 40
23	Great Houghton Halt	8 40
24	Grimethorpe Halt	8 40
25	Hampole	56 50
26	Harlington Halt	8 40
27	Heck	3 51
28	Hemsworth	56 41
29	Hemsworth + South Kirkby	7 41
30	HENSALL	1 52
31	Hickleton + Thurnscoe	7 40
32	Kippax	3 42
33	Kirk Smeaton	7 51
34	KNOTTINGLEY	1 42
35	Ledston	3 42
36	Monk Fryston	3 52
37	MONKHILL	1 42
38	Moorhouse + South Elmsall	7 40
39	MOORTHORPE + South Kirkby	34 41
40	Moss	3 51
41	Norton	1 51
42	Nostell	56 41
43	Pickburn + Brodsworth	7 50
	PONTEFRACT	42
44	BAGHILL	34 42
45	MONKHILL	1 42
46	Tanshelf	1 42
47	SNAITH	1 02
48	Snaith + Pollington	57 62

STATIONS + HALTS (continued)

No	Name	Ry Ref
A 49	SOUTH ELMSALL	56 41
50	Sprotborough	7 50
51	STAINFORTH + HATFIELD	5 61
52	Sykehouse	57 61
53	Tanshelf	1 42
54	Temple Hirst	3 62
55	Thorpe·in·Balne	57 61
56	Upton + North Elmsall	7 41
57	Wath + Bolton	4 40
58	Wath·on·Dearne	5 40
59	Wath·on·Dearne	7 40
60	WHITLEY BRIDGE	1 52
61	Wombwell	5 40
62	Womersley	1 51

GOODS ONLY STATIONS

No	Name/Location	Ry Ref
G 1	Ackworth Moor Top	33 41
2	Balne Moor	7 51
3	Bramwith	56 60
4	Cherry Tree Lane	4 50
5	Fryston	3 42
6	Grimethorpe	8 40
7	Harlington	8 40
8	Hickleton	8 40
9	Houghton	8 40
10	Houghton Colliery	8 40
11	Knottingley	1 52
12	Marsh Gate	5 50
13	Warmsworth Lime	5 50
14	York Road - Doncaster	57 50

SIDINGS ETC

No	Company/Name/Location	Ry Ref
P 1	Featherstone Colliery	4X 42
2	Ackton Hall Colliery	4X 42
3	Whitwood Colliery	X 42
4	Whitwood Colliery	X 42
5	Allerton Main Collieries	X 42
6	Hemsworth Colliery	3356X 41
7	Grimethorpe Colliery	458X 40
8	Houghton Colliery	458X 40
9	Hickleton Main Colliery	78 40
10	Frickley Colliery	347X 40
11	Brodsworth Main Colliery	7 50
12	Brodsworth Main Colliery	56 50
13	Bullcroft Colliery	57 50
14	Bentley New Colliery	57 50
15	Bentley New Colliery	6 50
16	Whitwood Branch	3 42

SHEDS

No	Location	Ry Ref
E 1	Doncaster	6 50

COMPANY WORKS

No	Location	Ry Ref
C 1	Doncaster	6 50

TUNNELS

No	Name/Location	Length Yards	Ry Ref
T 1	Brierley	685	7 41
2	Barnsdale	1226	7 41
			42

JUNCTIONS

No	Name/Location	Ry Ref	No	Name/Location	Ry Ref
J 1	Whitwood	3 42	J 41	Joan Croft	3 51
2	Whitwood Branch	3 42	42	Askern	136 50
3	Castleford East Branch	3 42	43	Applehurst	356 50
4	Castleford Old Station	3 42	44	Bullcroft Colliery	56 50
5	Don Pedro	4 42	45	Bullcroft	56 50
6	Featherstone	4 42	46	Castle Hills	56 50
7	Colliery Line	1X 42	47	Bentley New Colliery	6 50
8	Monkhill	1 42	48	Kirk Sandal	513456 60
9	Cutsyke	13 42	49	Bentley	5 50
10	Castleford New Station	3 42	50	Marsh Gate	5 50
11	Ferrybridge	334 42	51	Doncaster North Jcts	6565 50
12	For Ferrybridge	1 42	52	Doncaster S (St James)	65 50
13	For Doncaster	1 42	53	Balby	65 50
14	Goods Loop North	1 42	54	Decoy	6 50
15	Goods Loop South	1 42	55	Potteric Carr	613456 50
16	Pontefract Baghill	34 42	56	Low Ellers	13456 60
17	Burton Salmon	3 42	57	Black Carr	6611 60
18	Brayton East	3 62	58	Bessacarr	6118 60
19	Temple Hirst	30 62	59	Sprotboro North	575 50
20	Hensall	17 62	60	Sprotboro South	575 50
21	Gowdall	7 62	61	Sprotboro South	5 50
22	Aire	757 62	62	Sprotboro North	5 50
23	Brackenhill	3433 41	63	Hexthorpe	5 50
24	Hemsworth Colliery	56 41	64	Avoiding Line	5 50
25	Brierley	78 41	65	Cadeby Colliery	8 50
26	South Kirkby North	567 41	66	Mexborough West	345 40
27	South Kirkby East	7 41	67	Swinton	45 40
28	South Kirkby Main	3456 41	68	Bolton Line	54 40
29	Moorthorpe North	34 41	69	Dearne South	34 40
30	South Elmsall	3466 41	70	Dearne North	334 40
31	Moorthorpe South	34 41	71	Elsecar	5 40
32	Hinchcliffe	34X 40	72	Hickleton South	348 40
33	Hampole	56 40	73	Thurnscoe	8 40
34	Wranglebrook West	7 41	74	Hickleton Colliery	7 40
35	Wranglebrook East	7 41	75	Houghton Colliery	4X 40
36	Moorhouse North	756 40	76	Houghton Colliery	8 40
37	Moorhouse South	7X 40	77	Grimethorpe	8 40
38	Adwick	56 50	78	Grimethorpe Joint Line	45 40
39	Skellow	56 50	79	Starrs Mill	4 40
40	Carcroft	56 50	80	Grimethorpe	5 40

NOTES:

(1) REFERENCES - All in square SE

(2) BRITISH RAIL - New Main Line   Junction in Red is new BR Junct.

(3) JUNCTIONS - Not all identified but a fairly full selection has been included.

(4) AXHOLME EXT - Never completed.

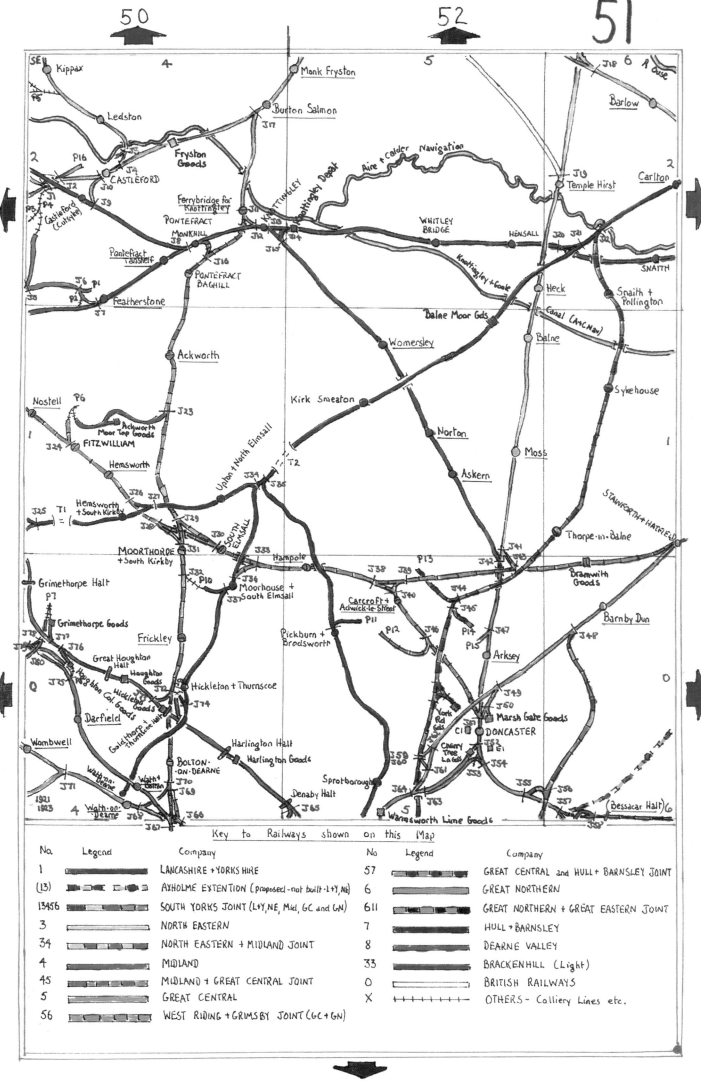

Key to Railways shown on this Map

No.	Legend	Company		No.	Legend	Company
1		LANCASHIRE + YORKSHIRE		57		GREAT CENTRAL and HULL + BARNSLEY JOINT
(13)		AXHOLME EXTENTION (proposed - not built - L+Y, NE)		6		GREAT NORTHERN
13456		SOUTH YORKS JOINT (L+Y, NE, Mid, GC and GN)		611		GREAT NORTHERN + GREAT EASTERN JOINT
3		NORTH EASTERN		7		HULL + BARNSLEY
34		NORTH EASTERN + MIDLAND JOINT		8		DEARNE VALLEY
4		MIDLAND		33		BRACKENHILL (Light)
45		MIDLAND + GREAT CENTRAL JOINT		0		BRITISH RAILWAYS
5		GREAT CENTRAL		X		OTHERS - Colliery Lines etc.
56		WEST RIDING + GRIMSBY JOINT (GC + GN)				

52
RAILWAYS

No	Name of Company
R3	NORTH EASTERN
22	DERWENT VALLEY
0	BRITISH RAIL

STATIONS + HALTS

No	Name	Ry Ref
A 1	Beningbrough	3 55
2	Bolton Percy	3 54
3	Cawood	3 53
4	CHURCH FENTON	3 53
5	Cliff Common	3 63
6	Cliff Common	22 63
7	Copmanthorpe	3 54
8	Cottingwith	22 64
9	Dunnington	22 65
10	Dunnington Halt (Kexby)	22 65
11	Earswick	3 65
12	Elvington	22 64
13	Escrick	3 64
14	Hambleton	3 53
15	Haxby	3 65
16	Hemingbrough	3 63
17	Hessay	3 55
18	Holtby	3 65
19	Layerthorpe	22 65
20	Marston Moor	3 55
21	Menthorpe Gate	3 63
22	Monk Fryston	3 53
23	Murton Lane	22 65
24	Naburn	3 64
25	POPPLETON	3 55
26	Riccall	3 63
27	(Rowntree Halt) (2)	3 65
28	SELBY	3 63
29	Sherburn-in-Elmet	3 53
30	Skipwith	22 63
31	SOUTH MILFORD	3 43
32	Thorganby	22 64
33	ULLESKELF	3 54
34	Warthill	3 65
35	Wheldrake	22 64
36	Wistow	3 53
37	YORK	3 55
38	York-Layerthorpe	3 63

GOODS

No	Name/Location	Ry Ref
G 1	Foss Islands	3 65
2	Thorp Gates	3 53
3	York Central	3 55

SIDINGS

No	Name/Location	Ry Ref
P 1	Rowntree Works	3 X 65

SHEDS

No	Location	Ry Ref
E 1	York	3 55
2	Selby	3 63

JUNCTIONS

No	Name/Location	Ry Ref
J 1	Poppleton (Skelton)	3 64
2	Severus	3 55
3	North	3 55
4	Holgate Bridge	3 55
5	Bootham	3 65
6	Burton Lane	3 53
7	Foss Islands	3 22 65
8	Layerthorpe	22 65
9	(York)	3 55
10	(York)	3 55
11	(York)	3 55
12	(York)	3 55
13	Rowntree	3 X 65
14	Church Fenton North	3 53
15	Church Fenton South	3 53
16	Sherburn	3 53
17	Gascoigne Wood	3 53
18	Milford	3 53
19	Thorp	3 53
20	Wistow-London Road	3 63
21	Wistow	3 63
22	Brayton North	3 63
23	Brayton East	3 63
24	Selby - Station	3 63
25	Selby - West	3 63
26	Selby - East No 1	3 63
27	Selby - East No 2	3 63
28	Cliff Common	3 22 63
29	Cliff Common DV	22 63
30	Colton	30 54
31	Hambleton - West	30 53
32	Hambleton - North	30 53
33	Hambleton - South	30 53
34	Hambleton - East	30 53
35	Chaloner's Whin	3 54

NOTES:

(1) REF - All in square SE

(2) Rowntree Halt - open for some casual passenger traffic

(3) British Rail New Main Line

Junctions in Red

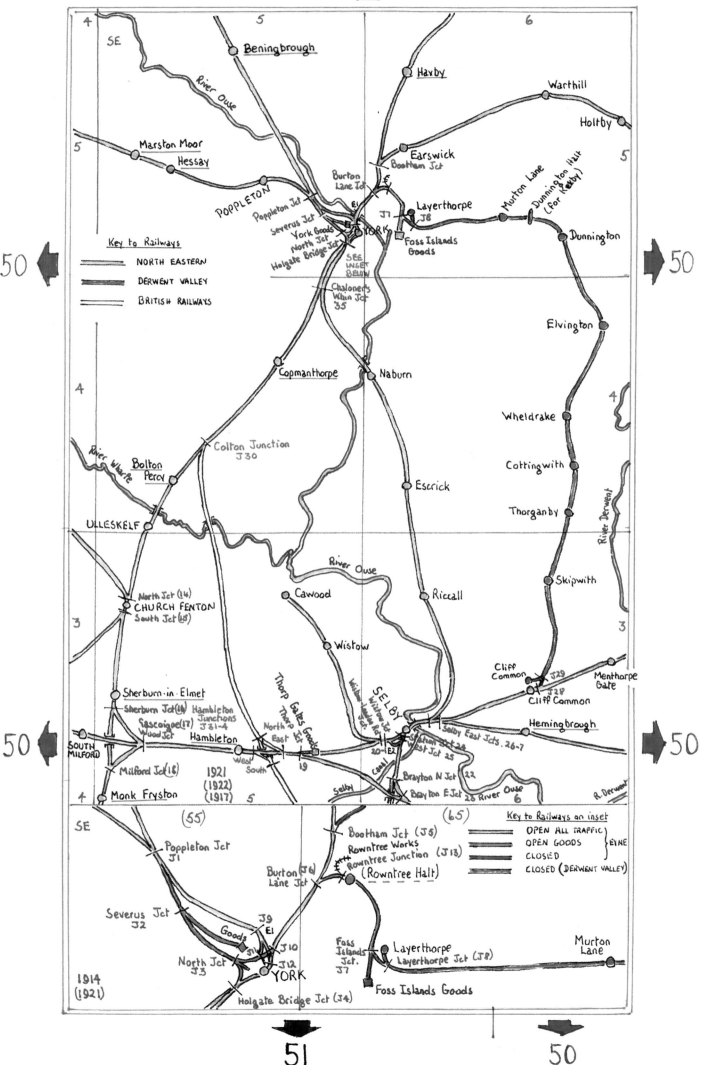

4   5   6

SE

Beningbrough

River Ouse

Haxby

Warthill

Holtby

Marston Moor
Hessay

Earswick

Bootham Jct

Murton Lane

Dunnington Halt
(for Kexby)

5   5

Burton
Lane Jct

POPPLETON

Poppleton Jct

Severus Jct
York Goods
North Jct
Holgate Bridge Jct

E1
J7
J8

YORK

Layerthorpe

Foss Islands
Goods

Dunnington

50   50

SEE
INSET
BELOW

Chaloners
Whin Jct
35

Elvington

Copmanthorpe

Naburn

4   4

Wheldrake

River Wharfe

Bolton
Percy

Colton Junction
J30

Cottingwith

Escrick

Thorganby

River Derwent

ULLESKELF

River Ouse

Skipwith

North Jct (14)
CHURCH FENTON
South Jct (15)

Cawood

Riccall

3   3

Wistow

Cliff
Common

J29

Menthorpe
Gate

Sherburn-in-Elmet

Thorp Gates Goods

Thorp Jct

SELBY

J28

Cliff Common

Sherburn Jct (16)
Gascoigne (17)
Wood Jct

Hambleton
Junctions
J31-4

North
East Jct

Wistow Leeds Jct

Wistow Jct

Selby East Jcts. 26-7

Hemingbrough

50   50

SOUTH
MILFORD

Hambleton

West
South

19

20-E2

Selby
West Jct 25

Selby North Jct 24

Milford Jct (18)

1921
(1922)
(1917)

West

Brayton N Jct   22

Monk Fryston   5

Selby

Canal

Brayton E Jct 23   River Ouse   6

R. Derwent

53

HUMBERSIDE

RAILWAYS

No	Company
R12	AXHOLME JOINT (Lancs + Yorks and NE)
2	NORTH EASTERN
23	NORTH EASTERN and HULL + BARNSLEY JT
3	HULL + BARNSLEY
5	GREAT CENTRAL
6	GREAT NORTHERN

STATIONS

No.	Name	Ry Ref
A 1	ALTHORPE	5 SE81
2	Appleby	5 SE91
3	ARRAM	2 TA03
4	Bainton	2 SE95
5	BARNETBY	5 TA00
6	BARROW HAVEN	5 TA02
7	BARTON (-ON-HUMBER)	5 TA02
8	BEVERLEY	2 TA03
9	Beverley Road	3 TA03
✳	(Boothferry Park)	3 TA02
11	Botanic Gardens	2 TA02
12	BRIDLINGTON	2 TA16
13	BRIGG	5 TA00
14	BROCKLESBY	5 TA11
15	BROOMFLEET	2 SE82
16	BROUGH	2 SE92
17	Burdale	2 SE86
18	Burton Agnes	2 TA16
19	Burton Constable	2 TA13
20	Cannon Street	3 TA02
21	Carnaby	2 TA16
22	Cherry Burton	2 SE94
23	CLEETHORPES	5 TA30
25	COTTINGHAM	2 TA03
26	DRIFFIELD	2 TA05
27	East Halton	5 TA12
28	ELSHAM	5 TA01
29	Enthorpe	2 SE94
30	Everingham	2 SE84
31	FERRIBY	2 SE92
32	Flamborough	2 TA16
33	Fockerby	12 SE81
34	Frodingham + SCUNTHORPE	5 SE81
35	Garton	2 SE95
36	GILBERDYKE §99	2 SE82
37	GOXHILL	5 TA02
37A	GREAT COATES	5 TA21
	GRIMSBY	
38	DOCKS	5 TA21
39	Pier	5 TA21
40	TOWN	5 TA20
41	HABROUGH	5 TA11
42	HEALING	5 TA21

No	Name	Ry Ref
43	Hedon	2 TA12
44	HESSLE	2 TA02
45	Holton-le-Clay	6 TA20
46	Hornsea	2 TA24
47	Hornsea Bridge	2 TA14
48	Howsham	5 TA00
	HULL	
49	Beverley Road	3 TA03
50	Botanic Gardens	2 TA02
51	Cannon Street	3 TA02
52	Newington ✳	2 TA02
53	PARAGON	2 TA02
54	Riverside Quay	2 TA02
55	Southcoates	2 TA12
56	Stepney	2 TA02
57	Wilmington	2 TA03
✳	(Boothferry Park)	3 TA02
58	HUTTON CRANSWICK	2 TA05
59	Immingham W Jetty	5 TA21
60	Keyingham	2 TA22
61	Killingholme	5 TA11
62	Kipling Cotes	2 SE94
63	KIRTON LINDSEY	5 SE90
64	Little Weighton	3 SE93
65	Lockington	2 TA04
66	Londesborough	2 SE84
67	Lowthorpe	2 TA06
68	Luddington	12 SE81
69	Marfleet	2 TA12
70	Market Weighton	2 SE84
71	(Melton)	2 SE92
72	Middleton-on-the-Wolds	2 SE95
73	Moortown	5 TA00
74	NAFFERTON	2 TA05
75	NEW CLEE	5 TA20
76	NEW HOLLAND	5 TA02
77	Newington ✳	2 TA02
78	Newport	3 SE83
79	North Cave	3 SE83
80	North Grimston	2 SE86
81	North Kelsey	5 TA00
82	Nunburnholme	2 SE84
83	Ottringham	2 TA22
84	PARAGON	2 TA02
85	Patrington	2 TA32
86	Riverside Quay	2 TA02
87	Rye Hill	2 TA22
88	Sandholme	3 SE83
89	Scawby + Hibaldstow	5 SE90
90	Scunthorpe	5 SE81
91	SCUNTHORPE (Frodingham +)	SE81
92	Settrington	2 SE86
93	Sigglesthorne	2 TA14

No	Name	Ry Ref
94	Skirlaugh	2 TA12
95	Sledmere + Fimber	2 SE96
96	Southburn	2 SE95
97	South Cave	3 SE93
98	Southcoates	2 TA12
99	STADDLETHORPE §36	2 SE82
100	STALLINGBOROUGH	5 TA21
101	Stepney	2 TA02
102	Sutton-on-Hull	2 TA13
103	Swine	2 TA13
104	THORNTON ABBEY	5 TA11
105	ULCEBY	5 TA11
106	Waltham	6 TA20
107	Wassand	2 TA14
108	West Halton	5 SE91
109	Wetwang	2 SE95
110	Wharram	2 SE86
111	Whitedale	2 TA14
112	Whitton	5 SE82
113	Willerby + Kirk Ella	3 TA03
114	Wilmington	2 TA03
115	Winteringham	5 SE92
116	Winterton + Thealby	5 SE91
117	Withernsea	2 TA32

GOODS

No	Name/Location	Ry Ref
G 1	Alexandra Dock	23 TA12
2	Grimsby - Coal	5 TA21
3	- Dock	5 TA21
4	- Gt. Northern	6 TA20
5	- Town	5 TA20
6	Guiness + Burringham	5 SE81
7	Immingham Dock	5 TA21
8	Keadby	5 SE81
9	Kilnwick Gate	2 TA04
10	King George Dock	23 TA12
11	Normanby Park	5 SE81
12	Neptune Street - Hull	3 TA02
13	Stoneferry	2 TA13
14	Winestead	2 TA22

SIDINGS ETC

No	Company/Location	Ry Ref
P 1	Gunhouse Wharf	5 SE81
2	New Holland Pier + Docks	5 TA02
3	Winteringham Haven	5 SE92

SHEDS

No	Location	Ry Ref
E 1	Immingham	5 TA11
2	Scunthorpe	5 SE91
3	Grimsby	5 TA20
4	New Holland	5 TA02
5	Bridlington	2 TA16

JUNCTIONS

No	Name/Location	Ry Ref
J 1	Keadby Goods	5 SE81
2	Goods Jcts (2)	5 SE81
3	Staddlethorpe	2 SE82
4	Market Weighton West	2 SE84
5	Market Weighton East	2 SE84
6	Frodingham	5 SE91
7	Wrawby South	5 TA00
8	Wrawby North	5 TA00
9	Docks Branch	5 TA02
10	Beverley	2 TA04
11	Driffield West	2 TA05
12	Driffield East	2 TA05
13	Brocklesby	5 TA11
14	Habrough	5 TA11
15	Ulceby North + South	5 TA11
16	Humber Road	5 TA11
17	Goods	5 TA11
18	East	5 TA11
19	Immingham West	5 TA11
20	Goxhill	5 TA12
21	Dock Lines West	5 TA20
22	Dock Lines North	5 TA20
23	Dock Lines East	5 TA20
24	Docks	5 TA21
25	Garden Street	5 TA20
26	Haven	5 SE92

NOTES:

(1) ✳ Boothferry Park is not located on this map - see map 54

(2) § Map name } Name Change
§ Modern name }

(3) ✳ Passenger Service discontinued before 1922

(4) ENLARGEMENT MAP - In the area covered by this map only passenger stations and a quite small selection of Goods stations. Other facilities - SEE 54

(5) NORTH EASTERN 'took over' the HULL + BARNSLEY PRIOR to grouping. Cannon Street - downgraded to a Goods only station in the 1920's. A new LMS connection was laid in Hull - details see Map 54

(6) Exact detail of all junctions in the Grimsby - Immingham area is NOT shown.

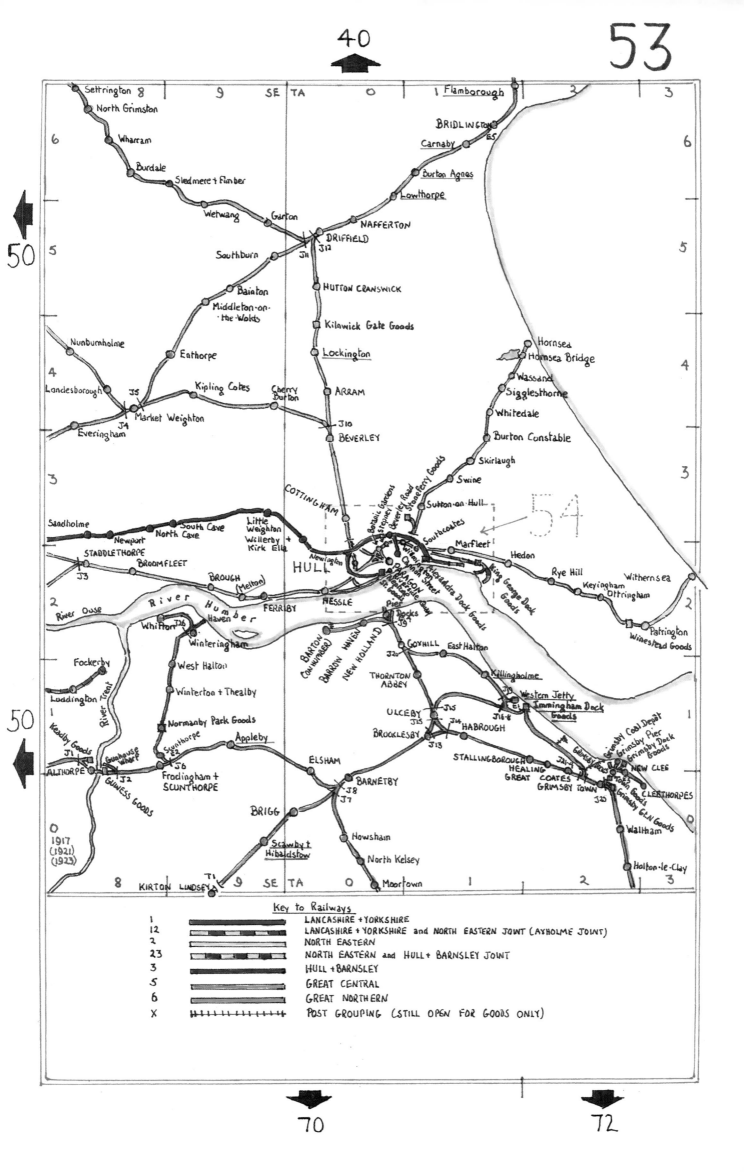

Key to Railways

1	▅▅▅	LANCASHIRE + YORKSHIRE
12	▅▅▅	LANCASHIRE + YORKSHIRE and NORTH EASTERN JOINT (AXHOLME JOINT)
2	▅▅▅	NORTH EASTERN
23	▅▅▅	NORTH EASTERN and HULL + BARNSLEY JOINT
3	▅▅▅	HULL + BARNSLEY
5	▅▅▅	GREAT CENTRAL
6	▅▅▅	GREAT NORTHERN
X	┼┼┼┼┼┼	POST GROUPING (STILL OPEN FOR GOODS ONLY)

RAILWAYS

No	Company
R 2	NORTH EASTERN
23	NORTH EASTERN and HULL + BARNSLEY
3	HULL + BARNSLEY
7	LMS (Post-grouping connections)
0	National Radiator Co (Private lines)

PASSENGER STATIONS

No	Name	Ry Ref
A 1	Beverley Road	3 O3
2	(Boothferry Park) ⚲	3 O2
3	Botanic Gardens	2 O2
4	Cannon Street ‡	3 O2
5	COTTINGHAM	2 O3
6	HESSLE	2 O2
7	Newington *	2 O2
8	PARAGON	2 O2
9	Marfleet	2 12
10	Riverside Quay	2 O2
11	Southcoates	2 12
12	Stepney	2 O2
13	Sutton-on-Hull	2 13
14	Wilmington	2 O3

ENGINE SHEDS

No	Name/Location	Ry Ref
E 1	Hessle Junction	2 O2
2	Botanic Gardens Jct	2 O2
3	Springbank	3 O2

BRIDGES + VIADUCTS

No	Name	Ry Ref
V 1	Hull Bridge	3 O3

GOODS STATIONS

No	Name/Location	Ry Ref
G 1	Albert Dock	2 O2
2	Alexandra Dock	3 12
3	Burleigh Street	3 12
4	Creek	2 O2
5	Dairycoates	3 O2
6	Dansom Lane Depot	2 12
7	Drypool	2 12
8	Drypool-Victoria Dock	2 12
9	Ella Street Coal	3 O3
10	Foreign Cattle Depot	2 12
11	King George Dock	23 12
12	Kingston Street	2 O2
13	Kingston Street (Central)	2 O3
14	Neptune Street	2 O2
15	St Andrews Dock	2 O2
16	Sculcoates	2 12
17	Sculcoates (Stepney)	2 O2
18	Stepney (Temple St.)	2 12
19	Stoneferry	2 O2
20	Wilmington	2 13

SIDINGS ETC

No	Company/Name/Location	Ry Ref
P 1	British Extracting Co	3 O3
2	Anglo-American Oil	2
3	Ashworth Kirk + Co	3 O3
4	Billingsgate Fish Mkt	23 O2
5	British Gas Light	3 O3
6	Bruce, J + Sons	2 O2
7	Co-op Wholesale	2
8	Corporation Waterworks	3
P 9	Earl's G+T	2 12
10	Earl's Shipbuilding	2 12
11	Earl's Shipbuilding	3 12
12	Hull Coal Supply	2 12
13	National Radiator Co	230 O2
14	National Wool Sheds	3 O3
15	Salt End Jetty	23 12
16	Fruit Warehouse	2 O2
17	St Andrews Timber Yard	2 O2
18	Railway Dock LNW +	2 O2
19	No 3 Quay -King George Dock	23 12
20	Timber Pools adj to Alexandra + Victoria Docks	O2 / 2 O2
21	Chalk Lane Sidings	3 O2

JUNCTIONS

No	Name/Location	Ry Ref
J 1	National Rad'r Co Siding	2 O2
2	National Rad'r Co Siding	O O2
3	National Wool Sheds Siding	3 O3
4	Goods	3 O3
5	Br Gas Light	3 O3
6	Br Extracting Co Siding	3 13
7	Withernsea Line	2 13
8	Stepney Goods	2 O2
9	Stepney Goods Temple St	2 O3
10	Goods	2 12
11	Dansom Lane	2 12
12	Southcoates North	2 12
13	Drypool	2 12
14	Southcoates South	2 12
15	Southcoates East	2 12
16	Dairycoates	2 O2
17	St Andrews Dock	2 O2
18	Boothferry Park	3 O2
19	New Curve	37 O2
20	Albert Dock	2 O2
21	Kingston Street	2 O2
22	Cottingham	2 O2
23	Springbank West	3 O2
24	Springbank North	3 O2
25	Springbank South	2 O2
26	Hessle	2 O2
27	(for Timber Yard)	2 O2
28	Liverpool Street	32 O2
29	Albert Dock	2 O2
30	Anlaby Road	2 O2
31	Victoria L.C	2 O2
32	Victoria Dock Branch	2 O2
33	West Parade	2 O2
34	Botanic Gardens	2 O2
35	Cottingham Branch	2 O2
36	Hessle Road	2 O2
37	Walton Street	27 O2
38	Ella Street	3 O3
39	Beverley Road	3 O3
40	Burleigh Street Goods	3 12
41	Bridges	32 12
42	Hedon Road	2 12
43	Alexandra Dock	3 12
44	Joint Dock	223 12
45	Joint Dock Boundary	323 12
46	Stoneferry	2 13

NOTES:

(1) * Newington closed before 1922.

(2) ⚲ Boothferry Park - not opened until 1939 or later. Still used for occasional passenger trains.

(3) ‡ Cannon Street - Goods only from mid 1920's. With opening of LMS New Curve passenger trains diverted into PARAGON

(4) TA All references in square TA

(5) P Sidings where even approximate location uncertain are not on the map and no map reference is given.

(6) P21 Crane facilities available at Chalk Lane sidings.

(7) NORTH EASTERN merged with HULL + BARNSLEY pre-grouping.

(8) STATIONS also existed at Anlaby Road and Cemetery Road, close to Chalk Lane Sidings. Closed before 1904.

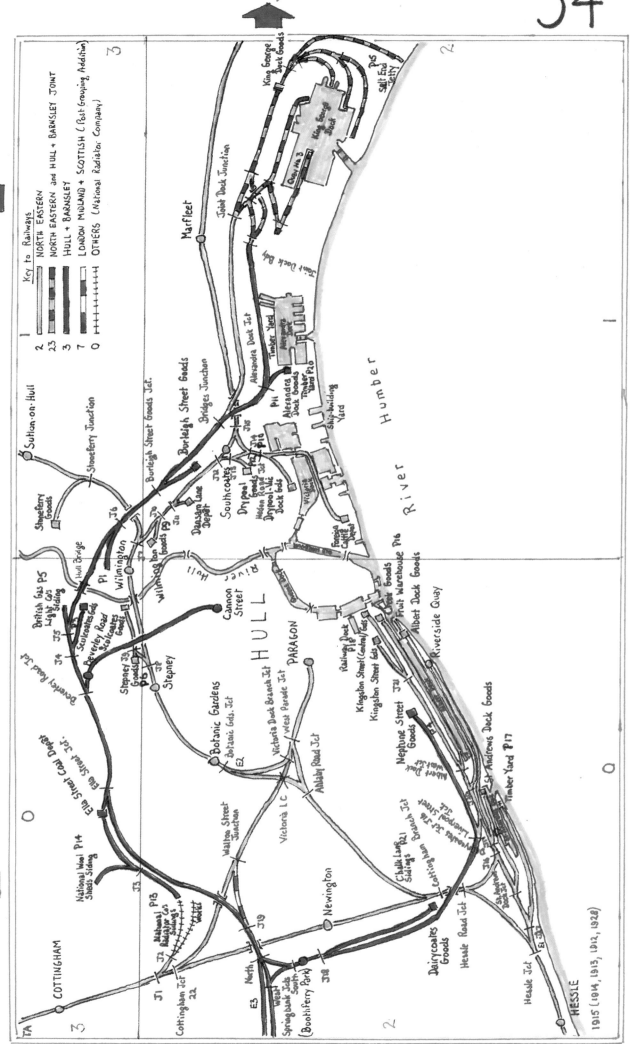

RAILWAYS

No.	Company	Gauge
R 1	LONDON + NORTH WESTERN	5
2	GREAT WESTERN	5
3	CAMBRIAN	5
4	FESTINIOG	1'11½"
5	NORTH WALES NARROW GAUGE	2'0"
6	PORTMADOC + CROESOR + BEDDGELERT	2'0"
7	WELSH HIGHLAND (See Note 2)	2'0"
8	SNOWDON MOUNTAIN	2'7½" Rack
X9	Other (Slate Tramways)	various

STATIONS

No.	Name	Ry Ref
A 1	Aber	1 67
2	ABERERCH	3 43
3	AFON WEN §70§	3 43
4	Amlwch	1 49
5	BANGOR	1 57
6	(Beddgelert)	7 54
7	Bethesda	1 66
8	Bettws Garmon	5 56
9	(Black Rock Halt)	1 53
10	BLAENAU FESTINIOG ‡	1 64
11	Blaenau Festiniog I	2 64
12	Blaenau Festiniog ‡	4 64
13	BODORGAN	1 37
14	BOSTON LODGE	4 53
15	Bryngwyn	5 45
16	Brynkir	1 44
17	Caernarvon	1 46
18	(CAMPBELL'S PLATFORM)	4 64
19	Cei Llydan	X 56
20	Ceint Halt	1 47
21	Chwilog	1 43
22	Clogwyn	8 65
23	CRICCIETH	3 43
24	Cwm-y-Glo	1 56
25	DDUALLT	4 64
26	Dinas	5 45
27	Dinas Junction	1 45
28	DUFFWS ‡	4 64
29	DYFFRYN (ANDUDWY)	3 52
30	Felin Hen	1 56
31	Festiniog	2 64
32	Gaerwen	1 47
33	Gilfach Ddu	X 56
34	Griffiths Crossing	1 46
35	Groeslon	1 45
36	(Hafod Garregog)	6 64
37	(Hafod Ruffydd)	7 55
38	(Hafolyllyn)	7 54
39	Halfway	8 65
40	HARLECH	3 53
41	Hebron	8 55
42	Holland Arms	1 47
43	HOLYHEAD	1 28
44	LLANBEDR	3 52
45	Llanbedr + PENSARN	3 52
46	Llanbedr Goch Halt	1 58
47	Llanberis	1 55
48	LLANBERIS	8 55
49	(LLANDANWG)	3 52
50	(LLANDECWYN)	3 63
51	Llanerchymedd	1 48
52	LLANFAIRFECHAN	1 67
53	LLANFAIR PG	1 57
54	Llangefni	1 47
55	Llangwyllog	1 48
56	Llangybi	1 43
57	Llanwnda	1 45
58	Maentwrog Road	2 63
59	Manod	2 64
60	Menai Bridge	1 57
61	MINFFORDD	3 53
62	MINFFORDD	4 53
63	Nantlle	1 45
64	(Nantmor)	7 54
65	Pant Glas	1 44
66	PENRHYNDEUDRAETH	3 63
67	PENRHYN (deudraeth)	4 63
68	PENSARN (Llanbedr)	3 52
69	Pentraeth	1 57
70	PEN-Y-CHAIN §3§	3 43
71	Pen-y-Groes	1 43
72	(Pitt's Head)	8 65
73	(PLAS HALT)	3 43
74	(Pont Groesor)	6 54
75	Pontrhythallt	5 56
76	Pont Rug (Halt)	1 46
77	Port Dinorwic	1 56
78	PORTMADOC	4 64
79	PORTMADOC	6 53
80	Portmadoc	6 53
81	PWLLHELI	3 33
82	Quellyn Lake	5 55
83	Red Wharf Bay + Benllech	1 58
84	Rhosgoch	1 48
85	RHOSNEIGR	1 37
86	Rhos Tryfan	5 45
87	Rhyd-y-Saint Halt	1 47
88	SNOWDON SUMMIT	8 65
89	(South) Snowdon	57 55
90	TALSARNAU	3 63
91	(TAL-Y-BONT)	3 52
92	TAN-Y-BWLCH	4 64
93	TAN-Y-GRISIAU	4 64
94	Tan-y-Manod	2 64
95	Trawsfynydd	2 63
96	Treborth	1 56
97	Tregarth	1 66
98	Tryfan Junction	5 45
99	TY-CROES	1 37
100	(TY-GWYN Halt)	3 63
101	VALLEY	1 27
102	Waenfawr	5 55
103	Ynys	1 44
104	(Ynys for)	6 64

GOODS

No.	Name/Location	Ry Ref
G 1	Holyhead	1 28
2	Holyhead Cattle	1 28
3	Pwllheli	3 33
4	Wern	3 53

SIDINGS

No.	Location	Ry Ref
P 1	Croesor	6 64
2	Nantlle	1X 45
3	Llanberis	X 56

ENGINE SHEDS

No.	Name/Location	Ry Ref
E 1	Holyhead	1 28
2	Bangor	1 57
3	Trawsfynydd	2 63

TUNNELS

No.	Name	Length	Ry Ref
T 1	Belmont		1 57
2	Bangor		1 57
3	Festiniog	3858	1 64

JUNCTIONS

No.	Name/Location	Ry Ref
J 1	Holyhead Goods	1 28
2	Holland Arms	1 47
3	Gaerwen	1 47
4	Afonwen Line	1 57
5	Bethesda	1 57
6	Llanberis Line	1 46
7	Afon Wen	31 43
8	Pen-y-Groes	1 45
9	Tryfan	5 45
10	Hafod Garregog	67 64

BRIDGES + VIADUCTS

No.	Name	Ry Ref
V 1	Stanley Embankment	1 28
2	Britannia Tubular Bridge	1 57

NOTES:

(1) REFERENCES - All in square SH

(2) RAILWAYS - 5+6 combined c. 1920 to become Welsh Highland. The new company built previous projected line to link the two systems and opened stations on the old North Wales section to Portmadoc. A small section near Portmadoc is preserved.

(3) LLANBERIS LAKE RAILWAY - This is a preserved slate tramway operating between Gilfach Ddu at Llanberis and Cei Llydan.

(4) BLAENAU FESTINIOG ‡ Many changes. Present BR station on site close to DUFFWS. Both stations are now known as BLAENAU.

(5) NAME CHANGE § Map name § Modern name

(6) SITE CHANGE ₤

(7) SPELLING - Welsh names. There are many minor changes to the spelling of present day names, but spellings current in the 1920s are used.

(8) PRESERVED RAILWAYS - On this map a station name in capitals and underlined in green, eg BOSTON LODGE does NOT on this map indicate a BR and preserved station. It indicates a preserved railway station that has remained open.

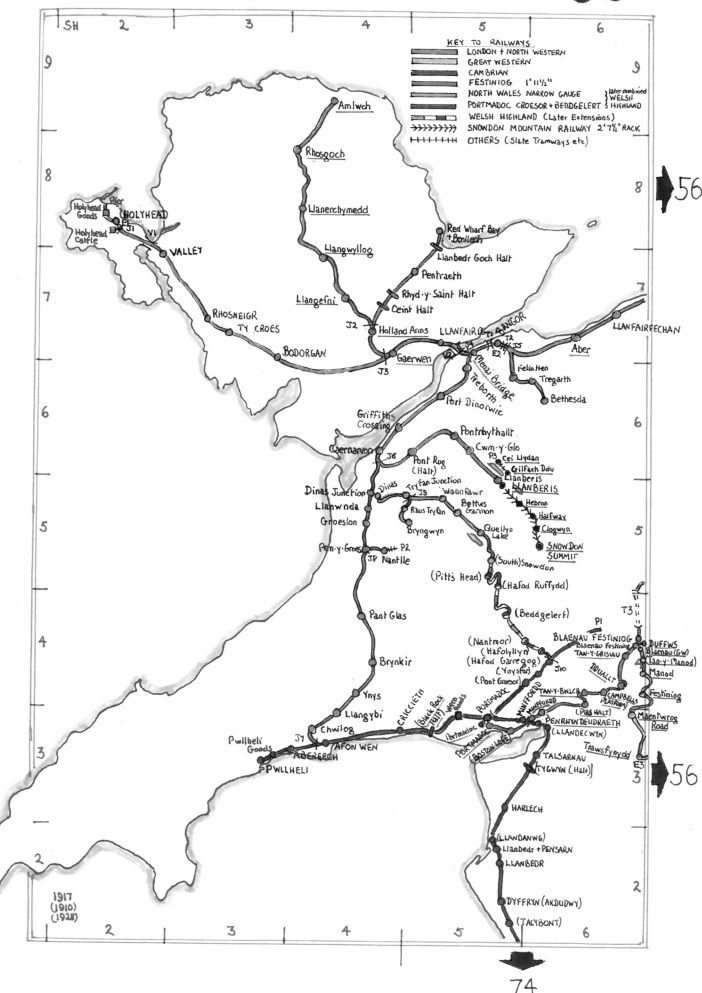

KEY TO RAILWAYS

LONDON + NORTH WESTERN
GREAT WESTERN
CAMBRIAN
FESTINIOG 1' 11½"
NORTH WALES NARROW GAUGE ⎱ later combined WELSH
PORTMADOC CROESOR + BEDDGELERT ⎰ HIGHLAND
WELSH HIGHLAND (Later Extensions)
SNOWDON MOUNTAIN RAILWAY 2' 7½" RACK
OTHERS (Slate Tramways etc)

SH 2 3 4 5 6

Amlwch
Rhosgoch
Llanerchymedd
Llangwyllog
Llangefni
Holland Arms
J2
RHOSNEIGR
TY CROES
BODORGAN
Gaerwen
J3
Red Wharf Bay + Benllech
Llanbedr Goch Halt
Pentraeth
Rhyd·y·Saint Halt
Ceint Halt
LLANFAIR C
BANGOR
Felin Hen
Tregarth
Bethesda
LLANFAIRFECHAN
Aber
Menai Bridge
Treborth
Port Dinorwic

HOLYHEAD
Holyhead Goods
Aber
Holyhead Cattle
VALLEY

Griffiths Crossing
Caernarvon
J6
Pont Rug (Halt)
Dinas Junction
Dinas
Tryfan Junction
J9
Waenfawr
Bettws Garmon
Rhos Tryfan
Bryngwyn
Quellyn Lake
Llanwnda
Groeslon
Pen·y·Groes
J8
Nantlle
P2
Pontrhythallt
Cwm·y·Glo
P3 Cei Llydan
Gilfach Ddu
Llanberis
LLANBERIS
Hebron
Halfway
Clogwyn
SNOWDON SUMMIT
(South) Snowdon
(Pitt's Head)
(Hafod Ruffydd)
(Beddgelert)

Pant Glas
Brynkir
Ynys
Llangybi
Chwilog
J7
AFON WEN
ABERERCH
PWLLHELI
Pwllheli Goods

(Nantmor)
(Hafolyllyn)
(Hafod Garregog)
(Ynysfor)
(Pont Croesor)
BLAENAU FESTINIOG
Blaenau Festiniog
TAN·Y·GRISIAU
J10
DDUALLT
DUFFWS
Blaenau (GW)
Tan·y·Manod
Manod
Festiniog
Maentwrog Road

P1
T3

CRICCIETH
(Black Rock Halt)
WERN Goods
PORTMADOC
PORTHMADOC
(Boston Lodge)
Portmadoc
MINFFORDD
Minffordd
TAN·Y·BWLCH
CAMPBELL'S PLATFORM
(Plas Halt)
PENRHYN DEUDRAETH
(Llandecwyn)
TALSARNAU
(Tygwyn (Halt))
E3

HARLECH
(Llandanwg)
Llanbedr + Pensarn
LLANBEDR
DYFFRYN (ARDUDWY)
(Talybont)

Trawsfynydd

1917
(1910)
(1928)

RAILWAYS

NORTH WALES

No	Company
R 1	LONDON + NORTH WESTERN
2	GREAT WESTERN
3	CAMBRIAN

STATIONS

No	Name	Ry Ref
A 1	ABERGELE (+PENSARN)	1 SH97
2	Arenig	2 SH83
3	Bala	2 SH93
4	Bala Junction	2 SH93
5	BETTWS·Y·COED	1 SH75
6	Bodfari	1 SJO7
7	Bont Newydd	2 SH72
8	Caerwys	1 SJ17
9	Carrog	2 SJ14
10	COLWYN BAY	1 SH87
11	Conway	1 SH77
12	Conway Marfa	1 SH77
13	Corwen	2 SJ04
14	Cwm Prysor	2 SH73
15	Cynwyd	2 SJ04
16	DEGANWY	1 SH78
17	Denbigh	1 SJ06
18	Derwen	1 SJ05
19	DOLWYDDELEN	1 SH75
20	Drws·y·Nant	2 SH82
21	Dyserth	1 SJ07
22	Eyarth	1 SJ15
23	Frongoch	2 SH93
24	Foryd	1 SH93
25	GLAN CONWAY	1 SH77
26	Glyndyfrdwy	2 SJ14
27	Gwyddelwern	1 SJ04
28	Holywell Junction	1 SJ27
29	Holywell Town	1 SJ17
30	Llandderfel	2 SH93
31	Llandrillo	2 SJ03
32	LLANDUDNO	1 SH78
33	LLANDUDNO JUNCTION	1 SH77
34	Llandulas	1 SH97
35	Llanfechain	3 SJ12
36	Llangedwyn	3 SJ12
37	Llangynog	3 SJ02
38	Llanrhaiadr	1 SJ06
39	Llanrhaiadr Monchnant	3 SJ12
40	LLANRWST (+Trefriw)	1 SH76
41	Llanuwychllyn	2 SH83
42	Llysfaen	1 SH87
43	Meliden	1 SJ08
44	Mochdre + Pabo	1 SH87
45	Mostyn	1 SJ18
46	Nannerch	1 SJ16
47	Nantclwyd	1 SJ15
48	Old Colwyn	1 SH87
49	Pedair·Ffordd	3 SJ12
50	PENMAENMAWR	1 SH77
51	Pentrefelin	3 SJ12
52	Penybontfawr	3 SJ02
53	PONT·Y·PANT	1 SH75
54	PRESTATYN	1 SJ08
55	Rhewl	1 SJ16
56	Rhuddlan	1 SJ07
57	Rhuddlan Road	1 SJ08
58	RHYL	1 SJ08
59	ROMAN BRIDGE	1 SH75
60	Ruthin	1 SJ15
61	St Asaph	1 SJ07
62	Talacre	1 SJ18
63	TAL·Y·CAFN (+Eglwys Bach)	1 SH76
64	Trawsfynydd	2 SH73
65	Trefnant	1 SJ07

GOODS

No	Location	Ry Ref
G1	Deganwy	1 SH77

ENGINE SHEDS

No	Location	Ry Ref
E1	Trawsfynydd	2 SH63
2	Llandudno Junction	1 SH87

SIDINGS ETC

No	Location	Ry Ref
P1	Rhyl Pier	1 SJ08

WATER TROUGHS

No	Location	Ry Ref
W1	Prestatyn	1 SJ08

BRIDGES

No	Name	Ry Ref
V1	Conway Tubular	1 SH77

JUNCTIONS

No	Location	Ry Ref
J1	St Georges	1 SH77
2	Llanrwst Line	2 SH87
3	Deganwy Goods	1 SH77
4	Rhyl - Denbigh Line	1 SJ08
5	Rhy - Pier Goods	1 SJ08
6	Dyserth	1 SJ08
7	Holywell	1 SJ27
8	Mold + Rhyl	1 SJ06
9	Corwen GW + LNW	21 SJ04
10	Corwen Station	2 SJ04
11	Bala	2 SH93

NOTES:

(1) SPELLING - Welsh place names shown as current 1920's

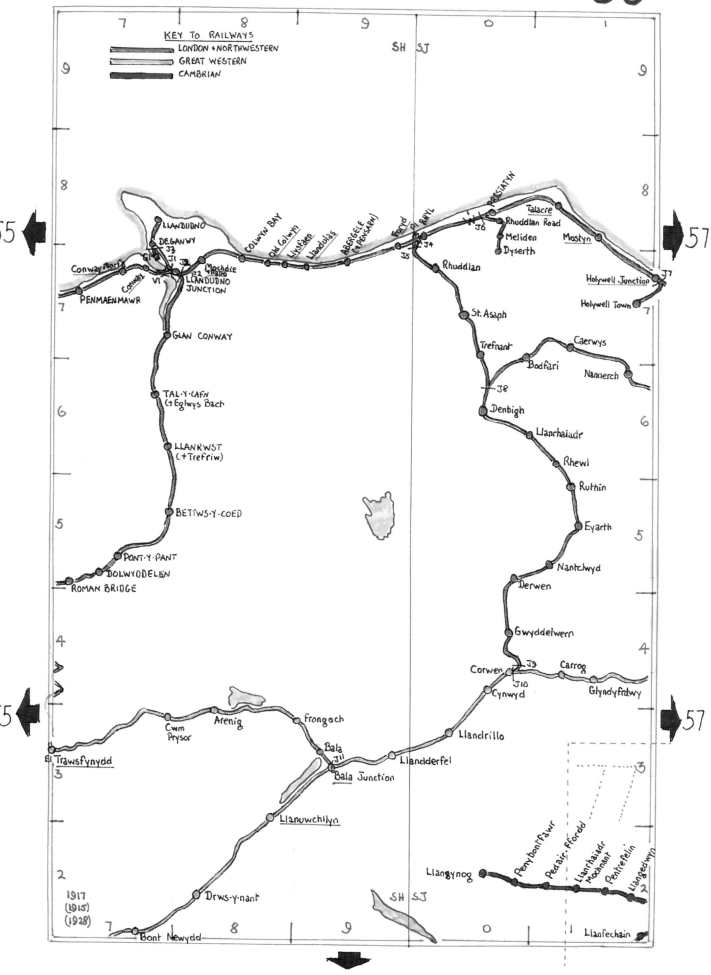

KEY TO RAILWAYS

LONDON + NORTHWESTERN
GREAT WESTERN
CAMBRIAN

SH SJ

55

57

LLANDUDNO
DEGANWY
Conway Morfa
Conway
PENMAENMAWR
COLWYN BAY
Old Colwyn
Llysfaen
Llandulas
ABERGELE (+PENSARN)
Foryd
RHYL
Talacre
Rhuddlan Road
Meliden
Dyserth
Mostyn
Holywell Junction
Holywell Town
J7
J8
J5
J4
Mochdre
LLANDUDNO JUNCTION
J3
J1
V1
E2
Rhuddlan

GLAN CONWAY
St. Asaph
Trefnant
Bodfari
Caerwys
Nannerch
J8
Denbigh

TAL·Y·CAFN
(+ Eglwys Bach)
Llanrhaiadr
Rhewl

LLANRWST
(+ Trefriw)
Ruthin

BETTWS·Y·COED
Eyarth

PONT·Y·PANT
DOLWYDDELEN
ROMAN BRIDGE
Nantclwyd
Derwen

Gwyddelwern

Corwen
Carrog
J9
J10
Glyndyfrdwy
Cynwyd

Cwm Prysor
Arenig
Frongoch
Llandrillo

El Trawsfynydd
Bala
J11
Llandderfel
Bala Junction

Llanuwchllyn

Llangynog
Penybontfawr
Pedair Ffordd
Llanrhaiadr Mochnant
Pentrefelin
Llangedwyn

Drws·y·nant

1917
(1915)
(1928)
Bont Newydd
Llanfechain

SH SJ

75

LIVERPOOL, OSWESTRY + CREWE

RAILWAYS

No	Company
R1	LANCASHIRE + YORKSHIRE
2	LONDON + NORTH WESTERN (LNW)
23	LNW + GW JOINT
25	M'CHESTER S JCT +A (LNW+GC)
3	GREAT WESTERN (GW)
4	MIDLAND (Mid)
45	SHEFFIELD + MIDLAND JT (Mid+GC)
456	CHESHIRE LINES C. (Mid, GC+GN)
5	GREAT CENTRAL (GC)
7	CAMBRIAN
8	NORTH STAFFORDSHIRE
9	MERSEY
11	WIRRAL
22	SHROPSHIRE + MONTGOMERY (Lgt)
33	GLYN VALLEY TRAMWAY (2'4½")
44	LIVERPOOL OVERHEAD

STATIONS

No 1–39

No	Name	Ry Ref
A1	Accrefair	3 24
2	ACTON BRIDGE	2 67
3	Adderley	3 64
4	AIGBURTH (Mersey Rd+)	456 38
5	AINTREE	1 39
6	Aintree	456 39
(58)	Alexandra Dock	44 39
7	Alexandra Dock	2 39
8	ALLERTON	2 48
(60)	Appleton	2 58
9	Arpley	2 68
10	Ashton-in-Makerfield	5 59
11	Audlem	3 64
12	(BACHE)	23 46
13	Bagillt	2 27
14	Balderton	3 36
(58)	Balliol Road	2 39
(58)	BANK HALL	1 39
15	Bangor-on-Dee	7 44
16	Barrow	456 47
17	Baschurch	3 42
18	BEBINGTON + New Ferry	23 38
19	Beeston Castle	2 56
20	Berwyn	3 24
21	Bettisfield	7 43
22	BIDSTON	115 29
23	(BIRCHWOOD)	456 69
	BIRKENHEAD	
(58)	CENTRAL	9 38
24	DOCKS §26	11 29
25	HAMILTON SQUARE	9 38
26	NORTH §24	11 29
27	PARK	911 38
(58)	Town	23 38
(58)	Woodside	23 38
28	Blacon	5 36
29	Blodwell Junction	7 22
30	BLUNDELLSANDS + CROSBY	1 39
(58)	BOOTLE	1 39
(58)	Balliol	2 39
(58)	NEW STRAND §163	1 39
(58)	ORIEL ROAD	1 39
* 31	BROAD GREEN	2 49
(58)	Brocklebank Dock	44 39
32	BROMBOROUGH	23 38
33	Broughton (+ Bretton)	2 36
34	Broxton	2 45
(58)	Brunswick Dock	44 38
35	Brymbo	3 35
(59)	Brymbo	5 35
36	BUCKLEY Junction	5 36
37	Burton Point	5 37
38	CAERGWRLE Castle	5 35
39	Caldy	23 28

No 40–104

No	Name
* (58)	Breck Road
40	Calveley
(58)	Canada Dock
41	CAPENHURST
42	Carr Mill
43	Castle Mill
44	Cefn
45	CEFN-Y-BEDD
	CHESTER
46	(BACHE)
47	GENERAL
48	Liverpool Road
49	Northgate
50	Childwall
51	CHIRK
52	Chirk
(58)	Clarence Dock
53	Clock Face
54	Caed Tallar
55	Collins Green
56	Cannah's Quay
57	Crank
58	CRESSINGTON
59	CREWE
60	CUDDINGTON
61	Culcheth
(58)	Custom House
62	Daresbury
63	DELAMERE
64	Dingle
65	DITTON Junction
66	Dolywern
67	Dunham Hill
68	EARLESTOWN
69	ECCLESTON PARK
70	EDGE HILL
(58)	Edge Lane
71	Ellesmere
72	ELLESMERE PORT
73	FARNWORTH §267
74	Farnworth + Bold
75	FAZAKERLEY
76	Fenn's Bank
77	Ffrith
78	Fiddlers Ferry + Penketh
79	FLINT
80	Ford
81	Frankton
82	FRODSHAM
83	GARSTON
(58)	Garston - Church Rd
(58)	Garston Dock
84	GARSWOOD
85	Gateacre for Woolton
86	Gerard's Bridge
(58)	Gladstone Dock
87	Glanyrafon
88	GLAZEBROOK
89	Glazebury
90	Glynceiriog
91	GOBOWEN
92	Golborne
93	Golborne
94	GREENBANK (Hartford+)
95	GREEN LANE
96	Gresford
97	GWERSYLLT
98	Hadlow Road
99	Hadnall
100	Halebank
101	Halewood
102	Halton
103	HARTFORD
104	Hartford + GREENBANK

No 105–171

Ry Ref	No	Name
2 39	105	HAWARDEN
2 56	106	(HAWARDEN BRIDGE)
44 39	107	Haydock
23 37	108	Haydock Park
2 59	109	HELSBY
33 23	(58)	Herculaneum Dock
3 24	111	Heswall
5 35	112	HESWALL Hills
	113	Hodnet
23 46	114	Holywell
23 46	115	HOOTON
5 46	116	Hope
456 46	117	Hope Exchange
456 48	(59)	Hope Junction
3 23	118	HOPE Village
33 23	119	HOUGH GREEN
44 39	120	HOYLAKE
2 59	121	HUNT'S CROSS
2 25	(58)	Huskisson Dock
2 59	122	HUYTON
2 37	123	Huyton Quarry
2 59	124	INCE + ELTON
456 38	(58)	James Street
2(8) 75	125	Johnstown + Hafod
456 67	126	Kenyon Junction
5 69	127	Kinnerley Junction
44 38	128	Kinnerton
23 58	129	Kirby Park
456 57	130	KIRKBY
44 38	(58)	KIRKDALE
2 48	131	Knotty Ash + Stanley
23 23	132	Latchford
23 47	133	Lea Green
2 59	134	LEASOWE
2 49	135	Ledsham
2 39	136	Legacy
2 39	137	Linacre Road
7 43	138	Liscard + Poulton
23 47	139	LITTLE SUTTON
456 58		**LIVERPOOL: (O=BR)**
2 58	140	CENTRAL
1 39	141	CENTRAL Low Level
7 57	142	Exchange
23 25	143	JAMES STREET
2 58	144	LIME STREET
1 27	(58)	(MOORGATE)
1 39	145	Llanfechain
7 33	146	Llanfynydd
23 57	147	Llangollen
456 48	148	Llansaintffraid
456 48	149	Llansilin Road
456 38	150	Llan-y-Blodwel
2 59	151	Llanynmech
456 48	152	Llanymynech Junct.
2 59	153	Llong
44 39	154	Llynclys
7 22	155	LOSTOCK GRALAM
456 69	156	Lowton
2 69	157	Lowton - St. Mary's
33 23	158	Lymm
3 23	159	Maesbrook
2 59	160	Malpas
5 59	161	(MANOR ROAD)
7	162	Marchwiel
9 38	163	Market Drayton
3 35	(58)	MARSH LN + STRAND RD §58
5 35	164	MEOLS
23 37	165	Mersey Rd + AIGBURTH
2 52	166	Mickle Trafford
2 48	167	Mickle Trafford
456 48	168	Minshull Vernon
23 57	169	Mold
2 67	170	Mollington
2 2	171	Moore

No 172–230

Ry Ref	No	Name
5 36	172	MORETON
5 37	173	Moss + Pentre
5 59	174	Moss Bank
2 38	175	MOSSLEY HILL
23 47	176	MOULDSWORTH
44 38	177	NANTWICH
23 28	(58)	Nelson Dock
5 28	177A	Neston
3 62	178	NESTON + Parkgate
2 27	179	NEW BRIGHTON
23 37	180	NEWTON-LE-WILLOWS
456(2) 67	181	NORTHWICH
23 58	182	NORTON §216
1 39	(58)	ORIEL ROAD
1 39	(58)	ORRELL PARK
456/45 48	(83)	Oswestry
11 28	184	Oswestry
456 48	185	Otters Pool
44 39	186	Over + Wharton
7 44	187	Overton-on-Dee
2 49	188	Padeswood + Buckley
23 47	189	PADGATE
7 22	190	Pant
3 34	191	Parkgate
2 69	192	Peasley Cross
22 32	193	Pennington
2 36	194	PEN-Y-FFORDD
23 28	195	Peplow
3 62	(58)	Pier Head
1 49	(59)	Plas Power
456 49	196	Plas Power
33 23	197	Pontfadog
2 68	198	Pontfaen
2 59	199	Porthywaen
7 22	(200)	(PORT SUNLIGHT)
23 38	201	PREES
2 53	202	Preesgweene
3 23	203	PRESCOT
2 49	204	Preston Brook
2 58	(58)	PRESTON ROAD §209A
1 39	(58)	Prince's Dock
44 39	205	Queensferry
2 36	(58)	Racecourse
1 39	206	RAINHILL
90 39	206A	Rednal + West Felton
3 32	207	Rhos
3 24	208	Rhostyllen
3 35	209	Rhydymwyn
2 26	(58)	(RICE LANE) §204A
1 39	(58)	Riverside
(2) 39	210	ROBY
2 49	211	ROCK FERRY
23(9) 38	212	Rookery
2 49	213	Rossett
3 35	214	RUABON
3 34	215	RUNCORN
2 58	216	RUNCORN EAST §182
23 58	217	ST HELENS
2 69	218	St Helens Central
5 59	219	ST HELENS JUNCTION
2 59	(58)	St James
2 54	220	ST MICHAELS
11 28	221	Saltney
2 36	222	Saltney Ferry
11 28	223	Sandycroft
2 58	224	Sankey Bridges
456 38	225	SANKEY (FOR PENKETH)
23 46	226	Saughall
11 39	227	Seacombe + Egremont
1 39	228	SEAFORTH + LITHERLAND
2 38	(58)	Sefton Park
2 36	229	Shotton
2 30	230	(SHOTTON)

No 231–276

No	Name	Ry Ref
231	SHOTTON + Connah's Quay	5 36
232	Speke	2 48
(58)	Spellow	2 39
233	SPITAL	23 38
(58)	Stanley	2 39
234	(STANLOW + THORNTON)	23 47
235	Storeton	5 28
(60)	Sutton Oak	2 59
236	Sutton Weaver	2 58
237	Tattenhall	2 45
238	Tattenhall Road	2 56
239	Tem Hill	3 63
240	THATTO HEATH	2 49
241	Thelwall	2 68
242	Thurstaston	23 28
(58)	Toxteth Dock	44 38
243	Trevor	3 24
(58)	Tue Brook	2 39
243A	Upton	5 28
244	WALLASEY GROVE RD	11 29
245	(WALLASEY VILLAGE)	11 29
(58)	Walton + Anfield	2 39
(58)	WALTON Junction	1 39
(58)	Walton-on-the-Hill	456 39
(58)	WALTON-PRESTON RD §	1 39
(58)	WALTON-RICE LANE §	1 39
(58)	Wapping	44 38
246	Warren	11 29
	WARRINGTON	
247	Arpley	2 68
248	BANK QUAY (High L)	2 68
(60)	Bank Quay Low Lev	2 68
249	CENTRAL	456 68
250	WATERLOO	1 39
251	Waverton	2 46
(58)	Wavertree	2 38
252	Welshampton	7 43
253	WEM	2 52
254	Wern Las	22 52
(58)	(WEST ALLERTON)	2 38
255	West Derby	456 39
256	WEST KIRBY	11 28
257	West Kirby	23 28
258	West Leigh + Bedford	2 69
259	WHITCHURCH	2(7) 54
260	Whitegate	456 66
261	Whitehurst	3 24
262	Whittington	3 33
263	Whittington	7 33
	WIDNES	
264	Central	45 58
265	LNW	2 58
266	Tanhouse Lane	2 58
267	(WIDNES) §73	456 58
268	Willaston	2 65
269	WINSFORD	2 66
270	Winsford + Over	456 66
271	Worleston	2 65
272	WRENBURY	2 64
273	WREXHAM CENTRAL	57 35
(59)	WREXHAM EXCHANGE	5 35
274	WREXHAM GENERAL	3 35
275	Wynn Hall (Halt)	3 24
276	YORTON	2 52

GOODS

No	Name / Location	Ry Ref
G1	Woodside	2 48
2	Helsby	456 47
3	Manley	456 57
4	Old Woods	3 42

NOTES:
See Gazetteer 58

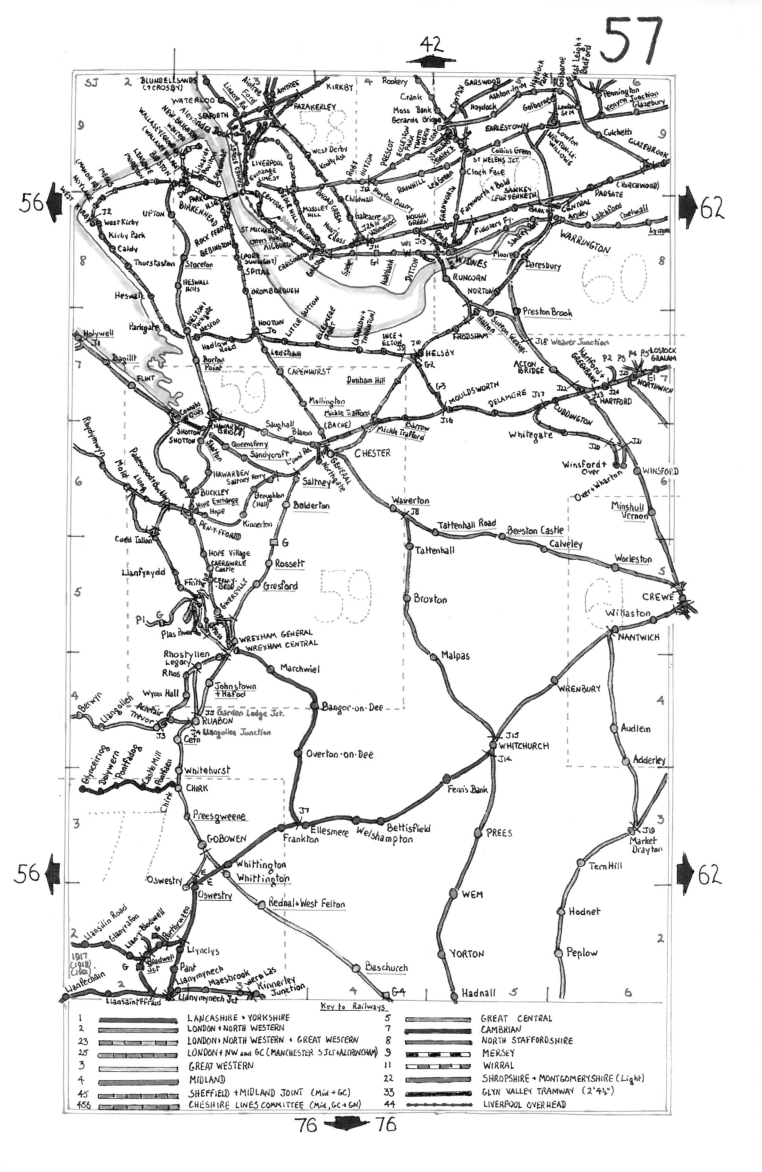

Key to Railways

1	LANCASHIRE + YORKSHIRE	5	GREAT CENTRAL
2	LONDON + NORTH WESTERN	7	CAMBRIAN
23	LONDON + NORTH WESTERN + GREAT WESTERN	8	NORTH STAFFORDSHIRE
25	LONDON + NW and GC (MANCHESTER S JCT + ALTRINCHAM)	9	MERSEY
3	GREAT WESTERN	11	WIRRAL
4	MIDLAND	22	SHROPSHIRE + MONTGOMERYSHIRE (Light)
45	SHEFFIELD + MIDLAND JOINT (Mid + GC)	33	GLYN VALLEY TRAMWAY (2'4½")
456	CHESHIRE LINES COMMITTEE (Mid, GC + GN)	44	LIVERPOOL OVERHEAD

LIVERPOOL + BIRKENHEAD

JUNCTIONS

No	Name/Location	Ry Ref
29	Jn Crown Street	2 139
30	Goods	1 139
31	Fazakerley West	456 139
32	Fazakerley South	456 139
33	Fazakerley North	456 139
34	Fazakerley	4564 139
35	Fazakerley	1 139
36	Aintree	1 139
37	Sefton	1 139
38	Walton	1 139
39	High Level Coal	1 139
40	Sandhills	1(2) 139
41	Bootle	1 139
42	Strand Road	1 139
43	Dock + Walton	1 139
44	Aintree Line	1 139
45	Lincare	1 139
46	Seaforth	1 139
47	Dock + Overhead	1 139
48	Lines Junctions	
49	(DISTRICT)	
50	Brassendale	456 38
51	Dock - West	2456 48
52	Dock - East	2 48
53	Speke	2 48
54	Hunts Cross West	456 48
55	Hunts Cross East	456 48
56	Allerton	2 48

No	Name/Location	Ry Ref
1	Rock Ferry	11 383
2	Mersey+Joint Line	11 383
3	Docks	25 383
4	Hamilton Square	9 383
5	Brook Street	23 383
6	Dee	5 293
7	Bidston - Neston	115 293
8	Bidston - West	11 293
9	Bidston - North	11 293
10	Bidston - East	11 293
11	Birkenhead Docks - North	11 293
12	Bidston - Goods	5 293
13	Seacombe	11 293
14	New Brighton No.1	11 293
15	New Brighton No.2	11 293
16	Slopes Branch	2 49
17	Seacombe Goods	1 293
18	Birkenhead Docks South	115 293
19	Dock Goods	11 293
20	(LIVERPOOL)	23 383
21	Egerton Street	4 139
22	Olive Mount	4 139
23	Derby Square	2 139
24	Paradise	1 139
25	Edge Lane	2 139
26	Wavertree	2 138
27	Goods	2456 138
28	Stanley Gattie	2 139

SIDINGS ETC

No	Comp/Name/Location	Ry Ref
P1	Wirral Foundry	X 383
2	Oil Depot	X 293
3	Gas + Water Works	X 393
4	Manure Works	X 393
5	Dukes Inlet	X 383
6	Vittoria Wharf Lines	456 393
7	Slopes Branch	5 393
8	Bibby + Sons	5 383
9	Blundell + Sons	23 383
10	Brown + Co	2 383
11	Hartleys Preserve Wks	456 383
12	Hulton Col Co	2 49
13	Leeds Fire Clay	1 293
14	Liverpool Corp Electric	2 393
15	Stubbs Flag Yard	2 138
16	Monks Ferry Shipbd Yd	23 383
17	Grain Storage Co	4 139
18	Lincare Gas Works	4 139
19	Wavertree Gas Works	2 139
20	Lord Derby's Yard	1 139
10	St Michaels	2 138
11	(Duke Street)	456 138
12	(Birkenhead Park)	2 139

SHEDS

No	Name/Location	Ry Ref
E1	Edgehill	4 139
2	Central	1 139
3	Aintree	1 139
4	Brunswick	2 138
5	Birkenhead	456 139
6	Birkenhead	2 383
7	Bidston	3 383
8	Walton-on-the Hill	5 293

WATER TROUGHS

No	Location	Ry Ref
W1	Kirkby	1 39

TUNNELS

No	Name (Location)	Ry Ref
T1	Mersey	4 39
2	Kirkdale	456 39
3	(Walton-on-Hill)	1 39
4	(Kirkdale)	2 39
5	Waterloo + Victoria	1 39
6	Russell Street	1 38
7	Mount Pleasant	2 38
8	Wapping	2 38
9	Dingle	1 38

NOTES (MAPS 57 + 58)

All stations in area covered are listed. Most are also located. Those not named are shown in BLUE; bracketed number (58) is reference to map on which it will be found.

(A) REFERENCES - all in square SJ
(B) LIVERPOOL OVERHEAD - Stations shown in red thus: Dingle
(C) NAME CHANGES - §Map Name §Modern Name; Part in small letters - that portion of name now dropped; Part in brackets - modern addition.
(D) LIVERPOOL STATIONS indexed only under own title except central area 139
(E) BIRKENHEAD STATIONS listed under own title shown thus 283
(F) DOCKS - Sketched in only - Gladstone Dock NOT SHOWN
(G) SIDINGS - Approximate site only is indicated; exact location uncertain. Information is as at 1904
(H) Names of some tunnels not known - no lengths available this area.

(1) MAP 57
(2) BOTH 57 + 58
(3) MAP 58

RAILWAYS

No	Company
R1	LANCASHIRE + YORKSHIRE
2	LONDON + NORTH WESTERN
23	BIRKENHEAD JOINT (LNW + GW)
3	GREAT WESTERN
4	MIDLAND
456	CHESHIRE LINES COM. (Mid, GC, LN)
5	GREAT CENTRAL
9	MERSEY
11	WIRRAL
44	LIVERPOOL OVERHEAD
0	BRITISH RAIL additions

STATIONS

No	Name	Ry Ref
A1	AIGBURTH (Mersey Rd)	456 38
2	AINTREE	1 139
3	Aintree	456 139
4	Alexandra Dock	44 139
5	Alexandra Dock	2 139
6	ALLERTON	2 48
7	Balliol Road	2 39
8	BANK HALL	1 39
9	BEBINGTON + New Ferry	23 38
10	BIDSTON	23 38
	BIRKENHEAD	
11	CENTRAL	383
12	DOCKS §14	9 383
13	HAMILTON SQUARE	9 383
14	NORTH §12	11 293
15	PARK	9 11 38
16	Town	23 38
17	Woodside	23 38
18	BLUNDELLSANDS + CROSBY	1 39
	BOOTLE	
19	Balliol Road	139
20A	NEW STRAND §	2 39
20B	MARSH LANE §	1 39
21	ORIEL ROAD	1 39
22	Breck Road	2 39
23	BROAD GREEN	2 49
24	Bracklebank Dock	44 38
25	Brunswick Dock	44 38
26	Canada Dock	44 39
27	Childwall	2 49
28	Clarence Dock	44 139
29	CRESSINGTON	456 38
30	Custom House	44 138
31	Dingle	44 138
32	EDGE HILL	2 39
33	Edge Lane	2 39
34	FAZAKERLEY	1 39
35	Ford	1 39
36	GARSTON	456 48
37	Garston - Church Rd	456 48
38	Garston - Docks	456 38
39	Gateacre for Woolton	456 48
40	Gladstone	
41	GREEN LANE	44 139
42	Herculaneum Dock	44 138
43	HUNT'S CROSS	456 48
44	Huskisson Dock	44 139
45	James Street	44 138
46	KIRKBY	1 39
47	KIRKDALE	1 139
48	Knotty Ash + Stanley	456 49
49	Lincare Road	1 39
50	Liscard + Poulton	11 39
	LIVERPOOL	
51	CENTRAL	456 139
52	CENTRAL Low Level	90 139
53	Exchange	1 139
54	JAMES STREET	90 139
55	LIME STREET	20 139
56	(MOORGATE)	0 139
57	MARSH LANE + STRAND RD §1	139
58	Mersey Road + AIGBURTH	456 38
59	MOSSLEY HILL	2 38
60	Nelson	44 139
61	NEW BRIGHTON	1 39
62	ORREL PARK	2 39
63	ORIEL ROAD	1 39
64	Otters Pool	1 39
65	Pier Head	1 39
66	PRESTON ROAD §69	2 39
67	Prince's Dock	2 49
68	Racecourse	44 139
69	RICE LANE §66	44 38
70	Riverside	44 139
71	ROBY	2 49
72	ROCK FERRY	23 383
73	St James	456 38
74	ST MICHAELS	456 38
75	SANDHILLS	1 139
76	Seacombe + Egremont	2 39
77	SEAFORTH + LITHERLAND	2 39
78	Sefton Park	1 39
79	Speke	1 39
80	Spellow	456 48
81	Stanley	456 48
82	Toxteth Dock	456 38
83	Tue Brook	456 48
84	(WALLASEY GROVE RD)	44 139
85	(WALLASEY VILLAGE)	9 383
	WALTON	
86	2nd Anfield	44 138
87	JUNCTION	44 139
88	on-the-Hill	44 139
89	PRESTON RD §90	1 49
90	RICE LANE	1 139
91	Wapping Dock	456 49
92	Warren	1 39
93	WATERLOO	11 39
94	Wavertree	139
95	(WEST ALLERTON)	456 139
96	West Derby	90 139

No	Name	Ry Ref
16	Crown Street	2 49
17	Wavertree + Edge Hill	23 383
18	Rathbone	456 38
19	Edge Hill	456 38
20	Stanley - Gattie	1 139
21	Brunswick	11 393
22	Garston	1 139
23	Garston Dock	2 38
30	Bidston	2 48
31	Birkenhead Dock	2 139
32	Seacombe	2 139
33	Great Float West	44 38
34	Dock Road	2 139
35	Duke Street	11 29
36	Cathcart Street	11 29
37	Egerton Dock	139
38	Shore Road	2 39
39	Monk Ferry	1 39
40	Tranmere Pool	456 139
41	Morpeth Dock	1 139

GOODS

No	Name	Ry Ref
G1	Alexandra Dock	4 139
2	North Mersey	1 139
3	Alexandra Dock	2 139
4	Alexandra + Canada Dock	5 139
5	Bankfield	1 139
6	Bootle Canada Dock	2 39
7	Sandon Dock	1 139
8	Huskisson	1 139
9	North Dock	456 38
10	Waterloo	44 139
11	Great Howard Street	1 139
12	Wapping/Salthouse	1 138
13	Park Lane	2 38
14	Brunswick Dock	2 38
15	South Docks	2 139

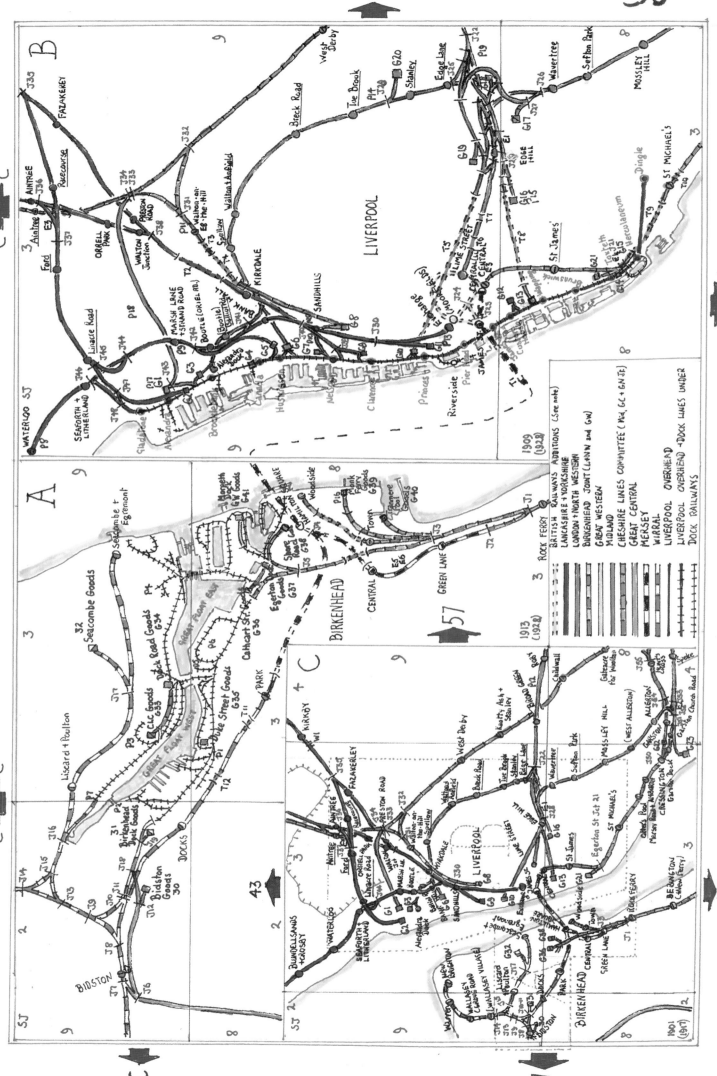

58

CHESTER + WREXHAM

RAILWAYS

No	Company (Owners)
R 2	LONDON + NORTH WESTERN
23	BIRKENHEAD JOINT (LNW + GW)
3	GREAT WESTERN
456	CHESHIRE LINES COMMITTEE (Mid, GC, GN)
5	GREAT CENTRAL
7	CAMBRIAN

NOTES:

(1) REFERENCES - All in Square SJ

(2) SHROPSHIRE UNION CANAL - owned by London + North Western

(3) SHOTTON STATIONS - 54 Origionally Goods station on this site as at map date (passenger station at that time was 53). 55 was known as Shotton + Connah's Quay.

(4) Hope Junction (29) also known as Hope + Pen·y·ffordd.

STATIONS

No	Name	Ry	Ref
A 1	(BACHE)	23	46
2	Balderton	3	36
3	Bangor·on·Dee	7	44
4	Barrow	456	47
5	Blacon	5	36
6	Broughton Hall	2	36
7	Brymbo	3	35
8	Brymbo	5	35
9	BUCKLEY Junction	5	36
10	Burton Point	5	37
11	CAERGWRLE Castle	5	35
12	CAPENHURST	23	37
13	CEFN·Y·BEDD	5	35
	CHESTER		46
14	(BACHE)	23	46
15	CHESTER General	23	46
16	Liverpool Road	5	46
17	Northgate	456	46
18	Coed Tallon	2	25
19	Connah's Quay	2	37
20	Dunham Hill	23	47
21	Ffrith	23	25
22	FLINT	2	27
23	Gresford	3	35
24	GWERSYLLT	5	35
25	HAWARDEN	5	36
26	(HAWARDEN BRIDGE)	5	37
27	Hope	2	36
28	Hope Exchange	5	36
29	Hope Junction	2	36
30	HOPE Village	5	35
31	Johnstown + Hafod	3	34
32	Kinnerton	2	36
33	Legacy	3	34
34	Llanfynydd	23	25
35	Llong	2	26
36	Marchwiel	7	34
37	Mickle Trafford	23	46
38	Mickle Trafford	456	46
39	Mollington	23	37
40	Moss + Pentre	5	35
41	Padeswood + Buckley	2	25
42	PEN·Y·FFORDD	5	36
43	Plas Power	3	35
44	Plas Power	5	35
45	Queensferry	2	36
46	Rhos	3	24
47	Rhostyllen	3	35
48	Rossett	3	35
49	Saltney	3	36
50	Saltney Ferry	2	36
51	Sandycroft	2	36
52	Saughall	5	36
53	Shotton	2	36
54	(SHOTTON)	2	36
55	SHOTTON + Connah's Quay	5	36
56	Waverton	2	46
57	WREXHAM CENTRAL	57	85
58	WREXHAM EXCHANGE	5	85
59	WREXHAM GENERAL	3	85
60	Wynn Hall	3	24
39A	Moss	3	45

GOODS

No	Name / Location	Ry	Ref
G 1	Brook Street	3	24
2	Buckley	5	26
3	Chester	3	46
4	Chester - Northgate	456	46
5	Coed Porth	3	25
6	Connah's Quay	5	37
7	Pulford	3	35
8	Saltney Wharf	2	36
9	Shotton (see note 3)	2	46
10	Wrexham Central	5	35

SIDINGS ETC

No	Company / Name / Location	Ry	Ref
P 1	Dee Oil Works	3	36
2	Saltney Wharf	3	36
3	Parry's Brick Works	5	26
4	Buckley Colliery	5	26
5	Brick + Tile Co. Works	5	26
6	Ashton's Brick Works	5	26
7	Lassell's Siding	5	35
8	Ffrwyd Iron Works	35	35
9	Minera Lime Works	3	25
10	Minera Lead Works	X	25
11	Ruabon Colliery	3	34
12	Vauxhall Colliery	3	34

SHEDS

No	Location	Ry	Ref
E 1	Chester	3	46
2	Chester	2	46
3	Saltney	2	36

TUNNELS

No	Name	Ry	Ref
T 1	Windmill Lane	2	46

BRIDGES

No	Name	Ry	Ref
V 1	Hawarden Bridge	5	37
2	Dee Bridge	2(3)	46
3	Bangor·on·Dee	7	44

JUNCTIONS

No	Name / Location	Ry	Ref
J 1	Connahs Quay West	25	27
2	Connahs Quay South	5	26
3	Connahs Quay East	2(5)	37
4	Shotton	5	36
5	Hawarden Bridge West	5	37
6	Hawarden Bridge North	5	37
7	Hawarden Bridge East	5	37
8	Chester West	5	46
9	Chester East	5456	46
10	Chester South	5456	40
11	Chester West	23	46
12	Chester South	23	46
13	Chester North	23	46
14	Manchester Line	232	46
15	New BR connections	0	46
16	Saltney	23	36
17	Dee	3	36
18	Saltney Ferry	2	36
19	Buckley	5	36
20	Mold	2	26
21	Ffrith	2	26
22	Hope West	25	26
23	Hope South	5	36
24	Coed Tallon West	2	26
25	Coed Tallon South	2	25
26	Coed Tallon East	2	26
27	Ffrwd	5	35
28	Plas Power	35	35
29	Brymbo Junction	323	35
30	Moss Valley	3	35
31	Wrexham North	35	35
32	Wrexham Colliery West	5	35
33	Wrexham Colliery East	5	35
34	Wrexham Colliery North	5	35
35	Wheatsheaf	3	35
36	Wrexham Mineral North	3	35
37	Wrexham Mineral West	3	35
38	Wrexham Mineral South	3	35
39	Wrexham South	3	35
40	Legacy	3	34
41	Wrexham Goods	5	35
42	Brymbo	5	35

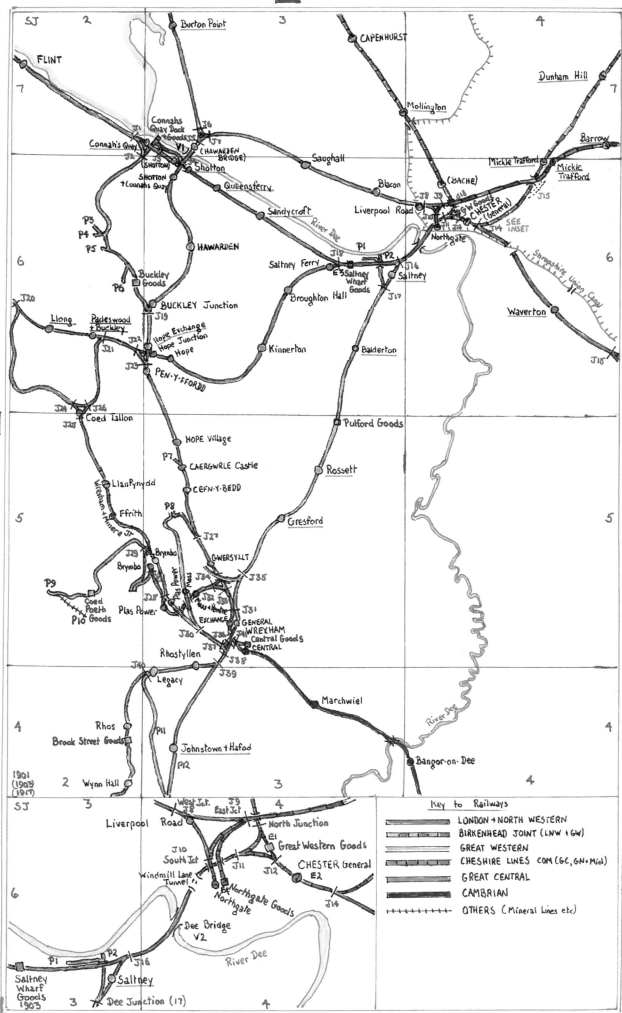

SJ   2   Burton Point   3   CAPENHURST   4

FLINT

Dunham Hill

7   Mollington   7

Connahs Quay Dock Goods   J6   Barrow

Connah's Quay   J1   V1   J7   Mickle Trafford

J2   (SHOTTON)   (HAWARDEN BRIDGE)   Saughall   (BACHE)   Mickle Trafford

SHOTTON + Connahs Quay   Shotton   Blacon   J8 J9   GW Goods   J15

         Queensferry   Liverpool Road   CHESTER (General)

P3   Sandycroft   Northgate   SEE INSET

P4   River Dee   J14

P5   HAWARDEN   P1   Shropshire Union Canal

6   Buckley Goods   Saltney Ferry   J18   E3 Saltney Wharf Goods   P2   Saltney   6

P6   Broughton Hall   J16   Waverton

J20   BUCKLEY Junction   J17

Llong   Padeswood + Buckley   J19   Kinnerton   Balderton   J15

         Hope Exchange   J22

J21   Hope Junction   Hope

J23   PEN-Y-FFORDD

J24   J26   Pulford Goods

57   J25   Coed Tallon   57

HOPE Village

P7   CAERGWRLE Castle   Rossett

Llanfynydd   CEFN-Y-BEDD

5   Ffrith   P8   Gresford   5

Wrexham + Minera Jt.   J27

      Brymbo   J29   GWERSYLLT

Brymbo   Plas Power Moss   J34   J35

P9   J28   J32 J33   J31

Coed Poeth   Plas Power   GW + Rhos   GENERAL

P10 Goods   EXCHANGE   WREXHAM

          J30   J36   Central Goods

Rhostyllen   J37   CENTRAL

4   Rhos   J40   J38   4

Brook Street Goods   Legacy   J39

        P11   Marchwiel

1901   Johnstown + Hafod   River Dee

(1907)   P12

(1917)   2   Wynn Hall   3   Bangor-on-Dee   4

SJ   3   West Jct.   J9   4

     J8   East Jct.

Liverpool Road   North Junction

              E1

      J10   Great Western Goods

   South Jct   J11   CHESTER General

Windmill Lane Tunnel   J12   E2

6   E3 Northgate Goods   J14   6

      Northgate

    Dee Bridge V2

           River Dee

P1   P2   J16

Saltney Wharf Goods 1903   Saltney

3   Dee Junction (17)   4

Key to Railways

	LONDON + NORTH WESTERN
	BIRKENHEAD JOINT (LNW + GW)
	GREAT WESTERN
	CHESHIRE LINES COM (GC, GN + Mid)
	GREAT CENTRAL
	CAMBRIAN
	OTHERS (Mineral Lines etc)

```
2 58
23,2 57
2 57
45,45 56 58
```

2 79 66 Runcorn
2 79 67 Frodsham
2 79 68 Weaver
2 58 69 Widnes

NOTES:-
All in square SJ
§ Map date name - number is cross-reference to the modern name
§ Modern name - number is cross-reference to the Map date name
Part of Name small letters shows this part of name now dropped
Part of Name in brackets shows a later addition to the title.
To show junction details more clearly in these areas.

(1) REFERENCES -
(2) NAME CHANGES
(3) ENLARGEMENTS

RAILWAYS

No.	Company	Ry Ref
R 2	LONDON + NORTH WESTERN (LNW + GW)	
23	BIRKENHEAD JT (LNW + GW)	
456	CHESHIRE LINES (Mid, GC, + GN)	
5	GREAT CENTRAL	
45	SHEFFIELD + MIDLAND JT. (Mid + GC)	
2.5	MANCHESTER SOUTH JUNCTION AND ALTRINCHAM (LNW + GC)	

STATIONS

No.	Name	Ry Ref
A 1	ALTRINCHAM + Bowden	2.5 78
2	Appleton	2.58
3	Arpley	2.68
4	ASHLEY	456 78
5	Ashton-in-Makerfield	5.59
6	Ashley	2.79
7	Baguley	456 78
8	Barton Moss	2.79
9	(BIRCHWOOD)	456 69
10	Broadheath	2.78
11	BROOKLANDS	2.5 79
12	Cadishead	456 79
13	Carr Mill	2.59
14	(CHASSEN ROAD)	456 79
15	Collins Green	2.59
16	Clock Face	2.59
17	Crank	2.59
18	Culcheth	2.69
19	(DANE ROAD)	2.5 79
20	Daresbury	23.58
21	(DERBYSHIRE LANE)	456 79
22	DITTON	2.48
23	Dunham Massey	2.78
24	EARLESTOWN	2.59
25	ECCLES	2.79
26	FARNWORTH §94	456.58
27	Farnworth + Bold	2.58
28	Fiddler's Ferry + Penketh	2.58
29	FLIXTON	456 79
30	FRODSHAM	23.57
31	GARSWOOD	2.59
32	Gerard's Bridge	2.59
33	GLAZEBROOK	456 69
34	Glazebury	2.69
35	Golborne	2.69
36	Golborne	5.69
37	HALE §62	456 78
38	Halton	23.57
39	Haydock	5.59
40	Haydock Park	5.59
41	Healey + Warburton	2.78
42	IRLAM	456 79
43	Kenyon Junction	2.69
44	KNUTSFORD	456 77
45	Latchford	2.68
46	Lea Green	2.59
47	Leigh + Bedford	2.69
48	Lowton	5.59
49	Lowton St Mary's	2.68
50	Lymm	456 78
51	MOBBERLEY	2.79
52	Manton Green	2.58
53	Moore	2.59
54	Mass Bank	2.59
55	(NAVIGATION ROAD)	2.5 79
56	NEWTON-LE-WILLOWS	456 79
57	NORTON §65	2.59
58	PADGATE	456 79
59	Partington	2.59
60	PATRICROFT	2.59
61	Peasley Cross	2.59
62	PEEL CAUSEWAY §57	2.69
63	Pennington	2.5 79
64	Preston Brook	23.58
65	RUNCORN EAST §57	456 79
66	RUNCORN	2.48
67	ST HELENS	2.78
68	St Helens Central	2.59
69	ST HELENS JUNCTION	2.79
70	SALE + Ashton-on-Mersey	456.58
71	Sankey Bridges	2.58
72	SANKEY (for PENKETH)	2.58
73	Seedley	456 79
74	STRETFORD	23.57
75	Sutton Oak	2.59
76	Sutton Weaver	2.59
77	Tanhouse Lane	456 69
78	Thelwall	2.69
79	TIMPERLEY	2.69
80	TRAFFORD PARK	5.69
81	URMSTON	456 78
	WARRINGTON	23.57
82	Arpley	5.59
83	BANK QUAY High L	5.59
84	Bank Quay Low L	2.78
85	CENTRAL	456 79
86	Weaste	2.69
87	West Leigh	456 77
88	West Leigh + Bedford	2.68
89	West Timperley	2.59
	WIDNES	2.69
90	Appleton	2.69
91	Central	5.69
92	LNW	2.68
93	Tanhouse Lane	456 78
94	(WIDNES) §26	2.79

No.		Ry Ref
12	Manchester Ship Canal Lines 58	
13	Partington Coal Basin §456 79	
14	Runcorn Dock	2.58
15	Diggles South Col	2.69
16	Hale Moss Siding §+456 78	

BRIDGES

No.	Name/Location	Ry Ref
V 1	Runcorn Bridge	2.58

TUNNELS

No.	Name	Length	Ry Ref
T 1	Sutton	1936	23.57

ENGINE SHEDS

No.	Name/Location	Ry Ref
E 1	Widnes	456 58
2	Warrington - Dallam	2.58
3	Warrington - Arpley	2.58
4	Tanhouse Lane	§456 58
5	Trafford Park	456 58
6	Warrington - CLC	456 68
7	Patricroft	2.79
8	Sutton Oak	2.59

GOODS

No.	Name/Location	Ry Ref
61	Leigh + Bedford	2.59
2	St Helens	23.58
3	Widnes	456 69
4	Warrington	456 79
5	Broadheath	2.79
6	Manchester Docks	2.59
7	Altrincham	456 78

SIDINGS ETC

No.	Company/Name/Location	Ry Ref
P1	Latchford Wharf	2.68
2	Gillers Green Colliery	5.59
3	Haydock Colliery	2.59
4	Havannah Colliery	2.59
5	(St. Helen's Jct)	2.59
6	Ditton Brook Iron	45.48
7	(Widnes Dock Lines)	2.58
8	(Widnes Dock Lines)	2.58
9	(Widnes Dock Lines)	2.58
10	Dallam Branch	2.68
11	Greengate Colliery	2.59

JUNCTIONS

No.	Name	Ry Ref
18	Widnes - West	2.58
19	Widnes - Station	2.58
20	Widnes - South	2.58
21	Widnes - Docks	2.58
22	Widnes - East	2.58
23	Carter House	2.58
24	Timperley - West	24.56 78
25	Deansgate	456,25 78
26	Skelton West	456 78
27	Skelton East	456 78
28	Timperley - North	2.52 78
29	Hale Moss	456 78
30		
31	Carr Mill	2.59
32	Gerard's Bridge	2.59
33	St Helens Goods	2.59
34	Ravenhead	2.59
35	Sherdley	2.59
36	Peasley	2.59
37	Sutton Oak West	2.59
38	Ashtons Green North	2.59
39	Ashtons Green South	2.59
40	Sutton Oak South	2.59
41	St Helens North	2.59
42	St Helens East	2.69
43	St Helens Jct - South	2.69
44	Earlestown West	2.59
45	Earlestown - Warrington	2.69
46	Earlestown - Newton	2.69
47	Winwick	2.59
48	Parkside West	2.69
49	Lowton - South	2.69
50	Parkside East	2.69
51	Lowton - Golborne	2.69
52	Lowton - St Helens	2.68
53	Pennington - South	2.69
54	Pennington - North	2.69
55	Diggles Branch	2.69
56	Kenyon	2.69
57	Dam Lane	456 69
58	Glazebrook Moss	5,456 69
59	Glazebrook West	456 69
60	Glazebrook East	456 69
61	Coal Basin	456 79

No.	Name/Location	Ry Ref
J 1	Acton Grange East	2.58
2	Acton Grange West	232.58
3	New South Walton	23.58
4	W+S	232.58
5	Old Main Line	2.69
6	New North Walton	232.58
1	Arpley Line	2.68
8	Chester Line	59
9	Arpley South	2.59
10	Arpley	2.59
11	Sankey	2.59
12	Old W+S	45.48
13	Dock Lines	2.58
14	Padgate	2.58
15	Ditton	2.58
16	Hutchinson	2.68
17	Moor Lane	2.59

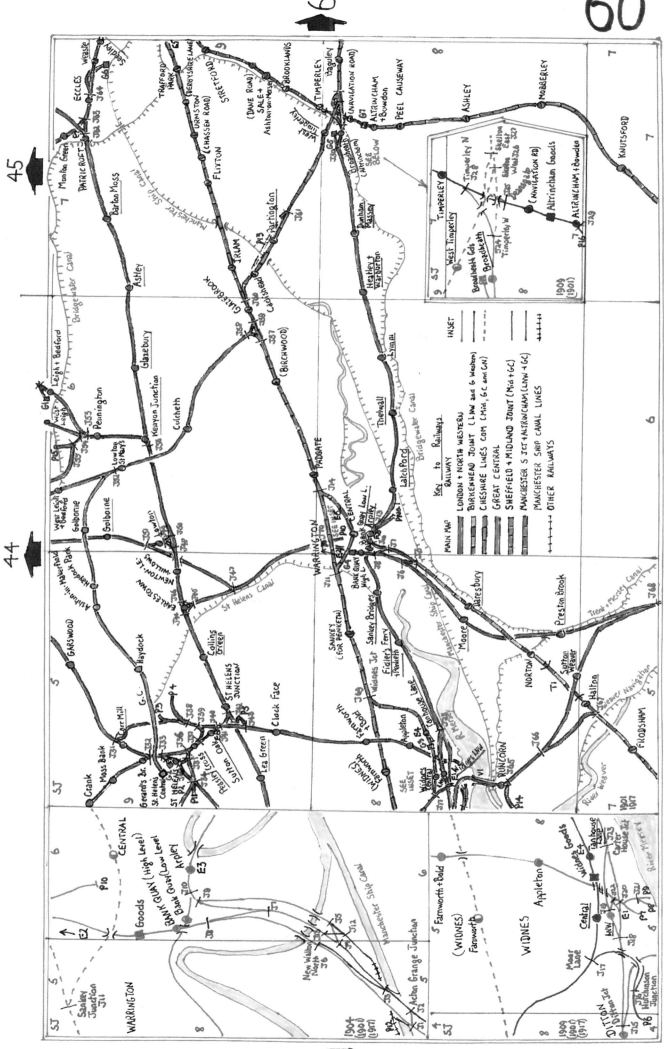

RAILWAYS

No	Company
R A	LONDON + NORTH WESTERN
3	GREAT WESTERN
8	NORTH STAFFORDSHIRE
8A	L,C+H (North Staffs) 2'6"

Lines

No	Name	Ry Ref
5	Chester Line	x 94
6	Shrewsbury Line	x 74
7	Crewe-North Staffs	8x 84
8	Crewe-Gresty Lane	8 85
9	Crewe-Curve	x 85
10	Madeley	8 85
11	Madeley Chord	8 85
12	Lawton	8 85
13	Audley Line	x 85
14	Congleton Lower	8x 85
15	Loop Line	8 84
16	Harecastle	8x 85
17	Bunkers Hill	8 84
18	Jamage Branch	x 84
19	Diglake	x 84
20	Talk o' th' Hill	x 84
21	Chatterley	x 84
22	Chesterton Branch	x 85
23	Halmerend	8 74
24	Keele	8 74
25	Silverdale	8 84
26	Pool Dam	8 84
27	Apedale	8 84
28	Etruria	0 74
29	Grange	0 74
30	Stoke North	8 85
31	Stoke South	8 85
32	Massfield West	8 85
33	Milton	8 85
34	Cheddleton	8 85
35	Tunstall Branch	8 85
36	Anner	8 85
37	Pinner Line	8 85
38	Newfields	8 85
39	Foxfield	8 84
40	Millfield	8 94

STATIONS + HALTS

No	Name	Ry Ref
A1	Adderley	3 64
2	ALSAGER	8 75
3	Alsager Road, (Talk +)	8 85
4	Audlem	3 6 38
5	Audley	8 85
6	Betley Road	2 7 40
7	Biddulph	8 85
8	Black Bull	8 85
9	BLYTH(E) BRIDGE	8 94
10	Bucknall + Northwood	8 84
11	Burslem	8 85
12	Chatterley	8 85
13	Cheddleton	8 95
14	Cobridge	8 84
15	CONGLETON	8 86
16	CREWE	2(8) 75
17	Endon	8 95
18	ETRURIA	8 84
19	Fenton	
20	Fenton Manor	8 84
21	Ford Green	8 85
22	Golden Hill (Newchapel)	8 86
23	Halmerend	8 74
24	Hanley	8 84
25	HARECASTLE §	8 85
16A	Consall	8 94
26	Keele	8 74
27	Keele Park	8 74
28	Kidsgrove	8 85
29	KIDSGROVE §	8 85
30	Kidsgrove Halt	8 85
31	Lawton	8 85
32	Leek	8 95
33	Leycett	8 74
34	LONGPORT	8 84
35	LONGTON	8 94
36	Madeley	2 74
37	Madeley Road	8 74
38	Meir	8 94
39	Milton	8 85
40	Minshull Vernon	2 66
41	Mow Cop	8 85
42	NANTWICH	2 65
43	Newcastle-under-Lyme	8 94
44	(Newchapel +) Golden Hill	8 84
45	Normacot	8 85
46	Pipe Gate	8 85
47	Pitts Hill	8 95
48	Radway Green	8 84
49	Rudyard	8 86
50	Rudyard Lake	2(8) 75
51	Rushton	8 95
52	SANDBACH	8 84
53	Silverdale	8 84
54	Stockton Brook	8 84
55	STOKE	8 85
56	(Talk +) Alsager Road	8 86
57	Tean (Totmanslow)	8 74
58	Trentham	8 84
59	Tunstall	8 85
60	Wall Grange for Cheddleton	8 95
61	Waterloo Road	8 74
62	(WEDGWOOD)	8 85
63	Wheelock + Sandbach	8 85
64	Whitmore	8 85
65	Willaston	8 85
66	Worleston	8 96

GOODS ONLY

Ry Ref	No	Name / Location	Ry Ref
	G1	Crewe Exchange	2 74
	2	Rookery Bridge	8 74
	3	Ettiley Heath	8 94
	4	Hanley	8 85
	5	Weston Coyney	2 66
	6	Longton	8 85
	7	Chesterton	2 65
	5	Massfield Colliery	8 95
	6	Crackley Pit	8 84
	7	Apedale Iron	8 84
	8	Talk Iron + Colliery	8 75
	9	Bunkers Hill Colliery	2 74
	10	Diglake Colliery	2 65
	11	Forge Colliery	2 65
	12	Newfields Branch	8 74
	13	Whitfield Colliery	8 84
	14	Chell Sidings	8x 85
	15	Pool Dam Wharf	8 84
	16	Jamage Colliery	8x 85
	17	Grange Branch	8 84
	18	Deep Pit Colliery	8 84
	19	Berry Hill Colliery	8 94
	20	Globe Colliery	8 94
	21	Oldfield Brickworks	8 84
	22	Birchenwood Cols.	8 76
	23	Sandbach Sidings	x 84
	24	Podmore Hall Col	x 84
	25	Sladderhill Colliery	x 94

COMPANY WORKS

Ry Ref	No	Location
8 85	C1	Crewe
8 94	C2	Crewe

ENGINE SHEDS

Ry Ref	No	Location
8 75	E1	Crewe
8 96	2	Alsager
8 96	3	Stoke

SIDINGS ETC

Ry Ref	No	Name / Company / Location	Ry Ref
8 95	P1	Foxfield Colliery	8 84
	2	Totmanslow Colliery	8 94
	3	Florence Colliery	8 84
	4	Great Fenton Colliery	8 85

TUNNELS

Ry Ref No	Name / Location	Length	Ry Ref
T1	Harecastle		2 75
2	Meir		8 85
3	Leek		8 94

JUNCTIONS

Ry Ref	No	Name / Location	Ry Ref
x 94	J1	Nantwich	23 64
x 94	2	Sandbach North	2 76
x 94	3	Sandbach North Staffs	2 8 76
x 84	4	Crewe-Mcr Line	2 75

NOTES

(1) REFERENCES: All in SJ

(2) NAME CHANGES: HARECASTLE § renamed KIDSGROVE § when the old Kidsgrove station on the Loop line was closed. BLYTH BRIDGE now BLYTHE BRIDGE

(3) CHEDDLETON: Though closed, used for passenger excursions from time to time

(4) JUNCTIONS: In red are new British Rail Junctions for Goods workings

(5) TEAN: Was to be known as Totmanslow and so shown when line projected. and on North Staffs' own maps and records.

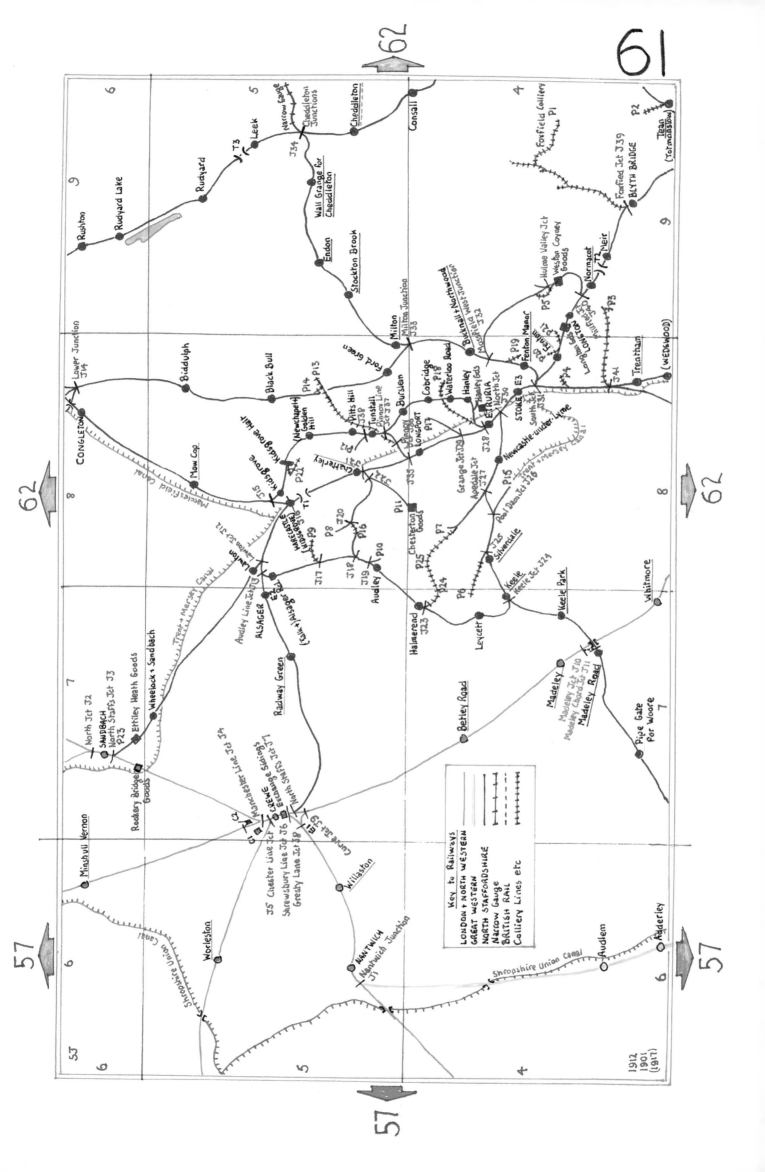

62 RAILWAYS

MANCHESTER + STAFFORD

No	Company
R1	LANCASHIRE + YORKSHIRE
2	LONDON + NORTH WESTERN
25	MANCHESTER SOUTH JUNCTION + ALTRINCHAM (LNW + GC) ⚡
4	MIDLAND
45	SHEFFIELD + MIDLAND (Mid + GC)
456	CHESHIRE LINES COMMITTEE (Mid, GC + GN)
5	GREAT CENTRAL
58	MACCLESFIELD COMMITTEE (GC + North Staffs)
8	NORTH STAFFORDSHIRE
8A	LEEK, CALDON + HARTINGTON (Light - 2'6" - N Staffs) X
0	BRITISH RAIL (Proposed 86)

STATIONS

No	Name	Ry Ref
A 1	ADLINGTON	2J97
2	ALDERLEY EDGE	2J87
(63)	Alexandra Park	5J89
4	ALSAGER	8J75
5	Alsager Road	8J85
6	Alsop-en-le-dale	2K15
7	Alton	8K04
8	ALTRINCHAM	25J78
9	ARDWICK	5J89
10	Ashbourne Joint	28K14
(63)	ASHBURYS for BELLE VUE	5J89
11	ASHLEY	456J78
12	ASHTON Charlestown ✱	1J99
13	Ashton-Oldham Rd	25AJ99
(63)	Ashton-Park Parade	5J99
14	Ashley	2J79
15	Aston-by-Stone	8J93
16	Audley	8J85
17	Baguley	456J78
18	BARLASTON	8J83
19	Barton Moss	2J79
20	Beeston Tor	8AK05
(63)	BELLE VUE	45J89
21	Betley Road	2J74
22	Biddulph	8J85
23	Birch Vale	45K08
24	Black Bull	8J85
25	BLYTH(E) BRIDGE ✱	8J94
26	Bollington	58J97
27	Bosley	8J96
28	Bradnop	8AK05
29	BRAMHALL	2J88
30	BREDBURY	45J99
(63)	(BRINNINGTON)	45J99
31	BROADBOTTOM Mottram+	5J99
32	Broadheath	2J78
33	BROOKLANDS	25J79
34	Bucknall+Northwood	8J84
35	Bugsworth	4K08
36	BURNAGE	2J89
37	Burslem	8J85
38	Butterton	8AK05
39	BUXTON	2K07
40	Buxton	4K07
41	Cadishead	456J79
42	CHAPEL-EN-LE-FRITH	2K07
43	Chapel-en-le-Frith	4K07
44	Chartley	6K02
45	(CHASSEN ROAD)	456J79
46	Chatterley	8J85
47	Cheadle	2J88
(63)	Cheadle	456J88
(63)	Cheadle Heath	4J88
48	CHEADLE HULME	2J88
49	Cheadle (Staffs)	8K04
50	Cheddleton †	8J95
51	CHELFORD	2J87
52	CHINLEY	4K08
53	Chorlton-cum-Hardy	456J89
54	Clayton Bridge	1J89
55	Clifton	8K14
(61)	Cobridge	8J84
56	Colwich	82K02
57	CONGLETON	8J86
58	Consall	8J94
59	Cresswell	8J93
60	Cross Lane	2J89
61	Crowden	5K09
62	(DANE ROAD)	25J79
63	DAVENPORT	2J88
64	Denstone	8K04
65	DENTON	2J99
66	(DERBYSHIRE LANE)	456J79
67	Didsbury	4J89
68	DINTING	5K09
69	DISLEY	2J98
70	DOVE HOLES	4K07
71	Droylsden	12J99
(64)	Dukinfield	5J99
(63)	Dukinfield+Ashton	2J99
72	Dunham Massey	2J78
73	EAST DIDSBURY	2J89
74	ECCLES	2J79
75	Ecton	8AK05
76	EDALE	4K18
77	Endon	8J95
78	ETRURIA	8J84
(63)	FAIRFIELD	5J99
(63)	Fallowfield	5J89
79	Fenton	8J84
80	Fenton Manor	8J84
81	FLIXTON	456J79
82	Ford Green	8J85
83	FURNESS VALE	2K08
84	GATLEY	2J88
85	GLOSSOP	5J09
86	Gnosall	2J82
87	GODLEY	5J99
88	Godley	456J99
89	Golden Hill	8J85
90	GOOSTREY	2J77
(63)	GORTON+Openshaw	5J89
91	Great Haywood	8K02
92	Great Longstone	4K17
93	Grindley	6K02
94	Grindon	8AK05
95	GUIDE BRIDGE	5J99
96	HADFIELD	5K09
97	HALE §J79	456J79
98	Halmerend	8J74
99	HANDFORTH	2J88
(61)	Hanley	8J84
100	Hartington	2K16
100A	HARECASTLE §126	8J85
100B	Haughton	2J82
101	Hayfield	45K08
102	HAZEL GROVE	2J98
103	Hazel Grove	4J98
104	HEALD GREEN	2J88
105	Heatley+Warburton	2J78
106	HEATON CHAPEL	2J89
107	Heaton Mersey	4J89
108	Heaton Norris	2J89
109	Hibel Road	2J97
110	Higher Buxton	2K07
111	High Lane	58J98
112	Hindlow	2K06
113	Hixon	8J93
114	HOLMES CHAPEL	2J76
115	HOPE (Derbyshire)	4K18
(63)	Hooley Hill	2J99
116	Hulme End	8AK05
117	Hurdlow	2K16
118	HYDE (CENTRAL)	45J99
119	HYDE (NORTH) Junction	45J99
(63)	Hyde Road	5J89
120	Ingestre for Weston	6J93
121	Ipstones	8AK05
122	IRLAM	456J79
123	Keele	8J74
124	Keele Park	8J74
125	Kidsgrove	8J85
126	(KIDSGROVE) §100A	8J85
127	Kidsgrove Halt	8J85
(63)	Knott Mill+DEANSGATE	25J89
129	Kingsley+Froghall	8K04
130	KNUTSFORD	456J77
131	Lawton	8J85
132	Leek	8J96
133	Leigh (Staffs)	8K03
(63)	LEVENSHULME	2J89
(63)	Levenshulme	2J89
134	Leycett	8J74
135	LONGPORT	8J84
136	LONGSIGHT	2J89
137	LONGTON	8J94
138	MACCLESFIELD Central	8J97
139	Madeley	2J74
140	Madeley Road	8J74

MANCHESTER

No	Name	Ry Ref
(63)	Central	456J89
(63)	DEANSGATE, Knott Mill+	25J89
(63)	Exchange	2J89
(63)	LONDON ROAD	25J89
141	OXFORD ROAD	25J89
(63)	PICCADILLY	25J89
142	VICTORIA	1J89
143	(MANCHESTER AIRPORT)‡	0J88
(63)	(MANCHESTER UNITED † FOOTBALL GROUND)	456J89
144	Marchington	8K03
145	MARPLE	45J98
(63)	MAUDLETH ROAD	2J89
146	Meir	8J94
147	Middlewich	2J76
148	Middlewood	58J88
149	MIDDLEWOOD	2J98
150	MILES PLATTING	1J80
151	Milford+Brocton	2J93
152	Miller's Dale	4K17
153	Milton	8J85
154	MOBBERLEY	456J78
154A	Monsal Dale	4K17
155	Monton Green	2J79
156	Mottram+BROADBOTTOM	5J99
157	(MOTTRAM-Staff Halt)	5K09
158	(NAVIGATION ROAD)	25J78
159	Mow Cop	8J85
160	Neston+Ingestre	8J92
161	Newcastle-under-Lyme	8J84
162	NEW MILLS (CENTRAL)	45J98
163	NEW MILLS (NEWTOWN)	2J98
(63)	NEWTON FOR HYDE	5J99
164	Narbury	8K14
165	Normacot	8J94
166	Northenden	456J88
167	North Rode	8J96
168	NORTON BRIDGE	2J83
169	Norton Bridge	8J83
170	Norton-in-Hales	8J73
171	Oakamoor	8K04
172	OLD TRAFFORD	25J89
173	Ordsall Lane	2J89
174	PARK	1J89
175	Parsley Hay	2K16
176	Partington	456J79
177	PATRICROFT	2J79
178	Peak Forest	4K07
179	PEEL CAUSEWAY	897, 456J89
180	Pendleton	1J89
181	PENDLETON Broad Street	1J89
182	Pipe Gate for Woore	8J74
183	Pitts Hill	8J85
184	PLUMBLEY	456J77
185	POYNTON	2J98
186	Poynton	58J98
187	PRESTBURY	2J97
188	Radway Green	8J75
189	REDDISH (NORTH)	45J89
(63)	REDDISH (SOUTH)	2J89
191	Rocester	8K03
192	ROMILEY	45J99
194	ROSE HILL (MARPLE)	58J97
195	Rudyard	8J95
196	Rudyard Lake	8J96
197	Rushton	8J96
198	SALE+Ashton-on-Mersey	25J79
199	SALFORD	1J89
200	Salt	6J93
201	SANDBACH	2J76
202	Sandon	8J93
203	Seedley	2J79
204	Silverdale	8J84
205	Sparrowlee	8AK05
206	STAFFORD (6)	2J93
207	Stafford Common	6J93
208	Staley+Millbrook	2J99
209	Staly bridge	1J99
210	STALYBRIDGE	25J99
211	Standon Bridge	2J83
212	STOCKPORT	2J88
213	Stockton Brook	8J95
214	STOKE	8J84
215	STONE	8J93
216	STRETFORD	25J79
217	STRINES	45J98
218	STYAL	2J88
219	Sudbury	8K03
220	Tean (Totmonslow) §	8J94
221	Thorpe Cloud	2K15
222	Thor's Cave	8AK05
223	TIMPERLEY	25J79
224	Tissington	2K15
225	Tiviot Dale	456J89
226	TRAFFORD PARK	456J79
227	Trentham	8J84
228	Trentham Park	8J83
229	Tunstall	8J85
230	URMASTON	456J79
231	UTTOXETER	8K03
232	Wall Grange	8J95
233	(WARWICK ROAD)	25J89
234	Waterhouse	8AK05
(61)	Waterloo Road	8J84
235	Weaste	2J79
236	(WEDGWOOD)	8J84
237	West Timperley	456J78
238	Wetton	8AK05
239	WHALEY BRIDGE	456J99
240	Wheeloch+Sandbach	8J75
241	Whitmore	2J74
242	Withington	4J89
243	WILMSLOW	2J88
244	Woodhead	5K10
245	WOODLEY	456J99

GOODS

No	Name/Location	Ry Ref
G1	Ladmanlow	2K07
2	Harpur Hill	2K07
3	Brunswick St-Congleton	8J86
4	Caldon	8K04
5	Friden	2K16
6	Fenny Bentley	2K15
7	Froghall	8K04
8	Badnall Wharf	2J83
9	Bromshall	8K03

ENGINE SHEDS

No	Location	Ry Ref
E1	Stafford	2J92
2	Uttoxeter	8K03

JUNCTIONS

No	Name/Location	Ry Ref
J2	Trent Valley	2J92
3	Norton Bridge	28J82
4	Stone	8J93
5	Cresswell	8J93
6	Bromshall	86K03
7	Uttoxeter E,W+N	8K13
8	Rocester	8K13
9	Froghall	8K04

NOTES:

(1) REFERENCES In SD, SJ, SK - the initial S is omitted

(2) ⚡ also OLDHAM, ASHTON + GUIDE BRIDGE (LNW + GC) - A-25A

(3) ✱ now known as ASHTON-UNDER-LYNE

(4) § Name changed - map name - number refers to modern name

(5) § Modern name - number refers to map name

(6) ✱ BLYTH BRIDGE is now BLYTHE BRIDGE

(7) † Station open but not for regular passenger service

(8) ‡ Proposed station at MANCHESTER AIRPORT

(9) X Although main source map shows gauge as 2'6", it is not so indicated elsewhere.

(10) § Totmonslow was proposed name prior to opening and it continued to be known by this name in the North Staffs official records!! Other sources shown as Tean

(11) Stations in BLUE not named number in brackets (61) shows the enlargement page on which it can be found

(12) Other features - only shown if in areas not covered by enlargements. Junctions listed are a selection only.

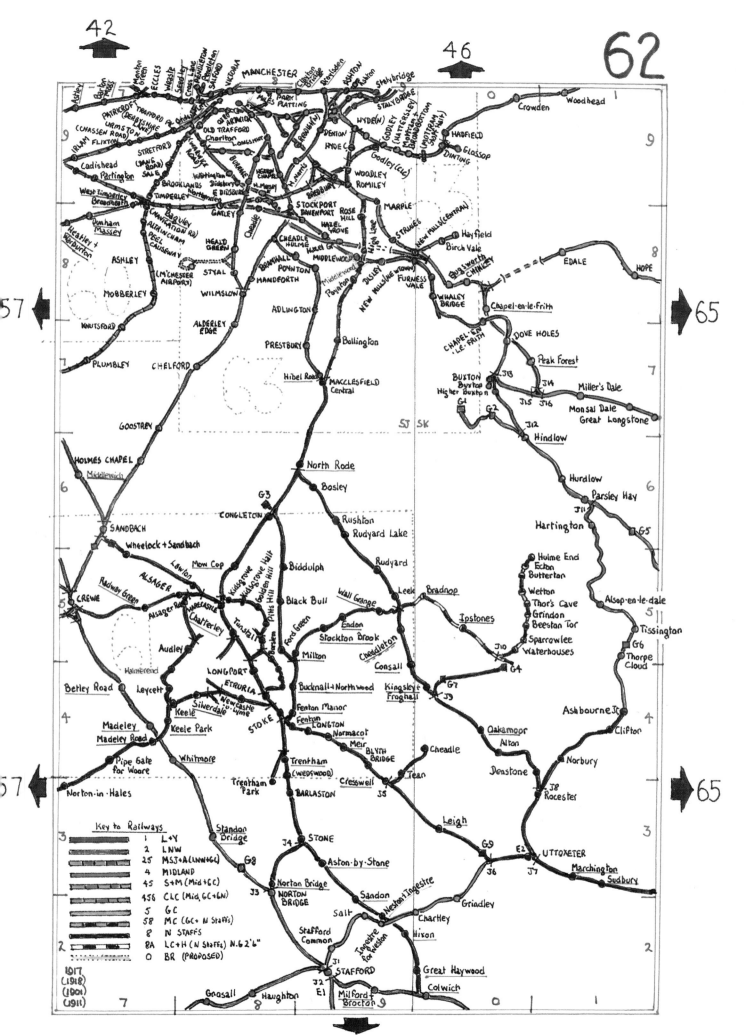

MANCHESTER + MACCLESFIELD

RAILWAYS

No	Company
R 1	LANCASHIRE+YORKSHIRE
2	LONDON+NORTH WESTERN
25	LONDON+N WESTERN+GREAT CENTRAL JT
A	OLDHAM, ASHTON + GUIDE BRIDGE
B	MANCHESTER S JCT+ALTRINCHAM
28	LNW +NORTH STAFFORDSHIRE
4	MIDLAND
45	SHEFFIELD + MIDLAND JOINT (Mid+GC)
456	CHESHIRE LINES COMMITTEE (Mid, GC,GN)
5	GREAT CENTRAL
58	MACCLESFIELD JOINT COM (GC+N.Staff)
8	NORTH STAFFORDSHIRE
0	BRITISH RAIL
X	COLLIERY RAILWAYS etc

STATIONS

No	Name	Ry Ref
A 1	ADLINGTON	2J97
2	ALDERLEY EDGE	2J87
3	Alexandra Park	5J89
4	ARDWICK	5J89
5	ASHBURYS FOR BELLE VUE	5J89
6	ASHTON (-UNDER-LYNE)-	J99
	Charlestown	1J99
7	Ashton-Oldham Road	25AJ99
8	Ashton-Park Parade	5J99
9	BELLE VUE	45J89
10	Birch Vale	45K08
11	Bollington	58J97
12	BRAMHALL	2J88
13	BREDBURY	45J99
14	(BRINNINGTON)	45J99
15	BROADBOTTOM, Mottram+	5J99
16	Bogsworth	4K08
17	BURNAGE	2J89
18	CHAPEL·EN·LE·FRITH	2K07
19	Chapel·en·le·Frith	4K07
20	Cheadle	2J88
21	Cheadle	456J88
22	Cheadle Heath	4J88
23	CHEADLE HULME	2J88
24	CHELFORD	2J87
25	CHINLEY	4K08
26	Chorlton-cum-Hardy	456J89
27	Clayton Bridge	1J89
28	Cross Lane	2J89
29	DAVENPORT	2J88
30	DEANSGATE, Knott Mill+	25BJ89
31	DENTON	2J99
32	Didsbury	4J89
33	DINTING	5K09
34	DISLEY	2J98
35	Droylsden	12J99
36	Dukinfield ✳	5J99
37	Dukinfield+Ashton	2J99
38	EAST DIDSBURY + Parr's Wood	J89 / 2J89
39	Exchange (Manchester)	2J89
40	FAIRFIELD	5J99
41	Fallowfield for Withington and Didsbury	J89 / 5J89
42	FURNESS VALE	2K08
43	GATLEY for Cheadle	2J88
44	GLOSSOP	5K09
45	GODLEY	5J99
46	Godley	456J99
47	GORTON + Openshaw	5J89
48	GUIDE BRIDGE	5J99
49	HADFIELD	5K09
50	HANDFORTH	2J88
51	Hayfield	45K08
52	HAZEL GROVE	2J98
53	Hazel Grove	4J98
54	HEALD GREEN	2J88
55	HEATON CHAPEL	2J89
56	Heaton Mersey	2J89
57	Heaton Norris	2J89
58	Hibel Road	2J97
59	High Lane	58J98
60	Hooley Hill	2J99
61	HYDE (CENTRAL)	45J99
62	HYDE (NORTH) Junction	45J99
63	Hyde Road	5J89
64	Knott Mill + DEANSGATE	25BJ89
65	LEVENSHULME	2J89
66	Levenshulme	5J89
67	LONDON ROAD	25J89
68	LONGSIGHT	2J89
69	MACCLESFIELD Central	8J97
	MANCHESTER	J89
70	Central	456J89
71	DEANSGATE (Knott Mill+	25BJ89
72	Exchange	2J89
73	LONDON ROAD	25J89
74	OXFORD ROAD	25BJ89
75	PICCADILLY	258J89
76	VICTORIA	1J89
77	(MANCHESTER AIRPORT) ✝	0J88
78	(MANCR UTD FC) ✝	456J89
79	MARPLE	45J98
80	MAULDETH ROAD	2J89
81	Middlewood	58J98
82	MIDDLEWOOD for High Lane	2J98
83	MILES PLATTING	1D80
84	Mottram + BROADBOTTOM	5J99
85	(MOTTRAM-Staff Halt) ✝	5K09
86	NEW MILLS (CENTRAL)	45J88
87	NEW MILLS (NEWTOWN)	2J98
88	NEWTON for HYDE	5J99
89	Northenden	456J88
90	OLD TRAFFORD	25BJ89
91	Ordsall Lane	2J89
92	OXFORD ROAD	25BJ89
93	PARK	1J89
94	Pendleton	1J89
95	PENDLETON Broad Street	1J89
96	PICCADILLY	25J89
97	POYNTON	2J98
98	Poynton	58J98
99	PRESTBURY	2J97
100	REDDISH (NORTH)	45J89
101	REDDISH (SOUTH)	2J89
102	ROMILEY	45J99
103	ROSE HILL (MARPLE)	58J97
104	SALFORD	1J89
105	Staley + Millbrook	2J99
106	Stalybridge	1J99
107	STALYBRIDGE	25J99
108	STOCKPORT	2J88
109	STRINES	45J98
110	STYAL	2J88
111	Teviot Dale	456J89
112	VICTORIA	1J89
113	(WARWICK ROAD FOR OLD TRAFFORD)	J89 / 25BJ89
114	WHALEY BRIDGE	2K08
115	Withington + Albert Park	4J89
116	WILMSLOW	2J88
117	WOODLEY	456J99

GOODS

No	Name/Location	Ry Ref
G 1	Dinting	5K09
2	New Mills	4K08
3	Bramhall Moor Lane	4J98
4	Stockport	2J88
5	Wellington Road	456J89
6	Portwood	456J89
7	Macclesfield	28J97
8	Macclesfield	58J97
9	Disley	2J88
10	Staley + Millbrook	2J99

SIDINGS

No	Company/Name/Location	Ry Ref
P 1	Poynton + Worth Colliery	X J98
2	Whaley Colliery	2 K08
3	Whaley Colliery	2 K07

ENGINE SHEDS

No	Location	Ry Ref
E 1	Stockport	2 J88

TUNNELS

No	Name/Location	Yds Long	Ry Ref
T 1	Stockport		2 J88
T 2	Wellington Road		456 J89
3	Teviot		456 J89
4	Prestbury		2 J97
5	Hibel Road		2 J97
6	Disley	3866	4 J98

JUNCTIONS

No	Name/Location	Ry Ref
J 1	Cheadle Village	2 J88
2	Exchange Sidings	456 J88
3	Cheadle	456 J88
4	Cheadle Heath South	4 J88
5	Heaton Mersey East	456 J89
6	Georges Road	456 J89
7	Heaton Mersey Station	4 J89
8	Heaton Norris	2 J89
9	Stockport Goods	2 J88
10	Stockport-Northenden	2 J88
11	Stockport -Buxton	2 J88
12	Davenport	2 J88
13	Goods	58 J97
14	Hibel	28 J97
15	Goods	2 J97
16	Central Station	858 J97
17	Marple Wharf	45/58 J88
18	Aqueduct	2 J98
19	Middlewood	258 J98
20	Dinting -East	5 K09
21	Dinting -West	5 K09
22	Dinting -Glossop	5 K09
23	New Mills	454 K08
24	New Mills South	4 K08
25	Chinley North	4 K08
26	Chinley South	4 K08
27	Chinley East	4 K08

NOTES

(1) REFERENCES in SD, SJ or SK - the S is omitted

(2) ✳ See map 64 for details

(3) ✝ Station open but not for regular service

(4) OTHER FEATURES (than stations) shown and listed only if not covered by enlargement.

(5) NAME CHANGES - Part of name in brackets and (CAPITALS) is modern addition. Part CAPITALS and part small shows modern deletion in name.

(6) ✝ Proposed Station (1986)

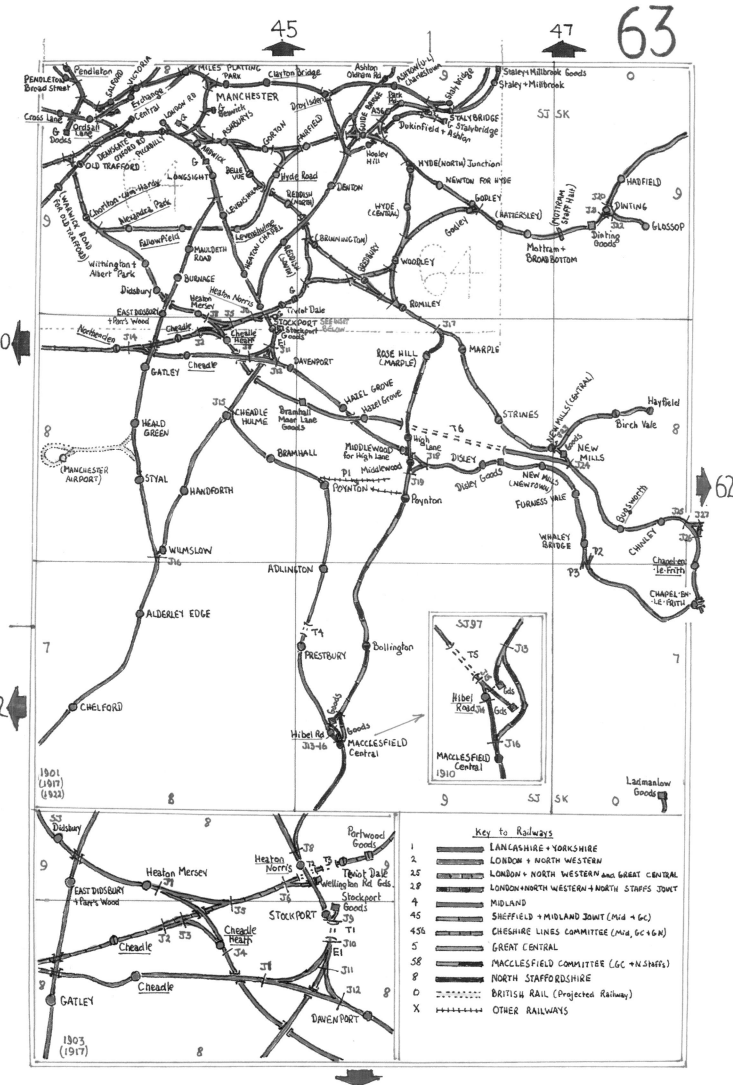

64

MANCHESTER

RAILWAYS

No	Company
R1	LANCASHIRE + YORKSHIRE
2	LONDON + NORTH WESTERN
25A	OLDHAM, ASHTON + GUIDE BRIDGE (LNW, GC)
25B	MANCHESTER S. JCT + ALTRINCHAM (LNW, GC)
4	MIDLAND
45	SHEFFIELD + MIDLAND (Mid + GC)
456	CHESHIRE LINES COM (Mid, GC, + GN)
5	GREAT CENTRAL
6	GREAT NORTHERN

STATIONS

Ry Ref	Grid	No	Name
5	89	A1	Alexandra Park
5	89	2	ARDWICK
5	89	3	ASHBURYS for BELLE VUE
5	99	4	ASHTON (UNDER LYNE)
1	99		Charlestown
25A	99	5	Ashton - Oldham Road
5	89	6	Ashton - Park Parade
45	89	7	BELLE VUE
45	99	8	BREDBURY
45	99	9	(BRINNINGTON)
2	89	10	BURNAGE
456	89	11	Charlton-cum-Hardy
1	89	12	Clayton Bridge
25B	89	13	Cross Lane
25B	89	14	DEANSGATE
2	99	15	DENTON
4	89	16	Didsbury
12	99	17	Droylsden
5	99	18	Dukinfield
2	99	19	Dukinfield + Ashton
2	89	20	East Didsbury + Parrs Wood
2	89	21	Exchange
5	99	22	FAIRFIELD
2	89	23	Fallowfield
5	99	24	GODLEY
456	99	25	Godley
5	89	26	GORTON + Openshaw
5	99	27	GUIDE BRIDGE
2	89	28	HEATON CHAPEL
4	89	29	Heaton Mersey
2	89	30	Heaton Norris
2	99	31	Hooley Hill
45	99	32	HYDE (CENTRAL)
45	99	33	HYDE (NORTH) Junction
5	89	34	Hyde Road
25B	89	35	Knott Mill + DEANSGATE
2	89	36	LEVENSHULME
5	89	37	Levenshulme
25	89	38	LONDON ROAD
5	89	39	LONGSIGHT
			MANCHESTER
1	99	40	Central
25A	99	41	DEANSGATE
5	89	42	Exchange
45	89	43	LONDON ROAD
45	99	44	OXFORD ROAD
45	99	45	PICCADILLY
2	89	46	VICTORIA
456 89	+456 89	47	(MANCHESTER UTD FC)
1	89	48	MAULDETH ROAD
2	89	49	MILES PLATTING
25B	89	50	NEWTON for HYDE
2	99	51	OLD TRAFFORD
4	89	52	Ordsall Lane
12	99	53	OXFORD ROAD
5	99	54	PARK
2	99	55	Pendleton
2	89	56	PENDLETON Broad Street
2	89	57	PICCADILLY
5	99	58	REDDISH (NORTH)
5	89	59	REDDISH (SOUTH)
5	99	60	ROMILEY
456	99	61	SALFORD
5	89	62	Staley + Millbrook
5	99	63	Staly bridge
2	89	64	STALYBRIDGE
4	89	65	STOCKPORT
2	89	66	Teviot Dale
2	99	67	VICTORIA
45	99	68	(WARWICK ROAD)
45	99	69	Withington + Albert Park
5	89	70	WOODLEY

SIDINGS

Ry Ref	Grid	No	Company/Name/Location
456	89	P1	Denton Colliery
1	89	2	Newton Wood Colliery
25B	89	3	Victoria Colliery
4	89	4	Broadoak Collieries
456	89	5	Limehurst Siding

GOODS

Ry Ref	Grid	No	Name/Location
2	89	G1	Ancoats
25	89	2	Ardwick
2	89	3	Ardwick
	89	4	Ardwick Coal
456	89	5	Ashton - Oldham Road
25B	89	6	Ashton Road
2	89	7	Beswick
25	89	8	Brindle Heath
25B	89	9	Central
25B	89	10	Cornbrook
1	89	11	Deansgate
+456	89	12	Dock
2	89	13	Dulcie Street
1	D80	14	Guide Bridge
5	99	15	Liverpool Road
25B	89	16	Liverpool Street
2	89	17	London Road
25B	89	18	Longsight
1	89	19	Mayfield
1	89	20	Oldham Road
1	89	21	Openshaw
25	89	22	Portwood
45	89	23	Salford
2	89	24	Staley + Millbrook
45	99	25	Stalybridge
1	89	26	Stockport
2	99	27	Wellington Road
1	99	28	Windsor Bridge

ENGINE SHEDS

Ry Ref	Grid	No	Location
4	89	E1	Trafford Park
2	89	2	Heaton Mersey
5	89	3	Openshaw
4	89	4	Longsight
2	99	5	Stockport

TUNNELS

Ry Ref	Grid	No	Name/Location
1	D80	T1	Cheetham Hill - Queens Rd.
456	89	2	Stalybridge
456	89	3	Stalybridge South
6	89	4	Brinnington

JUNCTIONS

Ry Ref	Grid	No	Name/Location
2	99	J1	Brindle Heath West
2	89	2	Brindle Heath East
1	89	3	Windsor Bridge North
1	89	4	Windsor Bridge South
2	89	5	Salford Goods
2	89	6	Victoria West Jcts
1	89	7	Victoria East Jcts
5	89	8	Cheetham Hill - North
456	89	9	Cheetham Hill - West
1	89	10	Cheetham Hill - South
2	99	11	Cheetham Hill - East
25	99	12	Thorps Bridge West
2	88	13	Thorps Bridge East
456	89	14	Oldham Road
1	89	15	Miles Platting Station
		16	Miles Platting East
		17	Miles Platting South
X	99	18	Park North
X	99	19	Park South
X	99	20	Park Station
X	D80	21	Beswick
X	D90	22	Ancoats
		23	Droylsden
456	79	24	Ashton West
456	89	25	Ashton East
456	89	26	Stalybridge L+Y
2	89	27	Stalybridge East
2	88	28	Ashton Moss
		29	Ashton West
		30	Ashton East
		31	Ashton - Stalybridge
1	D80	32	Dunkirk
2	99	33	Denton
2	99	34	Hyde Road
456	99	35	Gorton East
		36	Fairfield
1	D80	37	Gorton West
1	D80	38	Openshaw
1	D80	39	Whitworth
1	D80	40	Ashburys East
1	D80	41	Ashburys West
1	D80	42	Ardwick
1	D80	43	Ordsall + Liverpool Rd
1	D80	44	Castlefield
1	89	45	Thrastle Nest North
1	89	46	Thrastle Nest South
1	89	47	Cornbrook East
1	89	48	Cornbrook West
14	89	49	Trafford Park West
12	99	50	Trafford Park East
125	99	51	Chorlton
125	99	52	Heaton Mersey Station
15	99	53	Heaton Mersey East
2	99	54	Cheadle
2	99	55	Georges Road
525	99	56	Heaton Norris
525	99	57	Brinnington
45	99	58	Romiley
5	99	59	Bredbury
2	99	60	Woodley
5	89	61	Godley
5	89	62	Hyde
5	99	63	Rusholme
5	89	64	Reddish
2 52	99	64A	Crowthorn

NOTES:

(1) REFERENCES - Most in SJ - those in SD indicated D

(2) + Station open - but not for regular traffic

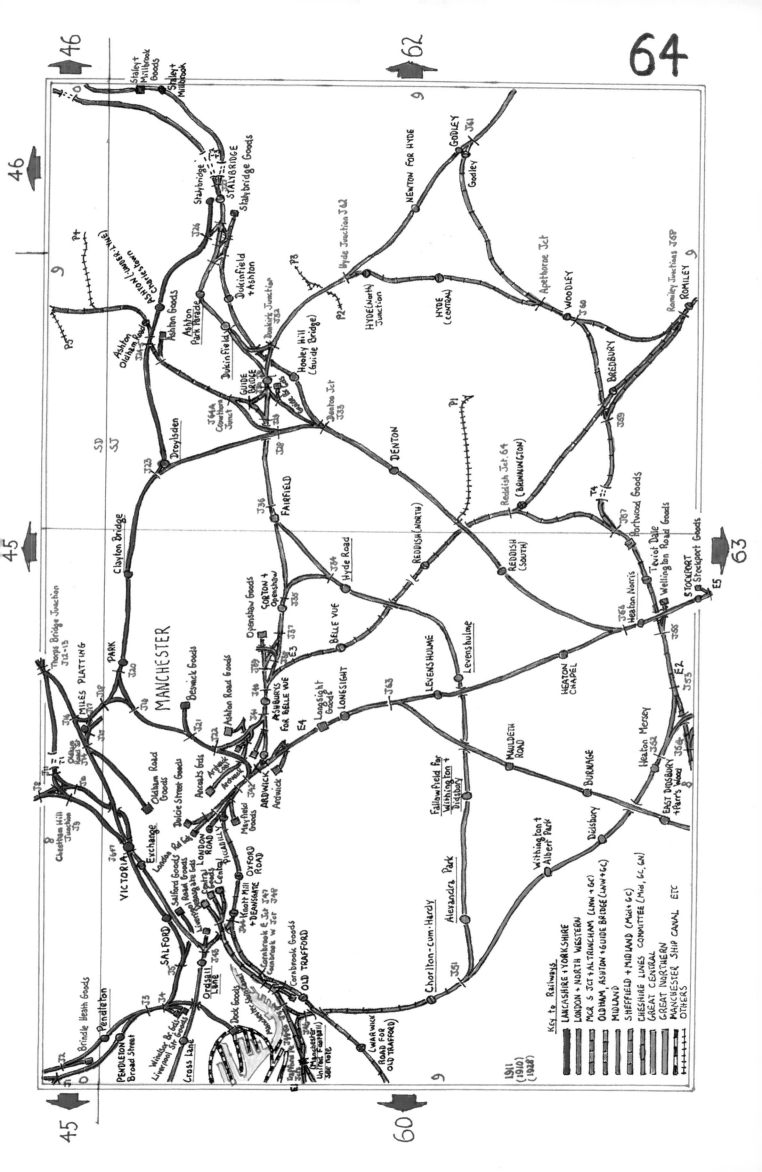

65

SHEFFIELD, DERBY + NOTTINGHAM

RAILWAYS

No.	Company
R 1	LANCASHIRE + YORKSHIRE
13456	SOUTH YORKSHIRE JOINT (LY, NE, Mid, GC + GN)
2	LONDON + NORTH WESTERN
26	LNW + GN JOINT
4	MIDLAND
45	MIDLAND + GREAT CENTRAL
457	MIDLAND, GC and HULL + BARNSLEY
5	GREAT CENTRAL
56	GREAT CENTRAL + GREAT NORTHERN
57	GREAT CENTRAL and HULL + BARNSLEY
6	GREAT NORTHERN
6A	GREAT NORTHERN (Light)
69	GREAT NORTHERN + GREAT EASTERN
7	HULL + BARNSLEY
8	NORTH STAFFORDSHIRE
95	SHEFFIELD DISTRICT see note ✗
11	DEARNE VALLEY
0	BRITISH RAILWAYS

STATIONS

No.	Name	Ry	Ref
A 1	ALFRETON + MANSFIELD PARKWAY §	4	45
2	ALFRETON + S. Normanton §	4	45
3	AMBERGATE	4	35
4	Annesley	4	55
5	Anston	45	58
6	Arkwright Street	5	53
(67)	Arkwright Town	5	47
6A	ATTENBOROUGH	4	53
7	Attercliffe	5	38
(66)	ATTERCLIFFE Road	4	38
8	Awsworth	6	44
9	Bakewell	4	26
10	BAMFORD	4	28
11	Barnby Moor + Sutton	6	68
12	Barrow Hill for Staveley Works	4	47
13	Basford	4	54
(68)	Basford + Bulwell	6	54
13A	Bawtry	6	69
14	Beauchief	4	29
15	BEESTON	4	53
16	Beighton	5	48
17	BELPER	4	34
18	Bessacar Halt	69	69
19	Bestwood Colliery	6	54
20	BINGHAM	6	63
21	Bingham Road	26	63
22	Blidworth + Rainworth	4	55
23	Bolsover ‡	4	47
24	Bolsover	5	46
25	Borrowash	4	43
26	Boughton	5	66
27	Branston	4	22
28	Breadsall	6	33
29	BRIGHTSIDE	4	39
(66)	Broughton Lane	5	38
30	Bulwell	4	54
(68)	Bulwell Common	5	54
31	Bulwell Forest	6	54
32	BURTON JOYCE	4	64
33	BURTON-ON-TRENT	4	22
34	Butler's Hill	6	54
35	Butterley	4	35
36	CARLTON + Netherfield	4	64
(68)	Carrington	5	54
37	Castle Donnington + Shardlow	4	42
38	Catcliffe	95	48
39	CHAPELTOWN	4	39
40	Chapeltown + Thorncliffe	5	39
41	Checker House	5	67
42	Chellaston + Swarkestone	4	33
43	CHESTERFIELD	4	37
44	Chesterfield Central	5	37
45	Chesterfield Market Pl.	5	37
46	Clay Cross	4	46
47	Clown	4	47
48	Clown	5	47
49	Codnor Park + Ironville	4	45
50	Codnor Park for Ironville + Jacksdale	6	45
51	CONISBOROUGH	5	59
52	Coxbench	4	34
53	Cresswell + Welbeck	5	57
54	CROMFORD	4	35
55	Crosshill + Codnor	4	44
56	Darley Dale	4	26
57	DARNALL	5	38
58	Daybrook	6	54
59	Deepcar	5	29
60	Denaby + Conisborough	7	58
61	Denby	4	34
62	DERBY	4	33
63	Derby	6	33
64	Derby-Nottingham Rd	4	33
65	Dinnington + Laughton	13456	58
66	Doe Hill	4	46
67	DORE + Totley	4	38
68	Draycott	4	43
69	DRONFIELD	4	37
70	DUFFIELD	4	34
71	East Leake	4	52
72	Eastwood + Langley Mill	6	44
73	Ecclesfield	4	39
74	Ecclesfield	5	39
75	Eckington + Renishaw	4	47
(66)	Eckington + Renishaw	5	47
76	Edlington Halt for Balby	11	59
77	Edwalton	4	53
78	Edwinstowe	5	66
79	Egginton	68	22
80	Elmton + Creswell	4	57
81	Etwall	6	23
82	Farnsfield	4	65
83	Finningley ‡	69	69
84	Gedling + Carlton	6	64
85	Glapwell	4	46
86	Grange Lane	5	39
87	Grassmoor	5	46
88	GRINDLEFORD	4	27
89	Hassop	4	27
90	Hathern	4	52
91	HATHERSAGE	4	28
92	Hazlewood †	4	34
93	Heanor	4	44
94	Heanor	6	44
95	Heath	5	46
96	Heeley	4	29
97	Hollin Well + Annesley	56	55
98	Holmes	4	49
99	Horninglow	8	22
100	Hucknall	4	54
(68)	Hucknall	6	54
101	Hucknall Town	5	54
102	Idridgehay	4	24
103	Ilkeston	6	44
104	Ilkeston Junction	4	44
104A	Ilkeston Town	4	44
105	Kegworth	4	52
106	Kilburn	4	34
107	Killamarsh	4	48
108	Killamarsh	5	48
109	Kilnhurst	4	49
110	Kilnhurst	5	49
111	Kimberley	6	44
112	Kirkby + Pinxton	5	45
113	Kirkby-in-Ashfield	4	55
114	Kirkby-in-A Central	5	45
115	Kirklington	4	65
116	(KIVETON BRIDGE)	5	48
117	KIVETON PARK	5	58
118	Langley Mill	4	44
(68)	Langley Mill + Eastwood	4	44
119	Langwith	4	56
120	Langwith Junction	5(46)	56
121	Linby	4	55
122	Linby	6	55
123	Little Eaton	4	34
(68)	London Rd High Level	6	53
(68)	London Rd Low Level	6	53
124	Long Eaton	4	43
125	(LONG EATON) §183	4	43
126	LOUGHBOROUGH	4	52
127	LOWDHAM	4	64
128	Maltby	13456	59
129	Mansfield	4	56
130	Mansfield	5	56
131	Mansfield Woodhouse	4	56
132	Marlpool	6	44
133	MATLOCK	4	26
134	MATLOCK BATH	4	25
(56)	Meadow Hall + Wincobank	5	39
135	Melbourne	4	32
136	MEXBOROUGH	5	49
137	Mickleover	6	23
138	Mill Houses + Ecclesall	4	38
139	Neepsend	5	38
140	NETHERFIELD + Colwick	6	64
141	New Basford	5	54
142	Newstead	4	55
143	Newstead	6	55
144	Newthorpe, Greasley + Shipley Gate	6	44

NOTTINGHAM

No.	Name	Ry	Ref
145	NOTTINGHAM	4	53
146	Arkwright Street	5	53
(68)	London Road HL	6	53
(68)	London Road LL	6	53
147	Racecourse	6	53
148	Victoria	56	53
149	Nottingham Road Derby	4	33
150	Old Dalby	4	62
151	Ollerton	5	62
152	Oughty Bridge	5	39
153	Palterton + Sutton	4	46
154	Parkgate + Aldwarke	5	49
155	Parkgate + Rawmarsh	4	49
156	PEARTREE + Normanton	4	33
157	Pilsley	5	46
158	Pinxton + Selston	4	45
159	Pinxton for South Normanton	6	45
160	Pleasley	6	56
(67)	Pleasley		46
161	Plumtree	4	63
162	Pye Bridge	4	45
163	Pye Hill + Somercotes	6	45
164	Racecourse, Nottingham	6	53
165	RADCLIFFE-on-Trent	6	63
166	Radford	4	53
167	Ranskill	6	68
168	Repton + Willington	4	22
169	RETFORD	6	67
170	Ripley	4	35
171	Rolleston-on-Dove	8	22
172	Rossington	6	69
173	Rotherham and Masborough	5	49
174	ROTHERHAM-Masborough	4	49
175	Rotherham Road	5	49
176	Rotherham Westgate	4	49
177	Rowsley	4	26
178	Rowthorn + Hardwick	4	46
179	Ruddington	5	53
180	Rushcliffe Platform	5	52
181	St Ann's Well	6	54
182	Sawley	4	43
183	SAWLEY JUNCTION §125	4	43
184	Scarcliffe	5	56
185	Scrooby	6	69
186	Sheepbridge + Brimmington	5	37
187	Sheepbridge + Whittington Moor	4	37

SHEFFIELD

No.	Name	Ry	Ref
188	Attercliffe	5	38
(66)	ATTERCLIFFE Road	4	38
189	POND STREET §✱	4	38
190	Victoria	5	38
(68)	Sherwood	6	54
191	Shipley Gate	4	44
192	Shirebrook	4	56
(67)	Shirebrook	6	56
193	SHIREOAKS	5	58
194	Shottle	4	34
195	(SINFIN CENTRAL)	4	33
196	(SINFIN NORTH)	4	33
197	Skegby for Stanton Hill	6	46
198	Spink Hill for Mount St. Mary	5	47
199	SPONDON	4	33
200	Stanton Gate	4	43
201	Stapleford + Sandiacre	4	43
202	Staveley Town	4	47
(67)	Staveley Town	5	47
(67)	Staveley Works for Barrow Hill	5	47
203	Stretton	4	36
204	Stretton + Clay Mills	8	22
205	Sutton-in-Ashfield Cent	5	55
206	Sutton-in-Ashfield Town	6	45
207	Sutton Junction	4	55
208	Swinton	4	49
209	Swinton	5	49
210	Teversall	4	46
(68)	Thorneywood	6	54
211	THURGARTON	4	64
212	Tibshelf + Newton	4	45
(67)	Tibshelf Town	5	46
213	Tickhill + Wadworth	13456	59
214	Tinsley	5	39
215	Tonge + Breedon	4	42
216	Treeton	4	48
217	Trent	4	43
218	Trowell	4	43
219	Tutbury	8	22
220	Unstone	4	37
221	Upper Broughton	4	62
222	Upperthorpe + Killamarsh	5	48
223	Wadsley Bridge ‡	5	39
224	Waleswood	5	48
225	Warsop	5	56
226	Wentworth for Hoyland Common	4	39
227	West Hallam	6	44
228	Westhouses + Blackwell	4	45
229	Weston-on-Trent	4	42
(66)	West Tinsley	95	39
230	Westwood	5	39
231	WHATSTANDWELL	4	35
232	Whiteborough	4	46
233	Whittington	4	47
234	Whitwell	4	57
235	Widmerpool	4	62
(66)	Wincobank + Meadow Hall	4	39
236	Wingfield	4	35
237	Wirksworth	4	25
238	WOODHOUSE	5	48
239	Woodhouse Mill	4	48
240	WORKSOP	5	57
241	Worthington	4	42
242	Wortley	5	29

GOODS

No	Name/Location	Ry	Ref
G 1	Steeplehouse	2	25
2	Longcliffe	2	25

SIDINGS

No	Name	Ry	Ref
P 1	Gotham Branch	5	52

TUNNELS

No	Name	Length yards	Ry	Ref
T 1	Totley	6230	4	27

JUNCTIONS

No	Name/Location	Ry	Ref
J 1	Willington	48	22
2	Stenson	4	32
3	Chellaston West	4	32
4	Chellaston East	4	32
5	Gotham Branch	5	52

NOTES:

(1) Stations in blue are not named on the map. See enlargements as indicated on page (67),(68) or (66).

(2) References all in SK

(3) Other features included on this page only if not shown on an enlargement

(4) Name Changes:
§ Map name
§ Modern name
† Hazlewood or Hazelwood
✱ POND STREET now just SHEFFIELD

Changes only shown as at map date (1917) and as at 1984 – intermediate changes are not indicated.

(5) Other Information:
‡ Closed station used for excursions only from time to time
✱ Closed early in 20th century.
✗ Independent but controlled by GE and GC.

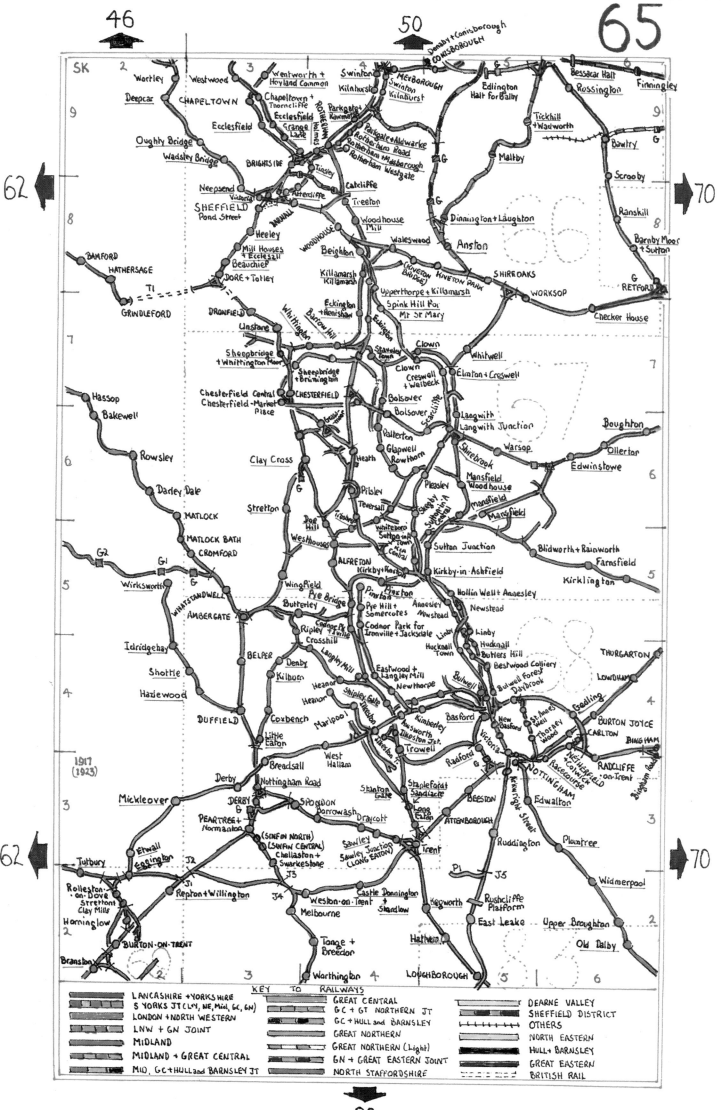

RAILWAYS

No.	Company
R 1	LANCASHIRE + YORKSHIRE
13456	SOUTH YORKS JT (LY, NE, Mid, GC + GN)
2	LONDON + NORTH WESTERN
4	MIDLAND
45	MIDLAND + GREAT CENTRAL
457	MIDLAND, GRAND HULL + BARNSLEY JOINT
5	GREAT CENTRAL
57	GREAT CENTRAL and HULL + BARNSLEY
6	GREAT NORTHERN
6A	GREAT NORTHERN (Light)
69	GT NORTHERN + GT EASTERN JOINT
7	HULL + BARNSLEY
95	SHEFFIELD DISTRICT (see note ⚹)
11	DEARNE VALLEY
O	BRITISH RAIL (New spurs)

STATIONS

No.	Name	Ry Ref
A1	Anston	5 39
2	Attercliffe	4 47
3	ATTERCLIFFE Road	5 47
4	Bawtry	11 59
5	Beauchief	69 69
6	Beighton	5 39
7	Bessacar Halt	4 29
8	BRIGHTSIDE	4 49
9	Broughton Lane	4 48
10	Catcliffe	5 48
11	CHAPELTOWN	4 49
12	Chapeltown + Thorncliffe	5 48
13	Checker House	5 67
14	CONISBOROUGH	5 59
15	DARNALL	5 38
16	Denaby + Conisborough	7 58
17	Dinnington + Laughton	13456 58
18	DORE + TOTLEY	4 38
19	DRONFIELD	4 37
20	Ecclesfield	4 39
21	Ecclesfield	5 39
22	Eckington + Renishaw †	4 47
23	Eckington + Renishaw †	5 47
24	Edlington Hall For Balby	11 59
25	Finningley ‡	69 69
26	Grange Lane	5 39
27	Heeley	4 29
28	Holmes	4 49
29	Killamarsh	4 48
30	Killamarsh	5 48
31	Kilnhurst	4 49
32	Kilnhurst	5 49
33	(KIVETON BRIDGE)	5 48
34	KIVETON PARK	5 58
35	Maltby	13456 59
36	Meadow Hall + Wincobank	5 39
37	MEXBOROUGH	5 49
38	Millhouses + Ecclesall	4 38
39	Neepsend	5 38
40	Oughty Bridge	5 39
41	Parkgate + Aldwarke	5 38
42	Parkgate + Rawmarsh	4 38
43	RETFORD	6 69
44	Rossington	4 29
45	Rotherham + Masborough	5 48
46	ROTHERHAM - Masborough	69 69
47	Rotherham Road	4 39
48	Rotherham Westgate	5 38
49	Scrooby	95 48
	SHEFFIELD	4 39
50	Attercliffe Road	5 39
51	ATTERCLIFFE Road	5 39
52	POND ST (now SHEFFIELD)	4 38
53	Victoria	5 58
54	SHIREOAKS	
55	Spink Hill for Mt. St. Mary	5 47
56	Swinton	5 39
57	Swinton	5 49
58	Tickhill + Wadworth	13456 59
59	Tinsley	5 39
60	Treeton	5 39
61	Unstone	4 47
62	Upper Hope + Killamarsh ‡	5 47
63	Wadsley Bridge ‡	11 59
64	Waleswood	69 69
65	Wentworth + Hoyland Common	5 39
66	West Tinsley	4 29
67	Westwood	4 49
68	Wincobank + Meadow Hall	4 48
69	WOODHOUSE	5 48
70	Woodhouse Mill	4 49
71	WORKSOP	5 49

COLLIERIES

No.	Name	Ry Ref
8	Kiveton Park Colliery	4 48
9	Birley Collieries	4 37
10	Tinsley Park Colliery	5 48
11	Treeton Colliery	5 39
12	Furnaces Siding	5 48
13	Silver Wood Colliery	4 39
14	Dinnington Main	95 39
15	Thurcroft Colliery	5 39
16	Maltby Main Colliery	4 39
17	Yorkshire Main Colliery	5 48
18	Yorkshire Main Colliery	4 48
19	Eastfield Tickhill	5 57
20	Rossington Main Colliery	
21	Canal Siding	5 58
22	Beighton Colliery	4 48

GOODS

No.	Name/Location	Ry Ref
G1	Attercliffe	5 39
2	Bridge houses	5 49
3	City	4 38
4	Edlington	5 38
5	Elsecar	5 39
6	Hellaby	5 49
7	Mission	4 49
8	Nunnery	6 67
9	Park	6 69
10	Pond Street	5 49
11	Queens Road	4 49
12	Thurcroft	5 49
13	Warmsworth	4 49
14	Wicker	6 69
15	Woodhouse	5 38

Goods stations with refs (right-hand column):

No.	Name	Ry Ref
9	Woodburn	4 48
10	Darnall	5 48
11	Attercliffe	95 48
12	Grimesthorpe	5 48
13	Brightside	5 49
14	Blackburn Valley	45 49
15	Tinsley South	13456 58
16	Tinsley West	457 58
17	Tinsley East	13456-59
18	Wincobank West	57 59
19	Wincobank North	11 x 59
20	Meadow Hall	6A 69
21	Grange Lane	6 69
22	Smithy Wood	5 58
23	Chapeltown	4 48
24	High Level Sidings	
25	Park Sidings	
26	Renishaw Iron Co	
27	Kiveton Park Branch	
28	Upper Hope	4 37
29	Beighton South	5 47
30	Beighton Station	
31	Birley Branch	
32	Halbrook	
33	Waleswood	
34	Orgreaves	
35	Treeton	
36	Tinsley Park Col Bch	
37	Holmes	
38	Masborough South	
39	Masborough North	
40	Roundwood	
41	Thrybergh	
42	Don Bridge East	
43	Silverwood West	
44	Silverwood East	
45	Swinton	
46	Mexborough No 1	
47	Mexborough No 2	
48	Mexborough East	

TUNNELS

No.	Name/Location	Length yards	Ry Ref
T1	Totley	6230	4 37
2	Bradway	2027	4 38
3	Spink Hill		5 47

ENGINE SHEDS

No.	Name/Location	Ry Ref
E1	Millhouses	4 38
2	Canklow	4 38
3	Grimesthorpe	45 38
4	Darnall	5 39
5	Mexborough Wath	4 38

JUNCTIONS

No.	Name/Location	Ry Ref
J1	Unstone Branch South	4 37
2	Unstone Branch North	4 39
3	Dore West	4 39
4	Dore South	4 39
5	Dore Station	5 39
6	Queens Road	X5 47
7	Pond Street Depot	X4 47
8	Tunnel	4 48

SIDINGS

No.	Company/Name/Location	Ry Ref
P1	Thorncliffe High Level	5 38
2	Smithy Wood Colliery	5 58
3	Thorncliffe Sidings	5 47
4	Grange Colliery	4 39
5	Harnthorpes Colliery	5 49
6	Eckington Iron Works	13456 59
7	Halbrook Colliery No.2	5 39

NOTES:

⚹ Refs. all in SK except J66-8 in SE

⚹⚹ Controlled by GE + GC

‡ Closed but used occasionally for passenger services

♀ Sheffield GOODS STATIONS

† Also known as Eckington

NAME CHANGES (stations still open): part in small letters now dropped.

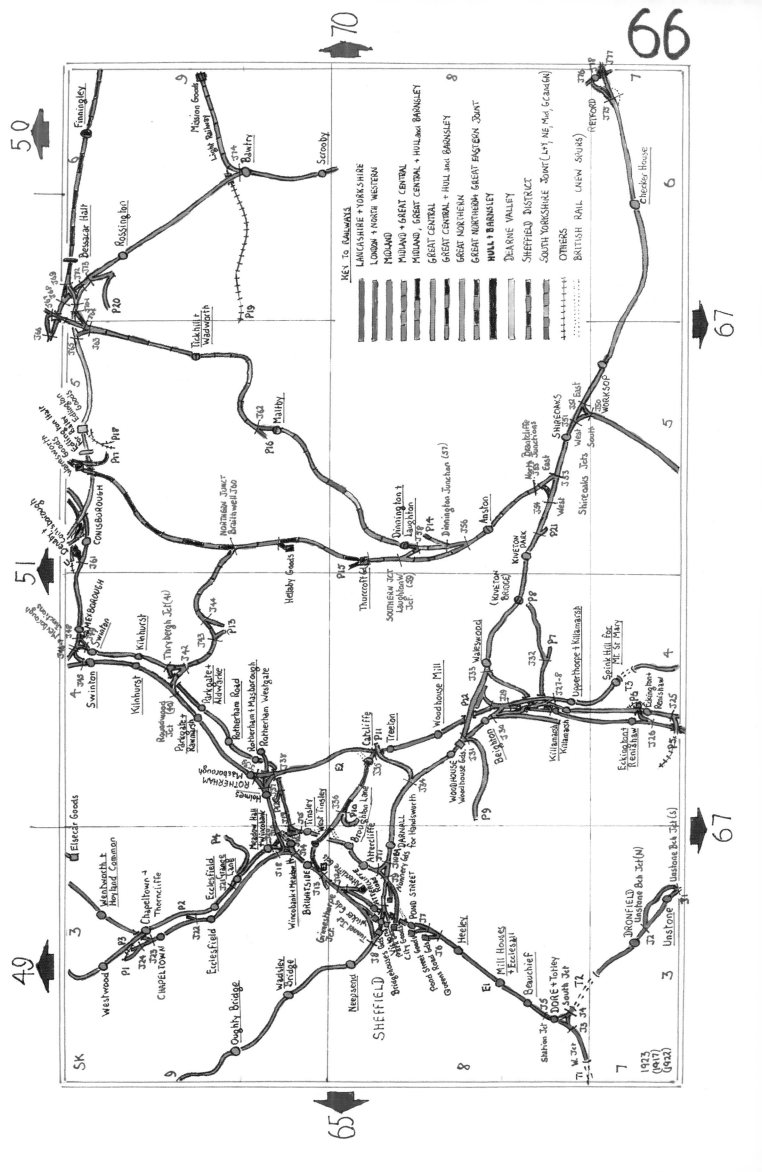

RAILWAYS

No	Company
R2	LONDON+NORTH WESTERN
4	MIDLAND
5	GREAT CENTRAL
6	GREAT NORTHERN
X	Colliery Lines

STATIONS

No	Name	Ry Ref
A1	ALFRETON+MANSFIELD PARKWAY	4(+6)5
2	ALFRETON+SOUTH NORMANTON §	
3	Annesley	4 55
4	Arkwright Town	5 47
5	Barrow Hill for Staveley Works	4 47
6	Bidworth + Rainworth	4 55
7	Bolsover ✝	4 47
8	Bolsover	5 46
9	Boughton	5 46
10	CHESTERFIELD	4 37
11	Chesterfield Central	5 37
12	Chesterfield Market Place	5 37
13	Clay Cross	4 36
14	Clown	4 46
15	Clown	4 47
16	Creswell + Welbeck	5 47
17	CROMFORD	4 35
18	Doe Hill	4 46
19	Edwinstowe	5 66
20	Elmton + Creswell	4 65
21	Farnsfield	4 46
22	Glapwell	5 46
23	Grassmoor	5 46
24	Heath	5 46
25	Hollin Well + Annesley	✳56 65
26	Kirkby + Pinxton	5 45
27	Kirkby-in-Ashfield	4 55
28	Kirkby-in-Ashfield Central	5 45
29	Kirling	4 65
30	Langwith Junction	5(+6)56
31	Langwith	4 56
32	Mansfield	4 56
33	Mansfield	5 56
34	Mansfield Woodhouse	4 56
35	Ollerton	5 66
36	Palterton + Sutton	4 46
37	Pilsley	5 46
38	Pinxton + Selston	4 45
39	Pinxton for South Normanton	6 45
40	Pleasley	4 46
41	Pleasley	6 50
42	Rowthorn + Hardwick	4 46
43	Scarcliffe	5 50
44	Sheepbridge + Brimington	5 37
45	Sheepbridge Whittington Moor	4 37
46	Shirebrook	4 56
47	Shirebrook	4 55
48	Skegby for Stanton Hill	5 47
49	Staveley Town	4 47
50	Staveley Town	4 55
51	Staveley Works for Barrow Hill	4 47
52	Stretton	5 46
53	Sutton-in-Ashfield Central	5 66
54	Sutton in Ashfield Town	4 37
55	Sutton Junction	5 37
56	Teversall	5 37
57	Tibshelf + Newton	4 46
58	Tibshelf Town	4 47
59	Warsop	5 47
60	Westhouses + Blackwell	5 57
61	WHATSTANDWELL	4 35
62	Whiteborough	4 46
63	Whittington	5 66
64	Whitwell	4 57
65	Wingfield	4 65

No	Name	Ry Ref
12	Whatstandwell	4 46 / 5 46
41	Creswell Colliery	4 35
42	Lord Saville's Sidings	4 55
43	Annesley Colliery Siding	4 55

ENGINE SHEDS

No	Name/Location	Ry Ref
E1	Westhouses	4 55
2	Hasland	4 35
3	Staveley (Barrow Hill)	4 37
4	Staveley	4 37
5	(Shirebrook)	4 45

SIDINGS

No	Company/Name/Location	Ry Ref
P1	Cliffe Quarry ♀	X 35
2	Crich Quarry ♀	X 35
3	Wingfield Manor Colliery	4X 35
4	Shirland Colliery	4 35
5	Nesfield Branch	4 37
6	Markswood Branch (disused) ✳	4 37
7	Swanick Branch - Langcroft	4X 45
8	Swanick Branch - Somercotes	4X 45
9	Pinxton Colliery	6X 45
10	Langton Colliery	4,5,X 45
11	Bentinck Colliery	4,5,X 45
12	New Hucknall Colliery	45X 45
13	Tibshelf Colliery	45X 46

TUNNELS

No	Name/Location	Yds
T1	Clay Cross	1784+
2	Rowtham	929

JUNCTIONS

No	Name/Location	Ry Ref
J1	High Peak	6 46
2	Wingfield	45 46
3	Shirland	45 46
4	Grassmoor Branch	4 46
5	Hollis Lane	45 46
6	Dunston + Barlow South	45 46
7	West	5 46
8	Dunston + Barlow North	4 46
9	Rye Bridge	54 47
10	Pinxton	45X 47
11	Colliery	5 47
12	Bentinck Branch No.1	45 47
13	Bentinck Branch No.2	4 47
14	Kirkby Colliery Branches	4 47
15	New Hucknall Colliery Branch	5 47
16	Blackwell South	45 57
17	Blackwell East	6 55
18	Blackwell Branch	4 56
19	Tibshelf South	5 56
20	Skegby Branch	4 56
21	Pilsley Branch	5 56
22	Clay Cross South	4+6 56
23	Clay Cross North	45X 56
24	Grassmoor	X 56
25	Heath	45 57
14	Silverhill Colliery	5 55
15	Silverhill Colliery	6 45
16	Teversall Colliery	4 55
17	Pilsley Colliery	4 46
18	Holmwood Colliery	45 45
19	Clay Cross Brick Works	5 46
20	Williamthorpe Colliery	5 56
21	Bond's Main Colliery	4 46
22	Glapwell Colliery	4 35
23	Glapwell Colliery	4 46
24	Bolsover Colliery	4 47
25	Markham Colliery	4 57
26	St Johns Colliery	4 35
27	Ireland Colliery	6 45
28	Springwell Branch	6 45
29	Oxcroft Colliery	4 45
30	Bartborough Colliery	5 45
31	Southgate Colliery	4 46
32	Kirkby Colliery Siding	6 55
33	King's Mill Siding	4 56
34	Mansfield Colliery	5 56
35	Mansfield Colliery	4 56
36	Clipstone Colliery	5 56
37	Shirebrook Colliery	5 56
38	Warsop Main Colliery	4 56
39	Warsop Main Colliery	4 56
40	Langwith Colliery	5 46

JUNCTIONS (continued)

No	Name/Location	Ry Ref
J26	Pleasley Colliery West	4 55
27	Arkwright Town	
28	Arkwright East	
29	Arkwright South	
30	Arkwright North	4 45
31	Glapwell Branch South	4 36
32	Glapwell Branch West	4 47
33	Glapwell Branch East	5 47
34	St John's Branch	6 56
35	Ireland	
36	Springwell Branch	
37	Staveley Passenger	
38	Hartington Midland	4 36
39	Hartington Great Central	4 46
40	Seymour	
41	Oxcroft	
42	Markham Colliery Sidings	42 35
43	Bartborough West	4 35
44	Bartborough East	4 35
45	Annesley North	4 36
46	Kirkby South	4 37
47	Sutton South	4 37
48	Mansfield South	4 37
49	Mansfield East	4 37
50	Mansfield North	4 45
J51	Mansfield Goods	4 46
52	Mansfield Colliery Branch	5 47
53	Rufford Colliery Branch	5 47
54	Mansfield Colliery	5 47
55	Clipstone Colliery	5 47
56	Lord Savilles Branch	5 47
57	Pleasley	5 47
58	Pleasley Colliery	5 47
59	Shirebrook Colliery	4 47
60	Shirebrook Colliery	4 47
61	Langwith North	4 47
62	Langwith Middle	4 47
63	Langwith South	5 47
64	Shirebrook Jcts.	5 47
65	Warsop	4 47
66	Warsop Main West	4 47
67	Warsop Main East	4 47
68	Langwith Colliery	5 47
69	Creswell Colliery	5 47
70	Creswell Colliery	56 55
71	Southgate Colliery	36 55
72	Creswell	4 55
73	Duke of Portlands	4 56
74	Clipstone West	4 56
75	Clipstone East	56 56

GOODS

No	Name/Location	Ry Ref
1	Brampton	56 55
2	Clay Cross	5 45
3	Clipstone	4 55
4	Cromford	5 45
5	Hasland	4 65
6	Mansfield	5(+6)56
7	Mansfield	4 56
8	Market Pl - Chesterfield	4 56
9	Sheepbridge	5 56
10	Sutton	4 56
11	Teversall	5 66

NOTES:

(1) REFERENCES - All in square SK
(2) NAME CHANGE ~ Name at map date
  Modern name
(3) STATION Closed - but open for excursions etc
(✝) Station Closed early 20th century
(5) Now Tramway (+ Tramway Museum) between these two points

§   ✝   ✳   ♀

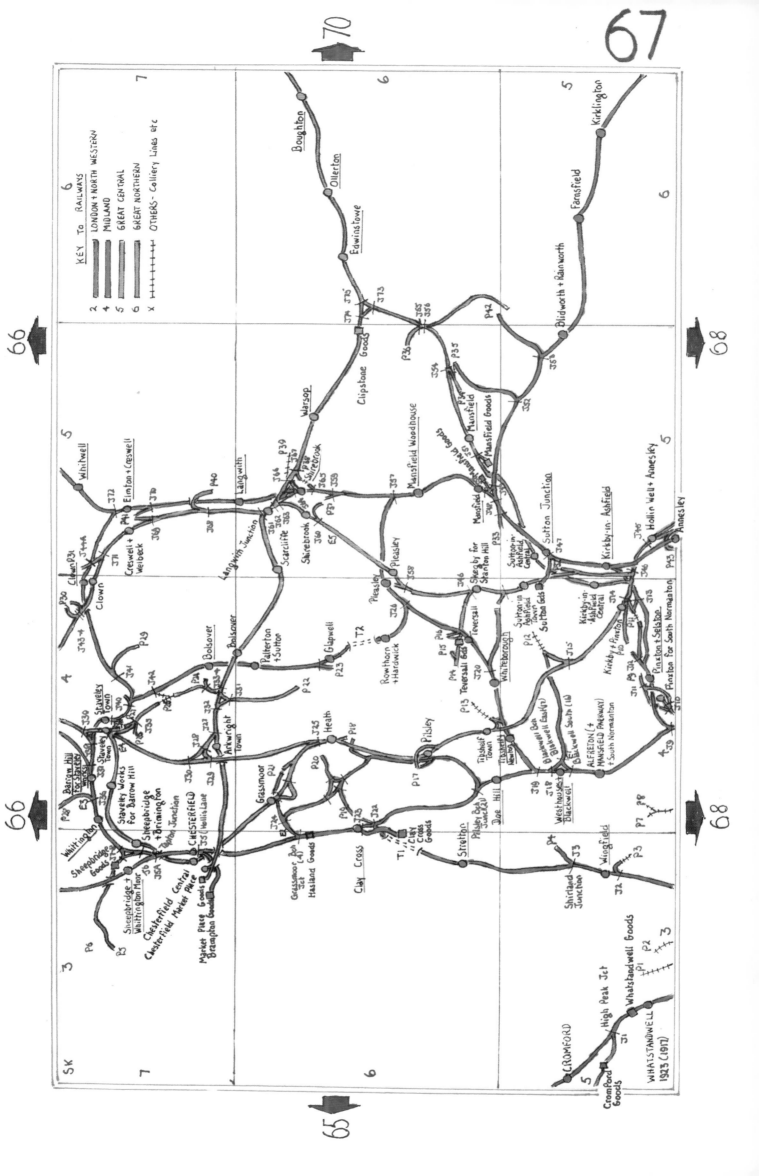

RAILWAYS

No	Company	Ry Ref
R2	LONDON + NORTH WESTERN	
26	LNW + GREAT NORTHERN JT	
4	MIDLAND	
5	GREAT CENTRAL	
56	GREAT CENTRAL + GREAT NORTHERN	
6	GREAT NORTHERN	
X	COLLIERY RAILWAYS ETC	

STATIONS + HALTS

No	Name	Ry Ref
A 1	AMBERGATE	4 35
2	Annesley	4 55
3	Arkwright Street	5 53
4	Awsworth	6 44
5	Basford	4 54
6	Basford + Bulwell	6 54
7	BELPER	4 34
8	Bestwood Colliery	6 54
9	BINGHAM	6 53
10	Bingham Road	26 63
11	Borrowash	4 43
12	Breadsall	6 33
13	Bulwell	4 54
14	Bulwell Common	5 54
15	Bulwell Forest	6 54
16	BURTON JOYCE	6 54
17	Butler's Hill	6 54
18	Butterley	4 35
19	CARLTON + Netherfield	4 64
20	Carrington	5 54
21	Chellaston + Swarkestone	4 33
22	Codnor Park for Ironville	4 45
23	Codnor Park for Ironville + Jacksdale	4 34
24	Corbench	4 44
25	Crosshill + Codnor	6 54
26	Daybrook	4 34
27	Denby	4 33
28	DERBY	4 43
29	Derby	6 33
30	Derby Nottingham Road	4 33
31	Draycott	4 43
32	DUFFIELD	4 34
32A	Eastwood + Langley Mill	6 44
33	Gedling + Carlton	4 43
34	Hazlewood	4 43
35	Heanor	6 54
36	Heanor	4 44
37	Heanor	4 34
38	Hucknall	4 33
39	Hucknall	4 33
40	Hucknall Town	4 33
41	Ilkeston	4 43
42	Ilkeston Junction	4 43
43	Ilkeston Town	4 43
44	Kilburn	4 34
45	Kimberley	6 44
46	Langley Mill	4 44
47	Langley Mill + Eastwood	4 44
48	Linby	4 34
49	Linby	6 44
50	Little Eaton	4 34
51	London Road	6 54
52	Long Eaton	4 34
53	(LONG EATON)	6 54
54	LOWDHAM	6 63
55	Marlpool	6 55
56	Mickleover	4 43
57	NETHERFIELD + Colwick	6 33
58	New Basford	4 54
59	Newstead	5 54
60	Newstead	6 54
61	Newthorpe, Greasley + Shipley Gate	4 64
	NOTTINGHAM	
62	Arkwright Street	4 64
63	London Road - High Level	5 54
64	London Road - Low Level	4 33
65	Racecourse	4 45
66	Victoria	4 35
67		
68	Nottingham Road Derby	4 34
69	PEARTREE + Normanton	4 44
70	Pye Bridge	6 54
71	Pye Hill + Somercotes	4 34
72	Racecourse - Nottingham	4 33
73	RADCLIFFE - on - Trent	6 33
74	Radford	4 33
75	Ripley	4 43
76	St Ann's Well	4 34
77	Sawley	6 64
78	SAWLEY JUNCTION	4 34
79	Sherwood	4 44
80	Shipley Gate	6 44
81	Shottle	4 54
82	(SINFIN CENTRAL)	6 54
83	(SINFIN NORTH)	5 54
84	SPONDON	6 44
85	Stanton Gate	4 44
86	Stapleford + Sandiacre	4 44
87	Thorneywood	4 34
88	THURGARTON	6 44
89	Trent	4 44
90	Trowell	4 44
91	West Hallam	4 55

GOODS

No	Name / Location	Ry Ref
5	Hartsay Colliery	4 43
6	Swanwick Branch + Colliery	4 43
7	Colliery Siding	6 54
8	Stanton Iron Works	4 44
9	Stanley Colliery	4 34
10	Mapperley Colliery	4 33
11	Nutbrook Colliery	4 33
12	Shipley Colliery	4 33
13	Eastwood Branch	4 43
14	Babbington Branch	4 43
15	Digby Colliery	6 54
16	Lodge Colliery	4 64
17	Plumtree Colliery	4 43
18	Beavale Works	4 43
19	New Brinsley Colliery	6 44
20	Riddings Colliery	
21	Britain Pit	
22	Beggarlee Branch	
23	Butterley Lines	4 34
24	Watnall Colliery	6 63
25	Cinderhill Collieries	6 33
26	Newcastle Colliery	6 33
27	Bestwood Colliery	6 33
28	Hucknall Branch	4 33
29	Hucknall Colliery Sidings	68 33
30	Newstead Colliery Sidings	4 33
31	Clifton Colliery Line	4 33
32	Sands + Sons	4 44
33	Nott's Sewage Farm	6 64
34	Gedling Colliery	5 53
35	Nuttall Sand Siding	5 53

No	Name / Location	Ry Ref
G1	Belper	4 43
2	Bingham	4 43
3	DERBY Duke Street	6 44
4	Gt Northern	6 33
5	GN Cattle	6 64
6	London Road	5 54
7	LNW + NS	4 55
8	Midland Cattle	6 55
9	St Mary's	6 44
10	Kimberley	6 44
11	Netherfield + Colwick	5 53
12	NOTTINGHAM - GC	4 53
13	GC Cattle	5 53
14	Lenton	5 53
15	LNWR	6 53
16	Midland	6 53
17	Mid Cattle	6 53
18	Mid Coal	56 53

SIDINGS

No	Company / Name / Location	Ry Ref
19	Ripley - Minerals	4 33
20	Trent (Sheet Stores)	4 33
P1	Cliffe Quarry	6 53
2	Criche Quarry	4 53
3	Salterwood Colliery	4 35
4	Marehay Main	6 54

COMPANY WORKS

No	Location	Ry Ref
30	Ripley	4 53
No		2 53
C1	DERBY	4 53

ENGINE SHEDS

No	Location	Ry Ref
E1	Derby	4 43
2	Nottingham	2 53
3	Derby	
4	Derby Friargate	6 33
5	Annesley	5 55
6	Netherfield + Colwick	6 64
7	Netherfield + Colwick	2 64
8	Stapleford + Sandiacre	4 34

JUNCTIONS

No	Name / Location	Ry Ref
X 35		4X 45
J1	Lenton South	6 44
2	Lenton North	6 43
3	Mansfield	6 44
4	Goods Yard East	4 44
5	London Road	4 44
6	Sneiton	X 44
7	Trent Lane West	4 44
8	Trent Lane East	6 44
9	Weekday Cross	6 44
10	Nottingham + Melton	6 44
11	Melbourne	X 44
12	Stenson	X 44
13	London Road Wharf	X 44
14	London Road	6 45
15	Spondon	X 45
16	Derby North	4 44
17	Derby South	X 43
18	Derby West	4X 54
19	St Mary's	X 54
20	GN Derby Goods	X 54
21	GN Derby Cattle	46 54
22	Little Eaton	5 54
23	Duffield	6 54
24	Ambergate South	6 54
25	Ambergate West	6 55
26	Ambergate North	6 53
27	Ambergate Crich	6 63
28	Buckland Hollow Branch	6 64
29	Butterley	6 64
30	Ripley	6 54
31	Trent Sheet Stores West	Ry Ref
32	Trent Sheet Stores East	4 33
33	Trent	
34	Trent Station South	
35	Sawley	Ry Ref
36	Trent Station North	4 33
37	Long Eaton	4 33
38	North Erewash	2 33
39	Attenborough	6 33
40	Meadow Lane	5 55
41	Stanton + Shipley Branch	6 64
42	Trowell	2 64
43	Ilkeston	4 43

No	Name / Location	Ry Ref
44	Bennerley	4 44
45	Ilkeston West	4 44
46	Ilkeston - Heanor Branch	6 44
47	West Hallam Colliery	6 44
48	Stanley Colliery	6 44
49	Langley Mill Curve	4 44
50	Heanor	4 44
51	Swanwick Branch	4 45
52	Ironville	4 45
53	Codnor Park	4 45
54	Great Northern	4 46
55	Riddings Colliery	4 45
56	Riddings	6 45
57	Pye Bridge	6 46
58	Brinsley	6 44
	(Colliery Lines)	4 35
59	Awsworth	4 35
60	Radford	4 35
61	Rectory	4 35
62	Netherfield North	4 35
63	Netherfield West	6 35
64	Swandale	6 33
65	Bagthorpe	6 33
66	Lee Valley	4 34
67	Ilkeston Branch (Basford)	4 35
68	Watnall Colliery Branch	6 35
69	Daybrook	4 35
70	Moorbridge	4 35
71	Bestwood Colliery	4 35
72	Bestwood Park Branch	4 35
73	Bulwell Common South	4 34
74	Bulwell Line	4 34
75		4 43

NOTES

(1) REFERENCES - All in square SK
(2) NAME CHANGE - Map name §
   - Modern name §
(3) ALTERNATIVE Spelling - Hazelwood †
(4) PASSENGER STATIONS also but closed as such early 20c †
(5) Closed early 20c ⊙
(6) A Midland line from Ilkeston to Kimberley abandoned in the early 20th century ✦

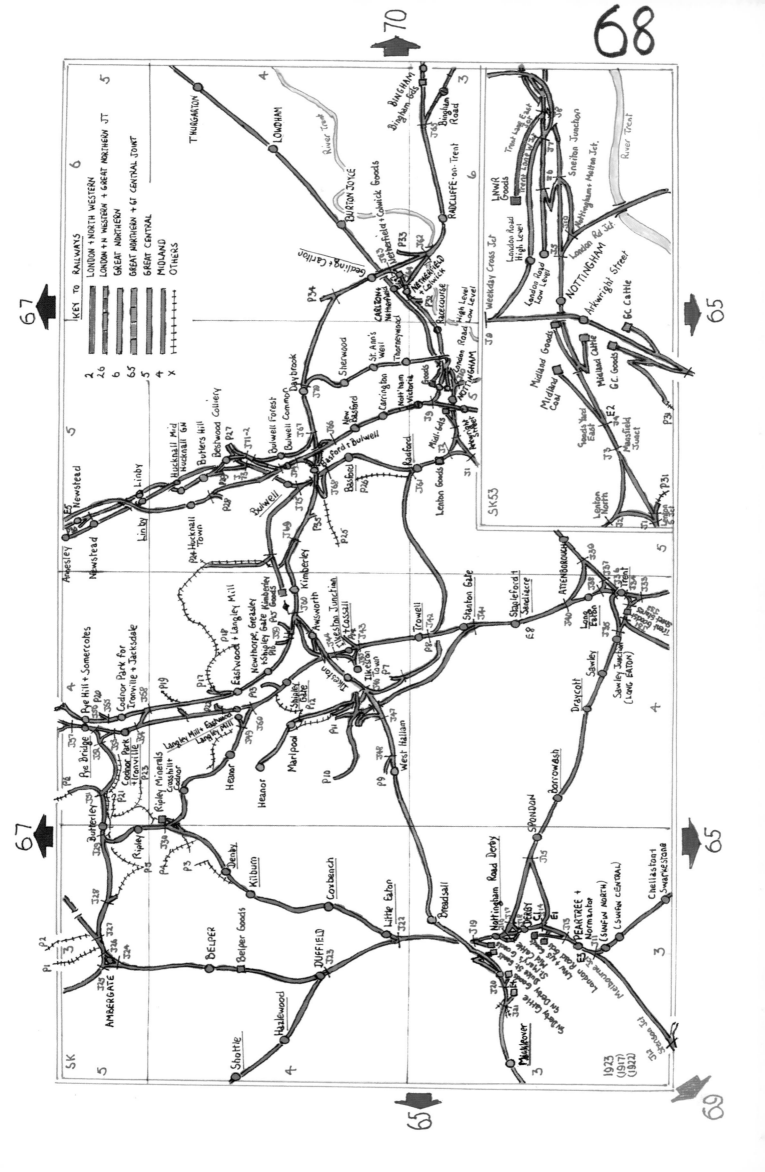

69 RAILWAYS

BURTON·ON·TRENT

Railways

No	Company
R2	LONDON + NORTH WESTERN
4	MIDLAND
6	GREAT NORTHERN
8	NORTH STAFFORDSHIRE
X	PRIVATE + WORKS LINES

STATIONS

No	Name	Ry Ref
A1	Branston	4 21 20
2	BURTON·ON·TRENT	4 23 23
3	Eggington	68 26 29
4	Horninglow	8 25 25
5	Repton + Willington	4 29 27
6	Rolleston·on·Dove	8 26 28
7	Stretton + Clay Mills	8 25 27
8	Tutbury	8 23 29

GOODS

No	Name	Ry Ref
G1	Bond End Wharf	4 24 21
2	Dallow Lane Wharf	4 23 24
3	Eggington	8 27 28
4	Hawkins Lane	6 26 24
5	Horninglow Streets	2 25 23
6	Moor Street Wharf	2 23 22
7	Shobnall Wharf	4 21 23
8	Station Street	4 23 23

SIDINGS

No	Company / Name / Location	Ry Ref
P1	Meakins Siding	4 22 21
2	Bass (Shobnall)	X 21 21
3	Bass (Shobnall)	X 21 22
4	Albion Brewery	X 21 23
5	Allsopps (Shobnall)	X 20 23
6	Eadies Siding	4 24 22
7	Eadies Brewery	X 24 22
8	Ind Coope (Mosley)	X 24 22
9	Robinsons Brewery	4X 25 22
10	Bindley's Sidings	4X 25 22
11	Hay Branch	4 26 22
12	Allsopps Cooperage	4 25 23
13	Bass + Allsopps Sidings	X 25 23
14	Bass (Guild Street)	X 25 23
15	Bretby Branch (Colliery)	4 29 20

ENGINE SHEDS

No	Name / Location	Ry Ref
E1	Burton (Leicester Jct)	4 22 22
2	Burton (North Staffs)	8 23 23
3	Burton (LNW)	2 25 23

JUNCTIONS

No	Name / Location	Ry Ref
J1	Branston ✳(Note 3)	4 21 20
2	Birmingham Curve	4 22 20
3	Leicester	4 22 22
4	Meakins Siding	4 22 22
5	Leicester South	4 22 21
6	Dale Street (North)	4 23 22
7	Dale Street (South)	24 23 22
8	Wellington Street	4 22 22
9	Shobnall	24 22 23
10	Mosley Street	4 23 22
11	Uxbridge Street	4 23 21
12	James Street	4 24 21
13	Brindley	4 25 22
14	Yeomans Siding	2X 22 23
15	Goods Yard	4 24 23
16	Guild Street	4 24 24
17	Horninglow	4 24 24
18	Allsopps Cooperage Bch	4 26 24
19	Hawkins Lane	2468 25 24
20	North	86 26 25
21	South	86 25 24
22	North Stafford (W)	48 25 25
23	North Stafford (S)	4 25 24
24	North Stafford (N)	4 25 25
25	Wetmore (S)	24 26 25
26	Stretton North	82 25 26
27	Stretton South	8 25 26
28	Willington	48 30 27
29	Dove	86 25 28
30	Marston	8 25 29
31	Eggington West	86 26 29
32	Eggington East	86 26 29

JUNCTIONS (continued)

No	Name / Location	Ry Ref
J33	Guild Street (Hay)	4 26 22
34	Wetmore	4 26 25

NOTES

(1) SCALE: Map is NOT to scale as can be seen from the Grid — the N-S distances are exaggerated

(2) REFERENCES: All in SK22 and, due to large scale, four-figure references are given

(3) BRANSTON JCT is actually some chains south of where shown + is close to Branston Station; the lines then ran side by side and then diverged at a point where the junction is shown ✳

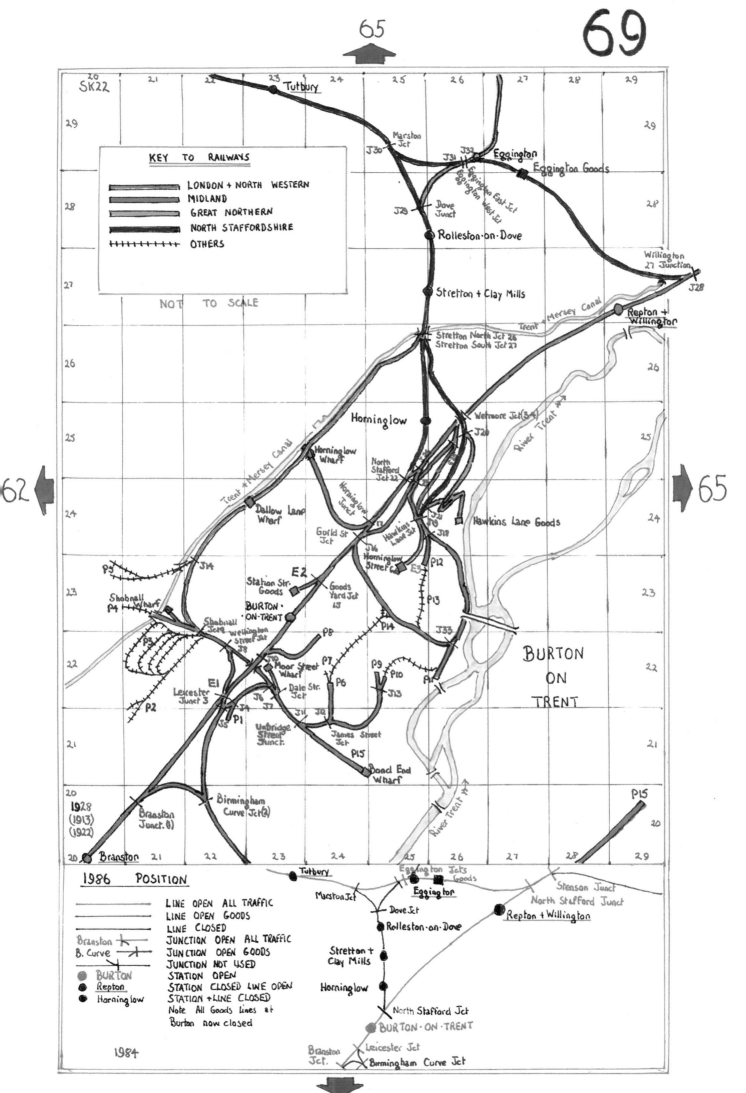

KEY TO RAILWAYS

LONDON + NORTH WESTERN
MIDLAND
GREAT NORTHERN
NORTH STAFFORDSHIRE
OTHERS

NOT TO SCALE

SK22

Tutbury

Marston Jct
J30
J31 J32 Eggington
Eggington East Jct   Eggington Goods
Eggington West Jct
J29   Dove Junct
Rolleston-on-Dove

Willington
Junction
J28

Stretton + Clay Mills

Trent + Mersey Canal   Repton +
Willington

Stretton North Jct 26
Stretton South Jct 27

Horninglow
Wetmore Jct (34)
J20
River Trent

Horninglow
Wharf
North Stafford
Jct 22

Trent + Mersey Canal

Dallow Lane
Wharf
Horninglow
Junct
J21   Hawkins Lane Goods
Gorild St   Hawkins Lane St
Jct   J18
J16   J10
P12
Horninglow
Street Gd   E3
P5   J14
Station Str.
Goods   E2
Goods
Yard Jct
15   P13
Shobnall
Wharf
P4
Shobnall   P8
Jct   Wellington
Street Jct
J8   P14   J33
P3   J10   Moor Street
E1   Wharf   P7   P9
Leicester
Junct 3   Dale Str.   P6   P10   BURTON
Jct   P1
J9   J7 J2 J11 Jq   J13   ON
J5 P1
Uxbridge   James Street
Street   Jct
Junct.   P15   TRENT
P2

Bond End
Wharf
River Trent

1928
(1913)
(1922)
Birmingham
Curve Jct (2)   P15
Branston
Junct. 8)
Branston   River Trent

62

65

1986 POSITION

LINE OPEN ALL TRAFFIC
LINE OPEN GOODS
LINE CLOSED
Branston   JUNCTION OPEN ALL TRAFFIC
B. Curve   JUNCTION OPEN GOODS
JUNCTION NOT USED
BURTON   STATION OPEN
Repton   STATION CLOSED LINE OPEN
Horninglow STATION + LINE CLOSED
Note All Goods lines at
Burton now closed

1984

Tutbury
Eggington Jcts
Goods
Marston Jct   Eggington   Stenson Junct
North Stafford Junct
Dove Jct
Rolleston-on-Dove   Repton + Willington

Stretton +
Clay Mills

Horninglow

North Stafford Jct

BURTON · ON · TRENT

Branston   Leicester Jct
Jct.   Birmingham Curve Jct

LINCOLN, NEWARK + SLEAFORD

RAILWAYS

No.	Company
R13	AXHOLME JOINT (LY+NE)
26	LONDON + NW and GN JOINT
4	MIDLAND
46	MIDLAND+GREAT NORTHERN JOINT
5	GREAT CENTRAL
6	GREAT NORTHERN
6A	GREAT NORTHERN (Light)
67	GT NORTHERN + GT EASTERN JOINT
O	BR + POST GROUPING additions

STATIONS

No.	Name	Ry Ref
A 1	ANCASTER	6 K94
2	ASLOCKTON	6 K74
3	Aswarby for Scredington	6 F04
4	Bardney	6 F16
5	Barkston	6 K94
6	Barnstone	26 K73
7	Beckingham	67 K78
8	Billingborough+Horbling	6 F13
9	BINGHAM	6 K74
10	Blankney+METHERINGHAM	67 F06
11	BLEASBY	4 K75
12	Blyton	5 K89
13	BOTTESFORD	6 K83
14	Branston + Heighington	67 F06
15	Carlton-on-Trent	6 K76
16	Caythorpe	6 K94
17	Claxby + Usselby	5 F19
18	Claypole	6 K84
19	Clifton-on-Trent	5 K87
20	COLLINGHAM	4 K86
21	Corby	6 K92
22	Cotham	6 K84
23	Cottam	5 K87
23A	Counter Drain	46 F12
24	Crow Park	6 K76
25	Digby	67 F05
26	Doddington + Harby	5 K87
27	Donington Road	67 F23
28	Dukeries Junction ✕	5 K76
29	Dukeries Junction ✕	6 K76
30	East Barkwith	6 F18
31	ELTON + ORSTON	6 K74
32	FISKERTON	4 K75
33	Five Mile House	6 F07
34	Fledborough	5 K77
35	GAINSBOROUGH (CENTRAL) †	5 K88
36	GAINSBOROUGH (LEA RD) †	67 K88
37	GRANTHAM	6 K93
38	Great Ponton	6 K92
39	Grimston	4 K72
40	Harby + Stathern	26 K73
41	Harmston	6 K96
42	Haxey + Epworth	67 K79
43	Haxey Junction	13 K79
44	Haxey Town	13 K79
45	HECKINGTON	6 F14
46	Helpringham	67 F14
47	Holton	5 F09
48	Honington	6 K94
49	Hougham	6 K94
50	HYKEHAM	4 K96
51	Kingthorpe	6 F17
52	Kirkstead	6 F16
53	KIRTON LINDSEY §	5 K99
54	Langworth	5 F07
55	Lea	67 K88
56	LEA ROAD	67 K88
57	Leadenham	6 K95
58	Leverton	5 K78
59	LINCOLN CENTRAL	6 K97
60	Lincoln St Marks	4 K97
61	Long Clawson + Hose	26 K72
62	MARKET RASEN	5 F18
63	METHERINGHAM, Blankney+	67 F06
64	Misterton	67 K79
65	Moortown	5 F09
66	Morton Road	6 F12
67	Navenby	6 K95
68	NEWARK (CASTLE) †	4 K75
69	NEWARK (NORTHGATE) †	6 K85
70	Nocton + Dunston	67 F06
71	Northorpe	5 K99
72	Park Drain	67 K79
73	Potter Hanworth	67 F06
74	RAUCEBY	6 F04
75	Redmile	26 K73
76	Reepham	5 F07
77	RETFORD	5 K78
78	RETFORD	6 K78
79	Rippingdale	6 F12
80	ROLLESTON Junction	4 K75
81	RUSKINGTON	67 F05
82	St Marks Lincoln	4 K97
83	SAXILBY	67 K87
84	Scalford	266 K72
85	Scopwick + Timberland	67 F05
86	Sedgebrook	6 K83
87	Skellingthorpe	5 K97
88	SLEAFORD	6 F04
89	Snelland	5 F08
90	Southrey	6 F16
91	Southwell	4 K75
92	Stixwould	6 F16
93	Stow Park	67 K88
94	Sturton	5 K78
95	SWINDERBY	4 K86
96	Thorpe-on-the-Hill	4 K96
97	Torksey	5 K87
98	Tuxford (Central) †	5 K76
99	Tuxford (North) †	6 K77
100	Waddington	6 K96
101	Walkeringham	67 K79
102	Washingborough	6 F07
103	Wickenby	5 F08
104	Woodhall Junction §	6 F16
105	Wragby	6 F17

No.	Name	Ry Ref
9	Tuxford North	56 K77
10	Whiskerhill East	5 K67
11	Retford North	56 K78
12	Retford	6 K78
13	Retford South	56 K78
14	Clarborough	5 K78
15	Haxey	136A K79
16	Stockwith	667 K79
17	Waltham	6 K82
18	Eastwell	6 K72
19	Belvoir	6 K83
20	Allington	6 K83
21	Lowfield	6 K85
22	Bottesford Line	6 K85
23	Newark Joint North	4466 K85
24	Newark Joint South	4466 K75
25	Sykes	567 K87
26	Trent Bridge North	567 K88
27	Trent Bridge South	567 K88
28	Gas Works	6 K93
29	Grantham	6 K93
30	Barkston South	6 K94
31	Barkston East	6 K94
32	Honington	6 K94
33	Pye Wipe North	567 K97
34	Pye Wipe	667 K97
35	Sleaford West	667 F04
36	Sleaford Station + East	6 F04
37	Sleaford South	67 F04
38	Sleaford North	67 F04
39	Woodhall	6 F16
40	Bardney	6 F16
41	Wycombe	64 K72
42	Newark Crossing East	6 0 K85
43	Newark Crossing South	6 0 K85
44	Whiskerhill North	5 0 K68
45	Whiskerhill East	5 0 K67

GOODS

No.	Name / Location	Ry Ref
6 1	Bracebridge	6 K96
2	Grantham	6 K93
3	Retford	6 K68
4	Waltham-on-the-Wold	6 K82

SIDINGS

No.	Name/Company/Location	Ry Ref
P 1	Eastwell	6 K72
2	Staveley + Oaks	6 K73
3	Denton Agricultural	6 K83
4	Woolsthorpe	6 K83
5	Stockwith	6 K79
6	Lowfield	6 K85

ENGINE SHEDS

No.	Name / Location	Ry Ref
E 1	Grantham	6 K93
2	Retford	6 K78

SUMMITS

No.	Name	Ht.	Ry Ref
S 1	Stoke	345	6 K92

TUNNELS

No.	Name	Yds	Ry Ref
T 1	Stoke		6 K92
2	Peascliffe		6 K94
3	Gonerby		6 K83

JUNCTIONS

No.	Name / Location	Ry Ref
J 1	Scalford	266 K72
2	Harby	26 K73
3	Bottesford West	6 K73
4	Bottesford South	26 K73
5	Bottesford East	266 K73
6	Bottesford North	266 K74
7	Rolleston	4 K75
8	Tuxford West	5 K76

NOTES:

REFERENCES - In SK or TF - initial letter not included

§ NAME CHANGE Pre-Grouping
§ After Grouping

✕ STATIONS same site but at different levels

† POST-GROUPING addition to station name (in brackets)

O Junctions in RED - Post-Grouping or BR

LINCOLN - full details of lines, junctions, goods, sidings, engine sheds and signal boxes see map 71

Some stations on or near margins are also shown on adjoining maps.

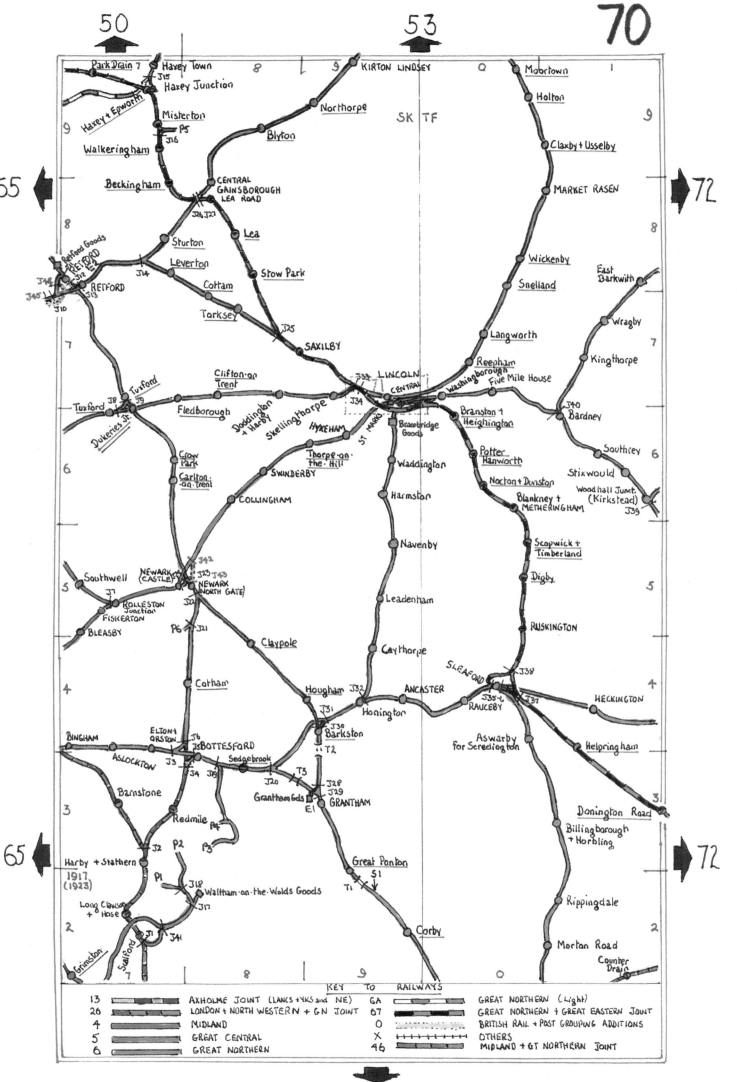

50

53

55

72

65

72

85

Park Drain 7
Haxey Town
J15
Haxey Junction
Haxey + Epworth
Misterton
P5
J16
Walkeringham
Beckingham
Kirton Lindsey
Northorpe
Blyton
SK TF
CENTRAL
GAINSBOROUGH
LEA ROAD
J26 J27
Sturton
Lea
Leverton
Stow Park
Cottam
Tarksey
SAXILBY
Retford Goods
RETFORD
J12
J44
J11
RETFORD
J45
J13
J10
Tuxford
J8
Tuxford
J9
Clifton-on-Trent
Fledborough
Doddington + Harby
Skellingthorpe
Hykeham
Thorpe-on-the-Hill
Swinderby
J33
LINCOLN
CENTRAL
J34
St Marks
Bracebridge Goods
Waddington
Dukeries Jr.
Crow Park
Carlton-on-Trent
COLLINGHAM
Harmston
Southwell
J7
Rolleston Junction
Fiskerton
Bleasby
NEWARK (CASTLE)
J42
J25 J43
NEWARK (NORTH GATE)
J22
P6
J21
Claypole
Cotham
Hougham
J32
Navenby
Leadenham
Caythorpe
ANCASTER
Bingham
Elton + Orston
J6
BOTTESFORD
J3
Aslockton
Sedgebrook
J4
J19
J20
T3
J31
T2
J30
Barkston
Honington
J28
J29
Grantham Gds
E1
GRANTHAM
Barnstone
Redmile
P4
J2
P2
P3
Harby + Stathern
1917
(1923)
P1
J18
Waltham-on-the-Wolds Goods
J17
Long Clawson + Hose
J5
J1
Grimston
Saxilby
Great Panton
51
T1
Corby
Mablethorpe
Holton
Claxby + Usselby
MARKET RASEN
Wickenby
Snelland
East Barkwith
Wragby
Kingthorpe
Langworth
Reepham
Washingborough
Five Mile House
J40
Bardney
Branston + Heighington
Potter Hanworth
Nocton + Dunston
Blankney + METHERINGHAM
Scopwick + Timberland
Digby
RUSKINGTON
Southrey
Stixwould
Woodhall Junct. (Kirkstead)
J39
Sleaford
J38
J35
RAUCEBY
J37
HECKINGTON
Aswarby for Scredington
Helpringham
Donington Road
Billingborough + Horbling
Rippingdale
Morton Road
Counter Drain

KEY TO RAILWAYS

13	AXHOLME JOINT (LANCS + YKS and NE)	
26	LONDON + NORTH WESTERN + GN JOINT	
4	MIDLAND	
5	GREAT CENTRAL	
6	GREAT NORTHERN	
GA	GREAT NORTHERN (Light)	
67	GREAT NORTHERN + GREAT EASTERN JOINT	
0	BRITISH RAIL + POST GROUPING ADDITIONS	
X	OTHERS	
46	MIDLAND + GT NORTHERN JOINT	

LINCOLN

(See colour key to Map B opposite)

NOTES

(1) **REFERENCES** - Are four figure numbers – those beginning with a 9 are in SK, those beginning with an O are in TF

(2) **SCALE:** The modern map is not to scale – there will be therefore some minor differences between references comparing the same point on each map

(3) **WATER TRANSPORT** Foss Dyke Navigation GN and GE, River Witham Navigation GN.

RAILWAYS

No	Company
R4	MIDLAND
5	GREAT CENTRAL
5A	LANCS, DERBY + E COAST (GC from 1906)
6	GREAT NORTHERN
67	GT NORTHERN + GT EASTERN JOINT
7	GREAT EASTERN
O	BRITISH RAIL
X	WORKS LINES ETC

STATIONS

No	Name	Ry Ref
A1	LINCOLN CENTRAL	6 9770
2	Lincoln St Marks	4 9770

GOODS

No	Name	Ry Ref
61	Holmes Yard	6 9671
2	East	5 9770
3	St Marks	4 9770
4	West	5 9671

SHEDS

No	Name Location	Ry Ref
41	GE (Pye Wipe)	4 9770
2	East Holmes	6 9770
3	St Marks	4 9770
4	Great Central	5 9871
5	Great Central	5 9871

SIGNAL BOXES

No	Name of Box	Ry Ref
B1	Rowland(s) Sidings	6 9472
2	Pye Wipe West	6 9472
3	Pye Wipe Junction	6 9571
4	West Holmes	6 9671
5	East Holmes	6 9671
6	High Street Crossing	6 9771
7	Pelham Street	6 9770
8	Sincil Bank	6 9870
9	Greetwell Junction	6 9870
10	Washingborough Junct.	6 0010
11	Monks Abbey Junction	5 9971
12	East Yard	5 9770
13	Boultham Junction	6 9570
14	Station	4 9770
15	Lincoln West	4 9670

SIGNAL BOXES (continued)

No	Name of Box	Ry Ref
B16	Gas Works Sidings	6 9770
17	Bracewell Sidings	6 9770

SIDINGS

No	Name/Company	Ry Ref
B1	Rowland(s) Sidings	5X 9971
P1	Smith Clayton Forge	5X 9971
2	Power Station	5X 9871
3	Lincoln Co-op	X 9670
4	R+H Timber Works	X 9670
5	Ruston + Hornsby Boiler	X 9670
6	Clark's Crank Forge Co	6X 9770
7	Robey + Co Ltd	X 9770
8	Lincoln Gas Works	6X 9770
9	Bracewell Sidings	6X 0769
10	Ruston - Bucyrus	X 9571
11	Stoneplace Siding	6 9571

SIDINGS (continued)

No	Name/Company	Ry Ref
12	Monks Abbey Quarry	X 0072
13	Bracewell Sidings	6 9770

JUNCTIONS

No	Name/Location	Ry Ref
J1	Pye Wipe North	567 9571
2	Pye Wipe	667 9571
3	Boultham	67 9570
4	West Holmes	667 9671
5	West Goods	56 9671
6	Lincoln East	56 9770
7	Durham Ox	5 9770
8	Pelham Street Crossing	56 9770
9	Sincil	6 9770
10	Greetwell West	667 9870
11	Greetwell East	667 9870
12	Washingborough	6 0071
13	Monks Abbey	5X 9971
14	Lincoln West	4 9670

UP-TO-DATE POSITION

STATIONS

No	Name	Ry Ref
1	Lincoln Central	9770
2	Lincoln St Marks	9770

GOODS

No	Name	Ry Ref
1	Holmes Yard	9671
2	Pelham Street Coal	9770

JUNCTIONS

No	Name	Ry Ref
1	Pye Wipe	9571
2	Boultham	9571
3	West Holmes	9671
4	East	9770
5	Durham Ox	9770
6	Pelham Street Crossing	0770
7	Greetwell West	9920
8	Greetwell East	9970

SHEDS

No	Name	Ry Ref
1	Maintenance Depot	9870

(See colour key to Map B opposite)

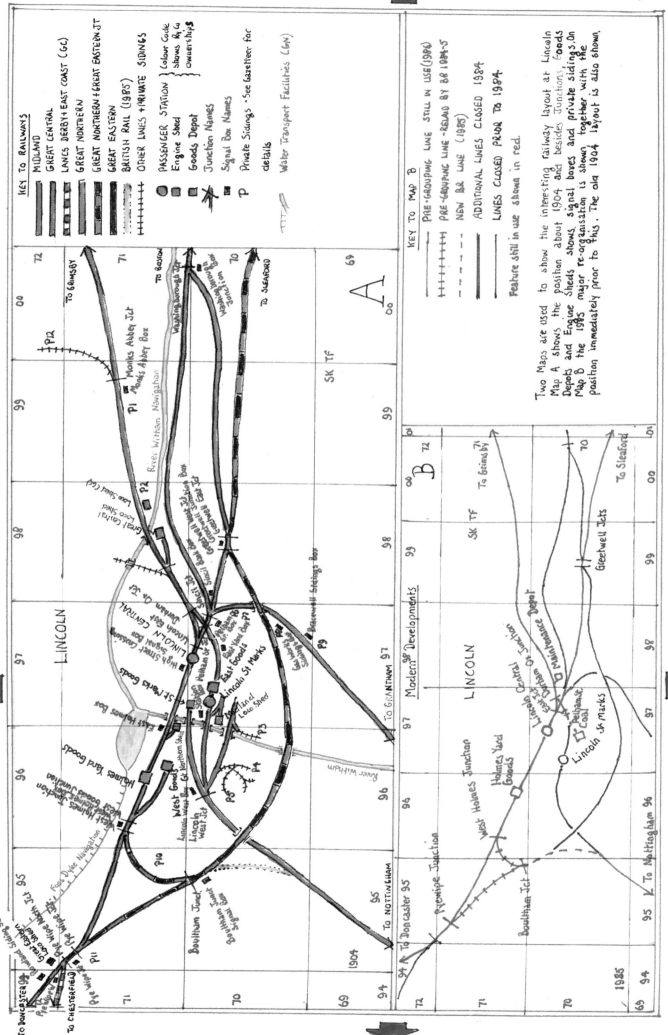

RAILWAYS

No	Company
R1	GREAT EASTERN
12	GREAT NORTHERN + GT EASTERN JT
2	GREAT NORTHERN
23	MIDLAND + GREAT NORTHERN JT
3	MIDLAND

STATIONS

No	Name	Ry Ref
A1	Aby	2 47
2	Alford	2 47
3	Algarkirk (+Sutterton)	2 23
4	Authorpe	2 48
5	BOSTON	2 34
6	Burgh	2 46
7	Clenchwarton ◇	23 51
8	Coningsby	2 25
9	Dersingham	1 63
10	Dogdyke	2 25
11	Donington-on-Bain	2 28
12	Donington Road	12 23
13	East Ville	2 45
14	Firsby	2 46
15	Fleet	23 32
16	Gayton Road ◇	23 61
17	Gedney	23 42
18	Gosberton	12 23
19	Grimoldby	2 48
20	Grimston Road	23 62
21	Hallington	2 38
22	Halton Holgate	2 46
23	HAVENHOUSE	2 56
24	Heacham	1 63
25	Holbeach	23 32
26	Horncastle	2 26
27	HUBBERT'S BRIDGE	2 24
28	Hunstanton	1 64
29	KINGS LYNN	1 62
30	Kirkstead §	2 16
31	Kirton	2 33
32	Langrick	2 24
33	Legbourne Road	2 38
34	Little Steeping	2 46
35	Long Sutton	23 42
36	Louth	2 38
37	Ludborough	2 39
38	Mablethorpe	2 58
39	Middleton	1 61
40	Midville	2 35
41	Moulton	23 32
42	Mumby Road	2 47
43	New Bollingbroke	2 35
44	North Drove	23 22
45	North Thoresby	2 39
46	North Wootton	1 62
47	Old Leake	2 35
48	Pinchbeck	12 22
49	Saltfleetby	2 49
50	Seacroft	2 56
51	Sedgeford	1 73
52	Sibsey	2 35
53	SKEGNESS	2 56
54	Snettisham	1 63
55	South Lynn ◇	23 61
56	South Willingham + Hainton	2 28
57	SPALDING	2 22
58	Spilsby	2 46
59	Stickney	2 35
60	Surfleet	2 22
61	Sutton Bridge	23 42
62	Sutton-on-Sea	2 58
63	SWINESHEAD	2 24
64	Tattershall	2 25
65	Terrington ◇	23 51
66	Theddlethorpe	2 48
67	THORPE CULVERT	2 46
68	Tumby Woodside	2 25
69	Tydd ◇	23 41
70	WAINFLEET	2 45
71	Walpole	23 51
72	Weston	23 22
73	Whaplode	23 32
74	Willoughby	2 47
75	Withcall	2 28
76	Wolferton	1 62
77	Woodhall Junction §	2 16
78	Woodhall Spa	2 26

GOODS

No	Name / Location	Ry Ref
G1	Boston Docks	2 34
	Kings Lynn	
2	(Main)	1 62
3	Dock	1 62
4	Hardwick Road	23 61
5	Harbour	1 62
6	Spalding	3 22

ENGINE SHEDS

No	Location	Ry Ref
E1	Hunstanton	1 64
2	Kings Lynn	1 61
3	Louth	2 38
4	Boston	2 34
5	South Lynn	23 61
6	Spalding	2 22

JUNCTIONS

No	Name / Location	Ry Ref
J1	Spalding North	2 12 22
2	Spalding Station (South)	123 22
3	Holbeach Line	223 22
4	Bourne Line	122 22
5	Cuckoo	23 22
6	Welland Bank	23 22
7	Kings Lynn Goods	1 62
8	Hunstanton	1 62
9	Ely + Norwich Lines	1 62
10	Harbour Branch	1 61
11	South Lynn North	123 61
12	South Lynn	23 61
13	Coningsby	2 25
14	Woodhall	2 16
15	Boston Docks	2 34
16	Boston South	2 34
17	Boston North	2 34
18	Mablethorpe Line	2 38
19	Louth	2 38
20	Sutton Bridge	23 42
21	Bellwater	2 45
22	Willoughby	2 47
23	Firsby - East	2 46
24	Firsby - North	2 46
25	Firsby - West	2 46
26	Firsby - Spilsby	2 46

NOTES:

(1) REFERENCES - All in **TF**

(2) CHANGE OF NAME Pregrouping §

Postgrouping §

(3) OVERLAP INTO 87 ◇

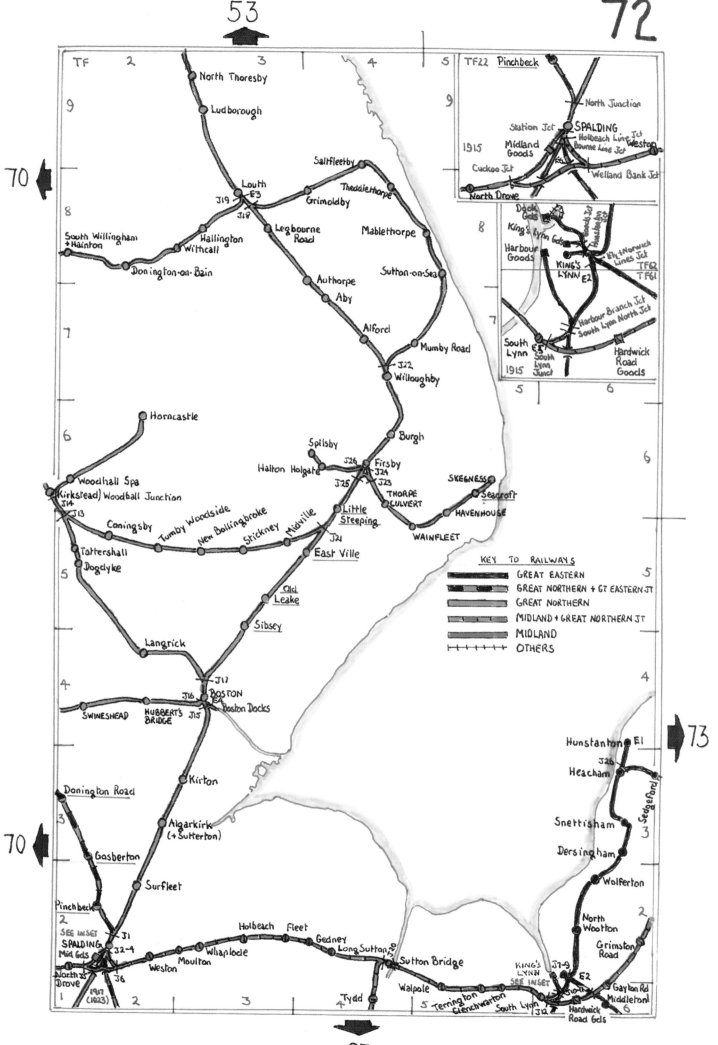

70
73
70

TF 2 3 4 5

North Thoresby
Ludborough
Saltfleetby
Theddlethorpe
Louth E3
J19
J18
Grimoldby
Mablethorpe
South Willingham + Hainton
Hallington
Withcall
Legbourne Road
Donington-on-Bain
Sutton-on-Sea
Authorpe
Aby
Alford
Mumby Road
J22
Willoughby
Horncastle
Burgh
Spilsby
Firsby
J26 J24
Halton Holgate
J25 J23
Woodhall Spa
Skegness
(Kirkstead) Woodhall Junction
J14
J13
THORPE CULVERT
Seacroft
Caningsby
Tumby Woodside
New Bollingbroke
Stickney
Midville
Little Steeping
HAVENHOUSE
Tattershall
Dogdyke
J21
East Ville
WAINFLEET
Old Leake
Sibsey
Langrick
J17
BOSTON
SWINESHEAD
J16 E4
HUBBERT'S BRIDGE J15
Boston Docks
Kirton
Donington Road
Algarkirk (+ Sutterton)
Gosberton
Surfleet
Hunstanton E1
J26
Heacham
Snettisham
Dersingham
Wolferton
Pinchbeck
SEE INSET
SPALDING Mid Gds
North Drove
1917 (1923)
J1
J2-4
J5
J6
Holbeach
Fleet
Gedney
Long Sutton
Whaplode
Weston Moulton
Sutton Bridge
Walpole
Tydd
Terrington Clenchwarton South Lynn
North Wootton
Grimston Road
KING'S LYNN
J7-9
SEE INSET
E2
Gayton Rd
Middleton
Hardwick Road Gds
J12

KEY TO RAILWAYS

GREAT EASTERN
GREAT NORTHERN + GT EASTERN JT
GREAT NORTHERN
MIDLAND + GREAT NORTHERN JT
MIDLAND
OTHERS

TF22 Pinchbeck
North Junction
Station Jct
SPALDING
Holbeach Line Jct
1915 Bourne Line Jct
Midland Goods
Weston
Cuckoo Jct
Welland Bank Jct
North Drove

Dock Gds
King's Lynn Gds
Goods Jct
Hunstanton Jct
Harbour Goods
Ely & Norwich Lines Jct
KING'S LYNN E2
TF62
TF61
Harbour Branch Jct
South Lynn
E5
South Lynn Junct
South Lynn North Jct
Hardwick Road Goods
1915

CROMER + NORTH·WALSHAM
WELLS·NEXT·THE·SEA + FAKENHAM

No	Company
R1	GREAT EASTERN
123	NORFOLK+SUFFOLK JT (GE, Mid +GC)
23	MIDLAND + GREAT NORTHERN JT
X	WELLS QUAY TRAMWAY

STATIONS

No	Name	Ry Ref
A1	Aylsham	1 G12
2	Aylsham	23 G12
3	Burnham Market	1 F84
4	Buxton Lamas	1 G22
5	Catfield	23 G32
6	Cawston	1 G12
7	Coltishall	1 G22
8	Corpusty + Saxthorpe	23 G02
9	County School	1 F92
10	Cromer	1 G24
11	CROMER Beach	23 G24
12	Docking	1 F73
13	East Rudham	23 F82
14	Fakenham	1 F92
15	Fakenham	23 F92
16	Felmingham	23 G22
17	Foulsham	1 G02
18	GUNTON	1 G23
19	Hillington	23 F72
20	Hindolvestone	23 G02
21	Holkham	1 F84
22	Holt	23 G03
23	Honing	23 G32
24	(Kelling Heath) X +	G04
25	Massingham	23 F72
26	Melton Constable	23 G03
27	Mundesley-on-Sea	123 G33
28	NORTH WALSHAM	1 G22
29	North Walsham	23 G22
30	Overstrand	123 G23
31	Paston + Knapton	123 G33
32	Raynham Park	23 F82
33	Reepham	1 G02
34	Ryburgh	1 F92
35	Sedgeford	1 F73
36	SHERINGHAM X ‡	23 G14
37	Stalham	23 G32
38	Stanhoe	1 F73
39	Thursford	23 F93
40	Trimingham	123 G23
41	Walsingham X	1 F93
42	(Warham Halt) X +	F94
43	Wells X	1 F84
44	WEST RUNTON	23 G14
45	Weybourne X	23 G14
46	Whitwell + Reepham	23 G02
47	(Wighton Halt) X +	F93
48	WORSTEAD	1 G22
49	WROXHAM	1 G31

SIDINGS

No	Name/Company	Ry Ref
P1	Wilson Stone Siding	23 F72
2	Wells Quay	X F94
3	Kelling Heath Siding	23 G14

ENGINE SHEDS

No	Location	Ry Ref
E1	Cromer Beach	23 G24
2	Wells	1 F94
3	Melton Constable	23 G03

JUNCTIONS

No	Name/Location	Ry Ref
J1	Wells	1 F94
2	Wells Tramway	1X F94
3	County School	1 F92
4	Melton Constable West	23 G03
5	Melton Constable East	23 G03
6	Wroxham	1 G21
7	North Walsham GE	1 G23
8	North Walsham Jt Line	23 G23
9	Antingham Road	123 G23
10	Cromer	1 G24
11	Roughton Road	1123 G24
12	Newstead Lane	12323 G14
13	Runton West	12323 G14
14	Runton East	23 G14

NOTES:

(1) REF - In TF or TG: TF = Fxx / TG = Gxx

(2) COMBINED GAZETTEER - Those on A shown BLACK, on B BLUE

(3) New Station opened by a preserved railway +

(4) Wells + Walsingham Railway 10¼" gauge X

(5) North Norfolk Railway X

(6) North Norfolk Railway station closely adjoins BR station ‡

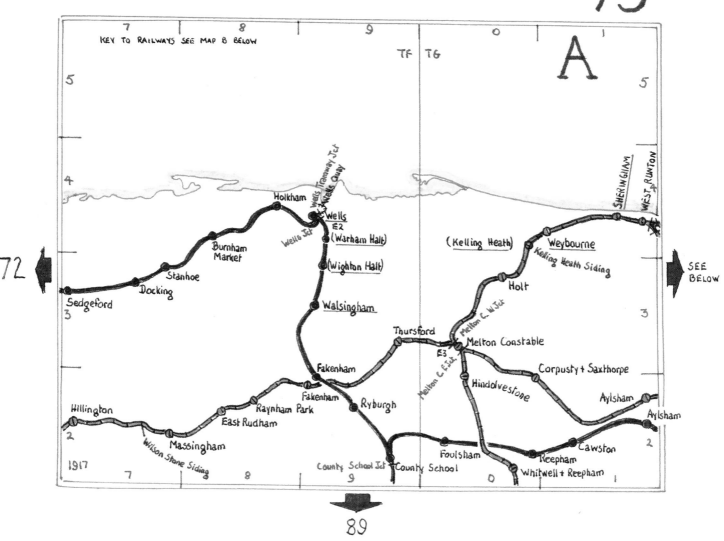

72 ←

SEE BELOW →

↓ 89

KEY TO RAILWAYS SEE MAP B BELOW

A

1917

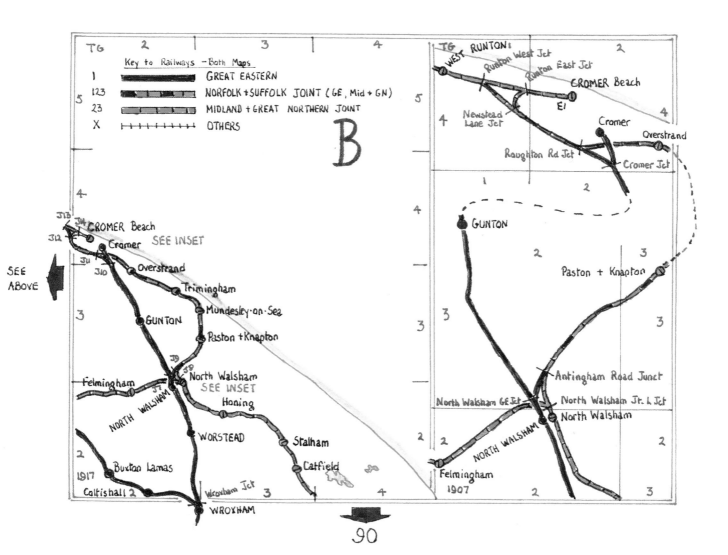

Key to Railways — Both Maps

1	▬▬▬	GREAT EASTERN
123	▬▬▬	NORFOLK + SUFFOLK JOINT (GE, Mid + GN)
23	▬▬▬	MIDLAND + GREAT NORTHERN JOINT
X	++++++	OTHERS

B

SEE INSET

SEE ABOVE ←

1917

1907

↓ 90

RAILWAYS

No	Company	Gauge
R 1	GREAT WESTERN	S
1 2	GREAT WESTERN + CAMBRIAN JT	S
2	CAMBRIAN	S
2A	VALE OF RHEIDOL (Cambrian)	1' 11½"
3	TALYLLYN	2' 3"
4	FAIRBOURNE	1' 3"
0	(BR + POST GROUPING ADDITIONS)	S

ABERYSTWYTH + HAVERFORDWEST

STATIONS

No	Name	Ry Ref
A 1	Aberayron	1 SN46
2	ABERDOVEY	2 SN69
3	ABERFFRW(Y)D †	2A SN67
4	ABERGYNOLWYN	3 SH60
5	(ABERTAFOL)	2 SN69
6	ABERYSTWYTH Joint	12 SN58
7	ABERYSTWYTH (V of RHEIDOL)	2A SN58
8	Arthog	2 SH61
9	BARMOUTH	2 SH61
10	Barmouth Ferry	4 SH61
11	BARMOUTH JUNCTION §6A	2 SH61
12	Blaenplwyf Halt	1 SN55
13	Boncath	1 SN13
14	BORTH	2 SN69
15	Bow Street	2 SN68
16	BRYN GLAS	3 SH60
17	Bryn Teify	1 SN43
18	CAPEL BANGOR	2A SN67
19	Cardigan	1 SN14
20	Ciliau Aeron	1 SN46
21	CLARBESTON ROAD	1 SN02
22	CLYNDERWEN	1 SN11
23	Crymmych Arms	1 SN13
24	Derry Ormond	1 SN55
25	DOLGOCH (FALLS)	3 SH60
26	DOVEY JUNCTION	2 SN69
27	FAIRBOURNE	2 SH61
28	Fairbourne	4 SH61
29	Felin Fach	1 SN55
30	Fishguard + Goodwick	1 SM93
31	FISHGUARD HARBOUR	1 SM93
32	Glandyfi	2 SN69
33	GLANRAFON	2A SN68
34	Glogue	1 SN23
35	(GOGARTH)	2 SN69
36	Golden Hill Platform	1 SM90
37	HAVERFORDWEST	1 SM91
38	Henllan	1 SN34
39	JOHNSTON	1 SM91
40	Kilgerran	1 SN14
41	KILGETTY	1 SN10
42	Lampeter	1 SN54
43	LAMPHEY	1 SN00
44	Letterston	1 SM92
45	(LLANABER)	2 SH51
46	LLANBADARN	2A SN58
47	Llandre §51	2 SN68
48	Llandyssil	1 SN44
49	Llanerch Ayron Halt	1 SN46
50	Llanfalteg	1 SN12
51	Llanfihangel §47	2 SN68
52	Llanfyrnach	1 SN23
53	(LLANGELYNIN)	2 SH50
54	Llanglydwen	1 SN12
55	Llangybi	1 SN65
56	Llanilar	1 SH67
57	Llanrhystyd Road	1 SN57
58	Llanybyther	1 SN54
59	Llan·y·Cefn	1 SN02
60	LLWYNGWRIL	2 SH50
61	Login	1 SN12
62	Lydstep	1 SS09
63	Maenclochog	1 SN02
64	Maesycrugiau	1 SN44
65	MANORBIER	1 SS09
66	MILFORD HAVEN	1 SM80
66A	MORFA MAWDDACH §11	2 SH61
67	(NANT GWERNOL)	3 SH60
68	NANTYRONEN	2A SN67
69	NARBERTH	1 SN11
70	Newcastle Emlyn	1 SN34
71	Neyland	1 SM90
72	PEMBROKE DOCK	1 SM90
73	PEMBROKE Town	1 SM90
74	PENALLY	1 SS19
75	PENDRE	3 SH50
76	(PENHELIG)	2 SN69
77	Penmaen Pool	2 SH61
78	Pentrecourt Platform	1 SN34
79	Pont Llanio	1 SN65
80	Puncheston	1 SN03
81	Rhydowen	1 SN12
82	RHYDYRONEN	3 SH60
83	Rosebush	1 SN02
84	SAUNDERSFOOT	1 SN10
85	Silian Halt	1 SN55
86	Strata Florida	1 SN76
87	Talsarn Halt	1 SN55
88	Templeton	1 SN11
89	TENBY	1 SN10
90	TONFANAU	2 SH50
91	TOWYN	2 SH50
92	TOWYN KINGS WHARF	3 SH50
93	Trawscoed	1 SN67
94	Tregaron	1 SN66
95	WHITLAND	1 SN11
96	Ynys Las	2 SN69
10	Aberayron	1 SN55
11	Aberystwyth Station	12 SN58
12	Cambrian + Joint Line	212 SN58
13	GW + Joint Line	112 SN58
14	Dovey	2 SN69
15	Barmouth	2 SH61

GOODS ✕

No	Location	Ry Ref
G1	Pembroke Docks	1 SM90
2	Pembroke Docks	1 SM90
3	Milford Haven Oil	O SM80
4	Milford Haven Oil	O SM90

ENGINE SHEDS

No	Location	Ry Ref
E1	Neyland	1 SM90
2	Milford Haven	1 SM90
3	Whitland	1 SN11
4	Pembroke	1 SM90
5	Cardigan	1 SN14
6	Fishguard	1 SM93
7	Newcastle Emlyn	1 SN34
8	Aberystwyth	1 SN58
9	Aberayron	1 SN46

BRIDGES

No	Name	Yds	Ry Ref
V1	Barmouth		2 SH61

JUNCTIONS

No	Name / Location	Ry Ref
J1	Herbrandston	(1) O SM90
2	Gulf Oil Branch	(1) O SM90
3	Milford Haven Branch	1 SM90
4	Letterston	1 SM93
5	Pembroke Docks	1 SM90
6	Clarbeston	1 SN02
7	N Pembrokeshire Branch	1 SN11
8	Cardigan Branch	1 SN11
9	Cardigan	1 SN11

NOTES:

(1) NAME CHANGES :
Not normally shown name is as at map date. Just two variations are indicated. —
§ Name at Map date
§ Earlier Alternative name to '05
† Shows alternative spellings in early source maps.

(2) GOODS ✕ – Detailed Information for most of the area re separate Goods stations – not available.

(3) Preserved – These station names in the main shown in capitals. NG and have tended to remain open, as distinct from lines closed by BR and then re-opened.

(4) Entire name changed – as distinct from modern welsh spelling alterations
§ Map Name
§ Modern Name

(5) Projected Railway was to go to Newquay

(6) Sketch to show relationship of Inset to Main Map 55

FISHGUARD HARBOUR
Fishguard + Goodwick
E6
Boncath
(LLANABER)

SM SN

5 1 6

BARMOUTH
Barmouth Ferry
Fairbourne
VI
Arthog
Barmouth Junct
BARMOUTH JUNCTION
FAIRBOURNE

Letterston Junction
Puncheston
Letterston
Crymmych Arms
Glogue
Llanfyrnach
Rhydowen
Rosebush
Maenclochog

LLYNGWRIL

(LLANGELYNIN)
ABERGYNOLWYN
2'3" gauge
(NANT GWERNOL)
TONFANAU
Talyllyn Rly
DOLGOCH(FALLS)
BRYNGLAS
RHYDYRONEN
PENDRE
TOWYN
TOWYN KINGS WHARF

Llanglydwen

Login

92

SH SN

Llan-y-Cefn

CLARBESTON ROAD
North Pembrokeshire Branch Junction
CLYNDERWEN
Llanfalteg
Cardigan branch Junction

Clarbeston Junction

WHITLAND
Cardigan Jct

ABERDOVEY (PENHELIG)
(ABERTAFOL)
(LLUGWARTH)
DOVEY JUNCTION
Dovey Junction

75

HAVERFORDWEST
NARBERTH

9

Glandyfi

9

Gulf Oil Branch Jct
Herbrandston Jct
Templeton
Ynys Las

JOHNSTON
Milford Haven Branch Junct.
BORTH

OIL TERMINAL BR
E2
Neyland
KILGETTY
Llandre

MILFORD HAVEN
Oil Terminal (BR)
E1
Docks
SAUNDERSFOOT
Bow Street

Dods
PEMBROKE DOCK
Golden Hill Platform
PEMBROKE Town
LAMPHEY
Docks Junct
E4
93

Glanrafon
GLANRAFON
CAPEL BANGOR
Vale Rheidol 1'11½"
ABERFFRWYD
NANTYRONEN

ABERYSTWYTH (Joint)
ABERYSTWYTH (VoR)
SEE INSET BELOW

LLANBADARN
Llanrhystyd Road

SM
MANORBIER
TENBY
PENALLY
Lydstep

SR SS

Llanilar

Trawscoed

1917 (1922)

Key to Railways
GREAT WESTERN
GREAT WESTERN + CAMBRIAN JOINT
CAMBRIAN
VALE OF RHEIDOL (Cambrian) 1'11½"
TALYLLYN 2'3"
FAIRBOURNE 1'3"
PROJECTED (Not Built)
POST GROUPING + BR

Strata Florida

Aberayron
E9
Llanerch Ayron Halt
Ciliau Aeron
Tregaron

Felin Fach
Lampeter + Aberayron (Light)
Talsarn Halt
Blaenplwyf Halt
Pont Llanio

Silian Halt
Llangybi
Derry Ormond
Aberayron Junction

Lampeter

SN58
ABERYSTWYTH

1917 (1922)

Cardigan
E5
Kilgerran
Llanybyther
JOINT
Station Junction
VALE OF RHEIDOL
Junction with Joint Line
E8
Newcastle Emlyn
E7
Henllan
Pentrecourt Platform
Llandyssil
Maesycrugiau
LLANBADARN
Jct with Jt Line
1915

Boncath
Bryn Teify

SEE INSET ABOVE

75 RAILWAYS

No	Company		Gauge
R 2	LONDON + NORTH WESTERN		'S'
3	GREAT WESTERN		'S'
4	CORRIS		2'3"
7	CAMBRIAN	✠	'S'
7A	WELSHPOOL + LLANFAIR (Cam)		2'6"
7B	VALE OF RHEIDOL (Cam)		1'11½"

STATIONS + HALTS

No.	Name		Ry Ref
A 1	Aberangell		7 H81
2	Aberedw		7 O04
3	Aberllefenny	§	4 H71
4	Abermule		7 O19
5	Bryngwyn		7 J11
6	BUILTH ROAD		2 O05
7	Builth Road		7 O05
8	Builth Wells		7 O05
9	CAERSWS		7 O09
10	Carno		7 N99
11	CASTLE CAEREINION		7A J10
12	Cemmaes		7 H80
13	Cemmaes Road		7 H80
14	CILMERY	§	2 O05
15	Corris		4 H70
16	CYFRONYDD		7A J10
17	CYNGHORDY		2 N84
18	DEVIL'S BRIDGE		7B N77
19	Dinas Mawddwy		7 H81
20	DOLAU		2 O16
21	Doldowlod		7 N96
22	Dolgelley		3 H71
23	Dolwen		7 N98
24	Erwood		7 O04
25	Esgairgeiliog		4 H70
26	Ffridd Gate		4 H70
27	Garneddwen		4 H70
28	GARTH		2 N94
29	Golfa		7A J10
30	HENIARTH		7A J10
31	Kerry		7 O19
32	LLANBISTER ROAD		2 O17
33	Llanbrynmair		7 H80
34	Llandinam		7 O08
35	LLANDRINDOD Wells		2 O06
36	LLANFAIR CAEREINION		7A J10
37	Llanfechain		7 J12
38	Llanfyllin		7 J11
39	LLANGAMMARCH Wells		2 N94
40	Llanidloes		7 N98
41	LLANWRTYD Wells		2 N84
42	Llwyngwern		4 H70
43	Machynlleth		4 H70
44	MACHYNLLETH		7 H70
45	Mallwyd		7 H81
46	Moat Lane Junction		7 O09
47	Newbridge-on-Wye		7 O05
48	NEWTOWN		7 O19
49	Pantydwr		7 N97
50	PEN-Y-BONT		2 O16
51	Pontdolgoch		7 O09
52	Rhayader		7 N96
53	RHEIDOL FALLS		7B N77
54	RHIWFRON		7B N77
55	St. Harmon's		7 N97
56	Strata Florida		3 N76
57	SYLFAEN	✱	7A J10
58	Taleddig	†	7 H90
59	Tylwch		7 N98

GOODS ONLY

No	Name/Location	Ry Ref
G1	Scafell	7 O09

SIDINGS ETC

No	Company/Name/Location	Ry Ref
P1	Abercwmieddaw Quarry	X H70
2	Ratgoed Quarry	X H71
3	Trewythan - Van Bch	7 O09
4	Red House - Van Bch	7 N99
5	Trefeglwys - Van Bch	7 N98
6	Cerist - Van Bch	7 N98
7	Garth Road - Van	7 N98
8	Van	7 N98
9	Penpontbren Siding	7 N98
10	Glanyrafon Siding	7 N97

ENGINE SHEDS

No	Name/Location	Ry Ref
E 1	Builth Wells	7 O05
2	Llanidloes	7 N98
3	Moat Lane	7 O09
4	Machynlleth	7 H70
5	Corris (Narrow Gauge)	4 H70
6	Llanfyllin	7 J11
7	Builth Road	2 O05

TUNNELS

No	Name/Location	Yds	Ry Ref
T 1	Pen-y-Bont	440	2 O16
2	Sugar Loaf	1000	2 N84

SUMMITS

No	Name/Location	Ht Fr.	Ry Ref
S 1	Talerddig	†	7 H90
2	Sugar Loaf	820	2 N84

JUNCTIONS

No	Name/Location	Ry Ref
J 1	Dolgelley GW/Cambrian	37 N71
2	Mawddwy	7 N80
3	Van Branch (Caersws)	7 O09
4	Moat Lane	7 O09
5	Kerry Branch (Abermule)	7 O19
6	Elan (Waterworks line) §	7 N96
7	Builth North	72 O05
8	Builth South	2 O05

NOTES:

(1) REF in SH, SJ, SN or SO - the initial S not included.

(2) NAME CHANGES - Names as at map date. & the final Y sometimes shown as an I even in pre-grouping. † alternative spellings for this place Taleddig — or Talerddig.

(3) Reduced to Halt ✱ before grouping

(4) PRESERVED LINES which are narrow gauge are on this page shown in CAPITALS and likewise on the map. It is thus possible to show that Golfa station is now closed

(5) Goods information for this area is somewhat limited. But it should be remembered that most stations handled goods. Those shown on the maps are always GOODS ONLY stations.

(6) § This junction connected with a private line serving the Elan Valley Waterworks during construction - most of the line was taken up when construction completed

(7) ✠ The Cambrian Railway was merged with the GWR BEFORE grouping.

(8) On pages 74 + 76 - either side this map - Gt Western is the main railway - but on this map it is barely represented having but two stations !!.

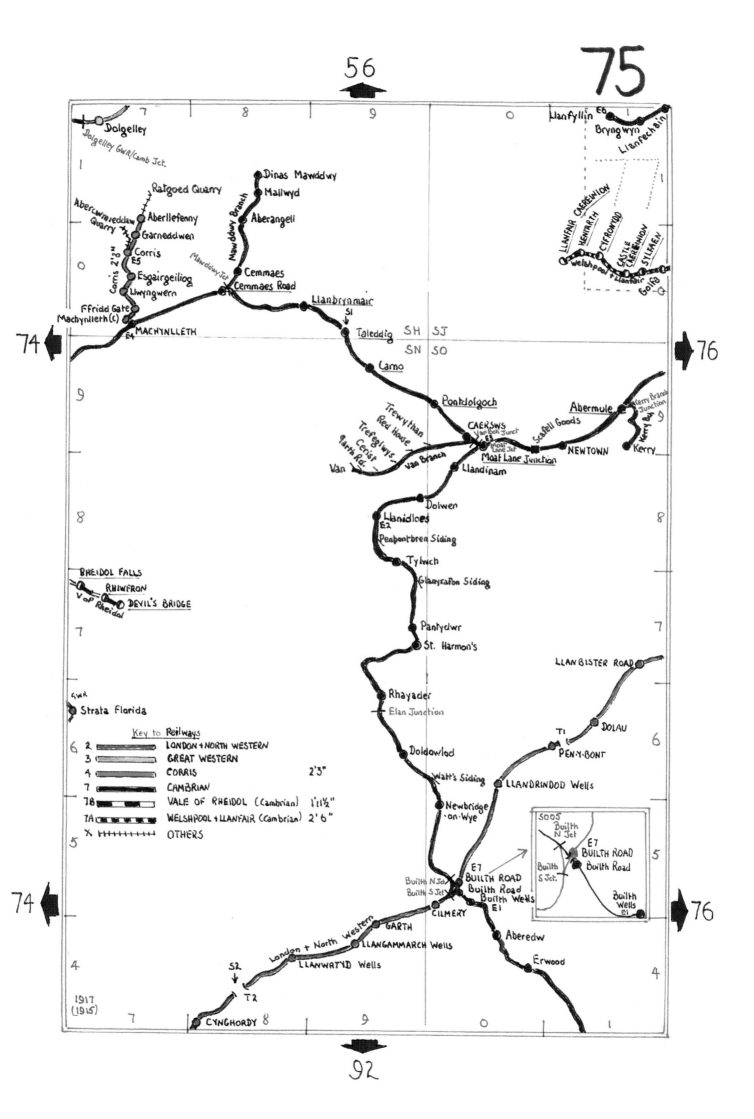

Dolgelley
Dolgelley GWR/Camb Jct.

Llanfyllin E6
Bryngwyn
Llanfechain

Dinas Mawddwy
Mallwyd
Aberangell

Ratgoed Quarry
Abercwmeiddaw Quarry
Aberllefenny
Garneddwen
Corris E5
Esgairgeiliog
Llwyngwern
Ffridd Gate
Machynlleth (c)
MACHYNLLETH E4

Mawddwy Branch
Mawddwy Jct.
Cemmaes
Cemmaes Road

Llanbrynmair
S1
Taleddig   SH SJ
                SN 50

Carno

LLANFAIR CAEREINION
NEWTOWN
CYFRONYDD
CASTLE CAEREINION
SYLFAEN
Welshpool Llanfair
Golfa

74

Pontdolgoch
Trewythan
Red House
Trefeglwys
Cerist
Garth Rd.
Van

Abermule
Kerry Branch Junction
CAERSWS
Van Bch Junct
E3
Moat Lane Jct.
Moat Lane Junction
Scafell Goods
NEWTON
Kerry Bch
Kerry

Van Branch
Llandinam

Dolwen
Llanidloes
E2
Penbontbren Siding

RHEIDOL FALLS
RHIWFRON
V of Rheidol
DEVIL'S BRIDGE

Tylwch
Glanyrafon Siding

Pantydwr
St. Harmon's

LLANBISTER ROAD

GWR
Strata Florida

Rhayader
Elan Junction

DOLAU
T1
PEN-Y-BONT

Key to Railways
2 ──── LONDON + NORTH WESTERN
3 ──── GREAT WESTERN
4 ──── CORRIS   2'3"
7 ──── CAMBRIAN
7B ─── VALE OF RHEIDOL (Cambrian) 1'11½"
7A ─── WELSHPOOL + LLANFAIR (Cambrian) 2'6"
X ──── OTHERS

Doldowlod
Watt's Siding
LLANDRINDOD Wells

Newbridge
·on·Wye

Builth N Jct.
Builth S Jct.
E7
BUILTH ROAD
Builth Road
Builth Wells
E1

SOO5
Builth N Jct
E7
BUILTH ROAD
Builth Road
Builth S Jct.
Builth Wells E1

CILMERY
GARTH
London + North Western
LLANGAMMARCH Wells
S2
LLANWRTYD Wells
T2

Aberedw
Erwood

1917
(1915)

CYNGHORDY

74

76

WELSHPOOL, WELLINGTON + HEREFORD

No	Company
R1	BISHOP'S CASTLE
2	LONDON+NORTH WESTERN
23A	SHREWSBURY+HEREFORD (LNW+GW)
23B	SHREWSBURY+WELSHPOOL (LNW+GW)
23C	SHREWSBURY+WELLINGTON (LNW+GW)
3	GREAT WESTERN
4	MIDLAND
5	CLEOBURY MORTIMER+DITTON PRIORS (Light) ‡
7	CAMBRIAN
7A	WELSHPOOL+LLANFAIR (Cambrian) 2'6" Gauge
22	SHROPSHIRE+MONTGOMERYSHIRE
X	OTHERS - Pte+Mines Lines

STATIONS + HALTS

No	Name	Ry Ref
A1	Abbey Foregate Platform *	23C J51
2	Admaston	23C J61
3	Almeley *	3 035
4	Arddleen	7 J21
5	Ashperton	3 064
6	Berrington	3 J50
7	Berrington+Eye	23A 046
8	Bishop's Castle	1 038
9	Bromyard	3 065
10	BROOME	2 038
11	Broomfield	23A 047
12	BUCKNELL	2 037
13	Buildwas	3 J60
14	Buttington	7(23) J21
15	Burwarton	5 068
16	Chapel Lane	22 J31
17	CHURCH STRETTON	23A 049
18	Cleobury Mortimer ✗	35 067
19	Cleobury Town	5 067
20	Clifford	3 024
21	Coalbrookdale	3 J60
22	Coalport	2 J60
23	Coalport	3 J60
24	Condover	23A J40
25	CRAVEN ARMS+Stokesay	23A 048
26	Credenhill	4 044
27	Cressage	3 J50
28	Crew Green	22 J31
29	Criggion	22 J21
30	Cruckton	22 J41
31	Crudgington	3 J61
32	Dinmore	23A 055
33	Ditton Priors	5 068
34	Dolyhir	4 025
35	Dorrington	23A J40
36	Dorstone	3 034
37	Eardisley	4 034
38	Easton Court	23A 056
39	Eaton	1 038
40	Fencote	3 065
41	Ford+Crossgates	22 J31
42	Ford Bridge	23A 055
43	Forden	7 J20
44	Four Crosses	7 J21
45	Hadley	2 J61
46	Hadnall	2 J51
47	Hanwood	23B J40
48	Hanwood Road	22 J41
49	Harton Road	3 048
50	Hay	4 024
51	HEREFORD Barr's Court	23A 054
52	HOPTON HEATH	2 037
53	Horderley	1 048
54	Horsehay	3 J60
55	Ironbridge+Broseley	3 J60
56	Ketley	3 J61
57	Kingsland	3 046
58	Kington	3 035
59	Kinnerley Junction	22 J32
60	Kinnersley	4 034
61	KNIGHTON	2 027
62	KNUCKLAS	2 027
63	Lawley Bank	3 J60
64	Leaton	3 J41
65	Leebotwood	23A 049
66	LEOMINSTER	23A 055
67	Lightmoor Junction	3 J60
68	Linley	3 079
69	Llandrinio Road	22 J31
70	LLANGUNLLO	2 027
71	Longville	3 059
72	LUDLOW	23A 057
73	Lydham Heath	1 039
74	Lyonshall	3 035
75	Madeley	3 J60
76	Madeley Market	2 J60
77	Malins Lee	2 J60
78	Marsh Brook	23A 048
79	Melverley	22 J31
80	Meole Brace	22 J40
81	Middletown	23B J21
82	Misterley	23B J30
83	Montgomery	7 029
84	Moorhampton	4 034
85	Moreton-on-Lugg	23A 054
86	Much Wenlock	3 J60
87	Neen Sollars	3 067
88	Nesscliff+Pentre	22 J31
89	(NEW HADLEY HALT) ♀3 (see note)	J61
90	Newnham Bridge	3 066
91	New Radnor	4 026
92	Oakengates	2 J71
93	OAKENGATES	3 J61
94	Onibury	23A 047
95	Pembridge	3 035
96	Plealey Road	23B J40
97	Plowden	1 038
98	Pontesbury	23B J30
99	Pool Quay	7 J21
100	Presteign	3 036
101	Presthope	3 059
102	RAVEN SQUARE	7A J20
103	Redhill	22 J40
104	Rowden Mill	3 065
105	Rushbury	3 059
106	Seven Stars	7A J20
107	Shrawardine	22 J31

SHREWSBURY

No	Name	Ry Ref
108	Abbey	22 J50
109	Abbey Foregate Platform *	23C J51
110	GENERAL §	23A J40
111	West	22 J41
112	Stanner	4 025
113	Steens Bridge	3 055
114	Stirchley	2 J60
115	Stoke Edith	3 064
116	Stottesdon	5 068
117	Stretford Bridge *	1 048
118	Tenbury Wells	23A 056
119	Titley	3 035
120	Trench Crossing	2 J61
121	Upton Magna	23C J51
122	Walcot	23C J51
123	WELLINGTON	23C J61
124	WELSHPOOL	7 J20
125	Welshpool	7A J20
126	RAVEN SQUARE	7A J20
127	Seven Stars	7A J20
128	Westbrook	3 024
129	Westbury	23B J31
130	Whitney-on-the-Wye	4 024
131	Withington	3 054
132	Woofferton	23A 056
133	Yockleton	23B J31

ENGINE SHEDS

No	Name/Location	Ry Ref
E1	Knighton	2 027
2	Kington	3 035

JUNCTIONS

No	Name/Location	Ry Ref
J1	Golden Valley Line	43 024
2	Eardisley	43 034
3	Titley	3 035
4	Lydham	1 039
5	Leominster-Bromyard	3 055
6	Leominster-Kington	3 055
7	Cleobury	35 067

SIDINGS

No	Name/Co/Location	Ry Ref
P1	Snailbeach (n.g)	X J30
2	Chilton *‡	5 067
3	Defton Ford *‡	5 067
4	Prescott *‡	5 068
5	Aston Botterell *‡	5 068
6	Cleobury North Crossing *‡	5 068

NOTES:

(1) REFERENCES - SO or SJ - the S is omitted

(2) STATIONS - all shown except Abbey Foregate (see 78) *

(3) OTHER FEATURES only shown if not in areas which are covered by enlargements

(4) CLOSED prior to grouping *

(5) CLEOBURY LINE - Sidings ‡ also served as Halts for a period *

(6) Now known as SHREWSBURY §

(7) Two stations at one time at this location - but reduced to one when control passed to Great Western ✗

(8) Opened post grouping and due to be closed by Br.R 1985-6 ♀

(9) RAVEN SQUARE is shown in CAPITALS as this is a narrow guage line - see note, map 75

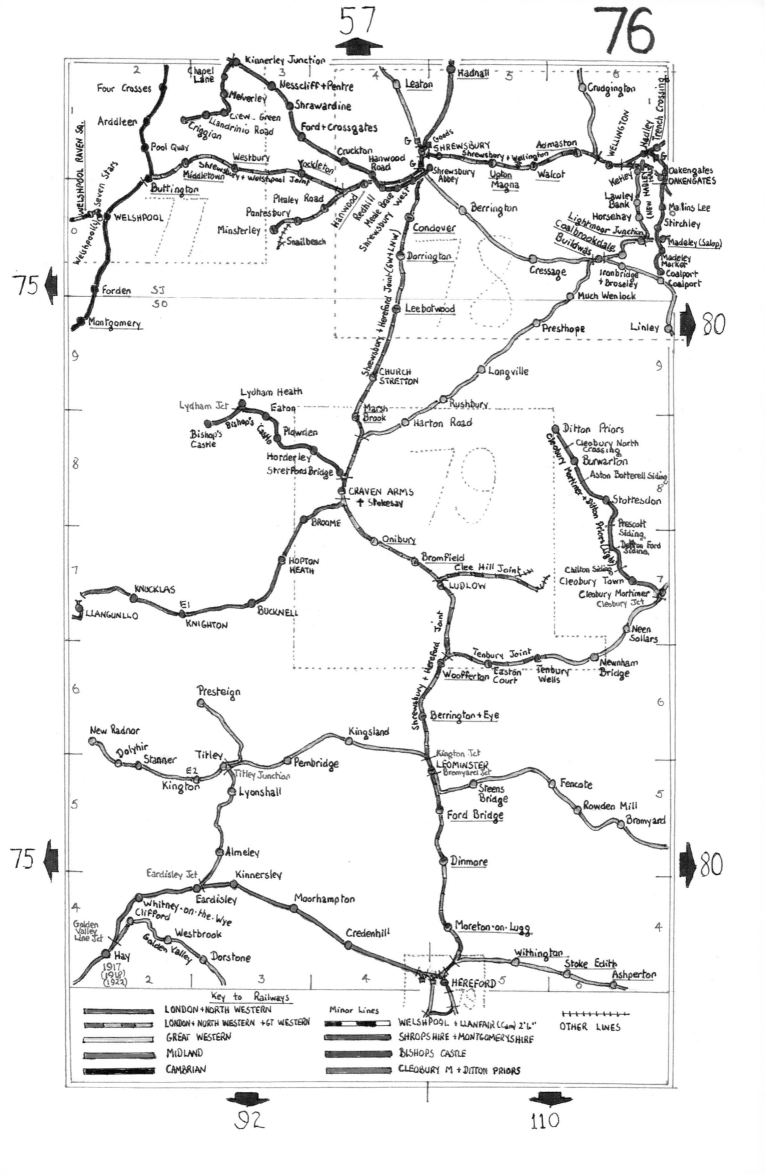

Four Crosses
Chapel Lane
Kinnerley Junction
Nesscliff + Pentre
Leaton
Hadnall
Crudgington
Melverley
Shrawardine
Arddleen
Crew Green
Llandrinio Road
Ford + Crossgates
WELLINGTON
Hadley
Trench Crossing
Criggion
Pool Quay
Cruckton
Hanwood Road
G
Goods
Shrewsbury
Admaston
Westbury
Yockleton
Shrewsbury + Welshpool Joint
Middletown
Hanwood
Redhill
Meole Brace
Shrewsbury West
G
Shrewsbury Abbey
Shrewsbury + Wellington
Walcot
Upton Magna
Ketley
OAKENGATES
Oakengates
Buttington
Plealey Road
(NEW MADELEY)
Lawley Bank
Mailins Lee
Pantesbury
Berrington
Lightmoor Junction
Horsehay
Stirchley
WELSHPOOL RAVEN SQ.
Welshpoo lly
Seven Stars
Minsterley
Snailbeach
Condover
Coalbrookdale
Buildwas
Madeley (Salop)
WELSHPOOL
Dorrington
Cressage
Ironbridge + Broseley
Madeley Market
Coalport
Coalport
Forden
SJ
SO
Leebotwood
Much Wenlock
Montgomery
Presthope
Linley
Shrewsbury + Hereford Joint (GW+LNW)
CHURCH STRETTON
Longville
Lydham Heath
Lydham Jct
Eaton
Rushbury
Marsh Brook
Harton Road
Ditton Priors
Bishop's Castle
Plowden
Cleobury North Crossing
Burwarton
Aston Botterell Siding
Horderley
Stretford Bridge
Stottesdon
CRAVEN ARMS
Stokesay
Cleobury Mortimer + Ditton Priors (Light)
Prescott Siding
Ditton Ford Siding
BROOME
Onibury
Bromfield
Chilton Siding
HOPTON HEATH
Clee Hill Joint
Cleobury Town
KNUCKLAS
LUDLOW
Cleobury Mortimer
Cleobury Jct
LLANGUNLLO
E1
BUCKNELL
Neen Sollars
KNIGHTON
Tenbury Joint
Newnham Bridge
Woofferton
Easton Court
Tenbury Wells
Presteign
Shrewsbury + Hereford Joint
Kingsland
Berrington + Eye
New Radnor
Kington Jct
Dolyhir
Stanner
Titley
Pembridge
LEOMINSTER
Fencote
Bromyard Jct
E2
Titley Junction
Steens Bridge
Rowden Mill
Kington
Lyonshall
Ford Bridge
Bromyard
Almeley
Dinmore
Kinnersley
Eardisley Jct
Moorhampton
Eardisley
Golden Valley Line Jct
Whitney-on-the-Wye
Clifford
Credenhill
Moreton-on-Lugg
Westbrook
Withington
Stoke Edith
Hay
1917
(1918)
(1922)
Golden Valley
Dorstone
HEREFORD
Ashperton

Key to Railways

LONDON + NORTH WESTERN	
LONDON + NORTH WESTERN + GT WESTERN	
GREAT WESTERN	
MIDLAND	
CAMBRIAN	

Minor Lines

WELSHPOOL + LLANFAIR (Cam) 2'6"
SHROPSHIRE + MONTGOMERYSHIRE
BISHOPS CASTLE
CLEOBURY M + DITTON PRIORS

OTHER LINES

75
80

WELSHPOOL + OSWESTRY

RAILWAYS

No.	Company	gauge
R23	SHREWSBURY + WELSHPOOL (GW+LNW)	S
3	GREAT WESTERN	S
7	CAMBRIAN	S
7A	WELSHPOOL + LLANFAIR (Cam)	2'6"
22	SHROPSHIRE + MONTGOMERYSHIRE	S
33	GLYN VALLEY TRAMWAY	2'4½"
X	Others	2'4½"

STATIONS

No.	Name	Ry Ref
A1	Arddleen	7 21
2	Blodwell Junction	7 22
3	Bryngwyn	7 11
4	Buttington	7(23) 21
5	Castle Caereinion	7A 10
6	Castle Mill	33 23
7	Chapel Lane	22 31
8	CHIRK	3 23
9	Chirk	33 23
10	Crew Green	22 31
11	Criggion	22 21
12	Cyfronydd	7A 10
13	Dolywern	33 23
14	Four Crosses	7 21
15	Frankton	7 33
16	Glanyrafon	7 22
17	Glynceiriog	33 23
18	GOBOWEN	3 23
19	Golfa	7A 10
20	Kinnerley Junction	22 32
21	Llandrinio Road	22 22
22	Llanfechain	7 12
23	Llanfyllin	7 11
24	Llangedwyn	7 12
25	Llanrhaiadr Mochnant	7 12
26	Llansaintffraid	7 22
27	Llansilin Road	7 31
28	Llan-y-Blodwell	7 22
29	Llanymynech	7 22
30	Llanymynech Junction	22 22
31	Llynclys	7 22
32	Maesbrook	33 22
33	Melverley	22 31
34	Middletown	23 31
35	Oswestry	3 22
36	Oswestry	7 22
37	Pant	7 22
38	Pentrefelin	7 12
39	Pontfadog	33 23
40	Pontfaen	33 23
41	Pool Quay	7 21
42	Porthywaen	7 22
43	Preesgweene	3 23
44	Raven Square	7A 20
45	Rednal + West Felton	3 32
46	Seven Stars	7A 20
47	Sylfaen	7A 10
48	WELSHPOOL	7 20
49	Welshpool	7A 20
50	Welshpool - Raven Square	7A 20
51	Welshpool - Seven Stars	7A 20
52	Wern Las	22 32
53	Westbury	23 31
54	Whittington	3 33
55	Whittington	7 33

GOODS

No	Name/Location	Ry Ref
G1	Rhydmeredydd	7 22
2	Nantmawr	7 22
3	Porthywaen	7 22

SIDINGS

No	Name/Company	Ry Ref
P1	New Cambrian Slate Quarry	X22 13
2	Pant-y-Neibion	X22 13
3	Rock Siding - Llanymynech	7 22

ENGINE SHEDS

No	Location	Ry Ref
E1	Oswestry	3 23
2	Oswestry	7 32
3	Welshpool	7 20
4	Llanfyllin	7 11

JUNCTIONS

No	Name/Location	Ry Ref
J1	Buttington	723 21
2	Kinnerley	22 31
3	Llynclys	7 22
4	Tanat Valley Line	7 22
5	Blodwell North	7 22
6	Blodwell South	7 22
7	Llanfyllin Line	7 22
8	Llanymynech East	722 22
9	Llanymynech South	7 22
10	Gobowen Line	7 22
11	Welshpool (Oswestry)	37 23
12	Oswestry Line	3 23

NOTES:

(1) REFERENCES: All in SJ

(2) CANAL is LNW owned

(3) On Welshpool + Llanfair ng railway, now partly preserved, all stations in lower case lettering - those still in use are underlined in green

(4) Spelling of Welsh place names is according to railway practice in period 1904-22

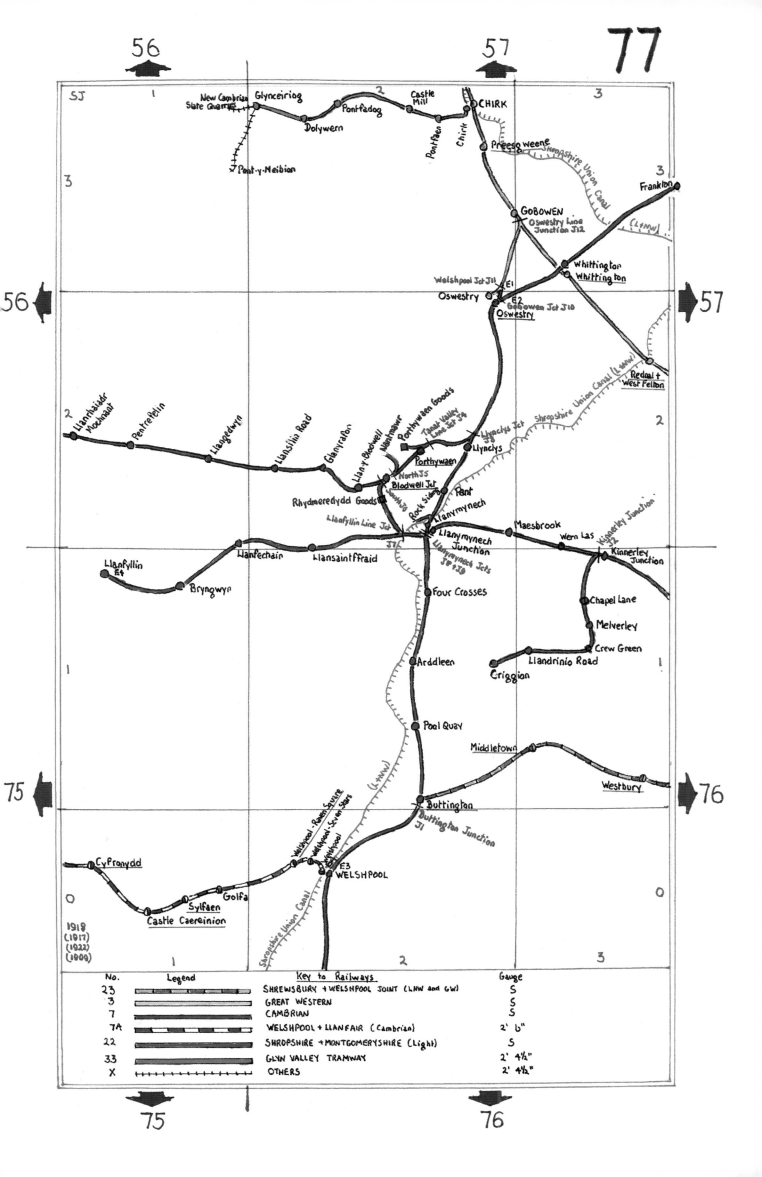

SJ

New Cambrian Slate Quarries
Glynceiriog
Pont-y-Meibion
Dolywern
Pontfadog
Castle Mill
Pontfaen
Chirk
CHIRK
Preesgweene
Shropshire Union Canal
Frankton
(LNW)
GOBOWEN
Oswestry Line Junction J12
Whittington
Whittington
Welshpool Jct J11
E1
E2
Oswestry
Gobowen Jct J10
Oswestry
Shropshire Union Canal (L+NW)
Redanlt
West Felton

2 Llanrhaiadr Mochnant
Pentrefelin
Llangedwyn
Llansilin Road
Glanyrafon
Llan-y-Blodwell
Nantmawr
Porthywaen Goods
Tanat Valley Line Jct J4
Llynclys Jct
Shropshire Union Canal
Porthywaen
Llynclys
North JS
Bloodwell Jct
Rhydmeredydd Goods
South JS
Rock Siding
Pant
Llanymynech
Maesbrook
Wern Las
Kinnerley Junction

Llanfyllin Line Jct
Llanfechain
Llansaintffraid
J7
Llanymynech Junction
Llanymynech Jcts J8 + J9
Kinnerley Junction

Llanfyllin E4
Bryngwyn
Four Crosses
Chapel Lane
Melverley
Crew Green
Llandrinio Road
Arddleen
Criggion
Pool Quay
Middletown
Westbury

Welshpool - Raven Square
Welshpool - Seven Stars
Welshpool
Buttington
Buttington Junction J1
Shropshire Union Canal
(L+NW)

Cyfronydd
Golfa
Sylfaen
Castle Caereinion
E3
WELSHPOOL

1918
(1917)
(1922)
(1900)

Key to Railways

No.	Legend		Gauge
23		SHREWSBURY + WELSHPOOL JOINT (LNW and GW)	S
3		GREAT WESTERN	S
7		CAMBRIAN	S
7A		WELSHPOOL + LLANFAIR (Cambrian)	2' 6"
22		SHROPSHIRE + MONTGOMERYSHIRE (Light)	S
33		GLYN VALLEY TRAMWAY	2' 4¼"
X		OTHERS	2' 4½"

56 57 75 76

RAILWAYS

No	Company	Ry Ref
R2	LONDON + NORTH WESTERN	23B J40
23A	SHREWSBURY + HEREFORD (LNW+GW)	22 J41
23B	SHREWSBURY + WELSHPOOL (LNW+GW)	3 J60
23C	SHREWSBURY + WELLINGTON (LNW+GW)	3 J60
3	GREAT WESTERN	3 J61
22	SHROPSHIRE + MONTGOMERYSHIRE	23A O49
X	Colliery Lines and Others	

STATIONS + HALTS

No	Name	Ry Ref
A1	Abbey Foregate Platform	23C J51
2	Admaston	23C J61
3	Berrington	3 J50
4	Buildwas	3 J60
5	Coalbrookdale	3 J60
6	Coalport	2 J60
7	Coalport	3 J60
8	Condover	23A J40
9	Cressage	3 J50
10	Cruckton	22 J22
11	Crudgington	3 J61
12	Donnington	2 J71
13	Dorrington	23A J40
14	Hadley	2 J61
15	Hadnall	2 J51
16	Hanwood	23B J40
17	Hanwood Road	22 J41
18	Horsehay	3 J60
19	Ironbridge + Broseley	3 J60
20	Ketley	3 J61
21	Lawley Bank	3 J60
22	Leaton	3 J41
23	Leebotwood	23A O49
24	Lightmoor Junction	3 J60
25	Linley	3 O79
26	Madeley (Salop)	3 J60
27	Madeley Market	2 J60
28	Malins Lee	2 J60
29	Meole Brace	22 J40
30	Much Wenlock	3 J60
31	(NEW HADLEY HALT) ♀	3 J61
32	Oakengates	2 J71
33	OAKENGATES	3 J61
34	Preshope	3 O59
35	Redhill	22 J40
	SHREWSBURY	
36	Abbey	2 J51
37	Abbey Foregate Plat^m	23C J51
38	GENERAL §	23A J41
39	West	22 J41
40	Strichley	2 J60
41	Trench Crossing	2 J61
42	Upton Magna	23C J51
43	Walcot	23B J40
44	WELLINGTON	22 J41
		3 J60

GOODS

No	Name/Location	Ry Ref
G1	Coleham	3 J41
2	Coton Hill	3 J41
3	Hadley	2 J61
4	Haybridge	2 J61
5	Hollinswood LNW	3 O79
6	Hollinswood GW	3 J60
7	Priors Lee	2 J60
8	Shrewsbury LNW	2 J60
9	Trench	22 J40
10	Wellington LNW	3 J60
11	Wellington GW	3 J61
12	Wombridge	2 J71
9	Radley Brickworks	23C J51
10	Haybridge Colliery	23C J61
11	Dowley Iron Works	3 J60
12	Ketley Siding	3 J61
13	Haybridge Siding	Ry Ref
14	Bradley Siding	23 J41
15	Greenfield Siding	3 J41
16	Allscott Siding	2 J61

SIDINGS ETC

No	Company/Name/Location	Ry Ref
P1	Shropshire Iron Co	22 J40
2	Hadley Lodge Siding	2 2 J51
3	Old Lodge Furnaces	23C J51
4	Granville Colliery	23A J41
5	Woodhouse Colliery	22 J41
6	Stafford Colliery	2 J60
7	Kemberton Colliery	2 J61
8	Foster's Siding	23C J51

TUNNELS

No	Name/Location	Ry Ref
T1	Preshope	3 O59

ENGINE SHEDS

No	Name/Location	Ry Ref
E1	Shrewsbury	2 J41
2	Shrewsbury	3 J41
3	Coalport	2 J70
4	Much Wenlock	3 J60
5	Wellington	3 J61

JUNCTIONS

No	Name/Locations	Ry Ref	Ry No Ref
J1	Cruck Meole	2 J61	23B J40
2	Shrewsbury West	X J71	23B22 J41
3	Stt H and Stt Wpool	X J71	23AB J41
4	Severn Valley	X J70	23A3 J41
5	Curve South	3 J70	23AC J41
6	Curve East	3 J70	23C J51
7	Stt H and Stt Wington	3 J70	23AC J41
8	Goods Line	3 J70	23A2 J41
9	For Crewe	3 J70	23A2 J41
10	GW and Joint Line	3 J60	23A3 J41
11	Market Drayton Line	3 J61	23C3 J61
12	Stafford	3 J61	23C J61
13	Joint Line + LNW	3 J60	23C2 J61
14	Joint Line + GW	3 J41	23C3 J61
15	Coalport	23C J61	2 J61
16	Ketley	2 J61	3 J61
17	Hollinswood	3 J70	3 J70
18	Madeley	3 J70	3 J70
19	Lightmoor	3 J60	3 J60
20	Buildwas West	3 J60	3 J60
21	Buildwas East	3 J60	3 J60

NOTES:

(1) REFERENCES - In SO or SJ: the S is omitted.

(2) § Now known as SHREWSBURY

(3) Opened post-grouping and due to be closed by British Rail 86

♀ . Exact site relative to Ketley Junction is uncertain

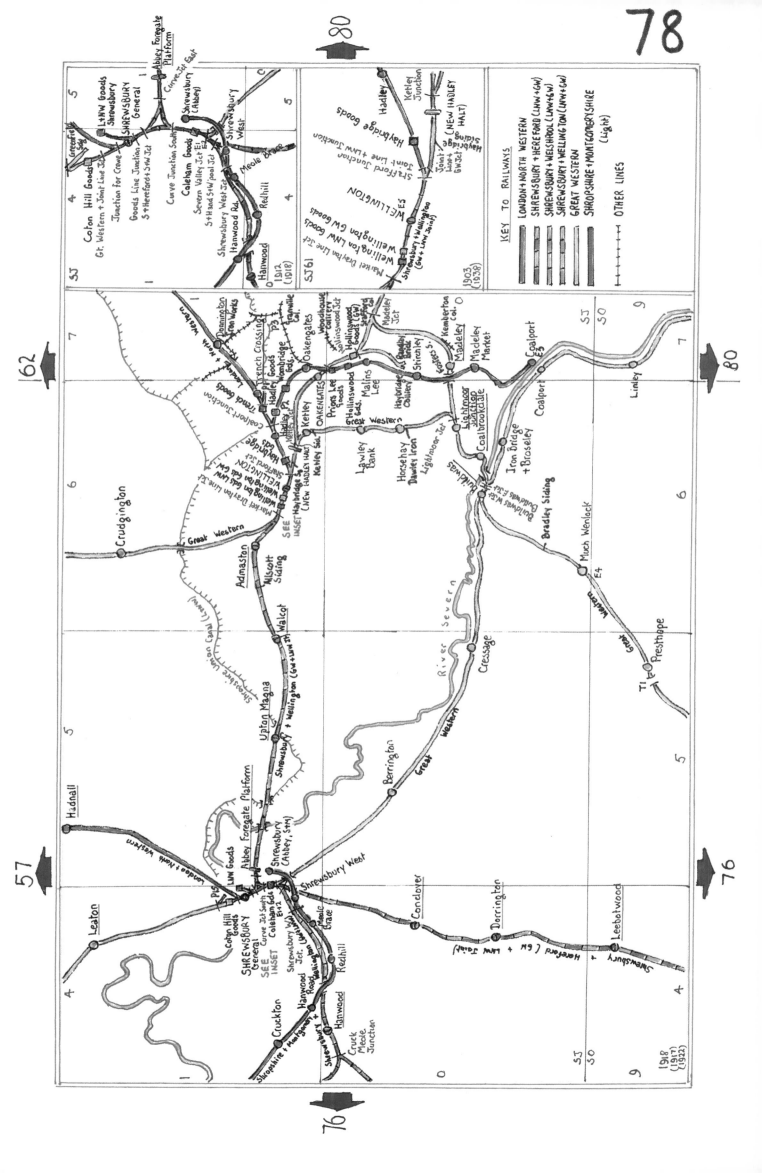

79   A) CRAVEN ARMS + LUDLOW   B) HEREFORD

A

RAILWAYS

No.	Company
R 1	BISHOPS CASTLE
2	LONDON + NORTH WESTERN
23A	SHREWSBURY + HEREFORD (LNW + GW)
3	GREAT WESTERN
5	CLEOBURY MORTIMER + DITTON PRIORS (Light) (GW)
X	Quarry and other lines

STATIONS

No.	Name	Ry Ref
A 1	BROOME	2 38
2	Broomfield	23A 47
3	CRAVEN ARMS + Stokesay	23A 48
4	Ditton Priors	5 68
5	Easton Court	23A 56
6	Harton Road	3 48
7	Horderley	1 48
8	LUDLOW	23A 57
9	Marsh Brook	23A 48
10	Newnham Bridge	3 66
11	Onibury	23A 47
12	Stretford Bridge *	1 48
13	Tenbury Wells	23A 56
14	Woofferton	23A 56

SIDINGS

No.	Company / Name / Location	Ry Ref
P 1	Middleton	23A 57
2	Bitterley	23A 57
3	Clee Hill	23A 57

ENGINE SHEDS

No.	Name / Location	Ry Ref
E 1	Craven Arms	2 48
2	Ludlow	2(3) 57

JUNCTIONS

No.	Name / Location	Ry Ref
J 1	Marsh Farm	23A3 48
2	Stretford Bridge	23A1 48
3	Craven Arms	23A2 48
4	Clee Hill	23A 57
5	Woofferton	23A 56
6	Tenbury Joint + GW	23A3 56

NOTES:
(1) REFERENCES – All in SO
(2) Closed pre-Grouping *

B

RAILWAYS

No.	Company
R 2	LONDON + NORTH WESTERN
23A	SHREWSBURY + HEREFORD (LNW + GW)
3	GREAT WESTERN
4	MIDLAND
X	Others

STATION

No.	Name	Ry Ref
A 1	HEREFORD Barr's Court	23A 54

SIGNAL BOXES

No.	Name	Ry Ref
B 1	Redhill Junction	3 43
2	Rotherwas Junction	3 53
3	Ayleston Hill	3 54
4	Brecon Curve	3 54
5	Barton Curve	3 54
6	Moorfields Junction	4 44
7	Barton	3 43
8	Station	3 54
9	Barr's Court Junction	3 54
10	Shelwick Junction	3 54

ENGINE SHEDS

No.	Name / Location	Ry Ref
E 1	Hereford LNW	2 54
2	Hereford GW	3 43
3	Hereford Mid	4 44

GOODS

No.	Name / Location	Ry Ref
G 1	Hereford LNW	2 54
2	Barr's Court	3 54
3	Barton	3 43
4	Moorfields	4 44

SIDINGS

No.	Company / Name / Location	Ry Ref
P 1	Gas Works	3X 54
2	Grooms Sidings	3 54
3	Corporation Siding	23A †
4	Moorfields Exchange	4(23) †
5	Show Yard Siding	3 †
6	Stone Siding	3 †
7	Wagon Works	3 †
8	Watkin Bros.	3 †

JUNCTIONS

No.	Name / Location	Ry Ref
J 1	Redhill	32 43
2	Shed	3 43
3	Goods Branch	4 44
4	Moorfields	4 44
5	Midland + GWestern	34 44
6	Rotherwas	32 53
7	Barr's Court South	23A3 54
8	Brecon Curve	23A 54
9	Barton Curve	23A3 54
10	Gas Works	3X 54
11	Barr's Court	23A3 54
12	Shelwick	23A3 54

NOTES:
(1) REFERENCES – All in SO
(2) LOCATION uncertain †
(3) SIGNAL BOXES on the joint line (GW + LNW) were subject to changes regarding working, manning and equipment. But in the main within this area were looked after by the GW

Map A

3 50
4
Marsh Brook
Harton Road
5
6
A
Ditton Priors
8

Horderley
Marsh Farm Junction

8
Stretford Bridge
Stretford Bridge Junction

E1 CRAVEN ARMS + Stokesay
Craven Arms Junction

6
BROOME

Shrewsbury + Hereford Joint (GW+LNW)
Onibury
Bromfield
Middleton
Incline
Dhustone Quarry

7
Clee Hill Joint
Bitterley

Clee Hill Junction
E2
LUDLOW
Clee Hill
7
76

KEY TO RAILWAYS (BOTH MAPS)

- LONDON + NORTH WESTERN
- SHREWSBURY + HEREFORD JT (LNW + GW)
- GREAT WESTERN
- MIDLAND
- BISHOP'S CASTLE
- OTHERS – Quarry lines + private lines
- CLEOBURY MORTIMER + DITTON PRIORS (Light) (GW)

Key to Other Features

- Passenger Station (may be also Goods)
- Engine Sheds (Colour – ownership)
- Goods Only (Colour – ownership)
- Junction Names
- Signal Boxes (Exact site questionable)
- | Goods only or private sidings etc
- To Destination of Lines (Map B)
- Water feature

6
3
1903 (1917)
4
Woofferton Junct
Tenbury Joint
Tenbury Jct ~ Jt + GW

Tenbury Wells
Newnham Bridge
6
6

Woofferton 5
Easton Court for Little Hereford

76 76

Map B

SO
4
B
Shelwick Junction S.B.
TO SHREWSBURY 5
Great Western
TO WORCESTER

TO SWANSEA

Gas Works
Barr's Court Junction Signal Box
Shrewsbury + Hereford (GW + LNW Joint)
Shelwick Junction

Gas Works Jct.
Grooms Sidg
Barton Curve
Barr's Court Junction

6
4
Midland
Midland + GW Jct
Midland & GW Moorfields Jct S.B.

Barton Curve S.B.
Barton Curve
Brecon Curve Signal Box
LNW Engine Shed
Brecon Curve Junction

4
76

Barton Curve Junction
Moorfields Junction Goods Branch Jct.
Brecon Curve
Hereford Goods (L + NW)

Midland Engine Shed
Barr's Court Goods GW Station S.B.
HEREFORD BARR'S COURT (Joint GW + LNW)
Ayleston Hill Signal Box
Barr's Court Junction South

Moorfields Goods

Barton Sig Box
Barton Goods
Shed Junction
GW Engine Shed

River Wye

2
3
L
L
C
Rotherwas Junction
Rotherwas Jct. S.B.
3
110

Great Western
Rotherwas Curve
London + North Western
Great Western

1913 (1921)
4
Red Hill Junction Signal Box
Redhill Junction
TO ABERGAVENNY
5
TO GLOUCESTER

WOLVERHAMPTON + EVESHAM

RAILWAY

No.	Company
R 1	STRATFORD-ON-AVON + MIDLAND JCT
2	LONDON + NORTH WESTERN
3	GREAT WESTERN
3A	GREAT WESTERN (Post Grouping)
34	HALESOWEN JOINT (GW + Mid)
4	MIDLAND
0	BRITISH RAIL

STATIONS

No.	Name	Ry Ref
A 1	ACOCK'S GREEN	3 P18
2	ADDERLEY PARK	2 P18
3	Albion	2 O99
4	ALBRIGHTON	3 J80
5	Alcester	4 PQ5
6	Aldridge	4 KOO
7	Alrewas	2 K11
8	ALVECHURCH	4 PO7
9	Arley	3 O77
10	Armitage	2 KOI
11	ASTON	2 PO9
12	Baptist End Halt	3 O98
13	BARNT GREEN	4 PO7
14	Barton + Walton	4 K11
15	BEARLEY	3 P16
16	Bengeworth	4 PQ4
17	BESCOT Junction	2 PO9
18	Bewdley	3 O77
19	Bidford-on-Avon	1 PO5
20	(BILBROOK)	3 J80
※	Bilston	3 O99
21	Bilston (Main Line)	3 O99
22	Binton	1 P15
23	Birchills	4 KOO
	BIRMINGHAM ※	
24	MOOR STREET	3 PO8
25	NEW STREET	2 PO8
※	Snow Hill	3 PO8
26	(BIRMINGHAM INTERN'L)	20 P18
26A	(BIRMINGHAM AIRPORT) ✈	0 P18
27	Blackwell	4 O97
28	BLAKEDOWN, Churchill +	3 O87
29	BLAKE STREET	2 K10
30	Bloxwich	2 KOO
31	BORDESLEY	3 PO8
32	BOURNVILLE	4 PO8
※	Bradley + Moxley ※	3 O99
33	Bransford Road	0 75
34	Bretfarton + Weston-sub-Edge	3 P14
35	Brettell Lane	3 O98
36	Bridgnorth	3 O79
37	Brierley Hill	3 O98
38	Brighton Road	4 PO8
39	Bramford Bridge	4 P19
40	(Bromley + Brockmore Halt)	3A O98
41	BROMSGROVE	4 O86
42	Broom (Junction)	4(1) PO5
43	Brownhills	2 KOO
44	Brownhills	4 KOO
45	(BUTLERS LANE)	2 P19
46	Campden	3 P14
※	Camp Hill	4 PO8
47	Cannock	2 J90
48	Castle Bromwich	4 P19
49	CHESTER ROAD	2 P19
50	Churchill + BLAKEDOWN	3 O87
※	Church Road	4 PO8
51	CLAVERDON	3 P26

No.	Name	Ry Ref
52	CODSALL	3 J80
53	COLWALL	3 O74
54	Combes Holloway Halt	3 O98
55	(Compton Halt)	3A O98
56	COSELEY, Deepfields +	2 O99
57	(COSFORD)	3 J70
58	Coughton	4 PO6
59	CRADLEY HEATH	3 O98
60	Croxall	4 K11
※	Daisy Bank	3 O99
61	DANZEY	3 P17
※	Darby End Halt	3 O98
※	Darlaston	2 O99
62	Deepfields + COSELEY	2 O99
63	Defford	4 O94
64	Donnington	2 J71
65	DORRIDGE, Knowle +	3 P17
66	DROITWICH (SPA)	3 O86
※	DUDDESTON, Vauxhall +	2 PO8
67	Dudley	2 O99
68	Dudley	3 O99
※	DUDLEY PORT High Level	2 O99
※	Dudley Port Low Level	2 O99
69	Dunstall Park	3 J70
70	Eardington	3 O78
71	EARLSWOOD LAKES	3 P17
72	Eckington	4 O94
73	Elford	4 K10
74	ERDINGTON	2 P19
75	Ettingshall Rd + Bilston	2 O99
76	EVESHAM	3 PO4
77	Evesham	4 PO4
78	Fernhill Heath	3 O85
※	FIVE WAYS	4 PO8
79	Fladbury	3 O94
80	Forge Mills	4 P19
81	Four Ashes	2 J90
82	FOUR OAKS	2 P19
83	Gailey	2 J91
84	(Gornal Halt)	3A O90
85	GRAVELLY HILL	2 P19
86	Great Alne	3 P15
87	GREAT BARR §94	2 PO9
※	Great Bridge	2 O99
※	Great Bridge	3 O99
88	GREAT MALVERN	3 O74
88A	Grimes Hill + WYTHALL	3 PO7
89	HAGLEY	3 O98
90	Hagley Road	2 PO8
91	Halesowen	3 O98
92	(HALL GREEN)	3 P18
93	Hammerwich	2 KOO
94	HAMPSTEAD §87	2 PO9
95	Hampton Loade	3 O78
※	Handsworth	2 PO8
※	Handsworth Wood	2 PO9
96	Harborne	2 PO8
97	HARTLEBURY	3 O87
※	Hartshill + Woodside	3 O98
98	Harvington	4 PO4
99	HATTON	3 P26
100	Hazelwell	4 PO8
101	Hednesford	2 J91
102	HENLEY-IN-ARDEN	3 P16
103	Henwick	3 O85
104	Highley	3 O78
※	High Street Halt	3 O98
105	(Himley)	3A O89
106	Hindon	4 PO4
107	Hockley	3 PO8
108	HONEYBOURNE	3 P14
109	Hunnington	34 O98

No.	Name	Ry Ref
※	Icknield Port Road	3 J80
110	KIDDERMINSTER	3 O74
111	King's Heath	3 O98
112	KING'S NORTON	3 O98
113	Knightwick	2 O99
114	Knowle + DORRIDGE	3 J70
115	LANGLEY GREEN	4 PO6
116	LAPWORTH	3 O98
117	(LEA HALL)	4 K11
118	Leigh Court	3 O99
119	LICHFIELD CITY	3 P17
120	Lichfield TV High L	3 O98
121	LICHFIELD TV Low L	2 O99
122	Lifford	4 PO8
123	Linley	3 O79
124	Littleton + Badsey	3 PO4
125	Long Marston	3 P14
126	(LONGRIDGE)	4 PO7
127	Lower Brierley Halt	3A O98
128	LYE	3 O98
129	Madeley	3 J70
130	MALVERN LINK	3 O74
131	Malvern Wells	3 O74
132	Malvern Wells	4 O74
133	MARSTON GREEN	2 P18
134	Milcote	3 P15
135	Manmore Green	2 O99
※	Monument Lane	2 PO8
136	MOOR STREET	3 PO8
137	Moseley	4 PO8
138	Netherton	3 O99
139	Newport	2 J71
140	NEW STREET	2 PO8
141	Newton Road	4 PO7
142	NORTHFIELD	4 PO7
143	North Walsall	4 KOO
144	(Northwood)	3 O77
145	Norton Junction	3 O85
※	Ocker Hill	2 O99
※	OLDBURY + Bramford L	2 O99
146	Oldbury (+ Langley Green)	3 O98
147	OLD HILL	3 O98
148	OLTON	3 P18
149	Pelsall	2 KOO
150	PENKRIDGE	2 J91
151	(Pen Halt)	3A O89
152	Penns	4 P19
153	(Pensnett Halt)	3A O98
154	PERRY BARR	2 PO9
155	PERSHORE	3 O94
※	Pleck	2 PO9
156	Priestfield	3 O99
※	Prince's End	2 O99
※	Prince's End	3 O99
157	REDDITCH	4 PO6
※	Rotton Park Road	2 PO8
※	Round Oak	3 O98
158	ROWLEY REGIS + Blackheath	3 O98
159	Rubery	4 PO4
160	Rugeley Town	2 KOI
161	RUGELEY (Trent Valley)	2 KOI
162	Salford Priors	4 PO5
※	Saltley	2 J91
※	SANDWELL + DUDLEY §	2 O99
163	SELLY OAK	4 PO8
164	SHENSTONE	2 K10
165	SHIFNAL	3 J70
166	SHIRLEY	3 P17
167	SHRUB HILL	3 O85
168	SMALLHEATH + Sparkbrook	3 P18
169	SMETHWICK §	2 PO8

No.	Name	Ry Ref
※	SMETHWICK JUNCTION §	3 PO8
※	SMETHWICK ROLFE ST §	2 PO8
※	SMETHWICK WEST §	3 PO8
※	Snow Hill	3 PO8
※	Soho	3 O75
169	Soho	3 PO8
170	Soho Road	2 PO8
171	SOLIHULL	3 P18
172	Somerset Road	4 PO8
※	Span Lane	3 O75
※	(SPRING ROAD)	3 P18
173	STECHFORD for Yardley	2 P18
174	Stoke Works	3 O96
175	Stoulton	3 O95
176	STOURBRIDGE JUNCTION	3 O98
177	STOURBRIDGE TOWN	3 O98
178	Stourport	3 O87
179	Stratford-on-Avon	1 P15
180	STRATFORD - (UP)ON-AVON	3 P15
181	Streetley	4 PO9
182	Studley + Astwood Bank	4 PO6
183	Suckley	3 O75
184	SUTTON COLDFIELD	2 P19
185	Sutton Coldfield	4 P19
186	Sutton Park	4 P19
187	Swan Village	3 O99
188	(Tettenhall)	3A J80
188A	(THE LAKES)	3 P17
※	TIPTON	2 O99
189	Tipton	3 O99
190	TYSELEY	3 P18
191	(UNIVERSITY)	4 PO8
192	Upton-on-Severn	4 O84
※	Vauxhall + DUDDESTON	2 PO8
193	Wadborough	4 O84
194	WALSALL	2 PO9
195	Walsall Wood	4 KOO
196	WATER ORTON	4 P19
197	Wednesbury	2 O99
※	Wednesbury	3 O99
198	Wednesfield	4 J90
199	West Bromwich	3 PO9
200	(WHITLOCK'S END)	3 P17
201	WIDNEY MANOR	3 P17
202	Willenhall	2 O99
203	Willenhall	4 O99
204	WILMCOTE	3 P15
205	Windmill End	3 O98
※	Winson Green	2 PO8
206	WITTON	2 PO9
207	Wixford	4 PO5
208	WOLVERHAMPTON HL	2 O99
※	Wolverhampton LL	3 O99
209	(Wombourn)	3A O89
210	WOOTTON WAWEN Platform	3 P16
211	WOOD END Platform	3 P17
※	Wood Green	2 PO9
	WORCESTER	
212	FOREGATE STREET	3 O85
213	SHRUB HILL	43 O85
214	WYLDE GREEN	2 P19
215	Wyre Forest	3 O77
216	Wyrley	2 J90
217	WYTHALL, Grimes Hill +	3 PO7
218	YARDLEY WOOD Platform	3 P18
	GOODS	
No.	Name / Location	Ry Ref
G1	Worcester	4 O85
2	Spetchley	4 O95
3	Dunhampstead	4 O95
4	Droitwich Road	4 O96
5	Stoke Works	4 O96

No.	Name / Location	Ry Ref
6	Stratford-on-Avon	3 P15
7	Healey	3 P16
8	Winchor	4 KOI
	SIDINGS	
No.	Company / Name / Loc	Ry Ref
P1	Hednesford Col	2 KOI
2	Five Ways Sdg	2 KOI
3	Cannock + Rugeley 1.	2 KOI
4	Chasetown Col	X KOO
5	Conduit Col	4 X KOO
	ENGINE SHEDS	
No.	Name / Location	Ry Ref
E1	Worcester	3 O85
2	Evesham	3 PQ4
3	Kidderminster	3 O87
4	Stratford-on-Avon	3 P15
5	Bromsgrove	4 O96
	JUNCTIONS	
No.	Name / Location	Ry Ref
J1	Malvern	34 O74
4	Honeybourne	3 P14
5	North Loop	3 P14
6	East Loop	3 P14
7	West Loop	3 P14
8	South Loop	3 P14
9	Bransford Road	3 O85
10	Norton	3 O85
11	Abbotswood	43 O85
12	Rainbow Hill	3 O85
13	Shrub Hill	3(34) O85
14	Tunnel	3(34) O85
15	Broom	41 PO5
16	Alcester	43 PO5
17	Stratford Goods	3 P15
18	Stratford-Evesham Rd	3 P15
19	Station	1 P15
20	Bearley West	3 P16
21	Bearley North	3 P16
22	Bearley East	3 P16
26	Rowington	3 P18
27	Stoke Prior	43 O96
28	Droitwich	3 O86
29	Henley-in-Arden	3 P16
30	Bewdley North	3 O77
31	Bewdley South	3 O77
32	Hartlebury	3 O87
33	Kidderminster	3 O87
34	Main Line	4 PO7
35	Halesowen	434 PO7
36	Norton Branch	2 KOO
39	Norton Branch	2 J91
41	Rugeley	2 KOI
42	City	2 K10
43	Lichfield West	2 K11
44	Lichfield East	2 K11
45	Wichnor	42 K11

NOTES:

※ All stations located but those in BLUE not named (see MAP 81).
Other features only shown if not in area covered by enlargements.
REF SJ, SK, SO or SP – 'S' omitted.
§ Map Name } NAME
§ Modern Name } CHANGE
✦ Proposed station.
※ Closed early 20th century.
✕ Central stations only.
X Other railway.
✦ Conjectural name.
J Selection only.

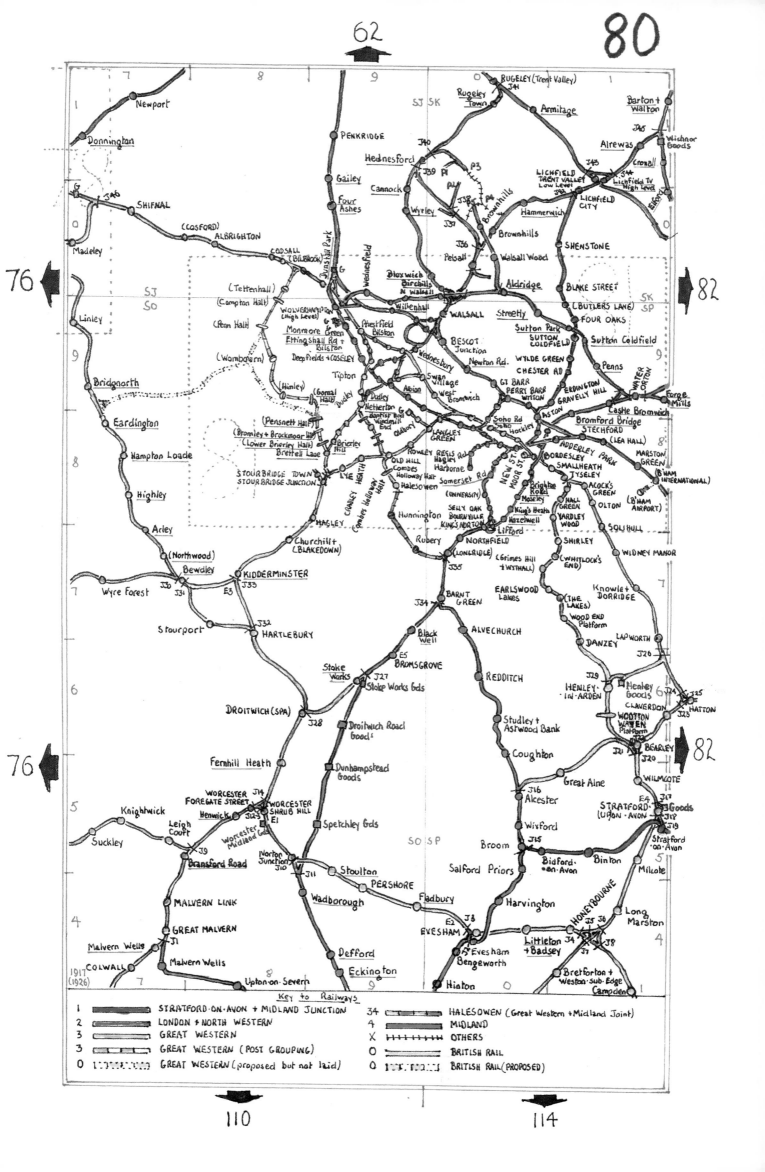

81

BIRMINGHAM + WOLVERHAMPTON

RAILWAYS

No.	Company
R2	LONDON + NORTH WESTERN
3	GREAT WESTERN
3A	GREAT WESTERN (Post Grouping)
34	HALESOWEN (GW + Midland)
4	MIDLAND
O	BRITISH RAIL (PROPOSED)
X	Others - Colliery Lines etc

STATIONS

No	Name	Ry Ref
1	ALCOCK'S GREEN	3 P18
2	ADDERLEY PARK	2 P18
3	Albion	2 099
4	Aldridge	4 K00
5	ASTON	2 P09
6	Baptist End Halt	3 098
7	BESCOT Junction	3 098
8	(DUBROOK)	3 J80
9	Bilston	3 099
9A	Bilston (Main Line)	3 099
10	Birchills	4 K00
11	(BIRMINGHAM) MOOR STREET	3 098
12	New Street	2 P08
13	Snow Hill	3 P08
14	(BIRMINGHAM AIRPORT) ♦	O P18
15	(BIRM HAM INTERNATIONAL)	2 P18
16	BLAKE STREET	2 K10
17	Bloxwich	2 K00
18	BORDESLEY	3 P08
19	BOURNVILLE	4 P08
20	Bradley + Moxley	3 099
21	Brettell Lane	3 098
22	Brierley Hill	3 098
23	Brighton Road	4 P08
2A	Bromford Bridge	4 P19
25	(Bromley + Brackmore Halt)	3A 098
26	(BUTLERS LANE)	2 P19
27	Camp Hill	4 P08
28	Castle Bromwich	3 099
29	CHESTER ROAD	2 P19
30	Church Road	4 P08
31	CODSALL	3 J80
32	Combes Holloway Halt	3 098
33	(Compton Halt)	3A 089
34	COSELEY, Deepfields +	2 099
35	CRADLEY HEATH + Cradley	3 098
36	Daisy Bank	3 099
37	Darby End Halt	3 098
38	Darlaston	2 099
39	Deepfields + COSELEY	2 099
40	DUDDESTON Vauxhall +	2 P08
41	Dudley	2 099
42	Dudley	3 098
43	DUDLEY PORT High Level	2 099
44	Dudley Port Low Level	2 099
45	Dunstall Park	3 J90
46	ERDINGTON	2 P19
47	Ettingshall Road + Bilston	
48	FIVE WAYS	2 099
49	Forge Mills	4 P08
50	FOUR OAKS	2 P19
51	(Gornal Halt)	3A D99
52	GRAVELLY HILL	2 P19
53	GREAT BARR §60	2 P09
54	Great Bridge	2 099
55	Great Bridge	3 099
56	HAGLEY	3 098
57	Hagley Road	2 099
58	Halesowen	3 098
59	(HALL GREEN) §53	2 P18
60	HAMPSTEAD	2 P08
61	Handsworth	2 099
62	Handsworth Wood	2 P09
63	Harborne	2 P08
64	Hartshill + Woodside	3 098
65	Hazelwell	4 P08
66	High Street Halt	3 098
67	(Himley)	4 P08
68	Hockley	4 P19
69	Hunnington	3 098
70	Icknield Port Road	2 P19
71	King's Heath	4 P08
72	KING'S NORTON	4 P19
73	LANGLEY GREEN	2 P19
74	(LEA HALL)	4 P08
75	Lifford	3 J80
76	(Lower Brierley Halt)	3A 098
77	LYE	3A 089
78	MARSTON GREEN	2 099
79	Monmore Green	3 098
80	Monument Lane	3 099
81	MOOR STREET	3 098
82	Moseley	2 099
83	Netherton	2 099
84	NEW STREET	2 P08
85	Newton Road	2 099
86	North Walsall	3 099
87	Ocker Hill	2 099
88	OLDBURY + Bromford Lane §105	2 099
89	Oldbury (+ Langley Green)	2 P19
90	OLD HILL	3 098
91	OLTON	2 099
92	Pelsall	4 P08
93	(Penn Halt)	4 P19
94	Penns	2 P19
95	(Peasnett Halt)	3A D99
96	PERRY BARR	2 P19
97	Pleck	2 P09
98	Priestfield	2 099
99	Prince's End	3 099
100	Prince's End	3 098
101	Rotton Park Road	2 P08
102	Round Oak	3 098
103	ROWLEY REGIS + Blackheath	3 P18
104	Saltley	2 P09
105	SANDWELL + DUDLEY §8§	4 P08
106	SELLY OAK	2 P09
107	Short Heath	2 P08
108	SMALL HEATH + Sparkbrook	3 098
109	SMETHWICK	4 P08
110	SMETHWICK JUNCTION §	3 098
111	SMETHWICK ROLFE ST §	3A 089
112	SMETHWICK WEST §	3 P08
113	Snow Hill	3A 098
114	Soho	2 P08
115	Soho	4 P08
116	Soho Road	2 P09
117	SOLIHULL	3 P08
118	Somerset Road	2 P18
119	Scott Lane	4 P08
120	(SPRING ROAD)	3A 098
121	STECHFORD for Yardley	3 098
122	STOURBRIDGE JUNCTION	2 P18
123	STOURBRIDGE TOWN	2 099
124	Streetley	2 P08
125	SUTTON COLDFIELD	3 P08
126	Sutton Coldfield	4 P08
127	Sutton Park	3 099
128	Swan Village	2 P08
129	(Tettenhall)	2 P09
130	TIPTON	4 K00
131	Tipton	2 099
132	TYSELEY	1 099
133	(UNIVERSITY)	2 099
134	Vauxhall + DUDDESTON	3 098
135	WALSALL	3 098
136	Walsall Wood	3 P18
137	WATER ORTON	2 K00
138	Wednesbury	3A 089
139	Wednesbury	4 P19
140	Wednesfield	3A 098
141	West Bromwich	2 P09
142	Willenhall	2 P09
143	Willenhall	3 099
144	Windmill End	2 099
145	Winson Green	3 099
146	WITTON	2 P08
147	WOLVERHAMPTON High Level	3 098
148	Wolverhampton Low Level	4 P08
149	(Worn bourn)	2 099
150	Wood Green	4 P08
151	WYLDE GREEN	4 J90
152	YARDLEY WOOD Platform	5 P18

TUNNELS

No	Name	Yds	Ry Ref
T1	Old Hill		4 P08
2	Dudley		2 099

ENGINE SHEDS

No	Location	Ry Ref
E1	Wolverhampton Stafford Rd	3 J90
2	Wolverhampton Oxley	3 J90

JUNCTIONS

No	Name / Location	Ry Ref
J1	Stourbridge South	3 098
2	Stourbridge North	3 098
4	Kingswinford	2 099
5	Halesowen	2 K00
6	Old Hill	2 K00
9	Withymoor Goods	3 098
10	Blowers Green	3 099
11	Dudley	2 K00
12	Sedgley	2 K00
13	Dudley Port	3 098
14	Great Bridge	3 098
15	Tipton East	3 098
16	Tipton North	2 P08
17	Tipton West	2 P09
18	Wednesbury South	3 098
19	Wednesbury Middle	3 098
20	Branch	2 099
21	Wednesbury North	3 099
26	Darlaston	3 099
27	Avoiding Line	4 P19
28	Crane Street	3 J90
29	Stafford Road	24 099
30	Oxley South	4 K00
31	Oxley East	3 P09
32	Oxley West	2 P08
33	Stour Valley	2 J90

SIDINGS

No	Company / Name / Location	Ry Ref
P1	Coppy Hall Col	2 K00
2	Aldridge Col 1+2	2 K00
3	Leighs Wood + Aldridge	4 K00
4	Thomas' Siding	2 K00
5	Amblecote Colliery	3 098
6	Shut End Siding	3X 089
7	Danels's Siding	3 098
8	Castle Mill Siding	3 098
9	Mitchell + Butlers Siding	2 P08
10	Hampstead Colliery	2 P09
11	Halesowen Basin	3 098
12	Cradley Colliery	3 098
13	Spring Vale Siding	2X 3 099
14	Bilston New Basin	3 099
15	Mornay Siding	3 099
16	Castle Bromwich Sidings	4 P19
17	Wolverhampton Co-op	3 J90
18	Himley Colliery	2 099
19	Walsall Wood Colliery	2 J90
20	Sandwell Park Col	4 K00
21	Soho Pool	4 P08
22	Birchill Furnaces	2 099

GOODS

No	Name / Location	Ry Ref
1	Albion	3 P08
2	Basin	3 P08
3	Birmingham Central	2 P08
4	Bloomfield	3 P08
5	Bushbury	3 P08
6	Camp Hill	3 P18
7	Curzon Street	4 P08
8	Darlaston	2 P09
9	Deepfields	3 P18
10	Herbert Street	2 P18
11	Lawley Street	3 098
12	Monmore Green	3 098
13	Oldbury	4 P08
14	Oldbury	2 P08
15	Old Hill	4 P08
16	Penns	4 P19
17	Soho	2 P08
18	Stourbridge	3A J80
19	Sutton Coldfield	2 099
20	Walsall LNW	3 099
21	Walsall Midland	3 P18
22	Walsall Street	4 P08
23	Water Orton	2 P08
24	Wednesbury	2 P09
25	Wednesfield Heath	4 K00
26	Windsor Street + Aston	4 P19
27	Withymoor	2 099
28	Wolverhampton Midland	3 099
35	S+B	3 J90
36	King's Norton	4 P08
37	Lifford West	4 P08
38	Lifford Station	4 P08
39	Lifford Canal Branch	4 P08
42	St Andrews	24 P08
40	Grand	4 P08
41	Saltley	4 P08
48	Aston - Stechford	3 J90
52	Sandwell	3 P18
53	Soho Pool	3 098
54	Handsworth	2 P08
55	Perry Barr North	2 P09
56	Perry Barr Station	2 P09
57	Aston - North	4 P08
59	South (Bescot)	4 P19
60	West (Bescot)	
61	East (Bescot)	24 P09
64	Rycroft	4 P19
65	Lichfield Line	2 099
66	North Walsall	2 099
68	Leighs Wood Branch	334 098
69	Norton Branch	3 098
75	Park Lane	3 098
76	Water Orton	3 099
80	Smethwick	23 P08
86	New Street	24 P08

NOTES:

(1) REF: In SJ, SK, SO or SP — the initial S is omitted.

(2) Line from Oxley to Brettell Lane projected pre-First World-War, but not built until mid 20's.

(3) JUNCTIONS - selection of names only is shown - others named from location.

§ Map date } NAME CHANGES
§ Modern }

✕ BIRMINGHAM - Central Stations

♦ Proposed Station

● Name conjectured

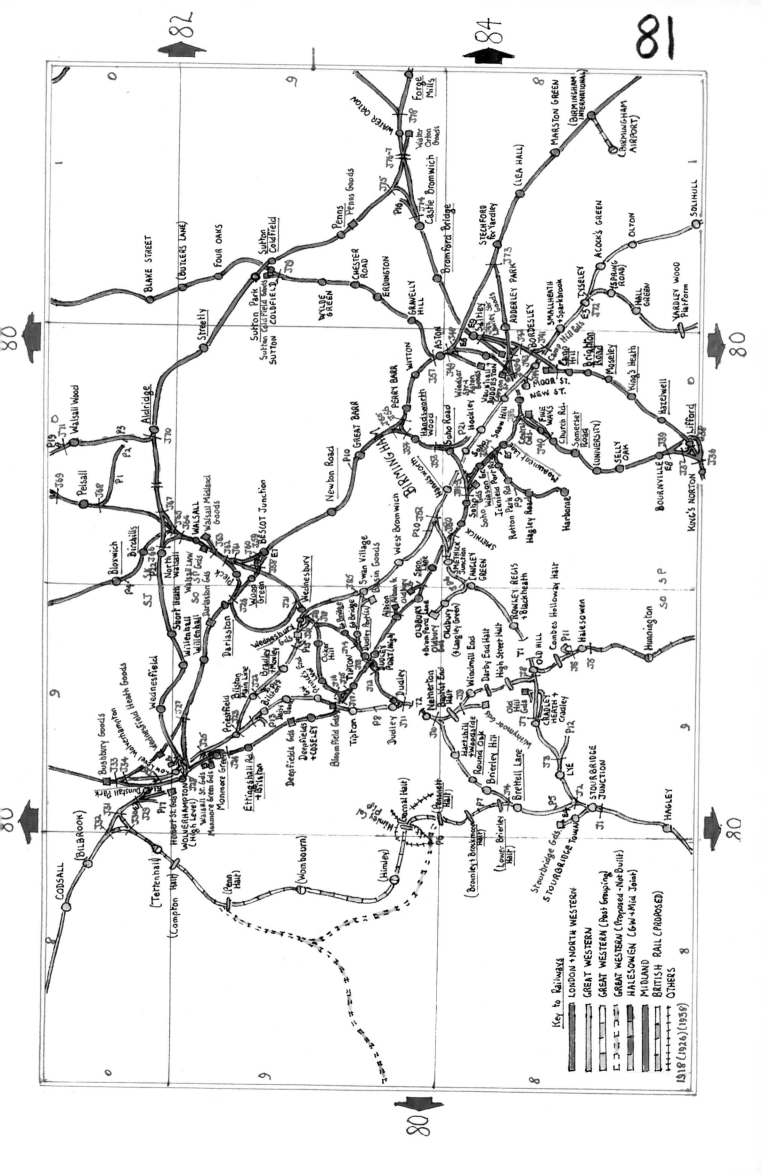

LEICESTER, RUGBY + BANBURY

RAILWAYS

No.	Company
R 1	STRATFORD-ON-AVON + MIDLAND JCT.
2	LONDON + NORTH WESTERN
24	LNW + MIDLAND JOINT
3	GREAT WESTERN
4	MIDLAND
5	GREAT CENTRAL
6	GREAT NORTHERN
0	LMS (POST-GROUPING)
X	Colliery lines etc

STATIONS

No	Name	Ry	Ref
A 1	Althorp Park	2	P66
2	Arley + Fillongley	4	P28
3	Ashby	4	K31
4	Ashby Magna	5	P59
5	ATHERSTONE	2	P39
6	Bagworth + Ellistown	4	K40
7	Banbury	2	P44
8	BANBURY	3	P44
9	Bardon Hill	4	K41
10	Barrow-on-Soar + Quorn	4	K51
11	Barton + Walton	4	K21
12	Bedworth	2	P38
13	Belgrave + Birstall	5	K50
14	BERKSWELL	2	P27
15	Birdingbury	2	P46
16	Blaby	2	P59
17	Blakesley	1	P64
18	Brandon + Wolston	2	P47
19	Braunston	2	P56
20	Braunston + Willoughby	5	P56
21	Brinklow	2	P48
22	Brooksby	4	K61
23	Broughton Astley	4	P59
24	Bulkington	2	P38
25	Byfield	1	P55
26	(CANLEY)	2	P37
27	Chalcombe Road Platform	5	P44
28	Charwelton	5	P65
29	Chilvers Coton	2	P39
30	CLAVERDON	3	P26
31	Clifton Mill	2	P57
32	Coalville	2	K41
33	Coalville	4	K41
34	Coleshill	4	P28
35	Coundon Road	2	P37
36	Countesthorpe	4	P59
37	COVENTRY	2	P37
38	Croft	2	P59
39	Cropredy	3	P44
40	Croxall	4	K11
41	Culworth	5	P54
42	Daventry	2	P56
43	Desford	4	K40
44	Donisthorpe	24	K31
45	Dunchurch	2	P47
46	Elford	2	K20
47	Elmesthorpe	2	P49
48	Ettington	1	P25
49	Eydon Road Platform	5	P54
50	Farthinghoe	2	P54
51	Fenny Compton	1	P45
52	Fenny Compton	3	P46
53	Flecknoe	2	P46
54	Foleshill	2	P38
55	Frisby	4	K61
56	Glenfield	4	K50
57	Glen Parva - Wigston	2	P59
58	Great Glen	4	P69
59	Gresley	4	K21
60	HAMPTON-IN-ARDEN	2	P28
61	Hampton-in-Arden	4	P28
62	HATTON	3	P26
63	Hawkesbury Lane	2	P38
64	Heather + Ibstock	24	K30
65	Helmdon	1	P54
66	Helmdon	5	P54
67	Higham-on-the-Hill	24	P39
68	HINCKLEY	2	P49
69	Hugglescote	24	K41
70	Humberstone	6	K60
71	Humberstone Road	4	K60
72	Ingersby	6	K60
73	Kenilworth	2	P27
74	Kibworth	4	P69
75	Kilsby + Crick	2	P57
76	Kineton	1	P35
77	Kingsbury	4	P29
78	Kirby Muxloe	4	K50
79	Leamington Spa	2	P36
80	LEAMINGTON SPA	3	P36
	LEICESTER		
81	Belgrave Road	6	K50
82	Central	5	K50
83	Humberstone Road	4	K50
84	LONDON ROAD §	4	K50
85	West Bridge	4	K50
86	Lilbourne	2	P57
87	LONG BUCKBY	2	P66
88	Longdon Road	3	P24
89	Longford + Exhall	2	P38
90	Loughborough Central	5	K51
91	Loughborough Derby Rd.	2	K51
92	Lutterworth	5	P58
93	Market Bosworth	24	K30
94	Marton	2	P46
95	Measham	24	K31
96	Milverton, Warwick	2	P36
97	Moira	4	K31
98	Morton Pinkney	1	P55
99	Napton + Stockton	2	P46
100	NARBOROUGH	2(24)	P59
101	NUNEATON	2	P39
102	Nuneaton	4	P39
103	Overseal ⚒	4	K21
104	POLESWORTH	2	K20
105	Quorn + Woodhouse	5	K51
106	Ratby	4	K50
107	Rearsby	4	K61
108	Rothley	5	K51
109	RUGBY	2	P57
110	Rugby Central	5	P57
111	Shackerstone	24	K30
112	Shenton	24	K30
113	Shepshed	2	K41
114	Shilton	2	P48
115	Shipston-on-Stour	3	P24
116	Shustoke	4	P29
117	Sileby	4	K61
118	Snarestone	24	K30
119	Southam + Long Itchington	2	P46
120	Southam Road + Harbury	3	P35
121	Stockingford	4	P39
122	Stoke Golding	24	P39
123	Swadlincote	4	K21
124	Swannington	4	K41
125	Syston	4	K61
126	TAMWORTH	2	K20
127	TAMWORTH	4	K20
128	Theddingworth	2	P68
129	Thurnby + Scraptoft	6	K60
130	TILE HILL	2	P27
131	Towcester	1	P64
132	Ullesthorpe + Lutterworth	4	P58
133	Wappenham	1	P64
134	WARWICK	3	P26
135	Warwick, Milverton	2	P36
136	Weedon	2	P65
137	Welford + Kilworth	2	P68
138	Welton	2	P56
139	West Bridge	4	K50
140	Whetstone	5	P59
141	Whitacre	4	P29
142	Whitwick	2	K41
143	Wigston	4	P59
144	Wigston - Glen Parva	2	P59
145	Wigston South	4	P59
146	WILNECOTE + Fazeley	4	K20
147	Woodford + Hinton	5	P55
148	Woodville	4	K31
149	Yelvertoft + Stanford Park	2	P57

GOODS

No.	Name / Location	Ry	Ref
G 1	Bell Green	2	P38
2	Gosford Green	2	P37
3	Wichnor	4	K11
4	Enderby	24	P59

SIDINGS

No	Company / Name / Location	Ry	Ref
P 1	Baxterley Park Colliery	4X	P29
2	Hall End Colliery	4X	P29
3	Baddesley Colliery Siding	4X	P29
4	Glascote Canal Wharf	4	K20
5	Netherseal Colliery	4	K21
6	Swannington Incline	4	K41
7	Coleorton Tramway ⌶	X	K31
8	Amington Colliery	X	K20

ENGINE SHEDS

No	Name / Location	Ry	Ref
E 1	Overseal	(4) 2	K31
2	Coalville	4	K41

JUNCTIONS

No	Name / Location	Ry	Ref
J 1	Kingsbury Branch	4	P29
2	Tamworth	2(4)	K20
3	Perry Crofts	(2) 4	K20
4	Wichnor	42	K11
5	Bretby Branch	4	K21
6	Swadlincote Branch	4	K21
7	Netherseal Branch	4	K21
8	Woodville	4	K21
9	Moira West	424	K21
10	Shackerstone	24	K30
11	Moira South	24	K31
12	Moira East	424	K31
13	Ashby	4	K31
14	Coleorton ⌶	4X	K31
15	Charnwood Forest	224	K41
16	Coalville	424	K41
17	Mantle Lane	4	K41
18	Towcester	1	P64

TUNNELS

No	Name	Length	Ry	Ref
T 1	Catesby	2997	5	P55

NOTES:

(1) REFERENCES: In SP or SK - 'S' omitted.

(2) Apart from stations, other features are, in the main, named only if in areas not covered by enlargements.

(3) Some Leicester stations are indexed both under Leicester and individual name.

§ Name change now LEICESTER.

⚒ Closed to passengers prior to 1904 - may have always been GOODS only.

⌶ Abandoned prior to 1920.

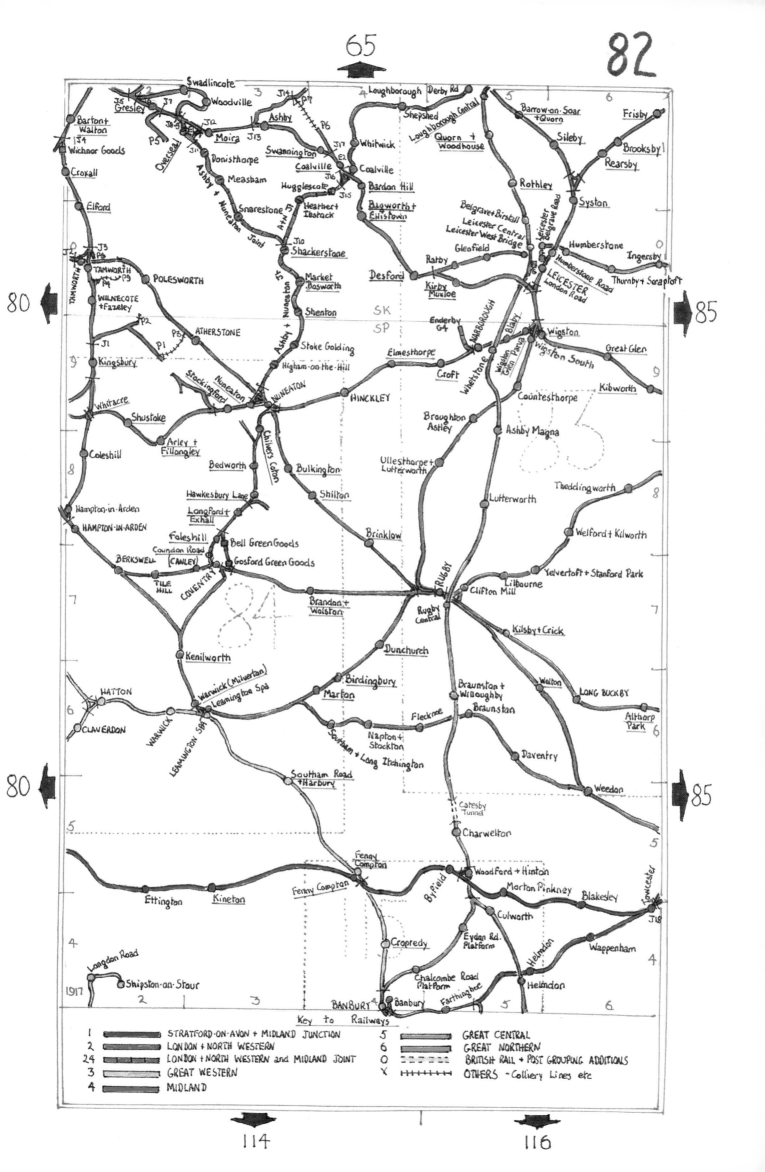

80

85

80

85

Key to Railways

1	STRATFORD-ON-AVON + MIDLAND JUNCTION	
2	LONDON + NORTH WESTERN	
24	LONDON + NORTH WESTERN and MIDLAND JOINT	
3	GREAT WESTERN	
4	MIDLAND	
5	GREAT CENTRAL	
6	GREAT NORTHERN	
O	BRITISH RAIL + POST GROUPING ADDITIONS	
X	OTHERS - Colliery Lines etc	

83

RAILWAYS

LOUGHBOROUGH, LEICESTER + RUGBY

No	Company
R2	LONDON + NORTH WESTERN
24	LONDON+NORTH WESTERN & MIDLAND JT.
4	MIDLAND
5	GREAT CENTRAL
6	GREAT NORTHERN
X	Others – Colliery Lines etc

STATIONS + HALTS

No	Name	Ry Ref
A 1	Althorp Park	2 P66
2	Ashby Magna	5 P59
3	Barrow-on-Soar + Quorn	4 K51
4	Belgrave + Birstall	5 K50
5	Blaby	2 P59
6	Braunston	2 P56
7	Braunston + Willoughby	5 P56
8	Brooksby	4 K61
9	Broughton Astley	4 P59
10	Church Brampton	2 P76
11	Clifton Mill	2 P57
12	Countesthorpe	4 P59
13	Croft	2 P59
14	Desford	4 K40
15	Daventry	2 P56
16	East Leake	5 K52
17	Flecknoe	2 P46
18	Frisby	4 K61
19	Glenfield	4 K50
20	Glen Parva, Wigston	2 P59
21	Great Glen	4 P69
22	Hathern	4 K52
23	Humberstone	6 K60
24	Humberstone Road †	4 K60
25	Ingersby	6 K60
26	Kibworth	4 P69
27	Kirby Muxloe	4 K50

LEICESTER

No	Name	Ry Ref
28	Belgrave Road	6 K50
29	Central	5 K50
30	Humberstone Road †	4 K60
31	LONDON ROAD §	4 K50
32	West Bridge †	4 K50
33	Lilbourne	2 P57
34	LONG BUCKBY	2 P66
35	LOUGHBOROUGH	4 K52
36	Loughborough Central	5 K51
37	Loughborough Derby Road	2 K51
38	Lubenham	2 P72
39	Lutterworth	5 P58
40	NARBOROUGH	2(24) P59
41	Old Dalby	4 K72
42	Quorn + Woodhouse	5 K51
43	Ratby	4 K50
44	Rearsby	4 K61
45	Rothley	5 K51
46	RUGBY	2/4 P57
47	Rugby Central	5 P57
48	Shepshed	2 K41
49	Sileby	4 K61
50	Syston	4 K61
51	Theddingworth	2 P68
52	Thurnby + Scraptoft	6 K60
53	Ullesthorpe + Lutterworth	4 P58
54	Upper Broughton	4 K62
55	Weedon	2 P65
56	Welford + Kilworth	2 P68
57	Welton	2 P56
58	West Bridge †	4 K50
59	Whetstone	5 P59
60	Wigston	4 P59
61	Wigston, Glen Parva	2 P59
62	Wigston South	4 P59
63	Yelvertoft + Stanford Park	P57

GOODS

No	Name/Location	Ry Ref
G 1	West Bridge	4 K50
2	Leicester GC	5 K50
3	Leicester LNW	2 K50
4	Leicester – East	4 K50
5	Leicester – Cattle	4 K50
6	Canal Basin Wharf – Rugby	4 P57
7	Enderby	24 P59

SIDINGS

No	Company/Name/Location	Ry Ref
P 1	Croft Granite + Brick	2 P59
2	Aylestone Wharf	4 K50
3	Soar Lane Wharf	4 K50
4	Leicester Corporation	6X K50
5	Heffords Siding	6 K60
6	Kilby Bridge Siding	4 P69
7	Groby Quarries	X K50
8	Mount Sorrel Quarries	X K51
9	Barrow Lime Works	4 K51
10	Barnstone Lime Company	5 K52
11	Canal Wharf Basin	4 P57
12	Dunmore Biscuits	4 P59
13	British Thomson	4 P57
14	Hunter's Siding	4 P57
15	The Br Electrical Works Sdg	4 K52

ENGINE SHEDS

No	Location	Ry Ref
E 1	Wigston	4 P69
2	Leicester	4 K50
3	Rugby	2 P57
4	Rugby	4 P57

TUNNELS

No	Name/Location	Yds	Ry Ref
T 1	Kilsby	2426	2 P56
2	Crick		2 P56

3	Ashby Magna	5 P58
4	Glenfield	1796 4 K50
5	(Ingersby)	6 K60

JUNCTIONS

No	Name/Location	Ry Ref
J 1	Wigston – Mkt Harboro' Line	42 P59
2	Wigston – Central West	4 P59
3	Wigston – Level Crossing	4 P59
4	Wigston – Central	4 P59
5	Wigston – Leicester Line	42 P59
6	Wigston – South	4 P69
7	Knighton – North	4 K50
8	Knighton – South	4 K50
9	Saffron Lane	4 K50
10	West Bridge Goods	4 K50
11	Leicester LNW Goods	42 K50
12	Leicester GC Goods	5 K50
13	Rugby – Leamington Branch	2 P47
14	Rugby – Trent Valley	2 P47
15	Rugby – Canal Wharf	4 P47
16	Rugby – Station	24 P57
17	Rugby – Stamford Branch	2 P57
18	Rugby – Northampton Line	2 P57
19	Weedon	2 P65
20	Desford	4 K50
21	Enderby	224 P59
22	Syston South	4 K60
23	Syston North	4 K61
24	Syston East	4 K61
25	Swithland	5X K51
26	Mount Sorrel	4x K51

NOTES

(1) REF – SK or SP – S is omitted
(2) Now known as LEICESTER §
(3) Leicester Stations – indexed † under Individual name also

East Leake
Upper Broughton
Hathern
Barnstone Lime Co's Siding
Old Dalby
Loughborough Derby Rd
LOUGHBOROUGH
Br Elect Wks
Loughborough Central
Shepshed
Barrow-on-Soar + Quorn
Frisby
Quorn + Woodhouse
Barrow Lime Works
Sileby
Brooksby
Mount Sorrell Jct
Rearsby
Swithland Jct
Mount Sorrel Quarries
Rothley
Syston North Jct
Syston East Jct
Syston South Jct
Syston
Groby Quarries
Belgrave + Birstall
Glenfield Tunnel 1796 yds
Desford Junction
Glenfield
Central
Belgrave Rd
Humberstone
Ingersby
West Bridge
Ratby
Desford
Kirby Muxloe
LEICESTER
SEE INSET
Thumby + Scraptoft
Tunnel
SK SP
Knighton Jct North
Knighton Jct South
SEE INSET

LEICESTER
Heffords Siding
Belgrave Road Corporation
Humberstone
West Bridge Gds Junct
Soar Lane Wharf
Humberstone Rd
LNW Goods Jct
West Bridge
Central LNW Gds
Leicester (Mid) Gds
West Bridge Gds
GC Gds
E2
LONDON ROAD
Goods Junction
Midland Cattle
Saffron Lane Jct
Knighton Jct North
Aylestone Wharf
Knighton Jct South
SK SP

Wigston
Wigston (Glen Parva)
Leicester Line Junction
Central Junction
Blaby
Mid Harboro line Jct
South Jct.
Whetstone
Central Jct the West
Wigston Level Crossing
E1
Wigston
1903
Dunmore Rd
Wigston South

Enderby Gt
Leicester Line Jct
Narborough
Blaby
South Jct
Croft Granite + Brick Siding
Wigston Glen Parva
Wigston
Kilby Bridge Siding
Whetstone
Wigston South
Great Glen
Croft
Countesthorpe
Grand Union Canal
Broughton Astley
Kibworth
Ashby Magna
Ashby Magna Tunnel
Ullesthorpe + Lutterworth
Lubenham
Lutterworth
Theddingworth
Welford + Kilworth

RUGBY
Canal Wharf Junction
Canal Basin Wharf
British Thomson
Hunters Sdg
Station Junction
E4
RUGBY
Trent Valley Junct
Stamford Branch Jct
E3
Leamington Branch Junction
Northampton Line Jct
Rugby Central
1909

Yelvertoft + Stanford Park
Canal Wharf Jct
Canal Wharf Basin
Rugby Wharf Sdg
SEE INSET
Rugby Central
Lilbourne
Clifton Mill
Kilsby + Crick
Crick Tunnel
Oxford Canal
Kilsby Tunnel 2426 yds
Welton
Braunston + Willoughby
Long Buckby
Althorp Park
Braunston
Flecknoe
Daventry
Church Brampton
1917
Weedon Junction
Weedon

Key to Railways

2	▬▬▬	LONDON + NORTH WESTERN
24	▬▬▬	LONDON + NORTH WESTERN & MIDLAND JOINT
4	▬▬▬	MIDLAND
5	▬▬▬	GREAT CENTRAL
6	▬▬▬	GREAT NORTHERN
X	+++++	OTHERS - Colliery Lines etc
0	‑‑‑‑‑	LMS - Post Grouping proposed

Key to other Features

⊤⊤⊤⊤	Canals
▣ Goods	Goods ONLY Stations
/ Junct	Junction Names
/ Siding	Sidings etc (often Private)
● STATION	Passenger Station still open in 1985
◑ Station	Closed - line open all traffic
◔ Station	Closed - line open goods only
○ Station	Closed - line closed

NUNEATON, COVENTRY + LEAMINGTON SPA

RAILWAYS

No.	Company
R 2	LONDON + NORTH WESTERN
24	LNW + MIDLAND JOINT
3	GREAT WESTERN
4	MIDLAND
X	Others - Colliery lines etc

STATIONS

No.	Name	Ry	Ref
A 1	Arley + Fillongley	4	28
2	Bedworth	2	38
3	BERKSWELL	2	27
• 4	Brandon + Wolston	2	47
5	Bulkington	2	38
6	(CANLEY)	2	37
7	Chilvers Coton	2	39
8	CLAVERDON	3	26
9	Coleshill	4	28
10	Coundon Road	2	37
11	COVENTRY	2	37
12	Foleshill	2	38
13	HAMPTON·IN·ARDEN	2	28
14	Hampton·in·Arden	4	28
15	HATTON	3	26
16	Hawkesbury Lane	2	38
17	Higham·on·the·Hill	24	39
18	HINCKLEY	2	49
19	Kenilworth	2	27
20	Kingsbury	4	29
21	Leamington Spa	2	36
22	LEAMINGTON SPA	3	36
23	Longford + Exhall	2	38
24	Marton	2	46

No.	Name	Ry	Ref
25	Milverton, Warwick	2	36
26	NUNEATON	2	39
27	Nuneaton	4	39
28	Shilton	2	48
29	Shustoke	4	29
30	Southam + Long Itchington	2	46
31	Southam Rd.+ Harbury	3	35
32	Stockingford	4	39
33	TILE HILL	2	27
34	WARWICK	3	26
35	Warwick, Milverton	2	36
36	Whitacre	4	29

GOODS

No.	Name / Location	Ry	Ref
G 1	Bell Green	2	38
2	Gosford Green	2	37
3	Coventry	4	37

SIDINGS

No.	Company / Name	Ry	Ref
P 1	Green's Wharf	4	39
2	Ansley Hall Colliery	4	39
3	Stockingford Colliery	4	39
4	Chapel End Siding	4	39
5	Judkin's	2	39
6	Mancetter	2	39
7	Stanley's Brick	2	39
8	Griff Colliery	2	38
9	Griffith's + Co	2	38
10	Charity Colliery	2	38
11	Forder's	2	38
12	Exhall Colliery	2X	38
13	Warwickshire Coal	2	38
14	Wyken Colliery	X	38
15	Coventry Corporation Gas	2	38
16	Bretts Patent	2	38
17	Webster's	2	38
18	Daimler	2	37
19	Cattle Sales	2	37
20	Binley Colliery	2	37
21	Lucas + Co	2	36
22	Haye + Co	2	46
23	Streets	2	27
24	Tunnel Pit	2	39
25	Imperial Stone Co	3	36
26	Greaves Lime Works	3	35

ENGINE SHEDS

No.	Name / Location	Ry	Ref
E 1	Leamington Spa	3	36
2	Coventry	2	37
3	Nuneaton	2	39

TUNNELS

No.	Name	Length yards	Ry	Ref
T 1	Berkswell		2	27
2	Arley	995	4	39

JUNCTIONS

No.	Name / Location	Ry	Ref
J 1	Hatton North	3	26
2	Hatton South	3	26
3	Hatton West	3	26
4	Kenilworth	2	27
5	Berkswell	2	27
6	Hampton·in·Arden	24	28
7	Whitacre - Hampton Line	4	29
8	Whitacre - Nuneaton Line	4	29
9	Kingsbury	4	29
10	Leamington West	2(3)	36
11	Leamington West	3(2)	36
12	Leamington East	2(3)	36
13	Leamington East	3(2)	36
14	Marton	2	36
15	Coventry - Nuneaton	2	37
16	Coventry - Midland Goods	24	37
17	Coventry - Leamington	2	37
18	Coventry - Humber Road	2	37
19	Three Spires	2	38
20	Wyken Colliery	2	38
21	Griff	2	38
22	Stockingford Branch	4	39
23	Nuneaton Loop	424	39
24	Nuneaton Abbey	4	39
25	Weddington	24	39
26	Ashby	4242	39
27	Nuneaton - Leicester Line	2	39
28	Nuneaton - Coventry Line	2	39
29	Nuneaton - South Leicester (also known as Midland Jct)	24	39

NOTE:
REF   All in SP

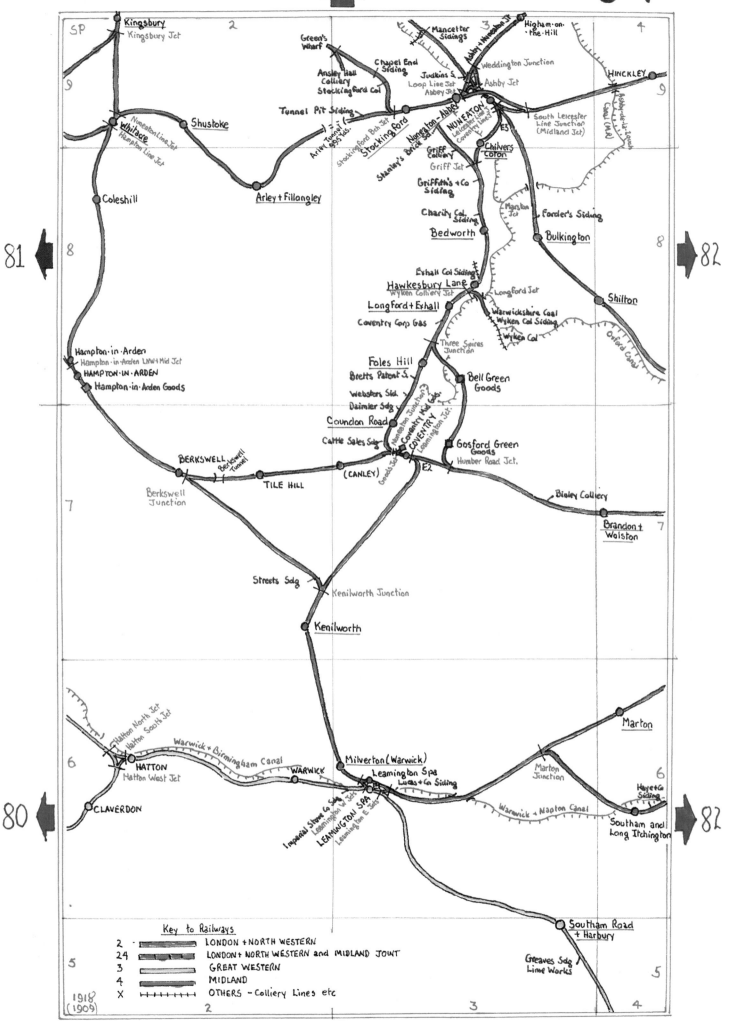

SP

Kingsbury
Kingsbury Jct.

Green's Wharf

Mancetter Sidings

Ashby + Nuneaton Jt.

Higham-on-the-Hill

HINCKLEY

Chapel End Siding

Ansley Hall Colliery Stockingford Col.

Weddington Junction

Shustoke

Tunnel Pit Siding

Judkins S.
Loop Line Jct.
Abbey Jct.

Ashby Jct.

NUNEATON
Leicester Line
Coventry Line

South Leicester Line Junction (Midland Jct)

Ashby-de-la-Zouch Canal (M&I)

Nuneaton Line Jct.
Whitacre
Hampton Line Jct.

Arley Tunnel 699 Yds.

Stockingford Bch Jct.
Stocking ford

Nuneaton-Abbey

Chilvers Coton

Stanley's Brick Co.

Griff Colliery

Griff Jct.

Coleshill

Arley + Fillangley

Griffith's + Co Siding

Charity Col. Siding

Bedworth

Marston Jct.

Forder's Siding

Bulkington

Exhall Col Siding

Hawkesbury Lane
Wyken Colliery Jct.

Longford Jct.

Warwickshire Coal
Wyken Col Siding

Shilton

Oxford Canal

Longford + Exhall

Coventry Corp Gas

Wyken Col

Hampton-in-Arden
Hampton-in-Arden LNW+Mid Jct.
HAMPTON-IN-ARDEN

Hampton-in-Arden Goods

Three Spires Junction

Foles Hill

Bretts Patent S.

Websters Sid.
Daimier Sdg

Bell Green Goods

Coundon Road

Cattle Sales Sdg

Nuneaton Junction?
Coventry Mid Jct.
COVENTRY
Leamington Jct.

Gosford Green Goods
Humber Road Jct.

BERKSWELL
Berkswell Tunnel

Goods Jct.
E2

Berkswell Junction

TILE HILL

(CANLEY)

Binley Colliery

Brandon + Wolston

Streets Sdg

Kenilworth Junction

Kenilworth

Marton

Hatton North Jct.
Hatton South Jct.

Warwick + Birmingham Canal

Milverton (Warwick)

HATTON
Hatton West Jct.

WARWICK

Leamington Spa
Lucas + Co Siding

Marton Junction

Haye+Co Siding

CLAVERDON

Imperial Stone Co Sdg
Leamington W Jct.
LEAMINGTON SPA
Leamington E Sds.

Warwick + Napton Canal

Southam and Long Itchington

Southam Road + Harbury

Greaves Sdg Lime Works

Key to Railways

2		LONDON + NORTH WESTERN
24		LONDON + NORTH WESTERN and MIDLAND JOINT
3		GREAT WESTERN
4		MIDLAND
X		OTHERS - Colliery Lines etc

1918
(1909)

RAILWAYS

No.	Company
R 1	STRATFORD-ON-AVON + MIDLAND JUNCT.
2	LONDON + NORTH WESTERN
26	LNW + GN JOINT
4	MIDLAND
46	MIDLAND + GT NORTHERN JOINT COM.
6	GREAT NORTHERN
7	GREAT EASTERN
0	BR + POST GROUPING additions
X	OTHERS - Tramways, Quarry lines etc

STATIONS

No.	Name	Ry Ref
A 1	Asfordby	4 SK71
2	Ashley + Weston	2 SP79
3	Ashwell	4 SK81
4	Barnack	6 TF00
5	Barnwell	2 TL08
6	BEDFORD MIDLAND	4 TL04
7	BEDFORD ST JOHNS	2 TL04
8	BIGGLESWADE	6 TL14
9	Billing	2 SP86
10	Blisworth	12 SP75
11	Blunham	2 TL14
12	Bourne	6 TF01
13	Braceborough Spa	6 TF01
14	Bradwell	2 SP84
15	Brixworth	2 SP77
16	Cardington	4 TL04
17	Castle Ashby + Earl's Barton	2 SP86
18	Castle Bytham	4 TF01
19	Castlethorpe	2 SP84
20	Castor ‡	2 TL19
21	Church Brampton	2 SP76
22	Clipston + Oxendon	2 SP78
23	Cranford	4 SP97
24	Deeping St James	6 TF10
25	Desborough + Rothwell	4 SP88
26	Ditchford	2 SP96
27	East Langton	4 SP79
28	East Norton	26 SK70
29	Edmondthorpe + Wymondham	4 SK81
30	Elton	2 TL09
31	Essendine	6 TF01
32	(Ferry Meadows) §	2 TL19
33	Finedon	4 SP87
34	Geddington	4 SP88
35	Glendon + Rushton	4 SP88
36	Grafham	4 TL16
37	Great Dalby	26 SK71
38	Great Linford	2 SP84
39	Gretton	4 SP99
40	Hallaton	26 SP79
41	Harringworth	4 SP99
42	Helpston	4 TF10
43	Higham Ferrers	4 SP96
44	Holme	6 TL18
45	Irchester	4 SP86
46	Irthlingborough	2 SP97
47	Isham + Burton Latimer	4 SP87
48	John o' Gaunt	26 SK70
49	Kelmarsh	2 SP78
50	(Kempston + Elstow Halt)	2 TL04
51	(KEMPSTON HARDWICK)	2 TL04
52	KETTERING (FOR CORBY)	4 SP87
53	Ketton	4 SK90
54	Kimbolton	4 TL07
55	Kingscliffe	2 TL09
56	Lamport	2 SP77
57	Little Bytham	6 TF01
58	Lowesby	6 SK70
59	Lubenham	2 SP78
60	Luffenham	4 SK90
61	Manton	4 SK80
62	Market Harborough ⚔	2 SP78
63	MARKET HARBOROUGH ⚔	4 SP78
64	Medbourne	26 SP89
65	Melton Mowbray	26 SK71
66	MELTON MOWBRAY	4 SK71
67	MILLBROOK	2 TL04
68	Morcott	2 SK90
69	Nassington	2 TL09
70	Newport Pagnall	2 SP84
71	Northampton	4 SP76
72	Northampton Bridge St.	2 SP75
73	NORTHAMPTON Castle	2 SP76
74	OAKHAM	4 SK80
75	Oakley	4 TL05
76	Olney	4 SP85
77	(Orton Mere) ♪	2 TL19
78	Orton Waterville §+	2 TL19
79	Oundle	2 TL08
80	Peakirk	6 TF10
81	PETERBOROUGH	6 TL19
82	Peterborough	7 TL19
83	Piddington	2 SP85
84	Pitsford + Brampton	2 SP76
85	Raunds	4 TL07
86	Ringstead + Addington	2 SP97
87	Roade	2 SP75
88	Rockingham	2 SP89
89	Rushden	4 SP86
90	Ryhall	6 TF01
91	St James, Deeping	6 TF10
92	ST NEOTS	6 TL16
93	Sandy ⚔	2 TL14
94	SANDY ⚔	6 TL14
95	Saxby	4 SK81
96	Seaton	2 SP99
97	Sharnbrook	4 TL05
98	Southill	4 TL14
99	South Witham	4 SK91
100	Spratton	2 SP77
101	STAMFORD	4 TF00
102	Stamford	6 TF00
103	(STEWARTBY)	2 TL04
104	Tallington	6 TF00
105	Tempsford	6 TL15
106	Thorpe	2 TL08
107	Thrapston	2 SP97
108	Thrapston	4 SP97
109	Thurlby	6 TF01
110	Tilton	26 SK70
111	Towcester	1 SP74
112	Turvey	4 SP95
113	Twenty	46 TF11
114	Twywell	4 SP97
115	Uffington	4 TF00
116	Ufford Bridge	6 TF00
117	Uppingham	2 SK80
118	Wakerley + Barrowden	2 SP99
119	Walton	4 TF10
120	Wansford	2 TL09
121	Wansford Road	6 TL09
122	Weldon + Corby	4 SP88
123	Wellingborough	2 SP96
124	WELLINGBOROUGH	4 SP96
125	Whissendine	4 SK81
126	Willington	2 TL14
127	WOLVERTON	2 SP84
128	Yaxley + Farcet	6 TL19

GOODS

No	Name/Location	Ry Ref
G1	Holwell	4 SK71
2	Fletton	6 TL19
3	Stoke Bruern	1 SP75
4	Long Stow	4 TL16

SIDINGS

No.	Company/Name/Location	Ry Ref
P1	Loddington	4 SP87
2	Cottesmore Wharf	4 SK81
3	BSC Corby	0 SP99
4	Stony Stratford Tramway	X SP84

JUNCTIONS

No	Name/Location	Ry Ref
J1	Mkt Harborough South	2 SP78
2	Mkt Harborough North	24 SP78
3	Welham	226 SP79
4	Hallaton	26 SP79
5	Marefield West	6 SK70
6	Marefield South	626 SK70
7	Marefield North	626 SK70
8	Holwell	4 SK71
9	Melton	4 SK71
10	Wolverton	2 SP84
11	Kettering	4 SP87
12	Cransley Branch	4 SP87
13	Glendon South	4 SP88
14	Drayton	226 SP89
15	Manton	4 SK80
16	Ashwell Branch	4 SK81
17	Saxby Station	4 SK81
18	Wansford Line	2 SP99
19	Uppingham Branch	2 SP99
20	Luffenham	42 SK90
21	Yarwell	2 TL09
22	Wansford	26 TL09
23	Stamford for GN	4(6) TF00
24	Stamford for Mid	6(4) TF00
25	Essendine + Wansford	6 TF00
26	Essendine	6 TF01
27	Little Bytham	446 TF01
28	Bourne West	646 TF01
29	Sandy	62 TL14
30	Holme	6 TL18
31	Bourne East	646 TF11

ENGINE SHEDS

No.	Name/Location	Ry Ref
E1	Kettering	4 SP87

NOTES:

All stations, including some goods only stations, are included in this gazetteer. Other features are included if in the area not covered by the enlargements on MAP 86.

⚔ One joint station in effect but each company had its own platforms

‡ Line preserved but station not.

§ Map date } Name changed.
§ Modern }

♪ Exact site relative to junction is unclear.

+ Earlier known as Overton.

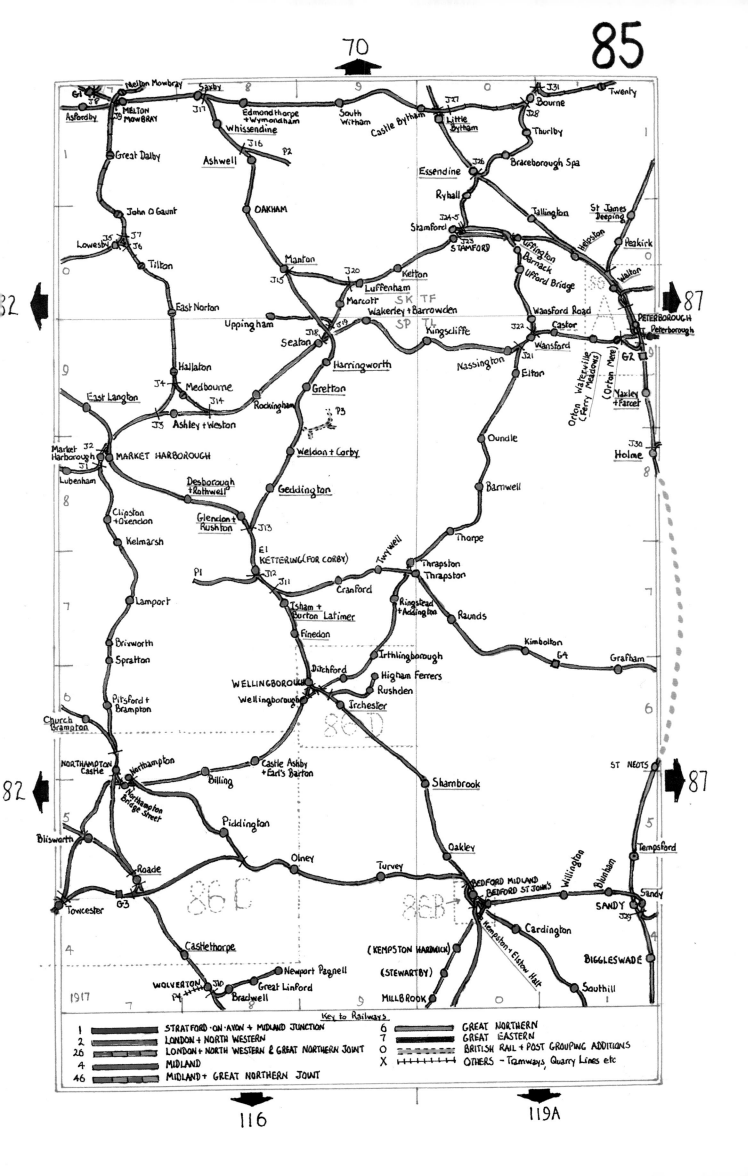

Panel B

RAILWAYS

No	Company
R2	LONDON + NORTH WESTERN
4	MIDLAND

ENGINE SHEDS

No	Name	Ry
E4	Bedford	4

STATIONS

No	Name	Ry
A1	BEDFORD - MIDLAND	4
2	BEDFORD - ST JOHN'S	2
3	Kempston + Elstow Halt	2

GOODS

No	Name	Ry
G1	Bedford LNW	2
2	Bedford Midland	4
3	Midland Coal Wharf	4

SIDINGS

No	Company/Name	Ry
P1	Bedford Gas Co	4X
2	Allen + Co	4X
3	Howard's Siding	4
4	Mitchell + Batler	4
5	Ballast Pits	4

JUNCTIONS

No	Name	Ry
J1	Bedford North	4
2	Bedford	4
3	Bedford South	4
4	Gas Siding	4X
5	LNW	4
6	Goods North	2
7	Goods Middle	2
8	Goods South	2
9	Goods East	2
10	Bed Ford Level Crossing	2+4
11	Ouse Bridge	4

NOTES:

No references shown - virtually the whole map is within TL04

B

Panel A

RAILWAYS

No	Company
R2	LONDON + NORTH WESTERN
4	MIDLAND
46	MIDLAND + GREAT NORTHERN JOINT
6	GREAT NORTHERN
7	GREAT EASTERN

STATIONS

No	Name	Ry	Ref
A1	(Ferry Meadows) §	2	TL19
2	(Orton Mere) +	2	TL19
3	Orton Waterville § ✗	2	TL19
4	PETERBOROUGH	6	TL19
5	Peterborough	7	TL19
6	Walton	4	TF10

GOODS

No	Name	Ry	Ref
G1	Fletton	6	TL19

SIDINGS

No	Company/Name	Ry	Ref
P1	Wisbech	46	TF10
2	Arktos	46	TF10
3	New England	6	TF10
4	Beebys	6	TF10
5	Sage + Co	6	TF10
6	Crescent Wharf	4	TL19
7	London Brick	6	TL19
8	Hicks + Co	6	TL19
9	Farrow + Co	6	TL19
10	Plowman's	6	TL19
11	New Peterborough Brick	6	TL19

ENGINE SHEDS

No	Name	Ry	Ref
E1	LNW	2	TL19
2	Midland	4	TL19
3	Great Northern ❗	6	TL10

JUNCTIONS

No	Name	Ry	Ref
J1	Werrington	6	TF10
2	Wisbech	46/4	TF10
3	GN+Mid Westwood	46	TF10
4	Westwood	6	TF10
5	Crescent	6	TL19
6	GN+Mid Peterborough	46	TL19
7	Nene	4	TL19
8	Longville	26	TL19
9	GE+LNW Peterborough	27	TL19
10	Fletton Road	74	TL19
11	Fletton	6	TL19
12	Fletton Sidings	6	TL19

NOTES:
Name change: § Map name —
§ Modern name ✗ Older name - Overton
+ Site relative to Jct uncertain. ❗
Shed site - New England

A

Panel C + D

RAILWAYS

No	Company
R1	STRATFORD-ON-AVON + MIDLAND JUNCT
2	LONDON + NORTH WESTERN
4	MIDLAND

STATIONS

No	Name	Ry	Ref
A1	Billing	2	86
2	Blisworth	12	75
3	Castlethorpe	2	84
4	Ditchford	2	96
5	Higham Ferrers	4	96
6	Irchester	4	96
7	Irthlingborough	2	97
8	Northampton	4	76
9	Northampton Bridge Street	2	75
10	NORTHAMPTON Castle	2	76
11	Olney	4	85
12	Piddington	2	85
13	Roade	2	75
14	Rushden	4	96
15	Towcester	1	74
16	Wellingborough	2	96
17	WELLINGBOROUGH	4	96

GOODS

No	Name/Location	Ry	Ref
G1	Stoke Bruern	1	75
2	Northampton Midland	4	76

SIDINGS

No	Name/Company/Location	Ry	Ref
P1	Stowe	2	65
2	Easton Neston	1	75
3	Towcester Ironstone	1	75
4	Blisworth Ironstone	1	75
5	Duston	2	75
6	Gas Co (Northampton)	2	76
7	Martins	2	76
8	Wellingborough Gas	4	96
9	Midland Brick	4	96
10	Stanton Iron	4	96
11	Rushden Brick	4	96
12	Clarks	4	96

ENGINE SHEDS

No	Name/Location	Ry	Ref
E5	Northampton	4	75
6	Northampton	2	75
7	Wellingborough	4	96
8	Blisworth	1	75

JUNCTIONS

No	Name/Location	Ry	Ref
J1	Towcester - Banbury Branch	1	74
2	Towcester - Olney Branch	1	74
3	Blisworth - Towcester Line	12	75
4	Blisworth - N'hampton Line	2	75
5	Roade	1	75
6	Towcester (Roade)	21	75
7	N'hampton Line (Roade)	2	75
8	Duston North	2	75
9	Duston East	2	75
10	Duston West	2	75
11	Hardingstone	24	75
12	Goods (N'hampton)	4	75
13	Rugby Line	2	76
14	Ravenstone Wood	41	85
15	Wellingborough Mid + LNW	24	96
16	Wellingborough	4	96
17	Irchester	4	96

NOTES:
(1) REF - All in SP
(2) COMBINED GAZETTEER FOR C+D

C + D

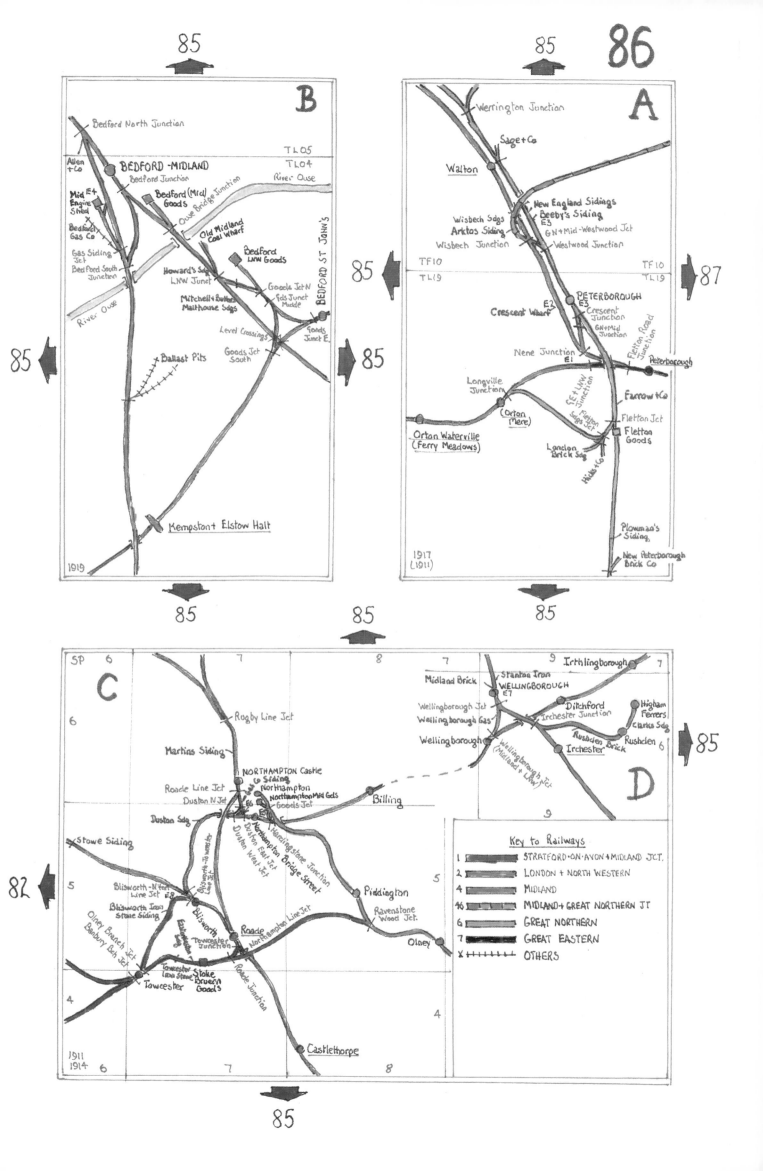

B

Bedford North Junction

TL 05
TL 04
River Ouse

Allen + Co
BEDFORD - MIDLAND
Bedford Junction
Mid E4 Engine Shed
Bedford (Mid) Goods
Ouse Bridge Junction
Bedford Gas Co
Old Midland Coal Wharf
Gas Siding Jct
Bedford South Junction
Howard's Sdg
LNW Junct
Bedford LNW Goods
Mitchell + Butlers Malthouse Sdgs
Goods Jct N
Fds Junct Muddle
BEDFORD ST JOHN'S
River Ouse
Level Crossings
Goods Junct E
Ballast Pits
Goods Jct South

Kempston + Elstow Halt

1919

A

Werrington Junction
Sage + Co
Walton
New England Sidings
Beeby's Siding
E3
Wisbech Sdgs
Arktas Siding
Wisbech Junction
GN + Mid - Westwood Jct
Westwood Junction
TF 10
TL 19
PETERBOROUGH
Crescent Wharf
E2
E3
Crescent Junction
GN + Mid Junction
Nene Junction
E1
Fletton Road Junction
Peterborough
Longville Junction
GE + LNW Junction
Fletton Sdgs Jct
Farrow + Co
(Orton Mere)
Fletton Jct
Fletton Goods
Orton Waterville (Ferry Meadows)
London Brick Sdg
Hicks + Co
Plowman's Siding
1917 (1911)
New Peterborough Brick Co

C

5P 6
7
8
7
9
Irthlingborough
7
Midland Brick
Stanton Iron
WELLINGBOROUGH
E7
Rugby Line Jct
Wellingborough Jct
Ditchford
Irchester Junction
Higham Ferrers
Martins Siding
Wellingborough Gas
Clarks Sdg
6
Wellingborough
Rushden Brick
Rushden
NORTHAMPTON Castle
Co Siding
Irchester
6
Roade Line Jct
Northampton
Wellingborough Jct (Midland + LNW)
Duston N Jct
Northampton Mid Gds
Billing
E6
Goods Jct
Duston Sdg
Harlingstone Junction
Northampton Bridge Street
9
Stowe Siding
Duston East Jct
Duston West Jct

D

82
5
Blisworth - N Yd Line Jct E8
Piddington
5
Blisworth Iron Stone Siding
Blisworth
Ravenstone Wood Jct.
Olney Branch Jct
Banbury Bch Jct
Roade
Northampton Line Jct
Olney
Easton Neston Sdg
Towcester Junction
Roade Junction
4
Towcester Iron Stone
Stoke Bruern Goods
Towcester
1911
1914
6
7
8
Castlethorpe

Key to Railways

1		STRATFORD - ON - AVON + MIDLAND JCT.
2		LONDON + NORTH WESTERN
4		MIDLAND
46		MIDLAND + GREAT NORTHERN JT
6		GREAT NORTHERN
7		GREAT EASTERN
X	+++++++	OTHERS

RAILWAYS

WISBECH   +   CAMBRIDGE

No	Company
R2	LONDON + NORTH WESTERN
3	COLNE VALLEY + HALSTEAD
4	MIDLAND
46	MIDLAND + GREAT NORTHERN JOINT
6	GREAT NORTHERN
67	GREAT NORTHERN + GREAT EASTERN JT.
7	GREAT EASTERN
7A	WISBECH + UPWELL TRAMWAY (GE)

STATIONS

No	Name	Ry Ref
A1	Abbey	7 F60
2	Abbot's Ripton	6 L27
3	Barnwell	7 L45
4	Bartlow	7 F54
5	Black Bank	7 L58
6	Bluntisham	7 L27
7	Bottisham + Lode	7 L56
8	Boyce's Bridge †	7A F40
9	Buckden	4 L26
10	Burwell	7 L56
11	CAMBRIDGE	7 L45
12	Chatteris	67 L38
13	Chettisham	7 L58
14	Clenchwarton	46 F51
15	Coldham	7 F40
16	Cowbit	67 F21
17	Denver	7 F50
18	DOWNHAM (MARKET)	7 F60
19	DULLINGHAM	7 L65
20	Earith Bridge	7 L37
21	East Winch	7 F61
22	Elm Bridge †	7A F40
23	ELY	7 L57
24	Emneth	7 F40
25	Eye Green	46 F20
26	Ferry	46 F41
27	Fordham	7 L66
28	FOXTON	7 L44
29	French Drove + Gedney Hill	F30 / 67 F30
30	Fulbourne	7 L55
31	Gamlingay	2 L25
32	Godmanchester	67 L27
33	Gayton Road	46 F61
34	GREAT CHESTERFORD	7 L54
35	Guyhirne	67 F30
36	Haddenham	7 L47
37	Harston	7 L45
38	Haverhill	3 L64
39	Haverhill	7 L64
40	Hilgay	7 L59
41	Histon	7 L46
42	Holme	6 L18
43	Huntingdon ⚒	4 L27
44	HUNTINGDON	6 L27
45	Huntingdon ⚒	67 L27
46	Islesham	7 L67
47	KENNETT	7 L66
48	Linton	7 L54
49	LITTLEPORT	7 L58
50	Littleworth	6 F21
51	Long Stanton	7 L36
52	Lord's Bridge	2 L35
53	MAGDALEN ROAD	7 F61
54	MANEA	7 L49
55	MARCH	7 L49
56	MELDRETH + Melbourn	6 L34
57	Middle Drove	7 F50
58	Middleton	7 F61
59	Mildenhall	7 L77
60	Murrow	46 F30
61	Murrow	67 F30
62	NEWMARKET	7 L66
63	Oakington	7 L46
64	Offord + Buckden	6 L26
65	Old North Road	2 L35
66	Outwell Basin †	7A F50
67	Outwell Village †	7A F50
68	Pampisford	7 L54
69	Postland	67 F21
70	Potton	2 L24
71	Quy	7 L58
72	Ramsey	6 L28
73	Ramsey	67 L28
74	ROYSTON	6 L34
75	Ryston	7 F60
76	St Ives	7 L37
77	St Mary's	6 L28
78	ST NEOTS	6 L26
79	SHELFORD	7 L45
80	SHEPRETH	6 L34
81	SHIPPEA HILL	7 L68
82	Six Mile Bottom	7 L55
83	Smeeth Road	7 F50
84	Soham	7 L57
85	Somersham	67 L37
86	South Lynn	46 F61
87	Stoke Ferry	7 L69
88	Stonea	7 L49
89	Stow	7 F60
90	Stretham	7 L57
91	Sturmer	7 L64
92	Sutton	7 L47
93	Swaffham Prior	7 L56
94	Swavesey	7 L36
95	Terrington	46 F51
96	Thorney	46 F20
98	Tydd	46 F41
99	Upwell †	7A F50
100	Walpole	46 F51
101	Warboys	67 L38
102	WATERBEACH	7 L56
103	WHITTLESEA	7 L29
104	WHITTLESFORD	7 L44
105	Wilburton	7 L47
106	Wimblington	7 L49
107	Wisbech	46 F40
108	Wisbech	7 F40
109	Wisbech St. Mary's	46 F40
110	Wryde	46 F30

GOODS

No	Name/Location	Ry Ref
G1	Benwick	7 L37
2	Burnt House	7 L37
3	Cambridge - Hills Road	2 L45
4	Cambridge - Mill Road	4 L45
5	Cambridge - GN	6 L45
6	Cambridge - GE	7 L45
7	Hardwick Road	46 F61
8	Jones Drove	7 L37
9	Quakers Drove	7 L37
10	Toft + Kingston	2 L35
11	West Fen Dyke	7 L37
12	White Fen	7 L37

JUNCTIONS

No	Name/Location	Ry Ref
J1	Holme	6 L18
2	Somersham	67 L37
3	Three Horse Shoes	7 L39
4	Bartlow	7 L54
5	Ely - St Ives	7 L57
6	Ely - Newmarket	7 L57
7	Ely - Loop South	7 L58
8	Ely - March	7 L58
9	Ely - Thetford	7 L58
10	Ely - Loop North	7 L58
11	Denver	7 F50
12	Haverhill - Colne Valley	7 L64
13	Haverhill - GE	3 L64
14	Warren Hill	7 L66
15	Snailwell	7 L66
16	Chippenham	7 L66
17	Fordham South	7 L66
18	Fordham North	7 L66
19	Magdalen Road	7 F61

NOTES:

(1) REFERENCES - All in TF or TL the T is omitted

(2) ENLARGEMENTS - All passenger stations are shown and listed together with some goods. But other features only shown if located in area not covered by an enlargement

(3) KINGS LYNN - Other features in this area, see inset on MAP 72

(4) Different platforms - same station ⚒ ⚒

(5) Passenger services on the Wisbech & Upwell Tramway were discontinued early in the 20th century. Goods discontinued in the '20's. †

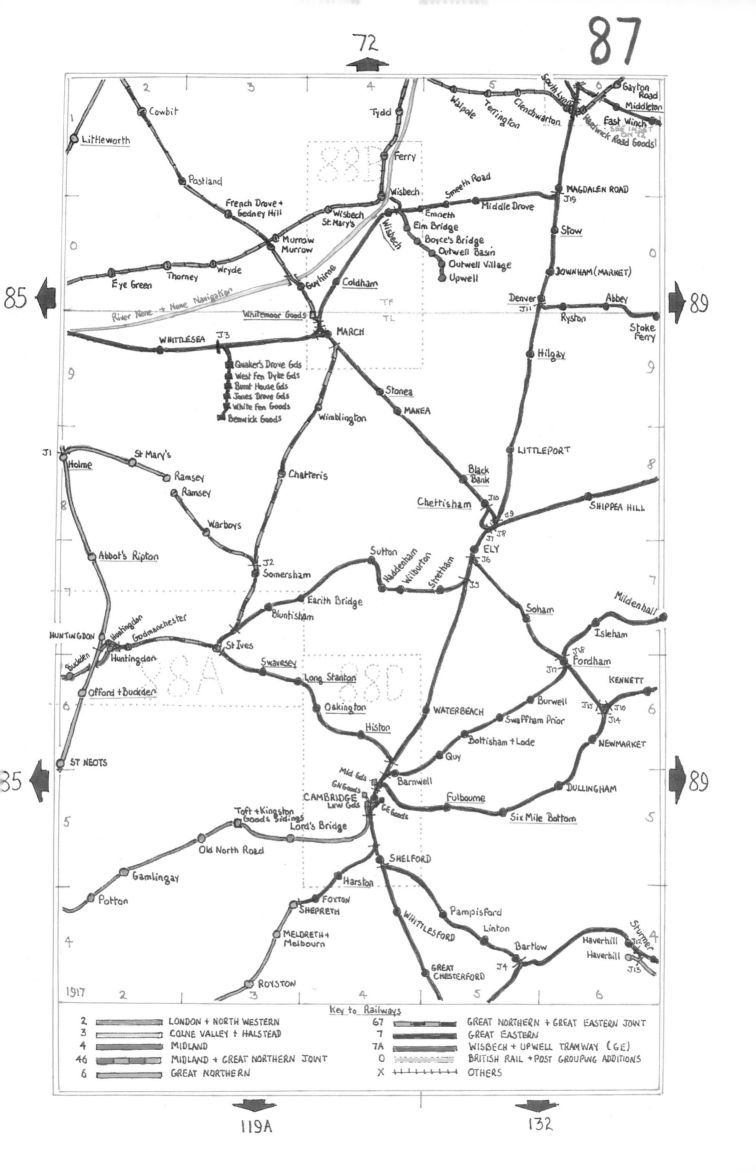

72

85

89

35

89

119A

132

1917

Littleworth

Cowbit

Postland

French Drove + Gedney Hill

Murrow Murrow

Eye Green

Thorney

Wryde

Guyhirne

River Nene + Nene Navigation

Coldham

Whitemoor Goods

MARCH

WHITTLESEA   J3

Quaker's Drove Gds
West Fen Dyke Gds
Burnt House Gds
Jones Drove Gds
White Fen Goods
Benwick Goods

Wimblington

Stonea

MANEA

Chatteris

St Mary's

Ramsey

Ramsey

Warboys

Abbot's Ripton

J1

Holme

J2

Somersham

Earith Bridge

Bluntisham

Huntingdon

Godmanchester

Huntingdon

St Ives

Swavesey

Long Stanton

Oakington

Histon

Buckden

Huntingdon

Offord + Buckden

ST NEOTS

Sutton

Haddenham

Wilburton

Stretham

ELY

J6

J5

J7   J8

J9

J10

Chettisham

Black Bank

LITTLEPORT

SHIPPEA HILL

Soham

Mildenhall

Isleham

J18

J17

Fordham

KENNETT

Burwell

Swaffham Prior

Bottisham + Lode

Quy

WATERBEACH

Barnwell

Mid Gds

GN Goods

CAMBRIDGE

LNW Gds

GE Goods

Fulbourne

Six Mile Bottom

DULLINGHAM

NEWMARKET

J15

J16

J14

Toft + Kingston Goods Sidings

Lord's Bridge

Old North Road

Gamlingay

Potton

SHELFORD

Harston

Foxton

SHEPRETH

MELDRETH + Melbourn

ROYSTON

WHITTLESFORD

Pampisford

Linton

Bartlow

GREAT CHESTERFORD

J4

Haverhill

Haverhill

Sturmer

J12

J13

Tydd

Ferry

Wisbech

Wisbech St. Mary's

Wisbech

Smeeth Road

Emneth

Middle Drove

Elm Bridge

Boyce's Bridge

Outwell Basin

Outwell Village

Upwell

MAGDALEN ROAD
J19

Stow

DOWNHAM (MARKET)

Denver
J11

Ryston

Abbey

Stoke Ferry

Hilgay

Walpole

Terrington

Clenchwarton

South Lynn

Gayton Road

Middleton

East Winch

Hardwick Road Goods!

SEE INSET ON 72

TF

TL

HUNTINGDON + ST IVES

RAILWAYS

No	Company
R4	MIDLAND
6	GREAT NORTHERN
67	GREAT NORTHERN + GREAT EASTERN
7	GREAT EASTERN

STATIONS

No	Name		Ry Ref
A1	Bluntisham		7 37
2	Buckden		4 26
3	Earith Bridge		7 37
4	Godmanchester		67 27
5	Huntingdon	⌘	4 27
6	HUNTINGDON	⌘	6 27
7	Huntingdon	⌘	67 27
8	Long Stanton		7 36
9	Offord + Buckden		6 26
10	St Ives		67 37
11	Swavesey		7 36

JUNCTIONS

No	Name/Location	Ry Ref
J1	Huntingdon South	6 27
2	Huntingdon East	674 27
3	St Ives	7 37
4	Needingworth	767 37

NOTES:

(1) REFERENCES – All in TL

(2) These two Huntingdon Stations – actually one – different platforms used by (a) Midland + (b) Great Northern + Great Eastern Joint ⌘

A

WISBECH + MARCH

RAILWAYS

No	Company
R46	MIDLAND + GREAT NORTHERN JOINT
67	GREAT NORTHERN + GREAT EASTERN
7	GREAT EASTERN
7A	WISBECH + UPWELL TRAMWAY (GE)

STATIONS

No	Name		Ry Ref
A1	Boyce's Bridge	†	7A F40
2	Coldham		7 F40
3	Elm Bridge	†	7A F40
4	Emneth		7 F40
5	Ferry		46 F41
6	MARCH		7 L49
7	Wisbech		46 F41
8	Wisbech		7 F40
9	Wisbech St Mary's		46 F40

GOODS

No	Name/Location	Ry Ref
G1	Twenty Foot River	67 F40
2	Whitemoor	7 L49
3	Wisbech Joint	46 F41
4	Wisbech GE	7 F40
5	Wisbech Joint Harbour	46 F41
6	Wisbech GE Harbour	7 F41

SIDINGS

No	Name	Ry Ref
P1	Waldersea Drove	7 F40

ENGINE SHEDS

No	Location	Ry Ref
E4	March	7 L49

JUNCTIONS

No	Name/Location	Ry Ref
J1	March – St Ives Line	767 L49
2	March – West	7 L49
3	March – South	7 L49
4	March – North	7 L49
5	March – Whitemoor	7 L49
6	Grassmoor	767 F40
7	Wisbech Goods	7 F40
8	Wisbech	7 F40
9	Harbour Branch	46 F41

NOTES:

(1) REF – In TF or TL (T omitted)

(2) Stations closed to passengers early 20th c, closed to Goods in 1920's †

B

CAMBRIDGE

RAILWAYS

No	Company
R2	LONDON + NORTH WESTERN
4	MIDLAND
6	GREAT NORTHERN
7	GREAT EASTERN

STATIONS

No	Name	Ry Ref
A1	Barnwell	7 45
2	CAMBRIDGE	7 45
3	Harston	7 45
4	Histon	7 46
5	Long Stanton	7 46
6	Lord's Bridge	2 45
7	Oakington	7 46
8	SHELFORD	7 45
9	WATERBEACH	7 46

GOODS

No	Location	Ry Ref
G1	Cambridge LNW	2 45
2	Cambridge – Mill Road	4 45
3	Cambridge – Hill Road	6 45
4	Cambridge – GE	7 45
5	Cambridge – Tenison Road	7 45

ENGINE SHEDS

No	Location	Ry Ref
E1	Cambridge	7 45
2	Cambridge	2 45

3	Cambridge	7 45

JUNCTIONS

No	Name/Location	Ry Ref
J1	Shelford	7 45
2	Shepreth Branch	7 45
3	Cambridge GE + LNW	27 45
4	Hills Road	7 45
5	(LNW) Goods	2 45
6	Tenison Road	74 45
7	Mill Road	7 45
8	Coldham Lane	7 45
9	Barnwell	7 45
10	Chesterton	7 45

NOTES:

(1) REF – All in TL

C

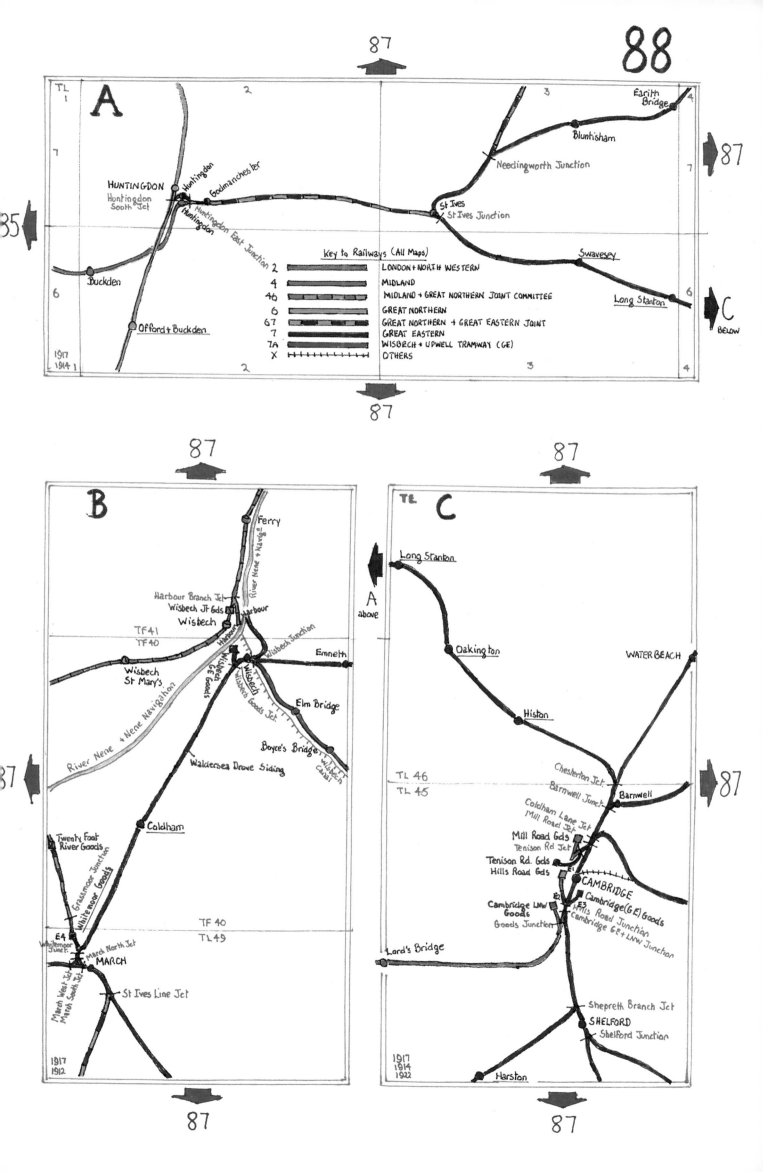

A

TL
1

7

Earith Bridge

Bluntisham

Needingworth Junction

Huntingdon

HUNTINGDON
Huntingdon South Jct

Godmanchester

Huntingdon East Junction

St Ives
St Ives Junction

87

7

85

Swavesey

Buckden

6

Key to Railways (All Maps)

2	LONDON + NORTH WESTERN
4	MIDLAND
46	MIDLAND + GREAT NORTHERN JOINT COMMITTEE
6	GREAT NORTHERN
67	GREAT NORTHERN + GREAT EASTERN JOINT
7	GREAT EASTERN
7A	WISBECH + UPWELL TRAMWAY (GE)
X	OTHERS

Long Stanton

6

C
BELOW

Offord + Buckden

1917
1914

87

B

Ferry

River Nene + Navign

Harbour Branch Jct
Wisbech Jt Gds
Wisbech
Harbour

TF41
TF40

Wisbech Junction

Emneth

Wisbech St Mary's

Wisbech GE Goods

Wisbech Goods Jct.

Elm Bridge

River Nene + Nene Navigation

Boyce's Bridge

Wisbech Canal

Waldersea Drove Siding

87

Coldham

Twenty Foot River Goods

Grassmoor Junction
Whitemoor Goods

TF 40
TL 49

E4
Whitemoor Junct.
March North Jct
MARCH

March West Jct
March South Jct

St Ives Line Jct

1917
1912

87

C

TL

Long Stanton

A
above

Oakington

WATER BEACH

Histon

Chesterton Jct.

TL 46
TL 45

Barnwell Junct.

Barnwell

87

Coldham Lane Jct
Mill Road Jct
Mill Road Gds
Tenison Rd Jct

Tenison Rd. Gds
Hills Road Gds

CAMBRIDGE

Cambridge (GE) Goods

Cambridge LNW Goods

E3
Hills Road Junction
Cambridge GE + LNW Junction
Goods Junction

Lord's Bridge

Shepreth Branch Jct

SHELFORD
Shelford Junction

1917
1914
1922

Harston

87

89
RAILWAYS

No	Company
R 2	MID SUFFOLK (Light)
3	COLNE VALLEY + HALSTEAD
46	MIDLAND + GREAT NORTHERN JOINT
7	GREAT EASTERN

WYMONDHAM + IPSWICH

STATIONS

No	Name	Ry Ref
A 1	Ashwellthorpe	7 M19
2	Aspall + Thorndon	2 M16
3	ATTLEBOROUGH	7 M09
4	Attlebridge	46 G11
5	Barnham	7 L87
6	Birdbrook	3 L74
7	BRANDON	7 L78
8	Brockford + Wetheringsett	2 M16
9	BURY ST EDMUNDS	7 L86
10	Capel	7 M04
11	Cavendish	7 L84
12	Clare	7 L74
13	Claydon	7 M15
14	Cockfield	7 L85
15	DERBY ROAD	7 M14
16	Dereham	7 F91
17	DISS	7 M17
18	Drayton	46 G11
19	Dunham	7 F81
20	ECCLES ROAD	7 M08
21	ELMSWELL	7 L96
22	Eye	7 M17
23	Flordon	7 M19
24	Forncett	7 M19
25	Fransham	7 F81
26	Glemsford	7 L84
27	Hadleigh	7 M04
28	Hardingham	7 G00
29	HARLING ROAD	7 L98
30	Haughley	2 M06
31	Haughley	7 M06
32	Hellesdon	46 G11
33	Hethersett	7 G10
34	Higham	7 L76
35	Holme Hale	7 F80
36	Ingham	7 L87
37	IPSWICH	7 M14
38	Kenton	2 M16
39	Kimberley	7 G00
40	LAKENHEATH	7 L78
41	Lavenham	7 L95
42	Lenwade	46 G01
43	Long Melford	7 L84
44	Mellis	7 M07
45	Mendlesham	2 M06
46	Mildenhall	7 L77
47	Narborough	7 F71
48	NEEDHAM (MARKET)	7 M05
49	North Elmham	7 F91
50	Pulham Market	7 M18
51	Raydon Wood	7 M04
52	Roundham Junction ✳	7 L98
53	Saxham + Risby	7 L76
54	SPOONER ROW	7 M09
55	Stoke	7 L74
56	Stow Bedon	7 L99
57	STOWMARKET	7 M05
58	SUDBURY	7 L84
59	Swaffham	7 F80
60	THETFORD	7 L88
61	Thetford Bridge	7 L88
62	Thuxton	7 G00
63	THURSTON	7 L96
64	Tivetshall	7 M18
65	Watton	7 F90
66	Welnetham	7 L85
67	Wendling	7 F91
68	WESTERFIELD	7 M14
69	Wretham + Hockham	7 L99
70	WYMONDHAM	7 G10
71	Yaxham	7 F90

GOODS

No	Location	Ry Ref
G 1	Ipswich	7 M14
2	Sudbury	7 L84

ENGINE SHEDS

No	Location	Ry Ref
E 1	Bury St Edmund's	7 L86
2	Ipswich	7 M14

WATERTROUGHS

No	Location	Ry Ref
W 1	Tivetshall	7 M18

JUNCTIONS

No	Name/Location	Ry Ref
J 1	Sudbury Goods	7 L84
2	Long Melford	7 L84
3	Bury St Edmunds	7 L86
4	Thetford	7 L88
5	Roundham	7 L98
6	Swaffham	7 F80
7	Dereham West	7 F91
8	Dereham North	7 F91
9	Dereham South	7 F91
10	Haughley - Bury	7 M06
11	Haughley - Exchange Sidings	7 M06
12	Haughley - Exchange Sdgs	2 M06
13	Mellis + Eye	7 M07
14	Goods + Harbour	7 M14
15	East Suffolk	7 M14
16	Westerfield	7 M14
17	Tivetshall	7 M18
18	Forncett	7 M19
19	Wymondham South	7 G10
20	Wymondham North	7 G10

NOTES:

(1) REF - In TF, TG, TL or TM the T is omitted

(2) Closed prior to grouping ✳

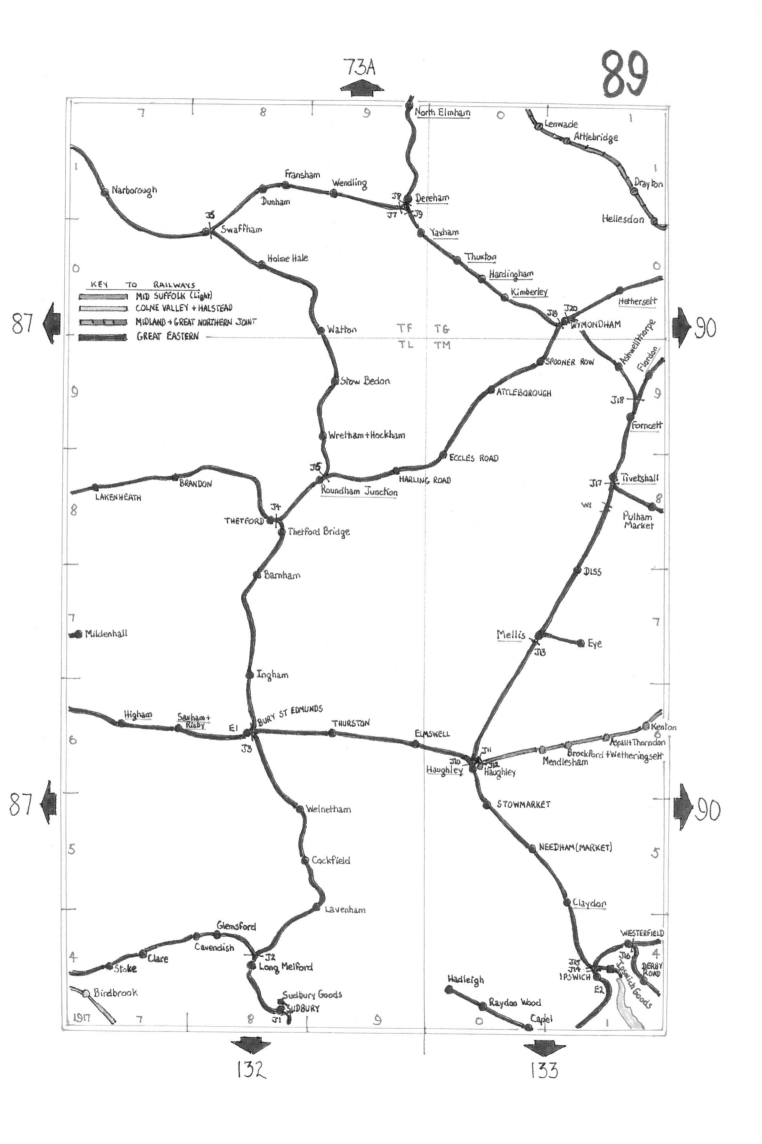

RAILWAYS

NORWICH, YARMOUTH + LOWESTOFT

No	Company
R2	MID SUFFOLK (Light)
3	SOUTHWOLD (3' Gauge)
46	MIDLAND + GREAT NORTHERN JOINT
467	NORFOLK + SUFFOLK JOINT (Mid, GN+GE)
7	GREAT EASTERN

STATIONS

No	Name	Ry Ref
A1	ACLE	7 G30
2	Aldeburgh	7 M45
3	Aldeby	7 M49
4	Bealings	7 M24
5	BECCLES	7 M49
6	Belton	7 G40
7	BERNEY ARMS	7 G40
8	Blythburgh	3 M47
9	BRAMPTON	7 M48
10	BRUNDALL	7 G30
11	(BRUNDALL GARDENS)	7 G30
12	BUCKENHAM	7 G30
13	Bungay	7 G38
14	Caister-on-Sea	46 G51
15	CANTLEY	7 G30
16	CARLTON COLVILLE §	7 M59
17	Coltishall	7 G21
18	Corton	467 M59
19	DARSHAM	7 G46
20	Ditchingham	7 G39
21	Earsham	7 G38
22	Ellingham	7 M39
23	Framlingham	7 M26
24	Geldeston	7 G39
25	Gorleston North	467 G50
26	Gorleston-on-Sea	467 G50
27	Great Ormesby	46 G41
28	Haddiscoe High Level	7 M49
29	HADDISCOE Low Level	7 M49
30	Halesworth	3 M37
31	HALESWORTH	7 M37
32	Harleston	7 M28
33	Hemsby	46 G41
34	Homersfield	7 M28
35	Hopton	467 M59
36	Horham	2 M27
37	Laxfield	2 M27
38	Leiston	7 G46
39	LINGWOOD	7 G30
40	LOWESTOFT Central	7 M59
41	Lowestoft North	467 M59
42	Marlesford	7 M35
43	Martham for Rollesby	46 G41
44	Melton	7 M25
45	Norwich City	46 G20
46	NORWICH THORPE	7 G20
47	Norwich Victoria	7 G20
48	Orwell	7 M24
49	OULTON BROAD (NORTH)	7 M59
50	OULTON BROAD SOUTH §	7 M59
51	Parham	7 M36
52	Potter Heigham	46 G41
53	Pulham St Mary	7 M28
54	REEDHAM	7 G40
55	St Olaves	7 M49
56	SALHOUSE	7 G21
57	SAXMUNDHAM	7 M36
58	SOMERLEYTON	7 M49
59	Southwold	3 M57
60	Stradbroke	2 M27
61	Swainsthorpe	7 G20
62	Trowse	7 G20
63	Walberswick	3 M47
64	Wenhaston	3 M47
65	Whitlingham	7 G20
66	WICKHAM MARKET	7 M35
67	Wilby	2 M27
68	WOODBRIDGE	7 M24
69	Worlingworth	2 M26
70	WROXHAM	7 G21
71	Yarmouth Beach	46 G50
72	Yarmouth South Town	467 G50
73	YARMOUTH Vauxhall	7 G50

GOODS

No	Location	Ry Ref
G1	Norwich Trowse	7 G20
2	Norwich Thorpe	7 G20
3	Snape	7 M35
4	Yarmouth	7 G50
5	Vauxhall Fish Market	7 G50
6	Haddiscoe	7 M49
7	Lowestoft Fish Market	7 M59
8	Lowestoft Harbour	7 M59
9	Kirkley	7 M59

ENGINE SHEDS

No	Location	Ry Ref
E1	Norwich	46 G20
2	Norwich	7 G20
3	Yarmouth	46 G50
4	Yarmouth	7 G50
5	Lowestoft	7 M59

JUNCTIONS

No	Name/Location	Ry Ref
J1	Victoria	7 G20
2	Trowse Lower	7 G20
3	Trowse Goods	7 G20
4	Trowse Swing Bridge	7 G20
5	Wensum	7 G20
6	Thorpe East	7 G20
7	Thorpe West	7 G20
8	Whitlingham	7 G20
9	Wickham Market	7 M35
10	Brundall	7 G30
11	Wroxham	7 G31
12	Snape	7 M35
13	Aldeburgh Line	7 M36
14	Lowestoft	7 M49

15	Oulton Broad South	7 M59
16	Oulton Broad North	7 M59
17	Harbour (Lowestoft)	7 M59
18	Coke Ovens	7467 M59
19	Fleet	7 M49
20	Haddiscoe	7 M49
21	Swing Bridge	7 M49
22	Marsh	7 M49
23	North Line	46467 7 G50
24	Lowestoft Line	7 G50
25	South Town Goods	7 G50
26	North Quay	746 G50
27	Lowestoft Line	46 G50
28	Caister Road	46 G50
29	Reedham	7 G40
30	Breydon	7 G51
31	Vauxhall	7 G50

NOTES:

(1) REF - In TG or TM the T is omitted

(2) NAME CHANGE - Map date §
                  - Modern §

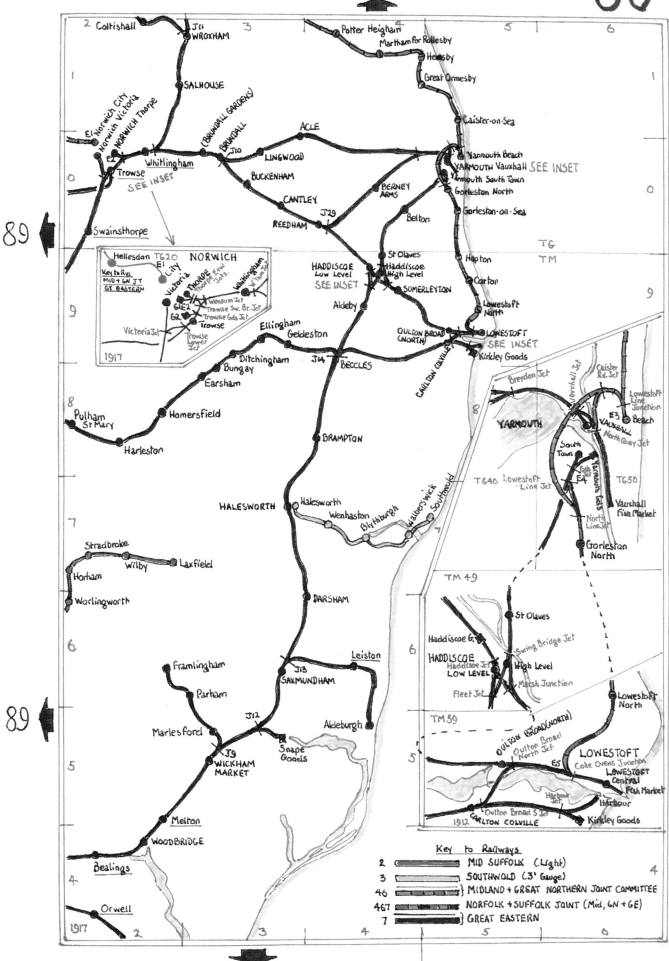

89

89

133

Key to Railways

2		MID SUFFOLK (Light)
3		SOUTHWOLD (3' Gauge)
46		MIDLAND + GREAT NORTHERN JOINT COMMITTEE
467		NORFOLK + SUFFOLK JOINT (Mid, GN + GE)
7		GREAT EASTERN

Coltishall
WROXHAM
J11
SALHOUSE
Potter Heigham
Martham for Rollesby
Hemsby
Great Ormesby
Caister-on-Sea
E, Norwich City
Norwich Victoria
NORWICH Thorpe
(BRUNDALL GARDENS)
BRUNDALL
J10
ACLE
LINGWOOD
Yarmouth Beach
YARMOUTH Vauxhall
SEE INSET
Whitlingham
Trowse
E1
SEE INSET
BUCKENHAM
Yarmouth South Town
Gorleston North
CANTLEY
BERNEY ARMS
Gorleston-on-Sea
Swainsthorpe
REEDHAM
J29
Belton
St Olaves
Hopton
TG
TM
HADDISCOE Low Level
SEE INSET
HADDISCOE High Level
Carlton
Hellesdan   TG20   NORWICH
E1   City
Key to Rys
MID + GN JT
GT EASTERN
Victoria
THORPE
Whitlingham
SOMERLEYTON
Lowestoft North
Aldeby
Wensum Jct
Trowse Sw. Br. Jct
Trowse Gds Jct
GtE2
G2
Victoria Jct
Trowse
Trowse Lower Jct
1917
Ellingham
Geldeston
BECCLES
J14
OULTON BROAD (NORTH)
LOWESTOFT
SEE INSET
Kirkley Goods
CARLTON COLVILLE
Ditchingham
Bungay
Earsham
Breydon Jct
Norwich Jct
Caister Rd. Jct
Lowestoft Line Junction
Pulham St Mary
Homersfield
YARMOUTH
VAUXHALL
E3
Beach
North Quay Jct
Harleston
BRAMPTON
South Town
Walberswick
Southwold
TG40   Lowestoft Line Jct
Fish Mkt Jct
E4
TG50
Vauxhall Fish Market
HALESWORTH
Halesworth
Wenhaston
Blythburgh
North Line Jct
Gorleston North
Stradbroke
Wilby
Laxfield
Horham
Worlingworth
DARSHAM
TM 49
St Olaves
Haddiscoe G.
Swing Bridge Jct
Leiston
Framlingham
Parham
J13
SAXMUNDHAM
HADDISCOE
LOW LEVEL
Haddiscoe Jct
High Level
Marsh Junction
Fleet Jct
Lowestoft North
J12
Aldeburgh
TM 59
OULTON BROAD (NORTH)
Marlesford
Snape Goods
Oulton Broad North Jct
E5
LOWESTOFT
Coke Ovens Junction
LOWESTOFT Central
Fish Market
J9
WICKHAM MARKET
Harbour Jct
Harbour
Melton
WOODBRIDGE
Oulton Broad S Jct
1912   CARLTON COLVILLE
Kirkley Goods
Bealings
Orwell
1917

SOUTH WALES INDEX MAP

Map		Scale Miles to an inch	Grid Ref SW Corner	Size in kms (East first)
79B	HEREFORD	1	SO4536	10 x 8
92A	CARMARTHEN + LLANDILO	5	SN2018	50 x 22
92B	LLANDOVERY + BRECON	5	SN7020	50 x 20
92C	PONTRILAS + HEREFORD	5	SO2020	40 x 22
92D	CARMARTHEN	Not to Scale	SN4018	
93	WHITLAND + KIDWELLY	2	SS1898	32 x 26
94	SWANSEA + PONTARDULAIS	2	SS5086	20 x 32
95	NEATH + BRYNAMMAN	2	SS7090	20 x 30
96	MERTHYR, ABERDARE + MOUNTAIN ASH	2	SS9090	20 x 30
97	EBBW VALE, ABERTILLERY, HENCOED + NEWBRIDGE	2	ST1090	20 x 30
98	ABERGAVENNY, USK + NEWPORT Newport	2	ST3090	20 x 30
99	PORT TALBOT + BRIDGEND	2	SS7068	30 x 22
100	PONTYPRIDD, LLANTRISANT, CARDIFF + PENARTH	2	ST0068	30 x 22
101	NEWPORT + WESTON-SUPER-MARE	2	ST3060	20 x 30
102	MERTHYR + ABERDARE	1	SN9700	16 x 10
103	EBBW VALE + ABERTILLERY	1	SO1300	16 x 10
104	NEATH + SWANSEA	1	SS6090	16 x 10
105	MOUNTAIN ASH + PONTYPRIDD	1	SS9790	16 x 10
106	HENCOED + NEWBRIDGE	1	ST1390	16 x 10
107	BRIDGEND DISTRICT	1	SS8575	10 x 16
108	PONTYPRIDD + LLANTRISANT	1	ST0274	10 x 16
109	CARDIFF + PENARTH	1	ST1274	10 x 16

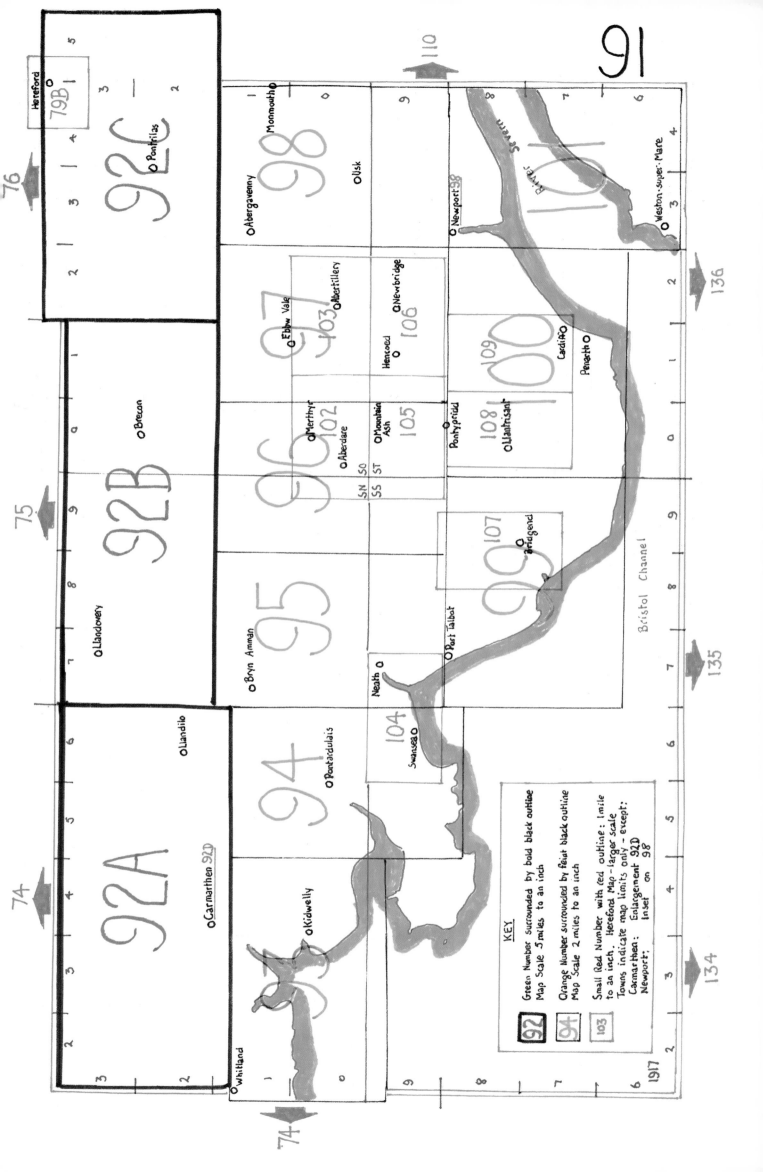

RAILWAYS

No	Company
R 1	BRECON + MERTHYR
2	LONDON + NORTH WESTERN
23	GREAT WESTERN + LNW JOINT
3	GREAT WESTERN
4	MIDLAND
5	NEATH + BRECON
7	CAMBRIAN

STATIONS + HALTS

No	Name		Ry Ref
A 1	Abbeydore	‡	3 O33
2	Aberbran	⁐	5 N92
3	Abergwili	X	2 N42
4	Bacton	‡	3 O33
5	Ballingham	‡	3 O53
6	Boncath	X	3 N23
7	Boughrood + Llyswen	⁐	7 O13
8	Brecon	⁐	15 NO2
9	Bronwydd Arms	X	3 N42
10	Bryn Teify	X	3 N43
11	Carmarthen Junction	X	3 N41
12	CARMARTHEN Town	X	3 N41
13	Conwil	X	3 N32
14	Cradoc	⁐	5 OO2
15	Cray	⁐	5 N82
16	Derwydd Road	X	2 N61
17	Devynock + Sennybridge	⁐	5 N92
18	Dryslwyn	X	2 N52
19	FAIRFACH §	X	3 N62
19A	FFAIRFACH §	X	3 N62
20	Fawley	‡	3 O52
21	Glanrhyd	X	23 N62
22	Glasbury-on-Wye	⁐	4 O13
23	Glogue	X	3 N23
24	Golden Grove	X	2 N52
25	HEREFORD Barr's Court	†	23 O54
26	Holme Lacy	‡	3 O53
27	Llanarthney	X	2 N52
28	LLANDILO	X	3 N62
29	Llandilo Bridge	X	2 N62
30	LLANDOVERY	⁐	23 N73
31	Llandyssil	X	3 N44
32	Llanfyrnach	X	3 N23
33	LLANGADOCK	X	23 N62
34	Llanpumpsaint	X	3 N42
35	Llanstephan Halt	X	3 N31
36	LLANWRDA	⁐	23 N73
37	Nantgaredig	X	2 N42
38	Pandy	‡	3 O32
39	Pencader	X	3 N43
40	Peterchurch	‡	3 O33
41	Pontrilas	‡	3 O32
42	Ross (-on-Wye)	‡	3 O62
43	St Clears	X	3 N21
44	St Devereux	‡	3 O43
45	Sarnau	X	3 N31
46	Talgarth	⁐	7 O13
47	Talley Road	X	23 N62
48	Talybont-on-Usk	⁐	1 O12
49	Talyllyn	⁐	1 O12
50	Three Cocks (Junction)	⁐	7 O13
51	Tram Inn	‡	3 O43
52	Trefeinon	⁐	7 O13
53	Vowchurch	‡	3 O33
54	WHITLAND	X	3 N11
55	Withington	‡	3 O54

ENGINE SHEDS †

No	Location		Ry Ref
E 1	Carmarthen	X	3 N42
2	Ross-on-Wye	‡	3 O62
3	Pontrilas	‡	3 O32

JUNCTIONS

No	Name/Location		Ry Ref
J 1	Towey Bridge	X	3 N41
2	Myrtlehill	X	3 N41
3	Carmarthen Station	X	3 N41
4	Abergwili	X	32 N42
5	Pencader	X	3 N43
6	Carmarthen Valley	X	32 N62
7	Vale of Towey	X	323 N62
8	Llandovery	⁐	223 N73
9	Brecon	⁐	15 OO2
10	Talyllyn Station	⁐	1 O12
11	Talyllyn North	⁐	7 O12
12	Talyllyn South	⁐	1 O12
13	Three Cocks for Llanidloes	⁐	7 O13
14	Mid Wales (Three Cocks)	⁐	74 O13
15	Golden Valley	‡	3 O32
16	Ross	‡	3 O62
17	Red Hill	† ‡	32 O53
18	Rotherwas	† ‡	32 O53
19	Barrs Court North	† ‡	23 O54
20			

NOTES:

(1) REF – SN or SO –S omitted

(2) Name changes not shown; exception altered before 1922

Map date	§
1922 and later	§

(3) HEREFORD – full details – see Map 79B †

(4) Map Location } A X
    in combined } B ⁐
    Gazetteer } C ‡
              } D X

(5) GWILI Railway runs from Bronwydd Arms to the North Stations .. Cwmdwyfran Penybont

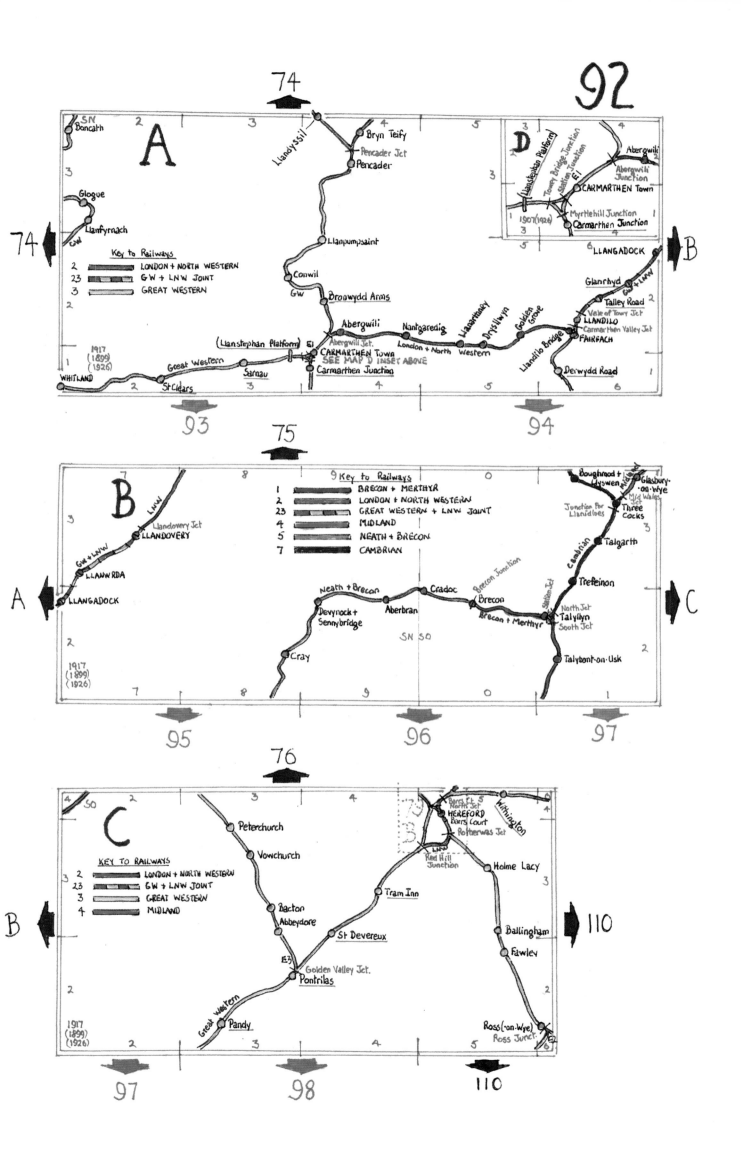

WHITLAND + KIDWELLY

ENGINE SHEDS

Ry Ref	No	Location
7 40	E1	Burry Port
3 11	2	Whitland

JUNCTIONS

Ry Ref	No	Name/Location
3 11	J1	Cardigan
34 40	2	Kidwelly
47 40	3	Tycoch
4X 40	4	Minkie Road
7 40	5	Kidwelly West
7 40	6	Kidwelly East
7 40	7	Kidwelly South
7 40	8	Trimsaran
7 40	9	Harbour
7 40	10	Cwn Capel Branch
37 40	11	Burry Port
67 40	12	Sandy
36 55 49	13	Llanelly

GOODS

Ry Ref	No	Name/Location
7 40	G1	Burry Port Harbour
6 40	2	Cynheidre
6 40	3	Horeb
4 40	4	Mynydd-y-Carreg
7 40	5	Trimsaran

SIDINGS

Ry Ref	No	Company/Name/Location
7 40	P1	Four Roads
3 31	2	Pentre Mawr Colliery
7 40	3	Gwendraeth Colliery
3 30	4	New Carway Colliery
3 40	5	Old Carway Colliery
7 40	6	Trimsaran Colliery
7 40	7	Cwn Capel Colliery
7 40	8	New Pool Colliery
7 40	9	Crown Colliery
7 41	10	Pwll Siding
3 21	11	Ponthenry Colliery
7 40	12	Sandy Siding
3 11	13	Achddu Brick Works

RAILWAYS

No	Company
R.3	GREAT WESTERN
4	GWENDRAETH VALLEYS
6	LLANELLY + MYNYD MAWR
7	BURRY PORT + GWENDRAETH VALLEYS
X	Colliery Lines etc

STATIONS

No	Name
A1	Burry Port
2	FERRYSIDE
3	Glyn Abbey Halt
4	KIDWELLY
5	PEMBREY + BURRY PORT
6	Pembrey Halt
7	Pinged Halt
8	Ponthenry
9	Pontyates
10	Pontyberem
11	St. Clear's
12	Trimsaran Road
13	WHITLAND

NOTES:

REF - All in SN except J13 marked SS

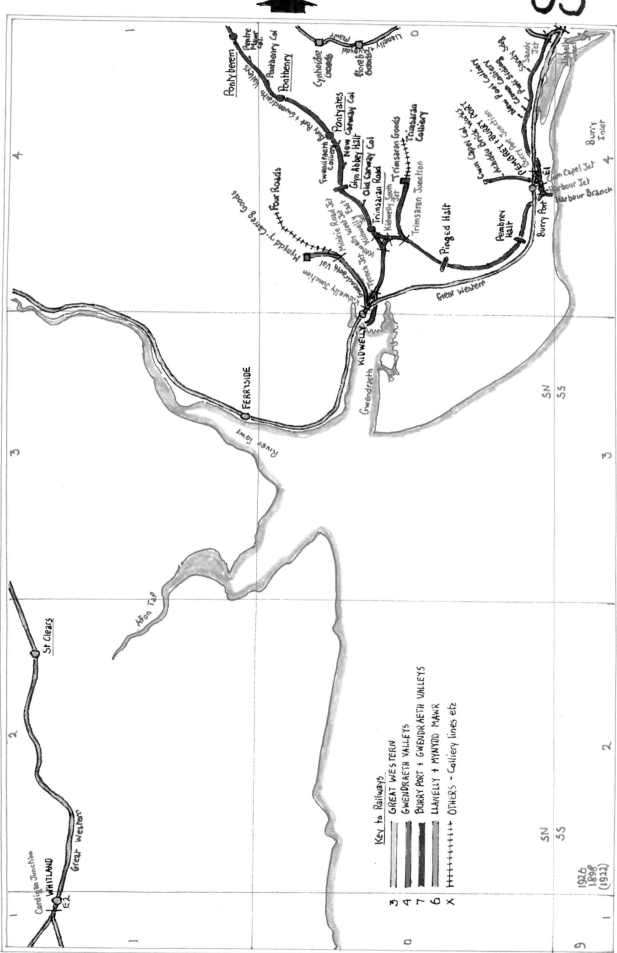

Key to Railways

3	━━━	GREAT WESTERN
4	━━━	GWENDRAETH VALLEYS
7	━━━	BURRY PORT + GWENDRAETH VALLEYS
6	━━━	LLANELLY + MYNYDD MAWR
X	++++++++	OTHERS - Colliery lines etc

1926
1898
(1912)

Cardigan Junction
WHITLAND
E2
Great Western
St Clears
Afon Tâf
River Towy
FERRYSIDE
KIDWELLY
Gwendraeth
Great Western
Kidwelly Junction
Gwendraeth Val
Mynydd-y-Garreg Goods
Four Roads
Mixtie Road Jct
West Jct
Kidwelly Jct
Kidwelly South Jct
Glanravon Goods
Trimsaran
Old Carway Col
Glyn Abbey Halt
New Carway Col
Pontyates
Fforest-fach Colliery
Pontyberem
Pontyberem Valleys
Ponthenry
Ponthenry Col
Pentre Mawr Col
Cynheidre Goods
Horeb Goods
Llanelly + Mynydd Mawr
Trimsaran Goods
Trimsaran Colliery
Trimsaran Junction
Pinged Halt
Pembrey Halt
Burry Port
Cwm Capel Col
Ashburnham Brick Works
PEMBREY + BURRY PORT
Burry Port Colliery
New Pool Colliery
Craig Colliery
Pool Siding
Burry Sidings
Sandy Jct
Cwm Capel Jct
Harbour Jct
Harbour Branch
Llanelly Dock
Llanelly Junction
Burry Inlet

SN
55

94
93
74
97A

RAILWAYS

No	Company
R 1	SWANSEA + MUMBLES
2	LONDON + NORTH WESTERN
3	GREAT WESTERN
30	GREAT WESTERN (Post Grouping) ⚒ 3
34	GREAT WESTERN + MIDLAND JOINT
4	MIDLAND
6	LLANELLY + MYNYDD MAWR
7	BURRY PORT + GWENDRAETH VALLEYS
8	RHONDDA + SWANSEA BAY
11	SWANSEA HARBOUR TRUST
X	OTHERS - Colliery lines etc

STATIONS + HALTS

No	Name	Ry Ref
A 1	Ammanford	3 N61
2	Ammanford Colliery Halt	3 N61
3	Blackpill	1 S68
4	Bryn Mill	1 S69
5	BYNEA	3 S59
6	Cockett	3 S69
7	Copper Pit Halt	3 S69
8	(Cwmgorse) ⚒	30 N60
9	(Cwm Mawr) ‡	7 N51
10	Dunvant	2 S59
11	Dan·y·Graig	8 S69
12	Derwydd Road	3 N61
13	East Dock ⚥	3 S69
14	Felin Fran Halt	3 S69
15	Garnant	3 N61
16	Glanamman	3 N61
17	Gorseinon	2 S59
18	Gors·y·Garnant Halt	3 N61
19	Gowerton	2 S59
20	GOWERTON	3 S59
21	Grovesend	2 N50
22	Gwaun·Cae·Gurwen Halt	3 N61
23	HIGH STREET ⚥	3 S69
24	Killay	2 S59
25	Landore High Level	3 S69
26	Landore Low Level ✳	3 S69
27	LLANDEBIE	3 N61
28	LLANELLY	3 S59
29	LLANGENNECH	3 N50
30	Llanmorlais	2 S59
31	Llansamlet	3 S69
32	Loughor	3 S59
33	Morriston	3 S69
34	Morriston	4 S69
35	Mumbles (Pier)	1 S68
36	Mumbles Road	2 S69
37	Oystermouth	1 S68
38	PANTYFFYNNON	3 N61
39	Penclawdd	2 S59
40	Plas Marl	3 S69
41	PONTARDULAIS	23 N50
42	Red Lion Crossing Halt	3 N61
43	Rutland Street ⚥	1 S69
44	St Gabriel's	1 S69
46	St Helen's	1 S60
48	St Thomas' ⚥	4 S69
	SWANSEA	S69
49	HIGH STREET ⚥	3 S69
50	East Dock	3 S69
51	(R+SB)	8 S69
52	St Thomas'	4 S69
53	Rutland Street	1 S69
54	Victoria	2 S69
55	Southend	1 S68
55A	Swansea (R+SB) ⚥	8 S69
56	Swansea Bay	2 S69
58	TIRYDAIL	3 N61
59	Upper Bank	4 S69
60	Victoria ⚥	2 S69
61	West Cross	1 S68

GOODS

No	Name/Location	Ry Ref
G 1	(Clydach) 3	30 N61
2	Cockett	3 S69
3	Cross Hands ◊	6 N51
4	Cross Hands (Penygroes) ⚒	3 N51
5	Cwm Blawd	6 N50
6	Dafen	3 S59
7	Felin Foel	6 N50
8	Felin Fran	3 S69
9	Gors·y·Garnant	3 N61
10	Llanelly Dock	3 S59
11	Llangyfelach	3 S69
12	Llansamlet	4 S69
13	Pont Lliw	3 N60
14	Queen Victoria Road	S59
	Llanelly	6 S59
15	Swansea Docks	2 S69
16	Swansea High Street	3 S69
17	Tumble	6 N51

SIDINGS

No	Name/Company/Location	Ry Ref
P 1	St George's Yard	3 S59
2	Glynea Colliery	3 S59
3	Ffasfach Colliery	3 S59
4	Holmes + Co's Killan Colliery	2 S59
5	New Dunvant Colliery	2 S59
6	Penprys Colliery	3 N50
7	Acorn Colliery	3 N50
8	Graig Merthyr Colliery	2 N50
9	Graig Merthyr Colliery	3 N50
10	Paton's Siding	3 N50
11	Glynhir Tin Plate Co	3 N50
12	Dynant Colliery	6 N50
13	Great Mountain Colliery	6 N51
14	Caerbryn Colliery	3 N51
15	Rhos Colliery	3 N61
16	Park + Blaina Colliery	3 N61
17	Gulston Siding	3 N61
18	Cylyrychen Lime Works	3 N61
19	Carmarthenshire Silica Co	3 N61
20	United Anthracite	3 N61

ENGINE SHEDS

No	Location	Ry Ref
E 1	Llanelly	3 S59
2	Pantyffynnon	3 N61

TUNNELS

No	Name/Location		Ry Ref
T 1	Cockett	789yds	3 S69

JUNCTIONS

No	Name/Location	Ry Ref
J 1	Gowerton	2 S59

2	Sandy	67 S59
3	Llanelly	6+36 S59
4	Llanelly Dock	3 S59
5	Llanelly St Davids	3 S59
6	Llanelly Morfa	3 S59
7	Llandilo West	3 S59
8	Llandilo East	3 S59
9	Bynea Tin Works	3 S59
10	Felin Fran West	3 S69
11	Felin Fran G·C·G West	30 S69
12	Felin Fran G·C·G East	30 S69
13	Felin Fran G·C·G North	30 S69
14	Morlais South	3 N50
15	Morlais East	3 N50
16	Hendy	3 N50
17	Pontardulais	23 N50
18	Pantyffynnon	3 N60
19	Tirydail	3 N61
20	Garnant West	3 N61
21	Garnant East	3 N61
22	G·C·G Colliery Branch	3 N61

NOTES:

(1) REF - SN or SS - S omitted

(2) ENLARGEMENT - Stations named and located including some goods - other features not included, see 104

(3) STATION located in abbreviated form on the map (LL) ✳

(4) Now known as SWANSEA ⚥

(5) Swansea stations - indexed both under Swansea + individual name ⚥

(6) Initially Goods only - opened to passengers in 1920's ‡

(7) Proposed - never opened. ⚒ This line never completed as a through connection. Latest extension ~1944

(8) Line - Northwards never 3 completed. - see also (7) above

(9) Possibly ultimately connected ◊

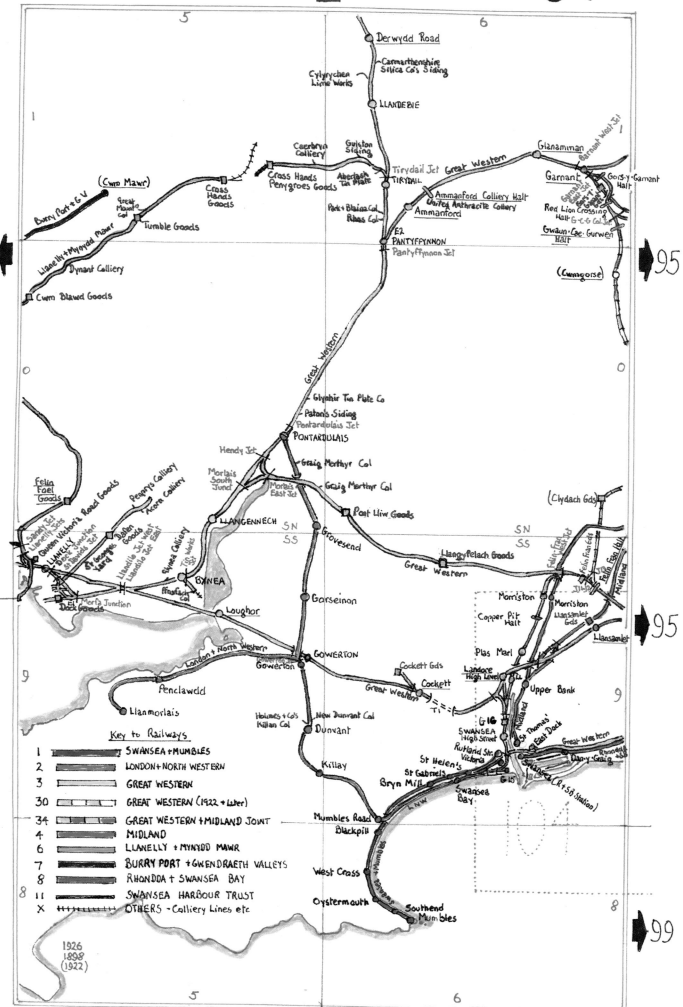

Derwydd Road
Carmarthenshire Silica Co's Siding
Cylyrychen Lime Works
LLANDEBIE
Caerbryn Colliery
Gulston Siding
Cross Hands Penygroes Goods
Aberlash Tin Plate
Tirydail Jct Great Western
TIRYDAIL
Glanamman
Garnant West Jct
Garnant
Gors-y-Garnant Halt
Ammanford Colliery Halt
United Anthracite Colliery
Park + Blaina Col Rhos Col
Ammanford
Red Lion Crossing Halt G-C-G Col Jct
Gwaun-Cae-Gurwen Halt
(Cwm Mawr)
Great Mountn Col
Cross Hands Goods
Burry Port + G V
Tumble Goods
E2
PANTYFFYNNON
Pantyffynnon Jct
Llanelly + Mynydd Mawr
Dynant Colliery
Cwm Blawd Goods
(Cwmgorse)
Great Western
Glynhir Tin Plate Co
Paton's Siding
Pontardulais Jct
PONTARDULAIS
Hendy Jct
Graig Merthyr Col
Felin Foel Goods
Penprys Colliery
Acorn Colliery
Morlais South Junct
Morlais East Jct
Graig Merthyr Col
(Clydach Gds)
Sandy Jct
Llanelly Jcts
Queen Victoria's Road Goods
Dafen Goods
Llandilo Jct West
Llandilo Jct East
LLANELLY
Dock Junction
St Davids Jct
St Georges Yard
Bynea Colliery
Tin Works
LLANGENNECH
SN SS
Grovesend
Post Lliw Goods
Great Western
Llangyfelach Goods
SN SS
Felin-Fran East Jct
Felin Fran Gds
Felin Fran Halt
TVR Jct
Midland
Ffosfach Col
BYNEA
Morfa Junction
Dock Goods
Loughor
Garseinon
Gowerton
Cockett Gds
Cockett
Great Western
Landore High Level
Morriston
Copper Pit Halt
Plas Marl
Morriston
Llansamlet Gds
Llansamlet
London + North Western
Gowerton
Gowerton
Penclawdd
Llanmorlais
Holmes + Co's Killan Col
New Dunvant Col
Dunvant
Upper Bank
G16
SWANSEA High Street
St Thomas'
Great Western
Dan-y-Graig
Killay
Rutland Str.
Victoria
Swansea East Dock
St Helen's
St Gabriels
Bryn Mill
Swansea Bay
G15
Swansea (R+SB Station)
Rhondda Jct
Mumbles Road
Blackpill
LNW
LNW
Swansea Bay
West Cross
Oystermouth
Southend Mumbles

Key to Railways
1 SWANSEA + MUMBLES
2 LONDON + NORTH WESTERN
3 GREAT WESTERN
30 GREAT WESTERN (1922 + later)
34 GREAT WESTERN + MIDLAND JOINT
4 MIDLAND
6 LLANELLY + MYNYDD MAWR
7 BURRY PORT + GWENDRAETH VALLEYS
8 RHONDDA + SWANSEA BAY
11 SWANSEA HARBOUR TRUST
X OTHERS - Colliery Lines etc

1926
1898
(1922)

93   95   95   99

NEATH + BRYNAMMAN

Company

No	Company
23	GREAT WESTERN
30	GREAT WESTERN (Post-Grouping) ⊗
4	MIDLAND
5	NEATH + BRECON
6	PORT TALBOT RAILWAY + DOCKS
7	SOUTH WALES MINERAL
8	RHONDDA + SWANSEA BAY
X	OTHERS – Collieries, Quarries etc

STATIONS + HALTS

No	Name	Ry Ref
A 1	Aberavon (Town)	8 S79
2	Abercrave	2 N81
3	Aberdylais	3 S79
4	Abergwynfi	3 S89
5	Blaengarw	3 S89
6	Blaengwynfi	8 S89
7	Briton Ferry East	8 S79
8	Briton Ferry Road	3 S79
9	Briton Ferry West	3 S79
10	Bryn	6 S89
11	Brynamman	3 N71
12	Brynamman	4 N71
13	Caerau	3 S89
14	(Cape Platform)	8 S79
15	Cardonnel Halt	3 S79
16	Cilfrew	5 N70
17	Clyne Halt	3 N80
18	Colbren (Junction)	5 N81
19	Court Sart	8 S79
20	Craig-y-Nos (Penwyllt)	5 N81
21	Crynant	5 N70
22	Cwm Avon	8 S79
23	Cwm Cymmer	8 S89
24	Cwmdu	6 S89
25	Cwmllynfell	4 N70
26	Cymmer (SWM)	7 S89
27	Cymmer (for Glyncorrwg)	3 S89
28	Cynon Platform §	8 S89
28A	Cynonville Halt §	8 S89
29	Duffryn Rhondda Halt	8 S89
30	Glais	4 N70
31	Glyncorrwg	7 S89
32	Glyn Neath	3 N70
33	Gwys	4 N71
34	Jersey Marine	8 S79
35	Maesteg – Castle Street	3 S89
36	Maesteg – Neath Road	6 S89
37	Melyncourt Halt	3 N80
38	Nanty Ffyllon	3 S89
39	Neath (CR+SB)	8 S79
40	Neath Abbey	3 S79
41	Neath Bridge Street	3 S79
42	NEATH GENERAL ‡	3 S79
43	Onllwyn	5 N81
44	(Pontardawe) ⊗	30 N70
45	Pontardawe	4 N70
46	Pontrhydyfen	8 S79
47	Pontwalby Halt	3 N80
48	Pont-y-Cymmer	3 S89
49	Resolven	3 N80
50	(Rhyd-y-Fro) ⊗	30 N70
51	Seven Sisters	5 N80
52	Skewen	3 S79
53	Troedyrhiew	6 S89
54	Ystalyfera	4 N70
55	Ystradgynlais	5 N70

GOODS

No	Name	Ry Ref
G 1	Duffryn Rhondda	8 S89
2	Briton Ferry	8 S79
3	Gurnos	4 N70
4	Glais	4 N70
5	Cadoxton	5 S79

SIDINGS

No	Name / Company / Location	Ry Ref
P 1	Briton Ferry Oil	X S79
2	Duffryn Branch Sidings	3 S89
3	Norths Navigation No 9 Col	3 S89
4	Llynvi Gas	3 S89
5	Maesteg UDC	6 S89

No	Name	Ry Ref
6	Llwyndu Colliery	4 N70
7	Glantawe Iron+Tin Plate	4 N70
8	Waen-y-Coed Colliery	4 N70
9	Tarini Colliery	4 N70
10	Varteg Anthracite Colliery	5 N70
11	South Wales Anthracite	4 N70
12	Ystalyfera Iron+Tin	4 N70
13	Pwllbach Colliery	4 N70
14	Phoenix Tin Plate	4 N71
15	Gilwen Colliery	4 N71
16	Brynmorgan Siding	4 N71
17	Gwaun Cae Gurwen Col	X N71
18	Blaen Waen Siding	4 N71
19	Rhosamman Colliery	4 N71
20	Blaen-Cae-Gurwen Col	4 N71
21	Black Mountain Col	X N71
22	Cefn Mawr Siding	3 N80
23	Ynisarwed Colliery	3 N80
24	Aberclwyd Colliery	3 N80
25	Cilfrew Tin Works	5 N70
26	Llycynon Colliery	5 N70
27	Crynant Colliery	5 N70
28	Crynant New Colliery	5 N70
29	Dillwyn Colliery	5 N80
30	Brynteg Colliery	5 N80
31	Seven Sisters Colliery	5 N80
32	Dulais Colliery	5 N81
33	Penthos Brick Co's Sdg	5 N81
34	Coll's Siding	5 N81
35	Dinas Brick Co's Sdg	5 N81
36	Gwaunclawdd Colliery	5 N81

ENGINE SHED

No	Location	Ry Ref
E 1	Glyn Neath	3 N80

TUNNELS

No	Name/Location	Yds	Ry Ref
T 1	Cymmer	1790	3 S89
2	Rhondda	3398	8 S89
3	Gyfylchi	1109	7 S79
4	Lon-Las		3 S79

JUNCTIONS

No	Name/Location	Ry Ref
J 1	Neath	3 S79
2	Cadoxton	5 S79
3	Cymmer Jct for Maesteg	73 S89
4	Station (Cymmer)	8 S89
5	Cymmer Middle	8 S89
6	Cymmer East	38 S89
7	Cymmer West	38 S89
8	Abercregan	7X S89
9	Cymmer-Glycorrwg	3 S89
10	Glais	4 N70
11	Ynys-y-Geinon	45 N70
12	Gurnos	4 N70
13	Brynhen Ilish	4 N71
14	Brynamman	43 N71
15	Colbren	5 N81
16	Duffryn Branch	3 S89
17	Pentmawr No1	4 N70
18	Pentmawr No2	4 N70

NOTES:

(1) REF – All in SN or SS – S omitted

(2) All stations included – other features only if not on area covered by enlargement (104)

(3) ⊗ Not completed – stations projected but not opened

(4) § Map date name (1926)
§ Earlier name

(5) Name or title changes are sometimes indicated by part of name being in (brackets)

(6) Now NEATH ‡

92A
94
96

CYMMER Junctions Detail

Avon Vale Col
Corrwg Vale Col
SS / S9
Jct for Maesteg
Cymmer (Swn)
Abercregan Jct
Station Jct
Cwm Cymmer
Cymmer (SW)
West Jct
East Jct
Glyncorrwg Junct.
Goods
Middle Junct.
Duffryn Rhondda Plat
T1

Black Mountain Colliery

Brynamman
Brynamman Junctions
Black Cae Gurwen Col
Rhosamman Col
Brynamman
Cwmllynfell
Midland
Blaen Nant Sdg
Gwaun Cae Gurwen Col
Brynhenllish Junction
Gwys

Penmawr No.1
Penmawr No.2
South Wales Anthracite
Cwmtwrclawdd Colliery
Abercrave
Colli Sdg
Colbren (Jct)
Colbren Junction

Brynmorgan Sdg
Gilwen Col
Phoenix Tin Plate Works
Gurnos Jct.
Gurnos Gds
Ystradgynlais
Penrhos Brick Co's Siding
Dulais Colliery
Onllwyn

Ystalyfera
Iron + Tin Wks
Pwllbach Col
Varteg Anthracite Colliery
Seven Sisters Col.
Seven Sisters

Ynys-y-Geinon Junction
Tareni Colliery
Waen-y-Coed Colliery
Bryateg Colliery
Dillwyn Colliery
Crynant New Colliery

Midland
Neath + Brecon
(Rhyd-y-fro)
Crynant Colliery
Crynant
Llwynon Colliery

Pontwalby Halt
Glyn Neath
E1
Great Western

Glantawe Iron + Tin Plate Works
Pontardawe
Aberclwyd Col
Resolven

(Pontardawe)
Llwyndu Colliery
Melyncourt Halt
Ynisarwed Colliery

Glais
Glais Junct.
Glais Goods
SN
SS
Cilfrew Tin Wks.
Cilfrew
Clyne Halt
Cefn Mawr Sdg

SN
SS

Cadoxton Junct.
Cadoxton Gds
Aberdylais
Glyncorrwg

Neath Junction
Neath Bridge Street
NEATH General
Neath (R+SB)
Cymmer (SWM)
Cwm Cymmer Rhondda
Blaengwynfi
Swansea Bay
T2

Skewen
GWR
Neath Abbey
Cardonnel Halt
South Wales Mineral
T3
Cymmer (for Glyncorrwg)
Abergwynfi

T4
Oil Depot
Court Sart
South Wales Mineral
Rhondda + SB
Cynon Platform
Duffryn Rhondda Goods
Duffryn Rhondda Platform
SEE INSET ABOVE

Cwrt Platform
Briton Ferry East
Briton Ferry West
Briton Ferry Goods
Pontrhydyfen
T1
Caerau

Briton Ferry Road
Jersey Marine
Duffryn Bch Jct
Blaengarw
Duffryn Bach Siding
Nantyffyllon
North's Navigation No.9 Col Sdg

Cwm Avan
Aberavon Town
Port Talbot
Bryn
Port Talbot
Maesteg Neath Road
Maesteg Castle Street
Cwmdu
Pont-y-Cymmer

1926
1898
(1938)
(1922)
Great Western
Rhondda + Swansea Bay
Maesteg UBC
 Llyn fach
Troedyrhiew

Craig-y-Nôs (Penwyllt)
Neath + Brecon
Dinas Brick Co's Siding

Key to Railways

3	GREAT WESTERN	
30	GREAT WESTERN (Proposed – not completed)	
4	MIDLAND	
5	NEATH + BRECON	
6	PORT TALBOT RAILWAY + DOCKS	
7	SOUTH WALES MINERAL	
8	RHONDDA + SWANSEA BAY	
X	OTHERS – Collieries, Quarries etc	

Inset

MERTHYR, ABERDARE + MOUNTAIN ASH

No.	Company
R 1	BRECON + MERTHYR
12	BRECON + MERTHYR and LNW JOINT
2	LONDON + NORTH WESTERN
3	GREAT WESTERN
30	GREAT WESTERN (Post Grouping)
34	GREAT WESTERN + TAFF VALE JOINT
36	GREAT WESTERN + RHYMNEY JOINT
4	TAFF VALE
5	BARRY
6	RHYMNEY
7	ALEXANDRA (Newport + South Wales) DOCK + RAILWAY
8	RHONDDA + SWANSEA BAY
X	Colliery Lines etc

STATIONS + HALTS

No	Name	Ry	Ref
A 1	Aberaman	4	S000
2	Abercanaid	36	S000
*2A	Abercwmboi Platform	4	ST09
3	ABERCYNON	4	ST09
	Aberdare		S000
4	Commercial Street Ptfm	4	S000
5	High Level	3	S000
6	Low Level	4	S000
7	Aberfan	36	S000
8	Abernant	3	S000
9	Bedlinog	36	S000
10	Berw Road Platform	4	ST09
11	Black Lion Crossing Halt	3	SN90
12	Blaengarw	3	SS89
13	Blaenrhondda	8	SS99
14	Cae Harris	36	S000
15	Cefn Coed	12	S000
16	Cilfynydd	4	ST09
17	Coedpenmaen	4	ST09
18	Cwmaman Colliery Halt	3	SS99
19	Cwmaman Crossing Halt	3	SS99
20	Cwm Bargoed	36	S000
21	Cwmnoel Halt ‡	3	S000
22	DINAS	4	ST09
23	Dolygaer	1	S001
	Dowlais		S000
24	Central	1	S000
25	Cae Harris	36	S000
26	High Street	2	S000
27	Top	1	S000
28	Ferndale	4	S000
29	Fochriw	1	S010
30	Gelli Platform	4	SS99
31	Glyn Taff Halt	7	ST09
32	Godreaman Halt	3	S000
33	Gyfeillon Platform	4	ST09
34	Hirwain	3	SN90
35	Llwydcoed	3	SN90
36	LLWYNYPIA	4	SS99
37	Maerdy	4	SS99
38	MERTHYR (TYDFIL)	3	S000
39	MERTHYR VALE	4	ST09
40	Mill Street Platform	4	SN90
41	Mountain Ash Cardiff Rd.	3	ST09
42	Mountain Ash Oxford St.	4	ST09
43	Nantymoel	3	SS99
44	Ogmore Vale	3	SS99
45	Old Ynysybwl Platform	4	ST09
46	Pant	1	S000
47	Pantysgallog	2	S000
48	Pantysgallog Halt	1	S000
49	Penrhiwceiber High Level	3	ST09
50	Penrhiwceiber Low Level	4	ST09
51	Pentir Rhiw Halt	1	S001
52	PENTREBACH	4	S000
53	Pentre Platform	4	SS99
54	Penygraig	3	SS99
55	Pontcynon Platform	4	ST09
56	Pont Sarn	12	S000
57	Pontsticill	1	S001
58	Pont-y-Cymmer	3	SS99
59	Pontygwaith Platform	4	ST09
60	PONTYPRIDD Central	4	ST09
61	Pontypridd Graig	5	ST09
62	Pontypridd Halt	7	ST09
63	PORTH	4	ST09
64	Quakers Yard High Level	3	ST09
65	QUAKERS YARD Low Level	4	ST09
66	Rhigos	3	SN90
67	Robertstown Platform	4	ST09
68	TONYPANDY + Trealaw	4	SS99
69	Torpantau	1	S001
70	Travellers Rest Halt	4	ST09
71	Trecynon Platform	3	SN90
72	Treforest Halt	7	ST09
73	TREHAFOD	4	ST09
74	Treharris	3	ST09
75	TREHERBERT	4	SS99
76	TREORCHY	4	SS99
77	TROEDYRHIW	4	S000
78	Troedyrhiw Halt	36	S000
79	Tylacoch Platform	4	SS99
80	Tylorstown	4	ST09
81	Ynishir	4	ST09
82	Ynysybwl	4	ST09
83	YSTRAD (RHONDDA)	4	SS99

GOODS

No	Name/Location	Ry	Ref
G1	Blaenclydach	4	SS99
2	Clydach Vale	4	SS99
3	Cwmaman	3	SS99
4	Merthyr - Plymouth Street	4	S000
5	Middle Duffryn	3	S000
6	Pontypridd - Maes-y-Coed	5	ST09
7	Pontypridd Town	4	ST09
8	Trecynon	4	SN90
9	Wattstown	4	ST09

SIDINGS

No	Name/Company/Location	Ry	Ref
P1	Blaengarw Ocean Col	3	SS99
2	Ffaldau Colliery	3	SS99
3	Davis Ocean Colliery	3	SS99
4	Aber Sidings	3	SS99
5	Caedu Colliery	3	SS99
6	Abergorchy Colliery	4	SS99
7	Lady Margaret Colliery	4	SS99
8	Nantdyrus Colliery	4	SS99
9	Fernhill Colliery	4	SN90
10	Blaenrhondda Colliery	4	SN90
11	Mynydd Colliery	4	SN90
12	Tower Pit	3X	SN90
13	Bwlch Colliery	3	SN90
14	Abercriban Quarry	1	S001
15	New Tylerbont Stone +		S001
	Asphalte	1	S001

ENGINE SHEDS

No	Name/Location	Ry	Ref
E1	Treherbert	30	SS99
2	Ferndale	4	SS99
3	Pwllyrhebog	4	SS99

TUNNELS

No	Name	Yds	Ry	Ref
T1	Rhondda	3398	8	SS99
2	Merthyr	2495	3	S000
3	Pencaedrain		3	SN90
4	Summit (Torpantau)		1	S001
5	Quakers Yard		3	ST09

JUNCTIONS

No	Name/Location	Ry	Ref
J1	Blaenrhondda Branch	4	SS99
2	Treherbert	48	SS99
3	Pontsticill	1	S001

NOTES:

(1) STATIONS - All shown except Abercwmboi (in code); see 102 and 105 Enlargements *

(2) OTHER FEATURES shown in full only in area not covered by enlargements. In areas covered by the enlargements shown — selectively only.

(3) NAME SPELLINGS - as used by RCH in 1926. ‡ Map and Gazetteer show alternative spellings in this case only.

(4) OVERLAP - Slight overlap at East, South + West margins

(5) WATER - Shore lines as at 1938.

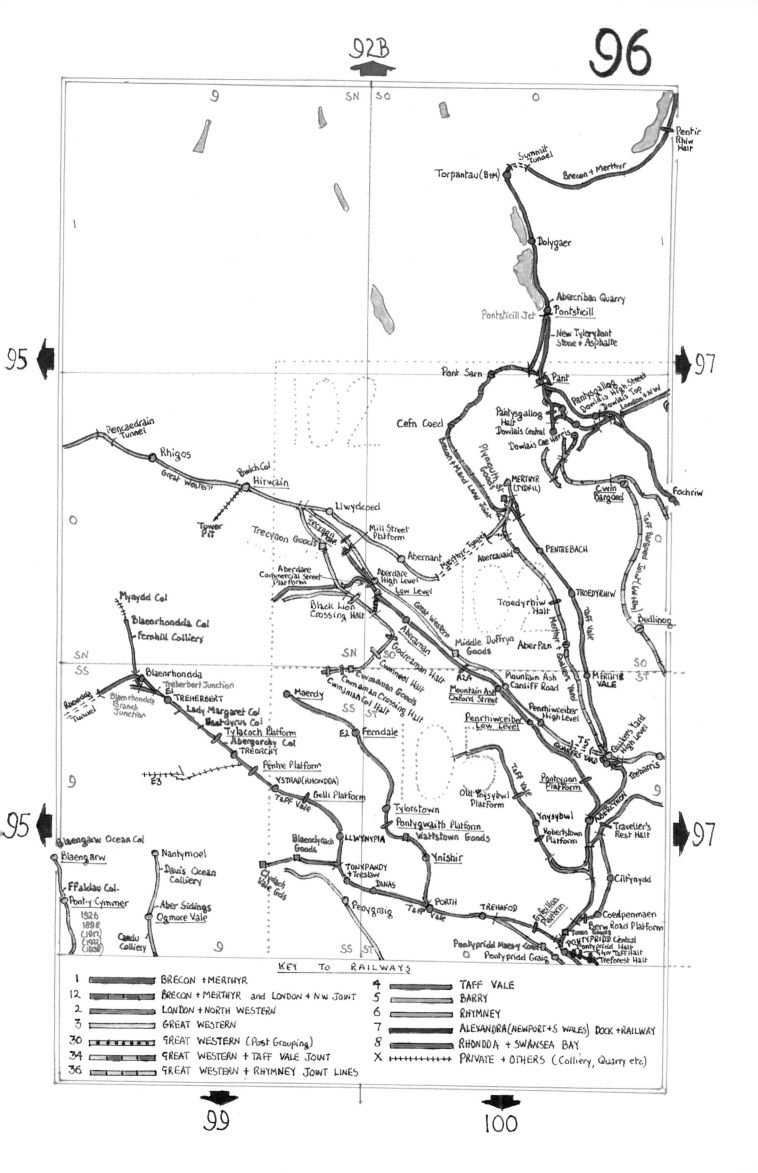

9 · SN · SO · O

Pentir Rhiw Halt

Summit Tunnel

Torpantau (B+M)

Brecon + Merthyr

Dolygaer

Abercriban Quarry

Pontsticill Jct · Pontsticill

New Tylerybont Stone + Asphalte

Pont Sarn · Pant

Pantysgallog High Street
Dowlais Top
London + NW

Cefn Coed

Pantysgallog Halt
Dowlais Central
Dowlais Cae Harris

Pencaedrain Tunnel

Rhigos

Bulch Col

Hirwain

Great Western

Brecon + Merthyr Goods

Plymouth St Goods

MERTHYR (TYDFIL)

Cwm Bargoed

Fochriw

Tower Pit

Trecynon Goods

Trecynon Halt

Llwydcoed

Mill Street Platform

Abernant

Merthyr Tunnel

Abercanaid

PENTREBACH

Taff Bargoed Joint (GW+RM)

Aberdare Commercial Street Platform

Aberdare High Level
Low Level

Great Western

Troedyrhiw Halt

TROEDYRHIW

Bedlinog

Mynydd Col

Blaenrhondda Col

Fernhill Colliery

Black Lion Crossing Halt

Aberaman

Godreaman Halt

Middle Duffryn Goods

Aberfan

Merthyr + Quakers Yard

Taff Vale

SN
SS

Blaenrhondda

Treherbert Junction

TREHERBERT

Cwmneol Halt

A2A

Mountain Ash Oxford Street

Mountain Ash Cardiff Road

MERTHYR VALE

SN SO
SS ST

Rhondda Tunnel

Blaenrhondda Branch Junction

Lady Margaret Col

Nantdyrus Col

Tylacoch Platform

Abergorchy Col

TREORCHY

Maerdy

Cwmaman Goods

Cwmaman Crossing Halt

Cwmaman Col Halt

E2 · Ferndale

SS ST

Penrhiwceiber High Level

Penrhiwceiber Low Level

Quakers Yard High Level

Pentre Platform

E3

YSTRAD (RHONDDA)

Gelli Platform

Taff Vale

Tylorstown

Old Ynysybwl Platform

Taff Vale

QUAKERS YARD

Treharris

Pontcynon Platform

9

Blaengarw Ocean Col

Blaengarw

Nantymoel

Davis Ocean Colliery

Clydach Vale Gds

Blaenclydach Goods

LLWYNYPIA

Pontygwaith Platform

Wattstown Goods

Ynishir

Ynysybwl

Robertstown Platform

Abercynon

Traveller's Rest Halt

Ffaldau Col.

Pont-y-Cymmer

1926
1898
(1912)
(1922)
(1858)

Aber Sidings
Ogmore Vale

Caedu Colliery

9

TONYPANDY + Trealaw

DINAS

Penygraig

Taff Vale

PORTH

TREHAFOD

Trehafod

Cilfynydd

Coedpenmaen

Berw Road Platform

Berw Goods

Town Goods

PONTYPRIDD Central

9

Pontypridd Maes y Coed

Pontypridd Halt
Rhondda Halt
Pontypridd Graig

Treforest Halt

KEY TO RAILWAYS

1	BRECON + MERTHYR
12	BRECON + MERTHYR and LONDON + NW JOINT
2	LONDON + NORTH WESTERN
3	GREAT WESTERN
30	GREAT WESTERN (Post Grouping)
34	GREAT WESTERN + TAFF VALE JOINT
36	GREAT WESTERN + RHYMNEY JOINT LINES
4	TAFF VALE
5	BARRY
6	RHYMNEY
7	ALEXANDRA (NEWPORT + S WALES) DOCK + RAILWAY
8	RHONDDA + SWANSEA BAY
X	PRIVATE + OTHERS (Colliery, Quarry etc)

No	Company
R 1	BRECON + MERTHYR
2	LONDON + NORTH WESTERN
2A	PENLLWYN TRAMWAY (L+NW)
23	LNW + GREAT WESTERN JOINT
3	GREAT WESTERN
36	GREAT WESTERN + RHYMNEY JOINT
4	TAFF VALE
6	RHYMNEY
26	LONDON + NORTH WESTERN + RHYMNEY
X	Colliery lines etc

STATIONS + HALTS

No	Name	Ry Ref
A 1	Aberbargoed	1 O10
2	Aberbeeg	3 O20
3	Abercarn	3 T19
4	Abersychan + Talywain	23 O20
5	Abersychan Low Level	3 O20
6	Abertillery	3 O20
7	Abertysswg	1 O10
8	Argoed	2 O10
9	BARGOED	6 O10
10	Beaufort	2 O11
11	Bedwellty Pits	2 O10
12	Blackwood	2 T19
13	Blaenavon	2 O20
14	Blaenavon	3 O20
15	Blaina	3 O10
16	Brecon Road	2 O21
17	BRAITHDIR	6 O10
18	Brynmawr	2 O11
19	Clydach	2 O21
20	Cross Keys	3 T29
21	Crumlin High Level	3 T29
22	Crumlin Low Level	3 T29
23	Cwm	3 O10
24	Cwm Avon	3 O20
25	CWMBRAN	3 T29
26	(Cwmcarn)	3 T29
27	Cwmsyfiog	1 O10
28	Darran + Deri	6 O10
29	Ebbw Vale	2 O10
30	Ebbw Vale	3 O10
31	(Fleur-de-Lis)	1 T19
32	Fochriw	1 O10
33	(Garndiffaith Halt)	2 O20
34	GILFACH FARGOED Halt	6 T19
35	Gilwern	2 O21
36	Govilon	2 O21
37	Hafodyrynys Platform	3 T29
38	Hengoed High Level	3 T19
39	HENGOED Low Level	6 T19
40	Holly Bush	2 O10
41	LLANBRADACH	6 T19
42	Llanfabon Road Platform	4 T10
43	Llanhilleth	3 O20
44	Lower Pontnewydd	3 T29
45	Maesycwmmer	1 T19
46	Markham Village	2 O10
47	Nantybwch	2 O11
48	Nantyglo	3 O10
49	Nelson	4 T19
50	Nelson + Llancaiach	3 T19
51	Newbridge	3 T19
52	New Tredegar	1 O10
53	Nine Mile Point	2 T29
54	(Oakdale Halt)	3 T19
55	Panteg + Griffithstown	3 T29
56	PENGAM (Glam.)	6 T19
57	Pengam (Mon.)	1 T19
58	(Penmaen Halt)	3 T19
59	Pentir Rhiw Halt	1 O01
60	(Pentwynmawr Halt)	3 T19
61	Pont Lawrence	2 T19
62	Pontllanfraith	2 T19
63	Pontllanfraith	3 T19
64	PONTLOTTYN	6 O10
65	Pontnewydd, Lower	3 T29
66	Pontnewydd, Upper	3 T29
67	Pontnewynydd	3 O20
68	Pontypool Clarence St	3 O20
69	Pontypool Crane Street	3 O20
70	PONTYPOOL Road	3 O20
71	Pontrhydyrun	3 T29
72	RHYMNEY	6 O10
73	Rhymney Bridge	26 O10
74	Rhymney (Pwll Uchaf)	1 O10
75	Risca	3 T29
76	Senghenydd	6 T19
77	Sirhowy	2 O10
78	TIR-PHIL	6 O10
79	Tredegar	2 O10
80	Trelewis Platform	36 T19
81	(Treowen Halt)	3 T29
82	Trevil	2 O11
83	(Troedyrhiwfwch Halt)	6 O10
84	Tylors Arms (Platform)	36 O20
85	Upper Pontnewydd	3 T29
86	Varteg	2 O20
87	Victoria	3 O10
88	Waenavon	2 O21
89	Ynysddu	2 T19
90	YSTRAD MYNACH	6 T19

GOODS

No	Name	Ry Ref
G 1	Blaendare	3 T29
2	Brynmawr	2 O11
3	Cwmbran	3 T29
4	Nine Mile Point	2 T19
5	Penmaen	3 T19
6	Penrhiw-Felin	6 T19
7	Wattsville	2A T19
8	Ynysddu Lower	2A T19
9	Ystrad Mynach	6 T19

SIDINGS ETC

No	Company/Name/Location	Ry Ref
P 1	Beaufort Iron Works	3X O11
2	Llwydcoed Colliery	2 O11
3	New Clydach Colliery	2 O21
4	Clydach Lime Works	2 O21
5	Govilon Canal Wharf	2 O21

JUNCTIONS

No	Name/Location	Ry Ref
J 1	Nantybwch Joint Line	226 O11
2	Sirhowy	2 O11
3	Ebbw Vale Line	2 O11
4	Western Valleys North	232 O11
5	Western Valleys South	223 O11
6	Brynmawr Goods	2 O11
7	Brynmawr-Waenavon	2 O11
8	Blain Iron Co	2X O11

TUNNELS

No	Name/Location	Ry Ref
T 1	Clydach	2 O21
2	New Clydach	2 O21

NOTES:

(1) REF In SO or ST, S omitted

(2) STATIONS - All shown AND included in this gazetteer.

(3) OTHER FEATURES - In the main, except for some Goods Depots, only shown if in an area NOT enlarged.

(4) SPELLING - Welsh place names have always been subject to minor alterations, often at frequent intervals. The names shown on the map are those in use in the early 20's.

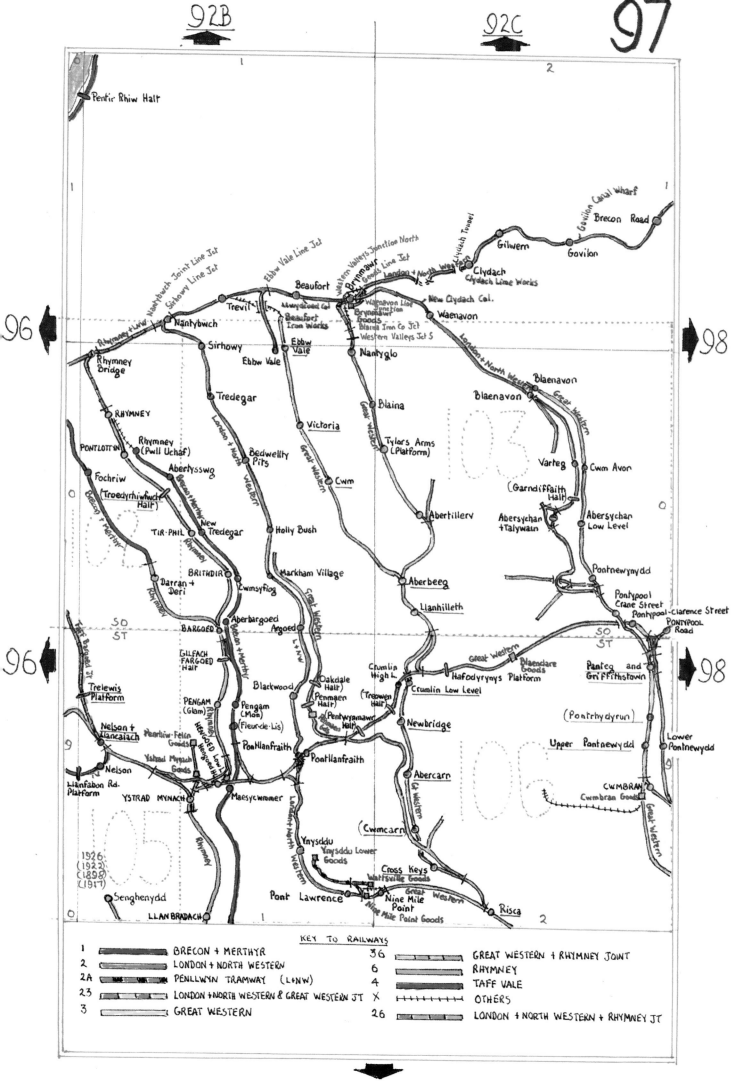

Pentir Rhiw Halt

Govilon Canal Wharf
Brecon Road
Gilwern
Govilon

Western Valleys Junction North
Naabybwrch Joint Line Jct
Sirhowy Line Jct
Ebbw Vale Line Jct
Beaufort
Goods Line Jct
London + North West
Clydach Tunnel
Clydach
Clydach Lime Works

Rhymney L.N.W.
Trevil
Brynmawr
Abbydcoed Col.
Waenavon Lied Junction
Brynmawr Goods
New Clydach Col.
Waenavon

Nantybwch
Beaufort Iron Works
Blaina Iron Co Jct
Western Valleys Jct S

Sirhowy
Ebbw Vale
Nantyglo

Rhymney Bridge
Ebbw Vale
Blaina
London + North Western
Blaenavon
Blaenavon
Great Western

RHYMNEY
Tredegar
Great Western
Victoria

PONTLOTTYN
Rhymney (Pwll Uchaf)
Abertysswg
Bedwellty Pits
Tylors Arms (L Platform)
Varteg
Cwm Avon

Fochriw
(Troedyrhiwfuch Halt)
London + North Western
Cwm
(Garndiffaith Halt)

Brecon + Merthyr
TIR-PHIL
New Tredegar
Holly Bush
Abertillery
Abersychan + Talywain
Abersychan Low Level

BRITHDIR
Darran + Deri
Cwmsyfiog
Markham Village
Aberbeeg
Pontnewynydd

Rhymney
Great Western
Llanhilleth
Pontypool Crane Street
Pontypool-Clarence Street

Taff Bargoed Jct
SO ST
BARGOED
Aberbargoed
Argoed
L+NW
Brecon + Merthyr
PONTYPOOL Road
SO ST

GILFACH FARGOED Halt
Crumlin High L.
Great Western
Blaendare Goods
Panteg and Griffithstown

Trelewis Platform
Blackwood
Oakdale Halt
Penmaen Halt
Hafodyrynys Platform
Crumlin Low Level

PENGAM (Glam)
Pengam (Mon)
(Fleur-de-Lis)
(Treowen Halt)
(Pontrhydyrun)

Nelson + Llancaiach
Penrhiw-Felin Goods
Pentwynmawr Halt
Newbridge
Upper Pontnewydd
Lower Pontnewydd

Ystrad Mynach Goods
Rhymney Low
Hengoed H.
Pontllanfraith
Pontllanfraith

Nelson
HENGOED Low
Abercarn
Gt Western
CWMBRAN
Cwmbran Goods

Llanfabon Rd. Platform
Maesycwmmer
London + North Western
Cwmcarn
Great Western

YSTRAD MYNACH
Rhymney
Ynysddu
Ynysddu Lower Goods

Senghenydd
Cross Keys
Wattsville Goods

LLANBRADACH
Pont Lawrence
Nine Mile Point
Great Western
Risca
Nine Mile Point Goods

1926 (1922) (1898) (1917)

KEY TO RAILWAYS

1	BRECON + MERTHYR	
2	LONDON + NORTH WESTERN	
2A	PENLLWYN TRAMWAY (L+NW)	
23	LONDON + NORTH WESTERN & GREAT WESTERN JT	
3	GREAT WESTERN	
36	GREAT WESTERN + RHYMNEY JOINT	
6	RHYMNEY	
4	TAFF VALE	
X	OTHERS	
26	LONDON + NORTH WESTERN + RHYMNEY JT	

98
RAILWAYS

No	Company
R 1	BRECON + MERTHYR
2	LONDON + NORTH WESTERN
3	GREAT WESTERN
7	ALEXANDRA DOCK + RAILWAY
O	(POST GROUPING ADDITIONS)
X	Others

STATIONS + HALTS

No	Name		Ry Ref
A 1	Abergavenny - Brecon Rd	2	021
2	Abergavenny Junction	(2) 3	031
3	ABERGAVENNY Monmouth Rd	3	031
4	Bassaleg	＊ 17	T28
5	Bassaleg Junction	＊ 31	T28
6	Brecon Road	2	021
7	Caerleon	＊ 3	T39
8	CWMBRAN	3	T29
9	Dingestow	3	041
10	Little Mill	3	030
11	Llandenny	3	040
12	Llantarnam	3	T39
13	Llanvihangel	3	031
14	Lower Pontnewydd	3	T39
15	Nantyderry	3	030
16	NEWPORT High Street	＊ 3	T38
17	Panteg + Griffithstown	3	T29
18	Penpergwm	3	031
19	Panthir	3	T39
20	PONTYPOOL Road	3	030
21	Raglan	3	040
22	Rogerstone	＊ 3	T28
23	Upper Pontnewydd	3	T29
24	Usk	3	030

GOODS

No	Name/Location	Ry Ref
G	NEWPORT ＊	T38
1	Dock Street	3 T38
2	High Street	3 T38
3	Mill Street	3 T38

SIDINGS

No	Name/Company/Location	Ry Ref
P 1	Abergavenny - Asylum	2 031
2	Nettlefolds ＊	1 T28
3	Rogerstone ＊	3 T28
S	NEWPORT ＊	T38
4	St Julians Brickworks	3 T38
5	Herbert's Siding	3 T38
6	Lliswerry Lime	3 T38
7	Healey + Pearl's	3 T38
8	Br. Mannesmann Tube	3 T38
9	Lysaght's Works	3 T38
10	Cardiff Channel Dry Dock + Pontoon Co	3 T38 / 3 T38

ENGINE SHEDS

No	Name/Location	Ry Ref
E 1	Newport Ebbw ＊	3 T38

No	Name		Ry Ref
2	Newport Pill	＊ 7	T38
3	Pontypool Road	3	030
4	Abergavenny		031

TUNNELS ＊

No	Name	Yds	Ry Ref
T 1	Newport Tunnel	(742)	30 T38
2	Gaer Tunnel		3 T38

BRIDGES ＊

No	Name	Ry Ref
V 1	Usk Bridge Newport	3 T38

JUNCTIONS

No.	Name/Location	Ry Ref
J 1	Abergavenny	32 031
2	Pontypool Jcts ♀	3 T29
3	Little Mill	3 030
＊	NEWPORT DISTRICT	
4	Bassaleg	31 T28
5	Bassaleg West	17 T28
6	Park West	3 T38
7	Park East	3 T38
8	Maesglas	37 T38
9	Ebbw	3 T38
10	Alexandra Dock	37 T38
11	Waterloo	3 T38
12	East Mendalgyf	7 T38
13	Pillbank	3 T38
14	Gaer	3 T38
15	High Street	3 T38
16	Nettlefolds Branch	3X T38
17	East Usk Branch	3 T38
18	Maindee North	3 T38
19	Maindee East	3 T38
20	Maindee West	3 T38
21	Cwmbran	3 T29
22	Llantarnam	3 T39

NOTES:

(1) REF - In SO or ST - S omitted

(2) PONTYPOOL JCTS SEE 106 ♀

(3) OVERLAPS - To the west + the South (Newport)

(4) ON INSET ＊＊＊＊

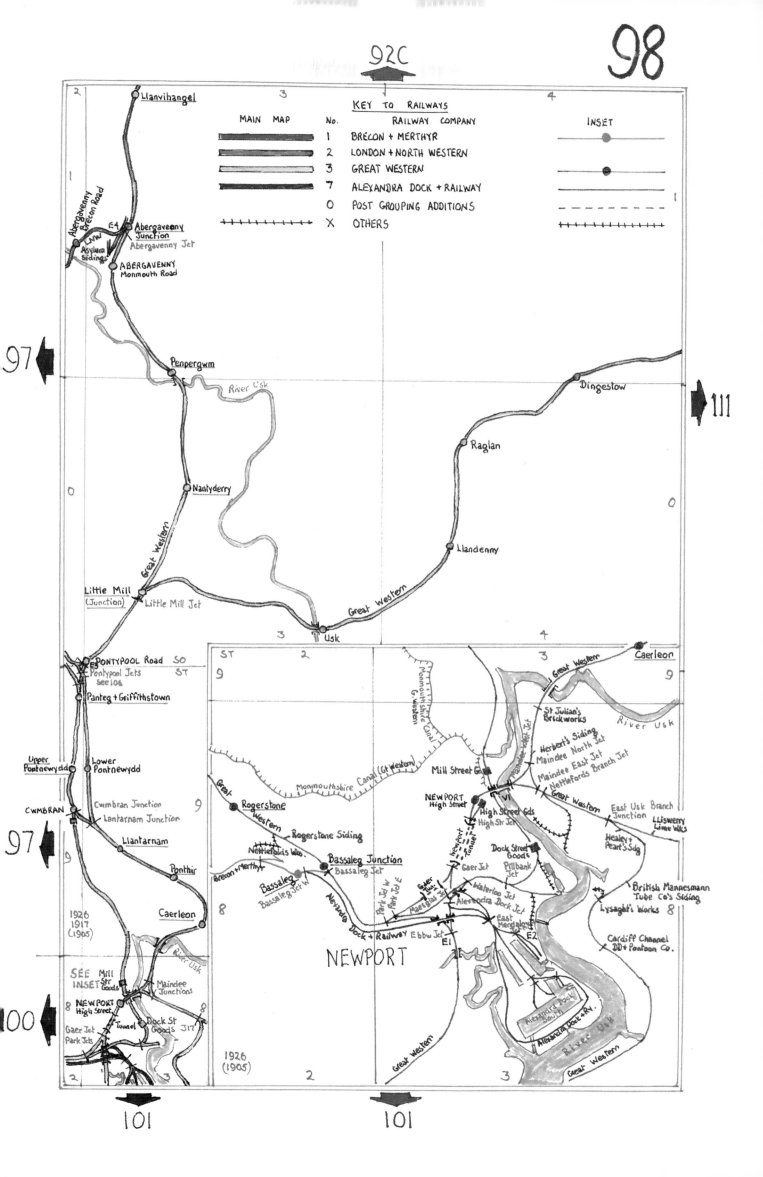

Llanvihangel

KEY TO RAILWAYS

MAIN MAP	No.	RAILWAY COMPANY	INSET
	1	BRECON + MERTHYR	
	2	LONDON + NORTH WESTERN	
	3	GREAT WESTERN	
	7	ALEXANDRA DOCK + RAILWAY	
	0	POST GROUPING ADDITIONS	
	X	OTHERS	1

Abergavenny Brecon Road
Abergavenny Junction
Abergavenny Jct
E4
L+NW
Asylum Sidings
ABERGAVENNY Monmouth Road

97

Penpergwm

River Usk

Dingestow

111

Raglan

Nantyderry

Great Western

Llandenny

Little Mill
(Junction)
Little Mill Jct

Great Western

Usk

Caerleon

Great Western

St Julian's Brickworks

Monmouthshire Canal (Gt Western)

Herbert's Siding
Maindee North Jct
Maindee East Jct
Nettlefords Branch Jct

River Usk

PONTYPOOL Road   SO
Pontypool Jcts   ST
See 106

Panteg + Griffithstown

ST
9

ST
2

3

4

9

Mill Street Gds

Maindee Loop Jct

Great Western

East Usk Branch Junction
Lliswerry Lime Wks

NEWPORT High Street
High Street Gds
High Str Jct

Upper Pontnewydd
Lower Pontnewydd

Great

Rogerstone

Western

Rogerstone Siding

Nettlefolds Wks.

Monmouthshire Canal (Gt Western)

Newport Tunnel

Dock Street Goods

Healey + Peart's Sdg

CWMBRAN

Cwmbran Junction
Lantarnam Junction

97

Llantarnam

Ponthir

Caerleon

1926
1917
(1905)

9

8

Brecon + Merthyr

Bassaleg
Bassaleg Jct W

Bassaleg Junction
Bassaleg Jct

Alexandra Dock + Railway

Gaer Jct

Park Jct W
Park Jct E

Maesglas Jct

Waterloo Jct

Alexandra Dock Jct

Ebbw Jct

East Mendalgief

E1   E2

Gaer Twn Jct

Pillbank Jct

British Mannesmann Tube Co's Siding

Lysaght's Works   8

Cardiff Channel DD + Pontoon Co.

NEWPORT

SEE Mill
INSET Str
Goods

NEWPORT High Street
Gaer Jct
Park Jcts

Tunnel
Dock St Goods J17

Maindee Junctions

River Usk

100

8

8

2   3

1926
(1905)

2

Alexandra Dock South
Alexandra Dock + Ry.

Great Western

Great Western

River Usk

Great Western

3

101

101

99

PORT TALBOT + BRIDGEND

RAILWAYS

No	Company		Ry Ref
R3	GREAT WESTERN		
5	BARRY		
6	PORT TALBOT		
8	RHONDDA + SWANSEA BAY		
X	Others - Colliery lines etc		

STATIONS + HALTS

No	Name	Ry Ref
A 1	Bettws	6 98
2	Black Mill	3 98
3	BRIDGEND	3 98
4	Brynmenyn	3 98
5	Gilfach	3 98
6	Hendreforgan	3 98
7	Kenfig Hill	3 88
8	Llandow Halt	5 97
9	Llangeinor	3 98
10	Llangonoyd	3 88
11	Llanharan	3 98
12	Llantwit Major	5 96
13	Lletty Brongu	6 88
14	Pencoed	3 98
15	Pont-y-Rhyll	3(6) 98
16	Porthcawl	3 87
17	Porthcawl-Golfers Platform	3 87
18	PORT TALBOT	3 78
19	Port Talbot Central	6 78
20	Pyle ✠	3 88
21	Pyle ✠	3 88
22	Southerndown Road	5 97
23	Tondu	3 88

GOODS

No	Name / Location	Ry Ref
G 1	Bridgend + Coity	5 98
2	Bryn · Gwynan	3 98
3	Dock (Port Talbot)	8 78
4	Margam	3 78
5	North Bank (Port Talbot)	6 78
6	South Rhondda	3 98

SIDINGS

No	Company / Name / Location	Ry Ref
P 1	Abbot Pit	6 X 78
2	Margam Moor Siding	6 78
3	Cornelly Siding	3 88
4	Pencoed Private Sidings	3 X 98
5	Cwm Cec Colliery	3 98
6	South Rhondda Colliery	3 X 98
7	Cardoc Vale Colliery	3 X 98
8	Glynogwr Colliery	3 98
9	Erna Colliery	3 98

JUNCTIONS

No	Name / Location	Ry Ref
J 1	Cefn	36 88
2	Cowbridge Road	5 97
3	Coity	35 98
4	Bryncethin	3 98
5	Gilfach	3 98
6	Llanharan	3 98

NOTES:

(1) REFERENCES — All in SS

(2) PYLE — Different platforms of the same station, originally being of differing gauges. Regarded as one station only from the 1920s - possibly earlier.

(3) ENLARGEMENTS — Apart from stations, other features only shown selectively in areas covered by enlargements.

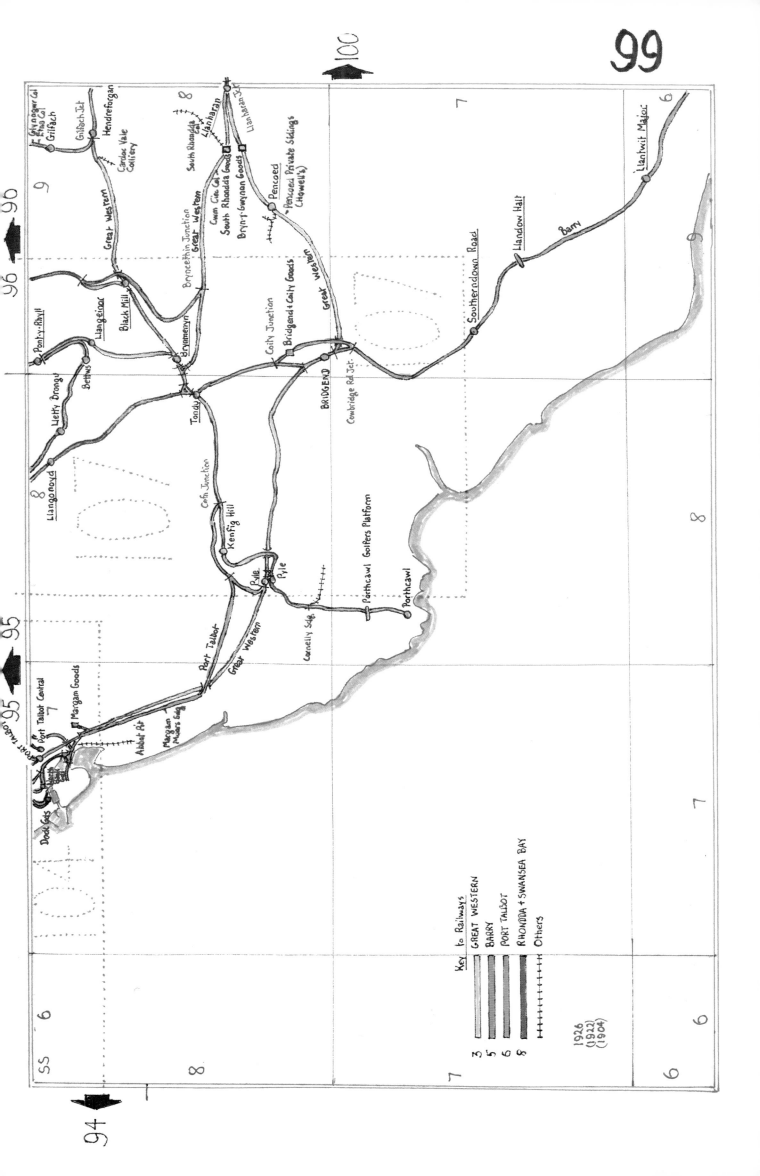

RAILWAYS

No.	Company	Ry Ref
R 1	BRECON + MERTHYR	§12
R 2	LONDON + NORTH WESTERN	
3	GREAT WESTERN	
4	TAFF VALE	
5	BARRY	
6	RHYMNEY	
7	ALEXANDRA DOCK + RAILWAY	
8	CARDIFF	
X	Colliery, Mineral, Harbour etc	

STATIONS

No.	Name	Ry	Ref
A 1	ABER §12	6	18
2	Aberthaw High Level	5	06
3	Aberthaw Low Level	4	06
4	Aberthin Platform	4	07
5	Aberthidwr	6	18
6	Alberta Place Platform	4	17
7	BARRY	5	16
8	BARRY DOCKS	5	16
9	BARRY ISLAND	5	16
10	Bassaleg	17	28
11	Bassaleg Junction	31	28
12	BEDDAU HALT §1	6	18
13	Beddau Halt (Llanwit)	4	08
14	Bedwas	1	18
15	(BIRCHGROVE)	8	18
16	CADOXTON	5	
17	CAERPHILLY	6	
	CARDIFF		
18	BUTE ROAD + §21	4	17
19	CENTRAL §22	3	17
20	Clarence Road	3	17
21	DOCKS +§18		
22	GENERAL §19		
23	Parade		
24	QUEEN STREET		
25	Riverside		
26	CATHAYS §18†		
27	(CEFN-ONN)		
28	Church Road		
29	Church Village		
30	Clarence Road		
31	Coedely		
32	COGAN		
33	CARYTON Halt		
34	Cowbridge	6	18
35	Creigiau	5	06
36	Cross Inn	5	06
37	DINAS POWIS	4	06
38	DINGLE ROAD Platform	4	07
39	Dynea Halt	6	18
40	Efail Isaf	4	17
41	Ely (Main Line) ‡	5	16
42	Fountain Bridge Halt	5	16
43	Gilfach *	5	16
44	Gileston	17	28
45	Glan-y-Llyn	31	28
46	GRANGETOWN	6	18
47	Groeswen Halt	4	08
48	Gwemydomen Halt	1	18
49	(HEATH HIGH LEVEL)	8	18
50	HEATH LOW LEVEL HALT	5	16
51	Hendre Fargan *	6	18
52	Lavernock		
53	Llanbethery Platform	4	17
54	LLANDAFF	3	17
55	Llanharan	3	17
56	Llanharry	4	17
57	LLANISHEN	3	17
58	Llantrisant	6	17
59	Llantrisant	4	17
60	Llanwit	3	17
61	Llanwit Major §10†	4	17
62	Lower Penarth	6	18
63	Machen	1	28
64	Maindy North Road Platform	4	08
	Platform	3	17
65	Marshfield	3	08
66	Nant Garw Halt High Level	5	17
67	Nant Garw Halt Low Level ♁	8	18
68	Parade	4	07
69	PENARTH	5	08
70	Penarth Dock	4	08
71	Pencoed ♁	5	17
72	Penyrheal	4	17
73	Peterston	7	08
74	QUEEN STREET ♁	5	08
75	RADYR	3	17
76	RHIWBA Halt	1	18
77	Rhiwderyn	3	98
78	Rhoose	5	06
79	Rhydfelin Halt	8	18
80	Rhydfelin Halt High Level	4	17
81	Riverside	7	18
82	Rogerstone	1	18
83	St Athan Road	6	18
84	St Fagan's	8	18
85	St Hilary Platform *	3	98
86	St Mary Church Road	4	16
87	Sully	4	07
88	Swanbridge Platform	4	18
89	TAFF'S WELL *	3	08
90	Tonteg Platform	4	08
91	Tanygwynlais	6	18
92	Tony refrail	3	08
93	(TREFOREST ESTATE)	4	08
94	Treforest High Level	4	08
95	Treforest Halt	5	96
96	TREFOREST Low Level	4	17
97	Trethyngyll + Maendy Platform	1	18
98	Trethomas	4	17
99	Upper Boat	3	28
100	Upper Boat Halt	5	17
101	Waterloo Halt	8	18
102	Wenvoe	6	17
103	WHITCHURCH (S.Glam)	4	17
104	WOODVILLE ROAD PLATFORM ♁	4	17
105	Ystradowen	6	18

GOODS

No.	Name/Location	Ry	Ref
1	Barry	8	18
2	Bryn-y-Gwnan	1	28
3	Cowbridge	5	06
4	South Rhondda	8	08
5	Treferig	7	08
6	Glynogwr Col. §26	4	17
7	Llanwit Rhondda Col	4	08
8	Coedely Col	8	18
9	Llanharry Iron Ore Mine	3	08
10	Llanharry Quarry	4	18
11	Beaupré	5	08
12	N Aberthaw Lime Works	7	08
13	St Athan Road Quarry	4	06
14	Portland Cement Works	4	06
15	Aberthaw Lim+Cement	4	07
16	(Rhoose) Station Cement	5	06
17	Barry Mineral	5	16
18	Syndicate	5	16
19	Armstrong Syndicate Smelting	5	17
20	Low' Penarth Cement Wks	4	16
21	Machen Lime Works	1	28
22	Garth Works	4	17
23	Rogerstone	3	28

TUNNELS

No.	Name	Length Yds	Ry	Ref
T 1	Caerphilly	1933	5	16
2	Barthkerry		3	98
3	Walnut Tree		4	07
4	Pontypridd	1373	3	98

SIDINGS

No.	Company/Name/Location	Ry	Ref
1	Glynogwr Col.	3(5)	17
2	Etna Col.	4	07
3	Cardac Vale Col	4	07
4	Cwm Circ Col	4	16
5	South Rhondda	4	16
6	Barry	4(6)	18
7	Cadoxton Docks	3	08

JUNCTIONS

No.	Name/Location	Ry	Ref
J 1	Gilfach *	3	98
2	Llanharan *	3	98
3	Cowbridge *	3	98
4	Mwyndy *	3	98
5	Gellyrhaidd *	3	98
6	Barry *	3x	98
7	Cadoxton Docks *	3	98
8	Cadoxton	5	16
9	Diglis	5x	16
10	Drope	5	17
11	Tyn-y-Caeau	5	17
12	Waterhall	4	17
13	Penarth Curve	3x	17
14	Crockherbtown	4(6)	17
15	Roath Branch	4	18
16	Heath	68	18
17	Pengam	3	27
18	Bassaleg West	17	28
19	Bassaleg	31	28

NOTES:

*** REF – In ST except for those marked (in ss) also on MAP 99

♠ CARDIFF Central stations also listed under CARDIFF

§ Map date } NAME CHANGE
§ Later or modern }

† Modern name from mid '20's

‡ Addition to Ely was in mid '20's when adjoining ex TV Goods used for passengers also

⊗ One station – originally worked as two due to mix of gauge – Dual working continued up to grouping.

* All stations shown on map – other features selective only in the areas covered by enlargements:
- INSET on 98
- MAP 108
- MAP 109

Key to Railways

1	BRECON + MERTHYR
2	LONDON + NORTH WESTERN
3	GREAT WESTERN
4	TAFF VALE
5	BARRY
6	RHYMNEY
7	ALEXANDRA DOCKS + RAILWAY
8	CARDIFF
X	OTHERS – Mineral, Harbour + Private

CARDIFF

Great Western

Rogerstone Sdg
Rogerstone
Bassaleg Junction
Bassaleg Jct
Brecon + Merthyr
Rhiwderin
Church Road
Garth Works Sdg
Machen Lime Works

Marshfield

Machen
Waterloo Halt
Gwernydomen Halt
Fountain Bridge Halt
Bedwas
Beddau Halt
CAERPHILLY

Trethomas

Caerphilly Tunnel
(GLAN-Y-NANT)
(LISVANE)
(HEATH HIGH LEVEL)
Heath Junction
Rhymney
Roath Branch Jct
WHITCHURCH (GLAM)
CORYTON HALT
Rhiwbina Halt
Heath Low Level Halt
Maindy North Road Platform
Woodville Road Platform
LLANDAFF
Cardiff
Tongwynlais
Taffs Well
Glan-y-Llyn
Nantgarw Halt High
Groeswen Halt
Upper Boat
Penyrheol
Nant Garw Halt High
TAFF VALE
RADYR
Ely (Main Line)
Waterhall Junct
Pen-y-Llan Jcts
St Fagans
Drope Junction
Wenvoe
Creigiau

Treforest New L
Treforest High L
Rhydfelin Halt
(TREFOREST ESTATE)
Nantgarw (Low)
Tonteg Plt
Edwin Isaf
Church Village
Llantwit
Taff Vale
Barry

Abertridwr

Pontypridd
Treforest

Cross Inn
Mwyndy Jct
Llantrisant
Llantrisant
Llanharry
Treferig Goods
Coedely
Coedely Col
Gilfach
Hendreforgan
Cardiac Vale Colliery
Bryn-y-Gruffydd Goods
Gyfeillion Col Ffos Col
Tonyrefail
Gilfach Junct
Llantwit Rhondda Col (High)
Gellihaidd Jct
South Rhondda Col Llanharan Jct
Llanharan
Llanharry Iron Ore Mine Sdg
Llanharry Quarry
Cwm Cae Col South Rhondda Goods
Pencoed
Howells Pencoed Private Sidings

Ystradowen
Aberthin Platform
Cowbridge Junction
Trerhyngyll + Maendy Platform
St Hilary Platform
North Aberthaw Lime Works
St Mary Church Road
Cowbridge
Cowbridge Gds
Beaupre Sdg

Llanblethien Platform
St Athan Road Quarry
St Athan Road
Pwllfrand Cement Works
Aberthaw + Bristol Channel Cement Wks
Aberthaw High Level
Station Cement Wks
Aberthaw Low Level
Aberthaw Lime + Cement
Gileston

Llantwit Major
1926
(1922)
(1904)

Peterston
Taff Vale
Great Western

Pengam Jct
CARDIFF
Crockherbtown Jct
Queen Street
General
Great Western
Taff Vale
Penarth Curve Junction
Grangetown
Clarence Road
Riverside
Bute Road
Cogan
Penarth Dock
Dinas Powis
Barry
Dingle Road Platform
PENARTH
Alberta Place Platform
Lower Penarth
Cement Works Sdg
Lavernock
Swanbridge Platform
Taff Vale
Sully
Biglis Junction
Armstrong Smelting
Cadoxton Jct
CADOXTON
Cadoxton Docks Jct
BARRY DOCKS
Syndicate Sdg
Minerals Sdg
Barry Goods
Barry Jct
BARRY
BARRY ISLAND

Rhoose
Barry

101

RAILWAYS

No	Company
R 2	WESTON CLEVEDON + PORTISHEAD
3	GREAT WESTERN
7	ALEXANDRA DOCK + RAILWAY

STATIONS

No	Name	Ry Ref
A 1	Bristol Road	2 36
2	Broadstone	2 36
3	Burrington	3 46
4	Cadbury Road §	2 47
5	(CALDICOT)	3 48
6	Clapton Road	2 47
7	Clevedon	2 47
8	Clevedon	3 47
9	Clevedon All Saints	2 47
10	Clevedon East	2 47
11	Colehouse Lane	2 46
12	Congresbury	3 46
13	Ebdon Lane	2 36
14	Ham Lane	2 36
15	Kingston Road	2 36
16	Langford	3 46
17	Llanwern	3 38
18	Magor	3 48
19	Milton Road	2 36
20	NAILSEA + BLACKWELL	3 46
21	NEWPORT High Street	3 38
22	Portbury	3 47
23	Portishead	2 47
24	Portishead	3 47
25	Portishead South	2 47
26	Puxton	3 36
27	Sandford + Banwell	3 46
28	SEVERN TUNNEL JUNCTION	3 48
29	Walton-in-Gordano	2 47
30	Walton Park	2 47
31	Weston-in-Gordano §	2 47
32	(WESTON MILTON)	3 36
33	Weston-super-Mare	2 36
34	WESTON·SUPER·MARE	3 36
35	Wick·St·Lawrence	2 36
36	Worle	3 36
37	Worle Town	2 36
38	Wrington	3 46
39	YATTON	3 46

GOODS

No	Name/Location	Ry Ref
G 1	Newport Dock Street	3 38
2	Newport Mill Street	3 38
3	Severn Tunnel	3 48
4	Portishead Dock	3 47

ENGINE SHEDS

No	Name/Location	Ry Ref
E 1	Severn Tunnel	3 48
2	Newport Ebbw	3 38
3	Newport Pill	7 38

4	Yatton	3 46
5	Weston·super·Mare	3 36

TUNNELS

No	Name	Yds	Ry Ref
T 1	Severn	7668	3 48

WATERTROUGHS

No	Name/Location	Ry Ref
W 1	Magor	3 48

BRIDGES

No	Name/Location	Ry Ref
V 1	Usk Bridge - Newport	3 38

JUNCTIONS

No.	Name/Location	Ry Ref
J 1	Ebbw	3 38
2	Park	3 38
3	Gaer	3 38
4	Pillbank	3 38
5	Maindee North	3 38
6	Maindee East	3 38
7	Maindee West	3 38
8	East Usk Branch	3 38
9	Severn Tunnel	3 48
10	Portishead	32 47
11	Worle	3 36
12	Yatton - Clevedon	3 46
13	Yatton - Cheddar	3 46
14	Wrington Valley	3 46

NOTES:

(1) REF - All in ST

(2) Alternative names for same station - for a period both used together §

(3) NEWPORT - Full details see Inset on Map 98

ST
Mill Str. Goods
North Maindee Junctions
East
West
NEWPORT High St.
V1
Dock St. Goods
East Usk Branch Jct
3
4
Severn Tunnel Goods
Severn Tunnel Jct.
E1
Severn Tunnel
Gaer Jct
Park Jcts
Ebbw Jct
E2
E3
Pillbank
8
8
SEE INSET PAGE 98
River Usk
Llanwern
Great Western
Magor
SEVERN TUNNEL JUNCTION
(CALDICOT)

Bristol Channel

Portishead Dock
Portishead
Portishead Jct
Portishead (W, C+P)
Portishead South
Portbury
Clapton Road
7
7
Cadbury Road
Weston-in-Gordano
Walton-in-Gordano
Walton Park
Clevedon All Saints
Clevedon East
Clevedon
Clevedon

113

Colehouse Lane
NAILSEA + BLACKWELL
Kingston Road
Broadstone
Great Western
Ham Lane
E4
Weston Clevedon + Portishead
Wick-St-Lawrence
YATTON
Yatton Junctions
6
6
Ebdon Lane
Warle Town
Congresbury
Wrington Valley Junction
Bristol Road
Milton Road
Puxton
Wrington Valley (Light)
Wrington
(Great Western)
Weston-super-Mare
E5
Worle Junction
Worle
(WESTON MILTON)
Langford
WESTON-SUPER-MARE
3
Sandford + Banwell
4
Burrington

Key to Railways

2		WESTON CLEVEDON + PORTISHEAD
3		GREAT WESTERN
7		ALEXANDRA DOCK + RAILWAY
X	+++++++++++	OTHER LINES

MERTHYR + ABERDARE

NOTES

(1) Ref — SN or SO; those starting with 9 are in SN, rest are in SO

(2) GREAT WESTERN + RHYMNEY JOINT ‡
   (A) Quakers Yard + Merthyr ‡
   (B) Taff Bargoed Joint ‡

(3) Aberdare Low Level — dotted red underlining indicates station is used for occasional passenger services.

(4) SPELLING — Names shown are the spellings used by Railways in the early 1920's.

RAILWAYS

No	Company
R.1	BRECON + MERTHYR
12	BRECON + MERTHYR and L+NW JOINT
2	LONDON + NORTH WESTERN
26	L+NW and RHYMNEY JOINT
3	GREAT WESTERN
30	GREAT WESTERN (Post Grouping)
34	GREAT WESTERN + TAFF VALE JOINT
36	GREAT WESTERN + RHYMNEY JOINT ‡
4	TAFF VALE
6	RHYMNEY
Z	DOWLAIS TRAMWAY
X	Other Private Lines etc

STATIONS

No	Name	Ry	Ref
A1	Aberaman	4	0101
2	Abercanaid	36	0404
3	Abercwmboi Platform	4	0200
	Aberdare		
4	Commercial St. Platform	4	9902
5	High Level	3	0002
6	Low Level	4	0002
7	Aberfan	36	0600
8	Abernant	30	0103
9	Abertysswg	1	1205
10	Bedlinog	36	0801
11	Black Lion Crossing Halt	3	9902
12	Cefn Coed	12	0207
13	Cwm Bargoed	36	0806
14	Cwmnoel Halt	3	0000
	Dowlais		
15	Cae Harris	36	0608
16	Central		
17	High Street		
18	Top		
19	Darran Deri		
20	Godreaman Halt		
21	Llwydcoed		
22	MERTHYR (TYDFIL)		
23	Mill Street Platform		
24	Pant		
25	Pantysgallog		
26	Pantysgallog Halt		
27	PENTREBACH		
28	PONTLOTTYN		
29	Pant Sam		
30	RHYMNEY		
31	Rhymney Bridge		
32	Rhymney (Pwll Ughaf)		
33	Trecynon Platform		
34	TROEDYRHIW		
35	Troedyrhiw Halt		
36	Troedyrhiwfuch Halt		

SIDINGS

No	Company/Name/Location	Ry	Ref
P1	Dyllas Drift Mine	X	9905
2	Dyllas Colliery	3X	9905
3	Bwllfa Dare Col.	4	9602
4	Bwllfa + Merthyr Dare Cols	3	9702
5	Cwmdare Colliery	3	9702
6	Llwynhelig Colliery	3	9802
7	Blaengwawr Siding	3	9802
8	Fforchaneol Siding	3	9902
9	Cwm Dare Col Sdg	4	9702
10	Duffryn Dare Col Sdg	4	9802
11	Upper Llwydcoed Sdg	3	0004
12	Werfa Dare Cols	3X	0103
13	Aberdare Iron Co	34X	0102
14	Abernant Col Sdg	4	0101
15	Old Duffryn Col Sdg	4X	0201
16	George Pit	X	0301
17	Cwmdu Drift	X	0205
18	Mountain Level	X	0106
19	Cyfarthfa Iron	12X	0307
20	Plymouth Cols	4X	0504
21	Plymouth Iron Wks	4X	0603
22	Penry-Darren Pits	X	0705
23	Naafy-Fan Colliery	36	0804
24	Bedlinog Quarry	36X	0802
25	Bedlinog Colliery	36X	0902
26	Nantwen Colliery	36	0901
27	Groesfaen Colliery	6	1201
28	Ogilvie Colliery	1	1203
29	Fochriw Colliery	36	0905
30	Tunnel Pit	36X	0906
31	Bute Iron Works	26X	1007
32	Maerdy Pits	6X	1107
33	Rhymney Iron Co	6X	1107
34	McLaren Cols	1X	1206
35	New Tredegar Cols	6	1305

JUNCTIONS

No	Name/Location	Ry	Ref
J1	Gelly Taw West	3	9705
2	Gelly Taw East	3	9705
3	Dare	3	9902
4	Blaengwawr	330	0001
5	Aberdare Low Level	430	0002
6	Dare Valley	4	9903
7	Gadlys South	43	9903
8	Gadlys North	34	9903
9	Cwmbach	4	0201
10	Brandy Bridge	4	0504
11	Joint Line	3	0405
12	Maerdy	334	0405
13	Cyfarthfa	12X	0405
14	Ynysfach	12	0405
15	Morlais	121	0510
16	Morlais East	1	0510
17	Ivor	12	0508
18	Penywern	2	0608
19	Dowlais Top	12	0708
20	Rhymney Bridge	26	1012
21	Rhydycar	123	0405
22	Fochriw	1X	0906
23	Dowlais Tramway	47	0405
24	Zig Zag Lines North	36	0607
25	Zig Zag Lines South	36	0607
26	Cwm Bargoed	36	0806
27	Pantywaen	17	0808
28	New Treclegar	6	1304
29	Deri	16	1202

ENGINE SHEDS

No	Location	Ry	Ref
E1	Aberdare	4	9802
2	Merthyr	3	0004
3	Dowlais	3X	0103
4	Cae Harris	34X	0102
5	Rhymney	4X	0201

TUNNELS

No	Name	Yds	Ry	Ref
T1	Merthyr	2495	3	0106

GOODS

No	Name	Ry	Ref
G1	Merthyr Plymouth St	4	0405
2	Middle Duffryn	12	0207
3	Trecynon	36	0806

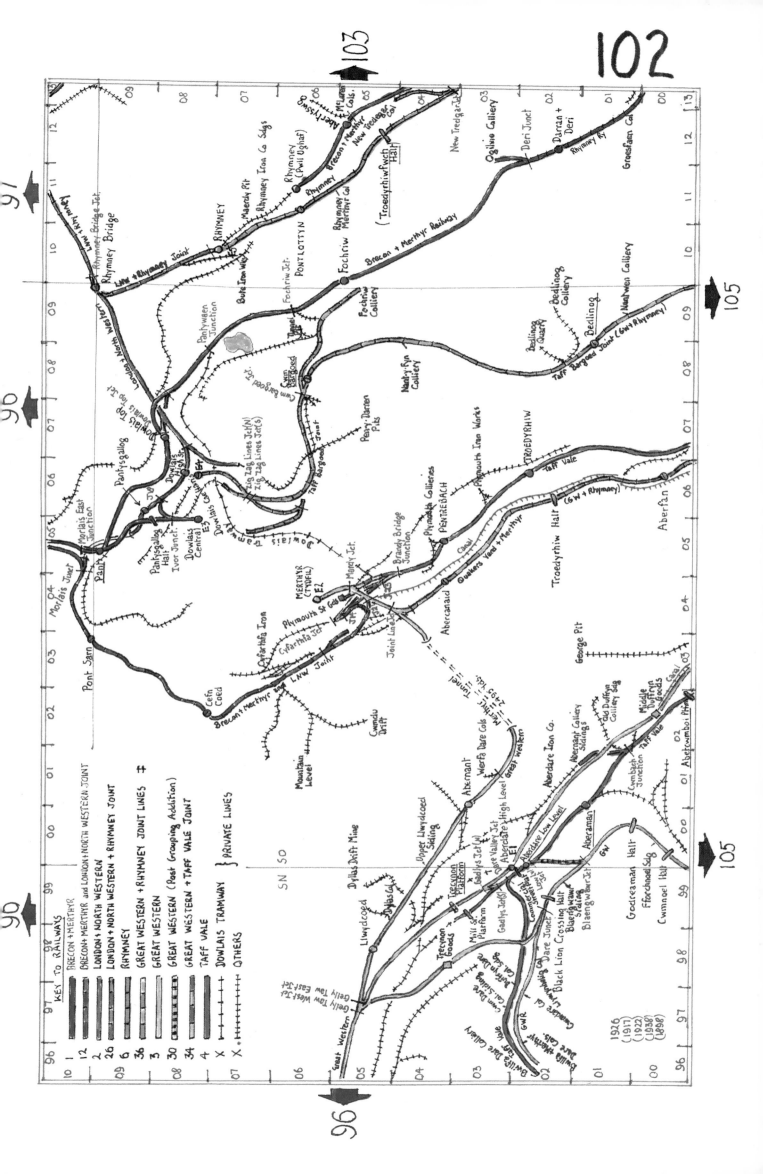

RAILWAYS

No	Company
R 1	BRECON + MERTHYR
2	LONDON + NORTH WESTERN
23	LNW + GW JOINT
3	GREAT WESTERN
6	RHYMNEY
X	Colliery Lines

STATIONS

No	Name	Ry	Ref
A 1	Aberbargoed	1	1400
2	Aberbeeg	3	2002
3	Abersychan + Talywain	23	2504
4	Abersychan Low Level	3	2604
5	Abertillery	3	2104
6	Argoed	2	1700
7	BARGOED	6	1400
8	Bedwellty Pits	2	1506
9	Blaenavon	2	2408
10	Blaenavon	3	2409
11	Blaina	3	1908
12	BRITHDIR	6	1402
13	Cwm	3	1805
14	Cwm Avon	3	2606
15	Cwmsyfiog	1	1502
16	Ebbw Vale	2	1610
17	Ebbw Vale	3	1610
18	Garndiffaith Halt	2	2605
19	Holly Bush	2	1603
20	Llanhilleth	3	2100
21	Markham Village	2	1602
22	Nantyglo	3	1810
23	New Tredegar	1	1303
24	Pontnewynydd	3	2702
25	Pontypool Clarence St.	23	2801
26	Pontypool Crane St.	3	2701
27	PONTYPOOL Road	3	2901
28	Sirhowy	2	1310
29	Tir Phil	6	1303
30	Tredegar	2	1408
31	Tylor Arms (Platform)	3	1907
32	Varteg	2	2606
33	Victoria	3	1707

GOODS

No	Location	Ry	Ref
6	1 Pontypool	3	2800

SIDINGS

No	Company / Location	Ry	Ref
P 1	Graesfaen Colliery	6	1301
2	New Tredegar Level	1	1304
3	New Tredegar Level	1	1304
4	Gwaelodywaen Sdg	1	1500
5	Abernant Siding	2	1602
6	Upper Bedwellty Cols	2X	1506
7	Trytrist Siding	2	1407
8	Deighton Iron	2	1308
9	Tredegar Iron (Tredegar)	2	1409
10	Tredegar Iron (Sirhowy)	2	1409
11	Markham Colliery	2	1602
12	Price Smith's Stone Q	3	1810
13	Marioel Colliery	3	1701
14	Llanover Colliery	3	1701
15	Westfield Colliery	3	1700
16	Daren Colliery	3	1800
17	Llanhilleth Colliery	3	2100
18	Craig Fawr Colliery	3	1803
19	Marine Colliery	3X	1804
20	Llandavel Siding	3	1804
21	Waun Llwyd Colliery	3	1707
22	Prince of Wales Colliery	3X	1608
23	Ebbw Vale Cols	23X	1609
24	Ebbw Vale Iron Works	3X	1609
25	Ebbw Vale Colliery	3X	1609
26	Griffin Colliery	X	1810
27	Jones + Co (Coalbrook)	3	1810
28	Coalbrookvale Siding	3	1809
29	Blaina Works + Cols	3X	1909
30	South Griffin Colliery	3X	1906
31	Rose Heyworth Siding	3X	2006
32	Vivians Colliery	3	2103
33	Six Bells Siding	3	2103
34	Arrai Griffin Colliery	3	2103
35	Milfraen Colliery	X	2110
36	Cwm Tillery Col	3X	2106
37	Tillery Colliery	3X	2205
38	Meadow Vein Level	V	2410
39	Blaenavon Iron Works	3V	2409
40	Tyre Mill Sidings	2	2309
41	New Slope Colliery	X	2407
42	Varteg Hill No.2 Col	X	2306
43	Lower Varteg Col	3X	2505
44	Golynos Colliery	3X	2505
45	Cwm Sychan Red Ash Col	X	2404
46	Llanerch Siding	3	2302
47	Craigddu Colliery	3X	2402
48	Cwmnantddu Cols	X	2403
49	Gellydeg Col	3	2401
50	Tir Pentwys Col	3X	2401
51	Ty-Gwyn Colliery	3X	2401
52	Glyn Collieries	V	2600
53	Mynyd Maen Col	3	2701
54	Blaendare Cols	V	2700
55	Newynydd Town Forge	3	2702
56	Elliot Pit	6	1402

No		Ry	Ref
6	Aberbeeg	3	2002
7	Abertillery	3	2104
8	Varteg Colliery	2	2408
9	Golynos	32	2505
10	Garndiffaith	2	2504
11	Abersychan Joint Line	323	2504
12	Oak Brick (Branches Fork)	3	2602
13	Pontnewynydd	3	2702
14	Trevethin	3	2702
15	Trosnant	3	2801
16	Pontypool North	3	2900
17	Pontypool East	3	2900
18	Pontypool West	32	2800
19	Pontypool Middle	3	2800
20	Pontypool South	3	2800

ENGINE SHEDS

No	Name / Location	Ry	Ref
E 1	Pontypool Road	3	2900
2	Aberbeeg	3	2002
3	Branches Fork	3	2602

JUNCTIONS

No	Name / Location	Ry	Ref
J 1	Bargoed North	6	1400
2	Bargoed South	61	1400
3	Brithdir Branch	1	1402
4	New Tredegar Branch	6	1303
5	Llanhilleth	3	2100

NOTES:

(1) REF - All in SO

(2) PONTYPOOL partly repeated on adjoining maps

(3) OVERLAP - West Margin repeated on 102. Slight extension to the North

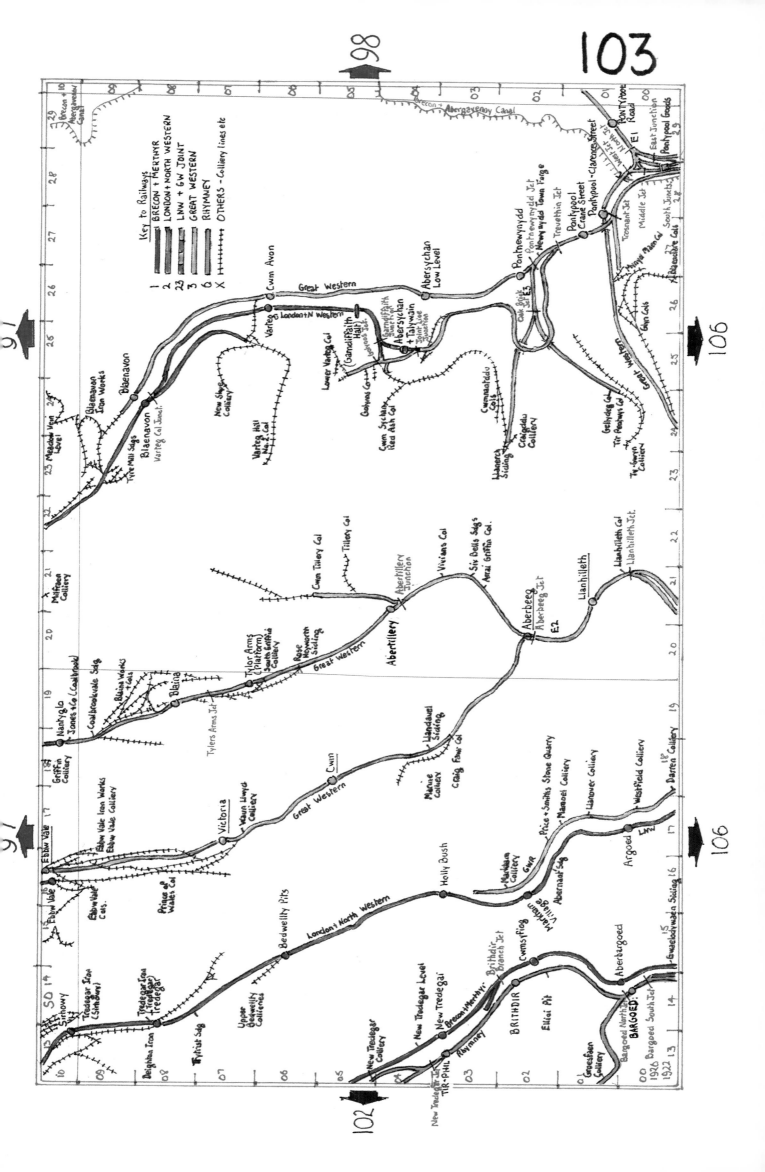

NEATH, SWANSEA + PORT TALBOT

RAILWAYS

No	Company
R1	SWANSEA + MUMBLES
2	LONDON + NORTH WESTERN
3	GREAT WESTERN
34	GREAT WESTERN + MIDLAND JOINT
4	MIDLAND
5	NEATH + BRECON
6	PORT TALBOT RAILWAY + DOCKS
7	SOUTH WALES MINERAL
8	RHONDDA + SWANSEA BAY
11	SWANSEA HARBOUR TRUST
X	OTHERS – Harbour + Colliery lines

STATIONS + HALTS

No	Name	Ry Ref
A1	Aberavon (Sea Side)	8 6589
2	Aberavon Town	8 6690
3	Briton Ferry East	8 7392
4	Briton Ferry Road	3 7193
5	Briton Ferry West	3 7392
6	(Cape Platform)	8 7294
7	Cardonnel Halt	3 7296
8	Copper Pit Halt	3 6796
9	Court Sart	8 7495
10	Cwm Avon	8 7892
11	Danygraig	8 6792
12	East Dock §✝	3 6692 G
13	HIGH STREET §✝	3 6593
14	Jersey Marine	8 7193
15	Landore High Level	3 6695
16	Landore Low Level	3 6695
17	Llansamlet	3 6996
18	Morriston	3 6797
19	Morriston	4 6797
20	Neath (R+SB)	8 7496
21	Neath Abbey	3 7396
22	Neath Bridge Street	3 7497
23	NEATH General	3 7497
24	Plas Marl	3 6695
25	Pontrhydyfen	8 7994
26	Port Talbot Central	6 7689
27	PORT TALBOT General	3 7689
28	Rutland Street ✝	1 6592 P
29	St Helen's	1 6491
30	St Thomas' ✝	4 6692
31	Skewen	3 7196
32	Swansea (R+SB) ✝	8 6692

SWANSEA

No	Name	Ry Ref
33	East Dock	69
34	HIGH STREET	
35	(R+SB)	
36	Rutland Street	
37	St Thomas'	
38	Victoria	
39	Upper Bank	§
40	Victoria	

GOODS

No	Name	Ry Ref
1	Dock	3 6593
2	East Depot	8 7193
3	High Street	3 6695
4	Wind Street	3 6695
5	Cadoxton	3 6996

SIDINGS

No	Name / Company	Ry Ref
1	Maliphant Siding ✝	1 6592 P
2	Foxhole Sidings	1 6491
3	Vivians Whitrock Works ✝	4 6692
4	Llanerch Slant Colliery	X 6693 E
5	Cwmfelin Tin	3 6594
6	Cwmburla Tin Works	3 6594
7	Mynydd Bach Colliery §	3 6692
8	Copper Pit Colliery	3 6593
9	Upper Forest Tin Plate	8 6692
10	Tir Isaf Colliery	1 6592
11	Pritchard's Siding	4 6692
12	National Oil Refineries	2 6592
13	New Melyn Colliery	4 6694
14	Pencae Slant Colliery ✝	2 6592
15	Neath Corpⁿ Electric	3x 7496
16	Eaglebush Colliery	X 7595
17	Ferry Tin Plate Works	8 7493
18	Wagon Repairs Ltd	8 7493
19	Blaenavon Branch	6 7997 J1
20	Llantwit Colliery	4 6692
21	Tongrugos Colliery	3 6693
22	Gwenffrwyd Quarry	3 6692
23	New Forest Colliery	5 7497
24	Whitworth Branch	3 6992
25	Craigddu Siding	8 7392
26	Eglaifach Mileage Sdg	4 6996
27	Cwm Avon Slant Col	78
28	Penstar Colliery	8 7588
29	Tewgoed Tramway	6 7689
30	Ynis Avon Siding	3 7888
31	Margam Forge Works	
32	Cwm Dyffryn Colliery	6 7689
33	Cwm Gwineu Colliery	6 8090
34	Dynevor Main Colliery	X 7297

ENGINE SHEDS

No	Name / Location	Ry Ref
E1	Swansea (LNW)	X 6893
2	Danygraig	3 6594
3	Swansea Dock	3 6594
4	Neath (N+B)	X 6497
5	Neath (Court Sart)	3 6696
6	Duffryn Yard	4 6797
7	Landore	X 6994
8	Upper Bank	3 6993

TUNNELS

No	Name	Yds	Ry Ref
T1	Lan-Las		3 7397
2	Gyfylchi	1109	

JUNCTIONS

No	Name / Location	Ry Ref
1	South Dock Branch	6 7997 J1
2	Rutland Street	6 7997
3	Wine Street	6 7997
4	High Street	6 7996
5	Hafod	7 7996
6	Landore North	6 8197
7	Landore South	6 8096
8	Landore West	6 7895
9	Swansea Valley	X 7792
10	Six Pit	6 7894
11	Upper Bank	X 7994
12	Harbour Branch	6 7892
13	Goods Branch	6 7190
14	East Dock	6 7889
15	King's Dock	6 8090
16	Lan-Las	X 7297
17	Skewen East	3 7196
18	Cardonnel	Ry Ref
19	Cardonnel East	2 6591
20	Jersey Marine North	8 6892
21	Jersey Marine South	3 6792
22	Canal West	5 7598
23	Canal East	3 7495
24	Cadoxton	6 7789
25	Neath	3 7694
26	Bridge Street	4 7794
27	S Wales + V of Neath	
28	Briton Ferry North	3 7497
29	Briton Ferry Middle	3 7396
30	Briton Ferry South	3 7394
31	Briton Ferry Docks	3 7393
32	Neath Loop	83 7295
33	Aberavon	86 7690
34	Burrows	86 7689
35	Plough	8 7689
36	Port Talbot East	38 7689
37	Tan-y-Groes North	6 7789
38	Tan-y-Groes South	6 7789
39	Dyffryn	3 6694
40	Margam	3 6694
41	Margam Goods	3 6594
42	Copper Works West	3436795
43	Copper Works East	434 6896
44	Copper Works North	4 6794
45	Loop	4 6693
46	Tymaen	4 6692
47	Ponthydyfen	1138 6892
48	Prossers	1138 6892
49	Blaenavon	3 7096
50	Tan Mawr West	3 7196
51	Tan Mawr East	83 7295
52	Court Sart	3 7295

NOTES:

(1) Ref – All in SS

(2) SWANSEA stations are indexed both under Swansea and under individual names indicated ✝

(3) Now known as SWANSEA §

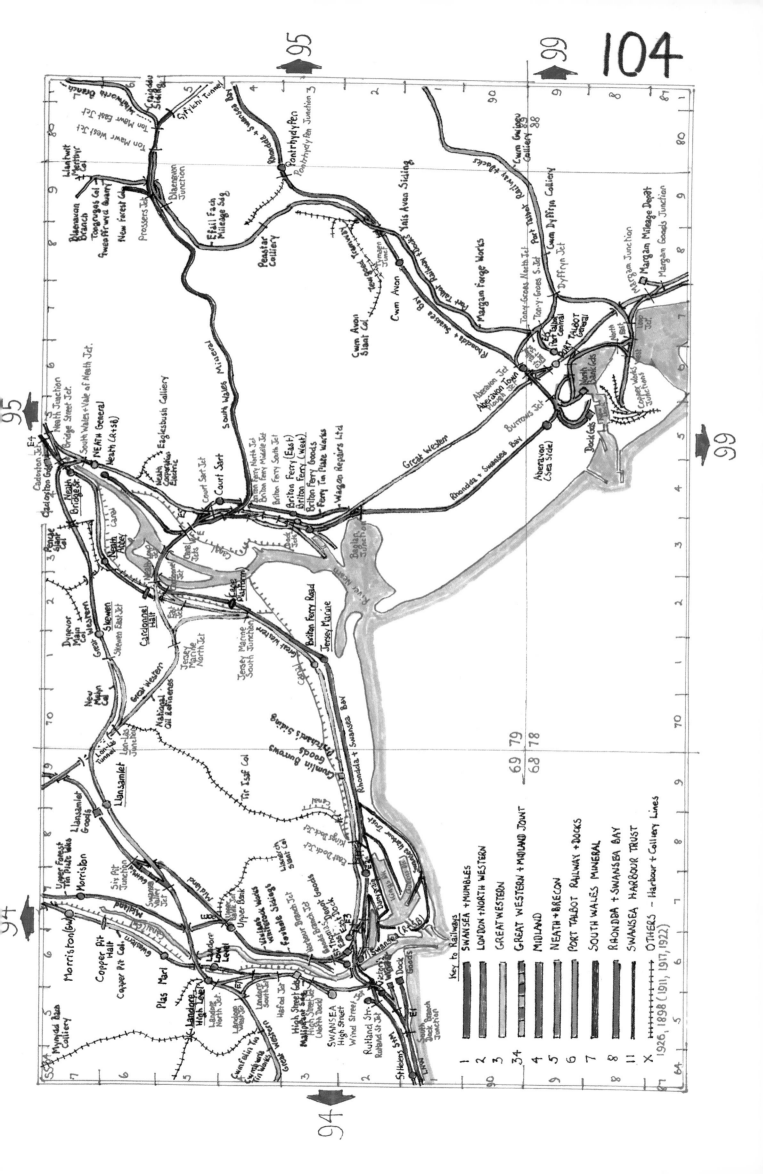

104

RAILWAYS

No.	Company
R3	GREAT WESTERN
36	GREAT WESTERN + RHYMNEY JOINT
4	TAFF VALE
5	BARRY
6	RHYMNEY
7	ALEXANDRA DOCK + RAILWAY
X	Others - Colliery lines etc

STATIONS + HALTS

No	Name	Ry Ref
A1	Abercwmboi Platform	4 0299
2	ABERCYNON	4 0795
3	Abertridwr	6 1189
4	Berw Road Platform	4 0791
5	Cilfynydd	4 0893
6	Coedpenmaen	4 0791
7	Cwmaman Colliery Halt	3 9999
8	Cwmaman Crossing Halt	3 9999
9	DINAS	4 0092
10	Ferndale	4 9997
11	Gelli Platform	4 9795
12	Glyn Taff Halt	7 0890
13	Gyfeillon Platform	4 0591
14	Llanfabon Road Platform	0995
15	LLWYNPIA	4 9994
16	Maerdy	4 9798
17	MERTHYR VALE	4 0799
18	Cardiff Road	3 0499
19	Oxford Street	4 0499
20	Nelson	4 1096
21	Nelson+Llancaiach	3 1096
22	Old Ynysybwl Platform	4 0595
23	Penrhiwceiber High Lev	3 0597
24	Penrhiwceiber Low Lev	4 0597
25	Pentre Platform	4 9696
26	Penygraig	3 9991
27	Pontcynon Platform	4 0796
28	Pontygwaith Platform	4 0094
29	PONTYPRIDD Central	4 0690
30	Pontypridd Graig	4 0795
31	Pontypridd Halt	6 1189
32	PORTH	4 0291
33	Quakers Yard High Lev	3 0897
34	QUAKERS YARD Low Level	4 0897
35	Robertstown Platform	4 0694
36	Senghenydd	6 1191
37	TONYPANDY + Trealaw	4 9992
38	Traveller's Rest Halt	4 0894
39	Trefforest Halt	7 0890
40	TREHAFOD	4 0491
41	Treharris	3 0997
42	Trelewis Platform	36 1097
43	Tylarstown	4 0094
44	Ynishir	4 0293
45	Ynysybwl	4 0594
46	YSTRAD (RHONDDA)	4 0499

GOODS

No	Location	Ry Ref
G1	Blaenclydach	3 1096
2	Clydach	4 0595
3	Cwmaman	3 0597
4	Pontypridd-Maesycoed	4 0597
5	Pontypridd-Town	4 9696
6	Porth	3 9991
7	Wattstown	4 0796
16	Duffryn Cols	4 9597
17	Nixons Navigation Col	3 0498
18	Penrhiwceiber Co	4 0597
19	Merthyr Vale Col	436 0798
20	Albion Colliery Sdg	4 9893
21	Griffith Main Quarry	3 9603
22	Ffaldcaiach Sidings	3 9999
23	Llancaiach Colliery	5 0690
24	Wernciaich Colliery	4 0691
25	Senghenydd Colliery	X6 1091

Quakers Yard:

No		Ry Ref
8	Joint Line	336 0897
9	Branch	3 0897
10	Low Level	43 0896
11	Penallta	36 1295
12	Abercynon	4 0794
13	Ynysydwr	4 0794
14	Dowlais Pits	4 0794
15	Stormstown	4 0794
16	Ynysybwl Branch	4 0793
17	Clydach Court Loop	4 0693
18	Clydach Court	4 0792
19	Pont Shon Norton	4 0791
	Pontypridd	

SIDINGS

No	Company/Name/Location	Ry Ref
P1	Dinas Maio Col	7 0790
2	Britannic Col	4 0291
3	Glamorgan Col	3 0897
4	Ffarchaman Col	4 0897
5	Cwmaman Col	4 0694
6	Ely Pits	6 1191
7	Dinas Isaf Col	4 9992
8	Citely Col	4 0894
9	National Col Sdg	7 0890
10	Tylarstown Lower	4 0491
11	Ferndale Pits	3 0997
12	Davis + Sons'	36 1097
13	Llanwonno Col	4 0094
14	Cum Siding	4 0293
15	Mynachty Col	4 0594

ENGINE SHEDS

No	Location	Ry Ref
E1	Ferndale	3 9890
2	Abercynon	3 9890

TUNNELS

No	Name	Yds	Ry Ref
T1	Quakers Yard	703	3 0797

JUNCTIONS

No	Name / Location	Ry Ref
J1	Pwllyrhebog Branch	4X 0193
2	Maerdy Branch	4 0094
3	Rhondda Fach	4 0095
4	Eirw Branch	4 0095
5	Trehafod	4 0397
6	Merthyr Vale Colliery	4 0496
7	Llancaiach	4 0496

NOTES:

(1) REF In SS a: ST - those starting 99 are in SS - the rest are in ST

(2) GREAT WESTERN + RHYMNEY Jt ‡

(A) Quakers Yard + Merthyr

(B) Taff Bargoed Joint

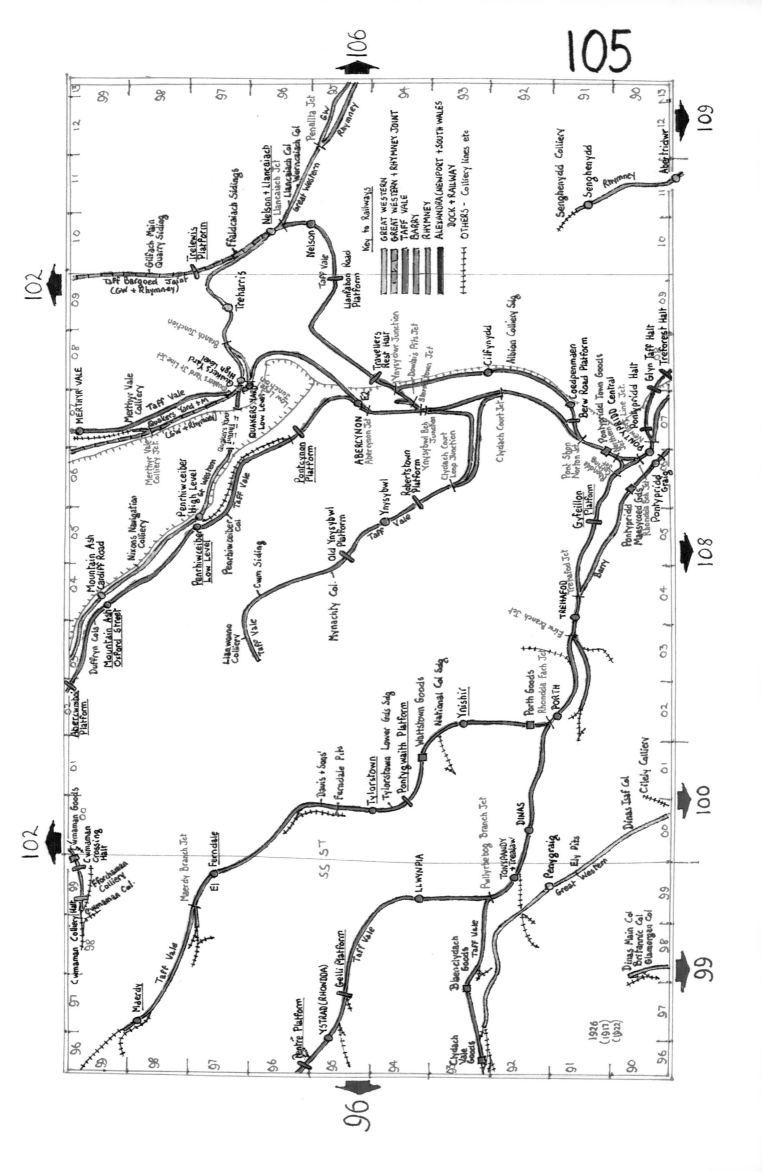

RAILWAYS

No	Company
R1	BRECON + MERTHYR
2	LONDON + NORTH WESTERN
2A	PENLLWYN TRAMWAY (LNW)
3	GREAT WESTERN
5	BARRY
6	RHYMNEY
X	OTHERS - Colliery lines etc

STATIONS + HALTS

No	Name	Ry Ref
A1	Abercarn	3 2196
2	Bedwas	1 1690
3	Blackwood	2 1798
4	Cross Keys	3 2193
5	Crumlin High Level	3 2098
6	Crumlin Low Level	3 2199
7	CWMBRAN	3 2995
8	(Cwmcarn)	3 2194
9	(Fleur-de-lis)	1 1597
10	Hafodyrynys Platform	3 2199
11	Hengoed High Level	3 1595
12	HENGOED Low Level	6 1595
13	LLANBRADACH	6 1490
14	Lower Ponthewydd	3 2997
15	Machen	1 2190
16	Maesycwmmer	1 1595
17	Newbridge	3 2097
18	Nine Mile Point	2 2081
19	(Oakdale Halt)	3 1798
20	Panteg + Griffithstown	3 2999
21	PENGAM (Glam)	6 1498
22	Pengam (Mon)	1 1598
23	(Penmaen Halt)	3 1797
24	(Penllwynmawr Halt)	3 1997
25	Pont Lawrence	2 1881
26	Pontllanfraith	2 1796
27	Pontllanfraith	3 1796
28	Ponthewydd, Lower	3 2997
29	Ponthewydd, Upper	3 2897
30	Pontrhydyrun	3 2998
31	Risca	3 2391
32	(Tirowen Halt)	3 2097
33	Trethomas	1 1890
34	Upper Ponthewydd	3 2897
35	Ynysddu	2 1793
36	YSTRAD MYNACH	6 1495

GOODS

No	Name/Location	Ry Ref
G1	Blaendare	3 2199
2	Cwmbran	3 1595
3	Nine Mile Point	6 1595
4	Penmaen	3 1797
5	Penrhiwfelin	6 1397
6	Wattsville	2A 1992
7	Ynysddu Lower	2A 1793
8	Ystradmynach	6 1495
9	(Pontypridd - see 103)	3 2999)

SIDINGS

No	Name/Company/Location	Ry Ref
P1	Grilfach Siding	1 1598
2	Pengam Brewery	1 1597
3	Gellyhaue Siding	1 1596
4	Gwerna Coke Ovens	1 1595
5	Bedwas Navigation Col	1 1890
6	Glyncwrn Siding	1 1890
7	Pands Rock Colliery	2 1799
8	Lewis's Cwm Gelly Sdg	2 2997
9	Budd + Co	2 1798
10	Marsh Siding	2 1798
11	Libanus Siding	2 1797
12	Pands Westlodge Col	2 1792
13	Cwmfelinfach Sdg	2A 1892
14	Nine Mile Point Col	2A 1992
15	Risca Colliery	3 2192
16	United Nat. Col.	3 2292
17	Danygraig Siding	3 2391
18	Tyn Cwm Brick Works	3 2491
19	Rogerstone Brick	3 2491
20	Pontymister Foundry	3 2491
21	Darran Brick Siding	3 2392
22	Cwmcarn Colliery	3 2294
23	Prince of Wales Col	3 2195
24	Gelynen Col Sdg	3 2196
25	Cwmdows Col Sdg	3 2096
26	Twyngwyn Col.	3 1997
27	Woodfield Col	3 1798
28	Oakdale Colliery	3 1899
29	Abercarn UDC	3 2098
30	Navigation Colliery	3 2099
31	Hafodyrynys Colliery	3 2399
32	Baldwins Steel	3 2999
33	Pontrhydyrun Tin	3 2998
34	Ponthewydd Tin	3X 2997
35	Cwmbran Iron	3X 2896
36	Cwmbran Colliery	X 2697
37	Healys Slope Col	X 2595
38	Oakfield Brick	3 2995
39	Cwmbran Brick	3 2995
40	Penallta Colliery	6 1396
41	Cylla Quarry	6 1396
42	Tir-Berth Sdg	6 1497
43	Bargoed Colliery	6 1598
44	Grilfach Colliery	6 1599

TUNNELS

No	Name/Location	Ry Ref
T1	Bryn	3 2391
2	Penar	3 2491
3	Hafodyrynys	3 2299

BRIDGES

No	Name	Ry Ref
V1	Crumlin Viaduct	3 2196

JUNCTIONS

No	Name/Location	Ry Ref	Ry Ref
J1	Aberbargoed	1 1599	
2	Maesycwmmer	13 1596	3 2098
3	Barry	15 1591 (1)	3 2099
4	Machen	1 2090 (2)	3 2399
5	Birch-in Hand N	2 1796	3 2999
6	Birch-in Hand Middle	23 1796	3 2998
7	Birch-in Hand South	2 1795	3X 2997
8	Nine Mile Point S	22A 1992	3X 2896
9	Nine Mile Point N	22A 1892	X 2697
10	Penllwyn Tramway	3 2X 2092	X 2595
11	Risca	3 2391	3 2995
12	Halls Road	3 2292	3 2995
13	Cwmcarn Colliery	3 2198	6 1396
14	Crumlin	3 2199	6 1396
15	Penar (Jcts)	3 1897	6 1497
16	Birch-in-Hand North	3 1796	6 1598
17	Birch-in-Hand South	3 1796	6 1599
18	Sirhowy	23 1795	
19	For Nine Mile Point	2 1795	
20	Hengoed Branch	6 1596	
21	Hengoed	36 1495	3 1695
22	Ystrad North	36 1495	3 1997
23	Ystrad South	6 1495	3 2299
24	Hengoed East	3 1595	
25	Bargoed Pits	6 1598	
26	Coed-y-bric North	3 2999	
27	Coed-y-bric South	3 2999	3 2099
28	Panteg	3 2999	
29	Cwmbran	3 2895	
30	Llantarnam	3 3085	
31	Penallta	6 1394	1 1599

NOTES

(1) REF - All in ST
(2) OVERLAP - Slight overlap to South (with 109)

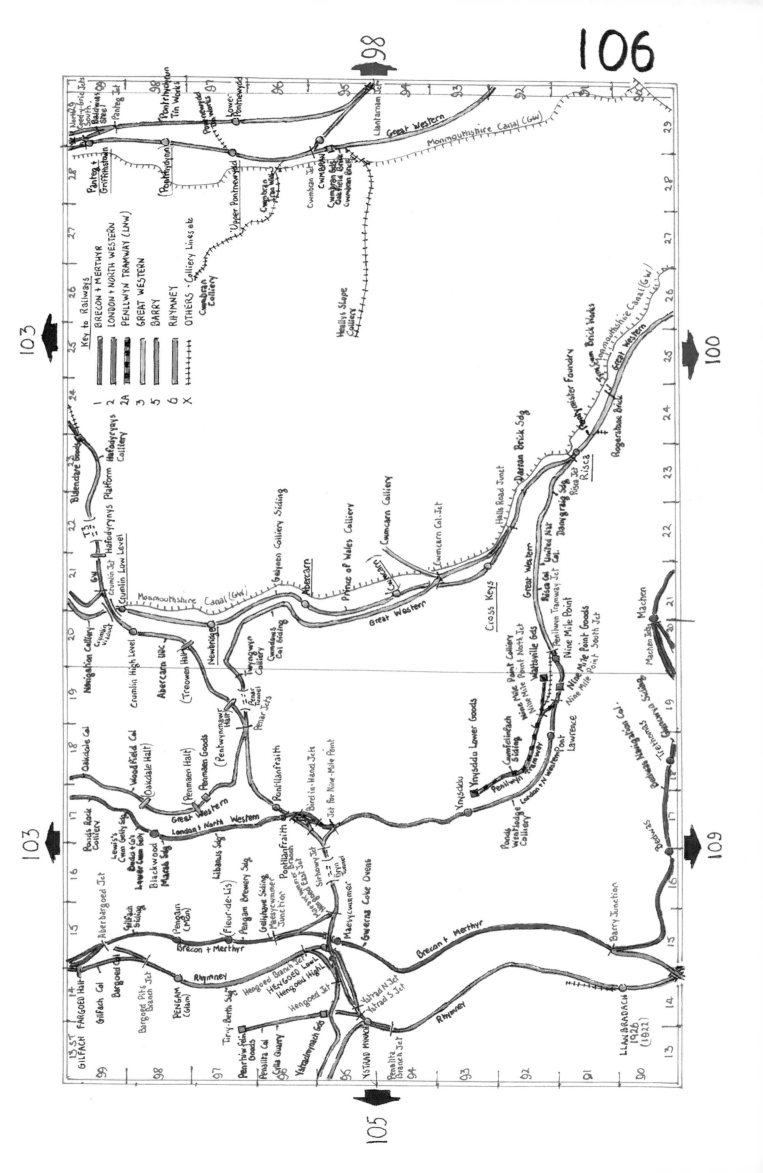

107
RAILWAYS

No.	Company
R 3	GREAT WESTERN
5	BARRY
6	PORT TALBOT
X	OTHERS - Colliery lines etc

STATIONS

No.	Name	Ry Ref
A 1	Bettws	6 98
2	Black Mill	3 98
3	BRIDGEND	3 98
4	Brynmenyn	3 98
5	Cwmdu	6 89
6	Kenfig Hill	3 88
7	Llangeinor	3 98
8	Llangonoyd	3 88
9	Lletty Brongu	6 88
10	Maesteg Castle Street	3 89
11	Maesteg Neath Road	6 89
12	Ogmore Vale	3 99
13	Pont-y-Cwmmer	3 99
14	Pont-y-Rhyll	3 98
15	Pyle ⚒	3 88
16	Pyle ⚒	3 88
17	Tondu	3 88
18	Troedyrhiew Garth	3 89

GOODS

No	Name	Ry Ref
G 1	Bridgend + Coity	5 98

SIDINGS

No	Name/Company/Location	Ry Ref
P 1	Pant Mawr Quarries	X 88
2	Bryndu Sidings	6X 88

No	Name	Ref
3	Aber Baiden Colliery	6X 88
4	Ton Phillip Colliery	6X 88
5	Tondu Gas Siding	3 88
6	Cedfyw Rhondda Colliery	6 88
7	Gelli Hir Colliery	6 88
8	Llynvi Valley Colliery	3X 88
9	Celtic Garth Colliery	3X 88
10	Cwm Cerwin East End Col	X 89
11	Norths Nav. No 9 Col Sdg	3X 89
12	Maesteg Deep Cols	X 89
13	Llynvi Gas Co	3 89
14	Oakwood Colliery Sdg	3X 89
15	Garth Colliery (Celtic)	6 89
16	Ffaldau Colliery	(3)X 89
17	Bridgend Aberthaw Lime	5 98
18	National Aberthaw Lime	5 98
19	Maendy Colliery	3 98
20	Bryncethin Colliery	3X 98
21	Bryncethin Milage Sdg	3 98
22	Lewis Merthyr Colliery	3 98
23	Rhondda Main Colliery	3 98
24	Llest Colliery	3X 99
25	New Briach-y-Cymmer Col	3X 99
26	Wyndham Pits	3 99
27	Aber Sidings	3 99

ENGINE SHEDS

No	Location	Ry Ref
E 1	Tondu	3 88
2	Bridgend	3 98

TUNNELS

No	Name	Yds	Ry Ref
T 1	Cwm Cerwin		3 89

JUNCTIONS

No	Name/Location	Ry Ref
J 1	Waterhall	6 88
	Pyle:	88
2	Great Western + Port Talbot	36 88
3	West	3 88
4	Middle	3 88
5	East	3 88
6	South	3 88
	Tondu:	88
7	North	3 88
8	Station	3 88
9	East	3 88
10	Cowbridge Road	5 97
11	Bridgend South	35 98
12	Bridgend North	3 98
13	Coity	3(5) 98
14	Bryncethin	3 98
15	Ynisawdre	3 98
16	Tynycoed	3 98
17	Brynmenyn	3 98
18	Black Mill	3 98
19	Ogmore Valley	3 98
20	Pont-y Rhyll	3 98
21	Aber Baiden Colliery	6X 88
22	Cefn	36 88

NOTES:

(1) REF All in SS

(2) Pyle ⚒ Operated as two stations as a legacy of the Broad Guage. Stations finally combined officially in the 20's

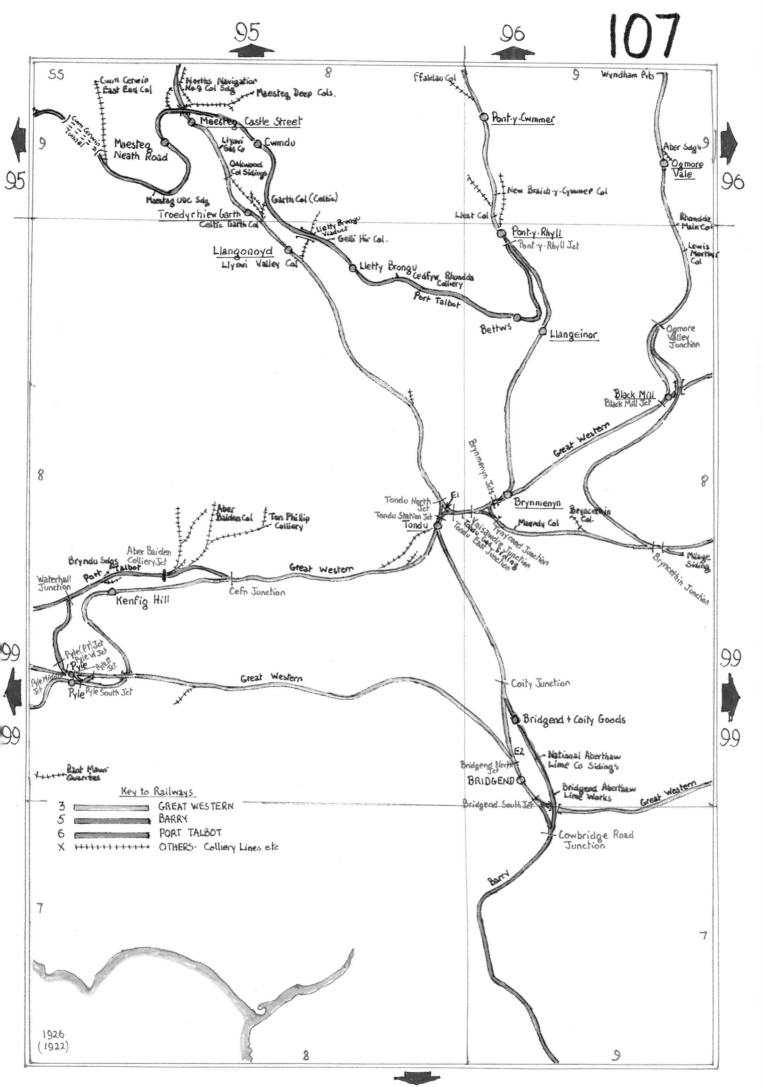

95

96

55

8

9

Cwm Cerwin
East End Col

Norths Navigation
No.9 Col Sdg

Maesteg Deep Cols.

Ffaldau Col

Wyndham Pits

9

Cwm Cerwin
Tunnel

Maesteg Castle Street

Pont-y-Cwmmer

Maesteg
Neath Road

Llynvi
Gas Co

Cwmdu

Aber Sdgs

9

9

Ogmore
Vale

Oakwood
Col Sidings

New Braich-y-Cymmer Col

95

96

Rhondda
Main Col

Maesteg UDC Sdg

Garth Col (Celtic)

Lliest Col

Lewis
Merthyr
Col

Troedyrhiew Garth

Celtic Garth Col

Lletty Brongu
Viaduct

Gelli Hir Col.

Pont-y-Rhyll

Pont-y-Rhyll Jct

Llangonoyd

Llynvi Valley Col

Lletty Brongu

Cedfyw
Colliery

Rhondda

Port Talbot

Ogmore
Valley
Junction

Bettws

Llangeinor

Black Mill

Great Western

Black Mill Jct

8

8

Aber
Baiden Col

Ton Phillip
Colliery

Tondu North
Jct

E1

Brynmenyn Jcts

Tondu Station Jct

Ynisawdre Junction

Brynmenyn

Tynycoed Junction

Tondu

Tondu East Junction

Maendy Col

Bryncethin
Col.

Aber Baiden
Colliery Jct

Great Western

Bryndu Sdgs

Port
Talbot

Bryncethin Junction

Milage
Siding

Waterhall
Junction

Cefn Junction

Kenfig Hill

99

Pyle (PT) Jct

Pyle W Jct

Pyle

Pyle Jct

99

Pyle Middle
Jct

Pyle South Jct

Pyle

Great Western

Coity Junction

99

99

Bridgend + Coity Goods

E2

National Aberthaw
Lime Co Sidings

Bridgend North
Jct

BRIDGEND

Bridgend Aberthaw
Lime Works

Great Western

Bridgend South Jct

Cowbridge Road
Junction

Pant Mawr
Quarries

Barry

Key to Railways

3 ————————— GREAT WESTERN
5 ————————— BARRY
6 ————————— PORT TALBOT
X ++++++++++ OTHERS· Colliery Lines etc

7

7

1926
(1922)

8

9

99

108
RAILWAYS

No	Company
R 3	GREAT WESTERN
4	TAFF VALE
5	BARRY
6	RHYMNEY
7	ALEXANDRA DOCK & RAILWAY
8	CARDIFF
X	OTHER - Colliery Lines etc

STATIONS & HALTS

No	Name	Ry Ref
A 1	Beddau Halt	4 0684
2	Church Village	4 0886
3	Creigiau	5 0881
4	Cross Inn	4 0583
5	Dynea Halt	7 0988
6	Efail Isaf	5 0885
7	Glan-y-Llyn	8 1185
8	Glyn Taff Halt	7 0889
9	Groeswen Halt	7 1187
10	Llanharry	4 0180
11	Llantrisant ⚒	3 0381
12	Llantrisant ⚒	4 0381
13	Llantwit	4 0785
14	Nant Garw Halt Low Lev	8 1186
15	Peterston	3 0776
16	PONTYPRIDD Central	4 0789
17	Pontypridd Graig	5 0689
18	Pontypridd Halt	7 0789
19	Rhydfelin Halt	8 0888
20	Rhydfelin Halt - High Level	7 0888
21	St Fagan's	3 1177
22	Tonteg Platform	4 0986

PONTYPRIDD + LLANTRISANT

No	Name	Ry Ref
23	(TREFFOREST ESTATE)	4 1086
24	Treforest Halt	7 0889
25	Treforest High Level	5 0788
26	TREFOREST Low level	4 0789
27	Upper Boat	8 0987
28	Upper Boat Halt	7 1087

GOODS

No	Name / Location	Ry Ref
G 1	St Fagan's	5 1177
2	Treferig	4 0387
3	Treforest - Llantwit Road	5 0788

SIDINGS

No	Name/Company/Location	Ry Ref
P 1	Mountford & Phillips Sdg	3 0282
2	Cambrian Works	3 0282
3	Cardiff Nav. Col. Siding	3 0381
4	Bute Siding	3 0582
5	Mwyndy Saw Mills	3 0582
6	Brofiskin Lime	3 X 0681
7	Cottage Siding	4 0582
8	Glyn Colliery	4 X 0288
9	Castellau Sdg	4 0486
10	Gelynog Colliery	X 0585
11	Cwm (Llantwit) 6 W Col	4 0684
12	Tarygoed Colliery	4 0683
13	South Cambria Colliery	4 X 0883
14	Creigiau Colliery & Quarry	4 0882
15	Pantycored Siding	4 0881
16	Treforest Tin Works	4 0887
17	Newbridge Works	7 0889
18	Pontypridd Gas Works	7 0889

ENGINE SHEDS

No	Location	Ry Ref
E 1	Llantrisant	3 0381

TUNNELS

No	Name/Location	YDS	Ry Ref
T 1	Pontypridd	1373	5 0789
2	Wenvoe	1868	5 1175

JUNCTIONS

No	Name / Location	Ry Ref
J 1	Llantrisant (TV)	43 0381
2	Llantrisant North	3 0381
3	Llantrisant South	3 0381
4	Mwyndy	3 0382
5	Maesraul	34 0482
6	Llantrisant Common	34 0285
7	Peterston West	35 0876
8	Peterston South	5 0877
9	Peterston East	35 0877
10	Tyn-y-Caeau for Penrhos	5 1078
11	Tyn-y-Caeau for St Fagan's	5 1077
12	St Fagan's North	5 1177
13	St Fagan's West	35 1177
14	St Fagan's East	35 1177
15	Drope	5 1176
16	Tonteg	5 0986
17	Llantwit Road	5 0888
18	Newport Line	47 0789
19	Treforest North	4 0888
20	Treforest South	48 0888
21	Llantrisant Branch	4 0987
22	Taffs Well Siding	4 X 1184
23	South Cambria	4 X 0882
24	Tarygoed	4 0583
25	Common Branch	4 0583
26	Gelynog Branch	4 X 0584
27	Treferig Railway	4 0484

NOTES:

(1) REF   All in ST

(2) Llantrisant - one station worked as two due to gauge - and in view of separate pre-grouping companies ⚒

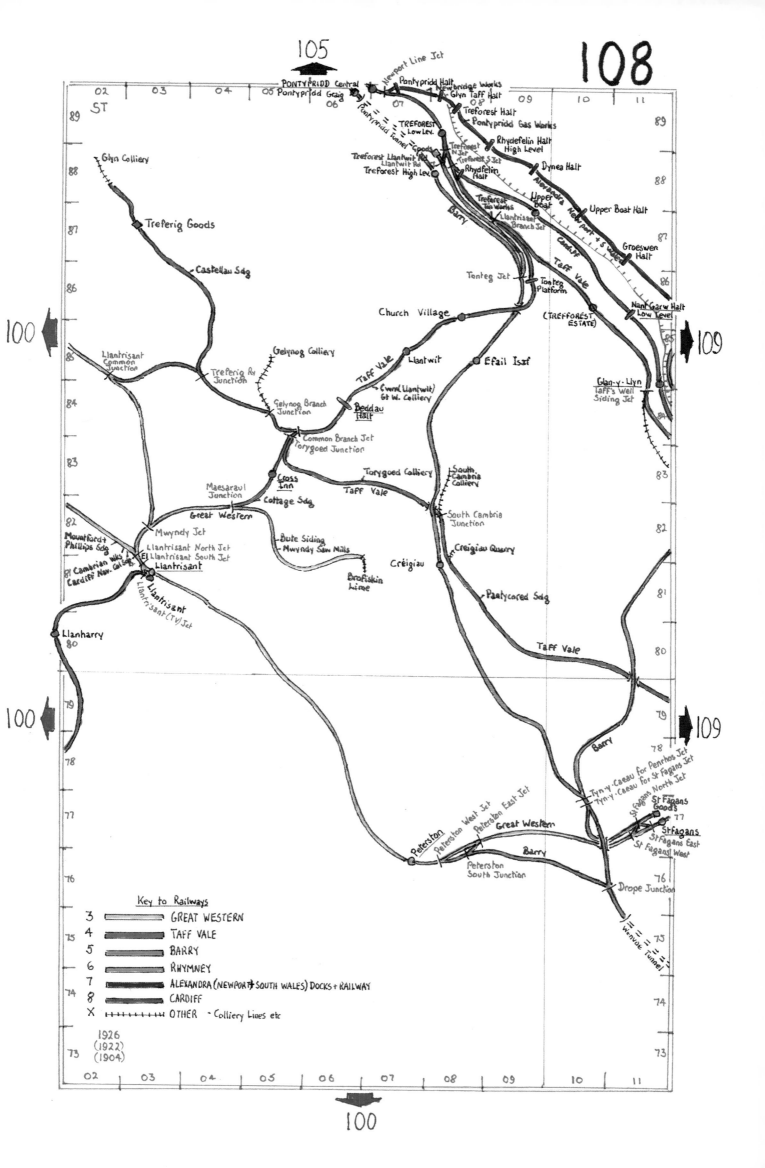

Glyn Colliery

Treferig Goods

Castellau Sdg

Pontypridd Graig
Pontypridd Central
Newport Line Jct
Pontypridd Halt
Newbridge Works
Glyn Taff Halt
Treforest Halt
Pontypridd Gas Works
TREFOREST Low Lev.
Rhydefelin Halt High Level
Treforest Goods
Pontypridd Tunnel
Treforest Llantwit Rd
Llantwit Rd
Treforest N Jct
Treforest S Jct
Rhydfelin Halt
Dynea Halt
Treforest High Lev.
Barry
Treforest Tin Works
Upper Boat
Upper Boat Halt
Llantrisant Branch Jct
Alexandra (Newport + S Wales)
Cardiff
Taff Vale
Groeswen Halt

Tonteg Jct
Tonteg Platform
(TREFFOREST ESTATE)
Nant Garw Halt Low Level

Church Village

Llantrisant Common Junction

Gelynog Colliery

Treferig Rv Junction

Taff Vale
Llantwit
Efail Isaf

Glan-y-Llyn
Taff's Well Siding Jct

Gelynog Branch Junction

Cwm (Llantwit) Gt W. Colliery
Beddau Halt

Common Branch Jct
Torygoed Junction

Maesaraul Junction

Cross Inn

Cottage Sdg
Great Western

Torygoed Colliery

South Cambria Colliery

Taff Vale

South Cambria Junction

Mountford + Phillips Sdg
Mwyndy Jct
Llantrisant North Jct
Llantrisant South Jct
Cambrian Wks
Cardiff New. Col Sdg
Llantrisant

Bute Siding
Mwyndy Saw Mills

Brofiskin Lime

Créigiau

Créigiau Quarry

Pantycored Sdg

Llantrisant (Ty) Jct

Llanharry

Taff Vale

Barry

Tyn-y-Caeau for Penrhos Jct
Tyn-y-Caeau for St Fagans Jct
St Fagans North Jct
St Fagans Goods
St Fagans
St Fagans East
St Fagans West

Peterston
Peterston West Jct
Peterston East Jct
Great Western
Barry

Peterston South Junction

Drope Junction

Wenvoe Tunnel

Key to Railways

3	GREAT WESTERN
4	TAFF VALE
5	BARRY
6	RHYMNEY
7	ALEXANDRA (NEWPORT + SOUTH WALES) DOCKS + RAILWAY
8	CARDIFF
X	OTHER - Colliery Lines etc

1926
(1922)
(1904)

109 RAILWAYS

No	Company
R 1	BRECON + MERTHYR
2	LONDON + NORTH WESTERN
3	GREAT WESTERN
38	GREAT WESTERN + CARDIFF JOINT
4	TAFF VALE
5	BARRY
6	RHYMNEY
7	ALEXANDRA DOCKS + RAILWAY
8	CARDIFF
X	OTHERS – Mineral + Private

STATIONS + HALTS

No	Name		Ry Ref
A 1	ABER	§3	6 1487
2	Abertridwr		6 1189
3	BEDDAU HALT	§1	6 1487
4	Bedwas		1 1689
5	(BIRCHGROVE)		8 1681
6	BUTE ROAD	⚥§11†	4 1975
7	CAERPHILLY		6 1587
	CARDIFF		
8	BUTE ROAD	⚥§11	4 1975
9	CENTRAL	§12	3 1876
10	Clarence Road		3 1875
11	DOCKS	⚥§8	4 1975
12	GENERAL	§9	3 1876
13	Parade		6 1877
14	QUEEN STREET		4 1877
15	Riverside		3 1876
16	CATHAYS	§48	4 1878
17	(CEFN-ONN)		6 1785
18	Clarence Road	†	3 1875
19	CORYTON Halt		8 1481
20	Ely (Main Line)	✗	3 1477
21	Fountain Bridge Halt		1 1889
22	Glan-y-Llyn		8 1185
23	GRANGETOWN		4 1775
24	Groeswen Halt		7 1187
25	Gwernydomen Halt		1 1788
26	(HEATH HIGH LEVEL)		6 1881
27	HEATH LOW LEVEL Halt		8 1881
28	LLANDAFF		4 1480
29	LLANISHEN		6 1782
30	Machen		1 2089
31	Maindy North Road Platform		1779 / 4 1779
32	Nant Garw Halt – High Lev	7	1286
33	Nant Garw Halt – Low Level	8	1186
34	Parade	†	6 1877
35	Penarth Dock		4 1773
36	Penyrheol		6 1338
37	QUEEN STREET	†	4 1877
38	RADYR		4 1381
39	RHIWBINA Halt		8 1581
40	Riverside	†	3 1876
41	St Fagan's		3 1271
42	TAFF'S WELL		4(6) 1283
43	Tongwynlais		8 1382
44	Trethomas		1 1889
45	Waterloo Halt		1 1988
46	Wenvoe		5 1274
47	WHITCHURCH (S Glam.)		8 1581
48	WOODVILLE ROAD PLATFORM		1878 / §16 4 1878

GOODS

No	Name / Location		Ry Ref
G 1	Adam Street	†	6 1977
2	Canton Coal + Goods	†	3 1677
3	Cardiff Dock	†	4 1876
4	Cardiff LNW	†	2 1876
5	Eneurglyn		5 1488
6	Fairwater Road	✗	4 1478
7	Newport Road	†	4 2078
8	Newtown	†	3 1977
9	Penarth Dock + Harbour		4 1873
10	Roath	†	3 2078
11	St Fagan's		5 1277
12	Waterhall		4 1478

SIDINGS

No	Name / Company / Location	Ry Ref
P 1	Bedwas Navigation Col	1 1789
2	Glyngwyn Siding	1 1889
3	Machen Forge	1X 2089
4	Pwllclu Colliery	1X 2088
5	Waterloo Tin Plate Works	1X 1988
6	Crosswells Brewery	3 1477
7	Penarth Tidal Harbour	4 1874
8	Windsor Slipway	4 1874
9	Gas Works (Grangetown)	4 1775
10	Llandough Lime + Brick	4 1774
11	Canton Siding	4 1676
12	Ely Paper Mills Sdg	4 1577
13	Star Fuel Works	4 1778
14	Maindy Fuel Works	4 1679
15	Dumballs Siding	3 1876
16	Cardiff Canal Sdg	3 1876
17	Alps Quarry Siding	5 1273
18	Trebur Quarry	1 1589
19	Cairn Street Siding	6 1878
20	Cathays Siding	6 1879
21	Wernddu Colliery	6X 1686
22	Rockwood Colliery	6 1284
23	Portobello Quarry	6 1284
24	Phoenix Brick Works	8 1681

COMPANY WORKS

No	Name / Location	Ry Ref
C 1	Rhymney – Caerphilly	6 1687

ENGINE SHEDS ⚇

No	Name		Ry Ref
E 1	Canton	‡	3 1776
2	Cathays	‡	4 1878
3	East Dock	‡	3 1976
4	Radyr		3 1380
5	Taff's Well		6 1284

TUNNELS

No	Name (Location)	Yds	Ry Ref
T 1	Caerphilly	1933	6 1785
2	Wenvoe	1868	5 1275
3	Walnut Tree		5 1282
4	Cogan		5 1673

BRIDGES ETC

No	Name	Ry Ref
V 1	Walnut Tree Viaduct	5 1283

JUNCTIONS

No	Name	Ry Ref
J 1	Machen Jcts	1 2089
2	Machen Forge Siding	1X 1989
3	Tin Works	1 1788
4	B+M and Rhymney	16 1587
5	Penarth Harbour (1)	4 1773
6	Penarth Barry (2)	45 1773
7	Penarth Dock (3)	4 1773
8	Grangetown	4 1775
	CARDIFF	
9	Penarth Curves North	34 1776
10	Penarth Curves South	34 1776
11	Penarth Curves East	3 1776
12	East Branch	4 1877
13	Crockherbtown	46 1877
14	Adam Street	6 1977
15	Long Dyke	3 1977
16	Tyndall Street	6 1977
17	Roath Basin	38 1976
18	Splott	38 2076
19	Roath Dock SE	48 2076
20	Roath Dock N	48 2076
21	GW + Joint Line	338 2077
22	Pengam	3 2078
23	Newport Road	4 1979
24	Roath Branch	4 1580
25	Waterhall	4 1478
26	Penarth Branch	4 1380
27	Pentyrch	4X 1282
28	Taffs Well / Walnut Tree	46 1283
29	Taffs Well Siding	4X 1184
30	Penrhos Lower	5 1285
31	Penrhos Upper	56 1386
32	Penrhos	67 1386
33	Beddau Loop	6 1386
34	Watford Crossing	6 1486
35	Caerphilly West Branch	6 1587
36	Caerphilly East Branch	6 1587
37	Caerphilly Loco Works	6 1586
38	Wernddu	6X 1686
39	Heath	68 1880
40	Beddau North	6 1487
41	Aber Branch	6 1487
42	Eneurglyn South	56 1488
43	Eneurglyn Goods	5 1488
44	Eneurglyn North	5 1488
45	St Fagans West	35 1177
46	St Fagans East	35 1177
47	St Fagans North	5 1177

NOTES:

(1) REF – All in ST

(2) NAME CHANGE – Modern §
              – Early §

(3) Change of name was in 20's ⚥

(4) CARDIFF – Central area station †

(5) CARDIFF Area Goods station †

(6) CARDIFF Engine Shed ‡

(7) SHEDS – see map for details ⚇

(8) Suffix added in 20's ✗ when new station near to Fairwater Goods also open to passengers

(9) Opened as Ely (to passengers) see Note 8 above ✗

(10) Alternative names to same Junction J28

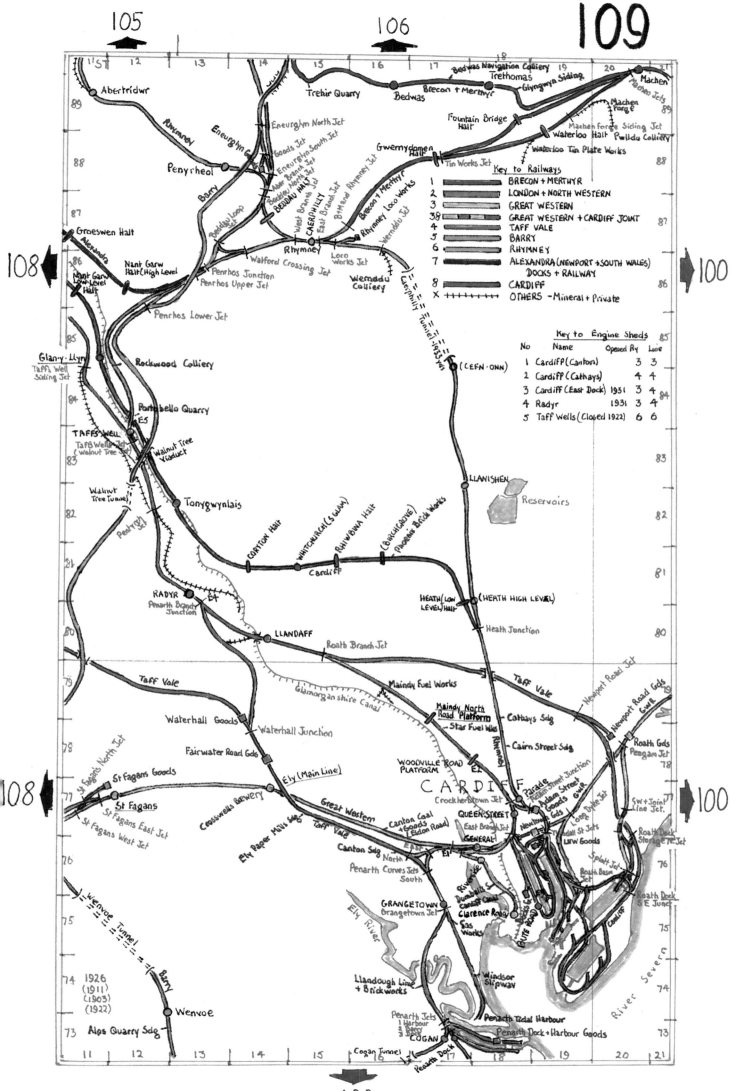

Abertridwr

Trehir Quarry

Bedwas

Bedwas Navigation Colliery

Trethomas

Brecon + Merthyr

Glynwyn Siding

Machen

Machen Jcts

Machen Forge

Machen Forge Siding Jct

Pwllda Colliery

Waterloo Halt

Waterloo Tin Plate Works

Fountain Bridge Halt

Rhymney

Eneuralyn C

Penyrheol

Barry

Eneurglyn North Jct

Goods Jct

Eneurglyn South Jct

Mar Branch Jct

Bedley North Jct

BEUDAU HALT

West Branch Jct

CAERPHILLY

East Branch Jct

B+M and Rhymney Jct

Brecon + Merthyr

Rhymney Loco Works

Gwernydomen Halt

Tin Works Jct

Key to Railways

1		BRECON + MERTHYR
2		LONDON + NORTH WESTERN
3		GREAT WESTERN
38		GREAT WESTERN + CARDIFF JOINT
4		TAFF VALE
5		BARRY
6		RHYMNEY
7		ALEXANDRA (NEWPORT + SOUTH WALES) DOCKS + RAILWAY
8		CARDIFF
X		OTHERS — Mineral + Private

Key to Engine Sheds

No	Name	Opened	By	Line
1	Cardiff (Canton)		3	3
2	Cardiff (Cathays)		4	4
3	Cardiff (East Dock)	1931	3	4
4	Radyr	1931	3	4
5	Taff Wells (Closed 1922)		6	6

Groeswen Halt

Alexandra

Nant Garw Halt (High Level)

Beddau Loop Jct

Watford Crossing Jct

Rhymney

Loco Works Jct

Rhymney Loco Works Jct

Wernddu Jct

Penrhos Junction

Penrhos Upper Jct

Wernddu Colliery

Nant Garw Low Level Halt

Penrhos Lower Jct

Caerphilly Tunnel 1953 yds

Glan-y-Llyn

Taffs Well Siding Jct

Rockwood Colliery

(CEFN-ONN)

Portobello Quarry

E5

TAFFS WELL

Taff B Well Jct (Walnut Tree Jct)

Walnut Tree Jct

Walnut Tree Viaduct

LLANISHEN

Reservoirs

Walnut Tree Tunnel

Tonygwynlais

Pentyrch Jct

CORYTON HALT

WHITCHURCH (LS QLAY)

RHIWBINA HALT

(BIRCHGROVE)

Phoenix Brick Works

Cardiff

HEATH (LOW LEVEL) HALT

(HEATH HIGH LEVEL)

RADYR

E4

Penarth Branch Junction

LLANDAFF

Roath Branch Jct

Heath Junction

Heath Junction

Taff Vale

Taff Vale

Newport Road Jct

Maindy Fuel Works

Newport Road Gds GWR

Glamorganshire Canal

Maindy North Road Platform

Cathays Sdg

Waterhall Goods

Waterhall Junction

Star Fuel Wks

Cairn Street Sdg

Roath Gds

Pengam Jct

Fairwater Road Gds

Rhymney

St Fagans North Jct

WOODVILLE ROAD PLATFORM

E2

CARDIFF

St Fagans Goods

Ely (Main Line)

Crosswells Brewery

Great Western

Crockherbtown Jct

Adam Street Goods GWR

Roath Branch Junction

St Fagans

Taff Vale

Canton Coal + Goods (Eldon Road)

QUEEN STREET

Parade

SW + Joint Line Jct.

St Fagans East Jct

St Fagans West Jct

Ely Paper Mills Sdg

Taff Vale

Canton Sdg North

GENERAL

East Branch Jct

NewTown

Adam Street Goods GWR

Long Dyke Jct

Roath Dock Storage Jct

East Jct

E1

Tyndall St Jcts

LNW Goods

Penarth Curves Jcts North

Roath Basin Jct

Splott Jct

GRANGETOWN

Grangetown Jct

Riverside

Bute Rd

Clarence Road

Cardiff Canal

Roath Dock SE Junc

Gas Works

Bute Road

Cardiff

Ely River

Llandough Line + Brickworks

Windsor Slipway

River Severn

Wenvoe Tunnel

1926 (1911) (1903) (1922)

Barry

Wenvoe

Penarth Jcts 1 Harbour 2 Barry 3 Barry

Penarth Tidal Harbour

Alps Quarry Sdg

COGAN

Penarth Dock + Harbour Goods

Cogan Tunnel

Penarth Dock

BRISTOL + CHELTENHAM

RAILWAYS

No.	Company
R14	SOMERSET + DORSET (LSW + Mid)
2	LONDON + NORTH WESTERN
3	GREAT WESTERN
34A	SEVERN + WYE (GW + Mid)
34B	CLIFTON EXTENSION (GW + Mid)
34C	GW + MIDLAND (other Joint Lines)
4	MIDLAND

STATIONS

No.	Name	Ry Ref
A 1	Ashchurch	4 093
2	Ashley Hill	† 3 T67
3	(Ashton Gate Platform	† 3 T57
4	Ashton-under-Hill	4 093
5	Avoncliff Halt	3 T86
6	AVONMOUTH Dock	34B T57
7	(AVONMOUTH - ST ANDREWS ROAD	3 T58
8	Awre (for Blakeney)	3 060
9	Badminton	3 T88
10	Ballingham	3 053
11	Barber's Bridge	3 072
12	BATH (SPA)	3 T76
13	Bathampton	3 T76
14	Bath Green Park	4 T76
15	Beanacre Halt	3 T96
16	Beckford	4 093
17	BEDMINSTER	† 3 T57
18	Berkeley	34A 060
19	Berkeley Road	434A 070
20	(Bilson Halt)	3 061
21	Bishop's Cleeve	3 092
22	Bitton	4 T67
23	Bowbridge Crossing Halt	3 080
24	Box	3 T86
25	BRADFORD (-ON-AVON)	3 T86
26	Bredon	4 093
27	Brimscombe	3 080
28	Brimscombe Bridge Halt	3 080
29	Brislington	† 3 T67

BRISTOL

No.	Name	Ry Ref
30	Ashley Hill	3 T67
31	Ashton Gate Platform	3 T57
32	BEDMINSTER	3 T57
33	Brislington	3 T66
34	Clifton Bridge	3 T57
35	CLIFTON DOWN	34B T57
✳	Hotwells	34B T57
36	LAWRENCE HILL	3 T67
37	MONTPELIER	34B T57
38	(PARSON STREET)	3 T57
39	REDLAND	34B T57
40	St. Anne's Park	3 T67
✳	St Philips §	4 T57
✳	STAPLETON ROAD	3 T67
✳	TEMPLE MEADS §	34C T57
41	(BRISTOL PARKWAY)	3 T68
42	Bromham + Rowde	3 T96
43	Bullo Cross Halt	3 060
44	Calne	3 T97
45	Cam	4 T79
46	Chalford	3 080
47	Charfield	4 T79
48	Charlton Halt	3 T58
49	Charlton King's	3 091

CHELTENHAM

No.	Name	Ry Ref
50	High Street Halt	3 092
51A	LANSDOWN §51B	4 092
52	Malvern Road	3 092
53	St James	3 092
54	South + Leckhampton	3 091
51B	SPA §51A	4 092
55	CHEPSTOW	3 T59
56	CHIPPENHAM	3 T97
57	Chipping Sodbury	3 T78
58	Churchdown	34 081
59	Cinderford	34A(3)061
60	Cleeve	4 092
61	Clifton Bridge	† 3 T57
62	CLIFTON DOWN	† 34B T57
63	Coaley (Junction)	4 070
64	Coalpit Heath	3 T68
65	Coleford	3 051
66	Coleford	34A 051
67	Corsham	3 T86
68	Culkerton	3 T99
69	Dauntsey	3 T98
70	Devizes	3 T96
71	Downfield Crossing Halt	3 080
72	Drybrook Halt	3 061
73	Drybrook Road	34A 061
74	Dudbridge	4 080
75	Dursley	4 T79
75A	Dymock	3 062
76	Ebley Crossing Halt	3 080
77	Fawley	3 052
78	Filton Halt (North)	3 T68
79	FILTON Junction	3 T67
80	Fish Ponds	4 T67
81	Flax Bourton	3 T57
82	FRESHFORD	3 T76
83	Frocester	4 070
84	GLOUCESTER	3 081
85	Gloucester	4 081
86	Gotherington	3 092
87	Grange Court	3 071
88	Great Somerford	3 T98
89	Gretton Halt	3 092
90	(Hallen Halt)	3 T58
91	Ham Mill Crossing Halt	3 080
92	(Hampton Row Halt)	3 T76
93	Haresfield	4 080
94	Henbury	3 T58
95	Holme Lacy	3 093
96	(Horfield)	3 T67
✳	Hotwells	† 34B T57
97	Holt Junction	3 T86
98	Hullavington	3 T98
99	Iron Acton	4 T68
100	Kelston for Saltford	4 T66
101	KEMBLE	3 T99
102	Kerne Bridge	3 051
103	KEYNSHAM	3 T66
104	Lacock Halt	3 T96
105	LANSDOWN ‡ §51B	4 092
106	LAWRENCE HILL †	3 T67
107	LEDBURY	3 073
108	Limpley Stoke	3 T76
109	Little Somerford	3 T98
110	Langhope	3 061
111	Lower Lydbrook Halt	34A 061
112	Lydbrook Junction	334A 051
113	LYDNEY	3 060

No.	Name	Ry Ref
114	Lydney Junction	34A 060
115	Lydney Town	34A 060
116	Malmesbury	3 T98
117	Malvern Road	‡ 3 092
118	Mangotsfield	4 T67
119	Melksham	3 T86
120	Midford	14 T76
121	Milkwall	34A 050
122	Mitcheldean Road	3 062
123	Monmouth May Hill	3 051
124	Monmouth Troy	3 051
125	MONTPELIER	† 34B T57
126	Nailbridge Halt	3 061
127	Nailsworth	4 T89
128	Newent	3 072
129	Newland	3 051
130	Newnham	3 061
131	(North) Filton Halt	3 T68
132	Oakle Street	3 071
133	(OLDFIELD PARK)	3 T76
134	Parkend	34A 060
135	(PARSON STREET)	† 3 T57
136	PATCHWAY	3 T68
137	Pensford	3 T66
138	Pill	3 T57
139	PILNING	3 T58
140	Portskewett	3 T58
141	Redbrook	3 050
142	REDLAND	† 34B T57
143	Ripple	4 083
144	Rodmarton Platform	3 T99
145	Ross	3 062
146	(Ruddle Road Halt)	3 061
147	Ruspidge Halt	3 061
148	Ryeford	4 080
149	St. Anne's Park	† 3 T67
150	St. Briavels + Llandogo	3 050
151	St James	‡ 3 092
152	St Mary's Crossing Halt	3 080
✳	St Philips §†	4 T57
153	Saltford	3 T66
154	SEA MILLS	34B T57
155	Seend	3 T96
156	Semington Halt	3 T96
157	SEVERN BEACH	3 T58
158	Severn Bridge	34A 060
159	Sharpness	34A 060
160	SHIREHAMPTON	34B T57
161	Speech House Road	34A 061
162	Staple Edge Halt	3 061
163	Staple Hill	4 T67
✳	STAPLETON ROAD	† 3 T67
164	Steam Mills Crossing Halt	3 061
165	Stonehouse Bristol Road	4 080
166	STONEHOUSE Burdett Road	3 080
167	STROUD	3 080
168	Stroud	4 080
169	Symonds Yat	3 051
✳	TEMPLE MEADS §†	34C T57
170	Tetbury	3 T89
171	Tewkesbury	4 083
172	Thornbury	4 T68
173	Tidenham	3 T59
174	Tintern	3 050
175	Tytherington	4 T68
176	Upper Lydbrook	34A 061
177	Upper Soudley Halt	3 061
178	Warmley	4 T67

No.	Name	Ry Ref
179	Weston	4 T76
180	Whimsey Halt	3 061
181	Whitecroft	34A 060
182	Wickwar	4 T78
183	Winterbourne	3 T68
184	Woodchester	4 080
185	Woolaston	3 T69
186	Yate	4 T78

GOODS

No.	Name/Location	Ry Ref
G1	Blakeney	3 060
2	Bullo Pill	3 061
3	Cheltenham High Street	4 092
4	Coates	3 T99

ENGINE SHEDS

No	Name/Location	Ry Ref
E1	Chippenham	3 T97
2	Malmesbury	3 T98

TUNNELS

No.	Name	Length yards	Ry Ref
T1	Ledbury	1323	3 073
2	Severn	7668	3 T58
3	Sodbury	4444	3 T78
4	Middle Hill	198	3 T86
5	Box	3212	3 T86
6	Sapperton Long	1860	3 090
7	Sapperton Short	352	3 090
8	Patchway Old	2003	3 T58
9	Patchway New	1760	3 T58

BRIDGES

No	Name	Ry Ref
V1	Severn Bridge	34A 060

JUNCTIONS

No	Name/Location	Ry Ref
J1	Wye Valley	3 T59
2	Red Hill	23 053
3	Rotherwas	23 053
4	Ledbury	3 073
5	Holt	3 T86
6	Thingley	3 T97
7	Calne Branch	3 T97
8	Dauntsey	3 T98
9	Westerleigh Junctions	3 T78

NOTES:

(1) REF In SO or ST -'S' omitted

(2) All stations in area included in this gazetteer. Other features only selectively except in the areas NOT covered by enlargements.

(3) Stations in BLUE located but:
- ✳ Not named see MAP 113.
- § Identified in code.
- § Map name ⎱ NAME CHANGE
- § Modern name ⎰
- † BRISTOL stations dual indexed.
- ‡ CHELTENHAM stations dual indexed.

North Filton used for occasional passenger trains.

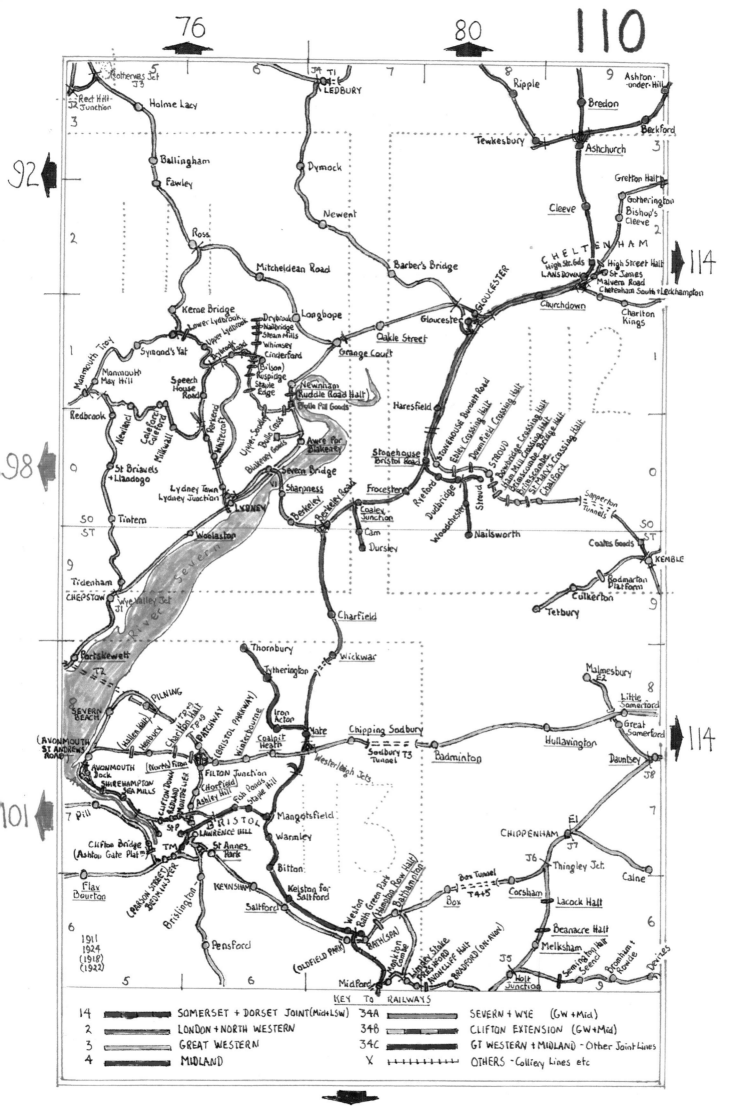

92

98

101

114

114

Rotherwas Jct
J3
Rect Hill Junction
J2
Holme Lacy
Ballingham
Fawley
Ross
Mitcheldean Road
Kerne Bridge
Lower Lydbrook
Upper Lydbrook
Lydbrook Road
Drybrook
Nailbridge
Steam Mills
Whimsey
Cinderford
Bilson
Ruspidge
Staple Edge
Symond's Yat
Monmouth Troy
Monmouth May Hill
Speech House Road
Redbrook
Newland
Coleford Coleford
Milkwall
Parkend
Whitecroft
St Briavels + Llandogo
Tintern
Lydney Town
Lydney Junction
LYDNEY
Sharpness
Berkeley
Berkeley Road
Woolaston
Tidenham
CHEPSTOW
Wye Valley Jct J1
Portskewett
T2
SEVERN BEACH
PILNING
TP+9
Charlton Halt
TP+9
PATCHWAY
(AVONMOUTH ST ANDREWS ROAD)
AVONMOUTH Dock
SHIREHAMPTON
SEA MILLS
(North) Filton
Wallen Halt
Henbury
CLIFTON DOWN
REDLAND
MONTPELIER
St P
(BRISTOL PARKWAY)
Winterbourne
FILTON Junction
(Horfield)
Ashley Hill
Fish Ponds
Staple Hill
Pill
Clifton Bridge (Ashton Gate Platm)
TM
CLIFTON HILL
LAWRENCE HILL
St Annes Park
(PARSON STREET BEDMINSTER)
Flax Bourton
Brislington
KEYNSHAM
Saltford
Mangotsfield
Warmley
Bitton
Keiston for Saltford
Pensford
Thornbury
Tytherington
Iron Acton
Coalpit Heath
Yate
Westerleigh Jcts
Chipping Sodbury
Sodbury Tunnel T3
Badminton
Hullavington
Malmesbury E2
Little Somerford
Great Somerford
Dauntsey J8
CHIPPENHAM
E1
J7
J6
Thingley Jct
Calne
Box Tunnel T4+5
Corsham
Lacock Halt
Beanacre Halt
Melksham
Seming Halt
Seend
Bromham + Rowde
Devizes
BRISTOL
Dymock
Newent
Barber's Bridge
GLOUCESTER
Gloucester
Oakle Street
Grange Court
Haresfield
Stonehouse Bristol Road
Frocester
Ryeford
Dudbridge
Stroud
Woodchester
Nailsworth
Coaley Junction
Cam
Dursley
Charfield
Wickwar
Stonehouse (Bunch) Road
Stonehouse Crossing Halt
Ebley Crossing Halt
Downfield Crossing Halt
STROUD
Brimscombe
Brimscombe Bridge Halt
St Mary's Crossing Halt
Chalford
Ham Mill Crossing Halt
Bowbridge Crossing Halt
Sapperton Tunnels
Coates Goods
KEMBLE
Rodmarton Platform
Culkerton
Tetbury
Ripple
Bredon
Beckford
Ashton-under-Hill
Tewkesbury
Ashchurch
Gretton Halt
Gotherington
Bishop's Cleeve
Cleeve
CHELTENHAM
High Str. Gds
LANSDOWN
High Street Halt
St James
Malvern Road
Cheltenham South + Leckhampton
Churchdown
Charlton Kings
Newnham (Ruddle Road Halt)
Bullo Pill Goods
Awre for Blakeney
Severn Bridge
Upper Soudley
Bullo Cross
Blakeney Goods
Coleford

River Severn

1911
1924
(1918)
(1922)

Monkton Combe
Midford
(OLDFIELD PARK)
BATH (SPA)
Limpley Stoke
FRESHFORD
AVONCLIFF Halt
BRADFORD (on-Avon)
J5
Holt Junction
Hampton Row (Halt)
Bathampton
Box
Weston
Bath Green Park

KEY TO RAILWAYS

1A	▬▬▬	SOMERSET + DORSET JOINT (Mid+LSW)	34A	▬▬▬	SEVERN + WYE (GW+Mid)
2	▬▬▬	LONDON + NORTH WESTERN	34B	▬▬▬	CLIFTON EXTENSION (GW+Mid)
3	▬▬▬	GREAT WESTERN	34C	▬▬▬	GT WESTERN + MIDLAND – Other Joint Lines
4	▬▬▬	MIDLAND	X	++++++	OTHERS – Colliery Lines etc

III RAILWAYS

No	Company
R 3	GREAT WESTERN
34	SEVERN + WYE (Gt Western + Midland Jt)
4	MIDLAND
X	OTHERS - Colliery lines etc

FOREST OF DEAN

STATIONS + HALTS

No	Name	Ry Ref
A 1	Awre for Blakeney	3 060
2	Ballingham	3 053
3	Berkeley	34 060
4	Berkeley Road	4(34) T79
5	(Bilson Halt)	3 061
6	Bullo Cross Halt	3 060
7	Cinderford	34(3) 061
8	Coleford	3 051
9	Coleford	34 051
10	Drybrook Halt	3 061
11	Drybrook Road	34 061
12	Fawley	3 052
13	Grange Court	3 071
14	Kerne Bridge	3 051
15	Longhope	3 061
16	Lower Lydbrook Halt	34 061
17	Lydbrook Junction	3(34) 051
18	LYDNEY	3 060
19	Lydney Junction	34 060
20	Lydney Town	34 060
21	Milkwall	34 050
22	Mitcheldean Road	3 062
23	Monmouth May Hill	3 051
24	Monmouth Troy	3 051
25	Nailbridge Halt	3 061
26	Newent	3 072
27	Newland	3 051
28	Newnham	3 061
29	Parkend	34 060
30	Redbrook	3 050
31	Ross	3 062
32	(Ruddle Road Halt)	. 3 061
33	Ruspidge Halt	3 061
34	St Briavels + Llandogo	3 050
35	Severn Bridge	34 060
36	Sharpness	34 060
37	Speech House Road	34 061
38	Staple Edge Halt	3 061
39	Steam Mills Crossing Halt	3 061
40	Symonds Yat	3 051
41	Tidenham	3 T59
42	Tintern	3 050
43	Upper Lydbrook	34 061
44	Upper Soudley Halt	3 061
45	Whimsey Halt	3 061
46	Whitecroft	34 060
47	Woolaston	3 T69

GOODS

No	Name / Location	Ry Ref
G 1	Bilson	3 061
2	Blakeney	3 060
3	Bullo Pill	3 061
4	Bullo Pill Dock	3 060
5	Lydney Harbour	34 060
6	Parkend	34 060
7	Sharpness Dock	34 060

SIDINGS ETC

No	Name / Company / Location	Ry Ref
P 1	Redbrook Iron Works	3 X 050
2	Tintern Wire Works	3 050
3	Soudley Stone	3 061
4	Meerbrook	3 061
5	Ruspidge Mill	3 061
6	Cinderford Iron Works	3 061
7	Churchway	3 061
8	Howbeach Colliery	3 060
9	Woorgreen Colliery	34 061
10	New Fancy Colliery	34 060
11	Van	34 060
12	Phipps	34 060
13	Norchard Colliery	34 060
14	Colour Works	34 060
15	Middle Forge	34 060
16	Princess Royal	34 060
17	Parkend Royal	34 060
18	Point Quarry	34 060
19	Futterhill	34 050
20	West Ham Pit	34 050
21	Easter Iron Ore Mining	34 050
22	Bixhead Quarry	X 061
23	Howlershill Quarry	X 061
24	Wimberry Quarry	X 061
25	Waterloo Colliery	34 061
26	Kidnalls Colliery	34 060

ENGINE SHEDS

No	Name / Location	Ry Ref
E 1	Lydney Junction	34(3) 060
2	Bullo Pill	3 061
3	Ross	3 062

TUNNELS

No	Name	Yds	Ry Ref
T 1	Bradley Hill	299	3 061
2	Bullo	1064	3 060
3	Redbrook Lower	264	3 051
4	Redbrook Upper	66	3 051
5	Newland	278	3 050
6	Severn Bridge	506	34 060
7	Mierystock	242	3 061
8	Symonds Yat	433	3 051
9	Lydbrook	630	3 051
10	Mitcheldean		3 062
11	Ballingham	1206	3 053
12	Tidenham	1190	3 T59
13	Newnham		3 061

BRIDGES

No	Name	Ry Ref
V 1	Severn Bridge	34 060

JUNCTIONS

No	Name / Location	Ry Ref
J 1	Wye Valley (Chepstow)	3 T59
2	Wye Valley (Monmouth)	3 051
3	Wire Works (Tintern)	3 050
4	Lydbrook	334 051
5	Ross	3 062
6	Hereford Line	3 071
7	Bullo Dock	3 061
8	Forest of Dean Branch	3 061
9	Awre	3 060
10	Lydney	3 060
11	Berkeley Road	434 070
12	Berkeley Road South	43 T79
13	Berkeley Loop	334 T79
14	Oldminster	34 060
15	North Docks Branch	34 060
16	Otters Pool	34 060
17	Engine Shed (Lydney)	34 060
18	Docks (Lydney)	34 060
19	Tufts South	34 060
20	Tufts North	34 060
21	Parkend (Goods)	34 060
22	Coleford Branch	34 060
23	Slings Branch	34 050
24	Bigslade	34 X 060
25	Howerslade	34 X 061
26	Wimberry	34 061
27	Serridge	34 061
28	Drybrook Road	34 061
29	Cinderford South Loop	334 061
30	Bilson North	334 061
31	Bilson South	334 061
32	Laymoor	34 061
33	Whimsey	3 061
34	Bilson	3 061
35	Wyesham	3 051

NOTES:

(1) REF In SO or ST - S omitted

(2) WESTWARD CONTINUATION OF 112 AND EASTWARD CONTINUATION OF THIS MAP AT SAME SCALE. THERE IS A SMALL GAP - DETAILS IN THIS AREA SEE 110

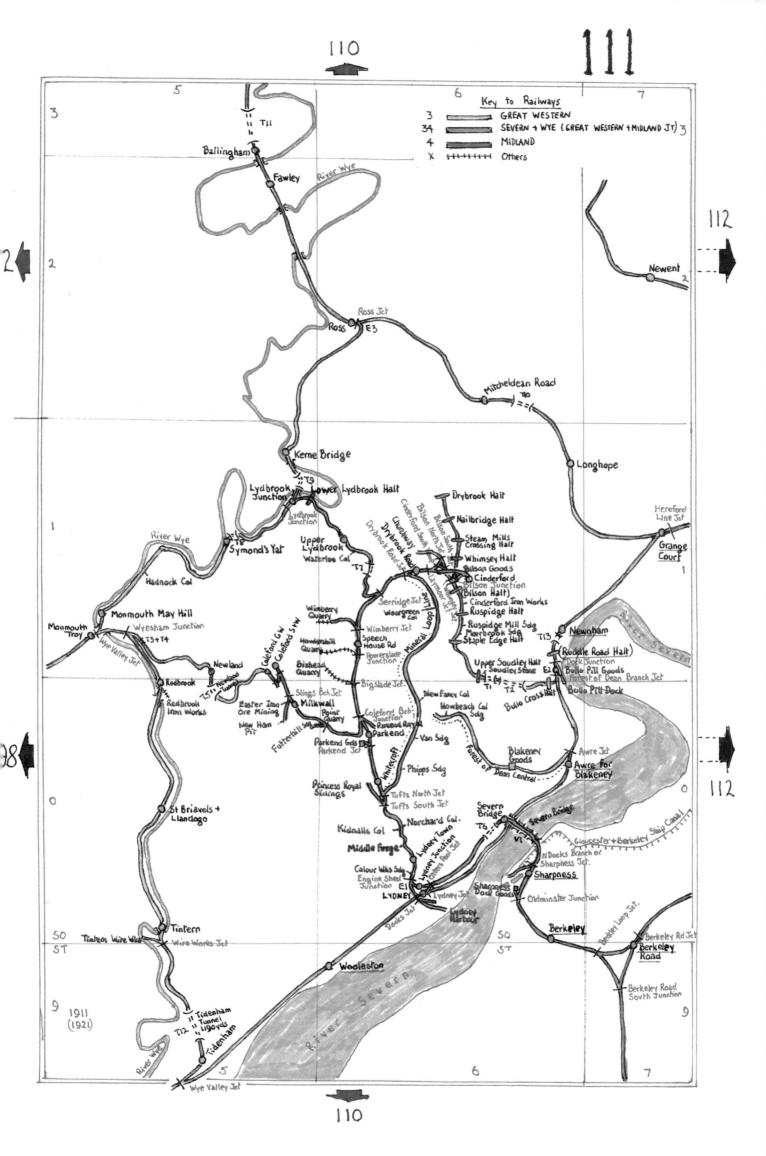

3

Key to Railways

3		GREAT WESTERN
34		SEVERN + WYE (GREAT WESTERN + MIDLAND JT)
4		MIDLAND
X	+++++++++	Others

T11

Ballingham

Fawley

River Wye

2

Newent

Ross Jct

Ross   E3

Mitcheldean Road   T10

Longhope

Kerne Bridge

T9

Lydbrook Junction   Lower Lydbrook Halt

Drybrook Halt

Nailbridge Halt

Lydbrook Junction

Steam Mills Crossing Halt

Hereford Line Jct

Grange Court

Upper Lydbrook
Waterloo Col

T8

Symond's Yat

Bilson North Jct
Cinderford South
Churchway
Bilson South

Drybrook Road Jct
Drybrook Road

Whimsey Halt
Bilson Goods
Cinderford
Bilson Junction
(Bilson Halt)
Cinderford Iron Works
Ruspidge Halt

Hadnock Col

T7

Serridge Jct
Woorgreen Col

Laxmoor Jct

Ruspidge Mill Sdg
Meerbrook Sdg
Staple Edge Halt

River Severn

Monmouth May Hill

Wyesham Junction

Wimberry Quarry

Wimberry Jct

Newnham

T13

Monmouth Troy

Wye Valley Jct   T3+T4

Howlerslill Quarry

Speech House Rd

Upper Soudley Halt
Soudley Stone   E2

(Ruddle Road Halt)

Dock Junction
Bullo Pill Goods
Forest of Dean Branch Jct

Coleford GW
Coleford S+W

Howlerslade Junction

Bishead Quarry

Big Slade Jct.

New Fancy Col

T1   (E)   T2   (

Newland

Redbrook

T5   Newland Tunnel

Slings Bch Jct

Easter Iron Ore Mining

New Ham Pit

Milkwall

Point Quarry

Fatterhill Sdg

Coleford Bch Junction
Parkend Royal
Parkend

Howbeach Col Sdg

Bullo Cross Halt

Bullo Pill Dock

Redbrook Iron Works

Parkend Gds
Parkend Jct

Van Sdg

Forest of Dean Central

Blakeney Goods

Awre Jct

Awre for Blakeney

Whitecroft

Phipps Sdg

St Briavels + Llandogo

Princess Royal Sidings

Tufts North Jct
Tufts South Jct

Severn Bridge

Severn Bridge

Kidnalls Col

Norchard Col.

T6   V1

Gloucester + Berkeley Ship Canal

Middle Forge

Lydney Town
Lydney Junction
Others Pool Jct

N Docks Branch or Sharpness Jct.

Colour Wks Sdg
Engine Shed Junction   E1

Sharpness

LYDNEY

Lydney Jct

Sharpness Dock Goods

Oldminster Junction

Berkeley Loop Jct.

Docks Jct

Lydney Harbour

Berkeley

Berkeley Road

Tintern

Tintern Wire Wks

Wire Works Jct

Woolaston

Berkeley Road South Junction

9   1911
(1921)

Tidenham Tunnel
T12   1,064yds

Tidenham

River Wye

Wye Valley Jct

River Severn

112
RAILWAYS

No	Company
R 3	GREAT WESTERN
4	MIDLAND
5	MIDLAND + SOUTH WESTERN JUNCT.
X	OTHERS

STATIONS + HALTS

No	Name	Ry Ref
A 1	Andoversford	3 P01
2	Andoversford + Dowdeswell	5 P01
3	Ashchurch	4 093
4	Barber's Bridge	3 072
5	Bishop's Cleeve	3 092
6	Bowbridge Crossing Halt	3 080
7	Brimscombe	3 080
8	Brimscombe Bridge Halt	3 080
9	Chalford	3 080
10	Charlton Kings	3 091
	CHELTENHAM	092
11	High Street Halt	3 092
12	LANSDOWN §15	4 092
13	Malvern Road	3 092
14	St James	3 092
15	SPA §12	4 092
16	South + Leckhampton	3 091
17	Churchdown	34 081
18	Cirencester	3 P00
19	Cleeve	4 092
20	Culkerton	3 T99
21	Downfield Crossing Halt	3 080
22	Dudbridge	4 080
23	Ebley Crossing Halt	3 080
24	Frocester	4 070
25	GLOUCESTER	3 081
26	Gloucester	4 081
27	Gotherington	3 092
28	Gretton Halt	3 092
29	Ham Mill Crossing Halt	3 080
30	Haresfield	4 080
31	KEMBLE	3 T99
32	LANSDOWN §15 ‡	4 092
33	Malvern Road ‡	3 092
34	Nailsworth	4 T89
35	Rodmarton Platform	T99
36	Ryeford	4 080
37	St James ‡	3 092
38	St Mary's Crossing Halt	3 080
39	Stonehouse Bristol Rd	4 080
40	STONEHOUSE Burdett Rd	3 080
41	STROUD	3 080
42	Stroud	4 080
43	Tewkesbury	4 083
44	Woodchester	4 080

GOODS

No	Name / Location	Ry Ref
G 1	Cheltenham - High St	4 092
2	Coates	3 T99
3	Stroud	4 080
4	Tewkesbury	4 083

SIDINGS

No	Name / Company / Location	Ry Ref
P 1	Cheltenham District	X 092
	Light Railway	X 092
2	Alstone Coal Wharf	4 092
3	Stonehouse Brick Works	3 080

ENGINE SHEDS

No	Location	Ry Ref
E 1	Gloucester	3 081
2	Gloucester	4 081
3	Cheltenham	3 092
4	Tewkesbury	4 083
5	Cirencester	3 P00
6	(Chalford) ⌖	3 080

TUNNELS

No	Name	Yds	Ry Ref
T 1	Tewkesbury	418	4 083
2	Sapperton Long	1860	3 090
3	Sapperton Short	352	3 090
4	Sandywell Park	400	3 P01

JUNCTIONS

No	Name / Location	Ry Ref
J 1	Kemble - Tetbury	3 T99
2	Kemble - Cirencester	3 T99
3	Dudbridge	4 080
4	Stonehouse	4 080
5	Standish GW	(4) 3 080
6	Standish Mid	(3) 4 080
7	Tuffley	4 081
8	Cheltenham Line	3 081
9	Engine Shed	3 081
10	Chequers Road	3 081
11	Over	3 081
12	Lansdown - Honeybourne	3(4) 092
13	Lansdown - Banbury	3(4) 092
14	Hatherley Curve	3 092
15	Gloucester Loop	3 092
16	Andoversford	35 P01
17	Alstone	4 092
18	Tewkesbury Quay Branch	4 083
19	Ashchurch - Tewkesbury	4 093
20	Ashchurch - Evesham Line	4 093
21	Ashchurch - Tewkesbury Line	4 093
22	Ashchurch - Evesham	4 093
23	Ashchurch - Level Crossing	4 093

NOTES:

(1) REF - In SO, SP, ST or SU, the S is omitted

(2) WESTWARD CONTINUATION - small gap in the same scale continuation (111) - details in this area see 110

(3) NAME CHANGE :-
§ LANSDOWN now known as
§ CHELTENHAM SPA

(4) ⌖ No actual shed here - this was just a railmotor stabling point, so far as can be ascertained

(5) ‡ Cheltenham stations - dual indexed

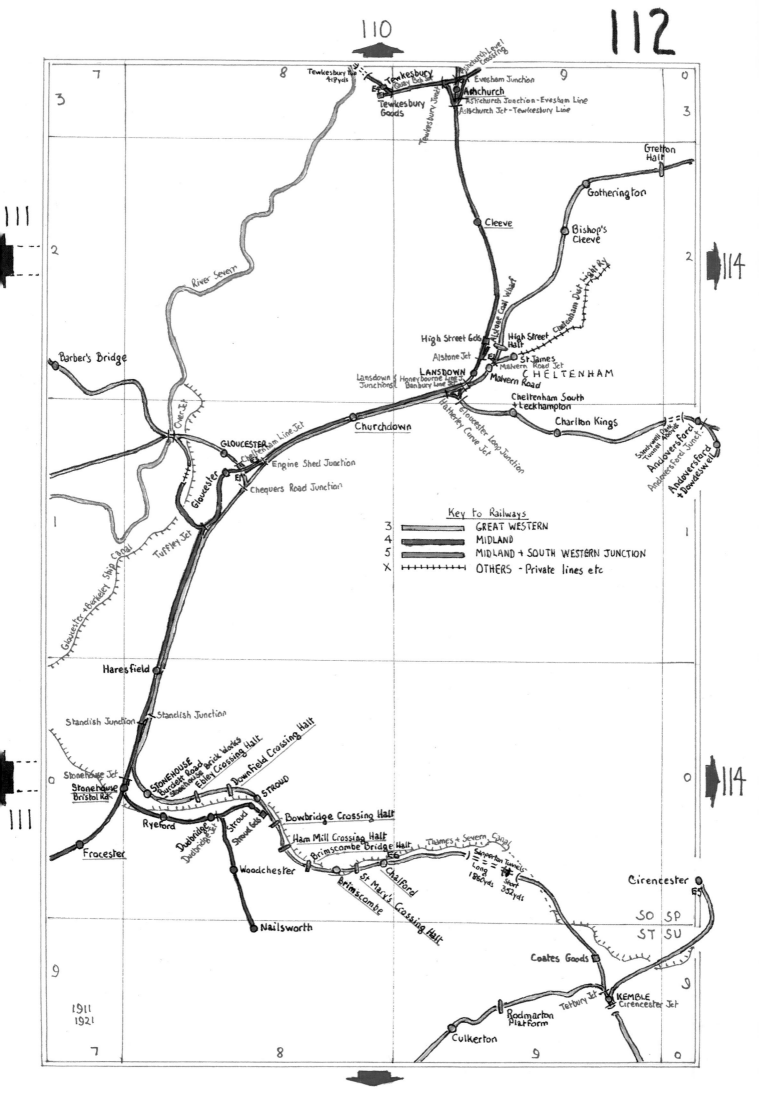

Tewkesbury Tun
418yds

Tewkesbury
Quay Bch Sdg

Tewkesbury
Tewkesbury Junct

Ashchurch Level
Crossing

Ashchurch

Evesham Junction
Ashchurch Junction-Evesham Line
Ashchurch Jct-Tewkesbury Line

Tewkesbury
Goods

Gretton
Halt

Gotherington

Cleeve

Bishop's
Cleeve

Cheltenham Dist Light Ry

River Severn

Barber's Bridge

High Street Gds

High Street
Halt

St James

Over Jct

Alstone Jct

LANSDOWN

Malvern Road Jct

CHELTENHAM

Lansdown
Junctions

Honeybourne Line Jt
Banbury Line Jct

Malvern Road

Cheltenham South
+Leckhampton

Charlton Kings

Sandywell Park
Tunnel 4068yds

Andoversford
Andoversford Junct.

Andoversford
+Dowdeswell

Churchdown

Cheltenham Line Jct

Gloucester Loop Junction

Hatherley Curve Jct

GLOUCESTER

Engine Shed Junction

Gloucester

Chequers Road Junction

Key to Railways

3			GREAT WESTERN
4			MIDLAND
5			MIDLAND + SOUTH WESTERN JUNCTION
X			OTHERS - Private lines etc

Tuffley Jct

Gloucester + Berkeley Ship Canal

Haresfield

Standish Junction

Standish Junction

Stonehouse Jct

STONEHOUSE
Burdett Road

Stonehouse Brick Works
Stonehouse

Ebley Crossing Halt

Downfield Crossing Halt

STROUD

Stonehouse
Bristol Rd

Ryeford

Dudbridge
Dudbridge Jct

Stroud
Stroud Gds Sdg

Bowbridge Crossing Halt

Ham Mill Crossing Halt

Brimscombe Bridge Halt

Thames + Severn Canal

Frocester

Chalford

Sapperton Tunnels
Long
1864yds

Short
352yds

Cirencester

Woodchester

Brimscombe

St Mary's Crossing Halt

SO SP
ST SU

Nailsworth

Coates Goods

1911
1921

Rodmarton
Platform

Tetbury Jct

KEMBLE
Cirencester Jct

Culkerton

BRISTOL + BATH

RAILWAYS

No	Company
R14	SOMERSET+DORSET JOINT (LSW+Mid)
3	GREAT WESTERN
3AB	CLIFTON EXTENSION (GW+Mid)
3AC	GREAT WESTERN + MIDLAND (Other Jt.)
4	MIDLAND
◇	BRITISH RAIL
X	OTHERS - Colliery Lines etc

STATIONS + HALTS

No	Name	Ry Ref
A1	Ashley Hill	† 3 67
2	(Ashton Gate Platform)	† 3 57
3	AVONCLIFF Halt	3 76
4	(AVONMOUTH - ST ANDREWS ROAD)	3 58
5	AVONMOUTH Dock	3AB 57
6	Badminton	3 78
7	BATH (SPA)	3 76
8	Bathampton	3 76
9	Bath Green Park	4(4) 76
10	BEDMINSTER	† 3 57
11	Bitton	4 67
12	Blagdon	3 56
13	Box	3 76
14	Brislington	† 3 67
	BRISTOL	
15	Ashley Hill	3 67
16	(Ashton Gate Platform)	3 57
17	BEDMINSTER	3 57
18	Brislington	3 67
19	Clifton Bridge	3 57
20	CLIFTON DOWN	3AB 57
21	Hotwells	3AB 57
22	LAWRENCE HILL	3 67
	BRISTOL (continued)	
23	MONTPELIER	3AB 57
24	(PARSON STREET)	3 57
25	REDLAND	3AB 57
26	St Anne's Park	3 67
27	St Philips	4 67
28	STAPLETON ROAD	3 67
29	TEMPLE MEADS	3AC 67
30	(BRISTOL PARKWAY)	30 68
31	(CALDICOT)	3A8 57
32	Charlton Halt	3 58
33	Chipping Sodbury	3 78
34	Clifton Bridge	† 3 57
35	CLIFTON DOWN	3 76
36	Clutton	3 66
37	Coalpit Heath	3 68
38	Combe Hay Halt	3 76
39	Dunkerton	3 76
40	Filton Halt North	3 68
41	FILTON Junction	3 68
42	Fish Ponds	4 67
43	Flax Bourton	3 57
44	FRESHFORD	† 3 57
45	(Hallen Halt)	4 67
46	(Hampton Row Halt)	3 56
47	Henbury	3 76
48	(Horfield)	† 3 67
49	Hotwells	3A8 57
50	Iron Acton	4 68
51	Kelston for Saltford	4 66
52	KEYNSHAM	3 66
53	LAWRENCE HILL	3 67
54	Limpley Stoke	3 57
55	Mangotsfield	4 67
56	Midford	14 76
57	Midford Halt	3 67
58	MONTPELIER	3A8 57
59	(North) Filton (Halt)	3 68
60	(OLDFIELD PARK)	3 76
61	(PARSON STREET)	3A8 57
62	PATCHWAY	3 67
63	Pensford	4 67
64	Pill	3 67
65	PILNING	3AC 67
66	Portskewett	30 68
67	REDLAND	3A8 57
68	St Anne's Park	3 58
69	St Philips	3 78
70	Saltford	† 3 57
71	SEA MILLS	† 3AB 57
72	SEVERN BEACH	3 66
73	SEVERN TUNNEL JUNCTION	3 68
74	SHIREHAMPTON	3 76
75	Staple Hill	3 76
76	STAPLETON ROAD	3 68
77	TEMPLE MEADS	3 68
78	Thornbury	4 67
79	Tytherington	3 57
80	Warmley	3 76
81	Weston	3 58
82	Wickwar	3 76
83	Winterbourne	3 58
84	Yate	3 67

TUNNELS

No	Name	Yds	Ry Ref
T1	Flax Bourton		† 3AB 57
2	Clifton Bridge		† 3 57
3	Pill		3 76
4	Clifton	1738	† 3AB 57
5	Severn	7668	3 58
6	St Annes Park		† 3 67
7	Patchway Old	2003	3 68
8	Patchway New	1760	3 68
9	Combe Down	1829	† 3 57
10	Sodbury	4444	† 3 78

Top-of-column listing (Temple Meads / Wapping Wharf / Avonmouth area):

No	Name	Ry Ref
7	Temple Meads	† 3AC 57
8	Wapping Wharf	† 3 58
9	Avonmouth	3 76
10	Avonmouth Docks	3 57
11	Bath	3 68

SIDINGS

No	Name (Company/Location)	Ry Ref
	No Name (Company/Location)	Ry Ref
P1	South Liberty	3 58
2	Ashton Vale Iron Co Col	† 3AB 57
3	Merchants Road	† 3 67
4	Galbraiths	† 4 67
5	Gas Works	3 66
6	Redcliff	3AB 57
7	United Gas Works	3 58
8	Kingswood Hill Col	3 48
9	Chittening HM Factory	3AB 57
10	Caldicot	4 67
11	Bramley Colliery	† 3 67
12	Foxes Wood	† 3AC 67
13	Shortwood Colliery	4 68
14	Parkfield	4 68
15	Victoria Brick + Tile	4 67
16	Bath + Twerton Coop	4 76
17	Mayshill Pit	4 78

JUNCTIONS

No	Name/Location	Ry Ref
J1	South Liberty ❋	4 67
2	Bedminster ❋	3 58
3	Ashton South	3 58
4	Ashton	3 66
5	Ashton Swing Bridge	3 67
6	Canons Marsh Crossing	4 67
7	Ashley Hill	4 67
8	Pylle Hill	14 76
9	Temple Meads West	14 76
10	Temple Meads East	4 68
11	Marsh Goods	
12	Days Bridge	3 67
13	Feeder Bridge	3 67
14	North Somerset	4 67
15	St Annes Park	414 76
16	Marsh North	3 67
17	Marsh South	3 76
18	Barrow Lane	3 48
19	Lawrence Hill	4 67
20	Stapleton Road	3 67
21	Kingswood	3 78
22	Sneyd Park	3 58
23	St Andrews	3 58
24	Hallen Marsh	3 58
25	Pilning South Wales	4 67
26	Mangotsfield Station	4 67
27	Mangotsfield North	4 67
28	Mangotsfield South	3 68
29	Filton West	3 68
30	Patchway	3 68
31	Stoke Gifford	3 68
32	Filton South	3 78
33	Westerleigh West	3 78
34	Westerleigh East	3 78
35	Westerleigh North	3 78
36	Yate South	43 78
37	Yale Main Line	4 78
38	Coal Pit Heath Branch	4 68
39	Bath (Mid and S+D)	A14 76
40	Bathampton	3 76
41	Camerton+Limpey Stoke	3 76

ENGINE SHEDS

No	Name/Location	Ry Ref
E1	Bristol Bath Road	† 3 67
2	Bristol St Philips	4 67
3	Bath Green Park	4 67
4	Bristol St Philips Marsh	3 67
5	Bath	3 76
6	Severn Tunnel Junction	3 48

GOODS

No	Name/Location	Ry Ref
G1	Bristol GW	† 3 57
2	Avonside Wharf	3 76
3	Canon's Marsh	4 67
4	Kingsland	14 76
5	Marsh	3 76
6	Pylle Hill	3 76

WATERTROUGHS

No	Location	Ry Ref
W1	Chipping Sodbury	† 3 57

NOTES:

(1) REF - In ST
(2) BRISTOL features an inset
(3) Name changed to Parson Street Junction

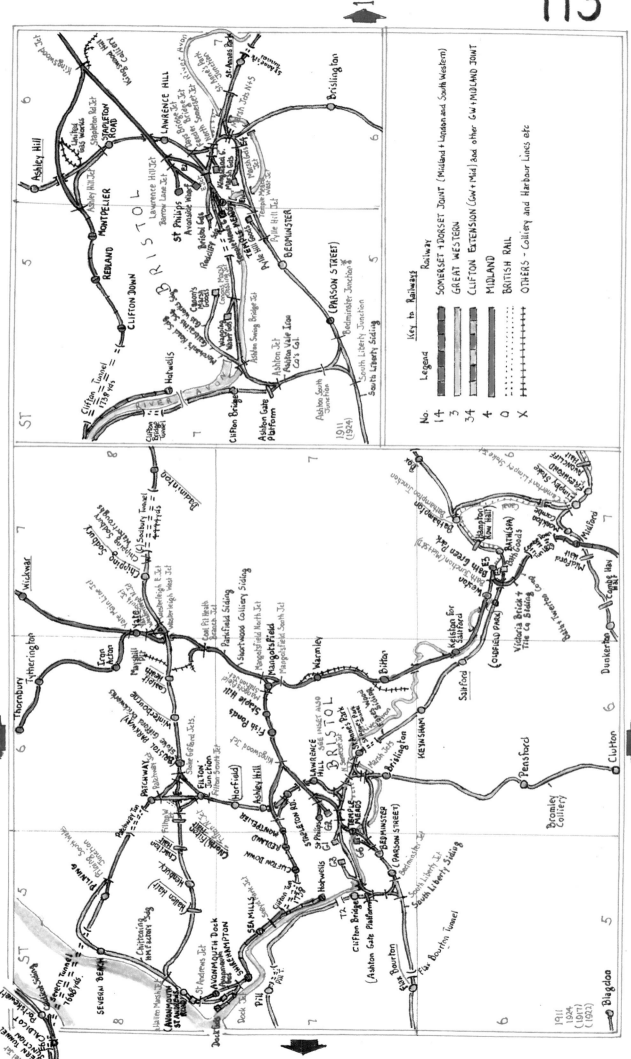

Key to Railways

Legend		No.	Railway
		14	SOMERSET + DORSET JOINT (Midland + London and South Western)
		3	GREAT WESTERN
		34	CLIFTON EXTENSION (GW + Mid) and other GW + MIDLAND JOINT
		4	MIDLAND
		0	BRITISH RAIL
		X	OTHERS – Colliery and Harbour Lines etc

BANBURY,   SWINDON   +   NEWBURY

No	Company
R 2	LONDON + NORTH WESTERN
3	GREAT WESTERN
3A	DIDCOT NEWBURY + SOUTHAMPTON (GW) ✳
4	WANTAGE TRAMWAY
5	MIDLAND + SOUTH WESTERN JUNCTION

STATIONS + HALTS

No	Name	Ry Ref
A 1	Abingdon	3 U49
2	Adderbury	3 P43
3	Adlestrop	3 P22
4	Alvescot	3 P20
5	Andoversford	3 P02
6	Andoversford + Dowdeswell	5 P01
7	ASCOTT·UNDER·WYCHWOOD	3 P31
8	Aynho (for Deddington)	3 P43
9	Aynho Park	3 P53
10	Bampton	3 P30
11	Banbury	2 P43
12	BANBURY	3 P43
13	BEDWYN	3 U26
14	Blenheim + Woodstock	3 P41
15	Bletchington	3 P41
16	Blockley	3 P13
17	Bloxham	3 P43
18	Blunsdon	5 U18
19	Bourton-on-the-Water	3 P12
20	Boxford	3 U47
21	Brinkworth	3 U08
22	Broadway	3 P02
23	Campden	3 P13
24	Cerney + Ashton Keynes	5 U09
25	CHARLBURY	3 P31
26	Chedworth	5 P01
27	Chipping Norton	3 P32
28	Chiseldon	5 U17
29	Cirencester	5 P00
30	Cirencester (Town)	3 P00
31	(COMBE)	3 P41
32	Cricklade	5 U09
33	Dauntsey	3 T98
34	Eastbury	3 U37
35	East Garston	3 U37
36	Eynsham	3 P40
37	Fairford	3 P10
38	Faringdon	3 U29
39	(FINSTOCK)	3 P31
40	Foss Cross	5 P02
41	Fritwell + Somerton	3 P42
42	Grafton + Burbage	5 U26
43	Great Shefford	3 U37
44	HANDBOROUGH	3 P41
45	Hannington	3 U19
46	HEYFORD	3 P42
47	Highclere	3A U46
48	Highworth	3 U19
49	Hook Norton	3 P33
50	HUNGERFORD	3 U36
51	Kelmscott + Langford Platform	P20
		3 P20
52	Kidlington	3 P41
53	KINGHAM	3 P22
54	KINGS SUTTON	3 P43
55	KINTBURY	3 U36
56	Lambourn	3 U37
57	Laverton Halt	3 P03
58	Lechlade	3 P20
59	Marlborough (High Level)	3 U16
60	Marlborough (Low Level)	5 U16
61	Milton Halt	3 P43
62	Minety + Ashton Keynes	3 U09
63	(Moredon Halt)	5 U18
64	MORETON·IN·MARSH	3 P23
65	NEWBURY	3 U46
66	Newbury Racecourse	3 U46
67	Newbury Westfields Halt	3 U46
68	Notgrove	3 P02
69	Ogbourne	5 U27
70	PEWSEY	3 U16
71	Purton	3 U08
72	Rollright Halt	3 P33
73	Sarsden Halt	3 P22
74	Savernake (High Level)	5 U26
75	Savernake (Low Level)	3 U26
76	SHIPTON for Burford	3 P21
77	Shrivenham	3 U28
78	South Leigh	3 P30
79	Speen	3 U46
80	Stanton	3 U19
81	Steventon	3 U49
82	Stockcross + Bagnor	3 U47
83	Stow-on-the-Wold	3 P12
84	Stratton	3 U18
85	Stretton-on-Fosse	3 P23
86	SWINDON	3 U18
87	Swindon Town	5 U18
88	(TACKLEY)	3 P42
89	Toddington	3 P03
90	Uffington	3 U39
91	Wantage	4 U38
92	Wantage Road	3 U49
93	Welford Park	3 U47
94	Winchcombe	3 P03
95	Withington	5 P01
96	Witney	3 P30
97	Wolvercot Platform	3 P40
98	Woodborough	3 U16
99	Woodhay	3A U46
100	Wootton Bassett	3 U08
101	Yarnton	3 P41
6	Kingham North †	3 P22
7	Kingham South †	3 P22
8	Kingham East †	3 P22
9	Kingham West †	3 P22

GOODS

No	Name/Location	Ry Ref
G 1	Burbage	3 U26
2	Rushey Platt	5 U18
3	Swindon	3 U18
4	Witney	3 P30

ENGINE SHEDS

No	Name/Location	Ry Ref
E 2	Fairford	3 P10
3	Abingdon	3 U49
4	Swindon	3 U18
5	Faringdon	3 U39
6	Kingham	3 P22
7	Cirencester	3 P00
8	Banbury	3 P43
9	Swindon	5 U18

COMPANY WORKS

No	Name	Ry Ref
C 1	Swindon	3 U18

SUMMITS

No	Name	Ht Ft.	Ry Ref
S 1	Notgrove	760'	3 P02

WATERTROUGHS

No	Location	Ry Ref
W 1	Aldermaston ‡	3 U56

JUNCTIONS

No	Name/Location	Ry Ref
J 1	Andoversford	35 P02
2	Faringdon Branch	3 U39
3	Witney Goods	3 P30
4	Blenheim Branch	3 P41
5	Shipston Branch	3 P23

NOTES:

(1) REF - In SP or SU - the S is omitted. Dauntsey is in ST.

(2) See Map 116   ‡

(3) Worked by Great Western   ✳

(4) Signal Box names   †

(5) ALL Stations shown on the map and included in this gazetteer, other features only selectively except in the areas NOT covered by enlargements.

(7) Newbury Racecourse - used for occasional passenger services

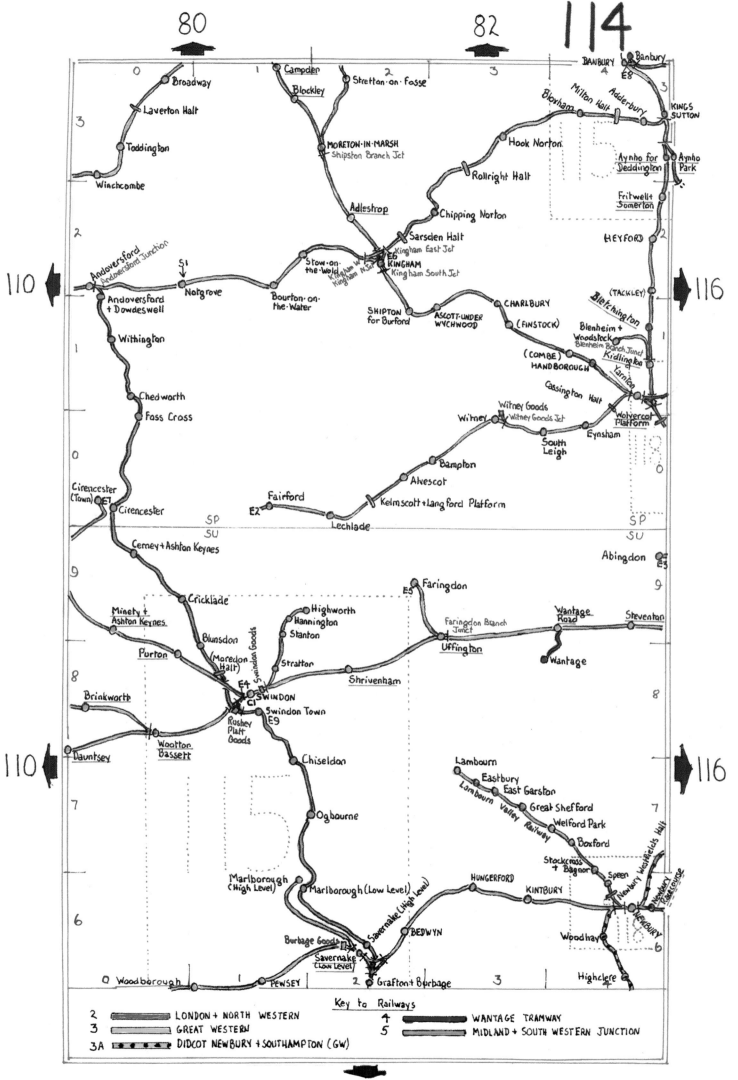

110

116

110

116

139

Broadway
Laverton Halt
Toddington
Winchcombe

Campden
Blockley
Stretton-on-Fosse

BANBURY
Banbury
E8

Bloxham
Milton Halt
Adderbury

KINGS
SUTTON

MORETON·IN·MARSH
Shipston Branch Jct

Hook Norton

Aynho for
Deddington
Aynho
Park

Rollright Halt

Fritwell+
Somerton

Adlestrop

Chipping Norton

HEYFORD

Andoversford
Andoversford Junction

S1

Sarsden Halt
Kingham East Jct
E6
KINGHAM
Kingham South Jct
Kingham W.
Kingham Nth Jct

(TACKLEY)

Andoversford
+ Dowdeswell

Notgrove

Stow-on-
the-Wold

Bletchington

Bourton-on-
the-Water

CHARLBURY

Withington

SHIPTON
for Burford

ASCOTT-UNDER
WYCHWOOD

(FINSTOCK)

Blenheim +
Woodstock
Blenheim Branch Junct

Chedworth

(COMBE)
HANDBOROUGH

Kidlington

Fosse Cross

Cassington Halt

Yarnton

Witney Goods
Witney Goods Jct
Witney

Wolvercot
Platform

Cirencester
(Town) E7
Cirencester

South
Leigh

Eynsham

Bampton

Alvescot

Fairford
E2

Kelmscott + Langford Platform

SP
SU

Lechlade

SP
SU

Abingdon
E3

Cerney + Ashton Keynes

Faringdon
E5

Cricklade

Highworth
Hannington
Stanton

Faringdon Branch
Junct

Wantage
Road

Steventon

Minety +
Ashton Keynes

Blunsdon

Uffington

Wantage

Purton

(Moredon
Halt)

Stratton

Brinkworth

E4
SWINDON
C1
Swindon Town
E9

Shrivenham

Dauntsey

Woolton
Bassett

Rushey
Platt
Goods

Chiseldon

Lambourn
Eastbury
East Garston
Great Shefford
Welford Park
Boxford

Newbury WestFields Halt

Ogbourne

Stockcross
+ Bagnor
Speen

Newbury
Racecourse

Marlborough
(High Level)

Marlborough (Low Level)

Savernake (High Level)

HUNGERFORD

KINTBURY

Newbury

Woodhay

Burbage Goods

Savernake
(Low Level)

BEDWYN

Woodborough

PEWSEY

Grafton + Burbage

Highclere

Key to Railways

2 LONDON + NORTH WESTERN
3 GREAT WESTERN
3A DIDCOT NEWBURY + SOUTHAMPTON (GW)
4 WANTAGE TRAMWAY
5 MIDLAND + SOUTH WESTERN JUNCTION

A

RAILWAYS

No	Company	Ry Ref
R3	GREAT WESTERN	3 16
5	MIDLAND + SOUTH WESTERN JUNCTION	5 18

GOODS

No	Name	Ry Ref
G1	Burbage	3 18
2	Rushey Platt	
3	Swindon	

STATIONS + HALTS

No	Name	Ry Ref
A1	BEDWYN	3 26
2	Blunsdon	5 18
3	Chiseldon	5 17
4	Cricklade	5 19
5	Grafton + Burbage	5 26
6	Hannington	3 19
7	Highworth	3 19
8	Marlborough (High Level)	3 16
9	Marlborough (Low Level)	5 16
10	Meredon Halt	5 18
11	Ogbourne	5 17
12	PEWSEY	3 16
13	Purton	3 18
14	Savernake (High Level)	5 26
15	Savernake (Low Level)	3 26
16	Shrivenham	3 28
17	Stanton	3 18
18	Stratton	3 18
19	SWINDON	3 18
20	Swindon Town	5 18
21	Woodborough	3 16
22	Wootton Bassett	3 08

SHEDS

No	Location	Ry Ref
E1	Swindon	3 18
2	Swindon	5 18

WORKS

No	Location	Ry Ref
C1	Swindon	3 18

SIDINGS

No	Name	Ry Ref
P1	Ogbourne St Andrew	5 17
2	Savernake Forest	5 16

JUNCTIONS

No	Name/Location	Ry Ref
J1	Marlborough Branch	3 16
2	Wolfhall	35 26
3	Grafton South	35 26
4	Grafton East	3 26
5	Rushey Platt	5 18
6	Swindon Exchange	35 18
7	Cheltenham Line	3 18
8	Highworth Branch	3 18
9	South Wales	3 08

NOTE: REF: All in SU

B

RAILWAYS

No	Company	Ry Ref
R1	STRATFORD-ON-AVON+MIDLAND JCT	
2	LONDON + NORTH WESTERN	
3	GREAT WESTERN	
5	GREAT CENTRAL	

ENGINE SHEDS

No	Location	Ry Ref
E1	Banbury	3 44

TUNNELS

No	Name	Ry Ref
T1	Ardley	3 42

STATIONS + HALTS

No	Name	Ry Ref
A1	Adderbury	3 43
2	Ardley	3 52
3	Aynho	3 43
4	Aynho Park	3 43
5	Banbury	2 44
6	BANBURY	3 44
7	Bloxham	3 43
8	Brackley	2 53
9	Brackley	5 53
10	Chalcombe Road Platform	5 44
11	Farthinghoe	2 54
12	Fritwell + Somerton	3 42
13	Helmdon	1 54
14	Helmdon	5 54
15	Kings Sutton	3 43
16	Milton Halt	3 43

JUNCTIONS

No	Name/Location	Ry Ref
J1	Aynho	3 43
2	Cheltenham (Line)	3 43
3	Banbury South	32 43
4	Banbury for GW	23 43
5	Banbury North	35 44
6	Cockley Brake	51 54

NOTES: REF: All in SP

SIDINGS

No	Name/Company/Location	Ry Ref
P1	Astrop Sidings	3 43
2	Sydenham Sidings	3 43
3	Milton Pits	3 43

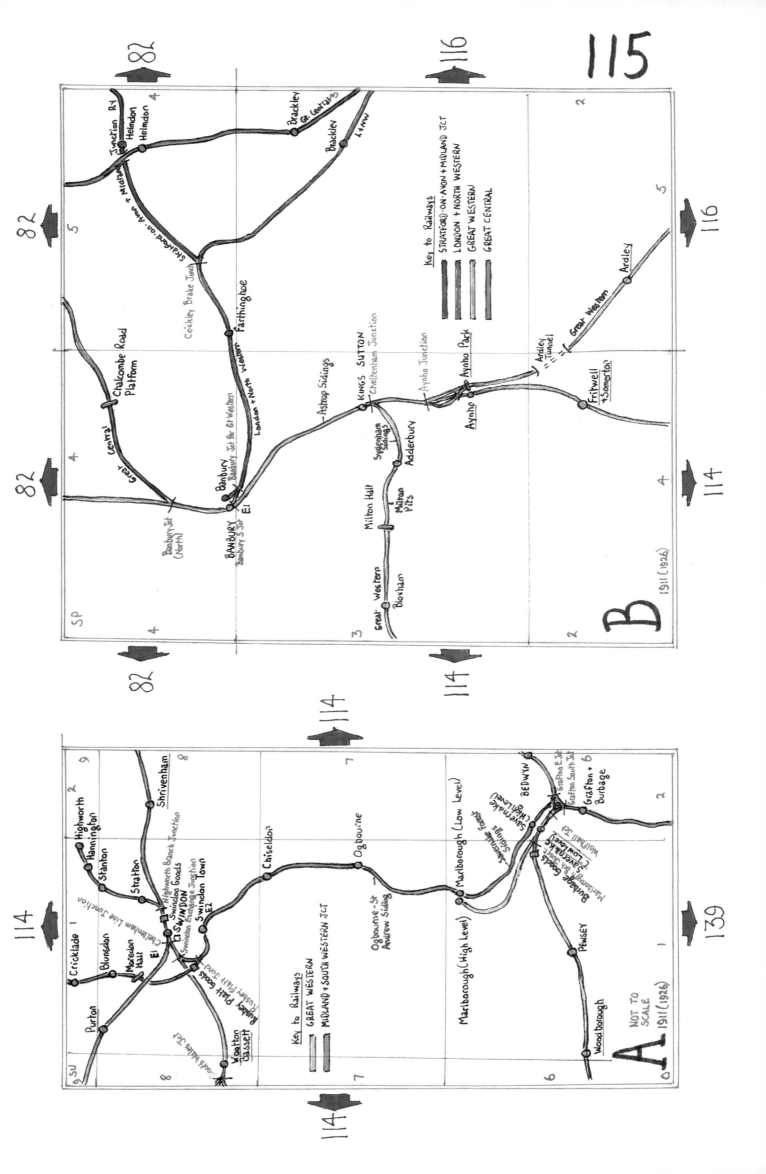

115

82

116

82

116

B 1911 (1926)

SP

Helmdon Junction Ry
Helmdon
Helmdon
4

Brackley Gt Central
Brackley
L + NW

Stratford-on-Avon + Midland Jct

Cockley Brake Junch

Chalcombe Road Platform

Farthinghoe

Great Central

Astrop Sidings

KINGS SUTTON
Cheltenham Junction

Aynho Junction

Aynho Park

Ardley Tunnel

Great Western
Ardley

Fritwell + Somerton

Aynho

Syderham Sidings
Adderbury

London + North Western

Banbury Jct for Gt Western

Banbury Jct (North)

BANBURY
Banbury S Jct
E¹

Milton Halt
Milton Pits

Great Western
Bloxham

Key to Railways
STRATFORD-ON-AVON + MIDLAND JCT
LONDON + NORTH WESTERN
GREAT WESTERN
GREAT CENTRAL

114

116

A NOT TO SCALE 1911 (1926)

SU

Highworth
Hannington
Stanton
Stratton

Shrivenham

Cricklade
Blunsdon
Moredon Halt

Purton

Highworth Branch Junction
Swindon Goods
SWINDON
Swindon Exchange Junction
Swindon Town
E²

Rushey Platt Goods
Rushey Platt Junch

Cheltenham Line Junction

South Wales Jct

Wootton Bassett

Chiseldon

Ogbourne

Ogbourne - St Andrew Siding

Key to Railways
GREAT WESTERN
MIDLAND + SOUTH WESTERN JCT

Marlborough (Low Level)

Marlborough (High Level)

Savernake (High Level)
Savernake Sidings

BEDWYN

Grafton E Jct
Grafton South Jct
Grafton + Burbage

Burbage Goods
Marlborough Jch Junct
Savernake (Low Level)
Wolfhall Jct

Pewsey

Woodborough

114

139

114

RAILWAYS

VERNEY JUNCTION, DIDCOT + READING

No	Company
R 1	LONDON + SOUTH WESTERN
2	LONDON + NORTH WESTERN
3	GREAT WESTERN
3A	DIDCOT NEWBURY + SOUTHAMPTON (GW)✕
35	GREAT WESTERN + GREAT CENTRAL JOINT
5	GREAT CENTRAL
57	GREAT CENTRAL + METROPOLITAN JOINT
6	SOUTH EASTERN + CHATHAM

STATIONS + HALTS

No	Name		Ry Ref
A 1	Abingdon	3	U49
1A	(Abingdon Road Halt)	3	P00
2	Akeman Street	5	P71
3	ALDERMASTON	3	U66
4	AMERSHAM	57	U99
5	(APPLEFORD)	3	U59
6	Ardley	3	P52
7	ASCOT	1	U96
8	(ASPLEY GUISE)	2	P93
9	Aston Rowant	3	U79
10	Aylesbury	2	P81
11	AYLESBURY	3557	P81
12	Aynho	3	P43
13	Aynho Park	3	P53
14	BAGSHOT	1	U96
15	BEACONSFIELD	35	U99
16	BERKHAMPSTEAD	2	P90
17	Bicester	2	P52
18	BICESTER	3	P52
19	Blackthorn	3	P61
20	BLACKWATER + Camberley	6	U86
21	Bledlow	3	P70
22	Bledlow Bridge Halt	3	P70
23	BLETCHLEY	2	P83
24	BOURNE END	3	U88
25	(BOW BRICKHILL)	2	P83
26	Brackley	2	P53
27	Brackley	5	P53
28	BRACKNELL	1	U86
29	Brill	57	P61
30	Brill + Ludgershall	3	P61
31	Buckingham	2	P63
32	BURNHAM Beeches	3	U98
33	Calvert	5	P62
34	CAMBERLEY + Yorktown	1	U86
35	CHALFONT + LATIMER	57	U99
36	Charlton Halt	2	P51
37	CHEDDINGTON	2	P91
38	CHESHAM	57	P90
39	Chinnor	3	P70
40	CHOLSEY + Moulsford	3	U58
41	Churn	3A	U58
42	Claydon	2	P72
43	Compton	3A	U58
44	COOKHAM	3	U88
44A	CROWTHORNE §128	6	U86
45	CULHAM	3	U59
46	DATCHET	1	U97
47	DIDCOT	3	U59
48	EARLEY	6	U77
49	Farthinghoe	2	P53
50	FENNY STRATFORD	2	P83
51	Finmere	5	P63
52	Fulwell + Westbury	2	P63
53	(FURZE PLATT)	3	U88
54	GERRARD'S CROSS	35	U98
55	GORING + STREATLEY	3	U68
56	Grandborough Road	57	P72
57	GREAT MISSENDEN	57	P80
58	Haddenham	35	P70
59	Hampstead Norris	3A	U57
60	HENLEY-ON-THAMES	3	U78
61	Hermitage	3A	U57
62	HIGH WYCOMBE	35	U89
62A	(Hinksey Halt)	3	P00
63	(Horspath Halt)	3	P50
64	(Iffley Halt)	3	P50
65	(Ilmer Halt)	35	P70
66	Islip	2	P51
67	KINGS SUTTON	3	P53
68	Kingston Crossing Halt	3	U79
69	Launton	2	P62
70	LEIGHTON BUZZARD	2	P92
71	Lewknor Bridge Halt	3	U79
72	LIDLINGTON	2	P93
73	LITTLE KIMBLE	35	P80
74	Littlemore	3	P50
75	(LONGCROSS)	1	U96
76	Loudwater	3	U89
77	MAIDENHEAD	3	U88
78	MARLOW	3	U88
79	Marsh Gibbon + Poundon	2	P62
80	Marston Gate	2	P81
81	MIDGHAM	3	U56
82	(MONK'S RISBOROUGH)	35	P80
83	(Morris Cowley)	3	P50
84	MORTIMER	3	U66
85	Oddington Halt	2	P51
86	OXFORD	3	P50
87	Oxford Rewley Road	2	P50
88	Oxford Road Halt	2	P51
89	Padbury	2	P72
90	PANGBOURNE	3	U67
91	Port Meadow Halt	2	P50
92	PRINCES RISBOROUGH	35	P80
93	Quainton Road	57	P71
94	RADLEY	3	U59
95	READING	3	U77
96	Reading	6(1)	U77
97	READING WEST	3	U77
98	RIDGMONT	2	P93
99	SANDHURST	6	U86
100	SAUNDERTON	35	U89
101	SEER GREEN Golf Platform	35	U99
102	(South Aylesbury Halt)	35	P81
103	SHIPLAKE	3	U77
104	SLOUGH	3	U98
105	Stanbridgeford	2	P92
106	STOKE MANDEVILLE	57	P81
107	SUNNINGDALE	1	U96
108	(SUNNYMEADS) ✳	1	Q07
109	Swanbourne	2	P82
110	TAPLOW	3	U98
111	Thame	3	P70
112	THATCHAM	3	U56
113	THEALE	3	U67
114	Tiddington	3	P60
115	TILEHURST	3	U67
116	(Towersey Halt)	3	P70
117	TRING	2	P91
118	TWYFORD	3	U77
119	Upton + Blewbury	3A	U58
120	Verney Junction	257	P72
121	VIRGINIA WATER ✳	1	Q06
122	Waddesdon	57	P71
123	Waddesdon Manor	57	P71
124	(Wainhill Halt)	3	P70
125	Wallingford	3	U58
126	WARGRAVE	3	U77
127	Watlington	3	U69
128	WELLINGTON COLLEGE	6	U86
129	Wendlebury Halt	2	P52
130	WENDOVER	57	P80
131	Westcott	57	P71
132	West Wycombe	35	U89
133	Wheatley	3	P50
	WINDSOR + ETON		U97
134	CENTRAL ‡	3	U97
135	RIVERSIDE ‡	1	U97
136	(WINNERSH)	6	U77
137	Winslow	2	P72
138	Winslow Road	57	P72
139	WOBURN SANDS	2	P93
140	WOKINGHAM	6(1)	U86
141	Wolvercote Halt ✳	2	P50
142	Wooburn Green	3	U98
143	Wotton	5	P61
144	Wotton	57	P61

ENGINE SHEDS

No	Name / Location		Ry Ref
E 1	Slough	3	U97
2	Watlington	3	U69
3	Aylesbury	(5)3	P81
4	Henley-on-Thames	3	U78
5	Marlow	3	U88
6	Wallingford	3	U58
7	Oxford	3	P50
8	Abingdon	3	U49
9	Reading	3	U77
10	Leighton Buzzard	2	P92
11	Bletchley	2	P83
12	Didcot ⚥	3	U59
13	Brill	57	P61
14	Oxford	2	P50

WATERTROUGHS

No	Location		Ry Ref
W 1	Aldermaston	3	U66

TUNNELS

No	Name		Ry Ref
T 1	Ardley	3	P02

JUNCTIONS

No	Name / Location		Ry Ref
J 1	Henley Branch	3	U77
2	Wokingham	61	U86
3	Ascot	1	U96
4	Maidenhead	3	U88
5	Slough West	3	U98
6	Slough South	3	U97
7	Slough East	3	U98
8	Bourne End	3	U88
9	High Wycombe	35	U89
10	Chesham	57	U99
11	Wallingford Branch	3	U58
12	Cheddington	2	P91
13	Dunstable Branch	2	P92
14	Bletchley - Bedford Line	2	P83
15	Bletchley - Oxford Line	2	P83
16	Aynho	3	P53

NOTES:

(1) REF - In SP or SU except those marked Q - in TQ ✳

(2) CHANGE of Name MAP date § / MODERN §

(3) Addition of designation is modern ‡

(4) Also spelt Wolvercot ✳

(5) Detail see 118 ⚥

(6) Worked by Gt Western ✕

(7) Quainton Road - utilised for occasional passenger services

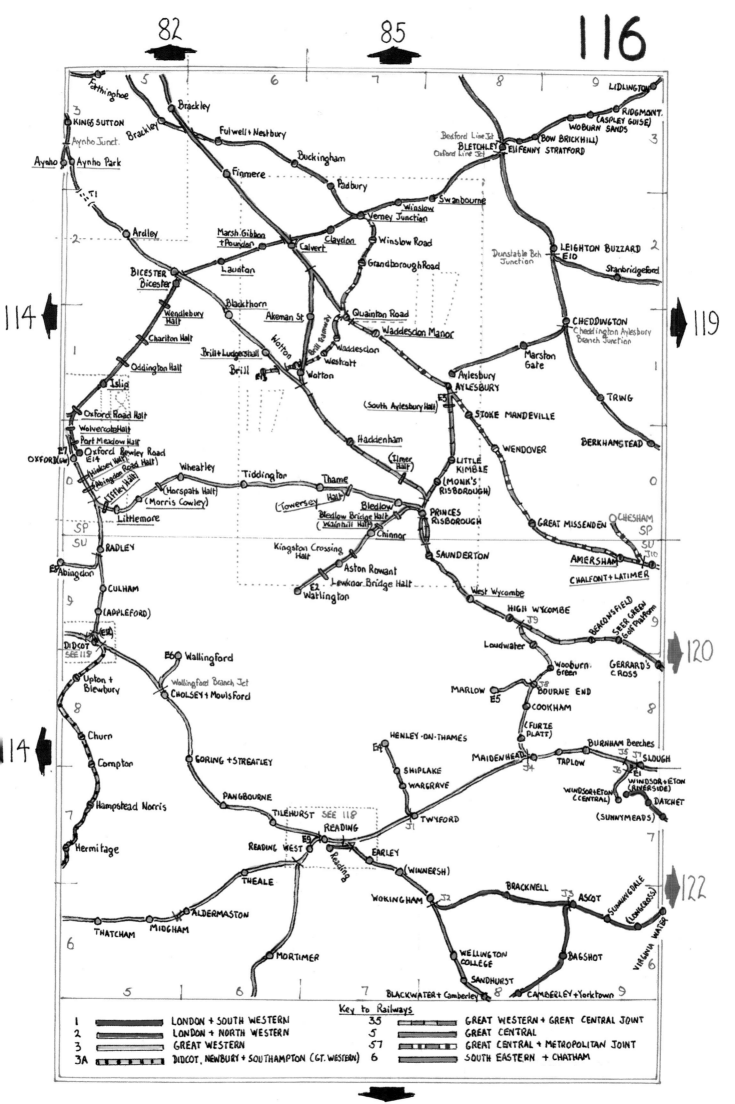

Farthinghoe
Brackley
Brackley
KINGS SUTTON
Aynho Junct.
Aynho   Aynho Park
Ardley
Fulwell + Westbury
Buckingham
Finmere
Padbury
Swanbourne
Winslow   Verney Junction
Marsh Gibbon + Pounden
Claydon   Winslow Road
Calvert
Launton
Grandborough Road
BICESTER
Bicester
Wendlebury Halt
Blackthorn
Akeman St
Quainton Road
Charlton Halt
Watton   Brill Tramway   Waddesdon Manor
Oddington Halt
Brill + Ludgershall   Westcott   Waddesdon
Islip   Brill   Wotton
Oxford Road Halt
Wolvercote Halt
Port Meadow Halt
Oxford Rewley Road   Wheatley
E14
OXFORD (G.W.)   (Hinksey Halt)   Tiddington   Thame
E7   (Abingdon Road Halt)   (Iffley Halt)   (Ilmer Halt)
(Horspath Halt)
(Morris Cowley)   (Towersey Halt)
Littlemore   Haddenham   South Aylesbury Halt
Bledlow   AYLESBURY   E5
RADLEY   Bledlow Bridge Halt   STOKE MANDEVILLE
(Wainhill Halt)
Kingston Crossing Halt   Chinnor   LITTLE KIMBLE   WENDOVER
E3   (MONK'S RISBOROUGH)
Abingdon   PRINCES RISBOROUGH
CULHAM   Aston Rowant   SAUNDERTON   GREAT MISSENDEN
(APPLEFORD)   Lewknor Bridge Halt
E2   AMERSHAM
DIDCOT   Watlington   West Wycombe   CHALFONT + LATIMER
SEE 118
E6   Wallingford   HIGH WYCOMBE
Upton + Blewbury   J9
Wallingford Branch Jct   Loudwater   BEACONSFIELD
CHOLSEY + MOULSFORD   SEER GREEN Golf Platform
Wooburn Green   GERRARD'S CROSS
Churn   MARLOW   BOURNE END
E5   COOKHAM
Compton   GORING + STREATLEY   (FURZE PLATT)
HENLEY-ON-THAMES   BURNHAM Beeches
Hampstead Norris   E4   J5 J7 SLOUGH
PANGBOURNE   MAIDENHEAD   TAPLOW   J6 E1
Hermitage   SHIPLAKE   J4   WINDSOR + ETON (RIVERSIDE)
WARGRAVE   WINDSOR + ETON (CENTRAL)   DATCHET
TILEHURST SEE 118   (SUNNYMEADS)
READING   J1
E9   Twyford
READING WEST   EARLEY
THEALE   (WINNERSH)   BRACKNELL   SUNNINGDALE
WOKINGHAM   J2   J3 ASCOT   (LONGCROSS)
ALDERMASTON   VIRGINIA WATER
THATCHAM   MIDGHAM   WELLINGTON COLLEGE   BAGSHOT
MORTIMER   SANDHURST
BLACKWATER + Camberley   CAMBERLEY + Yorktown

LIDLINGTON
RIDGMONT (ASPLEY GUISE)
WOBURN SANDS
Bedford Line Jct   BLETCHLEY   FENNY STRATFORD
Oxford Line Jct   (BOW BRICKHILL)
LEIGHTON BUZZARD E10
Dunstable Bch Junction   Stanbridgeford
CHEDDINGTON
Cheddington Aylesbury Branch Junction
Marston Gate
TRING
BERKHAMSTEAD
CHESHAM
SP
SU
J10

Key to Railways

1		LONDON + SOUTH WESTERN	35		GREAT WESTERN + GREAT CENTRAL JOINT
2		LONDON + NORTH WESTERN	5		GREAT CENTRAL
3		GREAT WESTERN	57		GREAT CENTRAL + METROPOLITAN JOINT
3A		DIDCOT, NEWBURY + SOUTHAMPTON (GT. WESTERN)	6		SOUTH EASTERN + CHATHAM

117 RAILWAYS

VERNEY JUNCTION, AYLESBURY + PRINCE'S RISBOROUGH

No	Company
R2	LONDON + NORTH WESTERN
3	GREAT WESTERN
35	GREAT WESTERN + GREAT CENTRAL JT
5	GREAT CENTRAL
57	GREAT CENTRAL + METROPOLITAN
57A	BRILL TRAMWAY (GC + Metropolitan)
3557	GW + GC and GC + MET. JOINT
0	(War time addition)

STATIONS + HALTS

No	Name		Ry Ref
A1	Akeman Street	5	P71
2	Aston Rowant	3	U79
3	Aylesbury	2	P81
4	AYLESBURY Joint	3557	P81
5	Bledlow	3	P70
6	Bledlow Bridge Halt	3	P70
7	Brill	57A	P61
8	Brill + Ludgershall	3	P61
9	Calvert	50	P62
10	Chinnor	3	P70
11	Claydon	2	P72
12	Grandborough Road	57	P72
13	Haddenham	35	P70
14	(Ilmer Halt)	35	P70
15	Kingston Crossing Halt	3	U79
16	Lewknor Bridge Halt	3	U79
17	LITTLE KIMBLE	35	P80
18	Marsh Gibbon + Poundon	2	P62
19	(MONK'S RISBOROUGH Halt)	35	P80
20	Padbury	2	P73
21	PRINCES RISBOROUGH	35	P80
22	Quainton Road	57/57A	P71
23	SAUNDERTON	35	U89
24	(South Aylesbury Halt)	35	P81
25	STOKE MANDEVILLE	57	P81
26	Swanbourne	2	P82
27	Thame	3	P70
28	Tiddington	3	P60
29	(Towersey Halt)	3	P70
30	Verney Junction	2	P72
31	Waddesdon	57A	P71
32	Waddesdon Manor	57	P71
33	(Wainhill Halt)	3	P70
34	Westcott	57A	P71
35	Winslow	2	P72
36	Winslow Road	57	P72
37	(Wood Siding) ✠	57A	P61
38	Wotton	5	P61
39	Wotton	57A	P61

SIDINGS

No	Name / Company	Ry Ref
P1	Benton's Siding	3 U79
2	Penn's Farm Siding	3 P70
3	Wood Siding ✠	57A P61
4	Church Siding	57A P61
5	Hartwell Siding	57 P81
6	Ilmers Siding	2 P62

ENGINE SHEDS

No	Location	Ry Ref
E1	Aylesbury	3(57) P81
2	Brill	57A- P61

JUNCTIONS

No	Name/Location	Ry Ref
J1	Princes Risborough South	35 P80
2	Princes Risborough North	335 P80
3	Aylesbury South	35/57/3557 P81
4	Aylesbury North	57/3557 P81
5	Brill Tramway	57/57A P71
6	Quainton Road	557— P71
7	Ashendon	3/5/35— P61
8	Grendon Underwood	5 P72
9	Shepherds Furze	50 P72
10	Claydon + LNE	20 P72
11	Buckingham Line	2 P72
12	Aylesbury Line	257 P72

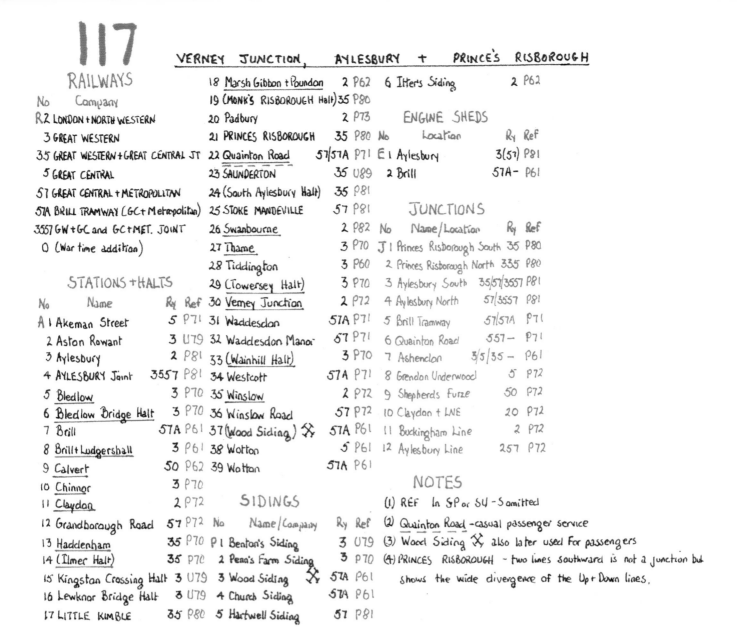

NOTES

(1) REF In SP or SU - S omitted

(2) Quainton Road - casual passenger service

(3) Wood Siding ✠ also later used for passengers

(4) PRINCES RISBOROUGH - two lines southward is not a junction but shows the wide divergence of the Up + Down lines.

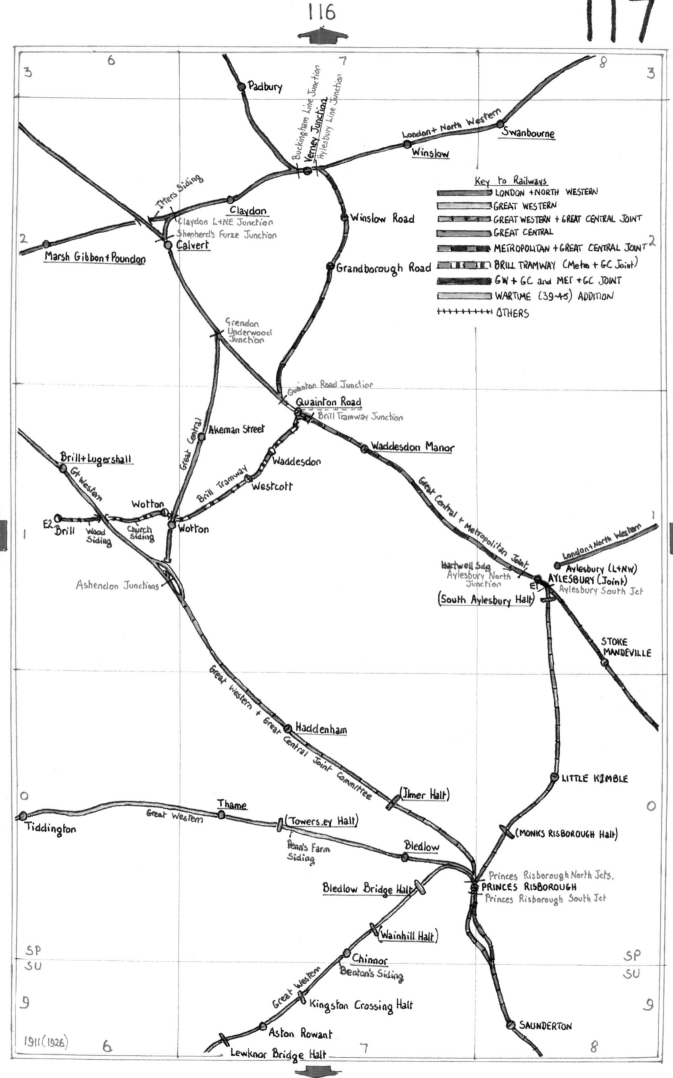

Key to Railways

LONDON + NORTH WESTERN
GREAT WESTERN
GREAT WESTERN + GREAT CENTRAL JOINT
GREAT CENTRAL
METROPOLITAN + GREAT CENTRAL JOINT
BRILL TRAMWAY (Metro + GC Joint)
GW + GC and MET + GC JOINT
WARTIME (39~45) ADDITION
OTHERS

Padbury

Buckingham Line Junction
Verney Junction
Aylesbury Line Junction

London + North Western
Swanbourne

Winslow

Titers Siding

Claydon

Claydon L+NE Junction
Shepherd's Furze Junction

Marsh Gibbon + Poundon
Calvert

Winslow Road

Grandborough Road

Grendon Underwood Junction

Quainton Road Junction
Quainton Road
Brill Tramway Junction

Great Central
Akeman Street

Waddesdon Manor

Brill + Lugershall
Gt Western

Waddesdon

Brill Tramway

Westcott

Great Central + Metropolitan Joint

London + North Western

Wotton

E2 Brill
Wood Siding
Church Siding
Wotton

Hartwell Sdg
Aylesbury North Junction
(South Aylesbury Halt)

Aylesbury (L+NW)
AYLESBURY (Joint)
Aylesbury South Jct

Ashendon Junctions

STOKE MANDEVILLE

Great Western + Great Central Joint Committee
Haddenham

(Ilmer Halt)

LITTLE KIMBLE

Thame
Great Western
(Towersey Halt)

Tiddington

(MONKS RISBOROUGH Halt)

Penn's Farm Siding

Bledlow

Bledlow Bridge Halt

Princes Risborough North Jcts.
PRINCES RISBOROUGH
Princes Risborough South Jct

(Wainhill Halt)

Chinnor
Beaton's Siding

Great Western
Kingston Crossing Halt

SAUNDERTON

Aston Rowant

Lewknor Bridge Halt

1911 (1926)

RAILWAYS

No	Company
R1	LONDON + SOUTH WESTERN
2	LONDON + NORTH WESTERN
2X	LNW (disused by early 20c)
3	GREAT WESTERN
3A	DIDCOT NEWBURY + SOUTHAMPTON (GW)
4	MIDLAND
5	SOUTH EASTERN + CHATHAM
6	GREAT NORTHERN
O	BRITISH RAIL (additions)

STATIONS + HALTS

No	Name	Ry Map
A1	(Abingdon Road Halt)	3 A
2	DIDCOT	3 C
3	EARLEY	5 D
4	Hill End	6 E
5	(Iffley Halt)	3 A
6	Islip	2 A
7	Kidlington	3 A
8	Littlemore	3 A
9	Napsbury	4 E
10	NEWBURY	3 B
11	Newbury Racecourse	3 B
12	Newbury Westfields Halt	3 B
13	OXFORD	3 A
14	Oxford Rewley Road	2 A
15	Oxford Road Halt	2 A
16	PARK STREET	2 E
17	Port Meadow Halt	2 A
18	READING	3 D
19	Reading	5(1) D
20	READING WEST	3 D
21	St Albans	6 E
22	ST ALBANS (ABBEY)	2 E
23	ST ALBANS (CITY)	4 E
24	Speen	3 B
25	Stockcross + Bagnor	3 B
26	Wolvercot Halt †	2 A
27	Wolvercot Platform	3 A
28	Woodhay	3A B
29	Yarnton	3 A

GOODS

No	Name/Location	Ry Map
G1	Oxford	3 A
2	Newbury	3 A
3	Didcot	4 E
4	Reading	3 B
5	Reading Central	3 B

SIDINGS

No	Name/Company/Location	Ry Map
P1	Wolvercot	3 A
2	Port Meadow	2 A
3	Oxford Gas Works	3 A
4	Cotland Siding	3A C
5	Rich's Siding	3A C
6	New Milton Trading	O C
7	CEGB	O C
8	Fleetville	6 E
7	Yarnton Loop	2X A
8	Oxford Road	2 A
9	Enborne	33A B
10	Lambourn Valley	3 B
11	Newbury East	33A B
12	Foxhall	3 C
13	Didcot West Curve	3 C
14	Didcot North	3 C
15	Didcot West	3 C
16	Didcot East	3 C
17	Didcot - Newbury Line	33A C
/	Didcot - BR Junctions	30 C

ENGINE SHEDS

No	Location	Ry Map
E1	Oxford GW	2 A
2	Oxford LNW	3 A
3	Didcot	3 C
4	Reading	3 D
18	Southcot	3 D
19	Coley Branch	3 D
20	Reading South	3 D
21	Reading West	3 D
22	Reading East	3 D
23	Reading Goods	3 D
24	Reading Main Line East	3 D
25	Reading - Earley Line	3(15) D
26	Reading - Low Level	31 D
27	Reading - For Goods	15 D
28	St Albans	26 E

JUNCTIONS

No	Name/Location	Ry Map
J1	Kennington	3 A
2	Oxford North	32 A
3	Wolvercot	3 C
4	Yarnton	3 D
5	Witney	3 D
6	Woodstock	2X A

NOTES:

(1) REF: Shown on maps but Gazetteer Reference is to MAP
(2) Newbury Racecourse – Used for passengers but not on a regular daily basis.
(3) JUNCTIONS + SIDINGS shown RED are BR additions.
(4) WOLVERCOT(E) † Different spelling used by each company !!

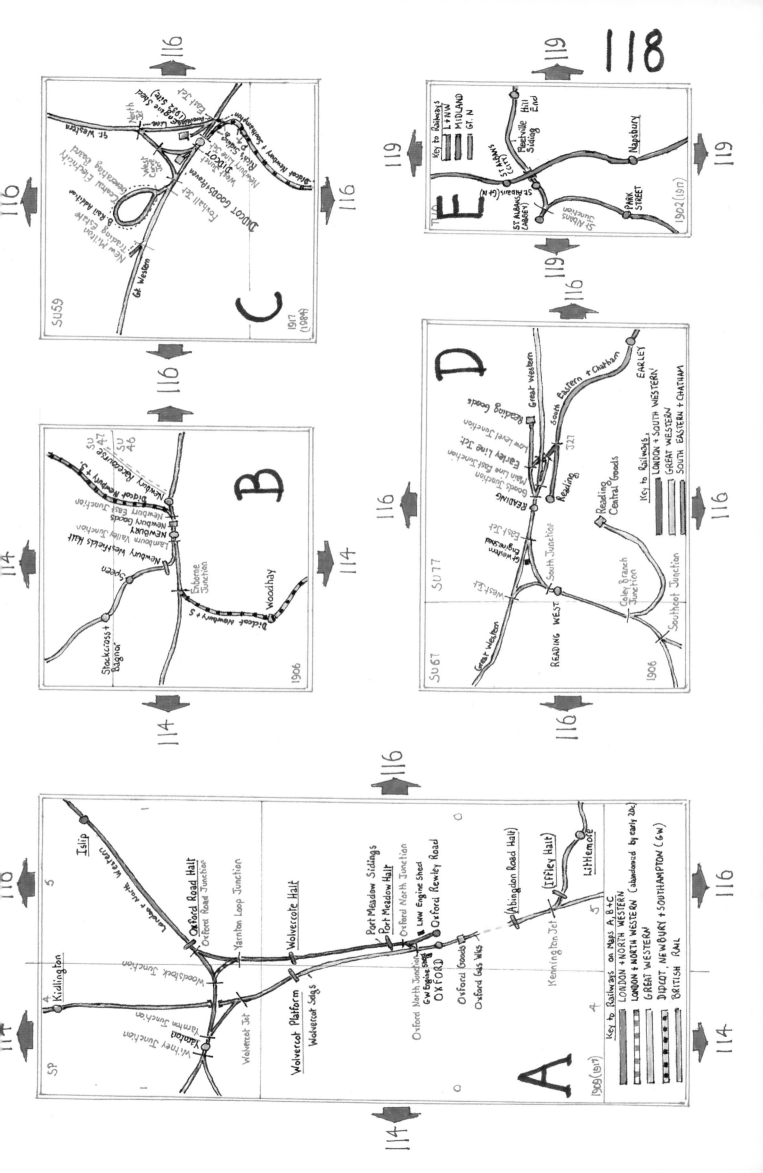

119A

HITCHIN + ST. ALBANS

RAILWAYS

No.	Company
R2	LONDON + NORTH WESTERN
4	MIDLAND
6	GREAT NORTHERN
7	GREAT EASTERN
2	LT - CENTRAL LINE (Ex GE)

STATIONS

No.	Name	Ry Ref
A1	Ampthill	4 03
2	(APSLEY)	2 00
3	Arlesey + Shefford Road	6 13
4	ASHWELL (+ MORDEN)	6 23
5	Ayot	6 21
6	BALDOCK	6 23
7	(BAYFORD)	6 30
8	BISHOP'S STORTFORD	7 42
9	BOXMOOR §32	2 00
10	Braughing	7 32
11	BRICKET WOOD	2 10
12	(BROOKMAN'S PARK)	6 20
13	BROXBOURNE	7 30
14	Buntingford	7 32
15	BURNT MILL §27	7 41
16	CHESHUNT	7 30
17	Chiltern Green	4 11
18	Cole Green	6 21
19	CREWS HILL	6 30
20	CUFFLEY + Goff's Oak	6 30
21	Dunstable	2 02
22	Dunstable	6 02
22A	EPPING	2 40
23	FLITWICK	4 03
24	(GARSTON)	2 10
25	Hadham	7 41
26	HARLINGTON	4 03
27	HARLOW TOWN §15	7 41
28	HARLOW (MILL)	7 41
29	HARPENDEN	4 11
30	Harpenden	6 11
31	HATFIELD	6 20
32	HEMEL HEMPSTEAD §9	2 00
33	Hemel Hempstead	4 00
34	Henlow	4 13
35	Hertingfordbury	6 31
36	Hertford	6 31
37	HERTFORD (EAST)	7 31
38	(HERTFORD NORTH)	6 31
39	Hill End	6 10
40	HITCHIN	6 12
41	KING'S LANGLEY + Abbot's Langley	2 00
42	KNEBWORTH	6 22
43	LEAGRAVE	4 02
44	LETCHWORTH Garden City	6 23
45	LUTON	4 02
46	Luton	6 02
47	Luton Hoo	6 11
48	Mardock	7 31
49	MILLBROOK	2 03
50	Napsbury	4 10
51	(NORTH) WELWYN	6 20
52	NORTH WEALD	2 40
53	PARK STREET	2 10
54	POTTERS BAR	6 20
55	RADLETT	4 10
56	Redbourn	4 11
57	ROYDON	7 41
58	RYE HOUSE	7 31
59	St Albans	6 10
60	ST ALBANS (ABBEY)	2 10
61	ST ALBANS (CITY)	4 10
62	ST MARGARET'S	7 31
63	SAWBRIDGEWORTH	7 41
64	Shefford	4 13
65	Smallford	6 10
66	Standon	7 32
67	Stapleford	6 31
68	STEVENAGE	6 22
69	THEOBALD'S GROVE	7 30
70	Three Counties	6 13
71	WALTHAM CROSS + Abbey	7 39 TQ
72	WARE	7 31
73	(WATTON-AT-STONE)	6 22
74	WELWYN, (NORTH)	6 20
75	(WELWYN GARDEN CITY)	6 20
76	Westmill	7 32
77	Wheathampstead	6 11
78	Widford	7 31

GOODS

No.	Name/Location	Ry Ref
G1	Langford	6 13
2	Hitchin	4 12
3	Dunstable	2 02
4	Dunstable-London Road	6 02
5	Letchworth	6 23
6	Theobald's Grove	7 30

SIDINGS

No.	Company/Location	Ry Ref
P1	London + Arlesey Brick	6 13
2	Luton Corporation	6 02
3	Heath Park	4 00

ENGINE SHEDS

No.	Name/Location	Ry Ref
E1	Hitchin	6 12
2	Hatfield	6 20
3	St. Albans	4 10

TUNNELS

No.	Name	Ry Ref
T1	Ampthill	4 03
2	Welwyn North	6 21
3	Welwyn South	6 21
4	Ponsbourne	6 30

VIADUCTS

No.	Name	Ry Ref
V1	Welwyn	6 21

WATERTROUGHS

No.	Name/Location	Ry Ref
W1	Langley	6 22

JUNCTIONS

No.	Name/Location	Ry Ref
J1	Dunstable	26 02
2	Hitchin Goods	4 13
3	Hitchin	46 13
4	Cambridge Line	6 12
5	Langley	6 22
6	Hemel Hempstead Branch	4 11
7	St Albans - Station	26 10
8	Hatfield - St Albans	6 20
9	Hatfield - Dunstable	6 20
10	Hatfield - Hertford	6 20
11	Cheshunt	7 30
12	Broxbourne	7 30
13	Hertford - New	6 31
14	Hertford - Station	6 31
15	Hertford - GN + GE	67 31
16	St Margaret's	7 31
17	Bishop's Stortford	7 42

NOTES:

(1) REF - All in TL

(2) Part of name in (BRACKETS) indicates post map date addition to name. Part of name in small letters has now been dropped from name.

(3) NAME CHANGE   Map date §
                            Modern §

(4) LONDON TRANSPORT open (CENTRAL LINE Ex GE)

119B

LONDON INDEX SHEET

Map No.	AREA	SCALE (Note1)	REF (Note2)	SIZE (Note3)
120	LONDON - NORTH·WEST	2	00 80	25 x 20
121	LONDON - NORTH·EAST	2	25 80	25 x 20
122	LONDON - SOUTH·WEST	2	00 60	25 x 20
123	LONDON - SOUTH·EAST	2	25 60	25 x 20
124	WILLESDEN JUNCTION, ACTON + HAMMERSMITH	½	18 77	6 x 9
125	PADDINGTON + MARYLEBONE	½	23 77	6 x 9
126	FINSBURY PARK AND LINES TO THE NORTH	½	28 84	9 x 5
127	CENTRAL LONDON - THE CITY	½	28 79	9 x 5
128	STRATFORD + POPLAR	½	37 77	6 x 9
129	CLAPHAM JUNCTION + WIMBLEDON	½	24 69	6 x 9
130	NEW CROSS	½	30 73	9 x 6
131	NORWOOD JUNCTION + THE SOUTHERN SUBURBS	½	30 67	9 x 6

NOTES:

1 SCALE   Miles to the inch approx.

2 REF   SW Corner. All in TQ

3 SIZE   In km s eastwards measurement is given first.

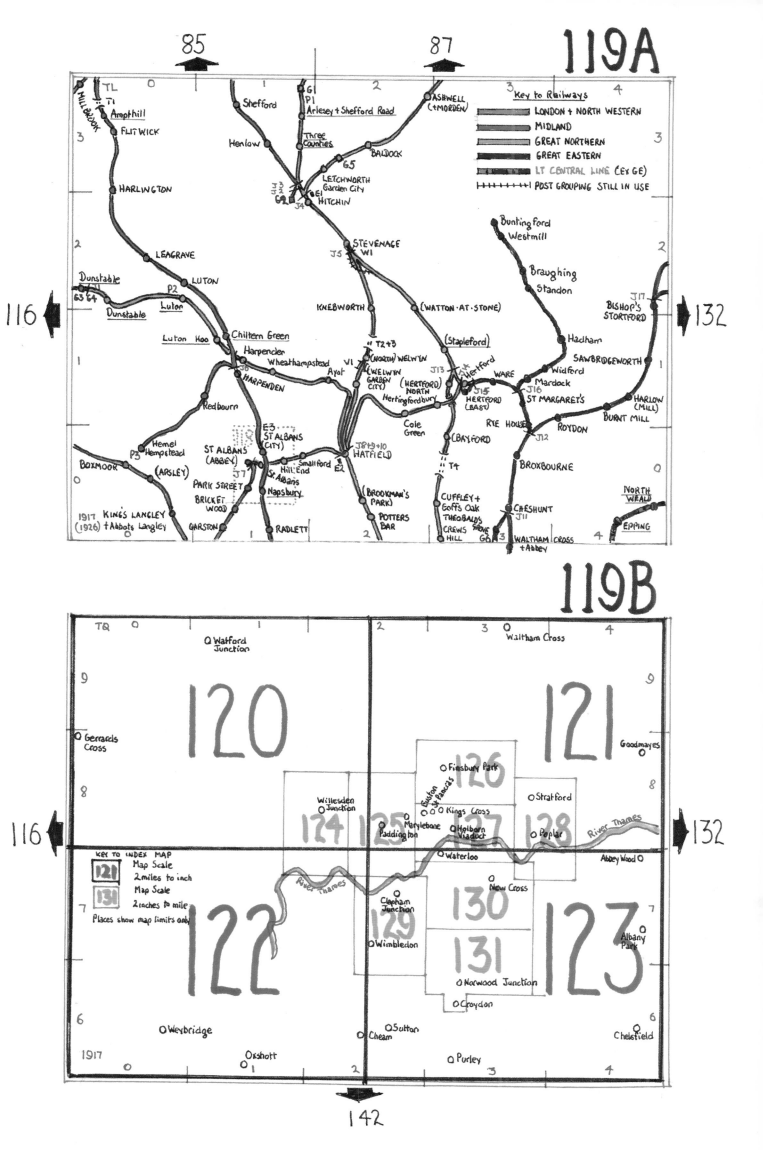

LONDON NORTH WEST

RAILWAYS +

No.	Company	Ry Ref	
R2	LONDON + NORTH WESTERN	3 18	3 18
3	GREAT WESTERN	353 18	353 18
35	GREAT WESTERN + GT CENTRAL JT	355 18	355 18
4	MIDLAND	55 18	
5	GREAT CENTRAL	2 18	
6	GREAT NORTHERN	2 19	
2	CENTRAL LINE	2 19	
5	METROPOLITAN LINE	2 19	
57	METROPOLITAN + PICCADILLY	2 19	
7	PICCADILLY LINE	4 28	
8	BAKERLOO LINE	4 28	
9	NORTHERN LINE	4 28	
11	JUBILEE LINE	57 18	

STATIONS + HALTS **

No.	Name	Ry Ref
A1	ACTON CENTRAL	12 4
2	ACTON (MAIN LINE)	12 4
3	(BELMONT)	2 19
4	(BRENT CROSS)	9 28
5	(BRENTHAM)	3 18
6	(BURNT OAK)	9 29
7	BUSHEY + Oxhey	2 19
8	Callowland §84	2 19
9	(CANONS PARK)	11 19
10	(CAPENDERS PARK)	2 19
11	CASTLE BAR PARK Halt	3 18
12	CHALFONT + LATIMER	55 09
13	CHORLEYWOOD + Chenies §84	55 09
14	(COLINDALE)	9 29
15	Cowley	4 28
16	CRICKLEWOOD	
17	CROXLEY Green	5 09
18	CROXLEY GREEN	2 09
19	DENHAM	35 08
20	DENHAM GOLF (CLUB) Platf	35 08
21	Drayton Green Halt	3 18
22	EALING BROADWAY	12 4
23	EASTCOTE	57 18
24	Edgware	6 19
25	(EDGWARE)	9 29
26	ELSTREE	4 19
27	GERRARDS CROSS	35 08
28	GREENFORD	32 18
29	HANWELL + Elthorne	3 18
30	HARROW + WEALDSTONE	28 19
31	HARROW-ON-THE-HILL	55 18
32	HATCH END	2 19
33	HAYES + HARLINGTON	3 18
34	(HEADSTONE LANE)	2 19
35	HENDON	4 28
36	(HENDON CENTRAL)	9 28
37	(HILLINGDON)	7 18
38	ICKENHAM	9 29
39	(IVER)	3 08
40	(KENSAL GREEN)	12 5
41	KENSAL RISE	12 5
42	KENTON	28 18
43	(KINGSBURY)	11 18
44	LANGLEY	3 08
46	MILL HILL (BROADWAY)	4 29
46	MILL HILL (EAST)	9 29
47	MOOR PARK + Sandy Lodge	55 09
48	NORTH HARROW	5 09
49	NORTHOLT	2 09
50	(NORTHOLT PARK)	35 08
51	NORTH WEMBLEY	35 08 / 28 18
52	(NORTHWICK PARK)	3 18
53	NORTHWOOD	12 4
54	NORTHWOOD HILLS	57 18
55	PERIVALE	6 19
56	PINNER	9 29
57	PRESTON ROAD	4 19
58	(QUEENSBURY)	35 08
59	RAYNERS LANE	32 18
60	RICKMANSWORTH	3 18
61	Rickmansworth	28 19
62	RUISLIP	55 18
63	RUISLIP GARDENS	2 19
64	RUISLIP MANOR	3 18
65	SOUTHALL	2 19
66	(SOUTH GREENFORD)	4 28
67	SOUTH HARROW	9 28
68	SOUTH KENTON	57 08
69	SOUTH RUISLIP + Northolt Junction	57 08 / 3 08
70	Stanmore	12 5
71	STANMORE	12 5
72	(STONEBRIDGE PARK)	28 18
73	SUDBURY + HARROW ROAD	11 18
74	SUDBURY HILL	3 08
75	SUDBURY HILL (+) HARROW	4 29
76	SUDBURY TOWN	9 29
77	The Hale Halt	6 29
78	UXBRIDGE	57 08
79	Uxbridge High Street	3 08
80	Uxbridge Vine Street	3 08
81	(WATFORD)	5 19
82	WATFORD HIGH STREET	28 18
83	WATFORD JUNCTION	5 18
84	(WATFORD NORTH) §8	5 09
85	(WATFORD STADIUM)	5 19
86	WATFORD WEST	2 18
87	WEMBLEY CENTRAL	5 19
88	WEMBLEY Hill (COMPLEX)	5 18
89	WEMBLEY PARK	11 19
90	Wembley Stadium	57 18
91	WEST DRAYTON + Yiewsley	55 09
92	WEST EALING	2 09
93	WEST HARROW	57 18
94	(WEST) RUISLIP + Ickenham	352 08 / 2 18
95	WILLESDEN JUNCTION	124- / 57 18

ENGINE SHEDS

No.	Location	Ry Ref	
E1	Southall	5 19	3 18
2	Watford	2 19	2 19

8	Drayton Green	3 18
9	Greenford South	3 18
10	Greenford West	353 18
11	Greenford East	353 18
12	Northolt	355 18
13	Harrow North	55 18
14	Stanmore Branch	2 18
15	Watford West Jcts	2 19

JUNCTIONS

No.	Name / Location	Ry Ref	
J1	West Drayton	2 19	3 08
2	Uxbridge Branch South	3 08	
3	Uxbridge Branch West	353 08	
4	Uxbridge Branch East	353 08	
5	Southall	3 18	
6	Hanwell	3 18	
7	West Ealing	3 18	
16	Bushey	2 19	
17	Rickmansworth Branch	2 19	
18	St Albans Branch	2 19	
19	Dudding Hill	4 28	
20	Brent Curve	4 28	
21	Cricklewood Curve	4 28	
22	Rayners Lane	57 18	
23	Preston Road	511 18	

GOODS

No.	Name	Ry Ref
G1	Watford	28 18 / 2 19

SIDINGS

No.	Name	Ry Ref
P1	Bushey Lodge Siding	11 9 / 2 19
2	Turner's Siding	12 4 / 2 19

TUNNELS

No.	Name	Yds	Ry Ref
T1	Watford East	5 18	2 19
	Watford Fast	7 18	1815

NOTES:

All in TQ

† LONDON TRANSPORT - Modern Line Names

Where lines used by both BR+LT (or an adjoining line) only shown if station or facility used by both. May be separate sta.

* Full details - see Maps 124 or +125

* LONDON TRANSPORT (also LT)

BRITISH RAIL

§ Name change MODERN NAME, Old Name. Part of Name in (CAPITALS + BRACKETS) is a modern addition. Part in small letters is an indication that portion now dropped.

See note on map.

See Key to railways on map.

(1) REFERENCES
(2) RAILWAYS
(3) STATIONS
(4) ENLARGEMENTS
(5) BR + LT JOINT

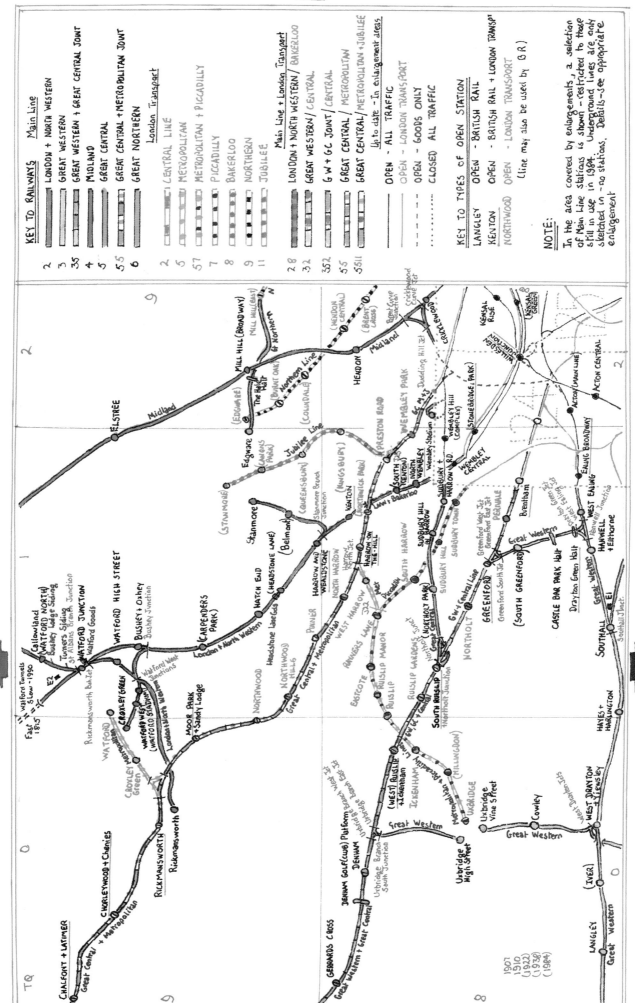

LONDON NORTH EAST

RAILWAYS †

No	Company
R4-7	TOTTENHAM + HAMPSTEAD (Mid + GE)
48	TOTTENHAM + FOREST GATE (Mid + LTS)
6	GREAT NORTHERN
7	GREAT EASTERN
8	LONDON TILBURY + SOUTHEND
2.2	PORT OF LONDON AUTHORITY
2	CENTRAL LINE
4	DISTRICT LINE
46	DISTRICT + METROPOLITAN
7	PICCADILLY LINE
9	NORTHERN LINE

STATIONS + HALTS ✳ ✳

No	Name	Ry Ref
A1	ALEXANDRA PALACE &1 48	6 39
2	ALEXANDRA PALACE	6 39
3	ANGEL ROAD	7 39
4	(ARNOS GROVE)	7 39
5	BARKING	8 45 48
6	BARKINGSIDE	2 48
7	BECKTON	7 48
8	(BECONTREE)	4 48
9	BETHNAL GREEN	12 7
10	BLACKFRIARS	12 7
11	BLACKHORSE ROAD	48 38
12	(BOUNDS GREEN)	7 39
13	BOWES PARK	6 39
14	BRIMSDOWN	7 39
15	BROAD STREET	12 7
16	BRUCE GROVE	7 39
17	BUCKHURST HILL	2 49
18	BUSH HILL PARK	7 39
19	CAMBRIDGE HEATH	12 7
20	CAMDEN ROAD	12 6
21	CANNING TOWN	12 8
22	CANNON STREET	12 7
23	CANONBURY	12 6
24	CHADWELL HEATH	7 48
25	CHARING CROSS	1 27
26	CHIGWELL	2 49
27	CHIGWELL LANE &3 38	2 49
28	CHINGFORD	7 49
29	CHURCHBURY &1 19	7 39
30	CLAPTON	12 6
31	(COCKFOSTERS)	7 29
32	CONNAUGHT ROAD	7 22 48
33	CRANLEY GARDENS	6 28
34	CUSTOM HOUSE - VICTORIA DOCK	12 8
35	DAGENHAM DOCK	8 48
36	(DAGENHAM HEATHWAY)	4 48
37	DALSTON JUNCTION	12 6
38	(DEBDEN) &2 7	2 49
39	DRAYTON PARK	12 6
40	EAST FINCHLEY	7 28
41	EAST HAM	45 48
42	ENFIELD CHASE	6 39
43	ENFIELD LOCK	7 39
44	ENFIELD TOWN	7 39
45	ESSEX ROAD	12 6
46	EUSTON	12 7
47	FAIRLOP	2 49
48	FENCHURCH STREET	12 7
49	FINCHLEY (CENTRAL)	12 7
50	FINSBURY PARK	12 6
51	FOREST GATE	7 39
52	FORTY HILL &1 29	6 39
53	GALLIONS	7 48
54	(GANTS HILL)	2 48
55	GEORGE LANE &1 21	2 49
56	GOLDERS GREEN	7 28
57	GOODMAYES	7 48
58	GORDON HILL	6 39
59	GRANGE HILL	2 49
60	GRANGE PARK	6 39
61	HACKNEY CENTRAL	12 6
62	HACKNEY DOWNS	12 6
63	HADLEY WOOD	6 29
64	(HAINAULT)	2 49
65	HAMPSTEAD	7 28
66	HARINGAY	7 39
67	HIGHAMS PARK	9 29
68	HIGH BARNET	7 28
69	HIGHGATE	12 6
70	HOLBORN VIADUCT	12 7
71	HOMERTON	7 22 48
72	HORNSEY	6 28
73	ILFORD	12 8
74	KENTISH TOWN	12 6
75	KILBURN HIGH ROAD	12 5
76	KINGS CROSS	12 7
77	LEA BRIDGE	12 6
78	LEYTON	2 49
79	LEYTON (MIDLAND ROAD)	12 6
80	LEYTONSTONE	7 28
81	LEYTONSTONE (HIGH ROAD)	45 48
82	LIVERPOOL STREET	6 39
83	LONDON BRIDGE	7 39
84	LONDON FIELDS	7 39
85	LOUGHTON	12 6
86	LOWER EDMONTON High Level	12 7
87	Lower Edmonton Low Level	2 49
88	MANOR PARK + Little Ilford	12 7
89	MANOR WAY	9 29
90	MARYLAND	12 6
91	MARYLEBONE	12 8
92	MILL HILL (EAST)	7 39
93	MOORGATE	22 48
94	MUSWELL HILL	2 48
95	NEW BARNET	2 49
96	NEWBURY PARK	7 28
97	NEW SOUTHGATE	7 48
98	NOEL PARK	6 39
99	(NORTHUMBERLAND) PARK	2 49
100	NORTH WOOLWICH	6 39
101	OAKLEIGH PARK	12 6
102	(OAKWOOD)	12 6
103	PADDINGTON	6 29
104	PALACE GATES	2 49
105	PALMERS GREEN &99	7 28
106	PARK	1 26
107	PONDERS END	7 39
108	QUEENS PARK	9 29
109	RECTORY ROAD	7 28
110	(REDBRIDGE)	1 27
111	(RODING VALLEY)	1 26
112	ST JAMES'S STREET	6 38
113	ST PANCRAS	7 48
114	SEVEN KINGS	1 26
115	SEVEN SISTERS	12 5
116	SILVER STREET	1 27
117	SILVER TOWN	1 26
118	SNARESBROOK	2 38
119	(SOUTHBURY) &29	48 38
120	(SOUTHGATE)	2 48
121	(SOUTH WOODFORD) &55	48 48
122	STAMFORD HILL	1 27
123	STEPNEY EAST	1 27
124	STOKE NEWINGTON	1 26
125	STRATFORD	2 49
126	THEYDON BOIS	7 39
127	TOTTENHAM (The Hale)	7 39
128	TOTTERIDGE + WHETSTONE	7 48
129	TURKEY HILL &52	22 48
130	(TURNPIKE ROAD)	12 8
131	UPNEY	12 5
132	VICTORIA DOCK, CUSTOM H.se	9 29
133	WALTHAMSTOW CENTRAL - Hoe Street	1 27
134	WALTHAMSTOW - QUEENS RD	6 29
135	(WANSTEAD)	2 48
136	WANSTEAD PARK	6 29
137	WATERLOO	7 39
138	WESTBOURNE PARK	7 39
139	(WEST FINCHLEY)	7 48
140	WEST GREEN	6 29
141	WEST HAM	7 39
142	WEST HAMPSTEAD	12 5
143	WHITE HART LANE	7 39
144	WINCHMORE HILL	7 39
145	WOODFORD	7 39
146	WOODGRANGE PARK	7 39
147	(WOOD GREEN)	12 5
148	Wood Lane &1	12 6
149	WOODSIDE PARK	2 48
150	WOOD STREET	2 49

Enlargement sub-entries:
11	Alexandra Palace	6 39
12	Finchley	LT 29
13	Park	6 28
14	Seven Sisters North	7 38
15	Seven Sister South	7 38

GOODS

No	Location	Ry Ref
G1	Barkingside	7 38
2	Enfield	7 39
3	Fairlop	7 48
4	Forest Gate	2 48
5	Grange Hill	7 39
6	Ilford	7 39
7	Loughton	2 49
8	Newbury Park	1 26
9	Queens Road	1 27
10	South Woodford	1 26
11	Temple Mills	12 8

ENGINE SHEDS

No	Location	Ry Ref
E1	Hornsey	7 39
2	Enfield	7 39

JUNCTIONS

No	Name / Location	Ry Ref
J1	Lower Edmonton	7 38
2	Bury Street	48 38
3	Angel Road	2 48
4	Ilford North	1 26
5	Ilford East	1 27
6	Ilford West	1 25
7	East Ham Loop North	9 29
8	East Ham West	7 38
9	East Ham East	1 28
10	Enfield Goods	12 5

NOTES:

(1) REF - All in TQ

(2) RAILWAYS - † LONDON TRANSPORT
Modern line names used, where lines used by both BR+LT (or an adjoining line) only shown if the actual station is used by both.
May be a SEPARATE closely - adjoining station

(3) STATIONS ✳ Passenger stations in blue for full detail see the numbered enlargement map-this is shown across Ry + Ref columns
✳ LONDON TRANSPORT (in RED)
BRITISH RAIL (also LT)
§ Name change - MODERN, Old.
( ) Part shows modern addition.
Part small letters shows that part of name now dropped

(4) ENLARGEMENTS - CENTRAL LONDON)
See notes on map page also.

(5) BR + LT Joint lines - See key to railways on the map.

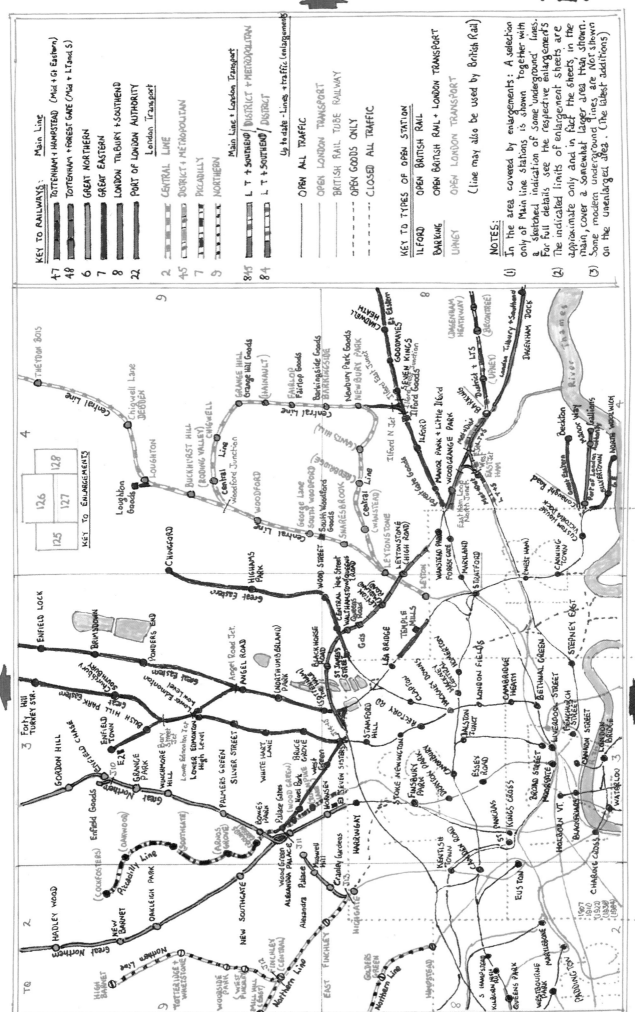

RAILWAYS +

No	Company
R1	LONDON + SOUTH WESTERN
144	L+SW AND LB+SC JOINT
3	GREAT WESTERN
44	LONDON BRIGHTON + SOUTH COAST
00	SOUTHERN (Post Grouping)
4	DISTRICT LINE
7	PICCADILLY LINE

STATIONS + HALTS

No	Name	Ry Ref
A 1	ADDLESTONE	1 06
2	ASHFORD	1 07
3	BANSTEAD	144 26
4	BARNES	1 27
5	(BARNES BRIDGE)	1 27
6	(BERRYLANDS)	1 26
7	BOSTON (MANOR) Road	7 17
8	BRENTFORD	1 17
9	Brentford	3 17
10	(BYFLEET + NEW HAW)	1 06
11	BYFLEET (WEST)	1 06
12	CHEAM	144 26
13	CHERTSEY	1 06
14	(CHESSINGTON NORTH)	00 26
15	(CHESSINGTON SOUTH)	00 16
16	CHISWICK + Grove Park	1 27
17	CLAYGATE	1 16
18	Colnbrook	3 07
19	Coombe + Malden §52	1 26
20	EAST PUTNEY	4 27
21	EGHAM	1 07
22	EPSOM	1 26
23	Epsom	44 26
24	ESHER + Claremont	1 16
25	EWELL (EAST)	44 26
26	EWELL (WEST)	1 26
27	FELTHAM	1 17
28	FULWELL + Hampton Hill	1 17
29	GUNNERSBURY *	124
30	HAMPTON	1 17
31	HAMPTON COURT	1 16
32	HAMPTON WICK	1 17
33	(HATTON CROSS)	7 17
34	HAYES + HARLINGTON	3 17
35	(HEATHROW TERMINALS 1-3)	7 07
36	(HEATHROW TERMINAL 4)	7 07
37	(HERSHAM)	1 16
38	Heston-Hounslow (Central)	7
39	(HINCHLEY WOOD)	1 16
40	HOUNSLOW + Whitton	1 17
41	(Hounslow Barracks) / (HOUNSLOW WEST)	7 17
42	(HOUNSLOW EAST)	7 17
43	Hounslow Town	7 17
44	ISLEWORTH + Spring Grove	1 17
45	Kempton Park	1 17
46	KEW BRIDGE *	124
47	KEW GARDENS	14 17
48	KINGSTON	1 16
49	(MALDEN MANOR)	00 26
50	MORTLAKE	1 27
51	(MOTSPUR PARK)	1 26
52	(NEW MALDEN) §19	1 07
53	NORTHFIELDS	1 26
54	(NORTH SHEEN)	44 26
55	OSTERLEY	1 16
56	OXSHOTT	44 26
57	(Poyle for Stanwell Moor Halt)	1 26
58	PUTNEY	1 17
59	(PUTNEY BRIDGE)	124
60	RAYNES PARK	1 17
61	RICHMOND	1 16
62	Runemede Range	1 17
63	ST MARGARETS	7 17
64	SHEPPERTON	3 17
65	SOUTH ACTON	7 07
66	SOUTHALL	7 07
67	SOUTH EALING	1 16
68	Staines	7
69	Staines High Street	1 16
70	STAINES JUNCTION	1 17
71	(STONELEIGH)	7 17
72	STRAWBERRY HILL	7 17
73	SUNBURY	7 17
74	(SUNNYMEADS)	7 17
75	SURBITON	1 17
76	(SYON LANE)	1 17
77	TEDDINGTON	1 17
78	THAMES DITTON	14 17
79	(TOLWORTH)	1 16
80	Trumpers Crossing Halt	00 26
81	TWICKENHAM	1 27
82	(UPPER HALLIFORD)	1 26
83	VIRGINIA WATER	126
84	WALTON (ON-THAMES)+Hersham	6
85	WEYBRIDGE	1 16
86	(WHITTON)	1 17
87	WIMBLEDON	144+27
88	WORCESTER PARK	1 26
89	WRAYSBURY	1 07
5	Virginia Water South	126
6	Virginia Water East	1 16
7	Staines	1 16
8	Staines West	1 06
9	Staines High Street	1 17
10	New Guildford Line	144+27
11	Hampton Court	1 26
12	Thames Valley	1 07
13	Shacklegate	
14	Fulwell	
15	Feltham	
16	Whitton	1 06
17	Hounslow	1 06
18	Lampton	LT 17
19	Epsom	144 26
20	Motspur Park	100 26
21	Raynes Park South	1 26
22	Raynes Park	1 26
23	New Malden	1 26
24	Barnes	1 26
25	Southall	1 27
26	Richmond	3 17

GOODS

No.	Location	Ry Ref
61	Brentford	3 17
62	Coombe + Malden	1 26
63	Kingston	1 17
64	Runemede *	3 07

SIDINGS

No	Name/Location	Ry Ref
P1	Cunliffe Siding	1 26
P2	Kingston Gas Works	1 17

ENGINE SHEDS

No	Location	Ry Ref
E1	Southall	3 17
E2	Feltham Junction	1 17

JUNCTIONS

No	Name/Location	Ry Ref
J1	Byfleet	1 06
2	Weybridge	1 06
3	Addlestone	1 06
4	Virginia Water North	1 06

NOTES:

(1)	REFERENCES	All in TQ
(2)	RAILWAYS	LONDON TRANSPORT - Modern Line names
(3)	STATIONS †	FULL DETAILS SEE MAP 124
(4)	NAME CHANGE §	MODERN, Old
(5)	ENLARGEMENTS	See notes on map.
(6)	BR+LT JOINT	See key to railways on map.
(7)	Kempton Park	Station open for some passenger trains but not on a daily basis

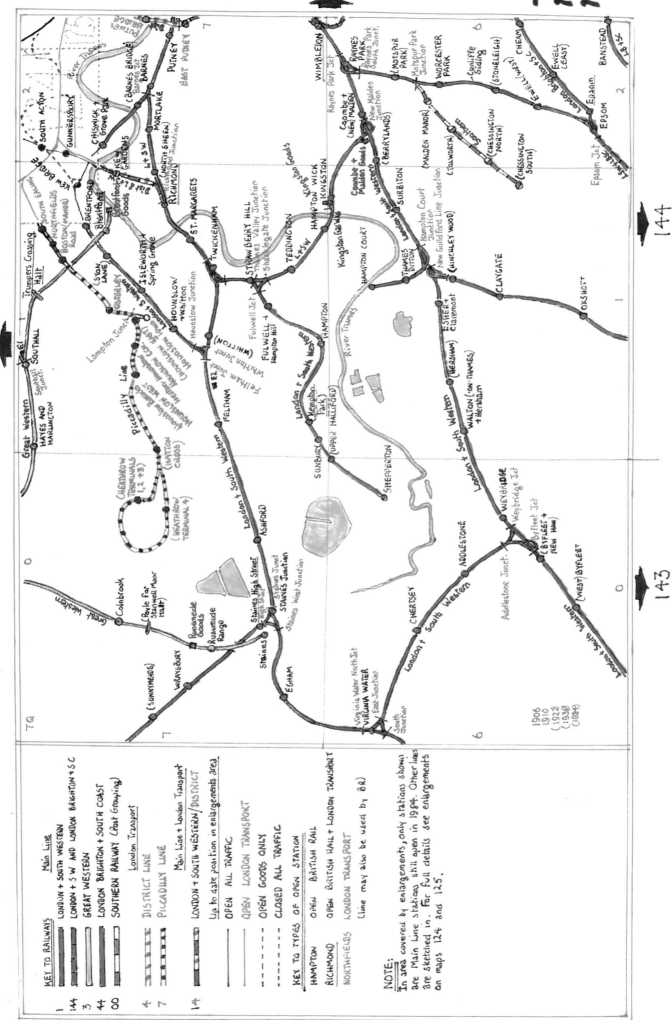

NOTES:
(1) REF: All in TQ
(2) MORDEN - LT Station +
(3) STATIONS In Blue - see enlargements
(4) NAME CHANGE $ NEW Old
(5) SEE ALSO NOTE ON MAP

RAILWAYS +

No	Company
R 7	GREAT EASTERN
11	SOUTH EASTERN + CHATHAM
1144	SE+CHATHAM and LB+SC JOINT
44	LONDON, BRIGHTON + SOUTH COAST
00	SOUTHERN (Post Grouping)
9	NORTHERN LINE

GOODS

No	Location	Ry Ref
G 1	Chislehurst	11 46
2	Orpington	11 46

SIDINGS

No	Location	Ry Ref
P 1	Hither Green Exchange	11 47

SUMMITS

No	Name	Ht	Ry Ref
S 1	Knockholt		11 47

JUNCTIONS

No	Name/Location	Ry Ref
J 1	Sutton-Wimbledon	4400 26
2	Sutton-Epsom	44 26
3	Sutton	44 26
4	Mitcham South	44 26
5	Mitcham North	44 26
6	Caterham Line	11 36
7	Selsdon	1144 36
8	South Croydon	44 36
9	West Croydon	44 36
10	Woodside	11 36
11	Chislehurst	11 46
12	Bickley	11 46
13	St Mary Cray	11 46
14	Orpington	44 36
15	Bromley Branch	11 47
16	Lee Spur	11 47
17	Lee	11 47
18	Blackheath	11 47

STATIONS + HALTS *

No	Name	Ry Ref
A 1	ABBEY WOOD	11 47
2	ADDISCOMBE Road	11 36
3	(ALBANY PARK) §11A	11 47
4	BALHAM	12 9
5	BANSTEAD	44 26
6	BATTERSEA PARK	12 9
7	BECKENHAM	13 1
8	BECKENHAM HILL	13 1
9	BEDLINGTON LANE	44 26
10	BELLINGHAM	13 1
11	BELMONT §3	44 26
11A	Bexley	11 47
12	BEXLEY HEATH	11 47
13	BICKLEY	11 46
14	Bingham Road Halt	1144 36
15	BIRKBECK	13 1
16	BLACKHEATH	11 47
17	BRIXTON	13 0
18	BROCKLEY	13 0
19	BROMLEY NORTH	11 46
20	BROMLEY SOUTH	11 46
21	CARSHALTON	44 26
22	CARSHALTON (BEECHES)	44 26
23	CATFORD	13 0
24	CATFORD BRIDGE	13 0
25	CHARLTON	12 8
26	CHEAM	44 26
27	CHELSFIELD	11 46
28	CHISLEHURST	11 46
29	CLAPHAM	13 0
30	CLAPHAM JUNCTION	12 9
31	CLOCK HOUSE	13 1
32	Coombe Lane	1144 36
33	Coulsdon	44 36
34	Coulsdon + Cane Hill	11 36
35	CROFTON PARK	13 0
36	CRYSTAL PALACE	13 1
37	DENMARK HILL	13 0
38	DEPTFORD	13 0
39	EARLSFIELD	12 9
40	EAST CROYDON	44 36
41	EAST DULWICH	13 0
42	EDEN PARK	13 1
43	ELEPHANT + CASTLE	12 7
44	ELMERS END	13 1
45	ELMSTEAD WOODS	11 47
46	(ELTHAM)	11 47
47	Eltham + MOTTINGHAM §77	11 47
48	Eltham Park (Shooters Hill)	44 26
49	(Eltham) Well Hall	13 1
50	(FALCON WOOD)	44 26
51	FOREST HILL	11 47
52	GIPSY HILL	11 47
53	GREENWICH	11 46
54	GROVE PARK	1144 36
55	HACKBRIDGE	13 1
56	HANDON'S ROAD	11 47
57	HAYES	13 0
58	HERNE HILL	13 0
59	HITHER GREEN	11 46
60	HONOR OAK PARK	11 46
61	KENLEY	44 26
62	KENT HOUSE	44 26
63	KIDBROOKE	13 0
64	KNOCKHOLT	13 0
65	LEE for Burnt Ash	12 8
66	LEWISHAM	44 26
67	LONDON BRIDGE	11 46
68	LOUGHBOROUGH JUNCTION	11 46
69	LOWER SYDENHAM	13 0
70	MAZE HILL	12 9
71	MERTON PARK	13 1
72	MITCHAM	1144 36
73	MITCHAM JUNCTION	44 36
74	MORDEN	11 36
75	MORDEN ROAD	13 0
76	(MORDEN SOUTH)	13 1
77	MOTTINGHAM §47	13 0
78	NEW BECKENHAM	13 0
79	NEW CROSS	12 9
80	NEW CROSS GATE	44 36
81	New Eltham + Pope Street	11 47
82	NORBURY	13 1
83	NORTH DULWICH	13 0
84	NORTH WOOLWICH	13 1
85	NORWOOD JUNCTION	11 47
86	NUNHEAD	11 47
87	ORPANGTON	11 47
88	PECKHAM RYE	11 47
89	(PETT'S WOOD)	11 47
90	PENGE EAST	11 47
91	PENGE WEST	13 1
92	PLUMSTEAD	13 1
93	PURLEY	13 0
94	PURLEY OAKS	11 47
95	QUEENS ROAD PECKHAM	44 26
96	QUEENSTOWN ROAD	12 9
97	RAVENSBOURNE	11 46
98	(REEDHAM)	13 0
99	(RIDDLESDOWN)	11 47
100	(ST HELIER)	13 0
101	ST JOHN'S	11 36
102	ST MARY CRAY	13 1
103	SANDERSTEAD	11 47
104	SELHURST	11 46
105	Selsdon (Road)	11 47
106	(Shooters Hill)+Eltham Park	11 47
107	SHORTLANDS	11 36
108	SIDCUP	11 47
109	SILVERTOWN	13 1
110	SMITHAM	12 8
111	SOUTH BERMONDSEY	12 9
112	SOUTH CROYDON	44 26
113	(SOUTH MERTON)	44 26
114	Spencer Road	9 26
115	STREATHAM	12 9
116	STREATHAM COMMON	00 26
117	STREATHAM HILL	11 47
118	SUNDRIDGE PARK	13 1
119	SUTTON	13 0
120	(SUTTON COMMON)	13 0
121	SYDENHAM	11 47
122	SYDENHAM HILL	13 1
123	THORNTON HEATH	13 0
124	TOOTING	7 47
125	TULSE HILL	13 1
126	VAUXHALL	13 0
127	VICTORIA	11 46
128	WADDON	13 0
129	(WADDON MARSH)	11 46
130	WALLINGTON	13 1
131	WANDSWORTH COMMON	13 1
132	WANDSWORTH ROAD	11 47
133	WANDSWORTH TOWN	44 36
134	WATERLOO	44 36
135	WELLING	13 0
136	WESTCOMBE PARK	12 9
137	WEST CROYDON	13 1
138	WEST DULWICH	11 36
139	WEST NORWOOD	1144 36
140	(WEST SUTTON)	00 26
141	WEST WICKHAM	13 0
142	WIMBLEDON	11 46
143	WIMBLEDON CHASE	1144 36
144	WOODSIDE + South Norwood	13 1
145	WOOLWICH ARSENAL	1144 36
146	WOOLWICH DOCKYARD	11 47

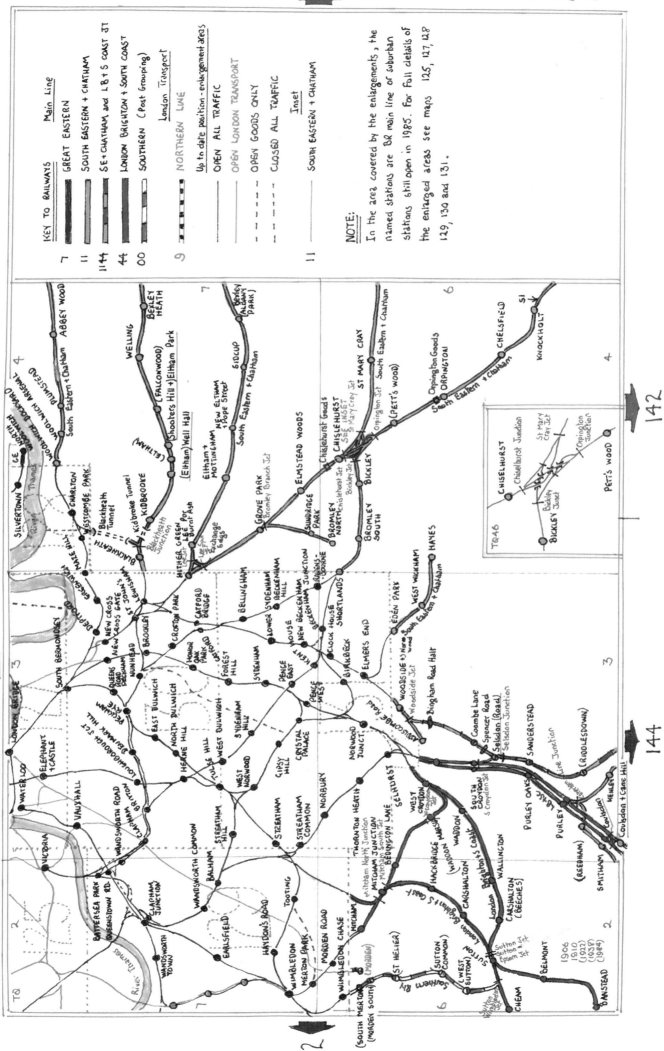

WILLESDEN JUNCTION, ACTON + HAMMERSMITH

RAILWAYS

No	Legend	Company/Line/Partners
R 1		LONDON + SOUTH WESTERN
2		LONDON + NORTH WESTERN
3		GREAT WESTERN
4		MIDLAND
5		GREAT CENTRAL
9		NORTH LONDON
00		LONDON MIDLAND + SCOTTISH
23		WEST LONDON (GW + LNW Joint)
249		NORTH + SOUTH WESTERN JCT JT (LNW, Mid + NL)
008		LMS + BAKERLOO LINE
2		CENTRAL LINE
4		DISTRICT LINE
5		METROPOLITAN LINE
7		PICCADILLY LINE
8		BAKERLOO LINE
11		JUBILEE LINE
24		CENTRAL + DISTRICT LINES
47		DISTRICT + PICCADILLY LINES
511		METROPOLITAN + JUBILEE LINES
4X		DISTRICT CLOSED
2X		CENTRAL CLOSED

NOTES:

(1) REFERENCES — All in TQ

(2) JOINT STATIONS — May be on different levels or closely adjoining sites

(3) JOINT LINES — May be on different levels eg - District + Piccadilly west from Earls Court. Where the stations shown as non-joint other line trains do not use, eg.- Dollis Hill (Jubilee) but line is Metropolitan + Jubilee.

(4) NAME CHANGES — § MODERN Old

Combination of LARGE and small letters in station title indicates portion of name in small letters is no longer used. A portion of the title written in (brackets) is a later addition to the name.

(5) UNDERGROUND — Modern line names are utilised - closed sections are related to modern line name also.

(6) DATE OF CHANGES — In most cases changes in name and new stations are before or AFTER 1910.

(7) STATION — LT

(8) STATION — LT + BR

(9) LMS addition — In the main in use under LNW, but post-map date.

STATIONS

No.	Name	Ry Ref
A1	ACTON CENTRAL	249 2080
2	ACTON (MAIN LINE)	3 2081
3	ACTON TOWN	47 1979
4	ALPERTON §31	7 1884
5	Bath Road Halt	249 2178
6	Brentham	3 1883
7	CHISWICK PARK	47 2078
8	DOLLIS HILL	11 2285
9	EALING BROADWAY	3 1881
10	EALING BROADWAY	24 1881
11	EALING COMMON	47 1980
12	(EAST ACTON)	2 2181
13	GOLDHAWK ROAD §36	5 2379
14	Grove Road	1 2378
15	GUNNERSBURY	14 1978
16	HAMMERSMITH	47 2378
17	Hammersmith + Chiswick	249 2178
18	HAMMERSMITH-Broadway	5 2378
19	(HANGER LANE)	2 1882
20	HARLESDEN	(2)008 2183
21	KEW BRIDGE	1 1978
22	Kew Bridge	1(249) 1978
23	NEASDEN + Kingsbury	11 2185
24	(NORTH ACTON)	2 2181
25	North Acton Halt	3 2082
26	NORTH EALING	7 1981
27	Old Oak Lane Halt	3 2181
28	Park Royal	3 2082
29	(PARK ROYAL)	7 1982
30	Park Royal + Twyford Abbey	7 1982
31	Perivale §34	7 1884
32	RAVENSCOURT PARK	47 2278
33	Rugby Road Halt	249 2179
34	St Quintin Park + Wormwood Scrubs	232381
35	Shepherd's Bush	12379
36	Shepherd's Bush §13	52379
37	SHEPHERD'S BUSH §51	5 2380
38	SOUTH ACTON	249 2079
39	South Acton	4X 2079
40	(STAMFORD BROOK)	47 2178
41	(STONEBRIDGE PARK)	008 1984
42	Sudbury + Wembley §44	2008 1885
43	Twyford Abbey Halt	3 1882
43A	TURNHAM GREEN	4 2178
44	WEMBLEY (CENTRAL) §42	2008 1885
45	WEMBLEY Hill (COMPLEX)	5 1985
46	(WEST ACTON)	2 1981
47	(WHITE CITY)	2 2380
47A	WILLESDEN JUNCTION	
48	High Level	2 2282
49	LOW LEVEL (MAIN LINE)	2 2282
50	(NEW)	28 2282
51	Wood Lane §37	5 2380
52	Woodstock Road Halt	249 2179

GOODS

No.	Name/Location	Ry Ref
G1	Acton Coal	249 2079
2	Dudding Hill	4 2285
3	Harlesden for West Willesden + Stonebridge Park	4 2183
4	Kew Bridge	249 1878
5	Kew Bridge Coal	249 1878
6	Mitre Bridge	2 2282
7	Neasden	5 2185
8	Old Oak Common	3 2181
9	Willesden	2 2183

SIDINGS

No	Company	Ry Ref
P1	Willesden + Acton Brick	3 2181
2	Metropolitan Electric Supply	2 2183

WORKS

No	Name	Ry Ref
C1	Neasden	Metrop'n 2185

ENGINE SHEDS

No.	Name/Location	Ry Ref
E1	Old Oak Common	3 2282
2	Willesden	2 2183
3	Neasden	5 2185

BRIDGES + VIADUCTS

No	Name/Location	Ry Ref
V1	Strand Green Bridge	1 1977
2	Brent Viaduct	2 1984

TUNNELS

No	Name	Ry Ref
T1	Honeypot Hill	2 2382

JUNCTIONS

No	Name/Location	Ry Ref
J1	Old Kew	1249 1878
2	New Kew	1 1978
3	Chiswick	1 1978
4	Kew East	249 1 1978
5	Brentford Road	1 + LT 1978
6	Acton Town North	LT 1979
7	Acton Town South	LT 1979
8	Acton West	3 1981
9	Hanger Lane	LT 1981
10	Acton Lane	1 LT 2078
11	Bollo Lane	1 2079
12	S. Acton - South	2491 2079
13	S. Acton - North	2492X1 2079
14	S. Acton - Hammersmith Bch	249 2079
15	Acton East Jcts	3 2081
16	North Acton	LT 2082
17	Canal	2 2083
18	Bedford Park	LT 2178
19	Acton Wells Jcts	2349 2181
20	Acton Wells Jcts	2349 2182
21	For High Wycombe	3 2181
22	Old Oak Jcts	2492 2182
23	Neasden	45 2185
24	Neasden South-West	5 2185
25	Neasden South-East	5 2185
26	Studland Road	1 LT 2278
27	Old Oak	3 2282
28	Willesden - Main Line	2 2282
29	Willesden - West London	2 2282
30	Mitre Bridge	2 2282
31	Mitre Bridge Goods	2 2282
32	Kensal Rise	2 2283
33	Church Lane	LT 2378
34	Richmond	1 LT 2379
35	North Pole	2323 2381
36	Dudding Hill	4 2386

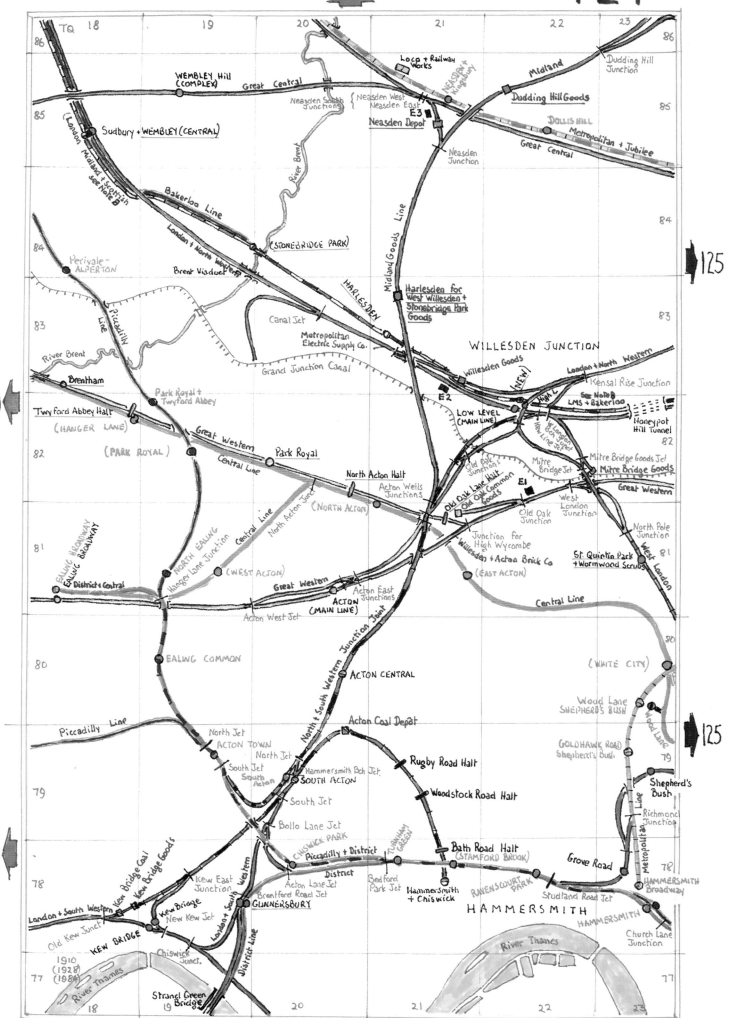

TQ 18   19   20   21   22   23
86   86
                                        Loco + Railway
                                        Works   Dudding Hill
                    WEMBLEY HILL   Junction
                    (COMPLEX)   Great Central   Midland
85   85
                                    Neasden West }
                              Neasden South { Neasden East
        Sudbury + WEMBLEY (CENTRAL)   E3   Dudding Hill Goods
                                    Neasden Depot   DOLLIS HILL
                                                Metropolitan + Jubilee
                                    Neasden   Great Central
                                    Junction

        Bakerloo Line
84   84
    Perivale-
    ALPERTON   London + North Western Line
            Brent Viaduct   (STONEBRIDGE PARK)
                        HARLESDEN   Midland Goods
83   Piccadilly   Line   83
    River Brent   Line   Canal Jct   Harlesden for
    Brentham   Metropolitan   West Willesden +
                    Electric Supply Co.   Stonebridge Park
                    Grand Junction Canal   Goods
                                        WILLESDEN JUNCTION
    Park Royal +   Willesden Goods   London + North Western
0   Twyford Abbey   Twyford Abbey Halt   (NEW)   Kensal Rise Junction
    (HANGER LANE)   E2   HIGH L.   See Note B
82   (PARK ROYAL)   Great Western   LOW LEVEL   LMS + Bakerloo   Honeypot   82
            Central Line   Park Royal   (MAIN LINE)   Kew Line Jct   Hill Tunnel
                                Old Oak Lane Halt   Mitre   Mitre Bridge Goods Jct
                        North Acton Halt   Old Oak Common   Bridge Jct   Mitre Bridge Goods
                    Acton Wells   Goods   E1   West   Great Western
                    Junctions   Old Oak   London
                North Acton Junc.   (NORTH ACTON)   Junction   Junction   North Pole
81   EALING BROADWAY   Central Line   Junction for   St. Quintin Park   Junction   81
    EALING BROADWAY   NORTH EALING   High Wycombe   + Wormwood Scrubs
    District + Central   Hanger Lane Junction   (WEST ACTON)   Willesden + Acton Brick Co   West
                            (EAST ACTON)   London
                    Great Western   Acton East
                    ACTON   Junctions   Central Line
80   Acton West Jct   (MAIN LINE)   (WHITE CITY)   80
    EALING COMMON   Wood Lane
                                        SHEPHERD'S BUSH
            ACTON CENTRAL   Wood Lane
    Piccadilly   Line   Acton Coal Depot   GOLDHAWK ROAD   125
                North Jct   Shepherd's Bush
                ACTON TOWN   Rugby Road Halt   79
79   North Jct   South Jct   Woodstock Road Halt   Shepherd's
    South Jct   South   Hammersmith Bch Jct.   Bush
    Acton   SOUTH ACTON   Richmond
        South Jct   Junction
        Bollo Lane Jct   TURNHAM GREEN   Bath Road Halt   Grove Road   78
2   Kew Bridge Coal   CHISWICK PARK   Piccadilly + District   (STAMFORD BROOK)   RAVENSCOURT   Metropolitan
    Kew Bridge Goods   District   Bedford   Hammersmith   PARK   HAMMERSMITH
78   Kew East   Acton Lane Jct   Park Jct   + Chiswick   Broadway   78
    London + South Western   Junction   Brentford Road Jct   Studland Road Jct
    Kew Bridge   GUNNERSBURY   HAMMERSMITH
    New Kew Jct   London + South   Church Lane
    KEW BRIDGE   Western   Junction
    Old Kew Junct.   River Thames
77   1910   Chiswick Junct.   River Thames   77
    (1928)   District Line
    (1964)   River Thames
    Strand Green
    Bridge   19
    18   20   21   22   23

125

PADDINGTON + MARYLEBONE

RAILWAYS

No	Legend	Company / Line
R 1		LONDON + SOUTH WESTERN
2		LONDON + NORTH WESTERN
3		GREAT WESTERN
4		MIDLAND
5		GREAT CENTRAL
9		NORTH LONDON
11		SOUTH EASTERN + CHATHAM
44		LONDON BRIGHTON + SOUTH COAST
23		WEST LONDON (GW + LNW)
12344		WEST LONDON EXTENSION (LSW, LNW, GW, +LBSC)
47		TOTTENHAM + HAMPSTEAD JOINT (Mid + GE)
35X		HAMMERSMITH + CITY JT (GW + Met) Now closed
2		CENTRAL
3		CIRCLE
4		DISTRICT
5		METROPOLITAN
7		PICCADILLY
8		BAKERLOO
9		NORTHERN
11		JUBILEE

London Transport Lines:
Modern names. Joint line
is shown by combining
the individual styles. In
addition, in most case the
railway or line name is also
shown on the map. Closed
sections are shown by
broad black stipple thus:
Closed District ▬▬▬▬▬

STATIONS + HALTS

No	Name		Ry Ref	No	Name	Ry Ref
A 1	Addison Road		23 2479	A 41	KILBURN	(5)11 2484
2	BAKER STREET		45811 2881	42	Kilburn + Maida Vale	2 2583
3	BARONS COURT		472478	43	(KILBURN HIGH ROAD)	2 2583
4	BAYSWATER		342580	44	(KILBURN PARK)	8 2583
5	BELSIZE PARK		9 2785	45	KNIGHTSBRIDGE	7 2779
6	Bishops Road	§56	5 2681	46	LADBROKE GROVE	5 2481
7	BOND STREET		211 2880	47	LANCASTER GATE	2 2680
8	Brompton	§24	347 2678	48	LATIMER ROAD	5 2380
9	Brompton Road		72779	49	Loudon Road	§72	2 2684
10	BRONDESBURY		2 2584	50	(MAIDA VALE)	8 2582
11	BRONDESBURY PARK		22484	51	MARBLE ARCH	2 2780
12	CAMDEN TOWN		92883	52	Marlborough Road §64	5 2683
13	Chalk Farm		2 2884	53	MARYLEBONE	58 2781
14	Chalk Farm	§58	9 2884	54	Notting Hill + LADBROKE	
15	CHALK FARM		9 2884		GROVE §46	5 2481
16	CRICKLEWOOD		4 2486	55	NOTTING HILL GATE	234 2580
17	Down Street		7 2879	56	PADDINGTON	85 §57/33458 2681
18	EARLS COURT		472578	57	(Praed Street) §56	34 2681
19	EDGWARE ROAD		345 2781	58	PRIMROSE HILL §14	9 2884
20	EDGWARE ROAD		8 2781	59	(QUEENS PARK)	2 82483
21	FINCHLEY ROAD		511 2684	59A	Queens Park + West Kilburn	2 82483
22	Finchley Road (Midland)		4 2684	60	Queens Road §61	22580
23	FINCHLEY ROAD + FROGNAL		2 2685	61	(QUEENSWAY) §60	22580
24	(GLOUCESTER ROAD) §8		347 2678	62	REGENT'S PARK	82881
25	GOSPEL OAK		247 2885	63	ROYAL OAK	5 2581
26	Grosvenor Road		11 2877	64	ST JOHNS WOOD §52	11(6)2683
27	HAMMERSMITH		47 2378	65	St Johns Wood Road	5 2782
28	HAMMERSMITH Broadway		5 2378	66	St Quintin Park + Wormwood	
29	HAMPSTEAD		9 2685		Scrubs	23 2381
30	HAMPSTEAD HEATH		2 2785	67	Shepherd's Bush	1 2379
31	Haverstock Hill		4 2885	68	Shepherd's Bush	232379
32	Highgate Rd High Level		47 2885	69	SHEPHERD'S BUSH	22379
33	Highgate Rd Low Level		42885	70	SHEPHERD'S BUSH §85	52380
34	HIGH ST KENSINGTON		342579	71	SLOANE SQUARE	342878
35	HOLLAND PARK		22480	72	SOUTH HAMPSTEAD §49	22684
36	HYDE PARK CORNER		72879	73	SOUTH KENSINGTON	234 2778
37	(KENSAL GREEN)		2 82383	74	SWISS COTTAGE	112684
38	KENSAL RISE		2 2383	75	(WARWICK AVENUE)	82682
39	KENSINGTON OLYMPIA		42478	76	WESTBOURNE PARK	352581
40	Kentish Town		2 2884	77	West Brompton	12344 2577

No	Name	Ry Ref	No	Name	Ry Ref
78	WEST BROMPTON	4 2577	10	Addison Road	123 2479
79	WEST HAMPSTEAD	2 2584	11	Cromwell Curve North	LT 2578
80	WEST HAMPSTEAD	511 2584	12	Cromwell Curve East	LT 2678
81	WEST HAMPSTEAD (MIDLAND)	4 2584	13	Kensington District Line	LT 2579
82	WEST KENSINGTON	4 2478	14	South Kensington	4x LT 2778
83	(WHITE CITY)	2 2380	15	Uxbridge Road	2335X 2379
84	WILLESDEN GREEN + Cricklewood		16	Shepherd's Bush Goods ✱§	23 2380
	(5)	112385	17	Portobello	3 2481
85	Wood Lane §70	5 2380	18	Subway	3 2581
86	Wood Lane	2 2380	19	Praed Street	LT. 2781
			20	Baker Street	LT. 2881
			21	Queens Park	2 LTO 2483
			22	Primrose Hill	2 2784
			23	Hampstead Road	92 2884
			24	Carlton Road	4 2885
			25	Cattle Dock	4 2885
			26	Mortimer Street	42 2885
			27	Engine Shed	4 2885
			28	West End	42 2486
			29	Cricklewood	4 2486

GOODS

No	Name/Location	Ry Ref
G 1	Brompton + Fulham	2 2577
2	Camden	2 2883
3	Kensington Coal	4 2579
4	Kensington - Lillie Bridge	12344 2578
5	Kentish Town Coal	4 2885
6	Kilburn + Maida Vale	2 2583
7	Marylebone	5 2782
8	Marylebone Coal	5 2781
9	Marylebone Regents Canal Wharf	5 2782
10	Paddington	3 2681
11	Shepherd's Bush LNW	2 2379
12	Shepherd's Bush GW	3 2379
13	Warwick Road LNW	2 2478
14	Warwick Road GW	3 2578
15	Westbourne Park Mileage	3 2581
16	West Kensington	4 2577

SIDINGS

No	Company/Name/Location	Ry Ref
P 1	Kensal Green Gas Works	3 2382
2	Saxby + Farmers	2 2583
3	Notting Hill	3 2581

BRIDGES

No	Name	Ry Ref
V 1	Victoria	1144 2877

TUNNELS

No	Name	Yds	Ry Ref
T 1	Primrose Hill		2 2784
2	Belsize Fast	1771	4 2685
3	Belsize Slow	1867	4 2685
4	Hampstead		2 2685
5	Park Street		2 2883
6	Honeypot Hill		2 2382

ENGINE SHEDS

No	Location	Ry Ref
E 1	Kentish Town	4 2885
2	Chalk Farm	2 2884

JUNCTIONS

No	Name/Location	Ry Ref
J 1	Church Lane	LT 2378
2	W London Goods ✱§	23 2380
3	Latimer Road	35x LT 2380
4	West Kensington Gds	4 LT 2478
5	Earls Court (end-on)	LT 2478
6	Olympia Goods Line	23 LT 2478
7	West Kensington East	LT 2478
8	Brompton Goods	2 2577
9	West Brompton South	12344 2577

NOTES:

(1) REF - All in TQ
(2) NAME CHANGE § NEW, Old
(3) LONDON TRASPORT Stations in red
(4) UNDERGROUND - Modern names
(5) DATE CHANGES - Post 1910
(6) JOINT LINES - may be on different levels
(7) BR + LT - CAPITALS UNDERLINED RED
(8) JOINT STATIONS - may be on different levels or closely adjoining sites - ie - different or separate stations.
(9) ✱ Goods Station - Name change

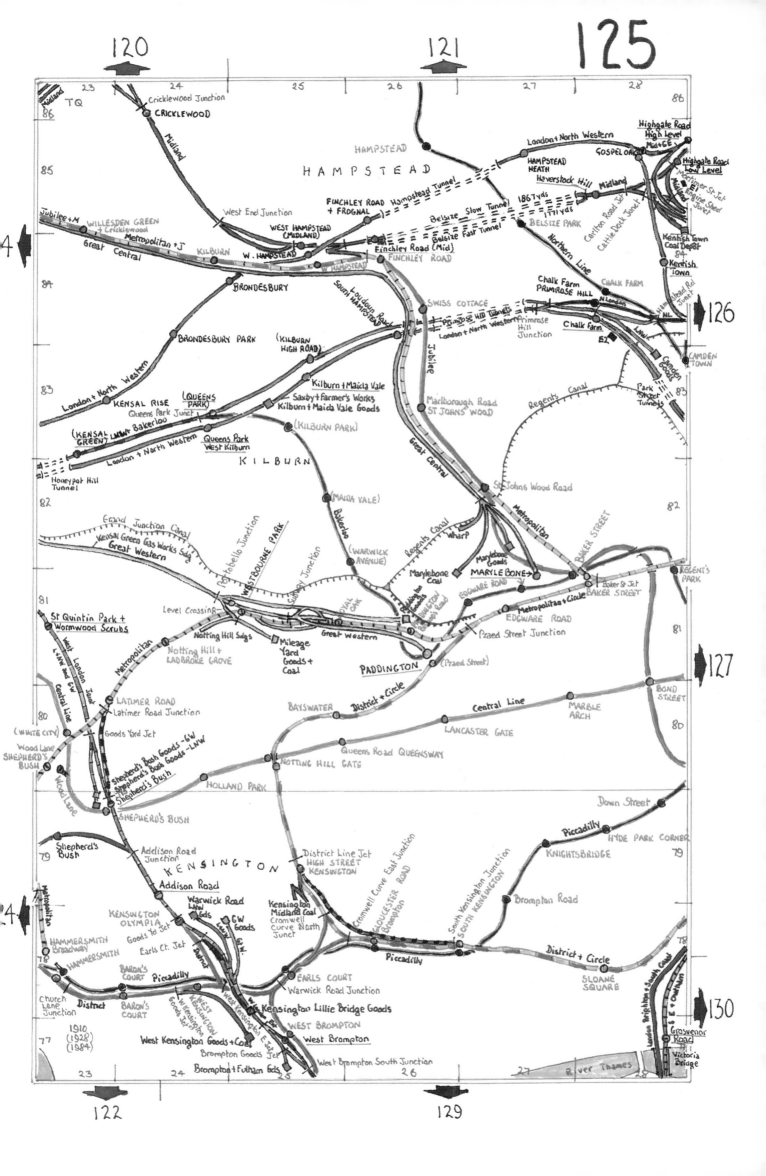

FINSBURY PARK + LINES TO THE NORTH

JUNCTIONS

No	Name/Location	Ry Ref
3	Clapton	7 3486
4	Queens Road	7 3485
1	Hampstead Road	92 2884
2	Kentish Town	92 2884
3	Carlton Road	4 2885
4	Mortimer Street	4 2885
5	Engine Shed	4 2885
6	Highgate Road	474 2885
7	Park	617 2888
8	Maiden Lane	92 2984
9	Copenhagen	6 3084
10	Harringay West	647 3187
11	Harringay Park	47 3187
12	Dalston	9 3384
13	Dalston Western	9 3384
14	Dalston Eastern	9 3384
15	South Tottenham West	747 3388
16	Seven Sisters South	7 3388
17	Seven Sisters North	7 3388
18	Hackney Downs	7 3485
19	South Tottenham East	{4 8 / 47} 3488
20	Tottenham Goods	474 3488
21	Tottenham West	747 3488
22	Tottenham North	7 3488
23	Clapton	7 3587
24	Copper Mills	7 3587
25	Hall Farm	7 3587
26	Lea Bridge	7 3087
27	Hackney Wick	7 3684

GOODS

No	Name/Location	Ry Ref
1	Ashburton Grove	6 3185
2	Caledonian Road Coal	2 3084
3	Caledonian Road Yard	6 3084
4	Camden	7 3085
5	Clapton	9 3584
6	Clarence Yard	6 3188
7	Hackney	47 3086
8	Hackney Coal	47 2986
9	Hackney Wick	2 2884
10	Highbury	49 2885
11	Highbury Vale	7 3686
12	Holloway Cattle	7 3687
13	Kentish Town Cattle	7 3484
14	Kentish Town Coal	9 2984
15	Kingsland	7 3287
16	Maiden Lane	9 3384
17	St Pancras	7 3486
18	Tottenham Coal	47 3388
19	Tufnell Park	7 3688

STATIONS

No	Name	Ry Ref
A 1	ARCHWAY §28	9 2986
2	ARSENAL §19	7 3186
3	BLACKHORSE ROAD	481 3688
4	CALEDONIAN ROAD	7 3084
5	CALEDONIAN RD + BARNSBURY	3084
6	Camden Road	9 3084
7	CAMDEN TOWN	4 2984
8	CAMDEN TOWN (ROAD)	9 2884
9	CANONBURY	9 3284
10	CLAPTON	7 3486
11	Cranley Gardens	6 2888
12	Crouch End	6 2987
13	CROUCH HILL	47 3087
14	DALSTON (JUNCTION)	9 3384
15	(DALSTON KINGSLAND)	9 3384
16	DRAYTON PARK	10T 3185
17	ESSEX ROAD	10T 3284
18	FINSBURY PARK §17	61 10T 3186
19	Gillespie Road §2	7 3188
20	GOSPEL OAK	247 2885
21	HACKNEY (CENTRAL)	7 3484
22	HACKNEY DOWNS	7 3484
23	HACKNEY WICK §56	9 3684
24	Haggerston	9 3393
25	HARRINGAY	6 3188
26	HARRING Park - Green	3288
	Lanes (STADIUM)	47 3288
27	HIGHBURY + ISLINGTON	3184
28	Highgate	9 2986
29	HIGHGATE	7 3186
30	Highgate Road High L.	472 2885
31	Highgate Road Low Level	4 2885
32	Holloway + Caledonian Rd	6 3085
33	HOLLOWAY ROAD	7 3085
34	HOMERTON	9 3584
35	HORNSEY	6 3188
36	Hornsey Road	47 3086
37	Junction Road	47 2986
38	Kentish Town (ROAD)	2 2884
39	KENTISH TOWN	49 2885
40	Lea Bridge	7 3686
41	(LEA BRIDGE)	7 3687
42	LONDON FIELDS	7 3484
43	Maiden Lane	9 2984
44	(MANOR HOUSE)	7 3287
45	Midmay Park	9 3384
46	RECTORY ROAD	7 3486
47	St Annes Road	47 3388
48	ST JAMES'S STREET	7 3688
49	SEVEN SISTERS	7 3388
50	SOUTH TOTTENHAM + Stamford Hill	4748 3388
51	STAMFORD HILL	7 3397
52	STOKE NEWINGTON	7 3386
53	Stroud Green	6 3087
54	TUFNELL PARK	0 2985
55	UPPER HOLLOWAY	47 2986
56	Victoria Park §23	9 3684
57	West Green	7 3289
58	York Road	7 3083

ENGINE SHEDS

No	Location	Ry Ref
E 1	Kentish Town	7 3397
2	Hornsey	7 3386
3	York Road	6 3087

TUNNELS

No	Name	Ry Ref
T1	Highgate	7 3289
2	Kingsland	7 3083

RAILWAYS

No.	Legend	Company
2		LONDON + NORTH WESTERN
4		MIDLAND
6		GREAT NORTHERN
7 GE		GREAT EASTERN
9 NL		NORTH LONDON
47		TOTTENHAM + HAMPSTEAD JUNCTION JT (Mid + GE)
48		TOTTENHAM + FOREST GATE (Mid + LTS)
10T		GREAT NORTHERN + CITY (BR Tube)
1		VICTORIA LINE } Shown as Modern
7		PICCADILLY LINE } Line names
9		NORTHERN LINE

OPEN STATIONS

NOTES

RECTORY ROAD	BR Station
SEVEN SISTERS	BR + LT Station
HIGHGATE	LT Station
ESSEX ROAD	BR Tube Station
HIGHBURY + ISLINGTON	BR, LT and BR Tube

REFERENCES	All in TQ
OPEN STATIONS	See above
NAME CHANGES §	NEW, Old

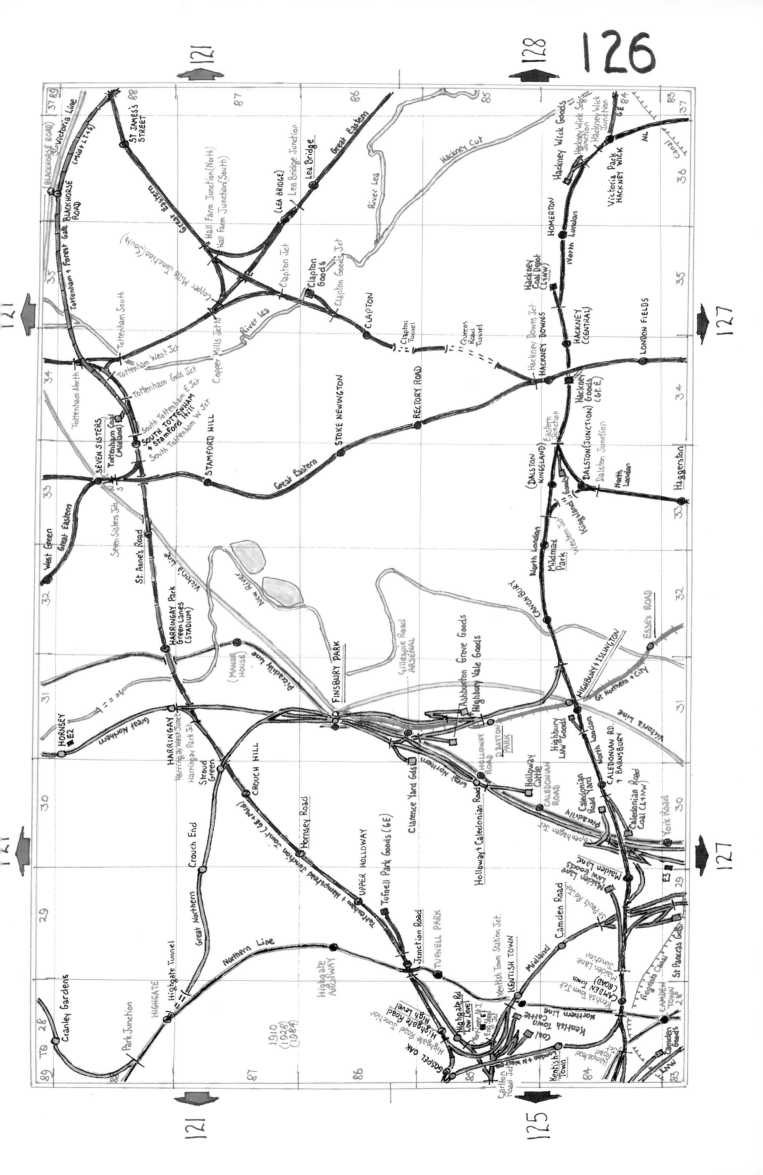

CENTRAL LONDON

RAILWAYS

Legend	Company / Line
R 1	LONDON + SOUTH WESTERN
2	LONDON + NORTH WESTERN
3	GREAT WESTERN
4	MIDLAND
5	GREAT NORTHERN
6	GREAT EASTERN
7	LONDON TILBURY + SOUTHEND
8	NORTH LONDON
9	METROPOLITAN (NOW BRITISH RAIL)
10	SOUTH EASTERN + CHATHAM
11	LONDON BRIGHTON + SOUTH COAST
1	VICTORIA
2	CENTRAL
3	CIRCLE
4	DISTRICT
5	METROPOLITAN
6	EAST LONDON
7	PICCADILLY
8	BAKERLOO
9	NORTHERN
11	JUBILEE
10T	GREAT NORTHERN + CITY } BRITISH RAIL TUBE RAILWAYS
20T	WATERLOO + CITY }

LONDON TRANSPORT
MODERN LINE NAMES
X INDICATES CLOSED LINE

STATIONS

No	Name	Ry Ref
A1	Aldersgate Street	
2	Aldgate	110 3181
3	Aldgate East	45 3381
4	(Aldwych) §84	7 3081
5	Angel	9 3183
6	Bank	2920T 3281
7	(Barbican)	45 3181
8	Bethnal Green	7 3492
9	Bethnal Green	2 3582
10	Bishopsgate	7 3382 3180
10A	Blackfriars	1134 3180 2881
11	Bond Street	9 3279
12	Borough	7 3582
13	Bow Road	453682
14	Bow Road	2 3081
15	British Museum	29 3381
16	Broad Street	
17	Burdett Road	7 3681
18	Cambridge Heath	7 3483
19	Camden Town	9 2883
20	Cannon Street	1134 3280
21	Chancery Lane	2 3081
22	Charing Cross	11891 3080
23	City Road	9 3182
24	Coburn Road for Old Ford	7 3682
25	Covent Garden	7 3081
26	Dover Street §40	1711 2880
27	Down Street	7 2880
28	Elephant + Castle	113179
29	Elephant + Castle	89 3179
30	Elephant + Castle	8 3179
31	Embankment	3489 3080
32	Essex Road	10T 3284
33	Euston	29 2982
34	Euston Square	45 2982
35	Farringdon Street	110 45 3181
36	Fenchurch Street	7 3380
37	Globe Road + Devonshire St	
38	Goodge Street	113479
39	(Gt Portland Street) §66	45 2882
40	Green Park §26	1711 2880
41	Haggerston	9 3383
42	Holborn	273081
43	Holborn Viaduct	113181
44	Kings Cross	614 579 3083
45	Kings Cross (Mid City)	110 3082
46	Kings Cross Suburban	6 3083
47	King William Street	9x 3280
48	(Lambeth North) §96	8 3179
49	Leicester Square	79 2980
50	Leman Street	7 3480
51	Limehouse	7 3680
52	Liverpool Street	7245 3381
53	London Bridge	11449 3280
54	London Fields	7 3484
55	Ludgate Hill	113181
56	Mansion House	34 3281
57	Mark Lane §87	34 3380
58	Mile End	2A5 3682
59	Monument	34 3280
60	Moorgate Street	110 459 T10 3281
61	Mornington Crescent	9 2883
62	Old Ford	9 3682
63	Old Street	9 T10 3282
64	Oxford Circus	128 2881
65	Piccadilly Circus	78 2980
66	Portland Road §39	45 2882
67	Post Office §75	2 3181
68	Regents Park	8 2882
69	Rotherhithe	6 3579
70	Russell Square	7 3082
71	St James's Park	34 2979
72	St Mary's	45 3481
73	St Pancras	2 2983
74	St Pauls	113180
75	St Pauls §67	2 3381
76	(Shadwell)	6 3481
77	Shadwell + St George's East	7 3480
78	Shoreditch	6 3882
79	Shoreditch	7 3380
80	Snow Hill	11 3181
81	Spa Road + Bermondsey	9 2981
82	Stepney (East)	45 2882
83	Stepney Green	2880
84	Strand §4	7 3081
85	Temple	
86	Tottenham Court Road	11 3181
87	Tower Hill §57	3083
88	Trafalgar Square	110 3082
89	Victoria	11A4 134 2879
90	(Wapping)	9x 3280
91	Warren Street	8 3179
92	Waterloo	79 2980
93	Waterloo Junction (East)	7 3480
94	West India Docks	7 3680
95	Westminster	7245 3381
96	Westminster Bridge Road §48	11449 3280
97	Whitechapel	113181
98	York Road	34 3281
99	York Road	34 3380

BRIDGES

No	Name	Ry Ref
V1	Charing Cross Bridge	19 2082
		1 89 20T 3080
2	Blackfriars Bridge	113180

ENGINE SHEDS

No	Location	Ry Ref
E1	York Road (King's X)	8 3179
2	Westminster Bridge Road LT3179	456 3481

TUNNELS

No	Name	Ry Ref
T1	Park Street	2 2883
2	(covered way)	2 2883

JUNCTIONS

No	Name/Location	Ry Ref
J1	Somers Town	42983
2	North London	4 2983
3	York Road	6 3083
4	Elephant + Castle Goods	116 3179
5	Charlotte Street	113179
6	Blackfriars	113180
7	Ludgate Hill	113181
8	Snow Hill	110 3181
9	Farringdon GN Goods	1106 3181
10	Farringdon Street	110 3181
11	Smithfield	3110 3181

GOODS

No	Name/Location	Ry Ref
1	Bishopsgate High Level	7 3382
2	Blackfriars Bridge	113180
3	Blackfriars Wharf	113180
4	Bow Depot	23683
5	Bow Road	73782
6	Broad Street	23281
7	Camden	22893
8	Commercial Road	83481
9	Devonshire Street	73582
10	Devonshire Street Coal	73682
11	Elephant + Castle Coal	6 3179
12	Farringdon Street	6 3181
13	Goodman's Yard	73380
14	Gravel Lane	113180
15	Haydon's Square	2 3381
16	Kings Cross	63081
17	London Docks	73480
18	Mint Street	7 3581
19	Old Ford	6 3882
20	St Pancras	9 3382
21	Shoreditch	11 3181
22	Smithfield	113479
23	Somers Town	7 3681
24	Spitalfields	45 3582
25	Spitalfields Coal	73081
26	Tower Hill	34 3080
27	West India Docks Coal	29 2981
28	Whitecross Street	343380
29	Worship Street	8 2980

No	Name	Ry Ref
17	Shoreditch Goods	4 2983
18	Haydon Square	2 3383
19	London Docks	3 3181
20	Commercial Road	4 2982
21	Stepney	7 3482
22	Limehouse	7 3481
23	Salmons Lane	6 3380
24	Bow GE+NL	4 3780
25	Bow Goods	110 3281
26	Bow GE+LTS	2 3382
27	Canal	
28	Old Ford Goods	
29	Bethnal Green West	
30	Bethnal Green East	
31	Shoreditch E London Jct	LT 3481
	St Marys	

NOTES:

(1) OPEN STATIONS STYLES
  (a) BRITISH RAILWAYS
  (b) BRITISH RAIL + LONDON TRANS
  (c) BR, LT and BR TUBE
  (d) LONDON TRANSPORT
  (e) LT and BR TUBE
  (f) BR TUBE
(2) REF All in TQ
(3) NAME CHANGE §§ NEW Old
(4) SOME STATIONS INDICATED AS JOINT May in fact be two or more stations at different levels or closely adjoining sites. Interchange facilities invariably exist
(5) UNDERGROUND - Modern system and all stations shown in the area which this map covers up-dated to 1984. However, continuations where these are at a smaller scale do not show some of the modern 'new lines'
(6) PROJECTED Openings and closing not shown 'Present' information as at 1984-5.
(7) JOINT LT Shown by combination of styles of individual partners.

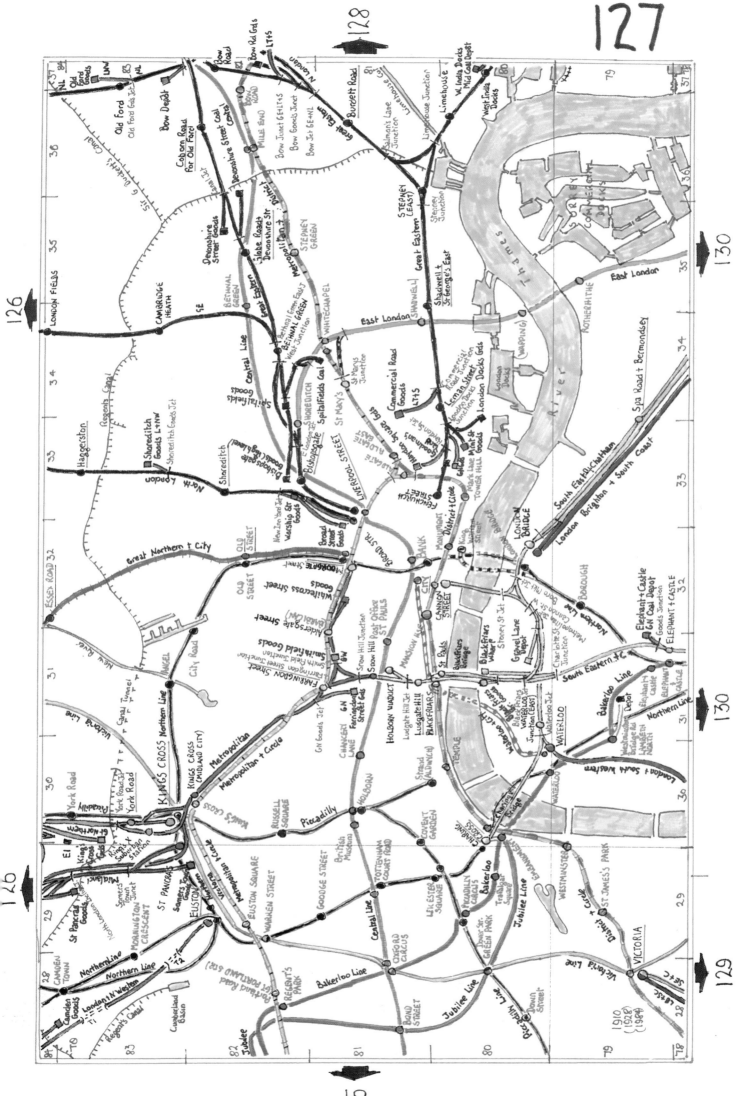

128

RAILWAYS

No	Legend	Company
R 2		LONDON + NORTH WESTERN
3		GREAT WESTERN
4		MIDLAND
6		GREAT NORTHERN
7		GREAT EASTERN
8		LONDON TILBURY + SOUTHEND
22		PORT OF LONDON AUTHORITY
11		SOUTH EASTERN + CHATHAM
9		NORTH LONDON
48		TOTTENHAM + FOREST GATE (Mid+LTS)
2		CENTRAL LINE
45		DISTRICT + METROPOLITAN LINES
X		OTHERS, Dock Lines etc

STATIONS

No	Name	Ry Ref
A 1	Blackwall	7 3880
2	Bow Road	7 3782
3	Bow Road	9 3782
4	BOW ROAD	45 3782
5	BROMLEY (·BY·BOW)	45 3782
6	CANNING TOWN	7 3981
7	CHARLTON	11 4078
8	Connaught Road	722 4180
9	CUSTOM HOUSE, VICTORIA DOCK	722 4080
10	EAST HAM	45 4283
11	FOREST GATE	7 4085
12	LEYTON	2 3885
13	MANOR PARK + Little Ilford	7 4185
14	MARYLAND Point	7 3984
15	MAZE HILL	11 3977
16	Millwall Docks	7 3779
17	Millwall Junction	7 3780
18	North Greenwich	7 3878
19	Old Ford	9 3783
20	PLAISTOW	45 4082
21	Poplar	7 3880
22	Poplar	9 3780
23	SILVERTOWN	7 4179
24	South Bromley	9 3781
25	South Dock	7 3879
26	STRATFORD Central·Low Lev	7 3884
27	STRATFORD Central Main Line	3884
	✳ 27	3884
28	Stratford Market	7 3883
29	Tidal Basin	7 3980
30	UPTON PARK	45 4483
31	VICTORIA DOCK, CUSTOM HOUSE	722 4080
32	WANSTEAD PARK	48 4085
33	WESTCOMBE PARK	11 3977
34	(WEST HAM)	7 3982
35	West Ham	8 3982
36	West India Docks	7 3780
37	WOODGRANGE PARK	8 4185

GOODS

No	Name/Location	Ry Ref
G 1	Angerstein Wharf	11 4078
2	Blackwall	7 3880
3	Bow (LNW)	2 3783
4	Bow (Midland)	4 3783
5	Bow Road	7 3782
6	Canning Town	2 3981
7	Carpenters Road	7 3883
8	Devon Road	2 3781
9	Forest Gate	7 4185
10	Lea Cut Coal	7 3781
11	Millwall Docks	7 3778
12	Old Ford	2 3783
13	Plaistow + West Ham	7 3982
14	Poplar (LNW)	2 3880
15	Poplar (GW)	3 3880
16	Poplar (GN)	6 3880
17	Poplar (NL)	9 3880
18	Poplar Coal	2 3880
19	Poplar Dock (Midland)	4 3880
20	Poplar Dock (GN)	6 3880
21	Stratford	7 3884
22	Stratford Market	7 3883
23	Stratford Market Coal	7 3883
24	TEMPLE MILLS †	7 3785
25	Thames Wharf (Mid)	4 3980
26	Thames Wharf (GE)	7 3980
27	Tidal Basin (Mid)	4 3980
28	Tidal Basin (GN)	6 4080
29	Tidal Basin (GE)	7 3980
30	Upton Park	2 4183
31	Victoria + Albert	3 4180
32	West India Docks Coal	4 3780
31	Plaistow	77 3982
32	Abbey Mills Lower	7 3982
33	Stratford Market Goods	7 3982
34	Beckton	722 4180
35	Upton Park Goods	82 4183
36	Forest Gate	78 4185
37	Woodgrange Park	848 4185

COMPANY WORKS

No	Name	Ry Ref
C 1	Plaistow	8 3982

ENGINE SHEDS

No	Name/Location	Ry Ref
E 1	Plaistow	8 3982

JUNCTIONS

No	Name/Location	Ry Ref
J 1	Millwall Goods	7 3778
2	Angerstein	11 4077
3	Charlton	11 4178
4	Harrow Lane	9 3780
5	(Poplar) High Street	9 3780
6	East India Dock Road	9 3780
7	Bow North (1)	78 3782
8	Bow Middle (2)	7 3781
9	Bow South (3)	79 3781
10	Lea Cut	92 3781
11	Campbell Road	8LT 3782
12	Bromley	89 3782
13	Tilbury	9 3782
14	Fenchurch Street Line	7 3783
15	Channelsea	7 3784
16	Lea	7 3784
17	High Mead	7 3784
18	Poplar Docks	7 3880
19	Upper Abbey Mills	87 3882
20	Stratford Western	7 3883
21	Stratford Southern	7 3883
22	Stratford Sheet Factory	7 3884
23	Stratford Central	7 3884
24	Stratford Eastern	7 3884
25	Cobham Farm	7 3884
26	Loughton North	7 3885
27	Loughton South	7 3885
28	Thames Wharf	7 3980
29	Blackwall	7 3981
30	Canning Town Goods	27 3981

SIDINGS

No	Name	Ry Ref
P 1	(Bow) Gas Works	9 3781

NOTES:

(1) REF All in TQ

(2) STRATFORD ✳ Two closely adjoining stations combined into one modern station

(3) TEMPLE MILLS - Still in use as a major BR depot. †

(4) Open station styles
OPEN BR
OPEN BR + LT
OPEN LT

(5) NAME CHANGES:- Some changes indicated by part of title in ( ) (LATER ADDITION). Part of title in small letters indicates that portion of name not in current use.

(6) DOCK LINES - 1910 position — later alterations NOT shown.

121
126
121
127
121
121
123
27
30
130
123

River Lea
TQ
37 38 39 40 41 42
85
TEMPLE MILLS YARD
Great Eastern
Central Line
LEYTON
Loughton Junction North
Loughton Junction South
Tottenham + Forest Gate Jt
(Midland + London Tilbury and Southend)
WANSTEAD PARK
Forest Gate Jct
MANOR PARK + Little Ilford
Forest Gate Goods
WOODGRANGE PARK
Woodgrange Park Junction
L T + S
85
Chobham Farm Junction
Great Eastern
FOREST GATE
S T R A T F O R D
High Meads Junction
Eastern Junction
MARYLAND Point
Hackney Cut
Gt Eastern
Sir Geodger's Canal
Great Eastern
Lea Junction
Channelsea Junction
Carpenters Road Goods
Stratford Goods
STRATFORD Central (Main Line)
Central Junction
STRATFORD Central (Low Level)
Sheet Fatory Junction
Southern Junction
EAST HAM
84
LNW
Old Ford Goods
Old Ford
Midland
Central Line
Western Junction
Stratford Market
Stratford Market (Goods) Coal
Stratford Market Goods
Stratford Market Goods Jct
Metropolitan + District
London Tilbury + Southend
UPTON PARK
Upton Park Depot LNW
Upton Park Gds Jct
83
83
Bow Depot (Mid)
Fenchurch Str Line Junction
River Lea
PLAISTOW
El
Loco Works LT + S
82
Bow
LNW
Bow Rd Goods
Bow Tcls
Bow Road
Tilbury Junction
B O W
Bow Rd
Bromley Junction
Upper Abbey Mills Jct
WEST HAM
West Ham (WEST HAM)
Abbey Mills Lower Jct
82
BOW ROAD
Bow Rd
Bow Jcts
Campbell Road Jct
Lea Cut Jct
BROMLEY (LNW-Bow)
Plaistow + West Ham Goods
Great Eastern
Plaistow Junction
3
Gas Works
Devon Rd Gds
Lea Cut Coal Dep.
Canning Town Goods Jct
81
81
Limehouse Cut
South Bromley
CANNING TOWN
Canning Town Goods
North London
P O P L A R
Blackwall Goods (GE) Coal
Blackwall Junction
Beckton Junction
Connaught Road
Thames Wharf Junction
Custom House
Victoria Dock Goods
CUSTOM HOUSE
Tidal Basin Gk Goods
Great Eastern
West India Docks Mid Coal Depot
E India Dock Rd J.
High St Jct
Harrow Lane Jct
Poplar Coal LNW
Poplar
STR
Tidal Basin
Tidal Basin Goods
Victoria + Albert Goods
Port of London Authority
80
West India Docks
Gt Eastern
Poplar
Blackwall
GE Mid
Thames Wharf Mid
Tidal Basin Mid Goods
Victoria Dock
Albert Dock
80
W India Docks
Millwall Jct
North London Poplar Gds
Poplar Dock (Midland)
Poplar Gt N Goods
Silvertown Tramway
SILVERTOWN
Great Eastern
South Dock
South Dock
79
River Thames
79
Millwall Docks
Royal Victoria
Millwall Docks
Millwall Goods Junction
Angerstein Wharf Goods
Charlton Tunnel
Maze Street Tunnel
Royal Dockyard
Dock St Tunnel
78
Millwall Docks
Millwall Docks Goods
Great Eastern
South Eastern + Chatham
CHARLTON
Charlton Junction
78
30
North Greenwich
77
1910 (1928) (1964)
WESTCOMBE PARK
Angerstein Junction
77
Greenwich MAZE HILL
37 38 39 40 41 42

CLAPHAM JUNCTION + WIMBLEDON

RAILWAYS

No	Legend	Company / Line
R 1	▬▬▬	LONDON + SOUTH WESTERN
2	▬▬▬	LONDON + NORTH WESTERN
3	▬▬▬	GREAT WESTERN
4	▬▬▬	MIDLAND
11	▬▬▬	SOUTH EASTERN + CHATHAM
44	▬▬▬	LONDON BRIGHTON + SOUTH COAST
12344	▬▬▬	WEST LONDON EXTENSION (LSW, LNW, GW, LBSC)
144	▬▬▬	L + SW AND L, B + SC JOINT
OO	▬▬▬	SOUTHERN (Post Grouping)
4	▬▬▬	DISTRICT LINE
9	▬▬▬	NORTHERN LINE
0	·········	OTHER POST GROUPING

STATIONS

No	Name	Ry Ref
A 1	(BALHAM)	9 2873
2	BALHAM + Upper Tooting	44 2873
3	Battersea	12344 2676
4	BATTERSEA PARK	44 2876
5	Battersea Park Road	11 2876
6	Chelsea + Fulham	12344 2677
7	CLAPHAM COMMON	9 2975
8	CLAPHAM JUNCTION SEE BELOW	2775
	1/12344/44/2	2775
9	Clapham Road	11 2975
10	(CLAPHAM SOUTH)	9 2874
11	(COLLIER'S WOOD)	9 2670
12	EARLSFIELD + Summers Town	1 2672
13	EAST PUTNEY	4 2474
14	(FULHAM BROADWAY) &30	4 2577
15	Grosvenor Road	11 2877
16	HAYDONS ROAD	144 2671
17	Merton Abbey	144 2669
18	MERTON PARK	144 2569
19	MORDEN (ROAD)	44 2569
20	PARSONS GREEN	4 2576
21	PUTNEY BRIDGE + Hurlingham	2475
		4 2475
22	QUEENS(TOWN) ROAD	44 2876
23	SOUTHFIELDS	4 2473
24	(SOUTH WIMBLEDON)	9 2570
25	STREATHAM	44 2970
26	STREATHAM COMMON	44 2970
27	TOOTING	144 2770
28	(TOOTING BEC)	9 2872
29	(TOOTING BROADWAY)	9 2771
30	Walham Green &14	4 2577
31	WANDSWORTH COMMON	44 2773
32	WANDSWORTH ROAD	11 2975
33	WANDSWORTH TOWN	1 2674
34	West Brompton	12344 2577
35	WEST BROMPTON	4 2577
36	WIMBLEDON	1444 2470
37	(WIMBLEDON CHASE)	OO 2469
38	WIMBLEDON PARK	4 2571
39	(Wimbledon Staff Halt)	1 2571

GOODS

No	Name/Location	Ry Ref
G 1	Battersea	44 2877
2	Battersea Coal	4 2976
3	Brompton + Fulham	2 2577
4	Clapham Goods + Coal	2 2775
5	New Wandsworth Coal	44 2774
6	South Lambeth	3 2977
7	Stewarts Lane	11 2976
8	West Kensington	4 2577

BRIDGES

No	Name	Ry Ref
V 1	Putney Bridge	4 2475
2	Battersea Bridge	12344 2676
3	Victoria Bridge	1144 2877

ENGINE SHEDS

No	Location	Ry Ref
E 1	Battersea	44 2877

TUNNELS

No	Name	Ry Ref
T 1	East Putney	14 2474

JUNCTIONS

No	Name/Location	Ry Ref
J 1	Wimbledon	144LT 2470
2	East Putney South	1 2474
3	East Putney North	1 2474
4	Merton Park	44144 2569
5	Point Pleasant	1 2574
6	Brompton Goods	2 2577
7	West Brompton South	212344 2577
8	Chelsea Dock	12344 2676
9	Tooting	144 2770
10	Balham	44 2873
11	Streatham South	44144 2970
12	Streatham Common	44 2970
13	Streatham	44 2970
14	Streatham Middle	44 2970
15	Streatham North	44 2971
16	Battersea Pier	44 2877

CLAPHAM JUNCTIONS

No	Name/Location	Ry Ref
17	Falcon (Clapham South)	44WL 2775
18	Coal Yard	2WL 2775
19	Ludgate	1WL 2775
20	Lavender Hill	111 2775
21	Latchmere S Western	WL 2776
22	Latchmere Main	WL 2776
23	Latchmere for Waterloo	WL 2776
24	Pouparts	44 2875
25	WL + LSW Line	1WL 2876
26	Longhedge Jcts	WL 2876
27	Goods	1 2876
28	Stewarts Lane	11 2976
29	Wandsworth Road	11 2976
30	Factory	11 2976
31	Battersea Park	44 2876

SIDINGS

No	Name	Ry Ref
P 1	Thorley's Siding	1 2574
2	Chelsea Dock	12344 2676

NOTES:

(1) REF - All in TQ
(2) NAME CHANGE (NEW Old)
(3) West London Ext 12344 WL
(4) OPEN STATIONS

(a) BRITISH RAIL
(b) BRITISH RAIL + LT
(c) LONDON TRANSPORT
(d) In use but not on daily basis

West Kensington Goods & Coal
TQ
West Brompton
Brompton Goods Junct
Brompton + Fulham Gds
WEST BROMPTON

26

27

28

29

West Brompton
South Junction

Grosvenor Road
Victoria Bridge

River Thames

Battersea Gds
+ Wharf

Battersea Pier Junction

77

77

Chelsea +
Fulham

E1

South
Lambett
Goods

Walham Green
(FULHAM BROADWAY)

C
L
A
P
H
A
M

J
U
N
C
T
I
O
N

Battersea Gds
+ Wharf

Battersea Park Jct
BATTERSEA PARK

Battersea Park Road Jct

Chelsea
Dock Jct

Canal

Chelsea
Dock

West London Extension Jt.

West London Ext 2nd
L+SW Waterloo Line Jct

Stewarts Lane Jct

76

District Line

PARSONS GREEN

Junction for Waterloo
Latchmere Main Junct
Latchmere S Western Jct

QUEENS(TOWN) ROAD (B4)
Goods Jct

Battersea
Midland Coal

76

Battersea
Bridge

Battersea

Longhedge Junctions

Factory Junction
Wandsworth Rd Jct

122

Ludgate Jct

Lavender Hill Junction

Popart's Junction

Stewarts Lane Goods

WANDSWORTH
ROAD

PUTNEY BRIDGE
+ Hurlingham

Putney
Bridge

Thorley's Siding

London + South Western

Coal Yard Junction
CLAPHAM JUNCTION

Clapham Goods + Coal Wharf

CLAPHAM Rd.

75

River Thames

WANDSWORTH TOWN

Falcon Junction / Clapham South

75

CLAPHAM
COMMON

130

East Potney North Jct
EAST PUTNEY
East Potney South Jct

Point Pleasant Junction

New Wandsworth Coal

Northern Line

74

74

East
Putney
Tunnel

London Brighton +
South Coast

(CLAPHAM SOUTH)

73

London + South Western

River Wandle

WANDSWORTH
COMMON

73

SOUTHFIELDS

District Line

(BALHAM)
BALHAM + Upper Tooting
Balham Junction

EARLSFIELD +
Summers Town

LB + SC

72

72

(TOOTING BEC)

London Brighton + South Coast

WIMBLEDON PARK

(Wimbledon Staff Halt)

71

Northern Line

(TOOTING BROADWAY)

71

131

LB+SC and L+SW Joint Jct.

Streatham North Jct

122

HAYDON'S
ROAD

Streatham Middle
Junction

STREATHAM

Wimbledon Jcts

WIMBLEDON

TOOTING

Streatham
Junction

Streatham Common Jct

70

(SOUTH
WIMBLEDON)

(COLLIERS
WOOD)

LB+SC 2nd L+SW Joint

Tooting
Junction

Streatham S Jct

STREATHAM
COMMON

Merton Park Jct
MERTON PARK

Merton Abbey

Southern Rly.

69

69

Q10
(Q28)
(1984)
(WIMBLEDON CHASE)

MORDEN (ROAD)

24

25

26

27

28

29

NEW CROSS

STATIONS

No	Name	Ry Ref
A1	Blackheath Hill	11 3776
2	BRIXTON	111 3074
3	BROCKLEY + Upper New Cross	44 3674
4	Brockley Lane	11 3615
5	Camberwell	11 3176
6	CATFORD	11 3773
7	CATFORD BRIDGE	11 3773
8	CLAPHAM Road (NORTH)	9 2975
9	CROFTON PARK	11 3674
10	DENMARK HILL	44 3275
11	DEPTFORD	11 3776
12	Deptford Road S4	6 3578
13	East Brixton	44 3174
14	EAST DULWICH	44 3374
15	ELEPHANT + CASTLE +	11 3178
16	ELEPHANT + CASTLE +	89 3178
17	GREENWICH	11 3776
18	Greenwich Park	11 3776
19	HERNE HILL	11 3173
20	HITHER GREEN	11 3873
21	Honor Oak	11 3473
22	HONOR OAK PARK	44 3573
23	(KENNINGTON)	9 3177
24	LADYWELL	11 3774
25	LEWISHAM	11 3875
26	Lewisham Road	11 3775
27	LOUGHBOROUGH JUNCTION	3175
28	NEW CROSS	11 6 3676
29	NEW CROSS GATE	44 6 3676
30	NORTH DULWICH	44 3275
31	North Greenwich	111 3074
32	NUNHEAD	11 3174
33	Old Kent Rd. + Hatcham	44 3576
34	(OVAL)	9 3077
35	PECKHAM RYE	44 3375
36	QUEENS ROAD PECKHAM	
37	ST JOHN'S	11 3775
38	SOUTH BERMONDSEY	44 3477
39	Southwark Park	11 3577
40	(STOCKWELL)	19 3076
41	(SURREY DOCKS) 8 12	6 3578
42	VAUXHALL	11 3077
43	Walworth Road	11 3277

SIDINGS

No	Name(s)/Location	Ry Ref
P1	Brixton Sorting Sidings	7 3877
2	Cambria Siding	44 3273
3	Martins Siding	11 3575

ENGINE SHEDS

No	Name/Location	Ry Ref
E1	Bricklayers Arms	11 3775
2	New Cross Gate	44 3477
3	Nine Elms	1 3077

TUNNELS

No	Name/Location	Ry Ref
T1	Knights Hill	44 3129
2	Grove	44 3275
3	Greenwich College	11 3877
4	Tanners Hill	1 2977
5	(Denmark Hill)	2 3675

JUNCTIONS

No	Name/Location	Ry Ref
1	Brixton	6 3635
2	Canterbury Road	11 3176
3	Barrington Road	44 3678
4	Herne Hill South	7 3778
5	Herne Hill North	2 3273
6	Brixton Sidings South	7 3676
7	Brixton Sidings North	24 3475
8	Knights Hill South	244 3173
9	Knights Hill North	244 3273
10	Cambria	44 3175
11	Cambria Road	1144 3176
12	Camberwell	11 3276
13	Walworth	11(4) 3177
14	Peckham Rye	44 3375
15	Cow Lane	42 44 3475
16	Nunhead West	11 3575
17	Nunhead East	11 3575
18	Ladywell	11 3774
19	Park Bridge	11 3774
20	Lewisham	11 3875
21	Tanners Hill	11 3775
22	Tanners Hill New	110 3775
23	Lewisham Vale	110 3775
24	Lewisham West	110 3775
25	Court Hill Loop North	110 3874
26	Court Hill Loop South	110 3874
27	New Cross (Gate) Up	44 3576
28	New Cross (Gate) Down	44 3576
29	New Cross	1133 3676
30	North Kent	11 3677
31	Surrey Canal	11 3577
32	Hither Green	11 3873
33	Old Kent Road	44 3476
34	Bricklayers Arms West	11 3477
35	Bricklayers Arms	11 3477
36	Corbetts Lane	1144 3577
37	Deptford Park	33LT 3578
38	Willow Walk	1144 3578

Junctions shown in red 22 to 26 are new British Rail Junctions

GOODS

No	Name/Location	Ry Ref
1	Nine Elms	11 3776
2	Brackley Lane	11 3776
3	Bricklayers Arms	11 3173
4	Brixton Coal	11 3873
5	Brockley Coal	11 3473
6	Camberwell	11 3573
7	Deptford Wharf	9 3177
8	Millwall Dock	11 3774
9	Knights Hill	11 3875
10	New Cross	11 3775
11	Peckhams Rye	3175
12	Walworth Coal	11 3175
13	Willow Walk	11 6 3676

RAILWAYS

No	Company Line	Legend
R 1	LONDON + SOUTH WESTERN	
2	LONDON + NORTH WESTERN	
4	MIDLAND	
6	GREAT NORTHERN	
7	GREAT EASTERN	
11	SOUTH EASTERN + CHATHAM	
33	EAST LONDON (Now closed) ⚡	
44	LONDON BRIGHTON + SOUTH COAST	
24	LONDON + NORTH WESTERN AND MIDLAND JT	
1	VICTORIA LINE	
6	EAST LONDON LINE	
9	NORTHERN LINE	
0	POST GROUPING ADDITIONS	

NOTES:

(1) REFERENCES - All in TQ

(2) NAME CHANGE § NEW Old

(3) ELEPHANT + CASTLE +. 8 is BAKERLOO LINE, terminates here.

(4) EAST LONDON ⚡ Jointly owned by Great Eastern, London, Brighton + South Coast, Metropolitan, Metropolitan District, and South Eastern + Chatham Railways. Portion as shown is now East London Line 6. Remainder now all closed (33).

(5) STYLES OF OPEN STATION
BRITISH RAIL
BRITISH RAIL + LONDON TRANSPORT
LONDON TRANSPORT

(6) PARTIAL NAME CHANGES (NEW ADDITION) portion discarded.

(7) Junctions in red BR additions

(8) Current usage of lines see Map 123

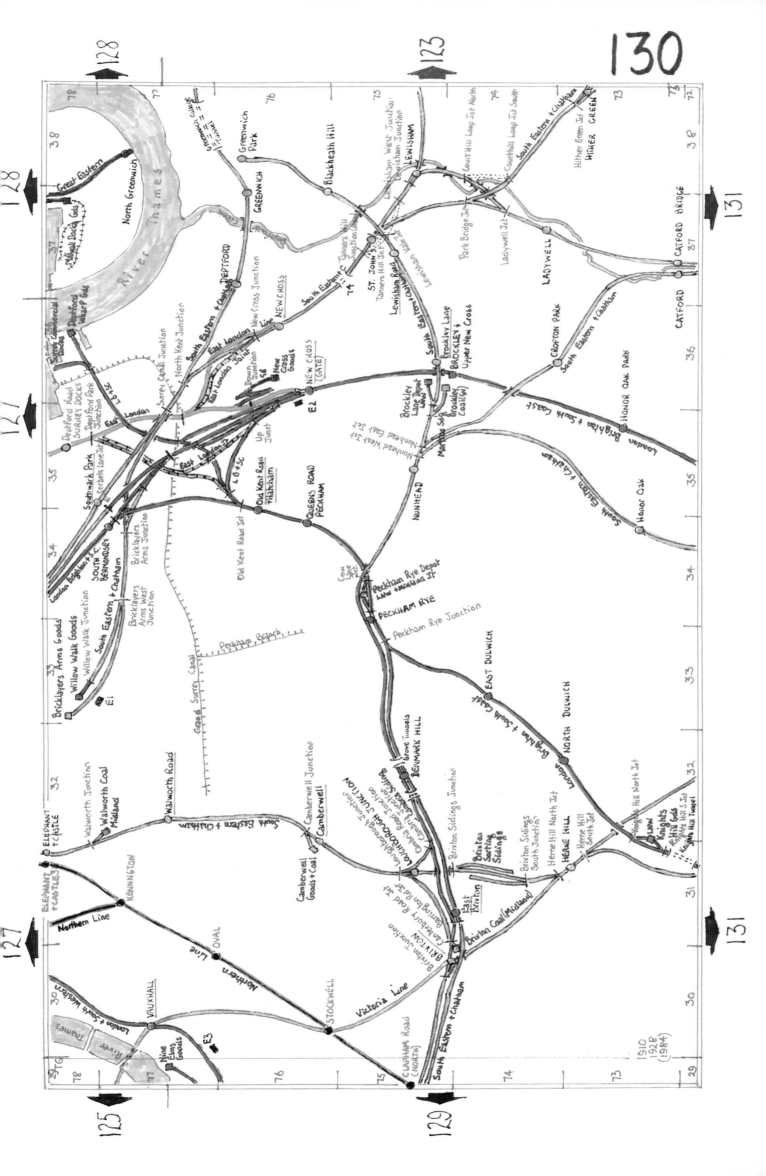

RAILWAYS

No	Company
R11	SOUTH EASTERN + CHATHAM
44	LONDON BRIGHTON + SOUTH COAST

STATIONS

No.	Name	Ry Ref
1	ANNERLEY	44 3470
2	BECKENHAM HILL	11 3771
3	BECKENHAM (JUNCTION)	11 3769
4	BELLINGHAM	11 3771
5	CLOCK HOUSE	11 3669
6	CRYSTAL PALACE	44 3370
7	Crystal Palace + Upper Norwood	11 3370
8	EAST CROYDON	44 3266
9	ELMERS END	11 3568
10	FOREST HILL	44 3572
11	GIPSY HILL	44 3271
12	KENT HOUSE	11 3569
13	Lordship Lane	11 3472
14	LOWER SYDENHAM	11 3671
15	NEW BECKENHAM	11 3670
16	New Croydon	44 3266
17	NORBURY	44 3069
18	NORWOOD JUNCTION	44 3368
19	PENGE (EAST)	11 3570
20	PENGE (WEST)	44 3470
21	RAVENSBOURNE	11 3870
22	SELHURST	44 3267
23	STREATHAM HILL	44 2972
24	SYDENHAM	11 3571
25	SYDENHAM HILL	11 3371
26	THORNTON HEATH	44 3168
27	TULSE HILL	44 3172
28	Upper Sydenham	11 3471
29	(WEST) DULWICH	11 3272
30	WEST NORWOOD	44 3171

JUNCTIONS

No	Name/Location	Ry Ref
J1	Crystal Palace Line South	44 3368
2	Crystal Palace Line North	44 3369
3	Crystal Palace Line	1144 3368
4	Spur	1144 3468
5	Northwood Station North	44 3368
6	Northwood Station South	44 3368
7	Windmill Bridge (Jcts)	44 {3266 {3267
8	Cottage	44 3267
9	Gloucester Road	44 3267
10	Norwood Fork (Jcts)	44 3267
11	Selhurst	44 3267
12	Crystal Palace	11 3471
13	Sydenham	44 3370
14	New Beckenham	44 3571
15	Penge	11 3670
16	Beckenham	11 3371
17	Shortlands	11 3471
18	Elmers End	44 3072
19	Leigham	44 3072
20	West Norwood	44 3172
21	Tulse Hill - Streatham Hill	44 3172
22	Tulse Hill - West Norwood	44 3172
23	Tulse Hill - Herne Hill	44 3172
24	Tulse Hill - SEC + LBSC	1144 3172

TUNNELS

No	Name/Location	Yds	Ry Ref
T1	Penge or Sydenham	2141	11 3569
2	Crystal Palace		11 3472
3	Streatham		11 3671
4	Leigham		11 3670
5	Upper Norwood		44 3266
6	Upper Sydenham		44 3069
7	Leigham Court		44 3368

NOTES

(1) REF   All in TQ

(2) NAME CHANGES:-

Portion of name in brackets thus:- (WEST) indicates modern addition to title

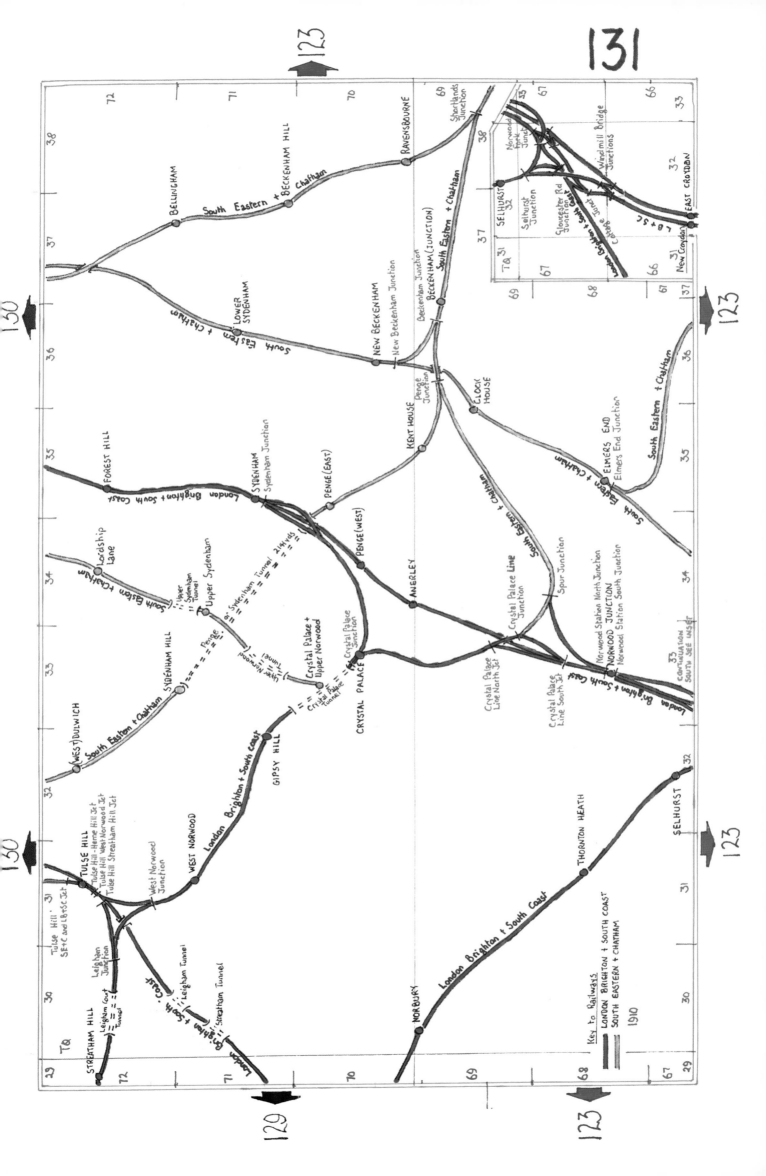

CHELMSFORD + ROCHESTER

No	Company
R 5	COLNE VALLEY + HALSTEAD
6	SOUTH EASTERN + CHATHAM
6A	SHEPPEY (Light) (SE+C)
7	GREAT EASTERN
7A	ELSENHAM + THAXTED (Light) (GE)
7B	KELVEDON TIPTREE + TOLLESBURY (Light) GE
8	LONDON TILBURY + SOUTHEND
27	CENTRAL LINE (EX GE)
48	DISTRICT / LONDON TILBURY + SOUTHEND

STATIONS

No	Name	Ry Ref
A 1	ALTHORNE	7 Q99
2	AUDLEY END	7 L53
3	(BASILDON)	8 Q78
4	BATTLESBRIDGE	7 Q79
5	BENFLEET (for CANVEY ISLAND)	8 Q78
6	BILLERICAY	7 Q69
7	Blake Hall ‡	7 L50
8	BRAINTREE + Bocking	7 L82
9	BRENTWOOD + Waley	7 Q59
10	BURES	7 L83
11	BURNHAM-ON-CROUCH	7 Q99
12	(CHALKWELL)	8 Q88
13	CHAPPEL + WAKES COLNE	73 L82
14	CHATHAM	6 Q76
15	Chatham Central	6 Q76
16	CHELMSFORD	7 L70
17	Cliffe	6 Q76
18	COLCHESTER	7 L92
19	Cold Norton	7 L80
20	CRAYFORD	6 Q57
21	CRESSING	7 L82
22	Cutlers Green Halt	7A L52
23	CUXTON	6 Q76
24	DAGENHAM EAST †	4 Q58
25	DARTFORD	6 Q57
26	Dunmow	7 L62
27	Earls Colne	3 L82
28	Eastchurch	6A Q97
29	East Minster-on-Sea	6A Q97
30	Easton Lodge	7 Q62
31	EAST TILBURY §64	8 Q67
32	ELM PARK †	4 Q58
33	ELSENHAM	7 L52
34	Elsenham	7A L52
35	EMERSON PARK	8 Q58
36	ERITH	6 Q57
37	EYNSFORD	6 Q56
38	FAMBRIDGE	7 Q89
39	FARNINGHAM ROAD + Sutton at Hone	6 Q56
40	Fawkham §63	6 Q56
41	Felstead	7 L62
42	GIDEA PARK	7 Q58
43	GILLINGHAM §70	6 Q76
44	GRAVESEND Central	6 Q67
45	Gravesend West Street	6 Q67
46	GRAYS	8 Q67
47	GREENHITHE	6 Q57
48	HALLING	6 Q76
49	Halstead	3 L83
50	HAROLD WOOD	7 Q59
51	HATFIELD PEVEREL	7 L81
52	HIGHAM	6 Q77
53	HOCKLEY	7 Q89
54	Hoo Halt	6 Q67
55	HORNCHURCH +	4 Q58
56	INGATESTONE	7 Q69
57	Inworth	7B L81
58	KELVEDON	7(7B) L81
59	(KEMSLEY)	6 Q96
60	Langford	7 L80
61	LAINDON	8 Q68
62	LEIGH-ON-SEA	8 Q88
63	LONGFIELD §40	6 Q56
64	Low Street §31	8 Q67
65	MALDON EAST + HEYBRIDGE	7 L80
66	Maldon West	7 L80
67	MARKS TEY	7 L92
68	MEOPHAM	6 Q66
69	Minster-on-Sea	6A Q97
70	New Brompton §43	6 Q76
71	NEWINGTON	6 Q86
72	NEWPORT	7 L53
73	NORTHFLEET	6 Q67
74	NORTH WEALD †	27 L50
75	OCKENDON	8 Q58
76	ONGAR †	27 L50
77	PITSEA	8 Q78
78	Port Victoria	6 Q87
79	PRITTLEWELL	7 Q88
80	PURFLEET	8 Q57
81	QUEENSBOROUGH	6 Q97
82	RAINHAM	6 Q86
83	RAINHAM	8 Q58
84	RAYLEIGH	7 Q79
85	Rayne	7 L82
86	ROCHESTER	6 Q76
87	Rochester Bridge	6 Q76
88	Rochester Central	6 Q76
89	ROCHFORD	7 Q88
90	ROMFORD	7 Q58
91	Romford	8 Q58
92	Rosherville	6 Q67
93	Saffron Walden	7 L53
94	Sharnal Street	6 Q76
95	Sheerness Dockyard	6 Q97
96	Sheerness East	6A Q97
97	SHEERNESS-ON-SEA	6 Q97
98	SHENFIELD + Hutton	7 Q69
99	SHOEBURYNESS	8 Q98
100	SHOREHAM	6 Q56
101	Sible + Castle Hedingham	3 L73
102	Sibleys for Chickney + Broxted	7A L52
103	SITTINGBOURNE + Milton Regis	6 Q96
104	SLADES GREEN	6 Q57
105	SNODLAND	6 Q76
106	SOLE STREET	6 Q66
107	SOUTHEND CENTRAL	8 Q88
108	(SOUTHEND EAST)	8 Q88
109	SOUTHEND-on-SEA (VICTORIA)	7 Q88
110	Southfleet	6 Q67
111	SOUTHMINSTER	7 Q99
112	STANFORD-LE-HOPE	8 Q68
113	STANSTED	7 L52
114	(STONE CROSSING Halt)	6 Q57
115	STROOD	6 Q76
116	(SWALE)	6 Q96
117	SWANLEY	6 Q56
118	(SWANSCOMBE)	6 Q67
119	Takerley	7 L52
120	TEYNHAM	6 Q96
121	Thames Haven	8 Q78
122	Thaxted	7A L62
123	THORPE BAY	8 Q98
124	TILBURY (RIVERSIDE)	8 Q67
125	TILBURY Dock (TOWN)	8 Q67
126	Tiptree	7B L81
127	Tollesbury	7B L90
128	Tolleshunt d'Arcy	7B L90
129	UPMINSTER ✳	84 Q58
130	UPMINSTER BRIDGE †	4 Q58
131	WESTCLIFF-ON-SEA	8 Q88
132	WEST HORNDON ✳	8 Q68
133	White Colne	3 L82
134	WHITE NOTLEY	7 L81
135	WICKFORD	7 Q79
136	Wickham Bishops	7 L81
137	WITHAM	7 L81
138	WOODHAM FERRERS	7 Q89
139	Yeldham	3 L73

GOODS

No	Name/Location	Ry Ref
G1	Romford	8 Q58
2	Erith Wharf	6 Q57
3	Rochester	6 Q76
4	Maldon	7 L80
5	Tollesbury Pier ◊	7B L90
6	Chelmsford	7 L70
7	Sheerness Dockyard Gates	6 Q97
8	Braintree	7 L72

SIDINGS

No	Name/Company/Location	Ry Ref
P1	Brambledown Sdg	6A Q97
2	Grove Sdg	6A Q97
3	Tudwick Road Sdg	7B L81
4	Ramsden Bellhouse	7 Q79
5	Cricksea Ferry Sdg	7 Q99
6	Baron's Lane Sdg	7 L80
7	Mountnessing Siding	7 Q69
8	Chatham Dockyard	6X Q76

ENGINE SHEDS

No	Name/Location	Ry Ref
E1	Colchester	7 L92
2	Shenfield	7 Q69
3	Gillingham	6 Q76

BRIDGES

No	Name	Ry Ref
V1	Queen's Bridge	6 Q96

JUNCTIONS

No	Name/Location	Ry Ref
J1	Swanley	6 Q56
2	Rosherville Line	6 Q56
3	Crayford Spur "B"	6 Q57
4	Dartford	6 Q57
5	Crayford Spur "A"	6 Q57
6	Crayford Creek	6 Q57
7	Perry Street Fork	6 Q57
8	Slade Green	6 Q57
9	Erith Wharf Branch	6 Q57
10	West Thurrock	8 Q57
11	Upminster East	8 Q58
12	Upminster West	8+LT Q58
13	Romford Goods	8 Q58
14	Romford - Southend Line	78 Q58
15	Elsenham	77A L52
16	Audley End	7 L53
17	Hoo	6 Q67
18	Tilbury West	8 Q67
19	Tilbury East	8 Q67
20	Tilbury South	8 Q67
21	Thames Haven	8 Q68
22	Shenfield	7 Q69
23	Strood	6 Q76
24	Bridge	6 Q76
25	Dockyard	6 Q76
26	Pitsea	8 Q78
27	Wickford	7 Q79
28	Chelmsford Goods	7 L70
29	Braintree Goods	7 L72
30	Sittingbourne West	6 Q86
31	Sittingbourne East	6 Q86
32	Sittingbourne Middle	6 Q86
33	Woodham	7 Q89
34	Maldon North	7 L80
35	Witham Branches	7 L81
36	Tollesbury Line	77B L81
37	Colne Valley	73 L82
38	Sheppey	66A Q97
39	Dockyard Gates	6 Q97
40	Marks Tey	L92

NOTES:

(1) REF: TL or TQ - T omitted
(2) NAME CHANGE - NEW Old §
(3) LONDON TRANSPORT †
(4) LT + BR OPEN STATION ✳
(5) Ex GE now closed line open LT ‡
(6) Originally Passengers also ◊
(7) Originally East Horndon - may have been different site. ✳

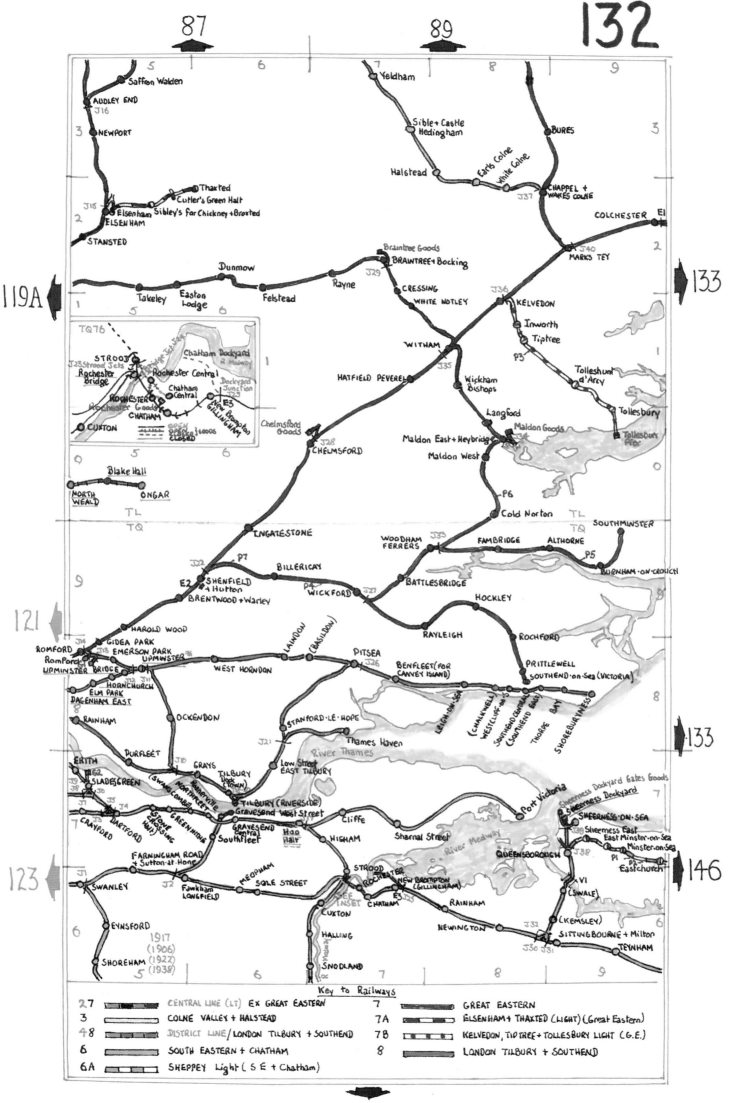

119A ◀   ▶ 133

121 ◀   ▶ 133

123 ◀   ▶ 146

Saffron Walden
AUDLEY END
J16
NEWPORT
Thaxted
Cutler's Green Halt
J15   Sibley's for Chickney + Broxted
Elsenham
ELSENHAM
STANSTED
Dunmow
Takeley   Easton Lodge   Felstead   Rayne
J29
Braintree Goods
BRAINTREE + Bocking
CRESSING
WHITE NOTLEY
WITHAM
J35
HATFIELD PEVEREL

Yeldham
Sible + Castle Hedingham
Halstead   Earls Colne   White Colne
J37
BURES
CHAPPEL + WAKES COLNE
COLCHESTER   E1
J40   MARKS TEY
KELVEDON
J36
Inworth
Tiptree
P3
Tolleshunt d'Arcy
Tollesbury
Tollesbury Pier
Wickham Bishops
Langford
Maldon Goods
J34
Maldon East + Heybridge
Maldon West
P6
Cold Norton
SOUTHMINSTER
WOODHAM FERRERS   J33   FAMBRIDGE   ALTHORNE   P5   BURNHAM-ON-CROUCH

TQ76
STROOD
J23 Strood Jcts
Rochester Bridge
ROCHESTER   Rochester Central
Rochester Goods
CHATHAM   Chatham Central
CUXTON   New Brompton
GILLINGHAM   J25
Dockyard Junction
Chatham Dockyard R.Medway
E3
OPEN
OPEN Goods
CLOSED

Chelmsford Goods
J28
CHELMSFORD

Blake Hall
NORTH WEALD   ONGAR
TL   TQ
INGATESTONE
J2   P7
BILLERICAY
E2   SHENFIELD + Hutton
BRENTWOOD + Warley
P4   WICKFORD   J27   BATTLESBRIDGE
LAINDON   (BASILDON)
HAROLD WOOD
J4   GIDEA PARK
ROMFORD   EMERSON PARK
Romford   UPMINSTER
UPMINSTER BRIDGE
J12 J11   HORNCHURCH
ELM PARK
DAGENHAM EAST
RAINHAM   OCKENDON
WEST HORNDON
PITSEA   J26
BENFLEET (for CANVEY ISLAND)
HOCKLEY
RAYLEIGH   ROCHFORD
PRITTLEWELL
SOUTHEND-on-SEA (VICTORIA)
(CHALKWELL)
WESTCLIFF-on-SEA
SOUTHEND CENTRAL
(SOUTHEND EAST)
THORPE BAY
SHOEBURYNESS
LEIGH-ON-SEA

STANFORD-LE-HOPE
J21
Thames Haven
River Thames
ERITH   J62
J9 SLADE GREEN   J38
J7   J5   J4
CRAYFORD   DARTFORD
PURFLEET   GRAYS
J10
TILBURY Dock (TOWN)
Low Street   EAST TILBURY
TILBURY (RIVERSIDE)
Gravesend West Street
(SWANSCOMBE)   NORTHFLEET
STONE CROSSING Halt
GREENHITHE   GRAVESEND Central
Southfleet   Hoo Halt
Cliffe
HIGHAM
Sharnal Street
River Medway
Port Victoria
Sheerness Dockyard Gates Goods
Sheerness Dockyard
SHEERNESS-ON-SEA
Sheerness East
East Minster-on-Sea
Minster-on-Sea
QUEENSBOROUGH   J38   P1
V1 (SWALE)   Eastchurch
J1
SWANLEY
J2   FARNINGHAM ROAD + Sutton-at-Hone
Fawkham   MEOPHAM   SOLE STREET
LONGFIELD
CUXTON
HALLING
STROOD
ROCHESTER
NEW BROMPTON (GILLINGHAM)
CHATHAM   E3
RAINHAM
SEE INSET
EYNSFORD
1917 (1906)
(1922)
(1938)
SHOREHAM
SNODLAND
NEWINGTON   J32   (KEMSLEY)
J30 J31   SITTINGBOURNE + Milton
TEYNHAM

Key to Railways

27	CENTRAL LINE (LT) EX GREAT EASTERN	7	GREAT EASTERN
3	COLNE VALLEY + HALSTEAD	7A	ELSENHAM + THAXTED (LIGHT) (Great Eastern)
48	DISTRICT LINE/LONDON TILBURY + SOUTHEND	7B	KELVEDON, TIPTREE + TOLLESBURY LIGHT (G.E.)
6	SOUTH EASTERN + CHATHAM	8	LONDON TILBURY + SOUTHEND
6A	SHEPPEY LIGHT (SE + Chatham)		

133

RAILWAYS

No	Company
R6	SOUTH EASTERN + CHATHAM
6A	SHEPPEY (Light) (SE+C)
7	GREAT EASTERN
OO	SOUTHERN (Post Grouping)
X	DOCK + Others

STATIONS

No	Name	Ry Ref
A 1	ALRESFORD	7 M02
2	Ardleigh	7 M02
3	Bentley	7 M13
4	BIRCHINGTON·ON·SEA	6 R26
5	Bradfield	7 M13
6	Brightingsea	7 M01
7	BROADSTAIRS †	6 R36
8	Capel	7 M03
9	(Chislet Colliery Halt)	6 R26
10	CLACTON·on·Sea+Southcliff	M11
		7 M11
11	COLCHESTER	7 M92
12	DOVERCOURT Bay	7 M23
13	(DUMPTON PARK)	OO R36
14	FAVERSHAM	6 R06
15	Felixstowe Beach	7 M23
16	Felixstowe Pier	7 M23
17	FELIXSTOWE Town	7 M23
18	FRINTON·ON·SEA	7 M22
19	GREAT BENTLEY	7 M12
20	Grove Ferry	6 R26
21	HARWICH PARESTON QUAY	7 M23
22	HARWICH TOWN	7 M23
23	HERNE BAY	6 R16
24	HYTHE	7 M02
25	KIRBY CROSS	7 M22
26	Leysdown	6A R06
27	MANNINGTREE	7 M03
28	Margate East †	6 R37
29	Margate Sands †	6 R37
30	MARGATE West †	6 R37
31	MINSTER	6 R36
32	MISTLEY	7 M13
33	RAMSGATE † 600	R36
34	Ramsgate Harbour †	6 R36
35	Ramsgate St Lawrence †	6 R36
36	Ramsgate Town †	6 R36
37	ST BOTOLPHS	7 M02
38	STURRY	6 R16
39	Thorington	7 M02
40	THORPE·LE·SOKEN	7 M12
41	TRIMLEY	7 M22
42	WALTON·ON·NAZE	7 M22
43	WEELY	7 M12
44	WESTGATE·ON·SEA	6 R37
45	Whitstable Harbour	6 R16
46	WHITSTABLE TOWN ✳	6 R16
47	WIVENHOE	7 M02
48	WRABNESS	7 M13

GOODS

No	Location	Ry Ref
G 1	Faversham Coal Wharf	6 R06
2	Graveney	6 R06
3	Whitstable Town ◊	6 R16
4	Hythe	7 M02
5	Harwich Pier	7 M23
6	Harwich	7 M23
7	Felixstowe Docks	7 M23

SIDINGS

No	Name	Ry Ref
P 1	Holford	6A R07
2	Harty Road See note 6	6A R06

ENGINE SHEDS

No	Location	Ry Ref
E 1	Colchester	7 M02
2	Clacton	7 M11
3	Faversham	6 R06

JUNCTIONS

No	Name / Location	Ry Ref
J 1	Faversham	6 R06
2	Minster West	6 R36
3	Minster East	6 R36
4	Minster South	6 R36
5	Ramsgate St Lawrence	6 R36
6	Ramsgate Town	6 R36
7	Ramsgate North	6 R36
8	Colchester	7 L92
9	Colne	7 M02
10	East Gate	7 M02
11	Hythe	7 M02
12	Hythe Goods	7 M02
13	Wivenhoe Wharf	7 M02
14	Brightlingsea Branch	7 M02
15	Manningtree South	7 M13
16	Manningtree North	7 M13
17	Manningtree East	7 M13
18	Mistley Tramway	7X M13
19	Dovercourt	7 M23
20	Felixstowe Docks	7 M23
21	Felixstowe Beach	7 M23
22	Felixstowe Town	7 M23
23	Trimley	7 M23
24	Thorpe	7 M12
25	Hadleigh Branch	7 M13

NOTES

(1) REF — In TL, TM or TR — the T is omitted

(2) KENT PORTION of the map is repeated on MAP no.146 and there is an enlargement of Ramsgate-Margate area; places marked are shown in greater detail on that inset †

(3) Origional passenger station converted to goods when new Town station opened ◊

(4) TOWN portion of name was dropped when Harbour sta closed ✳

(5) Also a halt

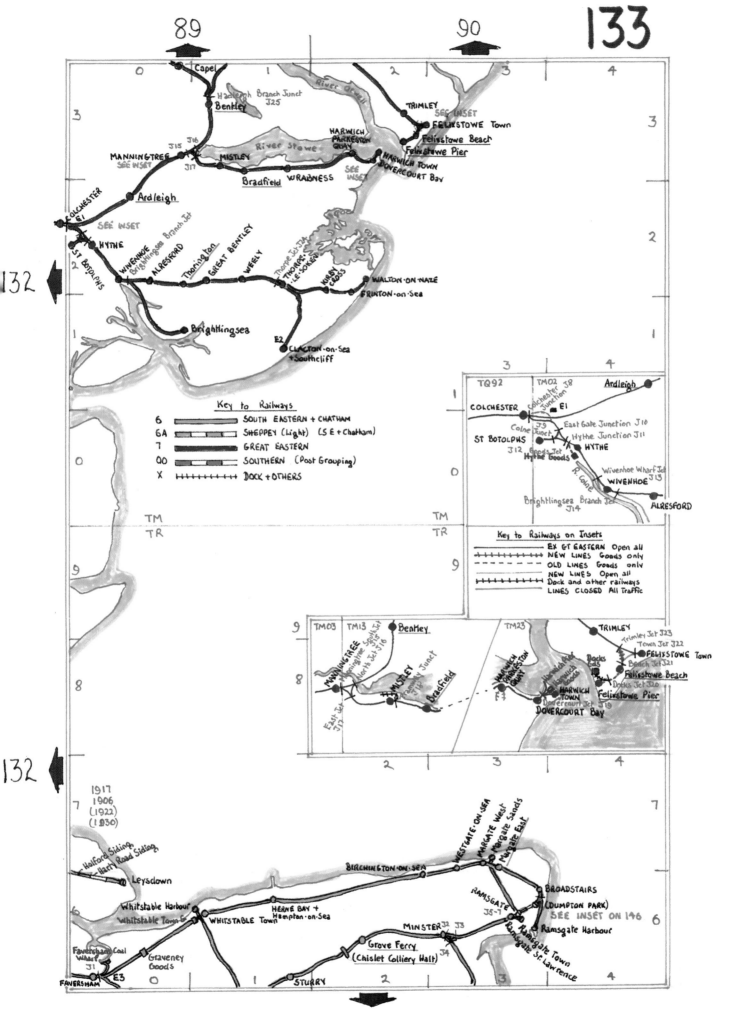

Capel

Hadleigh Branch Junct J25

Bentley

TRIMLEY

SEE INSET

FELIXSTOWE Town

Felixstowe Beach

Felixstowe Pier

J15 J16

MANNINGTREE
SEE INSET

River Orwell

River Stour

HARWICH
PARKESTON
QUAY

MISTLEY

J17

Bradfield WRABNESS

HARWICH TOWN
DOVERCOURT Bay

SEE INSET

COLCHESTER
E1

Ardleigh

SEE INSET

HYTHE

ST Botolphs

WIVENHOE
Brightlingsea Branch Jct

ALRESFORD

Thorrington

GREAT BENTLEY

WEELEY

Thorpe Jct J24

THORPE-
LE-SOKEN

KIRBY
CROSS

WALTON-ON-NAZE

FRINTON-on-Sea

Brightlingsea

E2

CLACTON·on·Sea
+ Southcliff

132

132

Key to Railways

6	SOUTH EASTERN + CHATHAM
6A	SHEPPEY (Light) (S E + Chatham)
7	GREAT EASTERN
00	SOUTHERN (Post Grouping)
X	DOCK + OTHERS

Inset (top right):

TQ92   TM02   J8   Ardleigh

COLCHESTER   Colchester Junction   E1

J9   East Gate Junction J10

Colne Junct   Hythe Junction J11

ST BOTOLPHS   Goods Jct   HYTHE

J12   Hythe Goods

R. Colne   Wivenhoe Wharf Jct

WIVENHOE   J13

Brightlingsea Branch Jct
J14   ALRESFORD

Key to Railways on Insets

	EX GT EASTERN Open all
+++	NEW LINES Goods only
---	OLD LINES Goods only
	NEW LINES Open all
+++	Dock and other railways
	LINES CLOSED All Traffic

Inset (lower middle):

TM03   TM13   Bentley   TM23   TRIMLEY   Trimley Jct J23

MANNINGTREE   Manningtree South Jct J15   Town Jct J22   FELIXSTOWE Town

Manningtree North Jct J16   Beach Jct J21

MISTLEY   Mistley Junct J17   HARWICH PARKESTON QUAY   Docks J25   Felixstowe Beach

Bradfield   Harwich Goods   Felixstowe Pier

East Jct J12   E7   Harwich Pier   Docks Jct J20

HARWICH TOWN

Dovercourt Jct J19   DOVERCOURT Bay

1917
1906
(1922)
(1930)

Halford Siding
Harty Road Siding

Leysdown

WESTGATE-ON-SEA

MARGATE-ON-SEA

Margate West

Margate Sands

Margate East

Whitstable Harbour

Whitstable Town

BIRCHINGTON-ON-SEA

RAMSGATE
J5-7

BROADSTAIRS
(DUMPTON PARK)

SEE INSET ON 146

HERNE BAY +
Hampton-on-Sea

WHITSTABLE Town

Ramsgate Harbour

MINSTER J2   J3

Ramsgate Town
Ramsgate St. Lawrence

Faversham Coal
Wharf

J1

Graveney
Goods

Grove Ferry
(Chislet Colliery Halt)

J4

FAVERSHAM

E3

STURRY

146

134

RAILWAYS

No	Company
R 1	LONDON + SOUTH WESTERN
2	BIDEFORD, WESTWARD HO + APPLEDORE
3	GREAT WESTERN
OO	NORTH DEVON + CORNWALL JCT (built post grouping)

STATIONS

No	Name	Ry Ref
A 1	Abbotsham Road	2 S42
2	Appledore	2 S42
3	Ashbury + North Lew	1 X40
4	Ashwater	1 X39
5	Bideford	1 S42
6	Bideford	2 S42
7	Braunton	1 S43
8	Brentor	1 X48
9	Bude	1 S20
10	Camelford	1 X08
11	Coryton	3 X48
12	Delabole	1 X08
13	(Dunsbear Halt)	OO S41
14	Dunsland Cross	1 S40
15	Egloskerry	1 X48
16	Halwill Junction	100 S40
17	(Hole)	OO S40
18	Halsworthy	1 S30
19	Instow	1 S42
20	Launceston	1 X39
21	Launceston	3 X39
22	Lifton	3 X48
23	Lydford	1 X58
24	Lydford	3 X58
25	Mortehoe	1 S44
26	Northam	2 S47
27	Otterham	1 X18
28	Torrington	100 S42
29	Tower Hill	1 X39
30	Tresmeer	1 X28
31	(Watergate Halt)	OO S41
32	Westward Ho	2 S42
33	Whitston + Bridgerule	1 S20
34	Wrafton	1 S43
35	(Yarde Halt)	OO S41

GOODS

No	Location	Ry Ref
G 1	Bideford	1 S42
2	Bude Quay	2 S20

SIDINGS

No	Name	Ry Ref
P 1	Bartlett's Siding	1 S42

ENGINE SHEDS

No	Location	Ry Ref
E 1	Launceston	1 X38
2	Bude	1 S20
3	Torrington	1 S41
4	Launceston	3 X38

JUNCTIONS

No	Name/Location	Ry Ref
J 1	Bude Quay	1 S20
2	Halwill Junctions	100 S40
3	Lydford	13 X58

NOTES

(1) REF In SS or SX - S omitted

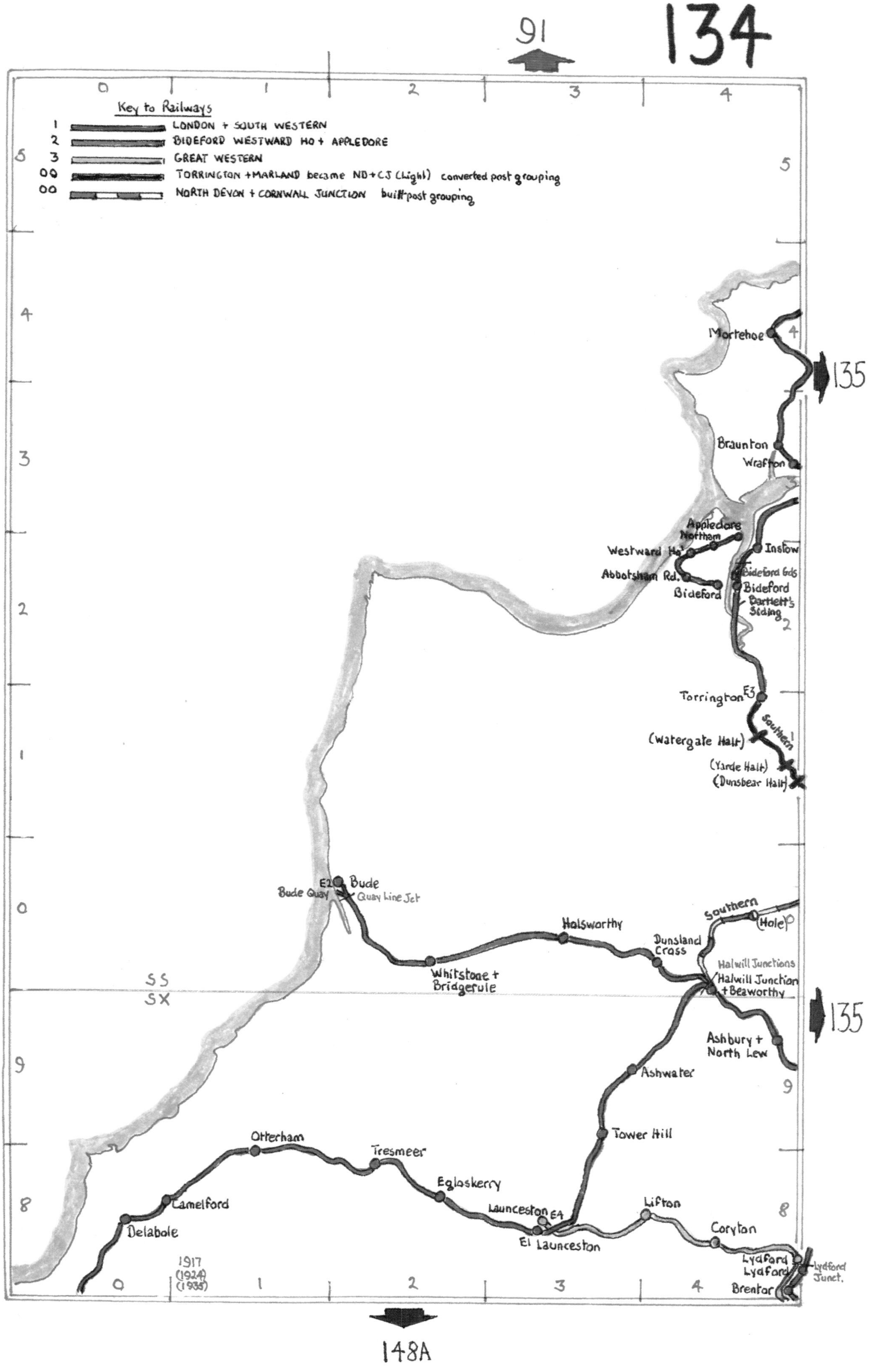

Key to Railways

1	▬▬▬	LONDON + SOUTH WESTERN
2	▬▬▬	BIDEFORD WESTWARD HO + APPLEDORE
3	▬▬▬	GREAT WESTERN
OO	▬▬▬	TORRINGTON + MARLAND became ND+CJ (Light) converted post grouping
OO	▬▬▬	NORTH DEVON + CORNWALL JUNCTION built post grouping

91

135

Mortehoe

Braunton
Wrafton

Appledore
Northam
Westward Ho
Instow
Abbotsham Rd.
Bideford Gds
Bideford
Bartlett's Siding
Bideford

Torrington E3
Southern
(Watergate Halt)
(Yarde Halt)
(Dunsbear Halt)

E2 Bude
Bude Quay ✕ Quay Line Jct.

Halsworthy
Southern
(Hole)
Dunsland Cross
Halwill Junctions
Halwill Junction
+ Beaworthy

135

Whitstone +
Bridgerule

Ashbury +
North Lew

Ashwater

S S
S X

Tower Hill

Otterham
Tresmeer
Egloskerry
Lifton
Camelford
Launceston E4
Corytan
Delabole
E1 Launceston
Lydford
Lydford
Lydford Junct.
Brentor

1917
(1924)
(1935)

148A

BARNSTAPLE + EXETER

RAILWAYS

No.	Company
R 1	LONDON + SOUTH WESTERN
2	LYNTON + BARNSTAPLE (1'11½")
3	GREAT WESTERN
6	WEST SOMERSET MINERAL ✳
OO	NORTH DEVON + CORNWALL JUNCT. (Light) (post-grouping)

STATIONS

No.	Name	Ry Ref
A 1	Ashton	3 X88
2	Bampton	3 S92
3	BARNSTAPLE Junction	1 S53
4	Barnstaple Town	1 S53
5	Barnstaple Town	2 S53
6	Barnstaple Victoria Rd.	3 S53
7	Bishop's Nympton+Molland	3 S72
8	Blackmoor	2 S64
9	Bow	1 S70
10	Bramford Speke	3 X99
11	Bratton Fleming	2 S63
12	Brentor	1 X58
13	Bridestowe	1 X58
14	Broad Clyst	1 X99
15	(Burn Halt)	3 S90
16	Cadeleigh	3 S90
17	Caffyn Halt	2 S74
18	CHAPELTON	1 S52
19	Chelfham	2 S63
20	Christow	3 X88
21	COPPLESTONE	1 S70
22	(Cove Halt)	3 S91
23	CREDITON	1 X89
24	Dulverton	3 S92
25	(Dunsbear Halt)	00 S51
26	Dunster	3 S94
27	East Anstey	3 S82
28	EGGESFORD	1 S61

EXETER

No.	Name	Ry Ref
29	(CENTRAL) Queen St	1 X99
30	(Lions Holt Halt)	1 X99
31	ST DAVIDS	3 X99
32	(ST JAMES PARK)✗	1 X99
33	ST THOMAS	3 X99
34	Exminster	3 X98
35	EXMOUTH	1 X98
36	EXTON §83	1 X98
37	Filleigh	3 S62
38	Fremington	1 S53
39	(Halberton Halt)	3 S91
40	(Hatherleigh)	00 S50
41	Hele + Bradninch	3 S90
42	Ide	3 X89
43	Ilfracombe	1 S54
44	KINGS NYMPTON §72	1 S61
45	LAPFORD	1 S70
46	Longdown	3 X89
47	Lustleigh	3 X78
48	Lydford	1 X58
49	Lydford	3 X58
50	LYMPSTONE	1 X98
51	(LYMPSTONE COMMANDO)	1 X98
52	Lynton	2 S74
53	(Meeth Halt)	00 S51
54	Minehead	3 S94
55	MORCHARD ROAD	1 S70
56	Morebath	3 S92
57	(Morebath Junction Halt)	3 S92
58	Moreton Hampstead	3 X78
59	Martehoe	1 S44
60	NEWTON · ST·CYRES	1 X89
61	North Tawton	1 X69
62	Okehampton †	1 X59
63	Parracombe Halt	2 S64
64	(Petrockstow)	00 S51
65	PINHOE	1 X99
66	(POLSLOE BRIDGE)	1 X99
67	PORTSMOUTH ARMS	1 S61
68	Sampford Courtenay	1 X69
69	Silverton	3 S90
70	Snapper (for Goodleigh) Halt	2 S53
71	South Molton	3 S72
72	South Molton Road §44	1 S61
73	STARCROSS	3 X98
74	Stoke Canon	3 X99
75	Swimbridge	3 S62
76	Thorverton	3 S90
77	Tiverton	3 S91
78	TOPSHAM	1 X98
79	Trusham	3 X88
80	UMBERLEIGH	1 S62
81	Up Exe Halt	3 S91
82	(West Exe Halt)	3 S90
83	Woodbury Road §36	1 X98
84	Woody Bay	2 S64
85	YEOFORD Junction	1 X79

GOODS

No.	Name/Location	Ry Ref
G 1	Alphington Road	3 X99
2	Canal Basin	3 X99
3	Queen Street	1 X99
4	Gupworthy	6 S93

SIDINGS

No.	Name/Company/Location	Ry Ref
P 1	North Devan Clay Co	00 S51
2	Meeth Clay Co	00 S51
3	Digby Siding	1 X99
4	Sander's Brick Works	1 X99
5	Odams Siding	1 X98
6	Rolle Quay	1 S53
7	Steam Cabinet Works	1 S53

ENGINE SHEDS

No.	Name/Location	Ry Ref
E 1	Barnstaple	1 S53
2	Ilfracombe	1 S54
3	Exmouth	1 (X98)
4	Exmouth Junction	1 X99
5	Okehampton	1 X59
6	Moreton Hampstead	3 X78
7	Minehead	3 S94
8	Barnstaple	3 S53

No.		Ry Ref
9	Exeter St Davids	3 X99

JUNCTIONS

No	Name/Location	Ry Ref
J 1	Meldon	1 X59
2	Lydford	13 X58
3	Coleford	1 X79
4	Budleigh Salterton	1 X98
	EXETER JUNCTIONS:	
5	for Queen Street	13 X99
6	Heathfield Branch	3 X99
7	Goods	3 X99
8	Basin Branch South	3 X99
9	Basin Branch	3 X99
10	Basin Branch North	3 X99
11	Goods Branch	1 X99
12	Exmouth Branch	1 X99
13	Cowley Bridge	31 X99
14	Stoke Canon-Exe Valley	3 X99
15	Barnstaple - Ilfracombe	1 S53
16	GW Junct	13 S53
17	South	3 S53
18	East Loop	3 S53
19	Station	3 S53
20	Exe Valley + Tiverton Bch	3 S91
21	Morebath	3 S92

VIADUCTS + BRIDGES

No.	Name	Ry Ref
V 1	Meldon	1 X59

NOTES:

REF - In SS or SX initial S omitted.

§ NAME CHANGE - NEW, Old

† Okehampton - open for occasional passenger trains

✳ Railway out of use prior to 1917

✗ Earlier name - Mount Pleasant Road Halt.

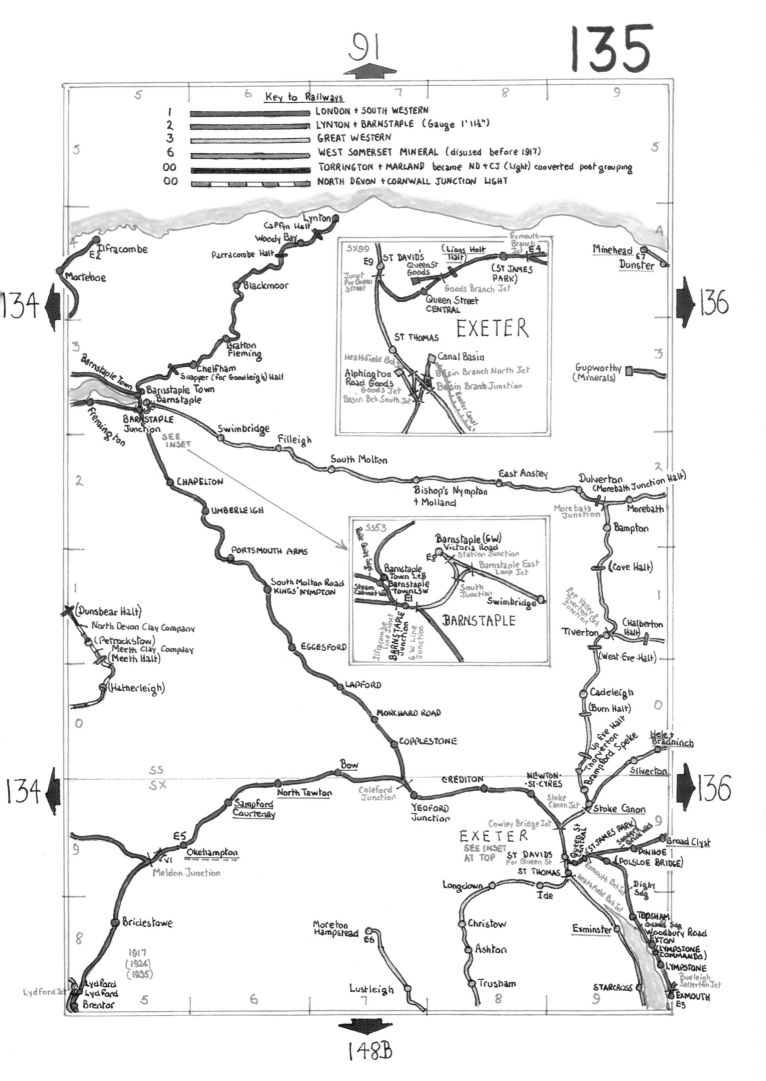

Key to Railways

1 LONDON + SOUTH WESTERN
2 LYNTON + BARNSTAPLE (Gauge 1' 11½")
3 GREAT WESTERN
6 WEST SOMERSET MINERAL (disused before 1917)
00 TORRINGTON + MARLAND became ND+CJ (Light) converted post grouping
00 NORTH DEVON + CORNWALL JUNCTION LIGHT

HIGHBRIDGE, TAUNTON + EXMOUTH

RAILWAYS

No	Company
R 1	LONDON + SOUTH WESTERN
1A	AXMINSTER + LYME REGIS (Light) L+SW
13	GW AND L+SW JOWT
14	SOMERSET + DORSET (L+SW and Midland)
3	GREAT WESTERN
6	WEST SOMERSET MINERAL ✳

STATIONS

No	Name	Ry	Ref
A 1	Ashcott	14	T43
2	Athelney	3	T32
3	Axbridge	3	T45
4	AXMINSTER	1	Y29
5	Bason Bridge	14	T34
6	(Bawdrip Halt)	14	T33
7	Bishops Lydeard ✳	3	T12
8	Blagdon	3	T45
9	Bleadon + Uphill	3	T35
10	Blue Anchor ✳	3	T04
11	Brent Knoll	3	T35
12	Bridgwater	14	T33
13	BRIDGWATER	3	T33
14	Bridport East Street	3	Y49
15	Bridport for Lyme Regis	3	Y49
16	Bridport West Bay	3	Y49
17	Budleigh Salterton	1	Y08
18	Burlescombe	3	T01
19	Burnham-on-Sea	14	T34
20	Burrington	3	T45
21	Chard	13	T30
22	Chard Junction	1	T30
23	Cheddar	3	T45
24	(Coldharbour Halt)	3	T01
25	Colyford †	1	Y29
26	Colyton Town †	1	Y29
27	Combpyne	1A	Y39
28	Cossington	14	T33
29	CREWKERNE	1	T40
30	Crowcombe ✳	3	T13
31	Cullompton	3	T00
32	Culmstock	3	T01
33	Draycott	3	T44
34	Dunball	3	T34
35	Dunster ✳	3	T04
36	Durston	3	T32
37	East Budleigh	1	Y08
38	Erdington Junction	14	T34
39	EXMOUTH	1	Y07
40	FENITON §67	1	Y09
41	Glastonbury + Street	14	T43
42	Hatch	3	T32
43	Hemyock	3	T11
44	Highbridge	14	T34
45	HIGHBRIDGE	3	T34
46	HONITON	1	T10
47	Ilminster	3	T31
48	Langford	3	T45
49	Langport East	3	T42
50	Langport West	3	T42
51	Littleham	1	Y08
52	Lodge Hill	3	T54
53	Long Sutton + Pitney Halt	3	T42
54	Lyme Regis	1A	Y39
55	Martock	3	T42
56	Milverton	3	T12
57	Montacute	3	T41
58	Newton Poppleford	1	Y09
59	Norton Fitzwarren	3	T12
60	Ottery St Mary	1	Y09
61	(Sampford Peverill Halt)	3	T01
62	Sandford + Banwell	3	T45
63	Seaton †	1	Y29
64	Seaton Junction	1	Y29
65	Shapwick	14	T44
66	Sidmouth	1	Y18
67	Sidmouth Junction §40	1	Y09
68	Somerton	3	T42
69	Stogumber ✳	3	T13
70	TAUNTON	3	T22
71	Thornfalcon	3	T22
72	Tipton St John's	1	Y09
73	TIVERTON JUNCTION ✕	3	T01
74	Uffculme	3	T01
75	Venn Cross	3	T02
76	Washford ✳	3	T04
77	Watchet ✳	3	T04
78	Wellington	3	T12
79	(WESTON MILTON)	3	T36
80	WESTON-SUPER-MARE	3	T36
81	WHIMPLE	1	Y09
82	(Whitehall Halt)	3	T11
83	Williton ✳	3	T04
84	Winscombe	3	T45
85	Wiveliscombe	3	T02
86	Worle	3	T36

GOODS

No	Location		Ry	Ref
G 1	Raleighs Cross	✳	6	T03
2	Combe Row	✳	6	T03
3	Roadwater	✳	6	T03
4	Washford	✳	6	T04
5	Watchet	✳	6	T04
6	Highbridge Wharf		14	T34
7	Bridgwater Docks S+D		14	T33
8	Bridgwater Docks GW		3	T33
9	Dunball Wharf		3	T33
10	Pitney Mileage Sidings		3	T42
11	Chard		1	T30

SIDINGS

No	Company / Name / Location	Ry	Ref
P 1	Warrens Sdg	1	X08
2	Collation Raleigh	1	X08
3	Poole Siding	3	T12
4	Victory Siding	3	T12
5	Somerville's Siding	3	T22
6	Bristol Waterworks	3	T45

ENGINE SHEDS

No	Location	Ry	Ref
E 1	Tiverton Junction	3	T01
2	Seaton	1	Y29
3	Lyme Regis	1	Y39
4	Highbridge	14	T34
5	Taunton	3	T22
6	Bridgwater	3	T33
7	Weston-super-Mare	3	T36
8	Bridport	3	Y49

COMPANY WORKS

No	Location	Ry	Ref
C 1	Highbridge	14	T34

TUNNELS

No	Name	Yds	Ry	Ref
T 1	Whiteball	1092	3	T01

SUMMITS

No	Name	Ht	Ry	Ref
S 1	Whiteball		3	T01
2	Honiton		1	T10

JUNCTIONS

No	Name / Location	Ry	Ref
J 1	Budleigh Salterton	1	Y08
2	Tipton	1	Y09
3	Sidmouth	1	Y09
4	Culm Valley Branch	3	T01
5	Tiverton Branch	3	T01
6	Minehead Branch	3	T12
7	Barnstaple Branch	3	T12
8	Seaton	1	Y29
9	Lyme Regis	1	Y29
10	Creech	3	T22
11	Cogload	3	T22
12	Chard Branch	1	T30
13	Goods + Joint Line	131	T30
14	Durston	3	T32
15	Athelney	3	T32
16	Bridgwater Docks SD	14	T33
17	Bridgwater Docks GW	3	T33
18	Dunball Wharf	3	T33
19	Highbridge Wharf	143	T34
20	S+D Loop	3	T34
21	Uphill	3	T35
22	Worle	3	T36
23	Edington	14	T34
24	Curry Rivel	3	T42
25	Wells Branch	14	T43

NOTES:

(1) REF All in ST or SY - S omitted

(2) WEST SOMERSET RLY ✳

(3) SEATON TRAMWAY (Colyton - Seaton) - additional intermediate halts; gauge 2'9" †

(4) Closed '86. Replaced by a new station TIVERTON PARKWAY approx site Sampford Peverill Halt ✕

(5) Railway out of use prior to 1917 ✳

(6) CHANGE OF NAME - NEW old §

(7) Flyover Junctions at Durston are not shown.

(8) SD + GW Crossing at Highbridge is on the level

(9) Some overlap for clarity at North and West margins

(10) Modern position as at March 1986.

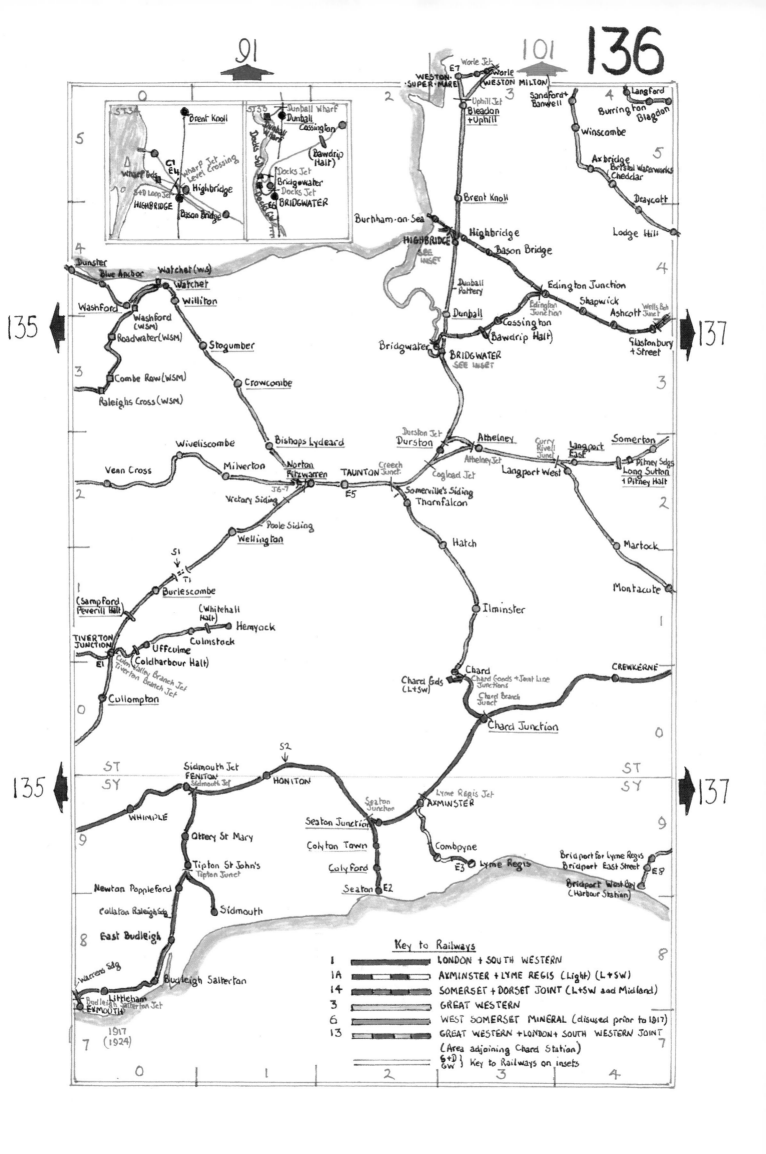

137
RAILWAYS

No	Company
R 1	LONDON + SOUTH WESTERN
13	WEYMOUTH + PORTLAND (GW+LSW)
14	SOMERSET + DORSET JT. (LSW+Midland)
2	EASTON + CHURCH HOPE
3	GREAT WESTERN
OO	GREAT WESTERN (Post Grouping)
X	OTHERS - Colliery lines etc

STATIONS + HALTS

No	Name	Ry Ref
A 1	Abbotsbury	3 Y58
2	(Alford Halt)	3 T63
3	Bailey Gate	14 Y99
4	Binegar	14 T64
5	Blandford (Forum)	14 T80
6	BRUTON	3 T63
7	Camerton	3 T65
8	CASTLE CARY	3 T63
9	Charlton Mackrell	3 T52
10	(Charlton Marshall Halt)	14 T90
11	(CHETNOLE)	3 T50
12	Chilcompton	14 T65
13	Clutton	3 T65
14	Cadford	3 T93
15	Cole	14 T63
16	(Combehay Halt)	3 T75
17	Corfe Castle	1 Y98
18	Coryates Halt	3 Y68
19	Cranmore	3 T64
20	(DILTON MARSH)	3 T85
21	DORCHESTER (SOUTH)	1 Y69
22	DORCHESTER (WEST)	3 Y69
23	Dunkerton	3 T75
24	Dunkerton Colliery Halt	3 T65
25	Easton ✳	2 Y67
26	Edington + Bratton	3 T85
27	Evercreech Junction	14 T63
28	Evercreech (New)	14 T63
29	Evershot	3 T50
30	FROME	3 T74
31	GILLINGHAM (Dorset)	1 T82
32	Grimstone + Frampton	3 Y69
33	Hallatrow	3 T65
34	HAMWORTHY	1 Y99
35	Henstridge	14 T71
36	Heytesbury	3 T84
37	HOLTON HEATH	1 Y99
38	Keinton Mandeville	3 T53
39	Lavington	3 T95
40	Lodge Hill	3 T54
41	MAIDEN NEWTON	3 Y59
42	Marston Magna	3 T62
43	Masbury	14 T64
44	Melcombe Regis	13 Y67
45	Mells Road	3 T75
46	Midford	14 T76
47	Midford Halt	3 T75
48	Midsomer Norton + Welton	14 T65
49	Midsomer Norton + Welton	3 T65
50	Milborne Port	1 T61
51	Mankton + Came Halt	3 Y68
52	Montacute	3 T51
53	MORETON	1 Y78
54	Paulton Halt	3 T65
55	Pennard, West ‡	14 T53
56	Polsham	14 T54
57	Portesham	3 Y68
58	Portland	(2)13 Y67
59	Powerstock	3 Y59
60	Pylle	14 T63
61	Radford + Timsbury Halt	3 T65
62	Radipole Halt	3 Y68
63	Radstock	14 T65
64	Radstock	3 T65
65	Rodwell	13 Y67
66	Semley	1 T82
67	Shepton Mallet	14 T64
68	Shepton Mallet	3 T64
69	SHERBORNE	1 T61
70	Shillingstone	14 T81
71	Sparkford	3 T62
72	Spetisbury	14 T90
73	Stalbridge	14 T71
74	(Stourpaine + Durweston Halt)	14 T80
75	Sturminster Newton	14 T71
76	Sutton Bingham	1 T51
77	TEMPLECOMBE (Upper)	1 T72
78	Templecombe	14 T72
79	(THORNFORD)	3 T51
80	TISBURY	1 T92
81	Toller	3 Y59
82	TROWBRIDGE	3 T85
83	Upwey	3 Y68
84	UPWEY Junction	3 Y68
85	Upwey Wishing Well Halt	3 Y68
86	Wanstrow	3 T74
87	WAREHAM	1 Y98
88	WARMINSTER	3 T84
89	Wellow	14 T75
90	Wells	14 T54
91	Wells	3 T54
92	WESTBURY	3 T85
93	Westham Halt	13 Y67
94	West Pennard ‡	14 T53
95	WEYMOUTH (QUAY) Harbour	13 Y67
96	WEYMOUTH Town	3 Y67
97	Wincanton	14 T72
98	Witham	3 T74
99	Wookey	3 T54
100	WOOL	1 Y88
101	Wyke Regis Halt	13 Y67
102	YEOVIL JUNCTION	1 T51
103	YEOVIL PEN MILL	3 T51
104	Yeovil Town	13 T51
105	YETMINSTER	3 T51

GOODS

No	Location	Ry Ref
G 1	Clifton Maybank	3 T51
2	Hendford	3 T51
3	Yeovil Town	1 T51
4	Portland	13 Y67
5	Hamworthy	1 Y99

SIDINGS

No	Name/Company/Location	Ry Ref
P 1	Grayfield Colliery	3 T65
2	Timsbury Colliery	3 T65
3	Dunkerton Colliery	3 T75
4	Claydown Colliery	14 T65
5	Writhlington Colliery	14 T75
6	Braysdown Colliery	14 T75
7	Norton Hill Colliery	14 T65
8	Welton, Old Colliery	14 T65
9	Moorewood Colliery	14 T65
10	Old Down Siding	14 T64
11	Old Mills Colliery	3 T65
12	Windsor Hill Sdgs	14 T64
13	Dulcot Siding	3 T54
14	Doulting Siding	3 T64
15	Norden Siding	1 Y98
16	Sandford Pottery	1 Y98
17	Vobster Colliery	3 T74

ENGINE SHEDS

No	Location	Ry Ref
E 1	Templecombe	14 T72
2	Templecombe Upper	1 T72
3	Wells	♀ 14 T54
4	Weymouth	3 Y68

JUNCTIONS

No	Name/Location	Ry Ref
J 1	Maiden Newton (Bridport)	3 Y59
2	Wells West	143 T54
3	Wells East	143 T54
4	Castle Cary	3 T63
5	Hallatrow	3 T65
6	Templecombe - S+D	1 T72
7	Templecombe 2+3	14 T72
8	Witham (Cheddar Line)	3 T74
9	Vobster	3 T74
10	Worgret	1 Y88

NOTES:

(1) REF: All in ST or SY, S omitted

(2) Dually indexed ‡

(3) Continuation see 138C ✳

(4) Junctions and engine sheds, etc not shown in the areas covered by enlargements - see Maps 138A, 138B, 138C, 138D

(5) Also GW Shed at Wells ♀

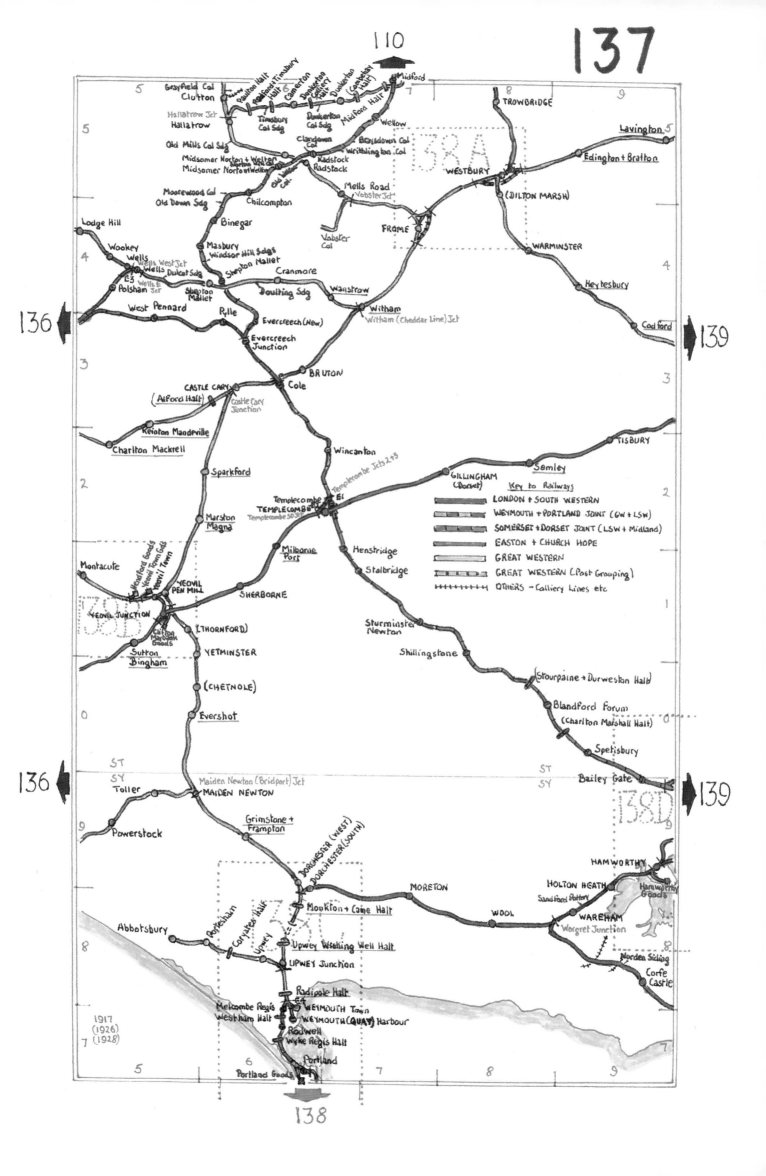

YEOVIL FROME + WESTBURY

Box B

RAILWAYS

No	Company
R 1	LONDON + SOUTH WESTERN
3	GREAT WESTERN

STATIONS

No	Name	Ry	Ref
A 1	Montacute	3	T51
2	SHERBORNE	1	T52
3	Sutton Bingham	1	T51
4	(THORNFORD)	3	T61
5	YEOVIL JUNCTION	1	T51
6	YEOVIL PEN MILL	3	T51
7	Yeovil Town	13	T51
8	YETMINSTER	3	T51

GOODS

No	Location	Ry	Ref
G 1	Clifton Maybank	3	T51
2	Hendford	3	T51
3	Town	1	T51

SIDINGS

No	Name	Ry	Ref
P 1	Bunford	3	T51

2	Hardington	1	T51

ENGINE SHEDS

No	Location	Ry	Ref
E 6	Yeovil Pen Mill	3	T51
7	Yeovil Town	1	T51

JUNCTIONS

No	Name / Location	Ry	Ref
J 1	Yeovil (Town Bch)	1	T51
2	Goods Branch (Clifton)	3	T51
3	Town	13	T51
4	Town Goods	13	T51
5	Hendford Goods	3	T51
6	Pen Mill	3	T51

NOTES

(1) REF : ST 51 or ST 52

(2) E7 is located close to Town Goods

Box A

RAILWAYS

No	Company
R 3	GREAT WESTERN
00	GREAT WESTERN (Post Grouping)

STATIONS

No	Name	Ry	Ref
A 1	(DILTON MARSH)	3	T85
2	Eddington + Bratton	3	T85
3	FROME	3	T74
4	WARMINSTER	3	T84
5	WESTBURY	3	T85

SIDINGS

No	Name	Ry	Ref
P 1	Frome Market Sdg	3	T74

ENGINE SHEDS

No	Location	Ry	Ref
E 8	Frome	3	T74
9	Westbury	3	T85

JUNCTIONS

No	Name / Location	Ry	Ref
J	FROME		T74
1	North	3	T74
2	South	3	T74

FROME — T74

No	Name	Ry	Ref
3	West	3	T74
4	Blatchbridge	300	T74
5	Clink Road	300	T74

WESTBURY — T85

No	Name	Ry	Ref
6	East	3	T85
7	West	3	T85
8	Loop	300	T85
9	Hawkerbridge Rd	300	T85
10	Heywood Road	300	T85
11	Fairwood	300	T85

NOTES

(1) REF - All in ST, S omitted

(2) JUNCTIONS Ry-300 are the post grouping cut-off lines

DORCHESTER WEYMOUTH POOLE BOURNEMOUTH

Box C

RAILWAYS

No	Company
R 1	LONDON + SOUTH WESTERN
13	WEYMOUTH + PORTLAND (GW+LSW)
2	EASTON + CHURCH HOPE (GW+LSW)
3	GREAT WESTERN
X	OTHERS

STATIONS + HALTS

No	Name	Ry	Ref
A 1	Coryates Halt	3	T68
2	DORCHESTER (SOUTH)	1	T69
3	DORCHESTER (WEST)	3	T69
4	Easton	2	T67
5	Melcombe Regis	13	T67
6	Monkton + Came Halt	3	T68
7	Portland	213	T67
8	Radipole Halt	3	T68
9	Rodwell	13	T67
10	Upwey	3	T68
11	UPWEY Junction	3	T68
12	Upwey Wishing Well Halt	3	T68
13	Westham Halt	13	T67
14	WEYMOUTH (QUAY) Harbour	13	T67
15	WEYMOUTH Town	3	T67
16	Wyke Regis Halt	13	T67

GOODS

No	Location	Ry	Ref
G 1	Dorchester ‡	1	Y69
2	Portland	13	Y67

SIDINGS

No	Name / Company	Ry	Ref
P 1	Castleton Stone	13	Y67
2	Sheepcroft Sidings	2	Y67
3	Whitehead Torpedo	13	Y67

ENGINE SHEDS

No	Location	Ry	Ref
E 1	Weymouth	3	Y67
2	Dorchester	1	Y69
3	Easton	‡ 1(3)	Y67

TUNNELS

No	Name	Ry	Ref
T 1	Bincombe	3	Y68
2	Dorchester	3	Y69

JUNCTIONS

No	Name / Location	Ry	Ref
J 1	Portland Goods	13	Y67
2	Tramway	13	Y67
3	Weymouth	313	Y67
4	Upwey	3	Y68
5	Dorchester	3	Y69
6	Station (Dorchester)	1	Y69

NOTES

(1) REF : All in SY, S omitted

(2) ‡ Worked by LSW

Box D

RAILWAYS

No	Company
R 1	LONDON + SOUTH WESTERN
14	SOMERSET + DORSET (LSW+Mid)

STATIONS

No	Name	Ry	Ref
A 1	Bailey Gate	14	Y99
2	Boscombe	1	Z09
3	BRANKSOME	1	Z09
4	Broadstone Junction	114	Z09
5	BOURNEMOUTH Central	1	Z09
6	Bournemouth West *	1	Z09
7	HAMWORTHY JUNCTION	1	Y99
8	PARKSTONE for Sandbanks	1	Z09
9	POOLE	1	Z09
10	Wimborne	114	Z09

GOODS

No	Location	Ry	Ref
G 1	Bournemouth Central	1	Z09
2	Hamworthy	1	Y99
3	Poole Quay	1	Y99

SIDINGS

No	Company	Ry	Ref
P 1	Stancrete Manufacturing	1	Y99

ENGINE SHEDS

No	Location	Ry	Ref
E 4	Hamworthy Junction	1	Y99
5	Bournemouth Central	1	Z09

JUNCTIONS

No	Name / Location	Ry	Ref
J 1	Hamworthy Goods	1	Y99
2	Holes Bay Curve	1	Y99
3	Corfe Mullen	14	Y99
4	Poole Quay	1	Z09
5	Holes Bay	1	Z09
	BROADSTONE		Z09
6	Poole + Hamworthy Lines	1	Z09
7	New S+D Line	114	Z09
8	Wimborne (Old S+D)	114	Z09
9	Gasworks	1	Z09
10	Bournemouth West	1	Z09
11	Bournemouth West (North)	1	Z09
12	Bournemouth Goods	1	Z09

NOTES

(1) REF In SY or SZ, S omitted

(2) * JUNCTION now dropped from title

(3) * RCH records show as goods but this was a fiction and was in fact part of LSW passenger station

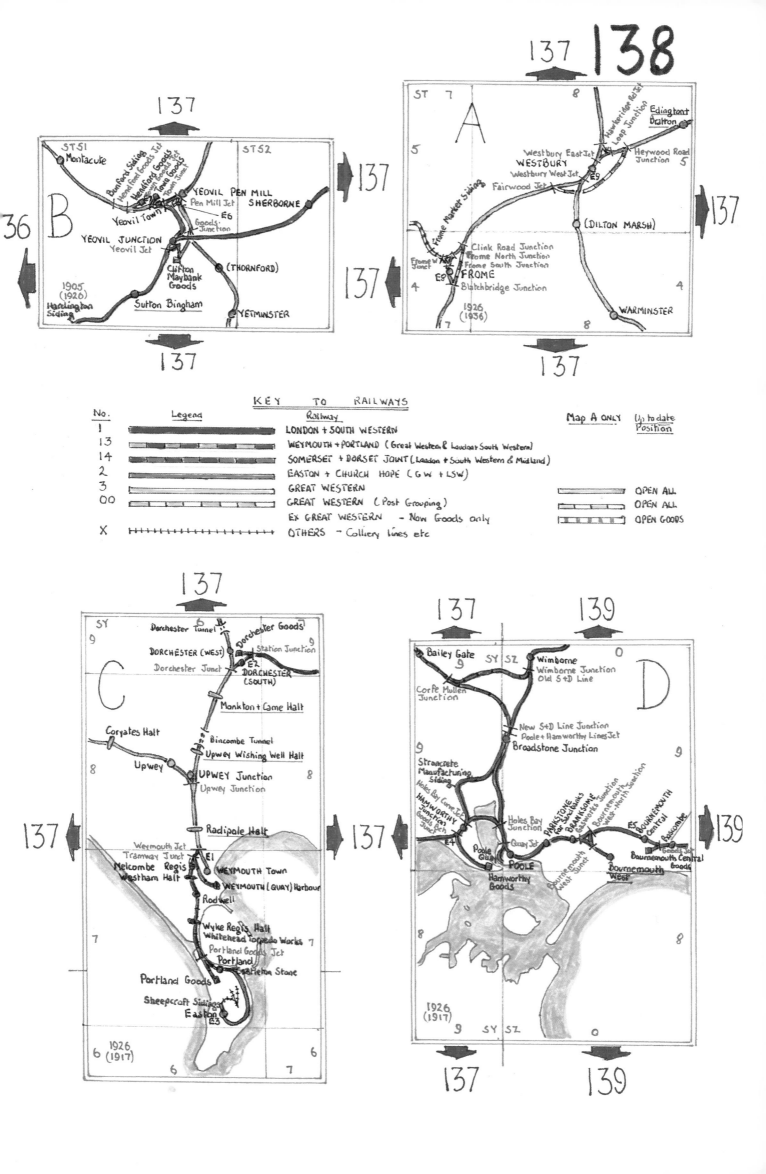

Map B:

137

36

ST 51 ST 52

Montacute

Benford Siding

Henford Goods Jct
Henford Goods
Jct

Goods
Town Goods

Town Junct

YEOVIL PEN MILL

Pen Mill Jct

E6

SHERBORNE

Yeovil Town

YEOVIL JUNCTION

Yeovil Jct

Goods
Junction

Clifton
Maybank
Goods

(THORNFORD)

1905
(1926)

Hardington
Siding

Sutton Bingham

YETMINSTER

137

137

Map A:

ST 7

A

5

8

Hawkeridge Rel Jct

Loop Junction

Edingtont
Dralton

Westbury East Jct

WESTBURY

Heywood Road
Junction

5

Westbury West Jct

E9

Frome Market Siding

Fairwood Jct

(DILTON MARSH)

Clink Road Junction

Frome North Junction

Frome South Junction

Frome W Jct

Frome Junct

E9

FROME

Blatchbridge Junction

WARMINSTER

1926
(1936)

7

4

4

8

137

137

KEY TO RAILWAYS

No.	Legend	Railway
1		LONDON + SOUTH WESTERN
13		WEYMOUTH + PORTLAND (Great Western & London + South Western)
14		SOMERSET + DORSET JOINT (London + South Western & Midland)
2		EASTON + CHURCH HOPE (GW + LSW)
3		GREAT WESTERN
00		GREAT WESTERN (Post Grouping)
		EX GREAT WESTERN - Now Goods only
X	+++++++++	OTHERS - Colliery lines etc

Map A only — Up to date Position

OPEN ALL
OPEN ALL
OPEN GOODS

Map C:

137

SY

9

Dorchester Tunnel

Dorchester Goods

DORCHESTER (WEST)

Station Junction

9

Dorchester Junct

Dorchester Junct

E2

DORCHESTER
(SOUTH)

C

Monkton + Came Halt

Coryates Halt

Bincombe Tunnel

Upwey Wishing Well Halt

8

Upwey

UPWEY Junction

Upwey Junction

Radipole Halt

137

Weymouth Jct

Tramway Junct

E1

Melcombe Regis

Westham Halt

WEYMOUTH Town

137

WEYMOUTH (QUAY) Harbour

Rodwell

Wyke Regis Halt

7

Whitehead Torpedo Works

7

Portland Goods Jct

Portland

Stone

Portland Goods

Sheepcroft Siding

Easton

E3

1926
(1917)

6

6

7

6

Map D:

137 139

Bailey Gate

SY SZ

Wimborne

0

9

Wimborne Junction

Old S+D Line

Corfe Mullen
Junction

New S+D Line Junction

Poole + Hamworthy Lines Jct

D

9

Broadstone Junction

9

Strancrete
Manufacturing
Siding

Holes Bay Curve Jct

HAMWORTHY
Junction

Holes Bay Curve Jct

PARKSTONE

BRANKSOME

Bournemouth Junction

137

for Sandbanks

Gasworks Junction

Bournemouth
West North Junction

139

Junction Goods Bch

Holes Bay
Junction

ES BOURNEMOUTH
Central

Junction Goods Jct

Quay Jct

Goods Jct

Bascombe

E4

POOLE

Poole Quay

Bournemouth Central
Goods

Bournemouth West Junct

Bournemouth
West

8

Hamworthy
Goods

POOLE

8

1926
(1917)

9 SY SZ 0

137 139

139
RAILWAYS

No	Company
R 1	LONDON + SOUTH WESTERN
14	SOMERSET + DORSET (LSW and Midland)
2	ISLE OF WIGHT CENTRAL
3	GREAT WESTERN
3A	DIDCOT NEWBURY + SOUTHAMPTON (GW)
5	MIDLAND + SOUTH WESTERN JUNCTION
7	FRESHWATER, YARMOUTH + NEWPORT
00	TOTTON HYTHE + FAWLEY (SR) (NOTE 3)
0	OTHER BR + SR (Postgrouping)

STATIONS + HALTS

No	Name	Ry Ref
A 1	Amesbury	1 U14
2	(Ampress Works)	1 Z39
3	ANDOVER Junction	1 U34
4	Andover Town	1 U34
5	BEAULIEU ROAD	1 U30
6	BITTERNE	1 U41
7	Boscombe	1 Z19
8	BOURNEMOUTH Central	1 Z19
9	Bournemouth West	1 Z09
10	BRANKSOME	1 Z09
11	Breamore	1 U11
12	Broadstone Junction	1(14) Z09
13	BROCKENHURST	1 U30
14	Bulford	1 U14
15	Bulford Camp	1 U24
16	Burghclere	3A U45
17	BURSLEDON	1 U40
18	Calbourne + Shalfleet	7 Z48
19	Carisbrooke	7 Z48
20	Chandler's Ford	1 U42
21	CHRISTCHURCH	1 Z19
22	Clatford	1 U34
23	Collingbourne	5 U25
24	Cowes	2 Z49
25	Daggons Road	1 U11
26	DEAN	1 U22
27	Dinton	1 U03
28	Downton	1 U12
29	DUNBRIDGE	1 U32
30	EASTLEIGH + Bishopstoke	1 U41
31	(Fawley)	00 U40
32	Fordingbridge	1 U11
33	Freshwater	7 Z38
34	Fullerton	1 U33
35	Grafton + Burbage	5 U25
36	GRATELEY	1 U24
37	(HAMBLE)	1 U40
38	HINTON ADMIRAL	1 Z29
39	Holmsley	1 U20
40	Horsebridge	1 U33
41	Hurn	1 Z19
42	Hurstbourne	1 U44
43	(Hythe)	00 U40
44	King's Worthy	3A U43
45	Litchfield	3A U45
46	Longparish	1 U44
47	Ludgershall	5 U25
48	LYMINGTON (TOWN)	1 Z39
49	LYMINGTON PIER	1 Z39
50	LYNDHURST ROAD	1 U31
51	(Marchwood)	00 U30
52	MILLBROOK	1 U41
53	Mill Hill	2 Z49
54	Mottisfont	1 U32
55	NETLEY	1 U40
56	NEW MILTON	1 Z29
57	Newport	2 Z58
58	Newport	7 Z48
59	Newton Tony	1 U24
60	Ningwood	7 Z48
61	Northam	1 U41
62	Nursling	1 U31
63	PARKSTONE for Sandbanks	1 Z09
64	Patney + Chirton	3 U05
65	PEWSEY	3 U15
66	POKESDOWN	1 Z19
67	POOLE	1 Z09
68	Porton	1 U13
69	REDBRIDGE	1 U31
70	Ringwood	1 U10
71	ROMSEY	1 U32
72	ST DENYS	1 U41
73	SALISBURY	1 U13
74	Salisbury	3 U13
75	SHAWFORD + Twyford	1 U42
76	SHOLING	1 U41
77	(SOUTHAMPTON AIRPORT)	1 U41
78	Southampton Ocean Terminal ✳	1 U41
79	Southampton Town	1 U41
80	SOUTHAMPTON WEST (Central)	1 U41
81	Stockbridge	1 U33
82	Sutton Scotney	3A U43
83	Swanage	1 Z07
84	SWAY	1 Z29
85	SWAYTHLING	1 U41
86	Tidworth	5 U24
87	TOTTON for Eling	1 U31
88	Verwood	1 U00
89	Watching Well	7 Z48
90	West Moors	1 U00
91	Weyhill	1 U34
92	Wherwell	1 U34
93	WHITCHURCH	1 U44
94	Whitchurch	3A U44
95	Wilton	1 U13
96	Wilton	3 U13
97	Wimborne	1(14) Z09
98	Winchester Chesil	3A U42
99	WINCHESTER City	1 U43
100	Wishford	3 U03
101	Woodborough	3 U15
102	WOOLSTON	1 U41
103	(Worthy Down)	3A U43
104	Wylye	3 U03
105	Yarmouth	7 Z38

GOODS

No	Location	Ry Ref
G 1	Salisbury	1 U13

SIDINGS

No	Name	Ry Ref
P 1	Uddens Siding	1 U00

ENGINE SHEDS

No	Location	Ry Ref
E 1	Swanage	1
2	Lymington	1
3	Newport	2

JUNCTIONS

No	Name / Location	Ry Ref
J 1	West Moors	1 U00
2	Patney	3 05
3	Christchurch	1 Z19
4	Ringwood	1 U10
5	Alderbury	1 U12
6	Amesbury Line	1 U23
7	Grateley	1 U24
8	Lymington Branch	1 U20
9	Ringwood Line	1 U20
10	Kimbridge	1 U32
11	Fullerton	1 U33
12	Hurstbourne	1 U44

NOTES:

(1) REF All in SU or SZ, S omitted

(2) SOUTHAMPTON - Present Name, previously known as:-
   (a) West - then later
   (b) Central

(3) Sanctioned 1903, but not built until mid 20's!

(4) Stations only shown in the areas covered by enlargements. For other details see 138 D and 140 A, B, C and D.

(5) ✳ Station not located - see Map 140 D.

(6) Stations underlined thus are still in use for some passenger services, but on an irregular basis. No daily service.

(7) OTHER BR etc (0), see the enlargement maps on 140.

137

141

137

141

Patney Jct
Woodborough
PEWSEY
Patney + Chirton
Grafton + Burbage
Burghclere
Litchfield
Collingbourne
Ludgershall
140A
Hurstbourne
WHITCHURCH
Whitchurch
Tidworth
Weyhill
ANDOVER Junction
Andover Town
Clatford
Longparish
Sutton Scotney
Hurstbourne Junction
Bulford Camp
Bulford
Amesbury
Grateley Jct
Newton Tony
GRATELEY
Wherwell
Fullerton
Fullerton Jct
Amesbury Line Jct
Porton
Stockbridge
(Worthy Down)
King's Worthy
Wylye
Wishford
Dinton
Wilton
Salisbury
SALISBURY
Salisbury Gds
Wilton
140C
WINCHESTER City
Winchester Chesil
Horsebridge
140B
Alderbury Junction
DEAN
DUNBRIDGE
Mottisfont
Kimbridge Junction
SHAWFORD + Twyford
Downton
ROMSEY
Chandler's Ford
EASTLEIGH + Bishopstoke
Breamore
Nursling
(SOUTHAMPTON AIRPORT)
SWAYTHLING
Fordingbridge
140D
REDBRIDGE
MILLBROOK
St DENYS
Northam
BITTERNE
Daggons Road
TOTTON
SOUTHAMPTON West
WOOLSTON
SHOLING
LYNDHURST ROAD
Southampton Town
(Marchwood)
NETLEY
BURSLEDON
(HAMBLE)
Verwood
Ringwood Junction
Ringwood
BEAULIEU ROAD
(Hythe)
(Fawley)
West Moors Junction
West Moors
Holmsley
BROCKENHURST
Lymington Branch Jct
Ringwood Line Jct
SU 57
Stl 52
Uddens Siding
Wimborne
Hurn
SWAY
(Ampress Works)
LYMINGTON (Town)
LYMINGTON PIER
COWES
Mill Hill
Broadstone Junction
BRANKSOME
Branksome
Parkstone
Baskome
NEW MILTON
HINTON ADMIRAL
Christchurch Jct
CHRISTCHURCH
POKESDOWN
BOURNEMOUTH Central
Newport
Yarmouth
Ningwood
Calbourne + Shalfleet
Watchingwell
Newport
POOLE
Bournemouth West
38D
PARKSTONE for Sandbanks
Freshwater
Yarmouth + Newport
Carisbrooke
Freshwater

E1
Swanage

KEY TO RAILWAYS

No.	Legend	Company
1		LONDON + SOUTH WESTERN
14		SOMERSET + DORSET (LSW + Midland)
2		ISLE OF WIGHT CENTRAL
3		GREAT WESTERN
3A		DIDCOT NEWBURY + SOUTHAMPTON (Great Western)
5		MIDLAND + SOUTH WESTERN JUNCTION
7		FRESHWATER, YARMOUTH + NEWPORT
00		TOTTON HYTHE + FAWLEY (Light) - SOUTHERN - Post Grouping

ANDOVER   SALISBURY   WINCHESTER
COMBINED GAZETTEER FOR MAPS A, B + C

RAILWAYS

No	Company
R1	LONDON + SOUTH WESTERN
3	GREAT WESTERN
3A	DIDCOT NEWBURY + SOUTHAMPTON (GW)
5	MIDLAND + SOUTH WESTERN JUNCTION
O	BR + POST GROUPING ADDITIONS

STATIONS + HALTS

No	Name	Ry	Ref
A1	ANDOVER Junction	1	A
2	Andover Town	1	A
3	King's Worthy	3A	B
4	Ludgershall	5	A
5	SALISBURY	1	C
6	Salisbury	3	C
7	SHAWFORD + Twyford	1	B
8	Tidworth	5	A
9	Weyhill	5	A
10	Wilton	1	C
11	Wilton	3	C
12	Winchester Chesil	3A	B
13	WINCHESTER City	1	B
14	(Worthy Down)	3A	B

GOODS

No	Location	Ry	Ref
G1	Salisbury	1	C
2	Winchester	‡ 3	B

SIDINGS

No	Name / Location	Ry	Ref
P1	Taskers – Andover	1	A

ENGINE SHEDS

No	Name / Location	Ry	Ref
E5	Andover Junction	1	A
6	Andover	5	A
7	Salisbury	1	C
8	Salisbury	3	C
9	Winchester City	1	B
10	Winchester	‡ 3	B

TUNNELS

No	Name	Ry	Ref
T1	Fisherton	1	C

JUNCTIONS

No	Name / Location	Ry	Ref
J1	Tidworth Branch	5	A
2	Red Posts	15	A
3	(Post Grouping Xover	O	A
4	Andover Town Branch	1	A
5	Winchester	1	B
6	Loop South	10	B
7	Loop North	3AO	B
8	Winchester Goods	3A	B
9	DNS + LSW	13A	B
10	Shaw Ford	1	B
11	Wilton	O	C
12	Salisbury	3(1)	C
13	Tunnel (Fisherton)	1	C
14	Laverstock North	10	C
15	Laverstock South	10	C
16	Milford	1	C

NOTES

(1) Although Grid References are shown on the maps, in view of the small area covered by each, reference simply indicates which map on this combined gazetteer.

(2) Ludgershall Still in use as a passenger station but NOT on a daily basis. See Note (6) on map 139

(3) Winchester ‡: although on DN+S these facilities were purely GW

EASTLEIGH + SOUTHAMPTON
D

RAILWAYS

No	Company
R1	LONDON + SOUTH WESTERN
OO	TOTTON HYTHE + FAWLEY (Light)
	Opened Post Grouping (Note3)
X	DOCK + OTHER

STATIONS

No	Name	Ry	Ref
A1	Bishop's Waltham	1	51
2	BITTERNE	1	41
3	BOTLEY	1	51
4	BURSLEDON	1	40
5	Chandler's Ford	1	42
6	EASTLEIGH + Bishopstoke	1	41
7	(HAMBLE)	1	40
8	(Hythe)	OO	40
9	(Marchwood)	OO	31
10	MILLBROOK	1	41
11	NETLEY	1	40
12	Northam	1	41
13	Nursling	1	31
14	REDBRIDGE	1	31
15	ROMSEY	1	32
16	ST DENYS	1	41
17	SHOLING	1	41
18	(SOUTHAMPTON AIRPORT)	1	41
19	Southampton Ocean Terminal		41
		1	41
20	Southampton Town	1	41
21	SOUTHAMPTON West (Central)		41
		1	41
22	SWANWICK	1	50
23	SWAYTHLING	1	41
24	TOTTON for Eling	1(OO)	31
25	WOOLSTON	1	41

GOODS

No	Location	Ry	Ref
G1	Southampton Town	1	41
2	Southampton Docks	1	41

SIDINGS

No	Name + Location	Ry	Ref
P1	Hospital (Netley)	1	40
2	Clay Wks (Bishops Waltham)	1	51

COMPANY WORKS

No	Name	Ry	Ref
C1	Eastleigh	1	41

ENGINE SHEDS

No	Name	Ry	Ref
E1	Eastleigh	1	41
2	Southampton Terminus †	1	41
3	Southampton Docks †	1	41
4	Southampton New Docks †	1	41

JUNCTIONS

No	Name / Location	Ry	Ref
J1	Fawley Line	1OO	31
2	Redbridge	1	31
3	Romsey	1	32
4	Northam North	1	41
5	Northam South	1	41
6	Northam West	1	41
7	Docks	1	41
8	St Denys	1	41
9	Eastleigh East	1	41
10	Eastleigh West	1	41
11	Bishop's Waltham Branch	1	51

NOTES:

(1) REF - All in SU

(2) Southampton Ocean Terminal open for passengers but not on a daily basis

(3) Authorised 1903. Not completed until mid 20's (Southern Ry)

(4) † Precise locations NOT shown.

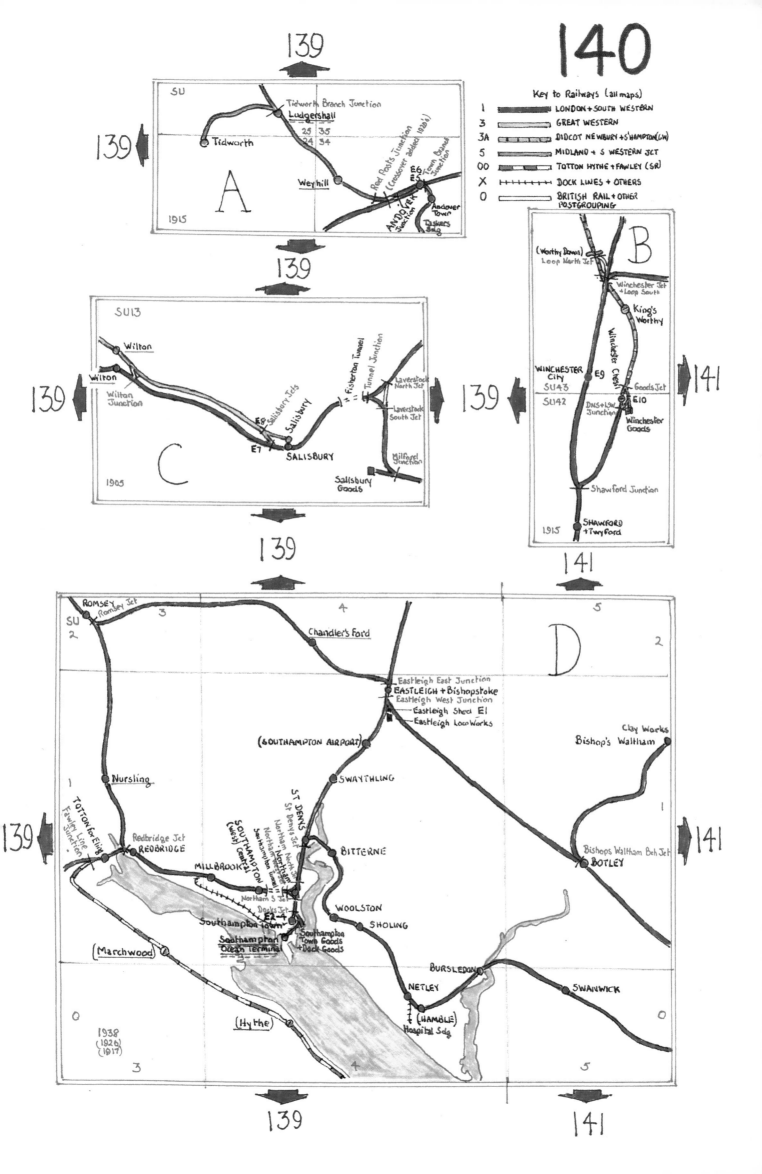

Key to Railways (all maps)

1		LONDON + SOUTH WESTERN
3		GREAT WESTERN
3A		DIDCOT NEWBURY + S'HAMPTON (LSW)
5		MIDLAND + S WESTERN JCT
00		TOTTON HYTHE + FAWLEY (SR)
X		DOCK LINES + OTHERS
0		BRITISH RAIL + OTHER POSTGROUPING

A

SU

139

Tidworth Branch Junction
Ludgershall
25 35
24 34

Tidworth

Weyhill

Red Posts Junction
(Crossover added 1926)

E6

Town Grand Junction

ANDOVER
Junction

Andover
Town

Taskers
Sdg

1915

B

(Worthy Down)
Loop North Jct

Winchester Jct
+ Loop South

King's Worthy

WINCHESTER
CITY
SU43
SU42

E9

Winchester Chesil

Goods Jct

E10

DNS + LSW
Junction

Winchester
Goods

Shawford Junction

SHAWFORD
+ Twyford

1915

141

C

SU13

Wilton

Wilton

Wilton
Junction

Salisbury Jcts

E8

Salisbury

E7

SALISBURY

Fisherton Tunnel

Tunnel Junction

Laverstock
North Jct

Laverstock
South Jct

Milford
Junction

Salisbury
Goods

1905

139

139

141

D

ROMSEY Jct
Romsey Jct

SU
2

3

4

Chandler's Ford

5

2

Eastleigh East Junction
EASTLEIGH + Bishopstoke
Eastleigh West Junction
Eastleigh Shed E1
Eastleigh Loco Works

(SOUTHAMPTON AIRPORT)

Clay Works
Bishop's Waltham

SWAYTHLING

Nursling

1

ST DENYS
St Denys Jct
Northam North Jct
Northam
Southampton Tunnel
Northam S Jct

SOUTHAMPTON
(West)

Southampton
Central

BITTERNE

1

Bishops Waltham Bch Jct
BOTLEY

TOTTON for Eling
Fawley Line
Junction

Redbridge Jct
REDBRIDGE

MILLBROOK

Docks Jct

E2-4
Southampton Town

Southampton
Ocean Terminal

Southampton
Town Goods
+ Dock Goods

WOOLSTON

SHOLING

BURSLEDON

SWANWICK

(Marchwood)

NETLEY

(HAMBLE)
Hospital Sdg

1938
(1926)
(1917)

0

(Hythe)

3

4

0

5

139

141

RAILWAYS

No	Company
R 1	LONDON + SOUTH WESTERN
1A	BENTLEY + BORDON (Light) L+SW
1B	LEE·ON·SOLENT (L+SW)
14	L+SW AND LB+SC JOINT
2	ISLE OF WIGHT CENTRAL
3	GREAT WESTERN
4	LONDON BRIGHTON + SOUTH COAST
5	ISLE OF WIGHT
6	SOUTH EASTERN + CHATHAM
7	FRESHWATER YARMOUTH + NEWPORT ⚥
8	HUNDRED OF MANHOOD + SELSEY (Tramway)

STATIONS + HALTS

No	Name	Ry Ref
A 1	ALDERSHOT TOWN	1 U85
2	Alresford	1 U53
3	ALTON	1 U73
4	Alverstone	2 Z58
5	Ash Green	1 U95
6	ASH	6 U95
7	Ashey	2 Z58
8	ASH VALE, North Camp +	1 U85
9	BARNHAM, Junction	4 U90
10	BASINGSTOKE ✳	1 U65
11	Basingstoke ✳	3 U65
12	(BEDHAMPTON)	4 U70
13	Bembridge	5 Z68
14	BENTLEY	1/1A U74
15	Bentworth + Lasham	1 U64
16	Bishop's Waltham	1 U51
17	Blackwater (IOW) ✳	2 Z58
18	BLACKWATER + York Town †	6 U85
19	BOGNOR (REGIS)	4 U90
20	Bordon	1A U73
21	BOSHAM	4 U80
22	BOTLEY	1 U51
23	BRADING	5 Z68
24	BRAMLEY	3 U65
25	BROOKWOOD	1 U95
26	Browndown	1B Z59
27	Chalder	8 Z89
28	CHICHESTER ✳	4 U80
29	Chichester ✳	8 U80
30	Cliddesden	1 U64
31	Cocking	4 U81
32	COSHAM	14 U60
33	Cowes	2 Z59
34	Droxford	1 U61
35	East Southsea	14 Z69
36	Elsted	1 U81
37	EMSWORTH	4 U70
38	FAREHAM	1 U50
39	Farlington	4 U60
40	FARNBOROUGH	1 U85
41	FARNBOROUGH NORTH	6 U85
42	FARNCOMBE	1 U94
43	FARNHAM	1 U84
44	Ferry Road	8 Z89
45	(FISHBOURNE)	4 U80
46	FLEET	1 U85
47	FORD Junction ⚥	4 00
48	Fort Brockhurst	1/1B U50
49	FRATTON + SOUTHSEA	14 U60
50	FRIMLEY	1 U85
51	GODALMING	1 U94
52	Godshill	2 Z58
53	Gosport	1 U60
54	Gosport Road	1 Z69
55	GUILDFORD	1 U95
56	GUILDFORD, LONDON ROAD	1 U95
57	HASLEMERE	1 U83
58	HAVANT	4(1) U70
59	Haven Street	1 Z58
60	Hayling Island	4 U70
61	Herriard	1 U64
62	(HILSEA)	14 U60
63	HOOK	1 U75
64	Horringford	2 Z58
65	Hunston	8 Z80
66	Itchen Abbas	1 U53
67	Kingsley Halt	1A U73
68	Langston	4 U70
69	Lavant	4 U80
70	Lee·on·the·Solent	1B U50
71	LIPHOOK	1 U83
72	LISS	1 U72
73	LONDON ROAD (GUILDFORD) ✳	1 U95
74	Medstead	1 U63
75	Merstone	2 Z58
76	MICHELDEVER	1 U54
77	Midhurst	1 U81
78	Midhurst	4 U81
79	MILFORD	1 U94
80	Mill Hill	2 Z59
81	Newchurch	2 Z58
82	Newport ✳	2 Z59
83	Newport ✳	7 Z49
84	NORTH CAMP	6 U85
85	North Camp + ASH VALE	1 U85
86	North Hayling	4 U70
87	(NUTBOURNE)	4 U70
88	Oakley	1 U55
89	OVERTON	1 U55
90	PETERSFIELD	1 U72
91	Petworth	4 U91
92	PORTCHESTER	1 U60
93	PORTSMOUTH + SOUTHSEA	14 U60
94	PORTSMOUTH HARBOUR	14 U60
95	Portsmouth Town	1 U60
96	Privet	1 U62
97	Privett	1B U50
98	Rogate	1 U82
99	Ropley	1 U63
100	Rowlands Castle	1 U71
101	RYDE ESPLANADE	14 Z69
102	RYDE PIERHEAD	14 Z69
103	RYDE ST JOHNS ROAD	145 Z69
104	St Helen's	5 Z68
105	St Lawrence	2 Z57
106	SANDOWN	52 Z68
107	Selham	4 U91
108	Selsey Beach	8 Z89
109	Selsey Town	8 Z89
110	SHALFORD	6 U94
111	SHANKLIN	5 Z58
112	Shide	2 Z58
113	Sidlesham	8 Z89
114	Singleton	4 U81
115	(SOUTHBOURNE)	4 U70
116	Stokes Bay ‡	1 Z69
117	SWANWICK	1 U50
118	Tisted for Selborne	1 U73
119	Tongham	1 U84
120	Ventnor	5 Z57
121	Ventnor Town	2 Z57
122	WANBOROUGH	1 U95
123	(WARDLINGTON)	4 U70
124	West Mean	1 U62
125	Whippingham	2 Z59
126	Whitwell	2 Z57
127	Wickham	1 U51
128	WINCHFIELD	1 U75
129	WITLEY + Chiddingfold	1 U93
130	WOKING	1 U95
131	Wootton	2 Z59
132	WORPLESDON	1 U95
133	Wroxall	5 Z57

GOODS

No	Location	Ry Ref
G 1	Medina Wharf (IOW) ✳	2 Z59
2	St Helen's Quay	5 Z68
3	Misling ford	1 U51
4	Faringdon	1 U73
5	Godalming	1 U94

SIDINGS

No	Name/Company	Ry Ref
P 1	Thorneycroft	1 U65
2	Bishop's Waltham Clay Works	1 U51

ENGINE SHEDS

No	Location	Ry Ref
E 1	Bognor	4 U90
2	Bordon	1A U73
3	Fratton	14 U60
4	Guildford	1 U94
5	Newport	2 Z58
6	St John's Road Ryde	2 Z69
7	Basingstoke	1 U65
8	Basingstoke	3 U65

TUNNELS

No	Name/Location	Yds	Ry Ref
T 1	Fareham		1 U50
2	West Mean	539	1 U62
3	Privet	1058	1 U62
4	Boniface Down		5 Z57

BRIDGES

No	Name	Ry Ref
V 1	Langston (Swing Bridge)	4 U70

JUNCTIONS

No	Name/Location	Ry Ref
J 1	Basingstoke - Alton	1 U65
2	Basingstoke - Bramley	13 U65
3	Basingstoke - Station	3 U65
4	Gosport Road South	1 Z69
5	Gosport Road North	1 U60
6	Gosport Road East	1 U60
7	Newport (South)	2 Z58
8	Newport - Freshwater Line	27 Z59
9	Merstone	2 Z58

10	Sandown	52 Z68
11	Brading	5 Z68
12	Smallbrook	5 Z68
13	Lee Solent	11B U50
14	Fareham (South)	1 U50
15	Mean Valley	1 U50
16	Knowle	1 U50
17	Battledown	1 U55
18	Blackfriars	14 U60
19	Fratton	14 U60
20	Portcreek	14 U60
21	Cosham	14 U60
22	Farlington	4 U60
23	Havant - Hayling Island	4 U70
24	Havant - Guildford	14 U70
25	Petersfield	1 U72
26	Butts	1 U73
27	Bordon Line (Bentley)	11A U74
28	Chichester - Selsey Line	4(8) U80
29	Chichester - Midhurst Line	4 U80
30	Midhurst LSW + LBSC	14 U81
31	Midhurst - Chichester Line	4 U81
32	Barnham	4 U90

NOTES:

(1) REF - SU or SZ - S omitted.
⚥ is in TQ

(2) Some of the stations shown as (NEW) may have been opened between 1906 and 1922

(3) ENLARGEMENT AREAS - In the main in these areas only stations are shown - other features see 140D and 143.

✳ Additions in brackets are to
✳ distinguish location.
† Name later changed to '+ Camberley' then suffix dropped.
‡ Name changed to Gosport Harbour.
⚥ Previously Isle of Wight Central Railway
✳ Stations at these places were closely adjoining and at Newport were different platforms of the same station.

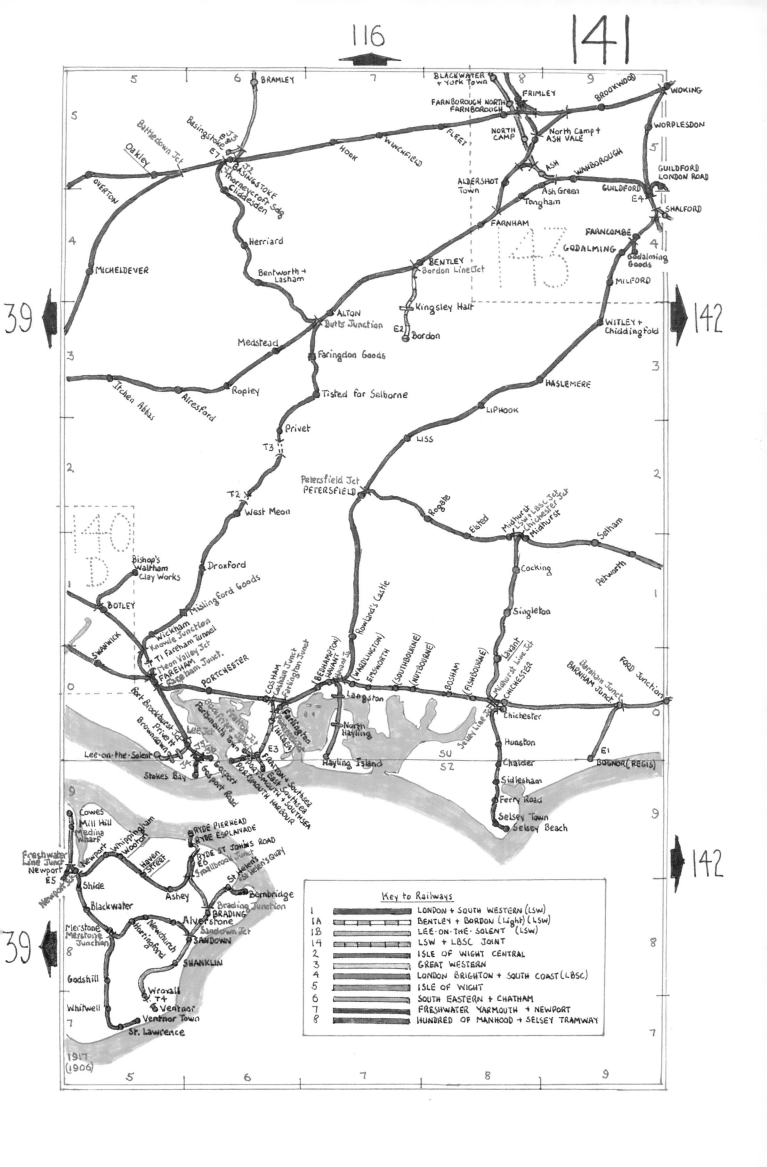

39

142

142

39

BRAMLEY

Battledown Jct
Oakley
OVERTON
Basingstoke BUS
Worting Jct
Basingstoke
Thorneycroft Sdg
Cliddesden
MICHELDEVER
Herriard
Bentworth + Lasham
ALTON
Butts Junction
Medstead
Faringdon Goods
Ropley
Tisted for Selborne
Itchen Abbas
Alresford
Privet
T3
T2
West Meon
Droxford
Bishop's Waltham
Clay Works
Mislingford Goods
BOTLEY
Wickham
Knowle Junction
T1 Fareham Tunnel
Meon Valley Jct
SWANWICK
FAREHAM
Fareham Junct.
PORTCHESTER
Port Brockhurst Jct
Portsmouth Jct
Fort Brockhurst
Priddy's
Browndown
Lee-on-the-Solent
Stokes Bay
Gosport Road
Gosport

BLACKWATER + York Town
FARNBOROUGH NORTH
FARNBOROUGH
FRIMLEY
BROOKWOOD
WOKING
WORPLESDON
HOOK
WINCHFIELD
FLEET
NORTH CAMP
North Camp + ASH VALE
ASH
WANBOROUGH
GUILDFORD LONDON ROAD
ALDERSHOT Town
Ash Green
Tongham
GUILDFORD
E4
SHALFORD
FARNHAM
FARNCOMBE
GODALMING
Godalming Goods
BENTLEY
Bordon Line Jct
MILFORD
143
Kingsley Halt
E2 Bordon
WITLEY + Chiddingfold
HASLEMERE
LIPHOOK
LISS
Petersfield Jct
PETERSFIELD
Rogate
Elsted
Midhurst
LSW + LBSC Jct
Chichester Jct
Midhurst
Selham
Cocking
Petworth
Singleton
Rowland's Castle
(BEDHAMPTON)
HAVANT
Havant Jct
(WARBLINGTON)
EMSWORTH
(SOUTHBOURNE)
(NUTBOURNE)
BOSHAM
(FISHBOURNE)
Lavant
Midhurst Line Jct
CHICHESTER
Barnham Junct
BARNHAM JUNCT.
FORD Junction
FORD
Chichester
Hunston
Chalder
E1
BOGNOR (REGIS)
Sidlesham
Ferry Road
Selsey Town
Selsey Beach
COSHAM
Cosham Junct
Farlington Junct
Langston
North Hayling
Hayling Island
SU
SZ
Selsey Line Jct

140
D

Farlington Jct
Portcreek Jct
FRATTON
Fratton
(SOUTHSEA)
PORTSMOUTH + SOUTHSEA
PORTSMOUTH TOWN
E3
PORTSMOUTH HARBOUR

Cowes
Mill Hill
Medina Wharf
Whippingham
Wootton
RYDE PIERHEAD
RYDE ESPLANADE
RYDE ST JOHNS ROAD
Smallbrook Junct
E6
Haven Street
St Helens
St Helen's Quay
Bembridge
Brading Junction
BRADING
Alverstone
Sandown Jct
SANDOWN
SHANKLIN
Wroxall
T4
Ventnor
Ventnor Town
St. Lawrence
Freshwater Line Junct
Newport
E5
Newport Jct
Shide
Blackwater
Merstone
Merstone Junction
Newchurch
Hortingford
Ashey
Godshill
Whitwell
1917 (1906)

Key to Railways		
1		LONDON + SOUTH WESTERN (LSW)
1A		BENTLEY + BORDON (Light) (LSW)
1B		LEE-ON-THE-SOLENT (LSW)
14		LSW + LBSC JOINT
2		ISLE OF WIGHT CENTRAL
3		GREAT WESTERN
4		LONDON BRIGHTON + SOUTH COAST (LBSC)
5		ISLE OF WIGHT
6		SOUTH EASTERN + CHATHAM
7		FRESHWATER YARMOUTH + NEWPORT
8		HUNDRED OF MANHOOD + SELSEY TRAMWAY

5   6   7   8   9

142

DORKING + BRIGHTON

RAILWAYS

No	Company/Undertaking
R 1	LONDON + SOUTH WESTERN
14	L+SW AND LB+SC JOINT
4	LONDON BRIGHTON + SOUTH COAST
46	LB+SC AND SE+C JOINT
6	SOUTH EASTERN + CHATHAM

STATIONS + HALTS

No	Name	Ry	Ref
A 1	(ALDRINGTON) §43	4	20
2	AMBERLEY	4	00
3	ANGMERING-on-Sea	4	00
4	Ardingly	4	32
5	ARUNDEL	4	00
6	ASHTEAD	14	15
6A	BALCOMBE	4	32
7	Barcombe	4	41
8	Barcombe Mills	4	41
9	Baynards	4	03
10	BETCHWORTH	6	25
11	BILLINGSHURST	4	02
12	BISHORSTONE	4	TV 49
13	BOOKHAM	1	15
14	Box Hill §38	4	14
15	BOX HILL *	4	15
16	Bramber	4	10
17	Bramley + Wonersh	4	04
18	Brasted	6	45
19	BRIGHTON Central	4	30
20	Brighton Lewes Road	4	30
21	BRIGHTON LONDON ROAD	4	30
22	Bungalow Town Halt	4	10
23	BURGESS HILL	4	31
24	CATERHAM	6	35
25	Chevening Halt	6	46
26	CHILWORTH + Albury	6	04
27	CHIPSTEAD	6	25
28	CHRIST'S HOSPITAL	4	12
29	CLANDON + Ripley	1	05
30	COBHAM+STOKE D'ABERNON	14	15
31	COOKSBRIDGE †A	4	41
32	Coulsdon *	4	35
33	Coulsdon + Cane Hill *	6	35
34	(COULSDON SOUTH)	6	35
35	COWDEN	4	44
36	Cranleigh	4	03
37	CRAWLEY	4	23
38	(DEEPDENE) §14	4	14
39	DORKING	4	15
40	DORKING (TOWN)	6	14
41	DORMANS	4	34
42	(DURRINGTON-ON-SEA)	4	10
43	Dyke Junction Halt §1	4	20
44	EARLSWOOD	4	24
45	EAST GRINSTEAD	4	33
46	(EAST WORTHING)	4	10
47	EDENBRIDGE	6	44
48	EDENBRIDGE TOWN	4	44
49	EFFINGHAM JUNCTION	1	15
50	EPSOM DOWNS	4	25
51	FALMER	4	30
52	FAYGATE	4	23
53	FISHERGATE	4	20
54	Fittleworth	4	01
55	FORD	4	00
56	Forest Row	4	43
57	(Freshfield Halt) 3	4	32
58	GATWICK AIRPORT, Tinsley Green for	4	24
59	Gatwick (Racecourse)	4	24
60	GLYNDE	4	50
61	Godstone	6	34
62	GOMSHALL + Shere †B	4	04
63	GORING-BY-THE-SEA	4	10
64	Grange Road	4	33
65	GUILDFORD, LONDON ROAD	1	05
66	Hartfield	4	43
67	HASSOCKS	4	31
68	HAYWARDS HEATH	4	32
69	Henfield	4	11
70	HEVER	4	44
71	Holland Road Halt	4	20
72	HOLMWOOD	4	14
73	HORLEY	4	24
74	HORSHAM	4	13
75	HORSLEY + Ockham	1	05
76	Horsted Keynes 3	4	32
77	HOVE	4	20
78	(HURST GREEN)	46	35
79	IFIELD	4	23
80	Isfield	4	41
81	Kemp Town	4	30
82	Kingscote	4	33
83	KINGSWOOD	6	25
84	LANCING	4	10
85	Leatherhead	1	15
86	LEATHERHEAD	4	15
87	LEWES	4	50
88	Lewes Road Brighton	4	30
89	LINGFIELD	4	33
90	LITTLEHAMPTON	4	00
91	(LITTLEHAVEN)	4	13
92	LONDON ROAD, GUILDFORD	1	05
93	LONDON ROAD, BRIGHTON	4	30
94	MERSTHAM	6	25
95	Monks Lane Halt	4	44
96	(MOULSECOOMB)	4	30
97	NEWHAVEN HARBOUR	4	40
98	(NEWHAVEN MARINE) †C	4	TV 49
99	NEWHAVEN TOWN	4	40
100	Newick + Chailey	4	42
101	NUTFIELD	6	24
102	OCKLEY	4	14
103	OXTED	46	35
104	Partridge Green	4	11
105	PLUMPTON	4	31
106	PORTSLADE	4	20
107	PRESTON PARK	4	20
108	PULBOROUGH	4	01
109	REDHILL †D	6	25
110	REIGATE	6	25
111	Rowfant	4	33
112	Rudgwick	4	03
113	SEAFORD	4	TV 49
114	SHALFORD For Godalming	6	04
115	Sheffield Park 3	4	42
116	SHOREHAM-BY-SEA †E	4	20
117	Slinfold	4	13
118	SMITHAM	6	25
119	(SOUTHEASE)	4	40
120	Southwater	4	12
121	SOUTHWICK	4	20
122	Steyning	4	11
123	TADWORTH + Walton-on-Hill	6	25
124	TATTENHAM CORNER	6	25
125	The Dyke	4	20
126	THREE BRIDGES	4	23
127	Tinsley Green for GATWICK AIRPORT	4	24
128	UCKFIELD	4	41
129	UPPER WARLINGHAM	46	35
130	Warlingham §137*	6	35
131	WARNHAM	4	13
132	Westerham	6	45
133	West Grinstead	4	12
134	West Hoathley	4	33
135	WEST WORTHING	4	10
136	WHYTELEAFE *	6	35
137	WHYTELEAFE SOUTH §130*	6	35
138	Withyham	4	53
139	WIVELSFIELD	4	31
140	WOKING	1	05
141	WOLDINGHAM	46	35
142	(WOODMANSTERNE)	6	25
143	WORTHING	4	10

GOODS

No	Location	Ry	Ref
G 1	Kingston-on-Sea	4	20
2	Holland Road	4	20
3	Brighton Central	4	30
4	Lewes	4	40

SIDINGS

No	Company/Name	Ry	Ref
P 1	Glynde Lime Works	4	40
2	Houghton Bridge Agricultural Lime Works	4	01

ENGINE SHEDS

No	Location	Ry	Ref
E 1	Brighton	4	30
2	Horsham	4	13
3	Newhaven	4	40
4	Three Bridges	4	23

TUNNELS

No	Name	Yds	Ry	Ref
T 1	Clayton	2259	4	21
2	Cliftonville		4	20
3	Hove		4	30
4	Kemp Hill	1024	4	30
5	Patcham		4	20

JUNCTIONS

No	Name/Location	Ry	Ref
J 1	Shoreham-Horsham Line	4	20
2	Hove	4	20
3	Preston Park (Lovers Walk)	4	20
4	Dyke Branch	4	20
5	Central Goods	4	30
6	Lewes Road	4	30
7	Lewes Station	4	40
8	Lewes Culver Line	4	40
9	Lewes Southerham	4	40
10	Lewes Goods South	4	40
11	Lewes Goods North	4	40
12	Lewes Goods West	4	40
13	Ford	4	00
14	Arundel	4	00
15	Littlehampton	4	00
16	Hardham	4	01
17	Itchingfield	4	12
18	Stammerham	4	12
19	Horsham	4	13
20	Three Bridges (Jcts)	4	23
21	Keymer	4	31
22	Haywards Heath	4	32
23	Copyhold	4	32
24	East Grinstead	4	33
25	St Margarets (E Grinstead)	4	33
26	Culver	4	41
27	Newhaven Harbour	4	40

NOTES:

(1) REF In TQ except those marked TV

(2) NAME CHANGES NEW Old §

(3) PARTIAL NAME CHANGES †
- A also COOKS BRIDGE
- B also spelt Sheire
- C also known as PIER
- D older version RED HILL
- E older version NEW SHOREHAM

(4) STATIONS LOCATED but full name details not shown on this map see MAP 144 *

(5) ENLARGEMENT AREA only passenger stations shown in this area – Other details see maps 143 + 144. See also note (4) above

(6) PRESERVED LINE - BLUEBELL RAILWAY 3

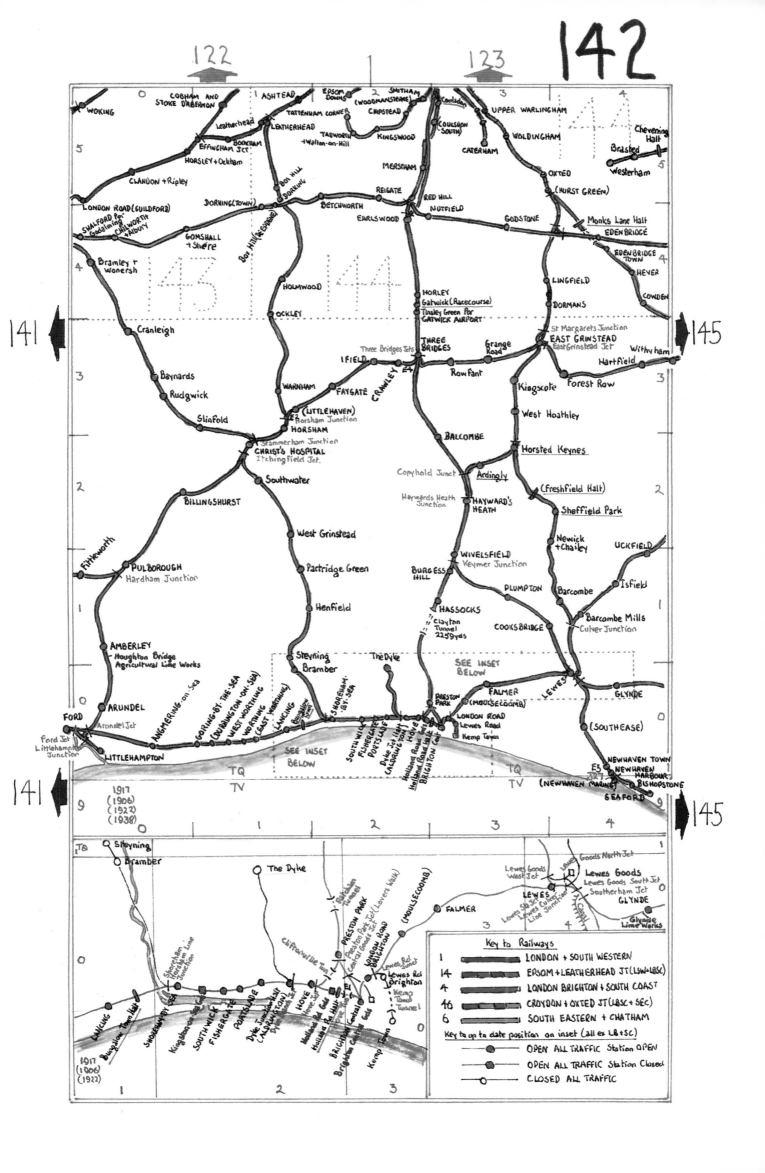

GUILDFORD + DORKING

RAILWAYS

No	Company	Ry Ref
R 1	London + South Western	
14	Ersom + Leatherhead Joint (LSW + LBSC)	
4	London Brighton + South Coast	
6	South Eastern + Chatham	
0	Southern Railway (Post Grouping)	
X	Bisley Military Railway	

NOTES

(1) Ref - Full Ref is shown
(2) Name changes - NEW, Old
(3) Name Alterations
  A Blackwater + York Town to Blackwater + Camberley
  B Boxhill + Burford Bridge to Box Hill + West Humble
(4) Appears to have been different platforms same station or very closely adjoining

TUNNELS

No	Name	Ry Ref
T 1	Norbury	4 TQ15

STATIONS

No	Name	Ry Ref
A 1	Aldershot Town	1 SU85
2	Ash	1 SU85
3	Ash	6 SU85
4	Ash Vale, North Camp +	1 SU85
5	Bisley Camp	X SU95
6	Blackdown Barracks	X SU95
7	Blackwater + York Town †A	6 SU85
8	Bookham	1 TQ15
9	Box Hill §17	6 TQ15
10	Box Hill + Burford Bridge (West Humble) †B	4 TQ15
11	Bramley + Wonersh	4 TQ04
12	Brookwood	1(X) SU95
13	Chilworth + Albury	6 TQ04
14	Clandon + Ripley	1 TQ05
15	Cobham + Stoke D'Abernon	1 TQ15
16	Deep Cut Barracks	X SU95
17	(Deepdene) §9	6 TQ15
18	Dorking	4 TQ15
19	Dorking (Town)	6 TQ15
20	Effingham Junction	1 TQ15
21	Farnborough (Main)	1 SU85
22	Farnborough (North)	6 SU85
23	Farncombe	1 SU94
24	Farnham	1 SU84
25	Frimley	1 SU85
26	Godalming	6 SU85
27	Gomshall + Shere †B	6 TQ04
28	Guildford	X SU95
29	Guildford London Road †A	6 SU85
30	Holmwood	4 TQ14
31	Horsley + Ockham	1 TQ05
32	Leatherhead *	1 TQ15
33	Leatherhead *	4 TQ15
34	London Road, Guildford	1 TQ05
35	Milford	1 SU94
36	North Camp	1(X) SU95
37	North Camp + Ash Vale	1 SU85
38	Ockley	4 TQ14
39	Shalford for Godalming	1 SU84
40	Tongham	1 SU95
41	Wanborough	6 TQ15
42	Woking	4 TQ15
43	Worplesdon	6 TQ15

JUNCTIONS

No	Name / Location	Ry Ref
J 1	Farnham	1 SU84
2	Aldershot North	1 SU85
3	Aldershot South	16 SU85
4	Ash Vale	1 SU85
5	Short	1 SU85
6	Short North	1 SU85
7	Short West	1/10 SU85
8	Farnborough Loop	60 SU85
9	Peasmarsh	14 SU94
10	Shalford	16 SU94
11	Guildford (Jcts)	1 SU94
12	Godalming Goods	1 SU94
13	Ash	16 SU85
14	Purbright	1 SU95
15	Brookwood Bisley MR	1X SU95
16	Woking	1 SU95
17	Effingham	1 TQ15
18	Leatherhead	1414 TQ15

GOODS

No	Location	Ry Ref
G 1	Godalming	1 SU94

SIDINGS

No	Name / Company	Ry Ref
P 1	Aldershot Military	1 SU85
2	North Camp	1 SU85
3	Peasmarsh	1 SU94
4	Goossmaker's	1 SU94
5	Merrow	1 TQ05

ENGINE SHEDS

No	Location	Ry Ref
E 1	Guildford	1 SU94

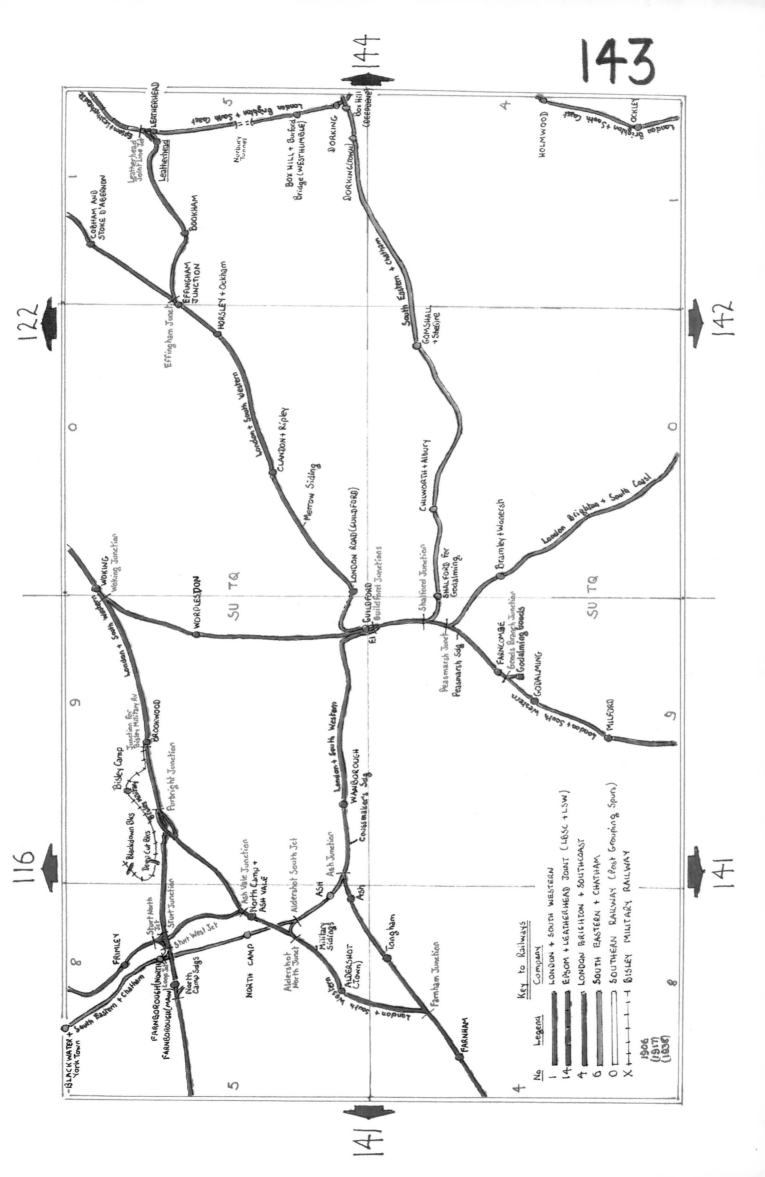

RAILWAYS

No	Company	Ry Ref
R1	London + South Western	
14	Epsom + Leatherhead Jt (LSW+LBSC)	
4	London Brighton + South Coast	
46	Croydon + Oxted Jt (LBSC+SEC)	
6	South Eastern + Chatham	

STATIONS

No	Name	Ry Ref
A1	ASHTEAD	14 15
2	BETCHWORTH	6 25
3	BOX HILL §13	6 15
4	Box Hill + Burford Bridge §4A	4 15
4A	BOX HILL (WESTHUMBLE) §4	4 15
5	Brasted	6 45
6	CATERHAM	6 35
7	Chevening Halt	6 45
8	CHIPSTEAD + Banstead Downs	6 25
9	Coulsdon	4 25
10	Coulsdon + Cane Hill	6 25
11	(COULSDON SOUTH)	6 25
12	COWDEN	4 44
13	(DEEPDENE) §3	6 15
14	DORKING	4 15
15	DORKING (TOWN)	6 15
16	DORMANS	4 34
17	EARLSWOOD	4 24
18	EDENBRIDGE	6 44
19	EDENBRIDGE TOWN	4 44
20	EPSOM DOWNS	4 25
21	GATWICK AIRPORT §42	4 24
22	Gatwick (Racecourse)	6 34
23	GODSTONE	4 44
24	HEVER	4 14
25	HOLMWOOD	6 24
26	HORLEY	46 35
27	(HURST GREEN) ‡	6 25
28	Kingswood + Burgh Heath	6 25
29	Leatherhead	6 45
30	LEATHERHEAD	6 35
31	LINGFIELD	6 45
32	MERSTHAM	6 25
33	Monks Lane Halt	4 25
34	NUTFIELD	6 24
35	OCKLEY	6 25
36	OXTED	4 44
37	Red Hill Junction §37A	6 15
37A	REDHILL §37	4 15 / 6 25
38	REIGATE	6 15
39	SMITHAM	4 34
40	TADWORTH + Walton-on-Hill	4 24 / 6 25
41	TATTENHAM CORNER	6 44 / 6 25
42	Tinsley Green for Gatwick AIRPORT §21	4 44 / 4 25
43	UPPER WARLINGHAM	4 24 / 46 35
44	Warlingham §47	4 24 / 6 35
45	Westerham	6 34 / 6 45
46	WHITELEAFE	4 44 / 6 35
47	(WHITELEAFE SOUTH) §44	4 14 / 6 35
48	WOLDINGHAM	6 24 / 46 25
49	(WOODMANSTERNE) ‡	46 35 / 6 25

ENGINE SHEDS

No	Location	Ry Ref
E1	Redhill	4 25

TUNNELS

No	Name / Location	Yds	Ry Ref
T1	BETCHWORTH §21		4 15
2	Kingswood No1		46 35
3	Kingswood No2		6 35
4	Merstham	1831	6 45
5	Merstham	1831	6 35
6	Betchingley	1327	6 34
7	Woldingham	2261	46 35
8	Kimpsfield		46 35
9	Edenbridge		4 44
10	Mark Beech		4 44

GOODS

No	Location	Ry Ref
G1	Red Hill	4 34 / 6 25

SIDINGS

No	Name / Company	Ry Ref
P1	Brockham	4 1A / 64 25
2	Nutfield Brick Works	46 35 / 46 25
3	Crowhurst	6 25 / 6 34

JUNCTIONS

No	Name / Location	Ry Ref
J1	Leatherhead Joint Line §14A	14 15
2	Earlswood	4 24
3	Redhill	6 15 / 64 25
4	Coulsdon - Stoats Nest	46 25
5	Crowhurst North	46 34 / 6 34
6	Hurst Green	446 35 / 6 25
7	Crowhurst East	6 44

NOTES:

(1) REF - All in TQ

(2) NAME CHANGE - NEW Old §

(3) (HURST GREEN) opened as a halt in pregrouping period ‡

(4) Stations close to each other; possibly different platforms of same station *

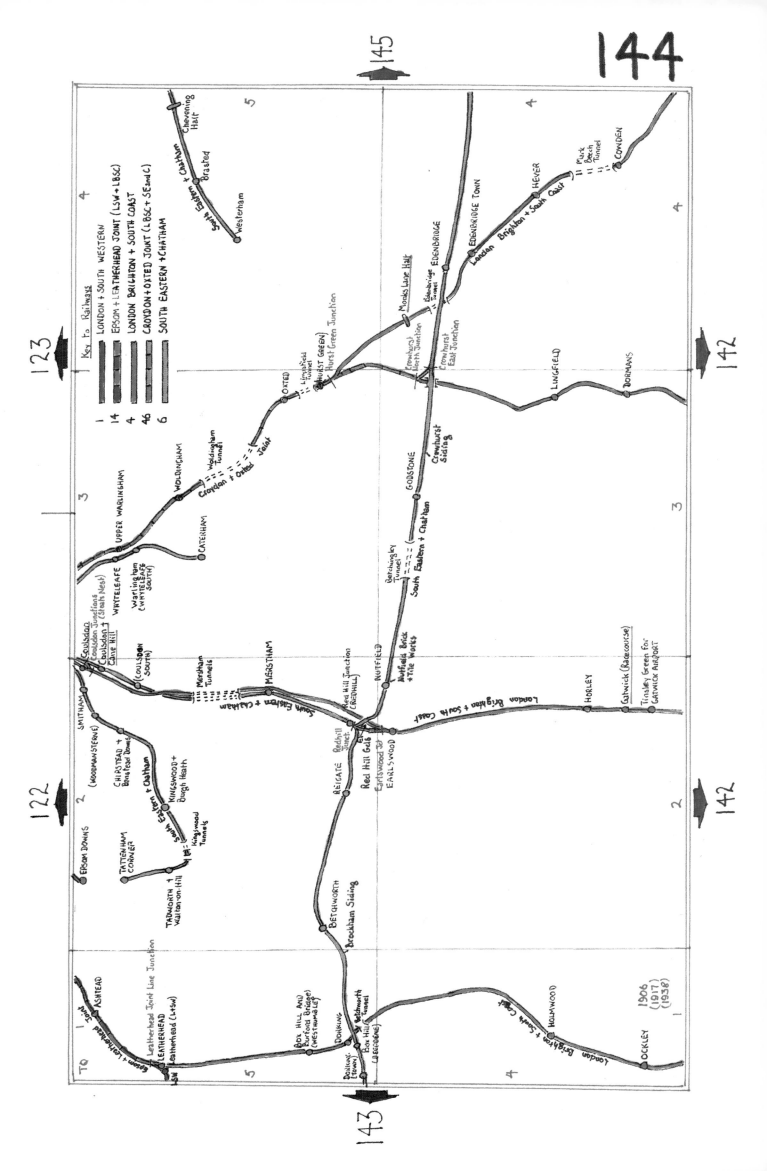

145

RAILWAYS

MAIDSTONE, TUNBRIDGE + HASTINGS

No	Company
R3	KENT + EAST SUSSEX (Light)
4	LONDON BRIGHTON + SOUTH COAST
6	SOUTH EASTERN + CHATHAM

STATIONS

No	Name	Ry Ref
A 1	APPLEDORE	6 92
2	ASHURST	4 53
3	AYLESFORD	6 75
4	BARMING	6 75
5	BAT + BALL	6 55
6	BATTLE	6 71
7	BEARSTED + Thurnham	6 75
8	(BELTRING)	6 64
9	BERWICK	4 50
10	BEXHILL-on-Sea (Central)	4 70
11	Bexhill West	6 70
12	Biddenden	3 83
13	Bodiham	3 72
14	(BOROUGH GREEN + WROTHAM) §976	65
15	Brookland	6 82
16	BUXTED	4 52
17	CHARING	6 94
18	(COLLINGTON)	4 70
19	(COODEN BEACH)	4 70
20	Cranbrook	6 73
21	CROWBOROUGH	4 52
22	CROWHURST Junction	6 71
23	(DOLEHAM)	6 81
24	DUNTON GREEN	6 55
25	EASTBOURNE	4 69 TV
26	EAST FARLEIGH	6 75
27	(EAST MALLING)	6 75
28	ERIDGE	4 53
29	ETCHINGHAM	6 72
30	FRANT	6 63
31	Frittenden	3 84
32	Goudhurst	6 73
33	GROOMBRIDGE	4 53
34	Hailsham	4 50
35	HAMPDEN PARK	4 60 TR
36	HAM STREET + Orlestone	6 03
37	HARRIETSHAM	6 85
38	HASTINGS	6 81
39	Hawkhurst	6 73
40	Headcorn	3 84

No	Name	Ry Ref
41	HEADCORN	6 84
42	Heathfield	4 51
43	Hellingly	4 51
44	(HIGH BROOMS)	§78 6 54
45	High Halden Road	3 83
46	HILDENBOROUGH	6 54
47	HOLLINGBOURNE	6 85
48	Horsmonden	6 73
49	Hothfield	6 94
50	Junction Road	3 72
51	KEMSING	6 55
52	(LEIGH) §52A	6 54
52A	Lyghe Halt §52	6 54
53	LENHAM	6 85
54	MAIDSTONE BARRACKS	6 75
55	MAIDSTONE EAST	6 75
56	MAIDSTONE WEST	6 75
57	MALLING, (WEST)	6 65
58	MARDEN	6 74
59	Mayfield	4 52
60	(NEW HYTHE)	6 75
61	(NORMANS BAY)	4 60
62	Northiam	3 82
63	ORE	6 81
64	OTFORD	6 55
65	PADDOCK WOOD	6 64
66	PENSHURST	6 54
67	PEVENSEY + WESTHAM	4 60
68	(PEVENSEY BAY)	4 60
69	PLUCKLEY	6 94
70	POLEGATE	4 50
71	ROBERTSBRIDGE	6(3) 72
72	Rolvenden	3 83
73	Rotherfield + Mark Cross	4 52
74	RYE	6 92
75	ST LEONARDS WARRIOR SQ	6 80
76	SEVENOAKS Tubs Hill	6 55
77	Sidley	6 70
78	Southborough §44	6 54
79	STAPLEHURST	6 74
80	(STONEGATE) §83	6 62
81	Tenterden Town	3 83
82	(THREE OAKS)	6 81
83	Ticehurst Road §80	6 62
84	TONBRIDGE	6 54
85	Tovil	6 75
86	TUNBRIDGE WELLS (CENTRAL)	6 53
87	TUNBRIDGE WELLS (WEST)	4 53

No	Name	Ry Ref
88	WADHURST	6 63
89	Waldron + Horeham Road	4 51
90	WATERINGBURY	6 65
91	(WEST) MALLING	6 65
92	West Marina	4 70
93	WEST ST LEONARDS	6 70
94	WINCHELSEA	6 81
95	Withyham	4 53
96	Wittersham Road	3 82
97	WROTHAM + BOROUGH GREEN §14	65
98	YALDING	6 65

GOODS

No	Location	Ry Ref
G 1	Tovil	6 75
2	Tunbridge Wells	6 54
3	Rye Harbour	6 91

SIDINGS

No	Name/Company/Location	Ry Ref
P 1	Teston Siding	6 75
2	High Brooms Siding	6 54
3	Crowhurst Park Sdg	6 71
4	Guestling Siding	6 81
5	Pluckley Brick + Tile Co	6 94
6	Kelly's Siding – Rye	6 91

ENGINE SHEDS

No	Name/Location	Ry Ref
E 1	Eastbourne	4 69 TV
2	St Leonards	4 70
3	Hastings	6 81
4	Tonbridge	6 54
5	Tunbridge Wells	4 53
6	Maidstone East	6 75
7	Maidstone West	6 75
8	Bat + Ball	6 55

TUNNELS

No	Name/Location	Yds	Ry Ref
T 1	Grove		4 53
2	Grove Hill		6 53
3	Wells	823	6 53
4	Strawberry Hill		6 53
5	Wheeler Street		6 75
6	Bopeep		6 70
7	Hastings		6 80

No	Name	Ry Ref
8	Ore	6 81
9	Mountfield	6 72
10	Heathfield	4 52
11	Best Beech Hill	6 63
12	Sevenoaks	2611 6 55

JUNCTIONS

No	Name/Location	Ry Ref
J 1	Polegate West	4 50
2	Polegate East	4 50
3	Redgate Mill	4 53
4	Birchden	4 53
5	Groombridge	4 53
6	Ashurst	4 53
7	Grove	64 53
8	Tonbridge West	6 54
9	Tonbridge East	6 54
10	Sevenoaks	6 55
11	Westerham Branch	6 55
12	Vestry North	6 55
13	Vestry East	6 55
14	Vestry South	6 55
15	Willingdon	4 60
16	Stone Cross	4 60
17	Paddock Wood – Maidstone Line	6 64
18	Paddock Wood – Hawkhurst Beh	6 64
19	Bopeep	64 70
20	Bexhill Line	6 71
21	Robertsbridge K+ES Line	63 72
22	Tovil Goods	6 75
23	Hastings Goods	6 81
24	Headcorn Station	3 84
25	Headcorn K + ES Line	63 84
26	Rye Harbour Branch	6 91
27	Lydd	6 92

NOTES:

(1) REF – All in TQ except those otherwise marked

(2) NAME CHANGE – Old §
(NEW) §

In some cases name changes are different stations and may be an adjoining site – changes are pre and post 1906 in most cases.

142 ←

142 ←

146 →

Key to Railways

3	KENT & EAST SUSSEX (Light)
4	LONDON BRIGHTON & SOUTH COAST
6	SOUTH EASTERN & CHATHAM

1906
(1917)
(1922)

(NEW HYTHE)
AYLESFORD
(WEST) MALLING
(EAST) MALLING
BARMING
MAIDSTONE EAST
Wheeler St. Tunnel
SEE INSET
BEARSTED + Thurnham
HOLLINGBOURNE
HARRIETSHAM
LENHAM
CHARING
Pluckley Brick & Tile Siding
HOTHFIELD
PLUCKLEY

OTFORD
Vestry North Jct
Vestry East Jct
KEMSING
Vestry South Jct
BAT + BALL
Sevenoaks Junction
SEVENOAKS Tubs Hill
Sevenoaks Tunnel 3861 yds
Westerham Bch Junct
DUNTON GREEN
WROTHAM + BOROUGH GREEN
MAIDSTONE
EAST
Tovil
E7
BARRACKS
WEST
Tovil Goods Junction
Tovil Goods
EAST FARLEIGH
WATERINGBURY
YALDING
(BELTRING)
HILDENBOROUGH
PENSHURST
LEIGH
TONBRIDGE
E4
Maidstone Line Junction
PADDOCK WOOD
Hawkhurst Bch Jct
MARDEN
STAPLEHURST
South Eastern + Chatham
Headcorn
HEADCORN Kent & East Sussex Line Jct
Headcorn Station Jct
Frittenden Road
Biddenden
High Halden Road
HAM STREET + Orlestone
APPLEDORE
Lydd Junction
Brookland
RYE
Rye Harbour
Kelly's Siding
WINCHELSEA
South Eastern + Chatham
Harbour Branch Junction

High Brooms Siding
Southborough (HIGH BROOMS)
Tunbridge Wells Goods
TUNBRIDGE WELLS (CENTRAL)
TUNBRIDGE WELLS (WEST)
SEE INSET BELOW
Tunbridge N Jct
Tonbridge East Jct
Grove Tunnel
E5
Grove Junction
ASHURST
GROOMBRIDGE
Groombridge Jct
Birchden Jct
Ashurst Jct
Withyham Jct
ERIDGE
FRANT
WADHURST
Best Beech Hill Tunnel
Redgate Mill Junction
Rotherfield + Mark Cross
CROWBOROUGH
Mayfield
BUXTED
London Brighton + South Coast
Heathfield Tunnel
HEATHFIELD
Waldron + Horeham Road
Hellingly
Hailsham
BERWICK
Polegate West
POLEGATE
Polegate East
Stone Cross Jct
Willingdon Junction
HAMPDEN PARK
E1
EASTBOURNE
TQ
TV

Horsmonden
Goudhurst
Cranbrook
Hawkhurst Tunnel
HAWKHURST
Ticehurst Road (STONEGATE)
ETCHINGHAM
Kent & East Sussex Line Junction
ROBERTSBRIDGE
Junction Road
Bodiam
NORTHIAM
Kent & East Sussex (Light)
Rolvenden
Wittersham Road
Tenterden Town
Mountfield Tunnel
BATTLE
CROWHURST
Crowhurst Junction
Bexhill Line Junction
Crowhurst Park Sidings
(DOLEHAM)
(THREE OAKS)
Guestling Sdg
WEST ST LEONARDS
ST LEONARDS WARRIOR SQ
Bopeep Tunnel
Hastings Tunnel
Ore Tunnel
ORE
Hastings Goods Jct
HASTINGS
Hastings Goods
West Marina
BEXHILL-on-Sea (Central)
Bexhill West
COLLINGTON
(COODEN BEACH)
(NORMANS BAY)
PEVENSEY + WESTHAM (PEVENSEY BAY)

Inset (lower left) 1906:

TQ
4
Tunbridge Wells Goods
Wells Tunnel
TUNBRIDGE WELLS (CENTRAL)
Grove Hill Tunnel
Grove Junction
E5 LB+SC
Grove Tunnel
TUNBRIDGE WELLS (WEST)
South Eastern + Chatham
Strawberry Hill Tunnel
FRANT

Inset (lower right) 1906:

TQ
AYLESFORD
(WEST) MALLING
BARMING
(EAST) MALLING
MAIDSTONE EAST
Wheeler Street Tunnel
MAIDSTONE BARRACKS
MAIDSTONE WEST
E6
Tovil Goods Junct
Tovil
South Eastern + Chatham
BEARSTED + Thurnham
HOLLINGBOURNE
Teston Sdg
Tovil Goods
EAST FARLEIGH
River Medway
WATERINGBURY

146

RAILWAYS

No	Company
R 1	ROMNEY HYTHE + DIMCHURCH (1'3" gauge)
3	EAST KENT (Light) ⚒
6	SOUTH EASTERN + CHATHAM
6A	SHEPPEY (Light) - SE+C
6X	SE+C (taken out of use before 1938)
O	SOUTHERN RAILWAY (post grouping)

STATIONS

No	Name	Ry Ref
A 1	ADISHAM	6 25
2	ASHFORD East	6 04
3	(Ash Town)	3 25
4	(AYLESHAM)	6 25
5	Barham	6 24
6	BEKESBOURNE	6 15
7	BIRCHINGTON-ON-SEA ‡	6 26
8	Bishopsbourne	6 15
9	Bridge	6 15
10	BROADSTAIRS ‡	6 36
11	(BURMARSH ROAD HALT)	1 13
12	CHILHAM	6 05
13	CANTERBURY EAST	6 15
14	Canterbury South	6 15
15	CANTERBURY WEST	6 15
16	(CHESTFIELD + SWALECLIFFE)	6 16
17	CHARTHAM	6 15
18	Chislet Colliery Halt ‡	6 26
19	DEAL	6 35
20	Dover Harbour	6 34
21	Dover Pier (Marine) §24	6 34
22	DOVER PRIORY	6 34
23	Dover Town	6 34
24	DOVER WESTERN DOCKS §21	6 34
25	(DUMPTON PARK) ‡	0 36
26	(DUNGENESS)	1 01
27	Dungeness	6 01
28	(DYMCHURCH)	1 02
29	(Eastry Junction)	3 25
30	Elham	6 14
31	(Eythorne)	3 24
32	FAVERSHAM ‡	6 06
33	FOLKESTONE CENTRAL	6 23
34	FOLKESTONE HARBOUR	6 23
35	Folkestone Junction (East)	6 23
36	Folkestone Warren	6 23
37	(FOLKESTONE WEST) §77	6 23
38	(Greatstone)	0 02
39	(GREATSTONE HALT)	1 03
40	Grove Ferry ‡	6 26
41	HAM STREET + Orlestone	6 03
42	HERNE BAY + Hampton-on-Sea	6 16
43	(HYTHE)	1 13
44	Hythe	6 13
45	(JEFFERSTONE LANE)	1 02
46	KEARSNEY	6 24
47	(Knowlton)	3 25
48	(LADE HALT)	1 02
49	Leysdown ‡	6A 06
50	Lydd ✱	6 02
51	(Lydd-on-Sea)	0 01
52	Lyminge	6 14
53	Margate East ‡	6 36
54	Margate Sands ‡	6 37
55	MARGATE West ‡	6 37
56	MARTIN MILL	6 34
57	MINSTER ‡	6 36
58	(NEW ROMNEY)	1 02
59	New Romney + Littleston-on-Sea	02 / 6 02
60	(PILOT HALT)	1 01
61	PRIORY, DOVER	6 34
62	(RAMSGATE) ‡	6 36
63	Ramsgate Harbour ‡	6 36
64	Ramsgate St Lawrence ‡	6 36
65	Ramsgate Town ‡	6 36
66	(ROMNEY SANDS)	1 02
67	(St Lawrence Halt)	6 36
68	St Lawrence, Ramsgate ‡	6 36
69	Sandgate	6 13
70	SANDLING Junction	6 13
71	SANDWICH	6 35
72	(Sandwich Road)	3 35
73	SELLING	6 05
74	(Shakespeare Staff Halt)	6 23
75	(Shepherd's Well)	3 24
76	SHEPHERDS WELL	6(3) 24
77	Shorncliffe Camp §37	6 23
78	Smeeth	6 03
79	(SNOWDOWN)	6 25
80	(Staple)	3 25
81	STURRY ‡	6 16
82	WALMER	6 35
83	WESTENHANGER	6 13
84	WESTGATE-ON-SEA ‡	6 36
85	Whitstable Harbour ‡	6 16
86	WHITSTABLE Town ‡	6 16
87	(Wingham)	3 25
88	(Woodnesborough)	3 25
89	(Woodnesborough Road)	3 35
90	WYE	6 04

GOODS

No	Location	Ry Ref
G 1	Ashford West	6 04
2	Faversham Coal Wharf	6 06
3	Graveney ‡	6 06
4	Whitstable Town ‡	6 16
5	Dover Town	6 34
6	Dover Pier	6 34

SIDINGS

No	Name / Location / Co	Ry Ref
P 1	Chartham	6 05
2	Ash Road	6 35
3	Guilford Colliery	3 24
4	Ashford Gas Works	6 TQ 94
5	Admiralty Siding	6X 01

COMPANY WORKS

No	Location	Ry Ref
C 1	Ashford	6 04

ENGINE SHEDS

No	Location	Ry Ref
E 1	Ashford	6 04
2	Faversham ‡	6 06
3	Dover	6 34
4	Folkestone	6 23
5	Canterbury West	6 15
6	Ramsgate	6 36

TUNNELS

No	Name / Location	Yds	Ry Ref
T 1	Harbour (Ramsgate)	1630	6 36
2	Archcliffe		6 34
3	Shakespeare		6 34
4	Abbotscliffe	1942	6 23
5	Lydden	2369	6 24
6	Martello		6 23
7	Harbour (Dover)		6 34
8	Priory		6 34
9	Charlton		6 34
10	Guston		6 34

JUNCTIONS

No	Name / Location	Ry Ref
J 1	Ashford Goods	6 TQ 94
2	Romney Old	6 02
3	Romney New	6 02
4	Ashford West	6 04
5	Ashford East	6 04
6	Faversham ‡	6 06
7	Sandling	6 13
8	Harbledown	6 15
9	Canterbury-Whitstable	6 15
10	Cheriton	6 13
11	Folkestone	6 23
12	Shepherds Well East Kent	63 24
13	Guilford Colliery Branch	3 24
14	Eastry	3 25
15	Dover - Archcliffe	6 34
16	Dover - Hawkesbury Street	6 34
17	Dover - Pier Goods	6 34
18	Dover - Pier (Marine)	6 34
19	Buckland	6 34
20	Kearsney Loop	6 34
21	Deal	6 34
22	Minster - West ‡	6 36
23	Minster - East ‡	6 36
24	Minster - South ‡	6 36
25	Ramsgate St Lawrence ‡	6 36
26	Ramsgate Town ‡	6 36
27	Ramsgate North ‡	6 36
28	(Temp¹ Jct) see note ⚲	0 36

NOTES:

(1) REF All in TR except where indicated otherwise

(2) NAME CHANGE Old §
                (NEW) §

(3) E KENT built post map date ⚒ (1911) - branches later

(4) Lydd is much nearer to the ✱ old Romney Junction than is shown

(5) Temp Junction - Harbour line closed shortly after new connection via DUMPTON PARK was opened.

(6) Also on Map 133 ‡

ADDITIONAL HALTS: In the early 1920's There were Halts open between CANTERBURY WEST + Whitstable Harbour at Blean + Tyler Hill, South Street and Tankerton

TR

Key to Railways
1 — ROMNEY HYTHE + DYMCHURCH (1'3" gauge built 1928-9)
3 — EAST KENT (Light) - Built 1911 - see note
6 — SOUTH EASTERN + CHATHAM
6. — SOUTH EASTERN + CHATHAM (Closed before 1939)
6A — SHEPPEY (Light) - (SE+C)
0 — SOUTHERN RAILWAY - New Ramsgate connection
0 — SOUTHERN RAILWAY - Lydd re-alignment

Leysdown
Whitstable Harbour
Whitstable Town Gds
Faversham Coal Wharf
Graveney Goods
Faversham Jct.
E2
SELLING
Chartham Siding
E5
STURRY
Canterbury-Whitstable Jct.
CANTERBURY WEST
CANTERBURY EAST
Harbledown Jct.
Canterbury South
CHARTHAM
CHILHAM
BEKESBOURNE
Bridge
ADISHAM
(AYLESHAM)
(SNOWDOWN)
Bishopsbourne
Barham
Shepherds Well - E Kent Junction
HERNE BAY + Hampton-on-Sea
(CHESTFIELD + SWALECLIFFE)
WHITSTABLE TOWN
Grove Ferry South Jct.
(Chislet Colliery Halt)
(Wingham)
(Staple)
(Ash Town)
(Woodnesborough)
(Sandwich Road)
Ash Road Sdg
SANDWICH
Eastry Junction
(Eastry Junction)
(Knowlton)
DEAL
WALMER
(Eythorne)
Guilford Col Bch J.
Guilford Col
SHEPHERDS WELL EK
Lydden Tunnel 2369 Yards
MARTIN MILL
BIRCHINGTON-ON-SEA
WESTGATE-ON-SEA
MARGATE WEST
Margate Sands
Margate East
MINSTER West Jct
East Jct
(RAMSGATE) SEE INSET
Jct
(E6)
Ramsgate Town
Ramsgate St Lawrence Halt
BROADSTAIRS
(DUMPTON PARK)
Ramsgate Harbour

KEARSNEY
Deal Junct.
Buckland Jct
Kearsney Loop Junction
DOVER PRIORY
SETON SET
E3
DOVER PIER (WESTERN DOCKS)
Archcliffe Junction
Shakespeare Tunnel
Abbotscliffe Tunnel 1942 yds
Shakespeare Staff Halt

WYE
Ashford Goods Jct
Ashford West Goods
ASHFORD EAST
Gas Works Sdg
Ashford W Junc
Ashford East Jct
C1
Smeeth
WESTENHANGER
Elham
Lyminge
Cheriton Junction
Martello Tunnel
E4
FOLKESTONE Junction (East)
Folkestone Warren
SHORNCLIFFE (FOLKESTONE Camp)
FOLKESTONE CENTRAL
FOLKESTONE HARBOUR
FOLKESTONE WEST
HAM STREET + Oelestone
SANDLING Junction
Sandling Junction
(HYTHE)
Sandgate
(BURMARSH ROAD HALT)
(DYMCHURCH)
(JEFFERSTONE LANE)
New Romney
Littlestone-on-Sea
(Greatstone)
(NEW ROMNEY)
(GREATSTONE HALT)
(ROMNEY SANDS)
(LADE HALT)
(PILOT HALT)
(DUNGENESS)
Lydd
Old Juncts for Romney
New
(Lydd-on-Sea)
1906
1911
(1930)
Dungeness Admiralty Sdg

KEY

Pre-Grouping Lines
——— Still in use
—|—|— out of use fr 1920's
—•—•— Now Goods only
—•—•— out of use but in use for period post 1920's

Post Grouping Lines
——— Still in use
—|—|— Goods only
—•—•— Closed
● Pre 20's OPEN
○ Post 20's OPEN } Stations
● Closed

1906
(1930)
(1984)

MARGATE
WESTGATE-ON-SEA
Margate Sands
Margate East
MARGATE WEST
TR37 TR47
TR36 TR46
BROADSTAIRS
Ramsgate North Junction
Temp Junction pending closure of Harbour Line
(DUMPTON PARK)
RAMSGATE
St. L. Jct.
E6
Ramsgate St. Lawrence
(St. Lawrence Halt)
(RAMSGATE)
Ramsgate Town
Ramsgate Harbour

TR34

Deal Junction
Kearsney Loop Junction
Buckland Junction
Guston Tunnel
Charlton Tunnel
Priory Tunnel
South Eastern & Chatham
PRIORY
Harbour Tunnel
DOVER
Harbour
Archcliffe Junct.
Archcliffe tunnel
Town
E3
Shakespeare Tunnel
Hawkesbury St Jct
Pier Goods Jct
Pier Junct
Admiralty Pier
1908
Pier (WESTERN DOCKS)

147

RAILWAYS

No	Company
R 1	LONDON + SOUTH WESTERN
2	Padstow Bedruthant Mawgan – proposed – not built
3	GREAT WESTERN

STATIONS

No	Name	Ry Ref
A 1	Burngullow	3 95
2	CAMBORNE	3 63
3	CARBIS BAY	3 53
4	Cam Brea	3 64
5	Chacewater	3 74
6	FALMOUTH	3 83
7	Goonbell Halt	3 75
8	Goonhavern Halt	3 75
9	Grampound Road	3 94
10	Gwinear Road	3 53
11	HAYLE	3 53
12	Helston	3 62
13	LELANT	3 53
14	(LELANT SIDINGS)	3 53
15	Marazion	3 43
16	(Mawgan)	2 86
17	Mitchell + Newlyn Halt	3 85
18	Mithian Halt	3 75
19	Mount Hawke Halt	3 74
20	Nancegollan	3 63
21	NEWQUAY	3 86
22	PENZANCE	3 43
23	(PENMERE)	3 73
24	PENRYN	3 73
25	Padstow	1 97
26	Perranporth	3 75
27	PERRANWELL	3 73

REDRUTH, TRURO + PENZANCE

No	Name	Ry Ref
28	Praze	3 63
29	Probus + Ladock Platform	3 84
30	QUINTREL DOWNS ✱	3 86
31	REDRUTH	3 74
32	ROCHE	3 96
33	St Agnes	3 75
34	ST COLUMB ROAD	3 95
35	ST ERTH	3 53
36	ST IVES	3 54
37	Scorrier	3 74
38	Shepherds	3 85
39	(THE DELL)	3 83
40	Trewerry + Trerice Halt	3 85
41	TRURO	3 84
42	Truthall Platform	3 62
43	Wadebridge	1 97

GOODS

No	Location	Ry Ref
G 1	Hayle Wharves	3 53
2	Portreath	3 64
3	Redruth	3 74
4	Newham	3 84
5	Newquay Harbour	3 86
6	Padstow Quay	1 97
7	Wadebridge Quay	1 97

SIDINGS

No	Company / Location	Ry Ref
P 1	Pansandane	3 43
2	Dakoath	3 63
3	Roskear	3 64
4	North Crofty	3 64
5	Tre Savean	3 73
6	Wheal Busy	3 74
7	Treamble	3 75

No	Name	Ry Ref
8	Gravel Hill	3 75
9	Trewerry Mill	3 85
10	High Street	3 95
11	Carpella New	3 95
12	Carpella Old	3 95
13	Meledor Mill	3 95
14	Burgotha	3 95
15	Treviscoe	3 95
16	Retew	3 95
17	Trerice	3 95
18	Drinnick Mill	3 95
19	Whitegate	3 95
20	Pochins	3 95

ENGINE SHEDS

No	Location	Ry Ref
E 1	Wadebridge	1 97
2	Truro	3 84
3	Penzance	3 43
4	Helston	3 62
5	St Ives	3 54

JUNCTIONS

No	Name / Location	Ry Ref
J 1	St Ives Branch	3 53
2	Hayle Wharves Branch	3 53
3	Helston Branch	3 63
4	Portreath Branch	3 64
5	Chacewater North	3 74
6	Chacewater South	3 74
7	Chacewater East	3 74
8	Penwithers for Falmouth	3 84
9	Penwithers for Newham	3 84
10	Treamble Branch	3 85
11	Harbour Branch	3 86
12	Tolcarn	3 80

No	Name	Ry Ref
13	Burngullow	3 95
14	St Dennis	3 96
15	Wadebridge East	1 97
16	Wadebridge West	1 97
17	Padstow Quay Branch	1 97

NOTES

(1) REF – All in SW

(2) SPELLING – Also shown by some authorities as QUINTRELL DOWNS ✱

In other cases, too, minor variations occur.

Key to Railways
1 ▬▬▬▬▬ LONDON & SOUTH WESTERN
2 ⊢-⊢-⊢-⊣ Padstow Bedruthan & Mawgan (Proposed – not built)
3 ▬▬▬▬▬ GREAT WESTERN
X ┼┼┼┼┼┼┼┼┼ Others – Mines etc

SW

Padstow
Padstow Quay
Wadebridge Quay E1
Padstow Quay Branch Junction
Wadebridge W.Jct
Wadebridge
Wadebridge East

(Mawgan)

Harbour
NEWQUAY
Harbour Branch Jct
Tolcarn Junction
QUINTREL DOWNS
ST COLUMB ROAD
St. Dennis Junction
ROCHE →148

Trewerry Mill Sdg
Gravel Hill
Trewerry & Trerice Halt
Treamble
J10
Mitchell & Newlyn Halt
Perranporth
Shepherds
Goonhavern Halt
Mithian Halt
Goonbell Halt
St Agnes

Trerice
Retew
Trevissoe Sdg
Burgotha Sdg
Meledor Mill

Pochins Siding
Whitegate Siding
Brianick Mill
Carpella Old Sdg

Carpella New Sdg
High Str. Sdg
Burngullow
Burngullow Junction

Grampound Road

Mount Hawke Halt
Chacewater North Jct
Wheal Busy Sdg
Portreath Gds
Chacewater
East Jct
South Jct
Scorrier
TRURO E2
Probus & Ladock Platform

Roskear Sdg
N Cross
Redruth Gds
REDRUTH
Newham Goods

Gwinear Road
Helston Branch Jct
Portreath Branch Junction
Tre Savan
PERRANWELL
For Falmouth
Repeater's Sidings
For Newham

ST IVES R5
CARBIS BAY
LELANT
(LELANT SIDINGS)
St Ives Bch Jct
ST ERTH
Hayle Wharves
Cam Brea
Dolcoath Sdg
CAMBORNE

HAYLE
Hayle Wharves Branch Jct

PENZANCE
Ponsandane Sdg
Marazion

Praze

Nancegollan

Truthall Platform

E4 Helston

PENRYN
(PENMERE)
(THE DELL)
FALMOUTH

1917
(1916)
(1926)

RAILWAYS

No.	Company
R 1	LONDON + SOUTH WESTERN
13	GREAT WESTERN + LSW JOINT
2	ST AUSTELL + PENTEWAN (2'6" gauge)
3	GREAT WESTERN
3A	LISKEARD + LOOE (GW)
3B	LISKEARD + CARADON (GW)
3C	PRINCETOWN (GW)
4	PLYMOUTH, DEVONPORT + SOUTH-WESTERN JUNCTION ⚒

STATIONS

No.	Name	Ry Ref
A1	Albert Road Halt ✳	1 45
2	Ashburton	3 77
3	Avonwick	3 75
4	BERE ALSTON	1 46
5	BERE FERRERS	1 46
6	Bickleigh	3 56
7	Billacombe	3 55
8	Bittaford Platform	3 65
9	Bodmin	1 06
10	Bodmin	3 06
11	BODMIN Road (PARKWAY)	3 16
12	Bovey	3 87
13	Brent	3 76
14	(Brimley Halt)	3 87
15	(BRITANNIA HALT) ⸨	3 85
16	Brixham	3 95
17	Brixton Road	3 55
18	Buckfastleigh	3 76
19	BUGLE	3 05
20	(Burrator Halt)	3C 56
21	Callington for Stoke Climsland	4 37
22	CALSTOCK	4 46
23	Camel's Head Halt ✳	1 45
24	CAUSELAND	3A 25
25	Chilsworthy	4 47
26	Chudleigh	3 87
27	Chudleigh + Knighton Halt	3 87
28	Churston Junction	3 85
29	COOMBE	3A 26
30	Cornwood	3 65
31	DAWLISH	3 97
32	DAWLISH WARREN	3 97
33	Defiance	3 45
34	DEVONPORT	3 45
35	Devonport + Stonehouse ✳	1 45
36	DOCKYARD Halt ✳	3 45
36A	Doublebois	3 26
37	Dousland	3C 56
38	Dunmere Halt	1 06
39	Elburton Cross	3 55
40	Ford ✳	1 45
41	Ford Platform ✳	3 45
42	Fowey	3 15
43	Friary	1 45
44	Gara Bridge	3 75
45	Golant	3 15
46	(GOODRINGTON SANDS) ⸨	3 85
47	Grogley Halt	1 00
48	GUNNISLAKE	4 47
49	Heathfield	3 87
50	Horrabridge	3 66
51	(Ingra Tor Halt)	3C 57
52	Ivybridge	3 65
53	KEYHAM	3 45
54	Kingsbridge	3 74
55	Kingskerwell	3 86
56	Kingswear	3 85
57	(King Tor Halt)	3C 57
58	Laira Halt ✳	3 55
59	Latchley	4 47
60	Lipson Vale Halt ✳	3 45
61	LISKEARD	3 26
62	Liskeard	3A 26
63	Loddiswell	3 74
64	LOOE	3A 25
65	LOSTWITHIEL	3 15
66	Lucas Terrace Halt	1 45
67	Luckett	4 37
68	LUXULYAN	3 05
69	Marsh Mills	3 55
70	Marytavy + Blackdown	3 47
71	MENHENIOT	3 26
72	Millbay	3 45
73	Moorswater	3AB 26
74	Mt. Gould + Tothill Halt ✳	3 55
75	Mutley	3 45
76	Nanstallon Halt	1 06
77	NEWTON ABBOT	3 87
78	North Road, PLYMOUTH	13 45
79	Oreston ✳	1 55
80	(RIVERSIDE, TOTNES) ⸨	(3) 86
81	PAIGNTON	3 86
82	(PAIGNTON QUEENS PARK) ⸨	(3) 86
83	PAR	3 05
84	Pentewan	2 04
85	Plym Bridge Platform	3 56
86	Plymouth Friary	1 45
87	PLYMOUTH North Road	13 45
88	Plymouth Millbay	3 45
89	Plymouth Mutley	3 45
90	Plympton	3 55
91	Plymstock	1(3) 55
92	Port Isaac Road	1 07
93	Princetown	3C 57
94	(RIVERSIDE, TOTNES)	(3) 86
95	St Austell	2 05
96	ST AUSTELL	3 05
97	St Blazey	3 05
97A	ST BUDEAUX (FERRY ROAD) §	3 45
98	ST BUDEAUX (VICTORIA ROAD)	1 45
99	ST GERMANS	3 35
100	St Kew Highway	1 07
101	ST KEYNE	3A 26
102	SALTASH	3 45
103	SANDPLACE	3A 25
104	(Seven Stones Halt)	4 37
105	Shaughbridge Platform	3 56
106	Staverton (BRIDGE) §	3 76
107	Steer Point	3 55
108	Tamerton Foliot	1 45
109	Tavistock	1 47
110	Tavistock	3 47
111	Teigngrace	3 87
112	TEIGNMOUTH	3 97
113	TORQUAY	3 96
114	TORRE	3 96
115	TOTNES	3 86
116	(TOTNES RIVERSIDE) ⸨	3 86
117	Turnchapel	1 45
118	Weston Mill Halt ✳	1 45
119	Whitchurch Down Platform	3 47
120	Wingfield Villas Halt	3 45
121	Wrangaton	3 65
122	Yealmpton	3 55
123	Yelverton	3 56

GOODS

No.	Name/Location	Ry Ref
G1	Par Dock	3 05
2	Game Dock	3 15
3	Fowey Docks	3 15
4	Totnes Quay	3 86
5	Newton Abbot	3 87

SIDINGS

No.	Company/Location	Ry Ref
P1	Carbean	3 05
2	Gunheath	3 05
3	Ruthern Bridge	1 06
4	Penargard	1 06
5	Helland	1 07
6	Stump Oak	1 07
7	Wenford	1 07
8	St Cleer	3B 26
9	Polwrath	3B 26
10	South Caradon	3B 26
11	Minions	3B 27
12	Cheesewring Quarry	3B 27
13	Kit Hill	4 37
14	Perry Spears	4 47
15	Cockings	4 47
16	Clitters	4 47
17	Eggworth	3C 57
18	Swell Tor Granite	3C 57
19	Redlake	3 65
20	Rattery	3 76
21	Gas House (Paignton)	3 85
22	Dainton	3 86
23	Aller	3 86

WORKS

No.	Name	Ry Ref
C1	Newton Abbot	3 87

JUNCTIONS

No.	Name/Location	Ry Ref
J1	Trenance Valley	3 05
2	Carbis	3 05
3	Gunheath	3 05
4	St Blazey	3 05
5	Par	3 05
6	Par Dock Line	3 05
7	Ruthern Bridge	1 06
8	Boscarne	13 06
9	Wenford Branch	1 06
10	Fowey Branch	3 15
11	Bodmin	3 16
12	for Liskeard (Moorswater)	3A 26
13	Liskeard Station	3/3A 26
14	Bere Alston	14 46
15	Princetown Branch	3/3C 56
16	Brent	3 66
17	Totnes-Ashburton Bch	3 86
18	Totnes-Quay Branch	3 86
19	Churston	3 85
20	Aller	3 87
21	Moretonhampstead Branch	3 87
22	Heathfield	3 87

ENGINE SHEDS

No.	Name/Location	Ry Ref
E1	Newton Abbot	3 87
2	Princetown	(c) 3 57
3	St. Blazey	3 05
4	Bodmin	3 06
5	Moorswater	(AB) 3 26
6	Kingsbridge	3 74
7	Ashburton	3 76
8	Callington	4 33

TUNNELS

No.	Name/Location	Length yds	Ry Ref
T1	Pinnock	1173	3 05

SUMMITS

No.	Name	Ry Ref
S1	Rattery (Wrangaton)	3 65
2	Dainton	3 86

BRIDGES + VIADUCTS

No.	Name	Ry Ref
V1	Royal Albert Bridge	3 45
2	Slade Viaduct	3 55
3	Blachford Viaduct	3 65
4	Tiddy Viaduct	3 35
5	Lynher Viaduct	3 35
6	Tresulgan + Coldrenick Viaducts	3 26

NOTES:

(1) REF — All in SX

(2) Combined Gazetteer Ref 0-4 are on map A. Ref 5-9 are on map B.

(3) Some stations in the enlarged area covered by MAP 149 are not on the map. These stations are shown in blue. Full details see map 149.

✳ Blue. Full details see map 149. All other features in this area - see map 149

⸨ (NEW PRESERVED STATIONS)

§ (BRIDGE) added to name when the station re-opened as a preserved railway.

§ Previously known as ST BUDEAUX Platform.

⚒ BERE ALSTON to DEVONPORT was also owned. This latter portion was however worked by LSW.

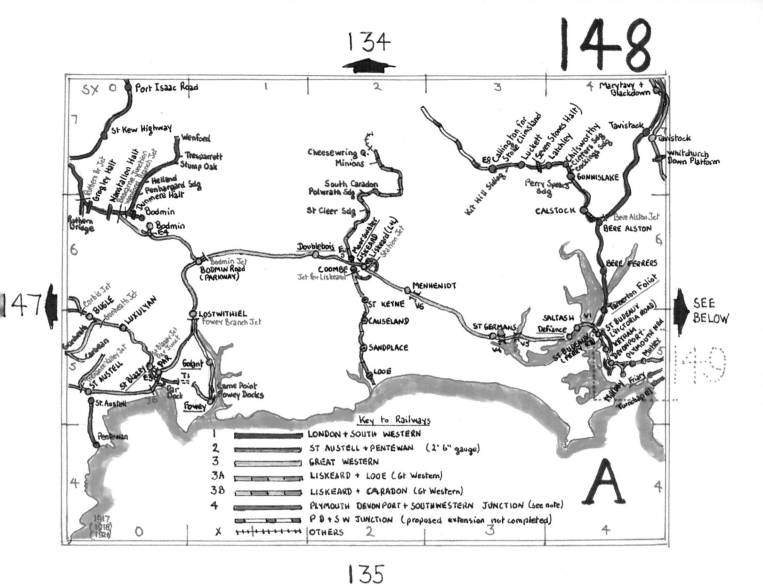

134

Map A

SX 0 — Port Isaac Road

1 2 3 4 Marytavy + Blackdown

7

St Kew Highway
Wenford
Wenfordbridge
Rothern Br Jct
Grogley Halt
Boscarne Junction
Wadebridge Junction
Wenford Branch Jct
Tresparrett
Stump Oak
Helland
Penhargard Sdg
Dunmere Halt
Bodmin

Cheesewring Q. Minions
South Caradon
Polwrath Sdg
St Cleer Sdg

Eg Callington for Stoke Climsland
Luckett
Seven Stones Halt
Latchley
Chilsworthy
Clitters Sdg
Cockings Sdg
GUNNISLAKE
Tavistock
Tavistock
Whitchurch Down Platform

Perry Spears Sdg

CALSTOCK

Ruthern Bridge
Bodmin
E4
Bodmin Jct
BODMIN ROAD (PARKWAY)

Doublebois
Moorswater
LISKEARD (LW)
Liskeard (LW)
Station Jct
COOMBE
Jct for Liskeard
MENHENIOT V6

Bere Alston Jct
BERE ALSTON
BERE FERRERS
Tamerton Foliot

SEE BELOW

147

Carbis Jct
BUGLE
Bunheath Jct
LUXULYAN
LOSTWITHIEL
Fowey Branch Jct

St Keyne
CAUSELAND
SANDPLACE
LOOE

St Germans
V4 V3
SALTASH V1
Defiance
St BUDEAUX (FERRY RD)
St BUDEAUX (VICTORIA ROAD)
KEYHAM
DEVONPORT
PLYMOUTH NRd
Mutley

149

Trenance Valley Jct
St AUSTELL
St Blazey Jct
PAR
St Blazey
E3
Par Dock
Carne Point
Fowey Docks

Golant
T1
Fowey

St. Austell

Pentewan

Millbay
Friary
Turnchapel

Key to Railways

1	LONDON + SOUTH WESTERN
2	ST AUSTELL + PENTEWAN (2' 6" gauge)
3	GREAT WESTERN
3A	LISKEARD + LOOE (Gt Western)
3B	LISKEARD + CARADON (Gt Western)
4	PLYMOUTH DEVONPORT + SOUTHWESTERN JUNCTION (see note)
	PD + SW JUNCTION (proposed extension not completed)
X	OTHERS

A

1917 (1918) (1926)

SX 0   1   2   3   4

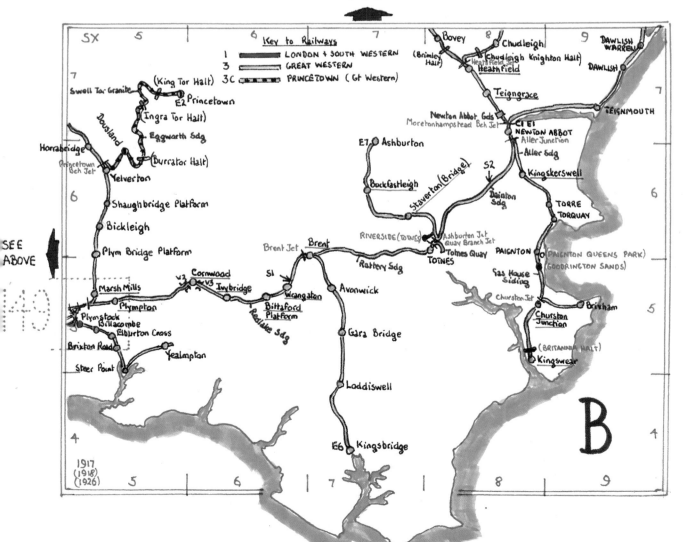

135

Map B

SX 5   6   7   8   9 DAWLISH WARREN

Bovey (Brimley Halt)
Chudleigh
Chudleigh Knighton Halt
Heathfield
DAWLISH

Key to Railways

1	LONDON + SOUTH WESTERN
3	GREAT WESTERN
3C	PRINCETOWN (Gt Western)

Teigngrace
TEIGNMOUTH

Swell Tor Granite
(King Tor Halt)
E2 Princetown
(Ingra Tor Halt)
Dousland
Eggworthy Sdg
Horrabridge
(Burrator Halt)
Princetown Bch Jct
Yelverton
Shaughbridge Platform
Bickleigh
Plym Bridge Platform

Newton Abbot Gds
Moretonhampstead Bch Jct
C1 E1
NEWTON ABBOT
Aller Junction
Aller Sdg
S2
Dainton Sdg
Kingskerswell
TORRE
TORQUAY

E7 Ashburton
Buckfastleigh
Staverton (Bridge)

SEE ABOVE

149

Marsh Mills
Plympton
V3 Cornwood
V3
Ivybridge
S1
Wrangaton
Bittaford Platform
Redlake Sdg
Brent Jct
Brent
Rattery Sdg
RIVERSIDE (Totnes)
Ashburton Jct
Quay Branch Jct
TOTNES
Totnes Quay

Gas House Siding
PAIGNTON
(PAIGNTON QUEENS PARK)
(GOODRINGTON SANDS)
Churston Jct

Plymstock
Billacombe
Elburton Cross
Brixton Road
Yealmpton
Steer Point

Avonwick
Gara Bridge

Churston Junction
(BRITANNIA HALT)
Kingswear
Brixham

Loddiswell

E6 Kingsbridge

B

1917 (1918) (1926)

SX 5   6   7   8   9

PLYMOUTH

RAILWAYS

No.	Company
R 1	LONDON + SOUTH WESTERN
13	GREAT WESTERN and LONDON + SOUTH WESTERN
3	GREAT WESTERN
0	BRITISH RAIL additions
X	Dock Lines etc

STATIONS

No.	Name	Ry Ref
A 1	Albert Road Halt	1 4555
2	Billacombe	3 5254
3	Brixton Road	3 6353
4	Camel's Head Halt	1 4657
5	DEVONPORT	3 4555
6	Devonport + Stonehouse	1 4655
7	DOCKYARD Halt	3 4555
8	Elburton Cross	3 5353
9	Ford	1 4556
10	Ford Platform	3 4556
11	Friary *	1 4854
12	KEYHAM	3 4556
13	Laira Halt	3 5056
14	Lipson Vale Halt	3 4955
15	Lucas Terrace Halt	1 4954
16	Marsh Mills	3 5257
17	Millbay	3 4754
18	Mount Gould + Tothill Halt *	3 5055
19	Mutley *	3 4865
20	North Road PLYMOUTH *	13 4755
21	Oreston	1 5053
	PLYMOUTH:	
22	Friary	1 4854
23	Millbay	3 4754
24	Mutley	3 4855
25	PLYMOUTH North Road	13 4755
26	Plympton	3 5357
27	Plymstock	1(3) 5054
28	ST BUDEAUX Platform (FERRY ROAD)	3 4457
29	ST BUDEAUX (VICTORIA ROAD)	1 4457
30	Turnchapel	1 4953
31	Weston Mill Halt	1 4557
32	Wingfield Villas Halt	3 4655

GOODS

No.	Name/Location	Ry Ref
G 1	Cattewater Harbour	
2	Devonport	
3	Friary	
4	Great Western Docks	
5	North Quay	
6	North Quay	
7	Stonehouse Pool	
8	Sutton Harbour	
9	Sutton Wharf	
10	Vauxhall Quay	

SIDINGS

No.	Company/Name/Location	Ry Ref
P 1	Bayly's Siding	
2	Northey's Siding	1 5053
3	Laira Exchange Sidings	

ENGINE SHEDS

No.	Name/Location	Ry Ref
E 1	Laira	
2	Friary	

TUNNELS

No.	Name	Ry Ref
T 1	Mutley	1 4953
2	Devonport	1 4557

BRIDGES + VIADUCTS

No.	Name	Ry Ref
V 1	Weston Mill Viaduct	3 4457

JUNCTIONS

No.	Name/Location	Ry Ref
J 1	Bull Point	3 4664
2	Keyham	1 4854
3	Devonport Goods	3 4854
4	Stonehouse Pool	1 4553
5	Devonport	3 4854
6	Plymouth West	1 4854
7	Plymouth South	1 4854
8	Plymouth North Road	3 4155
9	Friary Station	1 4954
10	Friary Goods	1 4954
11	for North Quay	3x 4954
12	Friary West	1 4954
13	Friary	31 4955
14	Mount Gould North	3 5055
15	Mount Gould South	3 5055
16	Cattewater	13 5054
17	Plymstock Line	1 5054
18	Turnchapel Branch	5054
19	Plymstock GW + LSW	13 5054
20	Lipson	3 5056
21	Laira	3 5056
22	Tavistock	3 5156
23	Marsh Mills	‡ 30 5256
24	for Gunnislake	‡ 30 4457

NOTES:

REF : All in SX.

* Plymouth Stations (central) dually indexed.

‡ New Br Junctions, RED on map.

148B

148B

148A

148A

St Budeaux (Victoria Road)
Weston Mill Halt
Camel's Head Halt
St Budeaux Platform
Bull Point Junction
Ford
Keyham Junction
KEYHAM
Ford (Platf)
DOCKYARD Halt
Albert Road Halt
Devonport Tunnel
DEVONPORT
Devonport + Stonehouse
Devonport Junction West Junct.
Wingfield Villas Halt
Stonehouse Pool Junction
Devonport Goods
Goods Junction
Stonehouse Pool Goods
PLYMOUTH North Road
North Road Junction
South Junction
Mutley
Mutley Tunnel
Lipson Vale Halt
Lipson Junction
Laira Junction
Laira Halt
Laira Exchange Sidings
Marsh Mills
Marsh Mills Junction
Tavistock Junction
Plympton
Friary Junct.
Friary West Junction
Station Junct.
Goods Junct.
North Quay
Cattle Wharf Jct.
Sutton Harbour Goods
Jct. for North Quay
North Quay Sdg.
Electric Lucas Halt
Mount Gould Junctions
Mount Gould + Tothill Halt
Cattewater Junction
Plymstock Line Junction
Turnchapel Branch Junction
London + SW and GW Junction
Plymouth Friary
Friary Goods
North Quay
Sutton Wharf
Vauxhall Quay
East water Harbour Goods
Plymouth Millbay
Gt Western Docks
Turnchapel
Oreston
Plymstock
Billacombe
Elburton Cross
Brixton Road

Weston Mill Viaduct

1918 (1928)

Key to Railways

	LONDON + SOUTH WESTERN
1	
3	GREAT WESTERN
0	BRITISH RAIL ADDITIONS
X	+++++++ DOCK LINES ETC

SX

BIBLIOGRAPHY

A RAILWAY CLEARING HOUSE PUBLICATIONS

(i) Country Maps

	Date	Miles to inch
England & Wales – Small	1915	11¼
England & Wales – Large	1917	7½
England & Wales – Large	1926	7½
Scotland	1907	7½
Scotland	1927	7½
Ireland	1912	7½

(ii) District Maps

Edinburgh & Glasgow Districts	1898	2
Cumberland & Westmorland District	1912	2
Durham & District	1914	2
Lancashire & Cheshire District	1901	2
Manchester District	1911	1
Yorkshire District North	1921	2
Yorkshire District South	1923	2
Staffordshire District	1918	2
South Wales	1899	2
South Wales	1926	1
Gloucestershire & Oxfordshire District	1911	2
East of England	1917	2
West of England (Airey)	1889	2
West of England	1918	2
West of England	1924	2
London & Environs	1910	½
South of England	1906	2

(iii) Other Publications

Railway Junction Diagrams	1914
Railway Junction Diagrams	1915
Railway Junction Diagrams	1915
Railway Junction Diagrams	1928
Handbook of Railway Stations	1904

B OTHER MAP SOURCES

(i) Railway Publications

GWR and Connections in the British Isles		1909
NER Newcastle + Dunston Districts		1908
NER Coalfields + Railways (Durham – Derby)		1913
N STAFFS Mineral District – Rlys + Minerals		1910
MID Midland Distance Diagrams		1922
Maps of British Railways Pre-grouping (I Allen)		1922
Rail Atlas Britain + Ireland	(OPC)	1984
Sectional Maps of British Railways (I Allen)		1947
British Rail – Main Line Gradient Profiles (I Allen)		

Track Layout Diagrams of GWR + BR (WR) – RA Cooke
Sections 10–18, 20, 26, 29, 30, 32, 36, 37, 39, 47A + B
49, 51–4, 56 + Supplement 1

(ii) Others

Bartholomew's Atlas of England + Wales	1938	2
The Ordnance Survey Atlas of Gt. Britain		4
Bartholomew Road Atlas of Britain		5
ABC – London Atlas – Ordnance Survey		¼
The Faber Atlas		
The Atlas of the Earth		
George Philip Modern Home Atlas		
AA Directory of Town Plans in Britain		
various Railway Gazette reprints		

(iii) Other Gazetteers

GWR – Towns, villages, outlying works	1938
The Railway + Commercial Gazetteer	1962

C OTHER RAILWAY BOOKS

(i) A Regional History of the Railways of Great Britain (D+C)

Vol	Region	Author
1	The West Country	St John Thomas
2	Southern England	White
3	Greater London	White
4	The North East	Hoole
5	The Eastern Counties	Gordon
6	Scotland – The Lowlands + Borders	Thomas
7	The West Midlands	Christiansen
8	South + West Yorkshire	Joy
9	The East Midlands	Leleux
10	The North West	Holt
11	North + Mid Wales	Baughan
12	South Wales	Barrie
13	Thames + Severn	Christiansen
14	The Lake Counties	Joy

(ii) Company Histories

1	GWR	1833–63	MacDermott
2	GWR	1863–1921	MacDermott
3	GWR	1923–47	Nock
	Southern Railway		Marshall
	Midland Railway North of Leeds		Baughan
	Londons Metropolitan Railway		Jackson

(iii) Historical Surveys

Forest of Dean Railways	Smith
Somerset + Dorset Railway	Judge + Potts
Lines to Torrington	Nicholas
Oxford – Cambridge Vols 1 + 2	Simpson
Chester – Holyhead Railway	Anderson + Fox
Great Western Stations Vols 1–3	Clark
Great Western Stations Vol 4	Potts
Southern Stations Vol 1	Pryer et al
LMS Stations Vols 1 + 2	Hendry + Hendry
Great Western Branch Line Termini	Karau
Didcot Newbury + Southampton Railway	Judge

(iv) Timetables

Bradshaw Reprints 1910, 1922, 1938	D+C	
GWR Service Timetable Appendices	1945	OPC
GWR Timetables	1947	OPC
GWR Appendix to Rule Book	1936	GWR
GWR Working Timetables – various		GWR
Somerset + Dorset Working Time Book 1920 + 31		OPC
London + North Western Timetables 1921		OPC
BR Passenger	1985–6	British Rail

(v) Engine Sheds (Historical Surveys)

GW	1947		Lyons
GW	1837–47		Lyons et al
LMS	Vol 1	LNWR	Hawkins + Reeve
LMS	Vol 2	Midland	Hawkins + Reeve
LMS	Vol 3	L + Y	Hawkins + Reeve
LMS	Vol 4	Other English	Hawkins + Reeve
Southern Sheds			Hawkins + Reeve

(vi) Miscellaneous

Main Lines to the West	Rocksborough-Smith
Railway History of Lincoln	Ruddock + Pearson
A Pictorial Record of LNWR Signalling	Vaughan

and many others for minor points + checking.

INDEX OF STATIONS

As mentioned in the Preface, the index includes passenger stations only. The following points should be noted:
(1) Where a place has two or more closely adjoining stations, there will usually be only one entry in this index, under the place name.
(2) Where a station is shown on two or more maps at differing scales, the index will normally direct to the map at the "smallest" scale. The central London area is the main exception to this treatment.
(3) Only the map number is shown.
(4) Some unusual station names – where the station is known by its designation alone – are included, for example: CITADEL (Carlisle), TEMPLE MEADS (Bristol) and the London Main Line Termini.
Full details for each station will be found on the facing page gazetter for the map indicated together with a reference to an enlargement if any.

Some selective additional information is, however, sometimes included:
(1) Name changes are usually indexed under old and new names – unless the change consists only of dropping part of the title.
(2) Some stations consisting of two elements may be indexed under each element. Inclusion depends upon the relative importance of the second element.
(3) Stations opened post grouping but now closed are sometimes included. The index is, however, in the main restricted to stations which were either open as at the relevant map date, or still in use in 1984. Other inclusions must be regarded as selective.

ABB   ALT

Station	Page
ALTRINCHAM + BOWDEN	62
ALVA	22
ALVECHURCH	80
ALVERSTONE	141
ALVERTHORPE	50
ALVES	15
ALVESCOT	114
ALYTH	17
ALYTH JUNCTION	17
AMBERGATE	65
AMBERLEY	142
AMBLE	33
AMERSHAM	116
AMESBURY	139
AMISFIELD	29
AMLWCH	55
AMMANFORD	94
AMMANFORD COLLIERY HALT	94
AMOTHERBY	40
AMPLEFORTH	40
AMPRESS WORKS	139
AMPTHILL	119
ANCASTER	70
ANDERSTON CROSS	20A
ANDOVER JUNCTION	139
ANDOVERSFORD	114
ANDOVERSFORD + DOWDESWELL	114
ANDOVER TOWN	139
ANERLEY	131
ANFIELD	58
ANGEL	127
ANGEL ROAD	121
ANGERTON	33
ANGMERING	142
ANGMERING-ON-SEA	142
ANNADALE	5
ANNAGHMORE	3
ANNAN	30
ANNBANK	28
ANNESLEY	65
ANNFIELD PLAIN	33
ANNITSFORD	33
ANSDELL + FAIRHAVEN	42
ANSTON	65
ANSTRUTHER	25
ANTRIM	3
APPERLEY BRIDGE + RAWDON	46
APPIN	16
APPLEBY (Lincs)	53
APPLEBY (Westmorland)	37
APPLEDORE (Kent)	145
APPLEDORE (Devon)	134
APPLEFORD	116
APPLETON	60
APPLEY BRIDGE	42
APSLEY	119
ARBIRLOT	17
ARBROATH	17
ARCHWAY	126
ARDAGH	9
ARDARA ROAD	1
ARDDLEEN	76
ARDEE	7
ARDFERT	8
ARDGAY	13
ARDGLASS	3
ARDGODED	97
ARDINGLY	142
ARD LEIGH	132
ARDLER	17
ARDLEY	114
ARDLUI	16
ARDMAYLE	9
ARDMORE	2
ARDRAHAN	5
ARDROSSAN	18
ARDROSSAN SOUTH BEACH	18
ARDROSSAN PIER	18
ARDSLEY	50
ARDSOLLUS + QUIN	9
ARDWICK	62
ARENIG	56
ARGOED	97
ARGYLE STREET	20A
ARIGNA	5
ARISAIG	16
ARKHOLME	37
ARKLOW	11
ARKSEY	51
ARKWRIGHT STREET	65
ARKWRIGHT TOWN	67
ARLESLEY + SHEFFORD ROAD	119
ARLEY	80
ARLEY + FILLONGLEY	82
ARMADALE	12
ARMAGH	2
ARMAGH IRISH STREET HALT	2
ARMATHWAITE	35
ARMITAGE	80
ARMLEY (CANAL ROAD)	48
ARMLEY + WORTLEY	46
ARMOY	3
ARNAGE	15
ARNOS GROVE	121
ARNSIDE	35
ARPLEY	57
ARRAM	53
ARROCHAR + TARBET	18
ARSENAL	126
ARTHINGTON	46
ARTHOG	74
ARUNDEL	142
ARVA ROAD	6
ASCOT	116
ASCOTT-UNDER-WYCHWOOD	114
ASFORDBY	85
ASH	141
ASHBOURNE	62
ASHBURTON	148
ASHBURY + NORTH LEW	134
ASHBURY'S	63
ASHBY	82
ASHBY MAGNA	82
ASHCHURCH	110
ASHCOTT	136
ASHEY	141
ASHFORD (Derby)	62
ASHFORD (Kent)	146
ASHFORD (Middlesex)	121
ASH GREEN	141
ASHINGTON	33
ASHLEY	62
ASHLEY + WESTON	85
ASHLEY HILL	110
ASHPERTON	76
ASHTEAD	142
ASHTON (Devon)	135
ASHTON (Lancs)	62
ASHTON GATE PLATFORM	110
ASHTON-IN-MAKERFIELD	57
ASHTON-UNDER-HILL	110
ASHTOWN	7
ASH TOWN	146
ASHURST	145
ASH VALE	141
ASHWATER	134
ASHWELL	85
ASHWELL + MORDEN	119
ASHWELLTHORPE	89
ASKAM	35
ASKEATON	9
ASKERN	50
ASKRIGG	37
ASLOCKTON	70
ASPALL + THORNDON	89
ASPATRIA	35
ASPLEY GUISE HALT	116
ASPULL	42
ASTLEY	62
ASTON	80
ASTON BOTTERELL SIDING HALT	76
ASTON-BY-STONE	62
ASTON ROWANT	116
ASWARBY + SCREDINGTON	70
ATHBOY	6
ATHELNEY	136
ATHENRY	5
ATHERSTONE	82
ATHERTON	42
ATHLONE	5
ATHY	10
ATTADALE	14
ATTANAGH	10
ATTENBOROUGH	65
ATTERCLIFFE	65
ATTERCLIFFE ROAD	66
ATTLEBOROUGH	89
ATTYMON JUNCTION	5
AUCHENDINNY	25
AUCHENGRAY	22
AUCHENHEATH	22
AUCHENMADE	18
AUCHINCRUIVE	28
AUCHINDACHY	15
AUCHINLECK	29
AUCHMACOY	15
AUCHNAGATT	15
AUCHNASHELLACH	14
AUCHTERARDER	17
AUCHTERHOUSE	17
AUCHTERLESS	15
AUCHTERMUCHTY	17
AUDLEM	57
AUDLEY	62
AUDLEY END	132
AUGHACASLA	8
AUGHER	2
AUGHNACLOY	2
AUGHRIM	11
AUGHTON	42
AUGHTON PARK HALT	42
AULDBAR ROAD	17
AULDEARN	15
AULDGIRTH	29
AULTMORE	15
AUNASCAUL	8
AUTHORPE	72
AVIEMORE	14
AVOCA	11
AVOCH	14
AVONBRIDGE	22
AVONCLIFF HALT	110
AVONMOUTH DOCK	110
AVONMOUTH ST. ANDREWS ROAD	110
AVONWICK	148
AWRE	110
AWSWORTH	65
AXBRIDGE	136
AXMINSTER	136
AYCLIFFE	38
AYLESBURY	116
AYLESFORD	145
AYLESHAM	146
AYLSHAM	73
AYNHO	114
AYNHO PARK PLATFORM	116
AYOT	119
AYR	28
AYSGARTH	38
AYTON	27
BACHE	57
BACKWORTH	33
BACTON	92
BACUP	46
BADMINTON	110
BADSEY	80
BAGENALSTOWN	10
BAGGROW	35
BAGILLT	57
BAGSHOT	116
BAGULEY	62
BAGWORTHY + ELLISTOWN	82
BAILDON	46
BAILEY GATE	137
BAILIFF BRIDGE	46
BAILLIESTON	18
BAINTON	53
BAKER STREET	125
BAKEWELL	65
BALA	56
BALADO	22
BALBRIGGAN	7
BALCOMBE	142
BALDERSBY	38
BALDERTON	57
BALDOCK	119
BALDOVAN	17
BALDOYLE + SUTTON	7
BALDRAGON	17
BALERNO	22
BALFRON	18
BALGOWAN	17
BALHAM + UPPER TOOTING	129
BALLA	4
BALLABEG	41

BALLACHULISH + GLENCOE	16	BALLYMONEY	3	BARDON MILL	32	BASIN	8
BALLACHULISH FERRY	16	BALLYMOTE	1	BARDOWIE	18	BASINGSTOKE	141
BALLAGHADERREEN	5	BALLYMURRY	5	BARDSEY	50	BASON BRIDGE	136
BALLASALLA	41	BALLYNAHINCH (Down)	3	BARE LANE	42	BASSALEG	100
BALLATER	15	BALLYNAHINCH (Galway)	4	BARGEDDIE	18	BASSENTHWAITE LAKE	35
BALLAUGH	41	BALLYNAHINCH JUNCTION	3	BARGOED JUNCTION	97	BAT + BALL	145
BALLINA	4	BALLYNASHEE	3	BARHAM	146	BATH	110
BALLINAMALLARD	2	BALLYNEEN + ENNISKEAN	12	BARKING	121	BATH ROAD HALT	124
BALLINAMORE (Donegal)	1	BALLYNOE	3	BARKINGSIDE	121	BATHAMPTON	110
BALLINAMORE (Leitrim)	6	BALLYNURE	3	BARKSTON	70	BATHGATE	22
BALLINASCARTHY	12	BALLYRAGGET	10	BARLASTON	62	BATLEY	46
BALLINASLOE	5	BALLYROBERT HALT	3	BARLOW	50	BATLEY CARR	49
BALLINASTEENING	8	BALLYRONEY	3	BARMBY	50	BATTERSBY	40
BALLINCOLLIG	12	BALLYSHANNON	1	BARMING	145	BATTERSEA	129
BALLINDALLOCH	15	BALLYSODARE	1	BARMOUTH	74	BATTERSEA PARK	129
BALLINDANGAN	9	BALLYVARY	4	BARMOUTH JUNCTION	74	BATTERSEA PARK ROAD	129
BALLINDERRY	3	BALLYWARD	3	BARNACK	85	BATTERSTOWN	7
BALLINDIKE	5	BALLYWILLAN	6	BARNAGH	8	BATTLE	145
BALLINDRAIT	2	BALLYWILLIAM	10	BARNARD CASTLE	38	BATTLESBRIDGE	132
BALLINGHAM	110	BALMORAL	3	BARNBY DUN	50	BATTYEFORD	46
BALLINGLEN	11	BALMORE	18	BARNBY MOOR + SUTTON	65	BAWNBOY ROAD + TEMPLEPORT	6
BALLINGRANE	9	BALMOSSIE	17	BARNES	122	BAWDRIP HALT	136
BALLINHASSIG	12	BALNACOUL	15	BARNES BRIDGE	122	BAWTRY	65
BALLINLOUGH	5	BALNE	50	BARNESMOOR HALT	1	BAXENDEN	42
BALLINLUIG	17	BALQUHIDDER	16	BARNETBY	53	BAYFORD	119
BALLINOSARE	8	BALSHAW LANE + EUXTON	42	BARNHAM	89	BAY HORSE	42
BALLINROBE	4	BALTIMORE	12	BARNHAM JUNCTION	141	BAYNARDS	142
BALLINTOGHER	1	BALTINGLASS	10	BARNHILL (Forfar)	17	BAYSIDE	7
BALLINTRA	1	BAMBER BRIDGE	42	BARNHILL (Lanark)	18	BAYSWATER	125
BALLOCH	18	BAMFORD	65	BARNOLDSWICK	46	BEACONSFIELD	116
BALLOCH PIER	18	BAMFURLONG	42	BARNSLEY	50	BEAL	27
BALLYARDS	2	BAMPTON (Devon)	135	BARNSTAPLE	135	BEALINGS	90
BALLYBAY	2	BAMPTON (Oxon)	184	BARNSTAPLE JUNCTION	135	BEAMISH	33
BALLYBEG	6	BANAGHER	5	BARNSTAPLE TOWN	135	BEANACRE HALT	110
BALLYBOFEY	2	BANAVIE	16	BARNSTONE	70	BEARLEY	80
BALLYBOLEY	3	BANAVIE PIER	16	BARNT GREEN	80	BEARSDEN	18
BALLYBRACK	8	BANBRIDGE	3	BARNTON FOR CRAMOND BRIG	22	BEARSTEAD + THURNHAM	145
BALLYBROPHY	10	BANBURY	82	BARNTON GATE	26	BEASDALE	16
BALLYBUNION	8	BANCHORY	15	BARNWELL (Cambs)	87	BEATTOCK	30
BALLYCAR NEWMARKET	9	BANDON	12	BARNWELL (Northants)	85	BEAUCHIEF	65
BALLYCARRY	3	BANFF BRIDGE	15	BARONS COURT	125	BEAUFORT	97
BALLYCASTLE	3	BANFF HARBOUR	15	BARRAS	37	BEAULIEU ROAD	139
BALLYCLARE	3	BANGOR (Caern)	55	BARRASFORD	32	BEAULY	14
BALLYCLARE JUNCTION	3	BANGOR (Down)	3	BARRHEAD	18	BEAUPARC	7
BALLYCLOUGHAN	3	BANGOR-ON-DEE	57	BARRHILL	28	BEBINGTON + NEW FERRY	57
BALLYCONNELL	6	BANGOR WEST	3	BARRMILL	18	BEBSIDE	33
BALLYCULANE	10	BANGOUR	22	BARROW (Cheshire)	57	BECCLES	90
BALLYCUMBER	6	BANK	127	BARROWDEN (See Wakerley)	85	BECKENHAM HILL	130
BALLYDEHOB	12	BANKFOOT	17	BARROWHAVEN	53	BECKENHAM JUNCTION	130
BALLYDOUGHERTY HALT	3	BANK HALL	58	BARROW HILL + STAVELEY WORKS	65	BECKERMET	35
BALLYDUFF (Leitrim)	5	BANKHEAD (Aberdeen)	15	BARROW-IN-FURNESS	35	BECKFOOT	35
BALLYDUFF (Waterford)	9	BANKHEAD (Lanark)	22	BARROW-ON-SOAR + QUORN	82	BECKFORD	110
BALLYGARVEY	3	BANKNOCK	22	BARRY	100	BECKINGHAM	70
BALLYGAWLEY	2	BANKS	42	BARRY DOCKS	100	BECKTIVE	6
BALLYGLUNIN	5	BANNOCKBURN	22	BARRY ISLAND	100	BECKTON	121
BALLYGOWAN	3	BANSHA	9	BARRY LINKS	17	BECONTREE	121
BALLYHAISE	6	BANSTEAD	122	BARTLOW	87	BEDALE	38
BALLYHALE	10	BANTEER	9	BARTON (Lancs)	42	BEDDAU HALT (Caerphilly)	100
BALLYHAUNIS	5	BANTRY	12	BARTON (Lincs)	53	BEDDAU HALT (Llantwit)	100
BALLYHEADY	6	BAPTIST END HALT	80	BARTON + BROUGHTON	42	BEDDGELERT	55
BALLYHOOLY	9	BARASSIE	18	BARTON + WALTON	89	BEDDINGTON LANE HALT	123
BALLYKELLY	2	BARBER'S BRIDGE	110	BARTON HILL	50	BEDFORD	85
BALLYLIFFIN	2	BARBICAN	127	BARTON-LE-STREET	40	BEDHAMPTON HALT	141
BALLYMAGAN	2	BARBON	37	BARTON MOSS	62	BEDLINGTON	33
BALLYMAGORRY	2	BARCOMBE	142	BASCHURCH	57	BEDLINOG	96
BALLYMARTLE	12	BARCOMBE MILLS	142	BASFORD	65	BEDMINSTER	110
BALLYMENA	3	BARDNEY	70	BASFORD + BULWELL	68	BEDWAS	100
BALLYMOE	5	BARDON HILL	82	BASILDON	132	BEDWELLTY PITS	97

Station	Pg	Station	Pg	Station	Pg	Station	Pg
BEDWORTH	82	BERWICK (Sussex)	145	BIRMINGHAM	80	BLAEN GWYNFY	95
BEDWYN	114	BERW ROAD PLATFORM	96	BIRMINGHAM AIRPORT	80	BLAENPLWYE HALT	74
BEECHBURN	38	BERWYN	57	BIRMINGHAM INTERNATIONAL	80	BLAENRHONDDA	96
BEECHES, CARSHALTON	123	BESCAR LANE	42	BIRNAM	17	BLAGDON	136
BEESTON (Notts)	65	BESCOT	80	BIRNIE ROAD SIDING	17	BLAINA	97
BEESTON (Yorks)	46	BESSACARR HALT	50	BIRR	5	BLAIRADAM	22
BEESTON CASTLE + TARPORLEY	57	BESSBROOK	3	BIRSTALL (Leics)	82	BLAIR ATHOLL	16
BEESTON TOR	62	BESSES·O'·TH'·BARN	46	BIRSTALL (Yorks)	49	BLAIRGOWRIE	17
BEIGHTON	65	BESTWOOD COLLIERY	65	BIRSTWITH	46	BLAIRHILL + GARTSHERRIE	24
BEITH	18	BETCHWORTH	142	BIRTLEY	33	BLAKEDOWN	80
BEKAN	5	BETHESDA	55	BISHOP AUCKLAND	38	BLAKE HALL	132
BEKESBOURNE	146	BETHNAL GREEN	127	BISHOPBRIGGS	18	BLAKESLEY	82
BELCOO	1	BETLEY ROAD	62	BISHOPSBOURNE	146	BLAKE STREET	80
BELFAST	3	BETTISFIELD	57	BISHOP'S CASTLE	76	BLANCHARDSTOWN	7
BELFORD	27	BETTWS	99	BISHOP'S CLEEVE	110	BLANDFORD FORUM	137
BELGRAVE + BIRSTALL	82	BETTWS GARMON	55	BISHOPSGATE	127	BLANEFIELD	18
BELLAHOUSTON	19	BETTWS·Y·COED	56	BISHOP'S LYDEARD	136	BLANKNEY + METHERINGHAM	80
BELLARENA	2	BEVERLEY	53	BISHOP'S NYMPTON +		BLANTYRE	18
BELL BUSK	46	BEVERLEY ROAD	53	MOLLAND	135	BLARNEY	12
BELLEEK	1	BEWDLEY	80	BISHOP'S ROAD	124	BLAYDON	33
BELLE VUE	63	BEXHILL-ON-SEA CENTRAL	145	BISHOP'S STORTFORD	119	BLEADON + UPHILL	136
BELL GREEN	82	BEXHILL WEST	145	BISHOPSTOKE	139	BLEAN + TYLER HILL HALT	146
BELLGROVE	19	BEXLEY	123	BISHOPSTONE	142	BLEASBY	70
BELLINGHAM (Kent)	130	BEXLEY HEATH	123	BISHOP'S WALTHAM	141	BLEDLOW	116
BELLINGHAM (Northumberland)	32	BICESTER	116	BISHOPTON	18	BLEDLOW BRIDGE HALT	116
BELLSHILL	22	BICKERSHAW + ABRAM	42	BISPHAM	42	BLENCOW	35
BELLURGAN	7	BICKLEIGH	148	BITTAFORD PLATFORM	148	BLENHEIM + WOODSTOCK	114
BELMONT (Middlesex)	120	BICKLEY	123	BITTERNE	139	BLENNERVILLE	8
BELMONT (Surrey)	123	BIDDENDEN	145	BITTON	110	BLESSINGTON	7
BELMONT + CLOGHAN	6	BIDDULPH	62	BLABY	82	BLETCHINGTON	114
BELPER	65	BIDEFORD	134	BLACK BANK	87	BLETCHLEY	116
BELSES	32	BIDFORD·ON·AVON	80	BLACK BULL	62	BLIDWORTH	65
BELSIZE PARK	125	BIDSTON	57	BLACKBURN	42	BLISWORTH	85
BELTON (Lincs)	50	BIELSIDE	15	BLACKDYKE	30	BLOCKLEY	114
BELTON (Suff)	90	BIGGAR	22	BLACKFORD	22	BLODWELL JUNCTION	57
BELTRING	145	BIGGLESWADE	85	BLACKFORD HILL	26	BLOOMFIELD	3
BELTURBET	6	BILBROOK	80	BLACKFRIARS	127	BLOWICK	43
BEMBRIDGE	141	BILBSTER	13	BLACKHALL ROCKS	38	BLOXHAM	114
BEMPTON	40	BILLACOMBE	148	BLACKHEATH	123	BLOXWICH	80
BENDERLOCH	16	BILLERICAY	132	BLACKHEATH HILL	130	BLUE ANCHOR	136
BENFLEET	132	BILLING	85	BLACKHILL	33	BLUNDELLSANDS + CROSBY	57
BENGEWORTH	80	BILLINGBOROUGH +		BLACK HORSE ROAD	121	BLUNHAM	85
BENINGBROUGH	50	HORBLING	70	BLACK LANE	42	BLUNSDON	114
BENLLECH	55	BILLINGHAM	38	BLACK LION CROSSING		BLUNTISHAM	87
BENNETTSBRIDGE	10	BILLINGSHURST	142	HALT	96	BLYTH	33
BEN RHYDDING	46	BILSON HALT	110	BLACKMILL	99	BLYTHBURGH	90
BENSHAM	33	BILSTON	80	BLACKMOOR	135	BLYTHE BRIDGE	62
BENTHAM	42	BINEGAR	137	BLACKPILL	94	BLYTON	70
BENTLEY (Hants)	141	BINGHAM	70	BLACKPOOL	42	BOARHILLS	17
BENTLEY (Suff)	133	BINGHAM ROAD	65	BLACKROCK (Cork)	12	BOAR'S HEAD	42
BENTON	33	BINGHAM ROAD HALT	123	BLACKROCK (Dublin)	7	BOAT OF GARTEN	15
BENTON SQUARE	33	BINGLEY	46	BLACKROCK HALT	55	BODDAM	15
BENTS	22	BINTON	80	BLACKROD	42	BODFARI	56
BENTWORTH + LASHAM	141	BIRCHFIELD PLATFORM	15	BLACKSBOAT	15	BODIHAM	145
BERAGH	2	BIRCHGROVE	100	BLACKSTON(E)	22	BODMIN	148
BERE ALSTON	148	BIRCHILLS	80	BLACKTHORN	116	BODMIN ROAD *	148
BERE FERRERS	148	BIRCHINGTON·ON·SEA	146	BLACKWALL	128	BODMIN PARKWAY *	148
BERKELEY	110	BIRCH VALE	62	BLACKWATER I.O.W	141	BODORGAN	55
BERKELEY ROAD	110	BIRCHWOOD	57	BLACKWATER + CAMBERLEY *	116	BOGNOR REGIS	141
BERKHAMPSTEAD	116	BIRDBROOK	89	BLACKWATER + YORK TOWN *	116	BOGSIDE (Ayr)	18
BERKSWELL	82	BIRDHILL	9	BLACKWEIR	8	BOGSIDE (Fife)	22
BERNEY ARMS	90	BIRDINGBURY	82	BLACKWELL	80	BOGSTON	18
BERRINGTON	76	BIRDWELL + HOYLAND		BLACKWOOD (Lanark)	22	BOHER	9
BERRINGTON + EYE	76	COMMON	50	BLACKWOOD (Mon)	97	BOLLINGTON	62
BERRY BROW	46	BIRKDALE	42	BLACON	57	BOLSOVER	65
BERRYLANDS	122	BIRKDALE PALACE	42	BLAENAU FESTINIOG	55	BOLTON	42
BERVIE	17	BIRKENHEAD	57	BLAENAVON	97	BOLTON ABBEY	46
BERWICK (Northumberland)	27	BIRKENSHAW + TONG	46	BLAENGARW	95	BOLTON-LE-SANDS	42

* Same station - different names at different periods

Station	Page	Station	Page	Station	Page	Station	Page
BOLTON·ON·DEARNE	50	BOXMOOR + HEMEL HEMPSTEAD	119	BRETTELL LANE	80	BROCK	42
BOLTON PERCY	50	BOYCE'S BRIDGE	87	BRICKET WOOD	119	BROCKENHURST	139
BONAR BRIDGE	13	BOYLE	5	BRIDESTOWE	135	BROCKETSBRAE	22
BONCATH	74	BRACEBOROUGH SPA	85	BRIDGE	146	BROCKFORD + WETHERINGSETT	89
BOND STREET	125	BRACKENHILLS	18	BRIDGE END	2	BROCKHOLES	46
BO'NESS	22	BRACKLEY	116	BRIDGEFOOT	35	BROCKLEBANK DOCK	58
BONNINGTON	26	BRACKNELL	116	BRIDGEND	99	BROCKLESBY	53
BONNYBRIDGE	22	BRADBURY	38	BRIDGE OF ALLAN	22	BROCKLEY	130
BONNYRIGG	25	BRADFIELD	133	BRIDGE OF DEE	29	BROCKLEY LANE	130
BONT NEWYDD	56	BRADFORD	46	BRIDGE OF DUN	17	BROCKLEY WHINS	33
BOOKHAM	142	BRADFORD·ON·AVON	110	BRIDGE OF EARN	17	BROCTON	62
BOOSBECK	40	BRADING JUNCTION	141	BRIDGE OF ORCHY	16	BRODIE	15
BOOT	35	BRADLEY	46	BRIDGE OF WEIR	18	BROIGHTER	2
BOOTERSTOWN	7	BRADLEY + MOXLEY	81	BRIDGETON CROSS	19	BROMBOROUGH	57
BOOTHFERRY PARK	54	BRADLEY FOLD	42	BRIDGETOWN (Donegal)	1	BROMFIELD (Cumb)	35
BOOTLE (Cumberland)	35	BRADNOP	62	BRIDGETOWN (Wexford)	11	BROMFIELD (Salop)	76
BOOTLE (Lancs)	57	BRADWELL	85	BRIDGNORTH	80	BROMFORD BRIDGE	80
BORDESLEY	80	BRAFFERTON	50	BRIDGWATER	136	BROMFORD LANE (See Oldbury)	81
BORDON	141	BRAIDWOOD	22	BRIDLINGTON	53	BROMHAM + ROWDE HALT	110
BOROUGH	127	BRAINTREE + BOCKING	132	BRIDPORT	136	BROMLEY + BROCKMORE HALT	80
BOROUGHBRIDGE	50	BRAITHWAITE	35	BRIERFIELD	46	BROMLEY·BY·BOW	128
BOROUGH GREEN + WROTHAM	145	BRAMBER	142	BRIERLEY HILL	80	BROMLEY CROSS	42
BORRIS	10	BRAMHALL	62	BRIGG	53	BROMLEY NORTH	123
BORROBOL PLATFORM	13	BRAMLEY (Hants)	141	BRIGHAM	35	BROMLEY SOUTH	123
BORROWASH	65	BRAMLEY (Yorks)	46	BRIGHOUSE	46	BROMPTON	38
BORTH	74	BRAMLEY + WONERSH	142	BRIGHTLINGSEA	133	BROMPTON ROAD	124
BORWICK	37	BRAMPFORD SPEKE	135	BRIGHTON	142	BROMSGROVE	80
BOSCOMBE	139	BRAMPTON (Suff)	90	BRIGHTON ROAD	80	BROMYARD	76
BOSHAM	141	BRAMPTON JUNCTION	32	BRIGHTSIDE	65	BRONDESBURY	125
BOSLEY	62	BRAMPTON TOWN	32	BRILL	116	BRONDESBURY PARK	125
BOSTON	72	BRANCEPETH	38	BRILL + LUDGERSHALL	116	BRONWYDD ARMS	92
BOSTON LODGE	55	BRANCHTON	18	BRIMLEY	148	BROOKEBOROUGH	2
BOSTON MANOR	122	BRANDON	89	BRIMSCOMBE	110	BROOKLAND	145
BOTANIC GARDENS (Glasgow)	19	BRANDON + WOLSTON	82	BRIMSCOMBE BRIDGE HALT	110	BROOKLANDS	62
BOTANIC GARDENS (Yorks)	53	BRANDON COLLIERY	38	BRIMSDOWN	121	BROOKMAN'S PARK	119
BOTHWELL	18	BRANKSOME	139	BRINKBURN	33	BROOKMOUNT	3
BOTLEY	141	BRANSFORD ROAD	80	BRINKLOW	82	BROOKSBY	82
BOTTESFORD	70	BRANSTON	65	BRINKWORTH	114	BROOKWOOD	141
BOTTISHAM + LODE	87	BRANSTON + HEIGHINGTON	70	BRINNINGTON	63	BROOME	76
BOUGHROOD + LLYSWEN	92	BRANTHWAITE	35	BRINSCALL	42	BROOMFLEET	53
BOUGHTON	65	BRASTED	142	BRISLINGTON	110	BROOMHILL (Inv)	15
BOUNDS GREEN	121	BRATTON FLEMING	135	BRISTOL	110	BROOMHILL (Nhumberland)	33
BOURNE	85	BRAUGHING	119	BRISTOL PARKWAY	110	BROOMHOUSE	18
BOURNE END	116	BRAUNSTON	82	BRISTOL ROAD	101	BROOMIEKNOWE	25
BOURNEMOUTH	139	BRAUNSTON + WILLOUGHBY	82	BRITANNIA	46	BROOMIELAW	38
BOURNEVILLE	80	BRAUNTON	134	BRITANNIA HALT	148	BROOM JUNCTION	80
BOURTON·ON·THE·WATER	114	BRAY	7	BRITHDIR	97	BROOMLEE	22
BOVEY	148	BRAYSTONES	35	BRITISH MUSEUM	127	BRORA	13
BOW	135	BRAYTON	35	BRITISH STEEL REDCAR	40	BROTTON	40
BOW BRICKHILL HALT	116	BREADSALL	65	BRITON FERRY	95	BROUGH	53
BOW BRIDGE CROSSING HALT	110	BREAMORE	139	BRITON FERRY ROAD	95	BROUGHTON (Peebles)	22
BOWDON	62	BRECHIN	17	BRITTAS	7	BROUGHTON + BRETTON	57
BOWER	13	BRECK ROAD	58	BRIXHAM	148	BROUGHTON ASTLEY	82
BOWES	38	BRECON	92	BRIXTON	130	BROUGHTON CROSS	36
BOWES PARK	121	BRECON ROAD	97	BRIXTON ROAD	148	BROUGHTON·IN·FURNESS	35
BOWHOUSE	22	BREDBURY	62	BRIXWORTH	85	BROUGHTON LANE	66
BOWKER VALE	46	BREDON	110	BROADBOTTOM	62	BROUGHTY FERRY	17
BOWLAND	25	BREICH	22	BROAD CLYST	135	BROWNDON	141
BOWLING	18	BRENT	148	BROADFIELD	46	BROWNHILLS	80
BOWLING JUNCTION	46	BRENT CROSS	120	BROAD GREEN	57	BROXBOURNE	119
BOWNESS	30	BRENTFORD	122	BROADHEATH	62	BROXTON	57
BOW ROAD	127	BRENTHAM	120	BROADLEY	46	BRUCE GROVE	121
BOW STREET	74	BRENT KNOLL	136	BROADSTAIRS	133	BRUCKLAY	15
BOX	110	BRENTOR	134	BROADSTONE (Dublin)	7	BRUCKLESS	1
BOXFORD	114	BRENTWOOD + WARLEY	132	BROADSTONE (Som)	101	BRUNDALL	90
BOX HILL	142	BRETFORTON + WESTON·SUB·EDGE	80	BROADSTONE JUNCTION	139	BRUNDALL GARDENS	90
BOX HILL + BURFORD BRIDGE	142			BROAD STREET	127	BRUNSWICK DOCK	58
				BROADWAY	114	BRUREE	9

Name	Pg	Name	Pg	Name	Pg	Name	Pg
BRUTON	137	BURNHAM BEECHES	116	CAHIR	9	CAPEL	89
BRYMBO	59	BURNHAM MARKET	73	CAHIRCIVEEN	8	CAPEL BANGOR	74
BRYN (Glam)	95	BURNHAM-ON-SEA	136	CAIRNBULG	15	CAPENHURST	57
BRYN (Lancs)	42	BURNHAM-ON-CROUCH	132	CAIRNEYHILL	22	CAPE PLATFORM	95
BRYNAMMAN	95	BURNHILL	38	CAIRNIE JUNCTION	15	CAPPAGH	10
BRYNGLAS	74	BURNLEY	46	CAISTER-ON-SEA	90	CAPPOQUIN	10
BRYNGWYN (Caern)	55	BURNMARSH ROAD HALT	146	CALBOURNE + SHALFLEET	139	CARAGH LAKE	8
BRYNGWYN (Mon)	75	BURNMOUTH	27	CALCOTS	15	CARBIS BAY	147
BRYNKIR	55	BURNTISLAND	25	CALDARVAN	18	CARBURY	6
BRYNMAWR	97	BURNT MILL (Cork)	12	CALDER	22	CARCROFT + ADWICK-LE-	
BRYNMENYN	99	BURNT MILL (Herts)	119	CALDERBANK	22	·STREET	50
BRYNMILL	94	BURNT OAK	120	CALDERCRUIX	22	CARDENDEN	25
BRYN TEIFY	74	BURRATOR HALT	148	CALDICOT	101	CARDIFF	100
BUBWITH	50	BURRINGTON	101	CALDWELL	18	CARDIFF DOCKS	100
BUCHLYVIE	18	BURRY PORT	93	CALDY	57	CARDIGAN	74
BUCKDEN	87	BURSCOUGH BRIDGE	42	CALEDON	2	CARDINGTON	85
BUCKENHAM	90	BURSCOUGH JUNCTION	42	CALEDONIAN ROAD	126	CARDONALD	19
BUCKFASTLEIGH	148	BURSELDON	139	CALEDONIAN ROAD +		CARDONNEL HALT	95
BUCKHAVEN	25	BURSLEM	62	BARNSBURY	126	CARDRONA	25
BUCKHURST HILL	121	BURTON (-ON-TRENT)	65	CALLANDER	18	CARDROSS	18
BUCKIE	15	BURTON + HOLME	37	CALLERTON	33	CARESTON	17
BUCKINGHAM	116	BURTON AGNES	53	CALLINGTON	148	CARFIN	22
BUCKLEY	57	BURTON CONSTABLE	53	CALLOWLAND	120	CARGAN	3
BUCKLEY JUNCTION	57	BURTON JOYCE	65	CALNE	110	CARGILL	17
BUCKNALL + NORTHWOOD	62	BURTON POINT	57	CALSTOCK	148	CARGO FLEET	40
BUCKNELL	76	BURTONPORT	1	CALTHWAITE	35	CARHAM	27
BUCKPOOL	15	BURTON SALMON	50	CALVELEY	57	CARISBROOKE HALT	139
BUCKSBURN	15	BURWARTON	76	CALVERLEY + RODLEY	46	CARK + CARTMEL	35
BUDDON	17	BURWELL	87	CALVERT	116	CARLINGFORD	7
BUDE	134	BURY	42	CAM	110	CARLINGHOW	49
BUDLEIGH SALTERTON	136	BURY ST EDMUNDS	89	CAMBERLEY + YORK TOWN	116	CARLISLE	30
BUGLE	148	BUSBY	18	CAMBERWELL	130	CARLOW	10
BUGSWORTH	62	BUSH	7	CAMBORNE	147	CARLTON (Durham)	38
BUILDWAS	76	BUSHEY + OXHEY	120	CAMBRIDGE	87	CARLTON (Yorks)	50
BUILTH ROAD	75	BUSHEY HILL PARK	121	CAMBRIDGE HEATH	127	CARLTON + NETHERFIELD	65
BUILTH WELLS	75	BUSHMILLS	3	CAMBUS	22	CARLTON COLVILLE	90
BULFORD	139	BUTLER'S HILL	65	CAMBUSAVIE PLATFORM	13	CARLTON-ON-TRENT	70
BULKINGTON	82	BUTLERS LANE	80	CAMBUSLANG	18	CARLUKE	22
BULLERS O' BUCHAN HALT	15	BUTTERLEY	65	CAMBUS NETHAM	24	CARMARTHEN	92
BULLGILL	35	BUTTERTON	62	CAMBUS O' MAY	15	CARMARTHEN JUNCTION	92
BULLO CROSS HALT	110	BUTTEVANT	9	CAMDEN TOWN	125	CARMYLE	18
BULWELL	65	BUTTINGTON	76	CAMELFORD	134	CARMYLLIE	17
BULWELL COMMON	68	BUTTS LANE HALT	43	CAMELON	18	CARNABY	53
BULWELL FOREST	65	BUXTED	145	CAMEL'S HEAD HALT	149	CARNAGH	2
BUNCHREW	14	BUXTON	62	CAMERON BRIDGE	25	CARNALEA	3
BUNCRANA	2	BUXTON LAMAS	73	CAMERTON (Cumb.)	35	CARNARVON (CAERNARVON)	55
BUNDORAN	1	BYERS GREEN	38	CAMERTON (Som)	137	CARN BREA	147
BUNDORAN JUNCTION	2	BYFIELD	82	CAMOLIN	11	CARNDONAGH	2
BUNGALOW TOWN HALT	142	BYFLEET	122	CAMPBELL'S PLATFORM	55	CARNFORTH	42
BUNGAY	90	BYKER	34	CAMPBELTOWN	28	CARNO	75
BUNTINGFORD	119	BYNEA	94	CAMPDEN	80	CARNOUSTIE	17
BURDALE	53			CAMP HILL	81	CARNTYNE	18
BURDETT ROAD	127			CAMPILE	10	CARNWATH	22
BURES	132			CAMPSIE GLEN	18	CARPENDERS PARK	120
BURFORD BRIDGE	142			CANADA DOCK	58	CARR BRIDGE	14
BURGESS HILL	142			CANE HILL (See Coulsden)	123	CARRICHUE	2
BURGH (Cumb)	30	CADBURY ROAD	101	CANLEY	82	CARRICKFERGUS	3
BURGH (Lincs)	72	CADELEIGH	135	CANNING TOWN	128	CARRICKMACROSS	6
BURGHCLERE	139	CADISHEAD	62	CANNOCK	80	CARRICKMINES	7
BURGHEAD	15	CADOXTON	100	CANNON STREET	127	CARRICKMORE	2
BURLESCOMBE	136	CAERAU	95	CANONBIE	30	CARRICK-ON-SHANNON	5
BURLEY-IN-WHARFEDALE	46	CAERGWRLE CASTLE + WELLS	57	CANONBURY	126	CARRICK-ON-SUIR	9
BURN (HALT)	135	CAERLEON	98	CANONS PARK	120	CARRIGALINE	12
BURNAGE	62	CAERNARVON	55	CANTERBURY EAST	146	CARRIGALOE	12
BURNBANK	18	CAERPHILLY	100	CANTERBURY SOUTH	146	CARRIGANS	2
BURNESIDE	37	CAERSWS	75	CANTERBURY WEST	146	CARRIGROHANE	12
BURNFOOT	2	CAERWYS	56	CANTLEY	90	CARRIGTWOHILL	12
BURNGULLOW	147	CAFFIN HALT	130	CAPE CASTLE	3	CARRINGTON	68

✱ Same station - alternative spellings

CREAGHANROE	2	CROWLE	50	CWM	97	DARESBURY	57
CREDENHILL	76	CROW PARK	70	CWMAMAN COLLIERY HALT	96	DARFIELD	50
CREDITON	135	CROW ROAD	20A	CWMAMAN CROSSING HALT	96	DARLASTON	81
CREESLOUGH	1	CROWTHORNE	116	CWMAVON (Glam)	95	DARLEY	46
CREETOWN	28	CROXALL	80	CWMAVON (Mon)	97	DARLEY DALE	65
CREEVY HALT	1	CROXDALE	38	CWM BARGOED	96	DARLINGTON	38
CREIGIAU	100	CROXLEY	120	CWMBRAN	97	DARNALL	65
CRESSAGE	76	CROXLEY GREEN	120	CWMCARN	97	DARRAN + DERI	97
CRESSING	132	CROY	22	CWM CYMMER	95	DARRAS HALL	33
CRESSINGTON + GRASSENDALE	57	CROYDON + ADDISCOMBE ROAD		CWMDU	95	DARSHAM	90
CRESSWELL	62	(See Addiscombe)	123	CWMLLYNFELL	95	DARTFORD	132
CRESWELL + WELBECK	65	CROYDON EAST	123	CWMMAWR	94	DARTON	50
CREW	2	CROYDON SOUTH	123	CWMNEOL HALT	96	DARVEL	18
CREWE	57	CROYDON WEST	123	CWM PRYSOR	56	DARWEN	42
CREW GREEN	76	CRUCKTON	76	CWMSYFIOG	97	DATCHET	110
CREWKERNE	136	CRUDEN BAY	15	CWM-Y-GLO	50	DAUNTSEY	110
CREWS HILL	119	CRUDGINGTON	76	CYFRONYDD	75	DAVA	15
CRIANLARICH	16	CRUMLIN (Antrim)	3	CYMMER	95	DAVENPORT	62
CRICCIETH	55	CRUMLIN (Mon)	97	CYNGHORDY	75	DAVENTRY	82
CRICKLADE	114	CRUMPSALL	46	CYNONVILLE HALT	95	DAVIOT	14
CRICKLEWOOD	120	CRUSHEEN	9	CYNWYD	56	DAWLISH	148
CRIEFF	16	CRYMMYCH ARMS	74			DAWLISH WARREN	148
CRIEFF JUNCTION	17	CRYNANT	95			DAYBROOK	65
CRIGGION	76	CRYSTAL PALACE	130			DDUALLT	55
CRIGGLESTONE	50	CRYSTAL PALACE + UPPER				DEADWATER	32
CROFT	82	NORWOOD	130			DEAL	146
CROFTFOOT	19	CUDDINGTON	57	DACRE	46	DEAN	139
CROFTON	50	CUDWORTH	50	DAGENHAM	121	DEAN LANE - NEWTON HEATH	46
CROLLY	1	CUFFLEY + GOFF'S OAK	119	DAGENHAM DOCK	121	DEARHAM	35
CROMARTY	14	CULBOKIE	14	DAGENHAM EAST	132	DEARHAM BRIDGE	35
CROMDALE	15	CULCHETH	57	DAGGONS ROAD	139	DEBDEN	121
CROMER	73	CULGAITH	37	DAILLY	28	DEELLS	8
CROMFORD	65	CULHAM	116	DAIRSIE	17	DEEPCAR	65
CROMPTON (See Shaw)	46	CULKERTON	110	DAISY BANK	81	DEEPDALE	42
CRONBERRY	29	CULLEEN	15	DAISY FIELD	42	DEEPDENE	142
CROOK	38	CULLERCOATS	33	DAISY HILL	42	DEEPFIELDS + COSELEY	80
CROOK-OF-DEVON	22	CULLINGWORTH	46	DALBEATTIE	29	DEEPING ST JAMES	85
CROOKSTOWN	19	CULLION	2	DALCROSS	14	DEFFORD	80
CROOKSTOWN ROAD	12	CULLODEN MOOR	14	DALEGARTH	35	DEFIANCE PLATFORM	148
CROOM	9	CULLOMPTON	136	DALGUISE	17	DEGANWY	56
CROPREDY	82	CULLOVILLE	6	DALHOUSIE	25	DEIGHTON	46
CROSBY	41	CULLYBACKEY	3	DALKEITH	25	DELABOLE	134
CROSBY GARRETT	37	CULMORE	2	DALKEY	7	DELAMERE	57
CROSSDONEY	6	CULMSTOCK	136	DALMALLY	16	DELNY	13
CROSSENS	42	CULRAIN	13	DALMARNOCK	20A	DELPH	46
CROSSFLATTS	46	CULROSS	22	DALMELLINGTON	28	DENABY HALT	50
CROSSFORD	29	CULTER	15	DALMENY	22	DENBIGH	56
CROSSGAR	3	CULTRA	3	DALMUIR	18	DENBY	65
CROSS GATES	50	CULTS	15	DALNASPIDAL	16	DENBY DALE + CUMBERWORTH	46
CROSSGATES	22	CULWORTH	82	DALREOCH	18	DENHAM	120
CROSS HAVEN	12	CUMBERNAULD	22	DALRY	18	DENHAM GOLF CLUB
CROSSHILL	19	CUMMERSDALE	30	DALRYMPLE	28	PLATFORM	120
CROSSHILL + CODNOP	65	CUMMERTREES	30	DALRY ROAD	26	DENHEAD	17
CROSSHOUSE	18	CUMNOCK	29	DALSERF	22	DENHOLME	46
CROSS INN	100	CUMWHINTON	30	DALSTON	30	DENMARK HILL	130
CROSS KEYS	97	CUNNINGHAMHEAD	18	DALSTON JUNCTION	126	DENNY	22
CROSS LANE	62	CUPAR	17	DALSTON KINGSLAND	126	DENNYLOANHEAD	22
CROSSMICHAEL	29	CURRAGH	6	DALTON	35	DENSTONE	62
CROSSMYLOOF	19	CURRAHEEN	8	DALWHINNIE	16	DENT	37
CROSS ROADS	3	CURRIE	22	DAMEMS	46	DENTON	62
CROSTON	42	CURRIE HILL	22	DANBY	40	DENVER	87
CROUCH END	126	CURRY	5	DANBY WISKE	38	DEPTFORD	130
CROUCH HILL	126	CURTHWAITE	35	DANDALEITH	15	DERBY	65
CROWBOROUGH + JARVIS		CUSTOM HOUSE (Liverpool)	58	DANE ROAD	62	DERBY ROAD	89
BROOK	145	CUSTOM HOUSE (London)	128	DAN-Y-CRAIG	94	DERBYSHIRE LANE	62
CROWCOMBE	136	CUTHLIE	17	DANZEY	80	DEREEN	6
CROWDEN	62	CUTLERS GREEN HALT	132	DARBY END HALT	81	DEREHAM	89
CROWHURST	145	CUXTON	132	DARCY LEVER	42	DERRIAGHY HALT	3

Station	Pg	Station	Pg	Station	Pg	Station	Pg
DYNEA HALT	100	EAST PUTNEY	122	ELHAM	146	ESHER	122
DYSART	25	EASTRINGTON	50	ELIE	25	ESHOLT	46
DYSERTH	56	EAST RUDHAM	73	ELLAND	46	ESKBANK	25
		EASTRY	146	ELLENBROOK	42	ESKBRIDGE	25
		EAST SOUTHSEA	141	ELLERBY (See Burton		ESKDALE GREEN	35
		EAST TILBURY	132	Constable)	53	ESKMEALS	35
		EAST VILLE	72	ELLESMERE	57	ESPLANADE (RYDE)	141
		EAST WINCH	87	ELLESMERE PORT	57	ESSENDINE	85
EAGLESCLIFFE	38	EASTWOOD	46	ELLINGHAM	90	ESSEXFORD	7
EALING	124	EASTWOOD + LANGLEY MILL	65	ELLIOT	17	ESSEX ROAD	126
EALING COMMON	124	EAST WORTHING	142	ELLIOT JUNCTION	17	ESSLEMONT	15
EARBY	46	EATON	76	ELLON	15	ESTON	40
EARDINGTON	80	EBBERSTON	40	ELMBRIDGE	87	ETCHINGHAM	145
EARDISLEY	76	EBBW VALE	97	ELMER'S END	130	ETHERLEY	38
EARITH BRIDGE	87	EBCHESTER	33	ELMESTHORPE	82	ETRURIA	62
EARLESTOWN JUNCTION	57	EBDON LANE	101	ELM PARK	132	ETTINGSHALL ROAD + BILSTON	80
EARLEY	116	EBLEY CROSSING HALT	110	ELMSTEAD WOODS	123	ETTINGTON	82
EARLS COLNE	132	ECCLEFECHAN	30	ELMSWELL	89	ETWALL	65
EARLS COURT	125	ECCLES	62	ELMTON + CRESWELL	65	EUSTON	127
EARLSFIELD	129	ECCLESALL (See Norton Bridge)	62	ELRINGTON	32	EUSTON SQUARE	127
EARLSHEATON	46	ECCLESFIELD	65	ELSECAR + HOYLAND	50	EUXTON	42
EARLSTON	25	ECCLESHILL	46	ELSENHAM	132	EVENWOOD	38
EARLSWOOD	142	ECCLES ROAD	89	ELSHAM	53	EVERCREECH	137
EARLSWOOD LAKES	80	ECCLESTON PARK	57	ELSLACK	46	EVERCREECH JUNCTION	137
EARSHAM	90	ECKINGTON	80	ELSTED	141	EVERINGHAM	53
EARSWICK	50	ECKINGTON + RENISHAW	65	ELSTREE	120	EVERSHOT	137
EASINGTON	38	ECTON	62	ELSWICK	33	EVESHAM	80
EASINGWOLD	50	EDALE	62	ELTHAM	123	EWELL	122
EASSIE	17	EDDERTON	13	ELTON	85	EWESLEY	33
EAST ALTON	124	EDDLESTON	25	ELTON + ORSTON	70	EWOOD BRIDGE + EDENFIELD	42
EAST ANSTEY	135	EDENBRIDGE	142	ELVANFOOT	29	EXETER	135
EAST BARKWITH	70	EDENBRIDGE TOWN	142	ELVET	38	EXMINSTER	135
EAST BOLDON	33	EDENBURY	6	ELVINGTON	50	EXMOUTH	135
EASTBOURNE	145	EDENFIELD (See Ewood Br.)	42	ELY	87	EXTON	135
EAST BRIXTON	130	EDEN PARK	123	ELY - MAIN LINE (Glam)	100	EYARTH	56
EAST BUDLEIGH	136	EDERMINE FERRY	11	EMBANKMENT (Ireland)	7	EYDON ROAD HALT	82
EASTBURY	114	EDGE HILL	57	EMBANKMENT (London)	127	EYE	89
EASTCHURCH	132	EDGE LANE	58	EMALOUGH	8	EYE GREEN	87
EASTCOTE HALT	120	EDGEWORTHSTOWN	6	EMBLETON	35	EYEMOUTH	27
EAST DIDSBURY + PARR'S		EDGWARE	120	EMBO	13	EYNSFORD	132
WOOD	62	EDGWARE ROAD	125	EMBSAY	46	EYNSHAM	114
EAST DULWICH	130	EDINBURGH	25	EMERSON PARK HALT	132	EYTHORNE	146
EASTERHOUSE	18	EDINGTON + BRATTON	137	EMLY	9		
EASTER ROAD	26	EDINGTON JUNCTION	136	EMNETH	87		
EAST FARLEIGH	145	EDLINGHAM	33	EMSWORTH	141		
EAST FINCHLEY	121	EDLINGTON HALT	65	ENDON	62		
EAST FORTUNE	25	EDMONDSTOWN	5	ENFIELD (Meath)	6		
EAST GARSTON	114	EDMONDTHORPE +		ENFIELD CHASE (Mx)	121	FACIT	46
EASTGATE	37	WYMONDHAM	85	ENFIELD LOCK	121	FAHAN	2
EAST GRANGE	22	EDROM	27	ENFIELD TOWN	121	FAILSWORTH	46
EAST GRINSTEAD	142	EDWALTON	65	ENNIS	9	FAIRBOURNE	74
EAST HALTON	53	EDWINSTOWE	65	ENNISCORTHY	11	FAIRFACH	92
EAST HAM	121	EDZELL	17	ENNISKILLEN	2	FAIRFIELD	63
EASTHAVEN	17	EFAIL ISAF + LLANTWIT VADRE	100	ENNISTYMON	8	FAIRFORD	114
EAST HORDON	132	EFFINGHAM JUNCTION	142	ENTHORPE	53	FAIRLIE	18
EAST KILBRIDE	18	EGGESFORD	135	ENTWISTLE	42	FAIRLOP	121
EAST LANGTON	85	EGGINGTON JUNCTION	65	ENZIE	15	FAKENHAM	73
EAST LEAKE	65	EGHAM	122	EPPING	119	FALCARRAGH	1
EASTLEIGH + BISHOPSTOKE	139	EGLINTON	2	EPSOM	121	FALCON WOOD	133
EAST LINTON	25	EGLINTON STREET	18	EPSOM DOWNS	142	FALKIRK	22
EAST MALLING	145	EGLOSKERRY	134	EPWORTH	50	FALKLAND ROAD	25
EAST MINSTER-ON-SEA	132	EGREMONT	35	ERDINGTON	80	FALLOWFIELD	63
EAST NEWPORT	17	EGTON	40	ERIDGE	145	FALLSIDE	18
EAST NORTON	85	ELBURTON CROSS	148	ERITH	132	FALMER	142
EASTOFT	50	ELDERSLIE	18	ERROL	17	FALMOUTH	147
EASTON	76	ELEPHANT + CASTLE	127	ERWOOD	75	FALSTONE	32
EASTON COURT	138	ELFORD	82	ESCRICK	50	FAMBRIDGE	132
EASTON LODGE	132	ELGIN	15	ESGAIRG EILIOG	75	FANGFOSS	50

GARTH	75	GLASGOW	18	GOGAR	22	GRANGE (Banff)	15
GARTLY	15	GLASGOW CROSS	20A	GOGARTH	74	GRANGE (Kilkenny)	10
GARTMORE	18	GLASGOW GREEN	20A	GOLANT	148	GRANGE CON	10
GARTNESS	18	GLASGOW SUBWAY	20A	GOLBORNE	57	GRANGE COURT	110
GARTON	53	GLASSAUGH	15	GOLCAR	46	GRANGE HILL	121
GARTSHERRIE	22	GLASSEL	15	GOLDEN GROVE	92	GRANGE LANE	65
GARVAGH	2	GLASSFORD	22	GOLDEN HILL	62	GRANGEMOUTH	22
GARVE	14	GLASSLOUGH	2	GOLDEN HILL PLATFORM	74	GRANGE-OVER-SANDS	35
GATEACRE	57	GLASSON	30	GOLDERS GREEN	121	GRANGE PARK	121
GATEHEAD	18	GLASSON DOCK	42	GOLDHAWK ROAD	124	GRANGE ROAD	142
GATEHOUSE-OF-FLEET	29	GLASTERLAW	17	GOLDSBOROUGH	50	GRANGETOWN (Glam)	100
GATESHEAD	33	GLASTONBURY + STREET	136	GOLDTHORPE + THURNSCOE		GRANGETOWN (Yorks)	40
GATESIDE	22	GLAZEBROOK	57	HALT	51	GRANTHAM	70
GATHURST	42	GLAZEBURY + BURY LANE	57	GOLF STREET	17	GRANTON	25
GATLEY	62	GLEMSFORD	89	GOLFA	75	GRANTON ROAD	26
GATWICK	142	GLENAGEARY	7	GOLLANFIELD JUNCTION	14	GRANTOWN-ON-SPEY	15
GAVELL	18	GLENAVY	3	GOLSPIE	13	GRANTSHOUSE	27
GAYTON ROAD	87	GLENBARRY	15	GOMERSAL	46	GRASSINGTON + THRESHFIELD	46
GEASHILL	6	GLENBEIGH	8	GOMSHALL + SHERE	142	GRASSMOOR	65
GEDDINGTON	85	GLEN BOIG	22	GOODGE STREET	127	GRATELEY	139
GEDLING + CARLTON	65	GLENBROOK	12	GOODRINGTON SANDS	148	GRAVELLY HILL	80
GEDNEY	72	GLEN BUCK	29	GOODMAYES	121	GRAVESEND	132
GELDESTON	90	GLENCARRON PLATFORM	14	GOODYEAR	3	GRAYRIGG	37
GELLI HALT	96	GLENCARSE	17	GOOLD'S CROSS	9	GRAYS	132
GEORGE LANE	121	GLEN CORSE	25	GOOLE	50	GREAT ALNE	80
GEORGEMAS	13	GLENDON + RUSHTON	85	GOONBELL HALT	147	GREAT AYTON	40
GERARDS BRIDGE	57	GLEN EAGLES	17	GOONHAVERN HALT	147	GREAT BARR	80
GERRARDS CROSS	116	GLENEALY	11	GOOSTREY	62	GREAT BENTLEY	133
GIANTS CAUSEWAY	3	GLEN FARG	17	GORAGHWOOD	3	GREAT BRIDGE	81
GIBBSTOWN	6	GLENFARNE	1	GORBALS	20A	GREAT BROUGHTON	35
GIDEA PARK + SQUIRRELS		GLENFIELD	82	GORDON	25	GREAT CHESTERFORD	87
HEATH	132	GLENFINNAN	16	GORDON HILL	121	GREAT COATES	53
GIFFEN	18	GLENGARNOCK	18	GOREBRIDGE	25	GREAT DALBY	85
GIFFNOCK	18	GLENLUCE	28	GORESBRIDGE	10	GREAT GLEN	82
GIFFORD	25	GLENMAQUIN	2	GOREY	11	GREATHAM	38
GIGGLESWICK	42	GLENMORE (Donegal)	2	GORGIE	26	GREAT HARWOOD	42
GILBERDYKE	53	GLENMORE (Kerry)	8	GORING + STREATLEY	116	GREAT HAYWOOD	62
GILDERSOME	46	GLENMORE AYLWARDSTOWN	10	GORING-BY-SEA	142	GREAT HORTON	46
GILESTON	100	GLEN PARVA	82	GORLESTON NORTH	90	GREAT HOUGHTON HALT	50
GILFACH	99	GLENSIDE	28	GORLESTON-ON-SEA	90	GREAT LINFORD	85
GILFACH FARGOED	97	GLENTIES	1	GORMANSTON	7	GREAT LONGSTONE	62
GILLESPIE ROAD	126	GLENWHILLY	28	GORNAL HALT	80	GREAT MALVERN	80
GILLING	40	GLOBE ROAD + DEVONSHIRE		GORSEINON	94	GREAT MISSENDEN	116
GILLINGHAM (Dorset)	137	STREET	127	GORS-Y-GARNANT HALT	94	GREAT ORMESBY	90
GILLINGHAM (Kent)	132	GLOGUE	74	GORT	5	GREAT PONTON	70
GILMERTON	25	GLOSSOP	62	GORTATLEA	8	GREAT PORTLAND STREET	127
GILNOCKIE	30	GLOUCESTER	110	GORTON	16	GREAT SHEFFORD	114
GILSLAND	32	GLOUCESTER ROAD	125	GORTON + OPENSHAW	62	GREAT SOMMERFORD	110
GILWERN	97	GLOUNAGALT BRIDGE	8	GOSBERTON	72	GREATSTONE	146
GIPSY HILL	131	GLYN ABBEY HALT	93	GOSFORD GREEN	82	GREAT WESTERN ROAD	18
GIRVAN	28	GLYNCEIRIOG	57	GOSPEL OAK	125	GREENBANK	57
GISBURN	46	GLYNCORRWG	95	GOSPORT	141	GREENCASTLE	3
GLADSTONE DOCK HALT	58	GLYNDE	142	GOSWICK	27	GREENFIELD (Eng)	46
GLAIS	95	GLYNDYFRDWY	56	GOTHERINGTON	110	GREENFIELD (Scot)	18
GLAISDALE	40	GLYNN	3	GOUDHURST	145	GREENFORD	120
GLAMIS	17	GLYN NEATH	95	GOURDON	17	GREEN HEAD	32
GLANAMMAN	94	GLYNTAFF HALT	96	GOUROCK	18	GREENHILL	22
GLAN CONWAY	56	GNOSALL	62	GOVAN	18	GREENHITHE	132
GLANDYFI	74	GOATHLAND	40	GOVILON	97	GREENISLAND	3
GLANRAFON	74	GOBOWEN	57	GOWERTON	94	GREEN LANE	57
GLANRHYD	92	GODALMING	141	GOWRAN	10	GREENLAW	25
GLANTON	33	GODLEY	62	GOXHILL	53	GREENLOANING	22
GLANWORTHY	9	GODMANCHESTER	87	GRACEHILL	3	GREENMOUNT	42
GLAN-Y-LLYN	100	GODNOW BRIDGE	50	GRAFHAM	85	GREENOCK	18
GLAN-Y-RAFON	57	GODREAMAN HALT	96	GRAFTON + BURBAGE	114	GREENODD	35
GLAPWELL	65	GODSHILL	141	GRAMPOUND ROAD	147	GREENORE	7
GLARRYFORD	3	GODSTONE	142	GRANBOROUGH ROAD	116	GREEN PARK	127
GLASBURY-ON-WYE	92	GOFF'S OAK (See Cuffley)	119	GRANDTULLY	16	GREEN ROAD	35

Station	No.	Station	No.	Station	No.	Station	No.
GREENWICH	130	HADDINGTON	25	HAMWORTHY JUNCTION	137	HATFIELD PEVEREL	132
GREENWICH PARK	130	HADDISCOE	90	HANDBOROUGH	114	HATHERN	65
GREETLAND	46	HADFIELD	62	HANDFORTH	62	HATHERLEIGH	135
GRESFORD	57	HADHAM	119	HANGER LANE	124	HATHERSAGE	65
GRESLEY	82	HADLEIGH	89	HANDSWORTH + SMETHWICK	81	HATTON (Aberdeen)	15
GRETNA	30	HADLEY	76	HANDSWORTH WOOD	81	HATTON (Warwick)	82
GRETNA GREEN	30	HADLEY WOOD	121	HANLEY	61	HATTON CROSS	122
GRETTON	85	HADLOW ROAD	57	HANNINGTON	114	HAUGHLEY	89
GRETTON HALT	110	HADNALL	57	HANWELL + ELTHORNE	120	HAUGHTON	62
GREYSTONES + DELGANY	7	HAFOD GARREGOG	55	HANWOOD	76	HAVANT	141
GRIFFITH'S CROSSING	55	HAFOD RUFFYDD	55	HANWOOD ROAD	76	HAVENHOUSE	72
GRIMES HILL + WYTHALL	80	HAFODYRYNYS PLATFORM	97	HAPTON	42	HAVEN STREET	141
GRIMETHORPE HALT	50	HAFOLYLLYN	55	HARBORNE	80	HAVERFORDWEST	74
GRIMOLDBY	72	HAGGERSTON	126	HARBURN	22	HAVERHILL	87
GRIMSARGH	42	HAGLEY	80	HARBY + STRATHERN	70	HAVERSTOCK HILL	125
GRIMSBY	53	HAGLEY ROAD	80	HARDINGHAM	89	HAVERTHWAITE	35
GRIMSTON	70	HAIGH	49	HARECASTLE	62	HAVERTON HILL	38
GRIMSTON ROAD	72	HAILSHAM	145	HARE PARK + CROFTON	50	HAWARDEN	57
GRIMSTONE + FRAMPTON	137	HAINAULT	121	HARESFIELD	110	HAWARDEN BRIDGE	57
GRINDLEFORD	65	HAIRMYRES	18	HARKER	30	HAWES	37
GRINDLEY	62	HALBEATH	22	HARLECH	55	HAWES JUNCTION +	
GRINDON	62	HALBERTON HALT	135	HARLESDEN	124	GARSDALE	37
GRINKLE	40	HALE	62	HARLESTON	90	HAWICK	30
GRISTHORPE	40	HALEBANK	57	HARLING ROAD	89	HAWKESBURY LANE	82
GROESLON	50	HALESOWEN	80	HARLINGTON	119	HAWKHEAD	19
GROESWEN HALT	100	HALESWORTH	90	HARLINGTON HALT	50	HAWKHURST	145
GROGLEY HALT	148	HALEWOOD	57	HARLOW	119	HAWORTH	46
GROOMBRIDGE	145	HALF WAY	55	HARMSTON	70	HAWSKER	40
GROOMSPORT ROAD	3	HALIFAX	46	HARMONSTOWN	7	HAWTHORN + ROSEWELL	25
GROSMONT	40	HALKIRK	13	HAROLD WOOD	132	HAXBY	50
GROSVENOR ROAD	129	HALLATON	85	HARPENDEN	119	HAXBY + EPWORTH	70
GROTTEN + SPRINGHEAD	46	HALLATROW	137	HARPERLEY	38	HAXEY JUNCTION	70
GROVE FERRY	133	HALLEN HALT	110	HARRIETSHAM	145	HAXEY TOWN	50
GROVE PARK	123	HALL GREEN	80	HARRINGAY	126	HAY	76
GROVESEND	94	HALLING	132	HARRINGAY PARK	126	HAYBURN WYKE	40
GUARD BRIDGE	17	HALLINGTON	72	HARRINGTON	35	HAYDOCK	57
GUAY	17	HALL ROAD	42	HARRINGWORTH	85	HAYDOCK PARK	57
GUIDE BRIDGE	62	HALMEREND	62	HARRISTOWN	7	HAYDON BRIDGE	32
GUILDFORD	141	HALSALL	42	HARROGATE	50	HAYDONS ROAD	129
GUISBOROUGH	40	HALSTEAD	132	HARROW + WEALDSTONE	120	HAYES	123
GUISELEY	46	HALTON (Ches)	57	HARROW·ON·THE·HILL	120	HAYES + HARLINGTON	120
GULLANE	25	HALTON (Lancs)	42	HARRYVILLE	3	HAYFIELD	62
GUNNERSBURY	124	HALTON HOLGATE	72	HARSTON	87	HAYLE	147
GUNNISLAKE	148	HALTWHISTLE	32	HART	38	HAYLING ISLAND	141
GUNTON	73	HALWILL JUNCTION	134	HARTFIELD	142	HAYMARKET	25
GURTEEN	12	HAMBLE	139	HARTFORD	57	HAYWARDS HEATH	142
GUTHRIE	17	HAMBLETON	50	HARTFORD + GREENBANK	57	HAYWOOD	22
GUYHIRNE	87	HAMILTON	22	HARTINGTON	62	HAZEL GROVE	62
GWAUN·CAE·GURWEN HALT	94	HAMILTON'S BRAWN	3	HARTLEBURY	80	HAZELWELL	80
GWEEDORE	1	HAM LANE	101	HARTLEPOOL	38	HAZELWOOD	65
GWERNYDOMEN HALT	100	HAMMERSMITH	124	HARTLEY	33	HAZLEHATCH + CELBRIDGE	7
GWERSYLLT	57	HAMMERTON	50	HARTON ROAD	76	HAZLEHEAD BRIDGE	46
GWINEAR ROAD	147	HAMMERWICH	80	HARTSHILL + WOODSIDE		HEACHAM	72
GWYDDELWERN	56	HAM MILL CROSSING HALT	110	HALT	81	HEADCORN	145
GWYS	95	HAMPDEN PARK	145	HARTWOOD	22	HEADFORD	8
GYFEILLON HALT	96	HAMPOLE	50	HARTY ROAD HALT	133	HEADINGLEY	46
GYPSY LANE	40	HAMPSTEAD (London)	121	HARVINGTON	80	HEADS NOOK	32
		HAMPSTEAD (Warwick)	80	HARWICH	133	HEADS OF AYR	28
		HAMPSTEAD HEATH	125	HASLEMERE	141	HEADSTONE LANE	120
		HAMPSTEAD NORRIS	116	HASLINGDEN	42	HEADWOOD	3
		HAMPSTHWAITE	46	HASSENDEAN	32	HEALD GREEN	62
		HAMPTON	122	HASSOCKS	142	HEALEY (See Shawclough)	46
HABROUGH	53	HAMPTON COURT	122	HASSOP	65	HEALEY HOUSE	46
HACKBRIDGE	123	HAMPTON·IN·ARDEN	82	HASTINGS	145	HEALING	53
HACKNEY	126	HAMPTON LOADE	80	HASWELL	38	HEALY'S BRIDGE	12
HACKNEY DOWNS	126	HAMPTON ROW HALT	110	HATCH	136	HEANOR	65
HADDENHAM (Bucks)	116	HAMPTON WICK	122	HATCH END	120	HEAPEY	42
HADDENHAM (Cambs)	87	HAM STREET + ORLESTONE	146	HATFIELD	119	HEATHER + IBSTOCK	82

HEATHY LANE HALT	43	HESLEDON	38	HINDLEY	42	HONOR OAK	130
HEATHFIELD (Devon)	148	HESLERTON	40	HINDLEY + PLATT BRIDGE	42	HONOR OAK PARK	130
HEATHFIELD (Sussex)	145	HESSAY	50	HINDLEY GREEN	42	HOO HALT	132
HEATH	100	HESSLE	53	HINDLOW	62	HOOK	141
HEATHROW	122	HEST BANK	42	HINDOLVESTONE	73	HOOK NORTON	114
HEATLEY + WARBURTON	62	HESTON-HOUNSLOW	122	HUNKSEY HALT	116	HOOLE	42
HEATON	34	HESWALL	57	HINTON	80	HOOLEY HILL	63
HEATON CHAPEL	62	HESWALL HILLS	57	HINTON ADMIRAL	139	HOOTON	57
HEATON MERSEY	62	HETHERSETT	89	HIPPERHOLME	46	HOPE (Derby)	62
HEATON NORRIS	62	HETTON	38	HIRWAIN	96	HOPE (Flint)	57
HEATON PARK	46	HEUSTON	7	HISTON	87	HOPE EXCHANGE	57
HEBBURN	33	HEVER	142	HITCHIN	119	HOPE JUNCT. + PENYFFORDD	59
HEBDEN BRIDGE	46	HEVERSHAM	35	HITHER GREEN	123	HOPEMAN	15
HEBRON	55	HEWORTH	34	IXION	62	HOPE VILLAGE	57
HECK	50	HEXHAM	32	HOCKLEY (Essex)	132	HOPTON	90
HECKINGTON	70	HEYBRIDGE (See Maldon E.)	132	HOCKLEY (Warwick)	80	HOPTON HEATH	76
HECKMONDWIKE	46	HEYFORD	114	HODNET	57	HORBURY + OSSETT	46
HEDDON-ON-THE-WALL	33	HEYSHAM	42	HOGHTON	42	HORBURY JUNCTION	50
HEDGELEY	33	HEYTESBURY	137	HOLBEACH	72	HORDEN	38
HEDNESFORD	80	HEYWOOD	46	HOLBECK	48	HORDERLEY	76
HEDON	53	HIBEL ROAD	62	HOLBORN	127	HOREHAM ROAD (See Waldron)	145
HEELEY	65	HICKLETON + THURNSCOE	50	HOLBORN VIADUCT	127	HORHAM	90
HEIGHINGTON	38	HIGHAM (Kent)	132	HOLBURN STREET	15	HORLEY	142
HELE + BRADNINCH	135	HIGHAM (Suff)	89	HOLCOMBE BROOK	42	HORNBY	42
HELENS BAY	3	HIGHAM FERRERS	85	HOLE	134	HORNCASTLE	72
HELLESDON	89	HIGHAM-ON-THE-HILL	82	HOLEHOUSE	28	HORNCHURCH	132
HELLIFIELD	46	HIGHAMS PARK	121	HOLKHAM	73	HORNINGLOW	65
HELLINGLEY	145	HIGH BARNET	121	HOLLAND ARMS	55	HORNSEA	53
HELMDON	82	HIGH BLAITHWAITE	35	HOLLAND PARK	125	HORNSEA BRIDGE	53
HELMSDALE	13	HIGH BLANTYRE	18	HOLLAND ROAD HALT	142	HORNSEY	121
HELMSHORE	42	HIGHBRIDGE	136	HOLLINGBOURNE	145	HORNSEY ROAD	126
HELMSLEY	40	HIGHBROOMS	145	HOLLINWELL + ANNESLEY	65	HORRABRIDGE	148
HELPRINGHAM	70	HIGHBURY + ISLINGTON	126	HOLLINWOOD	46	HORRINGFORD	141
HELPSTON	85	HIGHCLERE	114	HOLLOWAY ROAD	126	HORSE + JOCKEY	10
HELSBY	57	HIGHER BUXTON	62	HOLLY BUSH	28	HORSEBRIDGE	139
HELSTON	147	HIGH FIELD	50	HOLLYBUSH	97	HORSEHAY	76
HEMEL HEMPSTEAD	119	HIGHGATE	121	HOLLYHILL	12	HORSELEAP	6
HEMINGBROUGH	50	HIGHGATE ROAD	125	HOLLYMOUNT	4	HORSFORTH	46
HEMSBY	90	HIGH HALDEN ROAD	145	HOLME (Hunts)	85	HORSHAM	142
HEMSWORTH	50	HIGH HARRINGTON	35	HOLME (Lancs)	46	HORSLEY	142
HEMSWORTH + SOUTH KIRKBY	50	HIGHLANDMAN	16	HOLME (Yorks)	50	HORSMONDEN	145
HEMYOCK	136	HIGH LANE	62	HOLME HALE	89	HORSPATH HALT	116
HENBURY	110	HIGHLEY	80	HOLME LACY	110	HORSTED KEYNES	142
HENDON	120	HIGH SHIELDS	33	HOLMES	65	HORTON-IN-RIBBLESDALE	37
HENDREFORGAN	99	HIGH STREET (Glasgow)	19	HOLMES CHAPEL	62	HORTON PARK	46
HENFIELD	142	HIGH STREET KENSINGTON	125	HOLMFIELD	46	HORWICH	42
HENGOED	97	HIGH STREET HALT (Warw)	81	HOLMFIRTH	46	HOSCAR	42
HENIARTH	75	HIGHTOWN	42	HOLMSLEY	139	HOTHFIELD	145
HENLEY-IN-ARDEN	80	HIGH WESTWOOD	33	HOLMWOOD	142	HOTWELLS	110
HENLEY-ON-THAMES	116	HIGHWORTH	114	HOLSWORTHY	134	HOUGHAM	70
HENLLAN	74	HIGH WYCOMBE	116	HOLT (Norfolk)	73	HOUGH GREEN	57
HENLOW	119	HILDEN HALT	3	HOLT (Wilts)	110	HOUNSLOW	122
HENSALL	50	HILDENBOROUGH	145	HOLTBY	50	HOUNSLOW BARRACKS	122
HENSTRIDGE	137	HILGAY	87	HOLTON HEATH	137	HOUNSLOW TOWN	122
HENWICK	80	HILL END	119	HOLTON-LE-CLAY	53	HOUSTON	18
HEPSCOTT	33	HILLFOOT	18	HOLYHEAD	55	HOVE	142
HERCULANEUM DOCK	58	HILLINGDON	120	HOLYTOWN	22	HOVINGHAM SPA	40
HEREFORD	92	HILLINGTON (Glasgow)	19	HOLYWELL JUNCTION	56	HOWDEN	50
HERIOT	25	HILLINGTON (Norfolk)	73	HOLYWELL TOWN	56	HOWDEN CLOUGH	49
HERMITAGE	116	HILL OF DOWN	6	HOLYWOOD (Down)	3	HOWDON-ON-TYNE	33
HERNE BAY	133	HILLSBOROUGH	3	HOLYWOOD (Dumfr)	29	HOW MILL	32
HERNE HILL	130	HILLSIDE (Forfar)	17	HOMERSFIELD	90	HOWSHAM	53
HERRIARD	141	HILLSIDE (Lancs)	42	HOMERTON	126	HOWTH	7
HERSHAM	122	HILSEA	141	HONEYBOURNE	80	HOWTH JUNCTION	7
HERTFORD	119	HILTON HOUSE	42	HONING	73	HOWWOOD	18
HERTINGFORDBURY	119	HIMLEY	80	HONINGTON	70	HOY	13
HESKETH BANK + TARLETON	42	HINCKLEY WOOD	122	HONITON	136	HOYLAKE	57
HESKETH PARK	42	HINDERWELL	40	HONLEY	46	HUBBERT'S BRIDGE	72

Station	Page	Station	Page	Station	Page	Station	Page
HUCKNALL	65	ILKLEY	46	JAMES STREET (O'head)	58	KENNETHMOUNT	* 15
HUCKNALL TOWN	65	ILMER HALT	116	JAMES STREET (Wirral)	57	KENNETT	87
HUDDERSFIELD	46	ILMINSTER	136	JAMESTOWN	18	KENNINGTON	130
HUGGLESCOTE	82	IMMINGHAM	53	JARROW	33	KENNISHEAD	18
HULL	53	INCE	42	JEDBURGH	32	KENSAL GREEN	125
HULLAVINGTON	110	INCE + ELTON	57	JEDFOOT	32	KENSAL RISE	125
HULME END	62	INCH	11	JEFFERSTONE LANE	146	KENSINGTON	125
HUMBERSTONE	82	INCHBARE	17	JERSEY MARINE	95	KENTALLEN	16
HUMBERSTONE ROAD	82	INCHES	29	JERVAULX	38	KENT HOUSE	131
HUMBIE	25	INCH GREEN	18	JESMOND	33	KENTISH TOWN	126
HUNCOAT	42	INCH ROAD	2	JOHN O' GAUNT	85	KENTON (E Suff)	89
HUNDRED END	42	INCHTURE	17	JOHNSHAVEN	17	KENTON (Mx)	120
HUNGERFORD	114	INCHTURE VILLAGE	17	JOHNSTON	74	KENTON (Nhumberld)	33
HUNMANBY	40	INGATESTONE	132	JOHNSTONE	18	KENTS BANK	35
HUNNINGTON	80	INGERSBY	82	JOHNSTOWN + HAFOD	57	KENYON JUNCTION	57
HUNSLET	50	INGESTRE	62	JOPPA	25	KERNE BRIDGE	110
HUNSTANTON	72	INGHAM	89	JORDANHILL	19	KERRY	75
HUNSTON	141	INGLEBY	40	JORDANSTONE	17	KERSHOPE FOOT	30
HUNTINGDON	87	INGLETON	37	JORDANSTOWN	3	KESH	1
HUNTLY	15	INGRA TOR HALT	148	JUNCTION ROAD (Edinb.)	26	KESWICK	35
HUNT'S CROSS	57	INGROW	46	JUNCTION ROAD (Mx.)	126	KETLEY	76
HUNWICK	38	INNERLEITHEN	25	JUNCTION ROAD (Sussex)	145	KETTERING FOR CORBY	85
HURDLOW	62	INNERPEFFRAY	16	JUNIPER GREEN	22	KETTLENESS	40
HURLFORD	18	INNERWICK	27	JUSTINHAUGH	17	KETTON	85
HURN	139	INNISKEEN	7			KEW BRIDGE	124
HURSTBOURNE	139	INNY JUNCTION	6			KEW GARDENS (Lancs)	42
HURST GREEN HALT	142	INSCH	15			KEW GARDENS (Surrey)	122
HURWORTH BURN	38	INSTOW	134			KEYHAM	148
HUSKISSON DOCK	58	INVER	1			KEYINGHAM	53
HUSTHWAITE GATE	40	INNERAMSAY	15			KEYNSHAM	110
HUTCHEON STREET	15	INVERESK	25	KANTURK	9	KIBWORTH	82
HUTTON + HOWICK	42	INVERGARRY	14	KATESBRIDGE	3	KIDBROOKE	123
HUTTON CRANSWICK	53	INVERGORDON	14	KEADY	2	KIDDERMINSTER	80
HUTTON GATE	40	INVERGOWRIE	17	KEARSLEY + STONECLOUGH	70	KIDLINGTON	114
HUTTONS AMBO	50	INVERKEILOR	17	KEARSNEY	146	KIDSGROVE	62
HUYTON	57	INVERKEITHING	22	KEELE	62	KIDSGROVE HALT	62
HUYTON QUARRY	57	INVERKIP	18	KEELE PARK	62	KIDWELLY	93
HYDE	62	INVERNESS	14	KEGWORTH	65	KIELDER	32
HYDE JUNCTION	62	INVERSHIN	13	KEIGHLEY	46	KILBAGIE	22
HYDE PARK CORNER	125	INVERUGIE	15	KEINTON MANDEVILLE	137	KILBARCHAN	18
HYDE ROAD	62	INVERURIE	15	KEITH	15	KILBARRACK	7
HYKEHAM	70	INWORTH	132	KEITH TOWN	15	KILBIRNIE	18
HYLTON	33	IPSTONES	62	KELLS (Antrim)	3	KILBOWIE	18
HYNDLAND	19	IPSWICH	89	KELLS (Kerry)	8	KILBURN	65
HYTHE (Essex)	133	IRCHESTER	85	KELLS (Meath)	6	KILBURN + MAIDA VALE	125
HYTHE (Hants)	139	IRLAM	62	KELLSWATER	3	KILBURN (BRONDESBURY)	125
HYTHE (Kent)	146	IRISH STREET HALT	2	KELMARSH	85	KILBURN PARK	125
		IRON ACTON	110	KELMSCOTT + LANGFORD	114	KILCOCK	6
		IRON BRIDGE + BROSELEY	76	KELSO	27	KILCOE	12
		IRONGRAY	29	KELSTON	110	KILCONQUHAR	25
		IRTHLINGBOROUGH	85	KELTY	22	KILCOOL	7
		IRTON ROAD	35	KELVEDON	132	KILCREA	12
IBROX	18	IRVINE	18	KELVIN BRIDGE	19	KILDALE	40
IBSTOCK (See Heather)	82	IRVINESTOWN	2	KELVINHAUGH	20A	KILDANGAN	6
ICKENHAM HALT	120	ISFIELD	142	KEMBLE	110	KILDARE	6
ICKNIELD PORT ROAD	81	ISHAM + BURTON LATIMER	85	KEMNAY	15	KILDARY	13
IDE	135	ISLAND ROAD	5	KEMPSTON + ELSTOW HALT	85	KILDONAN	13
IDLE	46	ISLEHAM	87	KEMPSTON HARDWICK	85	KILDWICK + CROSSHILLS	46
IDRIDGEHAY	65	ISLEWORTH	122	KEMPTON PARK	122	KILFENORA	8
IFFLEY HALT	116	ISLINGTON (See Highbury)	126	KEMP TOWN	142	KILFREE	5
IFIELD HALT	142	ISLIP	116	KEMSING	145	KILGARVAN	12
ILDERTON	33	ITCHIN ABBAS	141	KEMSLEY	132	KILGERRAN	74
ILFORD	121	IVER	120	KENDAL	37	KILGETTY	74
ILFRACOMBE	135	IVYBRIDGE	148	KENFIG HILL	99	KILKEE	8
ILKESTON	65			KENILWORTH	82	KILKENNY	10
ILKESTON JUNCTION + COSSALL	65			KENLEY	123	KILKERRAN	28
ILKESTON TOWN	65			KENMARE	12	KILLAGAN	3
				KENNETHMONT	* 15	KILLALA	4

* Same station - alternative spellings

KILLALOE	9	KINGENNIE	17	KIRKBY STEPHEN	37	LADBROKE GROVE	125
KILLAMARSH	65	KINGHAM	114	KIRKBY STEPHEN +		LADE HALT	146
KILLARNEY	8	KINGHORN	25	RAVENSTONEDALE	37	LADYBANK	17
KILLAY	94	KINGSBARNS	17	KIRKBY THORE	37	LADY'S BRIDGE	15
KILLEAGH	12	KINGSBRIDGE (Devon)	148	KIRKCALDY	25	LADY WELL	130
KILLEARN	18	KINGSBRIDGE (Dublin)	7	KIRKCONNEL	29	LAFFAN'S BRIDGE	10
KILLESHANDRA	6	KINGSBURY (Leic)	82	KIRKCOWAN	28	LAGHEY	1
KILLESTER	7	KINGSBURY (Mx)	120	KIRKCUDBRIGHT	29	LAHINCH	8
KILLIECRANKIE	17	KING'S CLIFFE	85	KIRKDALE	58	LAINDON	132
KILLIN	16	KINGSCOTE	142	KIRKGUNZEON	29	LAIRA HALT	149
KILLINEY	7	KINGSCOURT	6	KIRKHAM ABBEY	50	LAIRG	13
KILLINGHOLME	53	KING'S CROSS	127	KIRKHAM + WESHAM	42	LAISTERDYKE	46
KILLINGWORTH	33	KING'S HEATH	80	KIRKHEATON	46	LAKE SIDE WINDERMERE	35
KILLINICK	11	KINGSHOUSE PLATFORM	16	KIRKHILL	19	LAKENHEATH	89
KILLIN JUNCTION	16	KING'S INCH	19	KIRKINNER	28	LAMANCHA	25
KILLOCHAN	28	KINGSKERSWELL	148	KIRKINTILLOCH	18	LAMB, THE	9
KILLONAN	9	KINGSKETTLE	25	KIRKLAND	29	LAMBEG	3
KILLORGLIN	8	KINGSKNOWE	25	KIRKLEE	19	LAMBETH	127
KILLOUGH	3	KINGSLAND	76	KIRKLINGTON	65	LAMBLEY	32
KILLUCAN	6	KING'S LANGLEY + ABBOT'S		KIRKLISTON	22	LAMBOURN	114
KILLURIN	11	LANGLEY	119	KIRKMICHAEL	41	LAMESLEY	33
KILLYBEGS	1	KINGSLEY + FROGHALL	62	KIRKNEWTON (Edinburgh)	22	LAMINGTON	22
KILLYGORDON	2	KINGSLEY HALT	141	KIRKNEWTON (N'umber'ld)	32	LAMPETER	74
KILLYLEA	2	KING'S LYNN	72	KIRKPATRICK	80	LAMPHEY	74
KILLYMARD HALT	1	KINGSMUIR	17	KIRK SMEATON	50	LAMPLUGH	35
KILLYRAN	6	KING'S NORTON	80	KIRKSTALL	46	LAMPORT	85
KILLYWHAN	29	KING'S NYMPTON	135	KIRKSTEAD	70	LANARK	22
KILMALCOM	18	KING'S PARK	19	KIRRIEMUIR	17	LANCASTER	42
KILMACOW	10	KING'S SUTTON	114	KIRTLEBRIDGE	30	LANCASTER GATE	125
KILMACRENAN	2	KINGSTON	122	KIRTON	72	LANCHESTER	38
KILMACTHOMAS	10	KINGSTON CROSSING HALT	116	KIRTON LINDSEY	53	LANCING	142
KILMAINHAM WOOD	6	KINGSTON ROAD	101	KITTYBREWSTER	15	LANDORE	94
KILMALLOCK	9	KINGSTOWN	7	KNETON BRIDGE	65	LANGBANK	18
KILMANY	17	KINGSWEAR	148	KIVETON PARK	65	LANGFORD (Essex)	132
KILMARNOCK	18	KINGSWOOD + BURGH HEATH	142	KNAPTON	40	LANGFORD (Som)	101
KILMAURS	18	KING'S WORTHY	139	KNARESBOROUGH	50	LANGHO	42
KILMEADAN	10	KINGTHORPE	70	KNEBWORTH	119	LANGHOLM	30
KILMESSAN	7	KINGTON	76	KNIGHTON	76	LANGLEY (Bucks)	120
KILMORNA	8	KING TOR HALT	148	KNIGHTSBRIDGE	125	LANGLEY (N'humberland)	32
KILMURRY (Clare)	8	KINGUSSIE	14	KNIGHTWICK	80	LANGLEY GREEN + ROOD END	80
KILMURRY (Cork)	12	KINLOSS	15	KNITSLEY	38	LANGLEY MILL	65
KILNHURST	65	KINNEGAR HALT	3	KNOCK (Banff)	15	LANGLEY MILL + EASTWOOD	68
KILPATRICK	18	KINNERLEY JUNCTION	57	KNOCK (Down)	3	LANGLOAN	22
KILRANE	11	KINNERSLEY	76	KNOCKANALLY	3	LANGPORT EAST	136
KILREA	3	KINNERTON	57	KNOCKANDO	15	LANGPORT WEST	136
KILROOT	3	KINNIEL	22	KNOCKANE	12	LANGRICK	72
KILRUSH	8	KINROSS	22	KNOCKCROGHERRY	5	LANGSIDE	19
KILSBY + CRICK	82	KINSALE	12	KNOCKHOLT	123	LANGSTON	141
KILSHEELAN	10	KINSALE JUNCTION	12	KNOCKLONG	9	LANGWATHBY	37
KILSYTH	22	KINTBURY	114	KNOCKLOUGHRIM	2	LANGWITH	65
KILTIMAGH	5	KINTORE	15	KNOTT END	42	LANGWITH JUNCTION	65
KILTOOM	5	KIPLING COTES	53	KNOTTINGLEY	50	LANGWORTH	70
KILTUBRID	5	KIPPAX	50	KNOTT MILL + DEANSGATE	62	LANSDOWN	110
KILUMNEY	12	KIPPEN	18	KNOTTY ASH + STANLEY	57	LANSDOWNE ROAD	7
KILWAUGHTER HALT	3	KIRBY CROSS	133	KNOWESGATE	32	LAPFORD	135
KILWINNING	18	KIRBY MOORSIDE	40	KNOWESIDE	28	LAPWORTH	80
KILWORTH (See Welford)	82	KIRBY MUXLOE	82	KNOWLE + DORRIDGE	80	LARBERT	22
KIMBERLEY (Norf)	89	KIRBY PARK	57	KNOWLTON	146	LARGO	25
KIMBERLEY (Notts)	65	KIRKANDREWS	30	KNUCKBUE	12	LARGS	18
KIMBOLTON	85	KIRKBANK	32	KNUCKLAS	76	LARKHALL	22
KINALDIE	15	KIRKBRIDE	30	KNUTSFORD	62	LARNE TOWN	3
KINBRACE	13	KIRKBUDDO	17	KYLE OF LOCHALSH	14	LARNE HARBOUR	3
KINBUCK	22	KIRKBURTON	46			LARTINGTON	38
KINCARDINE	22	KIRKBY	57			LASSWADE	25
KINCRAIG	14	KIRKBY + PINXTON	65			LATCHFORD	57
KINETON	82	KIRKBY·IN·ASHFIELD	65			LATCHLEY	148
KINFAUNS	17	KIRKBY·IN·FURNESS	35			LATIMER ROAD	125
KING EDWARD	15	KIRKBY LONSDALE	37	LACOCK HALT	110	LAUDER	25

LAUNCESTON	134	LENNOXTOWN	18	LISCOOLY	2	LLANERCH·AYRON HALT	74
LAUNTON	116	LENTRAN	14	LISDUFF	10	LLANERCHYMEDD	55
LAURENCEKIRK	17	LENWADE	89	LISELTON	8	LLANFABON ROAD PLATFORM	97
LAURENCETOWN	3	LENZIE	18	LISKEARD	148	LLANFAIR	55
LAURISTON	17	LEOMINSTER	76	LISMORE	9	LLANFAIR·CAEREINION	75
LAVANT	141	LESLIE	25	LISNAGRY	9	LLANFAIRFECHAN	55
LAVENHAM	89	LESMAHAGOW	22	LISNALINCHY	3	LLANFALTEG	74
LAVERNOCK	100	LETCHWORTH	119	LISNASKEA	2	LLANFECHAIN	56
LAVERTON HALT	114	LETHAM GRANGE	17	LISPOLE	8	LLANFIHANGEL	74
LAVINGTON	137	LETHENTY	15	LISS	141	LLANFYLLIN	75
LAWDERDALE	6	LETTERKENNY	2	LISTOWEL	8	LLANFYNYDD	57
LAW	22	LETTERSTON	74	LITCHFIELD	139	LLANFYRNACH	74
LAWLEY BANK	76	LEUCHARS JUNCTION	17	LITTLEBOROUGH	46	LLANGADOCK	92
LAWRENCE HILL	110	LEUCHARS OLD	17	LITTLE BYTHAM	85	LLANGAMMARCH WELLS	75
LAWTON	62	LEVEN	25	LITTLE EATON	65	LLANGEDWYN	56
LAXFIELD	90	LEVENSHULME	62	LITTLEHAM	136	LLANGEFNI	56
LAYERTHORPE	50	LEVERTON	70	LITTLEHAMPTON	142	LLANGEINOR	99
LAYTOWN	7	LEVISHAM	40	LITTLEHAVEN HALT	142	LLANGELYNIN	74
LAZONBY + KIRKOSWALD	37	LEWES	142	LITTLE HULTON	45	LLANGENNECH	94
LEA	70	LEWES ROAD HALT	142	LITTLE ISLAND	12	LLANGLYDWEN	74
LEA BRIDGE	126	LEWISHAM	130	LITTLE KIMBLE	116	LLANGOLLEN	57
LEADBURN	25	LEWISHAM ROAD	130	LITTLE MILL	33	LLANGONYD	99
LEADENHAM	70	LEWKNOR BRIDGE HALT	116	LITTLE MILL JUNCTION	98	LLANGUNLLO	76
LEADGATE	33	LEYBURN	38	LITTLEMORE	116	LLANGWYLLOG	55
LEADHILLS	29	LEYCETT	62	LITTLEPORT	87	LLANGYBI (Cardigan)	74
LEAGRAVE	119	LEYLAND	42	LITTLE SALKELD	37	LLANGYBI (Carnarvon)	55
LEA GREEN	57	LEYNY	1	LITTLE SOMERFORD	110	LLANGYNOG	56
LEA HALL	88	LEYSDOWN	133	LITTLE STEEPING	72	LLANHARAN	99
LEALHOLM	40	LEYSMILL	17	LITTLETON + BADSEY	80	LLANHARRY	100
LEAMINGTON SPA	82	LEYTON	121	LITTLE WEIGHTON	53	LLANHILLETH	97
LEAMSIDE	38	LEYTONSTONE	121	LITTLEWORTH	87	LLANIDLOES	75
LEA ROAD	42	LEZAYRE	41	LIVERPOOL	57	LLANILAR	74
LEASOWE	57	LHANBRYDE	15	LIVERPOOL STREET	127	LLANISHEN	100
LEATHERHEAD	142	LICHFIELD	80	LIVERSEDGE	46	LLANMORLAIS	94
LEATON	76	LIDLINGTON	116	LIVINGSTON	22	LLANPUMPSAINT	92
LECHLADE	114	LIFF	17	LIXNAW	8	LLANRHAIADR	56
LEDBURY	110	LIFFEY JUNCTION	7	LLANABER	74	LLANRHAIADR MOCHNANT	56
LEDSHAM	57	LIFFORD	80	LLAN ARTHNEY	92	LLANRHYSTYD ROAD	74
LEDSTON	60	LIFFORD HALT	2	LLAN BADARN	74	LLANRWST + TREFRIW	56
LEE	123	LIFTON	134	LLANBEDR	55	LLANSAMLET	94
LEEBOTWOOD	76	LIGHTCLIFFE	46	LLANBEDR + PENSARN	55	LLANSANTFFRAID	57
LEEDS	46	LIGHTMOOR JUNCTION	76	LLANBEDR GOCH HALT	55	LLANSILIN ROAD	57
LEEGATE	35	LILBOURNE	82	LLANBERIS	55	LLANSTEPHAN HALT	92
LEEK	62	LIMAVADY	2	LLANBETHERY PLATFORM	100	LLANTARNAM	98
LEEMING BAR	38	LIMAVADY JUNCTION	2	LLANBISTER ROAD	75	LLANTRISANT	100
LEEMOUNT	12	LIMEHOUSE	127	LLAN BRADACH	97	LLANTWIT	100
LEE·ON·THE·SOLENT	141	LIMERICK	9	LLAN BRYNMAIR	75	LLANTWIT MAJOR	99
LEES	46	LIMERICK JUNCTION	9	LLANDAFF	100	LLANUWCHYLLYN	56
LEGACY	57	LIMPEY STOKE	110	LLANDANWG	55	LLANVIHANGEL	98
LEGBOURNE ROAD	72	LINACRE ROAD	57	LLANDDERFEL	56	LLANWERN	101
LEICESTER	82	LINBY	65	LLANDERBIE	94	LLANWNDA	55
LEICESTER SQUARE	127	LINCOLN	70	LLANDECWYN	55	LLANWRDA	92
LEIGH (Kent)	145	LINDAL	35	LLANDENNY	98	LLANWRTYD WELLS	75
LEIGH (Lancs)	42	LINDEAN	25	LLANDILO	92	LLANYBLOODWELL	57
LEIGH (Staffs)	62	LINDORES	17	LLANDILO BRIDGE	92	LLANYBYTHER	74
LEIGH COURT	80	LINGFIELD	142	LLANDINAM	75	LLANYCEFEN	74
LEIGH·ON·SEA	132	LINGWOOD	90	LLANDOVERY	92	LLANYMYNECH	57
LEIGHTON BUZZARD	116	LINLEY	76	LLANDOW HALT	99	LLETTY BRONGU	99
LEISTON	90	LINLITHGOW	22	LLANDRE	74	LLONG	57
LEITH	25	LINTMILL HALT	28	LLANDRILLO	56	LLWYDCOED	96
LEITH WALK	26	LINTON	87	LLANDRINDOD WELLS	75	LLWYNGWERN	75
LEITRIM	3	LINTZ GREEN	33	LLANDRINIO ROAD	76	LLWYNGWRIL	74
LEIXLIP	7	LIONS HOLT HALT	135	LLANDUDNO	56	LLWYNYPIA	96
LELANT SIDINGS	147	LIPHOOK	141	LLANDUDNO JUNCTION	56	LLYNCLYS	57
LEMAN STREET	127	LIPSONVALE HALT	148	LLANDULAS	56	LLYSFAEN	56
LEMINGTON	33	LISBELLAW	2	LLANDYSSIL ✳	74	LOANHEAD	25
LENADERG	3	LISBURN	3	LLANDYSSUL ✳	74	LOCHAILORT	16
LENHAM	145	LISCARD + POULTON	57	LLANELLY	94	LOCHANHEAD	29

✳ Alternative Spellings same place

MORLEY'S BRIDGE	12	MULLINAVAT	10	NEILSTON	18	NEW HOLLAND	53
MORLEY TOP	49	MULLINGAR	6	NELSON (Glam)	97	NEWHOUSE	22
MORMOND	15	MULTIFARNHAM	6	NELSON (Lancs)	46	NEW HYTHE	145
MORNINGSIDE	22	MUMBLES PIER	94	NELSON + LLANCAIACH	97	NEWICK + CHAILEY	142
MORNINGSIDE ROAD	26	MUMBLES ROAD	94	NELSON DOCK	58	NEWINGTON (Edinburgh)	25
MORNINGTON CRESCENT	127	MUMBY ROAD	72	NENAGH	9	NEWINGTON (Kent)	132
MORPETH	33	MUMPS	46	NESSCLIFF + PENTRE	76	NEWINGTON (Yorks)	53
MORRIS COWLEY	116	MUNCASTER MILL	35	NESTON	57	NEWLAND	40
MORRISTON	94	MUNDESLEY-ON-SEA	73	NESTON + INGESTRE	62	NEW LANE	42
MORTEHOE	134	MUNLOCHY	14	NESTON + PARKGATE	57	NEWLAY + HORSFORTH	46
MORTIMER	116	MURRAYFIELD	25	NETHERBURN	22	NEW LUCE	28
MORTLAKE	122	MURROW	87	NETHERCLEUGH	30	NEWMACHAR	15
MORTON PINKEY	82	MURTHLY	17	NETHERFIELD	65	NEWMAINS	22
MORTON ROAD	70	MURTON	38	NETHERTON (Worc)	80	NEW MALDEN	122
MOSELEY	80	MURTON LANE	50	NETHERTON (Yorks)	46	NEWMARKET (Camb)	87
MOSES GATE	42	MUSGRAVE	37	NETHERTOWN	35	NEWMARKET (Cork)	9
MOSNEY	7	MUSSELBURGH	25	NETHY BRIDGE	15	NEW MILLS (Chesh)	62
MOSS	50	MUSWELL HILL	121	NETLEY	139	NEW MILLS (Derby)	62
MOSS + PENTRE	57	MUTHILL	16	NEWARK	70	NEW MILLS (Donegal)	2
MOSS BANK	57	MYTHOLMROYD	46	NEW BARNET	121	NEWMILNS	18
MOSSBRIDGE	42			NEW BASFORD	65	NEW MILTON	139
MOSSEND	22			NEW BECKENHAM	131	NEWNHAM	110
MOSS HALT	59			NEW BIGGIN	37	NEWNHAM BRIDGE	76
MOSSLEY (Antrim)	3			NEWBIGGIN	33	NEW PARK	22
MOSSLEY (Lancs)	46			NEWBIGGING	22	NEWPORT (Essex)	132
MOSSLEY HILL	57	NAAS	7	NEW BLISS	2	NEWPORT (Mayo)	4
MOSS ROAD HALT	28	NABURN	50	NEW BOLINGBROKE	72	NEWPORT (Mon)	98
MOSS SIDE	42	NAFFERTON	53	NEWBRIDGE (Kil)	6	NEWPORT (Salop)	80
MOSSTOWIE	15	NAILBRIDGE HALT	110	NEWBRIDGE (Mon)	97	NEWPORT (IOW)	139
MOSTON	46	NAILSEA + BACKWELL	101	NEWBRIDGE-ON-WYE	75	NEWPORT (Yorks E)	53
MOSTRIM	6	NAILSWORTH	110	NEW BRIGHTON	57	NEWPORT (Yorks N)	38
MOSTYN	56	NAIRN	14	NEW BROMPTON	132	NEWPORT PAGNELL	85
MOTHERWELL	22	NANCEGOLLAN	147	NEW BUILDINGS	2	NEW PUDSEY	46
MOTSPUR PARK	122	NANNERCH	56	NEWBURGH	17	NEWQUAY	147
MOTTINGHAM	123	NANSTALLON HALT	148	NEWBURN	33	NEW RADNOR	76
MOTTISFONT	139	NANTCLWYD	56	NEWBURY	114	NEW ROMNEY	146
MOTTRAM + BROAD BOTTOM	62	NANTGAREDIG	92	NEWBURY PARK	121	NEW ROMNEY + LITTLESTONE	146
MOULDSWORTH	57	NANTGARW HALT	100	NEWBURY RACECOURSE	114	NEW ROSS	10
MOULSECOOMB	142	NANTGWERNOL	74	NEWBURY WESTFIELDS HALT	114	NEWRY	3
MOULTON (Lincs)	72	NANTLLE	55	NEWBY BRIDGE	35	NEWSEAT	15
MOULTON (Yorks)	38	NANTMOR	55	NEWBY WISKE	38	NEWSHAM	33
MOUNTAIN ASH	96	NANTWICH	57	NEWCASTLE (Down)	3	NEWSHOLME	46
MOUNTAIN STAGE	8	NANTYBWCH	97	NEWCASTLE (Limerick)	9	NEW SOUTHGATE	121
MOUNTCHARLES	1	NANTYDERRY	98	NEWCASTLE (Wicklow)	7	NEWSTEAD	65
MOUNT FLORIDA	19	NANTYFFYLLON	95	NEWCASTLE-EMLYN	74	NEW THORPE	65
MOUNT GOULD + TOTHILL HALT	149	NANTYGLO	97	NEWCASTLE-ON-TYNE	33	NEWTON (Chesh)	62
		NANTYMOEL	96	NEWCASTLETON	30	NEWTON (Lanark)	18
MOUNT HAWKE HALT	147	NANTYRONEN	74	NEWCASTLE-UNDER-LYME	62	NEWTON ABBOT	148
MOUNTMELLICK	6	NAPSBURY	119	NEWCHAPEL + GOLDEN HILL	61	NEWTON AIRDS	29
MOUNT MELVILLE	17	NAPTON + STOCKTON	82	NEWCHURCH	141	NEWTON AYCLIFFE	38
MOUNT PLEASANT ROAD HALT	7	NARBETH	74	NEW CLEE	53	NEWTONDALE HALT	40
		NARBOROUGH (Leics)	82	NEWCOURT	12	NEWTON HEATH	46
MOUNT VERNON	18	NARBOROUGH (Norf)	89	NEW CROSS	130	NEWTON HILL	15
MOURNE ABBEY	9	NARROW WATER	3	NEW CROSS GATE	130	NEWTON KYME	50
MOW COP	62	NASSINGTON	85	NEW CUMNOCK	29	NEWTON-LE-WILLOWS	57
MOY	14	NATEBY	42	NEW CUT LANE HALT	43	NEWTONMORE	14
MOYASTA JUNCTION	8	NAVAN	6	NEW ELTHAM + POPE STREET	123	NEWTON-ON-AYR	26
MOYCULLEN	4	NAVENBY	70	NEWENT	110	NEWTON POPPLEFORD	136
MOYVALLEY	6	NAVIGATION ROAD	62	NEW GALLOWAY	29	NEWTON ROAD	80
MUCHALLS	15	NAWORTH	32	NEW HADLEY HALT	76	NEWTON ST CYRES	135
MUCH WENLOCK	76	NAWTON	40	NEW HAILES	25	NEWTON-STEWART	28
MUCKAMORE HALT	3	NEASDEN + KINGSBURY	124	NEWHALL	14	NEWTON TONY	139
MUINE BHEAG	10	NEATH	95	NEWHAM	33	NEWTOWN	75
MUIREND	18	NEATH ABBEY	95	NEW HAVEN	26	NEWTOWNARDS	3
MUIRKIRK	29	NEEDHAM MARKET	89	NEWHAVEN HARBOUR	142	NEWTOWN BUTLER	2
MUIR OF ORD	14	NEEN SOLLARS	76	NEWHAVEN MARINE	142	NEWTOWNCUNNINGHAM	2
MULBEN	15	NEEPSEND	65	NEWHAVEN TOWN	142	NEWTOWN FORBES	6
MULLAFERNACHAN	3	NEILL'S HILL	3	NEW HEY	46	NEWTOWNSTEWART	2

† Shown as Goods on map - see note

PATELEY BRIDGE	46	PENTRAETH	55	PITSEA	132	PONTNEWYDD	97
PATNA	28	PENTRE	96	PITSFORD + BRAMPTON	85	PONTNEWYNYDD	97
PATNEY + CHIRTON	139	PENTREBACH	96	PITTENWEEM	25	PONTRHYDYFEN	95
PATRICK'S WELL	9	PENTRECOURT PLATFORM	74	PITTINGTON	38	PONTRHYDYRUN	97
PATRICROFT	62	PENTREFELIN	56	PITT'S HEAD	55	PONTRHYTHALLT	55
PATRINGTON	53	PENTWYNMAWR HALT	97	PITTS HILL	62	PONTRILAS	92
PATTERTON	19	PENYBONT	75	PLAIDY	15	PONT RUG	55
PAULTON HALT	137	PENYBONTFAWR	56	PLAINS	22	PONTSARN	96
PEAKE	12	PENYCHAIN	55	PLAISTOW	128	PONTSTICILL JUNCTION	96
PEAK FOREST	62	PEN-Y-FFORDD	57	PLANTATION HALT	28	PONTWALBY HALT	95
PEAKIRK	85	PENYGRAIG + TONYPANDY	96	PLAS HALT	55	PONTYATES	93
PEAR TREE + NORMANTON	65	PENYGROES	55	PLASHETTS	32	PONTYBEREM	93
PEASLEY CROSS	57	PENYRHEOL	100	PLAS MARL	94	PONTYCYMMER	95
PECKHAM RYE	130	PENZANCE	147	PLAS POWER	57	PONT-Y-PANT	56
PEDAIR FFORDD	56	PEPLOW	57	PLATT BRIDGE	44	PONTYPOOL	97
PEEBLES	25	PERCY MAIN	33	PLAWSWORTH	38	PONTYPOOL ROAD	97
PEEL	41	PERIVALE	120	PLEALEY ROAD	76	PONTYPRIDD	96
PEEL CAUSEWAY	62	PERRANPORTH	147	PLEAN	22	PONTYRHYLL	99
PEEL ROAD	41	PERRANWELL	147	PLEASINGTON	42	POOL	46
PEGSWOOD	33	PERRY BAR	80	PLEASLEY	65	POOLE	139
PELAW	33	PERSHORE	80	PLECK	81	POOL QUAY	76
PELLON	46	PERSLEY	15	PLESSEY	33	POPLAR	128
PELSALL	80	PERTH	17	PLEX MOSS LANE HALT	43	POPPLETON	50
PELTON	33	PETERBOROUGH	85	PLOCKTON	14	PORT HALT	1
PEMBERTON	42	PETERCHURCH	92	PLODDER LANE	45	PORTADOWN	3
PEMBREY	93	PETERHEAD	15	PLOWDEN	76	PORTARLINGTON	6
PEMBREY + BURRY PORT	93	PETERSFIELD	141	PLUCK	2	PORTBURY	101
PEMBRIDGE	76	PETERSTON	100	PLUCKLEY	145	PORT CARLISLE	30
PEMBROKE	74	PETROCKSTOW	135	PLUMBLEY	62	PORTCHESTER	141
PENALLY	74	PETTIGO	2	PLUMPTON (Cumb)	35	PORT CLARENCE	40
PENARTH	100	PETT'S WOOD	123	PLUMPTON (Sussex)	142	PORT DINORWIC	55
PENCADER	92	PETWORTH	141	PLUMSTEAD	123	PORT ELPHINSTONE	15
PENCAITLAND	25	PEVENSEY + WESTHAM	145	PLUMTREE	65	PORT ERIN	41
PENCLAWDD	94	PEVENSEY BAY HALT	145	PLYM BRIDGE PLATFORM	148	PORTESHAM	137
PENCOED	99	PEWSEY	114	PLYMOUTH	148	PORTESSIE	15
PENDLEBURY	45	PHILORTH	15	PLYMPTON	148	PORT GLASGOW	18
PENDRE	74	PHILPSTOUN	22	PLYMSTOCK	148	PORT GORDON	15
PENGAM (Glam)	97	PICCADILLY CIRCUS	127	POCKLINGTON	50	PORTH	96
PENGAM (Mon)	97	PICKBURN + BRODSWORTH	50	POINT PLEASANT	34	PORTHALL	2
PENGE	131	PICKERING	40	POKESDOWN	139	PORTHCAWL	95
PENHELIG	74	PICKHILL	38	POLEGATE	145	PORTHYWAEN	57
PENICUIK	25	PICKTON	38	POLESWORTH	82	PORT ISAAC ROAD	148
PENISTONE	46	PIDDLINGTON	85	POLLOKSHAWS	19	PORTISHEAD	101
PENKETH (See Fiddler's Ferry)	57	PIEL	35	POLLOKSHIELDS	19	PORTKNOCKIE	15
PENKRIDGE	80	PIERCEBRIDGE	38	POLMONT	22	PORTLAND	137
PENMAEN HALT	97	PIER HEAD	58	POLSHAM	137	PORTLAND ROAD	127
PENMAENMAWR	56	PIERSHILL	25	POLSLOE BRIDGE PLATFORM	135	PORTLAOISE	6
PENMERE	147	PILL	110	POLTON	25	PORTLETHEN	15
PENNARD	137	PILLING	42	POMATHORN	25	PORTMADOC	55
PENMAEN POOL	74	PILMOOR	38	POMEROY	2	PORTMARNOCK	7
PENN HALT	80	PILNING	110	PONDERS END	121	PORT MEADOW HALT	116
PENNINGTON	57	PILOT HALT	146	PONFEIGH	22	PORTOBELLO	25
PENNS	80	PILSLEY	65	PONTARDAWE	95	PORT OF MENTEITH	18
PENPERGWM	98	PINCHBECK	72	PONTARDULAIS	94	PORTON	139
PENRHIWCEIBER	96	PINCHINTHORPE	40	PONTCYNON PLATFORM	96	PORTPATRICK	28
PENRHYNDEUDRAETH	55	PINGED HALT	93	PONTDOLGOCH	75	PORTRUSH	2
PENRITH	37	PINHOE	135	PONTEFRACT	50	PORT ST MARY	21
PENRUDDOCK	35	PINMORE	28	PONTELAND	33	PORTSKEWETT	110
PENRYN	147	PINNER	120	PONTESBURY	76	PORTSLADE	142
PENSARN	55	PINWHERRY	28	PONTFADOG	57	PORTSMOUTH (Lancs)	46
PENSFORD	110	PINXTON	65	PONTFAEN	57	PORTSMOUTH + SOUTHSEA	141
PENSHAW	33	PINXTON + SELSTON	65	PONT GROESOR	55	PORTSMOUTH ARMS	135
PENSHURST	145	PIPE GATE	62	PONTHENRY	93	PORTSMOUTH HARBOUR	141
PENSNETT HALT	80	PITCAPLE	15	PONTHIR	98	PORT SODERICK	41
PENTEWAN	148	PITFODELS	15	PONT LAWRENCE	97	PORTSOY	15
PENTIR RHIW	96	PITLOCHRY	17	PONTLLANFRAITH	97	PORTSTEWART	2
PENTON	30	PITLURG	15	PONT LLANIO	74	PORT SUNLIGHT	57
		PITMEDDEN	15	PONTLOTTYN	97	PORT TALBOT	99

Station	Page
PORT VICTORIA	132
POSSIL PARK	19
POSTLAND	87
POST OFFICE	127
POTTERHANWORTH	70
POTTER HEIGHAM	90
POTTERHILL	18
POTTER'S BAR	119
POTTO	38
POTTON	87
POULAPHOURCA	7
POULTON-LE-FLYDE	42
POWDERHALL	26
POWERSTOCK	137
POYLE	122
POYNTON	62
POYNTZ PASS	3
PRAED STREET	125
PRAZE	147
PREES	57
PREESALL	42
PREESGWEENE	57
PRESCOT	57
PRESCOTT SIDING	76
PRESTATYN	56
PRESTBURY	62
PRESTEIGN	76
PRESTHOPE	76
PRESTON	42
PRESTON BROOK	57
PRESTON JUNCTION	42
PRESTON PANS	25
PRESTON PARK	142
PRESTON ROAD (Lancs)	58
PRESTON ROAD (Mx)	120
PRESTWICH	46
PRESTWICK	28
PRIESTFIELD	80
PRIMROSE HILLS	125
PRINCE'S DOCK	58
PRINCE'S END	80
PRINCE'S RISBOROUGH	116
PRINCETOWN	148
PRITTLEWELL	132
PRIVET	141
PRIVETT	141
PROBUS + LADOCK PLATFORM	147
PRUDHOE	33
PUDSEY GREENSIDE	46
PUDSEY LOWTON	46
PUDSEY, NEW	46
PULBOROUGH	142
PULHAM MARKET	89
PULHAM ST MARY	90
PUNCHESTON	74
PURFLEET	132
PURLEY	123
PURLEY OAKS	123
PURTON	114
PUTNEY	122
PUTNEY BRIDGE + HURLINGHAM	122
PUXTON	101
PWLLHELI	55
PYE BRIDGE	65
PYE HILL + SOMERCOATS	65
PYLE	99
PYLLE	137

Station	Page
QUAINTON ROAD	116
QUAKERS YARD	96
QUARTER ROAD	22
QUEENSBOROUGH	132
QUEENSBURY (Mx)	120
QUEENSBURY (Yorks)	46
QUEEN'S FERRY	57
QUEEN'S PARK (Lanark)	19
QUEEN'S PARK (London)	125
QUEEN'S ROAD (Battersea)	129
QUEEN'S ROAD (Bayswater)	125
QUEEN'S ROAD (Peckham)	130
QUEENSTOWN	12
QUEENSTOWN JUNCTION	12
QUELLYN LAKE	55
QUILTY	8
QUINTREL DOWNS	147
QUORN + WOODHOUSE	82
QUY	87
RACECOURSE (Liverpool)	58
RACECOURSE (Nottingham)	65
RACKS	30
RADCLIFFE	42
RADCLIFFE BRIDGE	42
RADCLIFFE-ON-TRENT	65
RADFORD	65
RADFORD + TIMSBURY HALT	137
RADIPOLE HALT	137
RADLETT	119
RADLEY	116
RADSTOCK	137
RADWAY GREEN	62
RADYR	100
RAFFEEN	12
RAGLAN	98
RAHENY	7
RAINFORD JUNCTION	42
RAINFORD VILLAGE	42
RAINHAM (Essex)	132
RAINHAM (Kent)	132
RAINHILL	57
RAMPSIDE	35
RAMSDEN DOCKS	35
RAMSBOTTOM	42
RAMSEY (Hunts)	87
RAMSEY (IOM)	41
RAMSGATE	133
RAMSGILL	38
RANDALSTOWN	3
RANELAGH	7
RANKINSTON	28
RANNOCH	16
RANSKILL	65
RAPHOE	2
RASHENRY	2
RASKELF	50
RATBY	82
RATHDRUM	11

Station	Page
RATHDUFF	9
RATHEN	15
RATHGAROGUE	10
RATHKEALE	9
RATHKENNY	3
RATHLURIC	9
RATHMINES + RANELAGH	7
RATHMORE	8
RATHNEW	11
RATHO	22
RATHVEN	15
RATHVILLY	10
RAUCEBY	70
RAUNDS	85
RAVELRIG	22
RAVENGLASS	35
RAVENSBOURNE	131
RAVENSCAR	40
RAVENSCOURT PARK	124
RAVENSCRAIG	18
RAVEN SQUARE	76
RAVENSTHORPE	49
RAVENSTHORPE + THORNHILL	46
RAVENSTONEDALE	37
RAWCLIFFE (See Airmyn)	50
RAWMARSH (See Parkgate)	65
RAWTENSTALL	46
RAWYARDS	22
RAYDON WOOD	89
RAYLEIGH	132
RAYNE	132
RAYNERS LANE	120
RAYNES PARK	122
RAYNHAM PARK	73
READING	116
REARSBY	82
RECESS	4
RECTORY ROAD	126
REDBOURN	119
RED BRIDGE (Hants)	139
REDBRIDGE (London)	121
REDBROOK	110
REDCAR	40
REDCASTLE	14
REDDISH NORTH	62
REDDISH SOUTH	63
REDDITCH	80
RED HILL (Shrewsbury)	76
RED HILL (Surrey)	142
REDHILLS	6
REDLAND	110
RED LION CROSSING HALT	94
REDMILE	70
REDMIRE	38
REDNAL + WEST FELTON	77
RED ROCK	42
REDRUTH	147
RED WHARF BAY + BENLLECH	55
REEDHAM	90
REEDHAM HALT	123
REEDNESS	50
REEDSMOUTH	32
REEPHAM (Lincs)	70
REEPHAM (Norf)	73
REGENTS PARK	125
REIGATE	142
RENFREW	18
RENISHAW (See Eckington)	65

Station	Page
RENTON	18
REPTON + WILLINGTON	65
RESOLVEN	95
RESTON	27
RETFORD	70
RHAYADER	75
RHEIDOL FALLS	75
RHEWL	56
RHIGOS HALT	96
RHIWBWA HALT	100
RHIWDERYN	100
RHIWFRON	75
RHOOSE	100
RHOS	57
RHOSGOCH	55
RHOSNEIGR	55
RHOSTRYFAN	55
RHOSTYLLEN	57
RHUDDLAN	56
RHUDDLAN ROAD	56
RHYDOWEN	74
RHYDYFELIN HALT	100
RHYDYFRO	95
RHYDYMWYN	57
RHYDYRONEN	74
RHYD-Y-SAINT	55
RHYL	56
RHYMNEY	97
RHYMNEY BRIDGE	97
RHYMNEY-PONTLOTTYN	97
RIBBLEHEAD	37
RIBBLETON	42
RICCALL	50
RICCARTON JUNCTION	32
RICE LANE	58
RICHHILL	3
RICHMOND (Surrey)	122
RICHMOND (Yorks)	38
RICKMANSWORTH	120
RIDDINGS	30
RIDDLESDOWN	123
RIDGMONT	116
RIDING MILL	33
RIGG	30
RILLINGTON	40
RIMINGTON	42
RINGLEY ROAD	42
RINGSTEAD + ADDINGTON	85
RINGWOOD	139
RIPLEY	65
RIPLEY VALLEY	46
RIPON	38
RIPPINGDALE	70
RIPPLE	110
RIPPONDEN + BARKISLAND	46
RISBY (See Sarham)	89
RISCA	97
RISHTON	42
RISHWORTH	46
RIVERSIDE (Liverpool)	58
RIVERSIDE (Totnes)	148
ROADE	85
ROBERTSBRIDGE	145
ROBERTSTOWN PLATFORM	96
ROBIN HOOD'S BAY	40
ROBROYSTON	19
ROBY	57
ROCESTER	62

✳ Same station used by two companies - each used a different name.

Station	Pg	Station	Pg	Station	Pg	Station	Pg
SAUGHTON	22	SELBY	50	SHERBURN HOUSE	38	SILVERTOWN	121
SAUGHTREE	32	SELHAM	141	SHERBURN-IN-ELMET	50	SIMONSTONE	42
SAUNDERSFOOT	74	SELHURST	131	SHERE (See Gomshall)	142	SINCLAIRTOWN	25
SAUNDERTON	116	SELKIRK	30	SHERINGHAM	73	SINDERBY	38
SAVERNAKE	114	SELLAFIELD	35	SHERWOOD	68	SINFIN	65
SAWBRIDGEWORTH	119	SELLING	146	SHETTLESTON	18	SINGLETON (Lancs)	42
SAWDON	40	SELLY OAK	80	SHIDE	141	SINGLETON (Sussex)	141
SAWLEY	65	SELSDON ROAD	123	SHIELDHILL	30	SINNINGTON	40
SAWLEY JUNCTION	65	SELSEY	141	SHIELD ROW	33	SION MILLS	2
SAXBY	85	SELSTON (See Pinxton)	65	SHIELDS	20A	SIRHOWY	97
SAXHAM + RISBY	89	SEMINGTON HALT	110	SHIELDS ROAD	20A	SITTINGBOURNE + MILTON REGIS	132
SAXILBY	70	SEMLEY	137	SHIELMUIR	22	SIX MILE BOTTOM	87
SAXMUNDHAM	90	SENGHENYDD	97	SHIFNAL	80	SIXMILEBRIDGE	9
SCALBY	40	SESSAY	38	SHILDON	38	SIXMILECROSS	2
SCALFORD	70	SETTLE	46	SHILLELAGH	11	SKARES	29
SCARBOROUGH	40	SETTRINGTON	53	SHILLINGSTONE	137	SKEAF	12
SCARCLIFFE	65	SEVEN KINGS	121	SHILTON	82	SKEGBY	65
SCARVA	3	SEVENOAKS	145	SHINCLIFFE	38	SKEGNESS	72
SCAWBY + HIBALDSTOW	53	SEVEN SISTERS (Glam)	95	SHIPLAKE	116	SKELBO	13
SCHOLES	50	SEVEN SISTERS (Mx)	121	SHIPLEY	46	SKELLINGTHORPE	70
SCHOOLHILL	15	SEVEN STARS	76	SHIPLEY GATE	65	SKELMANTHORPE	46
SCHULL	12	SEVERN BEACH	110	SHIPPEA HILL	87	SKELMERSDALE	42
SCOPWITH + TIMBERLAND	70	SEVERN BRIDGE	110	SHIPTON	114	SKERRIES	7
SCORRIER	147	SEVERN TUNNEL JUNCTION	101	SHIPTON-ON-STOUR	82	SKEWEN	95
SCORTON (Lancs)	42	SEXHOW	38	SHIRDLEY HILL	42	SKIBBEREEN	12
SCORTON (Yorks)	38	SHACKERSTONE	82	SHIREBROOK	65	SKINNINGROVE	40
SCOTBY	30	SHADWELL	127	SHIREHAMPTON	110	SKIPTON	46
SCOTCH DYKE	30	SHADWELL + ST GEORGE'S EAST	127	SHIREOAKS	65	SKIPWITH	50
SCOTSCALDER	13	SHAKESPEARE STAFF HALT	146	SHIRLEY	80	SKIRLAUGH	53
SCOTSGAP	33	SHALFORD	141	SHOEBURYNESS	132	SLADES GREEN	132
SCOTSTOUN	19	SHALLEE	9	SHOLING	139	SLAGGYFORD	32
SCOTSTOUNHILL	19	SHANDON	18	SHOOTERS HILL + ELTHAM PARK	123	SLAITHWAITE	46
SCOTSWOOD	33	SHANKEND	32	SHOREDITCH	127	SLAMANNAN	22
SCRAPTOFT (See Thurnby)	32	SHANKHILL	7	SHOREHAM	132	SLATEFORD	25
SCREMERSTON	27	SHANKLIN	141	SHOREHAM-BY-SEA	142	SLEAFORD	70
SCROOBY	65	SHAP	37	SHORNCLIFFE CAMP	146	SLEDMERE + FIMBER	53
SCRUTON	38	SHAPWICK	136	SHORT HEATH	81	SLEIGHTS	40
SCUNTHORPE	53	SHARLSTON	50	SHORTLANDS	123	SLIGO	1
SEACOMBE + EGREMONT	57	SHARNAL STREET	132	SHOTLEY BRIDGE	33	SLINFOLD	142
SEABURN	33	SHARNBROOK	85	SHOTTLE	65	SLINGSBY	40
SEACROFT	72	SHARPNESS	110	SHOTTON	57	SLOANE SQUARE	125
SEAFORD	142	SHAUGH BRIDGE	148	SHOTTON BRIDGE	38	SLOUGH	116
SEAFORTH + LITHERLAND	57	SHAW + CROMPTON	46	SHOTTS	22	SMALLFORD	119
SEAHAM	38	SHAWCLOUGH + HEALEY	46	SHRAWARDINE	76	SMALL HEATH + SPARKBROOK	80
SEAHAM COLLIERY	33	SHAWFORD + TWYFORD	139	SHREWSBURY	76	SMARDALE	37
SEAHILL	3	SHAWFORTH	46	SHRIVENHAM	114	SMEAFIELD	27
SEAHOUSES	27	SHAWLANDS	19	SHUSTOKE	82	SMEATON	25
SEAMER	40	SHEEPBRIDGE + BRIMMINGTON	65	SIBLE + CASTLE HEDINGHAM	132	SMEETH	146
SEA MILLS	110	SHEEPBRIDGE + WHITTINGTON MOOR	65	SIBLEY'S	132	SMEETH ROAD	87
SEAPOINT	7	SHEERNESS	132	SIBSEY	72	SMETHWICK	81
SEASCALE	35	SHEFFIELD	65	SIDCUP	123	SMETHWICK JUNCTION	81
SEATON (Cumb)	35	SHEFFIELD PARK	142	SIDDICK	35	SMITHAM	123
SEATON (Devon)	136	SHEFFORD	119	SIDLESHAM	141	SMITHBOROUGH	2
SEATON (Durham)	38	SHELFORD	87	SIDLEY	145	SMITHY BRIDGE	46
SEATON (Rutland)	85	SHENFIELD + HUTTON	132	SIDMOUTH	136	SNAINTON	40
SEATON CAREW	38	SHENSTONE	80	SIDMOUTH JUNCTION	136	SNAITH	50
SEATON DELAVAL	33	SHENTON	82	SIDNEY PARADE (See Sydney)	7	SNAITH + POLLINGTON	50
SEATON JUNCTION	136	SHEPHERD'S	147	SIGGLESTHORNE	53	SNAPPER	135
SEDBERGH	37	SHEPHERD'S BUSH	124	SILEBY	82	SNARESBROOK	121
SEDGEBROOK	70	SHEPHERD'S WELL	146	SILECROFT	35	SNARESTONE	82
SEDGEFIELD	38	SHEPLEY + SHELLEY	46	SILIAN HALT	74	SNELLAND	70
SEDGEFORD	73	SHEPPERTON	122	SILKSTONE	46	SNETTISHAM	72
SEEDLY	62	SHEPRETH	87	SILLOTH	30	SNODLAND	132
SEEND	110	SHEPSHED	82	SILVERDALE (Lancs)	35	SNOWDON SOUTH	55
SEER GREEN HALT	116	SHEPTON MALLET	137	SILVERDALE (Staffs)	52	SNOWDON SUMMIT	55
SEFTON	42	SHERBORNE	137	SILVER STREET	121	SNOWDOWN	146
SEFTON PARK	58	SHERBURN COLLIERY	38	SILVERTON	135	SNOW HILL (Birm)	81
SEGHILL	33						

SNOW HILL (London)	127	SOUTHWATER	142	STANDON	119	STOKE (Staffs)	62
SOHAM	87	SOUTHWELL	70	STANDON BRIDGE	62	STOKE (Suff)	89
SOHO (Birm)	80	SOUTHWICK (Sussex)	142	STANFORD-LE-HOPE	132	STOKE CANON	135
SOHO + WINSON GREEN	80	SOUTHWICK (Kirkcudbr)	29	STANHOE	73	STOKE EDITH	76
SOHO ROAD	80	SOUTH WILLINGHAM +		STANHOPE	38	STOKE FERRY	87
SOLE STREET	132	HAINTON	72	STANLEY (Lancs)	58	STOKE GOLDING	82
SOLIHULL	80	SOUTH WIMBLEDON	129	STANLEY (Perth)	17	STOKE MANDEVILLE	116
SOMERLEYTON	90	SOUTH WITHAM	85	STANLEY (Yorks)	50	STOKE NEWINGTON	126
SOMERSET ROAD	80	SOUTHWOLD	90	STANLOW + THORNTON	58	STOKESAY (See Craven Arms)	76
SOMERSHAM	87	SOUTH WOODFORD	121	STANMORE	120	STOKES BAY	141
SOMERTON	136	SOWERBY BRIDGE	46	STANNER	76	STOKESLEY	40
SORBIE	28	SPA	8	STANNINGLEY	46	STOKE WORKS	80
SOUTH ACTON	124	SPALDING	72	STANNINGTON	33	STONEA	87
SOUTHALL	120	SPARMOUNT	2	STANSFIELD HALL	46	STONEBRIDGE PARK	124
SOUTHAM + LONG		SPA ROAD + BERMONDSEY	127	STANSTED	132	STONE CROSSING HALT	132
ITCHINGTON	82	SPARKFORD	137	STANTON	114	STONEGATE	145
SOUTHAMPTON	139	SPARROWLEE	62	STANTON GATE	65	STONEHAVEN	17
SOUTHAMPTON AIRPORT	139	SPEAN BRIDGE	16	STAPLE	146	STONEHOUSE (Glos)	110
SOUTHAM ROAD + HARBURY	82	SPEECH HOUSE ROAD	110	STAPLE EDGE HALT	110	STONEHOUSE (Lanark)	22
SOUTH AYLESBURY HALT	116	SPEEN	114	STAPLEFORD + SANDIACRE	65	STONE JUNCTION	62
SOUTH BANK	40	SPEETON	40	STAPLE HILL	110	STONELEIGH	122
SOUTH BERMONDSEY	130	SPEKE	57	STAPLEHURST	145	STONEYWOOD	15
SOUTHBOROUGH	145	SPELLOW	58	STAPLETON ROAD	113	STORETON	57
SOUTHBOURNE HALT	141	SPENCER ROAD HALT	123	STARBECK	50	STOTTESDON	76
SOUTH BROMLEY	128	SPENNITHORPE	38	STARCROSS	135	STOULTON	80
SOUTHBURN	53	SPENNYMOOR	38	STAVELEY	35	STOURBRIDGE JUNCTION	80
SOUTHBURY	121	SPETTISBURY	137	STAVELEY TOWN	65	STOURBRIDGE TOWN	80
SOUTH CAMP (See Aldershot)	141	SPILSBY	72	STAVELEY WORKS	67	STOURPAINE + DURWESTON	
SOUTH CANTERBURY (See		SPINK HILL	65	STAVERTON	148	HALT	137
Canterbury	146	SPITAL	57	STAWARD	32	STOURPORT	80
SOUTH CAVE	53	SPOFFORTH	50	STEAM MILLS CROSSING		STOW (Edinburgh)	25
SOUTHCOATES	53	SPONDON	65	HALT	110	STOW (Norfolk)	87
SOUTH DOCK	128	SPON LANE	81	STECHFORD	80	STOW BEDON	89
SOUTH EALING	122	SPOONER ROW	89	STEELE ROAD	32	STOWMARKET	89
SOUTHEASE + ROOMELL HALT	142	SPRATTON	85	STEENS BRIDGE	76	STOW-ON-THE-WOLD	114
SOUTH ELMSALL	50	SPRINGBURN	20A	STEER POINT	148	STOW PARK	70
SOUTHEND (Glam)	94	SPRINGFIELD	17	STEETON + SILSDEN	46	STRABANE	2
SOUTHEND-ON-SEA	132	SPRING ROAD	81	STEPFORD	29	STRADBROKE	90
SOUTHERNDOWN ROAD	99	SPRINGSIDE	18	STEPNEY (London)	127	STRAFFAN	7
SOUTHFIELDS	129	SPRING VALE	42	STEPNEY (Yorks)	53	STRAND	127
SOUTHFLEET	132	SPROTBOROUGH	50	STEPNEY GREEN	127	STRANOCUM	3
SOUTHGATE	121	SPROUSTON	27	STEPS ROAD	18	STRANOLAR	2
SOUTH GOSFORTH	33	SQUIRES GATE	42	STEVENAGE	119	STRANRAER	28
SOUTH GREENFORD	120	STACKSTEADS	46	STEVENSTON	18	STRATA FLORIDA	25
SOUTH HAMPSTEAD	125	STADDLETHORPE	53	STEVENTON	114	STRATFORD	128
SOUTH HARROW	120	STAFFORD	62	STEWARTBY	85	STRATFORD MARKET	128
SOUTH HETTON	38	STAFFORD COMMON	62	STEWARTON	18	STRATFORD-ON-AVON	80
SOUTHILL	85	STAFFORDSTOWN	3	STEWARTSTOWN	2	STRATHAVEN	18
SOUTH KENSINGTON	125	STAINCLIFFE + BATLEY CARR	49	STEYNING	142	STRATHBLANE	18
SOUTH KENTISH TOWN	125	STAINCROSS	50	STICKNEY	72	STRATHBUNGO	20A
SOUTH KENTON	120	STAINES	122	STILLINGTON	38	STRATHCARRON	14
SOUTH LEIGH	114	STAINES JUNCTION	122	STILLORGAN	7	STRATHMIGLOW	17
SOUTH LEITH	25	STAINFORTH + HATFIELD	50	STIRCHLEY	76	STRATHORD	17
SOUTH LYNN	87	STAINLAND + HOLYWELL GREEN	46	STIRLING	22	STRATHPEFFER	14
SOUTH MERTON	123	STAINTONDALE	40	STIXWOULD	70	STRATHYRE	16
SOUTH MILFORD	50	STAIRFOOT	50	STOBCROSS	19	STRATTON	114
SOUTHMINSTER	132	STAITHES	40	STOBO	22	STRAVITHIE	17
SOUTH MOLTON	135	STALBRIDGE	137	STOBS	32	STRAWBERRY HILL	122
SOUTH MOLTON ROAD	135	STALEY + MILLBROOK	62	STOCKBRIDGE	139	STREAMSTOWN	6
SOUTHPORT	42	STALHAM	73	STOCKCROSS + BAGNOR	114	STREATHAM	129
SOUTH RENFREW (See Renfrew)	18	STALLINGBOROUGH	53	STOCKINGFORD	82	STREATHAM COMMON	129
SOUTHREY	70	STALYBRIDGE	62	STOCKPORT	62	STREATHAM HILL	131
SOUTHSEA (See Portsmouth)	141	STAMFORD	85	STOCKSFIELD	33	STREET + RATHOWEN	6
SOUTH SHIELDS	33	STAMFORD BRIDGE	50	STOCKSMOOR	46	STREETLY	80
SOUTH STREET HALT	146	STAMFORD BROOK	124	STOCKTON	38	STRENSALL	50
SOUTH TOTTENHAM	126	STAMFORD HILL	126	STOCKTON-BROOK	62	STRETFORD	62
SOUTHWAITE	35	STANBRIDGEFORD	116	STOCKWELL	130	STRETFORD BRIDGE	76
SOUTHWARK PARK	130	STANDISH	42	STOGUMBER	136	STRETHAM	87

Name	Page
STRETTON	65
STRETTON + CLAY MILLS	65
STRETTON · ON · FOSSE	114
STRICHEN	15
STRINES	62
STROME FERRY	14
STROOD	132
STROUD	110
STROUD GREEN	126
STRUAN	16
STUBBINS	42
STUDLEY + ASTWOOD BANK	80
STURMER	87
STURMINSTER NEWTON	137
STURRY	133
STURTON	70
STYAL	62
SUCKLEY	80
SUDBURY (Derby)	62
SUDBURY (Suff)	89
SUDBURY + HARROW ROAD	120
SUDBURY HILL	120
SUDBURY TOWN	120
SULBY BRIDGE	41
SULBY GLEN	41
SULLY	100
SUMMER LANE	50
SUMMERSEAT	42
SUMMERSTON	18
SUNBURY	122
SUNDERLAND	33
SUNDRIDGE PARK	123
SUNILAWS	27
SUNNINGDALE	116
SUNNYMEADS	116
SURBITON	122
SURFLEET	72
SURREY DOCKS	130
SUTTON (Cambs)	87
SUTTON (Surrey)	123
SUTTON + BALDOYLE (See Baldoyle)	7
SUTTON BINGHAM	137
SUTTON BRIDGE	72
SUTTON COLDFIELD	80
SUTTON COMMON	123
SUTTON · IN · ASH	65
SUTTON JUNCTION	65
SUTTON OAK	60
SUTTON · ON · HULL	53
SUTTON · ON · SEA	72
SUTTON PARK	80
SUTTON SCOTNEY	139
SUTTON WEAVER	57
SWADLINCOTE	82
SWAFFHAM	89
SWAFFHAM PRIOR	87
SWAINSTHORPE	90
SWALE	132
SWALWELL	33
SWANAGE	139
SWANBOURNE	116
SWANBRIDGE PLATFORM	100
SWANLEY JUNCTION	132
SWANNINGTON	82
SWANSCOMBE HALT	132
SWANSEA	94
SWANSEA BAY	94
SWAN VILLAGE	80

Name	Page
SWANWICK	141
SWAVESEY	87
SWAY	139
SWAYTHLING	139
SWIMBRIDGE	135
SWINDERBY	70
SWINDON	114
SWINDON TOWN	114
SWINE	53
SWINESHEAD	72
SWINFORD	5
SWINTON (Lancs)	42
SWINTON (Yorks)	65
SWISS COTTAGE	125
SYDENHAM (Down)	3
SYDENHAM (Kent)	131
SYDENHAM HILL	131
SYDNEY PARADE	7
SYKEHOUSE	50
SYLFAEN HALT	75
SYMINGTON	22
SYMONDS YAT	110
SYON LANE	122
SYSTON	82

Name	Page
TACKLEY	114
TADCASTER	50
TADWORTH + WALTON · ON · HILL	142
TAFFS WELL	100
TAIN	13
TAKERLEY	132
TALACRE	56
TALEDDIG	75
TALGARTH	92
TALLAGHT	7
TALLEY ROAD	92
TALLINGTON	85
TALLOW ROAD	9
TALSARNAU	55
TALSARN HALT	74
TALYBONT HALT	55
TALYBONT · ON · USK	92
TAL · Y · CAFN + EGLWYSBACH	56
TALYLLYN JUNCTION	92
TAMERTON FOLIOT	148
TAMWORTH	82
TANDERAGEE	3
TANFIELD	38
TANHOUSE LANE	60
TANKERTON HALT	146
TANNADICE	17
TANSHELF	50
TAN · Y · BWLCH	55
TAN · Y · GRISIAU	55
TAN · Y · MANOD	55
TAPLOW	116
TARBOTTOM	28
TARFF	29
TARSET	32
TASSAGH	2
TATTENHALL	57
TATTENHALL ROAD	57
TATTENHAM CORNER	142
TATTERSHALL	72

Name	Page
TAUNTON	136
TAVISTOCK	148
TAYNUILT	16
TAYPORT	17
TEAN	62
TEBAY	37
TEDDINGTON	122
TEES-SIDE AIRPORT	38
TEIGNGRACE	148
TEIGNMOUTH	148
TEMPLE	127
TEMPLECOMBE	137
TEMPLE HIRST	50
TEMPLE MEADS	113
TEMPLEMORE	19
TEMPLEOGUE	7
TEMPLEPATRICK	3
TEMPLE SOWERBY	37
TEMPLETON	74
TEMPSFORD	85
TENBURY WELLS	76
TENBY	74
TENTERDEN TOWN	145
TERENURE	7
TERN HILL	57
TERRINGTON	87
TETBURY	110
TETTENHALL	80
TEVERSALL	65
TEWKESBURY	110
TEYNHAM	132
THACKLEY	46
THAME	116
THAMES DITTON	122
THAMES HAVEN	132
THANKERTON	22
THATCHAM	116
THATTO HEATH	57
THAXTED	132
THEALE	116
THEDDINGWORTH	82
THEDDLETHORPE	72
THE DELL	147
THE DYKE	142
THE HALE HALT	120
THE LAKES	80
THE LAMB	7
THELWALL	57
THE MOUND	13
THE OAKS	42
THEOBALD'S GROVE	119
THETFORD	89
THETFORD BRIDGE	89
THEYDON BOIS	121
THIRSK	38
THOMASTOWN	10
THOMES BRIDGE	46
THOREANBY	50
THORINGTON	133
THORNABY	38
THORNBURY	110
THORNE	50
THORNER	50
THORNEY	87
THORNEYBURN	82
THORNEYWOOD	68
THORN FALCON	136
THORNFORD	137

Name	Page
THORNHILL (Dumf)	29
THORNHILL (Yorks)	46
THORNIELEE	25
THORNLEY	38
THORNLIEBANK	18
THORNTON (Fife)	25
THORNTON (Lancs)	42
THORNTON (Yorks)	46
THORNTON ABBEY	53
THORNTON DALE	40
THORNTONHALL	18
THORNTON HEATH	131
THORNTON · IN · CRAVEN	46
THORP ARCH	50
THORPE	85
THORPE BAY	132
THORPE CLOUD	62
THORPE CULVERT	72
THORPE · IN · BALNE	50
THORPE · LE · SOKEN	133
THORPE · ON · THE · HILL	70
THORPE THEWLES	38
THOR'S CAVE	62
THORVERTON	135
THRAPSTON	85
THREE BRIDGES	142
THREE COCKS JUNCTION	92
THREE COUNTIES	119
THREE OAKS	145
THRELKELD	35
THROSK PLATFORM	22
THRUMSTER	13
THURGARTON	65
THURLBY	85
THURLES	10
THURNBY + SCRAPTOFT	82
THURNSCOE (See Hickleton)	50
THURSFORD	73
THURSO	13
THURSTASTON	57
THURSTON	89
THUXTON	89
THWAITES	46
TIBBERMUIR	17
TIBSHELF + NEWTON	65
TIBSHELF TOWN	67
TICEHURST ROAD	145
TICKHILL + WADWORTH	65
TIDDINGTON	116
TIDENHAM	110
TIDWORTH	139
TILBURY	132
TILBURY DOCKS	132
TILE HILL	82
TILEHURST	116
TILLICOULTRY	22
TILLIETUDLEM	22
TILLYFOURIE	15
TILLYNAUGHT	15
TILLYSBURN HALT	3
TILTON	85
TIMOLEAGUE	12
TIMPERLEY	62
TWAHELY	11
TINGLEY	46
TINSLEY	65
TINSLEY GREEN FOR GATWICK AIRPORT	142

Station	No.	Station	No.	Station	No.	Station	No.
WHATSANDWELL	65	WICKHAM	141	WINSLOW	116	WOODHOUSE MILL	65
WHAUPHILL	28	WICKHAM BISHOPS	132	WINSLOW ROAD	116	WOODKIRK	46
WHEATHER HAMPSTEAD	119	WICKHAM MARKET	90	WINSON GREEN	81	WOODLANDS	12
WHEATLEY	116	WICKLOW	11	WINSTON	38	WOODLANDS ROAD HALT	46
WHEELOCK (Sandbach)	62	WICK ST LAWRENCE	101	WINTERBOURNE	110	WOOD LANE	124
WHELDRAKE	50	WICKWAR	110	WINTERINGHAM	53	WOODLAWN	5
WHERWELL	139	WIDDRINGTON	33	WINTERTON + THEALBY	53	WOODLESFORD	50
WHETSTOWE	82	WIDFORD	119	WINTON	25	WOODLEY	62
WHIFFLET	24	WIDMERPOOL	65	WIRKSWORTH	65	WOODMANSTERNE	142
WHIMPLE	136	WIDNES	57	WISBECH	87	WOODNESBOROUGH	146
WHIMSEY HALT	110	WIDNEY MANOR	80	WISBECH-ST-MARY	87	WOODNESBOROUGH ROAD	146
WHIPPINGHAM	141	WIGAN	42	WISHAW	22	WOODSIDE	15
WHISSENDINE	85	WIGSTON	82	WISHFORD	139	WOODSIDE + BURRELTON	17
WHISTLEFIELD	18	WIGSTON SOUTH	82	WISTOW	50	WOODSIDE + SOUTH NORWOOD	123
WHITACRE	82	WIGTON	28	WITHAM (Essex)	132	WOODSIDE BIRKENHEAD	58
WHITBORN	22	WIGTOWN	35	WITHAM (Som)	137	WOODSIDE PARK	121
WHITBY	40	WILBURTON	87	WITHCALL	72	WOOD SIDING	117
WHITCHURCH (Glam)	100	WILBY	90	WITHERNSEA	53	WOODSTOCK ROAD HALT	124
WHITCHURCH (Hants)	139	WILKINSTOWN	6	WITHINGTON (Glos)	114	WOOD STREET	121
WHITCHURCH (Salop)	57	WILLASTON	57	WITHINGTON (Hereford)	76	WOODVALE	42
WHITCHURCH DOWN PLATFORM	148	WILLBROOK	8	WITHINGTON + ALBERT PARK	62	WOODVILLE	82
WHITE ABBEY	3	WILLENHALL	80	WITHNELL	42	WOODVILLE ROAD PLATFORM	100
WHITE BEAR	42	WILLERBY + KIRK ELLA	53	WITHYHAM	142	WOODY BAY	135
WHITEBOROUGH	65	WILLESDEN GREEN + CRICKLEWOOD	125	WITLEY	141	WOOFFERTON	76
WHITECHAPEL	127	WILLESDEN JUNCTION	124	WITNEY	114	WOOKEY	137
WHITE CITY	124	WILLIAMWOOD	19	WITTERSHAM	145	WOOL	137
WHITE COLNE	132	WILLINGTON (Beds)	85	WITTON	80	WOOLASTON	110
WHITECRAIGS	18	WILLINGTON (Derby See Repton)	65	WITTON GILBERT	38	WOOLER	33
WHITECROFT	110	WILLINGTON (Durham)	38	WITTON-LE-WEAR	38	WOOLFOLD	42
WHITEDALE	53	WILLINGTON QUAY	33	WIVELISCOMBE	136	WOOLSTON	139
WHITE FIELD	46	WILLITON	136	WIVELISFIELD	142	WOOLWICH	123
WHITEGATE	57	WILLOUGHBY	72	WIVENHOE	133	WOOPERTON	33
WHITEHALL HALT	136	WILMCOTE	80	WIXFORD	80	WOOTTON	141
WHITE HART LANE	121	WILMINGTON	53	WOBURN SANDS	116	WOOTTON BASSETT	114
WHITEHAVEN	35	WILMSLOW	62	WOKING	141	WOOTTON WAWEN PLATFORM	80
WHITEHEAD	3	WILNECOTE	82	WOKINGHAM	116	WORCESTER	80
WHITEHOUSE (Aberdeen)	15	WILPSHIRE	42	WOLDINGHAM	142	WORCESTER PARK	122
WHITEHOUSE (Antrim)	3	WILSDEN	46	WOLFERTON	72	WORKINGTON	35
WHITEINCH	19	WILSONTOWN	22	WOLSINGHAM	38	WORKINGTON BRIDGE	35
WHITE NOTLEY	132	WILSTROP SIDING ‡	50	WOLVERCOTE HALT	116	WORKSOP	65
WHITERIGG	22	WILTON	139	WOLVERCOT PLATFORM	114	WORLESTON	57
WHITHORN	28	WIMBLEDON	122	WOLVERHAMPTON	80	WORLE	101
WHITLAND	74	WIMBLEDON CHASE	129	WOLVERTON	85	WORLE TOWN	101
WHITLEY BAY	33	WIMBLEDON PARK	129	WOMBOURN	80	WORLINGWORTH	90
WHITLEY BRIDGE	50	WIMBLINGTON	87	WOMBWELL	50	WORMALD GREEN	46
WHITLINGHAM	90	WIMBORNE	139	WOMERSLEY	50	WORMIT	17
WHITLOCKS END	80	WINCANTON	137	WONERSH (See Bramley)	142	WORPLESTON	141
WHITMORE	62	WINCHBURGH	22	WOOBURN GREEN	116	WORSLEY	42
WHITNEY-ON-THE-WYE	76	WINCHCOMBE	114	WOODBOROUGH	114	WORSTEAD	73
WHITRIGG	30	WINCHELSEA	145	WOODBRIDGE	90	WORTHING	142
WHITSTABLE	133	WINCHESTER	139	WOODBURN	32	WORTHINGTON	65
WHITSTONE + BRIDGERULE	134	WINCHFIELD	141	WOODBURY ROAD	135	WORTHY DOWN	139
WHITTINGHAM	33	WINCHMOOR HILL	121	WOODCHESTER	110	WORTLEY	65
WHITTINGTON (Derby)	65	WINCOBANK + MEADOW HALL	66	WOODENBRIDGE	11	WOTTON	116
WHITTINGTON (Salop)	57	WINDER	35	WOODEND	35	WRABNESS	133
WHITTLESEA	87	WINDERMERE	35	WOOD END PLATFORM	80	WRAFTON	134
WHITTLESFORD	87	WINDERMERE LAKESIDE	35	WOODFORD	121	WRAGBY	70
WHITTON (Lincs)	53	WINDMILL END	80	WOODFORD + HINTON	82	WRANGATON	148
WHITTON (Surrey)	122	WINDSOR + ETON	116	WOODGRANGE PARK	121	WRAYSBURY	122
WHITWELL (Derby)	65	WINGATE	38	WOOD GREEN (Mx)	121	WREA GREEN	42
WHITWELL (IOW)	141	WINGFIELD	65	WOOD GREEN (Staffs)	81	WREAY	35
WHITWELL + REEPHAM	73	WINGFIELD VILLAS HALT	149	WOODHALL	18	WRENBURY	57
WHITWICK	82	WINGHAM	146	WOODHALL JUNCTION	70	WRESSLE	50
WHITWORTH	46	WINNERSH	116	WOODHALL SPA	72	WRETHAM + HOCKHAM	89
WHYTELEAFE	144	WINSCOMBE	136	WOODHAM FERRERS	132	WREXHAM	57
WICK	13	WINSFORD	57	WOODHAY	114	WRINGTON	101
WICKENBY	70	WINSFORD + OVER	57	WOODHEAD	62	WROTHAM + BOROUGH GREEN	145
WICKFORD	132			WOODHOUSE	65		

‡ Goods – occasional passenger service

WRO

WROXALL	141
WROXHAM	73
WRYDE	87
WYCOMBE (HIGH)	116
WYCOMBE (WEST)	116
WYE	146
WYKE + NORWOOD GREEN	46
WYKEHAM	40
WYKE REGIS HALT	137
WYLAM	33
WYLDE GREEN	80
WYLYE	139
WYMONDHAM	89
WYNN HALL HALT	57
WYNYARD	38
WYRE DOCK	92
WYRE FOREST	80
WYRLEY + CHESLYN HAY	80

YALDING	145
YARDE HALT	134
YARDLEY WOOD PLATFORM	80
YARM	38
YARMOUTH (I.OW)	139
YARMOUTH (Norfolk)	90
YARNTON	114
YATE	110
YATTON	101
YAXHAM	89
YAXLEY + FARCET	85
YEADON ‡	46
YEALMPTON	148
YEATHOUSE	35
YELDHAM	132
YELVERTOFT + STAMFORD PARK	82
YELVERTON	148
YEOFORD JUNCTION	135
YEOVIL	137
YETMINSTER	137
YNYS	55
YNYSBWL	96
YNYSDDU	97
YNYSFOR	55
YNYSHIR	96
YNYSLAS	74
YOCKLETON	76
YOKER	18
YORK	50
YORK ROAD (Belfast)	3
YORK ROAD (London)	126
YORKHILL	19
YORTON	57
YOUGHAL	10
YSTALYFERA	95
YSTRADGYNLAIS	95
YSTRAD MYNACH	97
YSTRADOWEN	100
YSTRAD RHONDDA	96

‡ Goods — occasional passenger service

KEY TO SYMBOLS USED ON MAPS

STATION - on some large scale maps actual shape MAY be shown.

HALT/UNSTAFFED STATION - shown as at map date, unless recently opened and still open - then current position shown.

J1   JUNCTION - may be named - or 'J' followed by number; for details see facing gazetteer.

VIADUCT OR BRIDGE - if 'V' and number, identified in gazetteer.

↓ S2   LINE SUMMIT - Number refers to gazetteer where height may be given

P3   SIDING - may be shown by letter - for details see facing gazetteer

W   WATER TROUGHS

G6   C1   E10   GOODS DEPOTS, ENGINE SHEDS, COMPANY WORKS - code letter shows which and colour indicates ownership. This style used on large scale plans and for Goods Depots on most maps.

E11   ENGINE SHEDS, COMPANY WORKS, GOODS DEPOTS - small scale maps. These features are sometimes indicated by code letter and number only

T8   TUNNEL - number refers to gazetteer, where length may be shown

OPEN TO PASSENGERS

EXETER

(CROSSFLATTS)   Opened post-grouping or post main map date and still open (may apply to part of name added later).

KEIGHLEY   Open and used by both BR and preserved line services.

Tiverton   Closed.

Norton Fitzwarren   Closed but line still open for all traffic.

Elland   Closed but line still open for goods only.

Oxenhope   Closed by BR but now open for preserved line services only

(Halberton Halt)   Opened post-grouping or post main map date and now closed (underline shows current line position as above)

Page of Continuation Map   At same scale

At a larger scale   } Only shown if there
is no continuation at
At a smaller scale   } the same scale

| NV | NW |
| SA | SB |

Green letters in pairs - National Grid reference.

Abbreviations used for features on the map sometimes shown in code, and colour codes used on maps and/or gazetteers. Entry in main colour used. (Variations in brackets):

A STATION/HALT (Gazetteer entries not on map)   Railway Names on maps

B SIGNAL BOX   P SIDINGS (sometimes blue or black)

C RAILWAY WORKS   S LINE SUMMIT

E ENGINE SHED   T TUNNEL

G GOODS DEPOT (sometimes in black)   V BRIDGE OR VIADUCT

J JUNCTION (sometimes in black)   W WATER TROUGHS (sometimes darker blue)

L NAME FOR SECTION OF LINE dotted arrows may indicate limits   Water features, canals thus ┬┬┬┬┬┬┬┬┬┬

93   Area surrounded by a fine dotted line in red and dotted number in red shows there is an enlargement of the area on the map page indicated by the number.

Other symbols used occasionally - explained on appropriate map or gazetteer